THE SS

ALIBI OF A NATION

THE SS
ALIBI OF A NATION
1922–1945

GERALD REITLINGER

With a new Foreword by
MARTIN GILBERT

ARMS AND ARMOUR PRESS
London Melbourne

Published in 1981 by
Arms and Armour Press, Lionel Leventhal Limited,
2–6 Hampstead High Street, London NW3 1QQ,
and in Australasia at
4–12 Tattersalls Lane, Melbourne, Victoria 3000.

Originally published
in 1956 by William Heinemann Limited.

British Library Cataloguing in Publication Data
Reitlinger, Gerald The SS.
1. Nationalsozialistiche Deutsche Arbeiter-Partei.
Schutzstaffel – History
943.085   DD253.6
ISBN 0–85368–187–2

Printed and bound in Great Britain
by Billing and Sons Limited, Guildford, London
and Worcester.

Foreword

BY MARTIN GILBERT

As a lifelong admirer of the works of Gerald Reitlinger, which have certainly served me well in twenty years of teaching and learning, I am very glad to see *The SS: Alibi of a Nation* reprinted.

Despite all that has been written about the SS since the first edition was published in 1956, and despite a quarter of a century of continuing researches, this book remains one of great importance, a model of historical presentation and a classic.

The SS: Alibi of a Nation was Gerald Reitlinger's fourth book on the Nazi period. Tracing the origin and rise of the SS and the career of its master, Heinrich Himmler, Reitlinger analyses the part taken by the SS in Hitler's rise to power and in the years leading up to the outbreak of war in September 1939. The rôle of the SS in the war itself is then told with chilling historical detail and compelling narrative skill, while the story of the part played by the SS at the time of the bomb plot against Hitler is a masterpiece of historical writing. So too are the sections on Nazi euthanasia programmes, and on the concentration camps – chapters that will remain of particular value for as long as this evil episode continues to be of such considerable public interest, and has now become the object of increasing study.

Reitlinger is particularly impressive in his searching out of essential material from the vast mass of documents prepared for the Nuremberg Trials. The end of the SS story is bizarre, Himmler himself opening negotiations with the Red Cross and trying to make peace with the Allies over Hitler's head, hoping to the last to turn the British and American armies against the Russians.

Reitlinger himself died in 1978, at the age of 78. As a pioneer historian of the Nazi era, he made a substantial contribution to our knowledge. This book is a monument both to his achievement and to his memory.

Contents

Glossary of Abbreviations

BdS – *Befehlshaber der Sicherheitspolizei* – Commander of the Security Police.

Gestapo – *Geheime Staatspolizei* – Secret State Police.

HIWI – *Hilfsfreiwillige* – Auxiliary (Russian) Volunteers.

HSPF (plural HSPFF) – *Hoehere SS und Polizei Fuehrer* – Higher SS and Police Leader.

KRIPO – *Kriminalpolizei* – Criminal Police.

NSDAP – *Nationalsozialistische Deutsche Arbeitspartei* – National Socialist German Workers' Party (The Nazis).

NSFO – *Nationalsozialistische Fuehrungsoffizier* – National Socialist Leadership Officer (in the armed forces).

Ob – *Oberbefehlshaber* – Commander-in-Chief.

OKH – *Oberkommando des Heeres* – High Command of the Army.

OKW – *Oberkommando der Wehrmacht* – High Command of the Armed Forces.

RAM – *Reichssaussenminister* – Reich Foreign Minister (Ribbentrop's title).

RKFDV – *Reichskommissar fuer die Festigung des Deutschen Volkstums* – Reich Commissioner for the Strengthening of German Nationhood.

RFSS – *Reichsfuehrer SS* – Reich Leader of the SS (Himmler's title).

RSHA – *Reichs-Sicherheitshauptamt* – Reich Security Main Office.

RUSHA – *Rasse und Siedlungshauptamt* – Race and Settlement Main Office.

SA – *Sturmabteilungen* – Assault Sections.

SD – *Sicherheitsdienst* – Security Service.

SIPO – *Sicherheitspolizei* – Security Police.

SS – *Schutzstaffeln* – Protection Squads.

SSFHA – *SS Fuehrungshauptamt* – SS Leadership Main Office.

VOMI – *Volksdeutsche Mittelstelle* – Racial German Transfer Agency.

WVHA – *Wirtschafts und Verwaltungshauptamt* – Economic and Administrative Head Office (of the SS).

Acknowledgements for Illustrations

Thanks are due to the following for permission to reproduce illustrations: SLOVAKIA FEDERATION OF JEWISH COMMUNITIES for the pictures of the massacre of Jews and Auschwitz, all taken from their publication Tragédia Slovenskych Židov, Bratislava, 1949; PICTURE POST LIBRARY for the photographs of Himmler and Roehm in 1934, Leeb, Von Fritsch etc in 1935, Heydrich, Himmler etc, and that of Kaltenbrunner; KEYSTONE PRESS AGENCY, LTD. for the pictures of Himmler in 1930, Dietrich, Blomberg, Berger and that of Goering at Rastenburg; WIDE WORLD for the photograph of Popitz; NEW YORK TIMES for that of Keitel; ASSOCIATED PRESS LTD. for the pictures of Heydrich, von Reichenau and Skorzeny; COPRESS for the photographs of the SS in 1923, Ohlendorf and Goerdeler; THE IMPERIAL WAR MUSEUM for the pictures of Wolff and Himmler's body; and AFTENPOST for that of Mueller.

The commissioned ranks of the Waffen SS

AND THEIR ARMY EQUIVALENTS

Untersturmfuehrer – 2nd Lieutenant
Obersturmfuehrer – Lieutenant
Hauptsturmfuehrer – Captain
Sturmbannfuehrer – Major
Obersturmbannfuehrer – Lieutenant-Colonel
Standartenfuehrer – Colonel (Oberst)
Oberfuehrer – Brigadier-General
Brigadefuehrer – Major-General
Gruppenfuehrer – Lieutenant-General
Obergruppenfuehrer – General
Oberstgruppenfuehrer – Colonel-General (General Oberst)

There were no field-marshals in the SS, but Himmler held the special supreme rank of Reichsfuehrer, equivalent to Goering's rank of Reichsmarschall as senior officer of the Armed Forces. Many of the higher SS officers had double ranks as members both of the SS and the Police, e.g., 'Obergruppenfuehrer and General of the Police'. In this book the SS ranks are used only in quoted speech in order to lighten the burden on the reader who is not used to these cumbrous names. It must be understood that, when an SS Major-General is mentioned, he would in fact have been called a Brigadefuehrer.

FOR VENETIA

'Through Charlemagne Christianity and with it Jewry got a foothold in our regions. (Ten minutes ago another alert was sounded in Munich.) I explained all this to Eike and Gertrud. Let's hope they grasped it.' GERDA BORMANN to her husband, 12 September 1944

THE SS
ALIBI OF A NATION

I

The SA and the SS 1920-1933

1. THE PARTY ARMY

There is a common pattern in all revolutions, whether they herald real social and economic transformation like the French and Russian revolutions or merely brief aberrations from the democratic pattern, like the military dictatorships of Latin America. All reach a stage when mob enthusiasm becomes too unwieldy and an inner bodyguard is called in to the protection of the new state at the cost of some heads. But the inner bodyguard has itself stepped out of the ranks of the revolutionary armed mob, not the most fanatical or idealistic part but the most disciplined and the most reliable, the part most acceptable to the professional army. Such originally was the SS.

But this is not the simple story of a revolutionary militia which became a dictator's Pretorian Guard. At the time of the capitulation of Germany there were half a million men, the greater part of them foreigners, wearing the insignia of the SS on their German uniforms. In addition to the *armed* SS, there were tens of thousands of office employees who belonged to the 'General SS' and there were hundreds of high-placed German officials who belonged to the 'honorary SS' and who had the right to wear the uniform of what had once been simply Hitler's bodyguard. This bodyguard was a very different thing at the end of the Second World War. Among the grotesque and unrelated activities of the SS there were offices whose concern was Germanic archæology and ancestral research, collecting the skeletons of 'sub-human races' and running baby farms. There were other SS offices devoted to forging foreign bank-notes, to collecting information on alchemy and astrology. There were institutes for the cultivation of medicinal herbs and wild rubber roots, for the acclimatisation of the wild horse of the steppes. The SS also controlled a mineral water and a porcelain factory, numerous night clubs in foreign capitals and a publishing firm.

What, then, was the general purpose of the complicated SS of the last years of Hitler's Reich? It had ceased to be the security force of a revolutionary militia; it had ceased to be the Pretorian Guard of a dictator; and it had spread its net far beyond the function of an inner political police in a one-party state like the NKVD in Russia. Often the SS has been described as a 'state within a state', but that had been the ideal of its creators and had never become an achievement. In the nineteen-forties the SS no longer possessed any unified purpose at all.

In June 1934 this small party police force had established itself as the political police of Hitler's so-called revolution. Within the next two years it dominated the regular police forces of the Reich, but even in a régime of total war the leaders of the SS never secured control of the judiciary arm. Even Gestapo rule, the pressure of the terrorist on the bureaucrat which had provided the standard excuse for every tyranny of the Nazi régime, had the most peculiar limitations. It is true that for eleven years everybody in Germany was afraid of the Gestapo, but the Gestapo certainly did not run Germany. In the welter of competing authorities that marked the decline of Hitler's personal dictatorship the Gestapo possessed the advantage of its own armed executive, but it was only a part of the huge SS organisation and at the head was a man too hesitant and too colourless in personality to exploit that advantage.

And so, too, with the armed Field SS. Originally this 'army within an army' had been the price paid by the German officer corps for their rescue from service in a citizen army, which might have been dominated by political commissars and party fanatics. In June 1934 the High Command and the General Staff believed that at any moment they would be thrown out of their jobs by a political captain called Roehm. Then Hitler's inner bodyguard had stepped in and carried out the requisite executions on their behalf. So the inner bodyguard had to be rewarded with the right to retain their military equipment and the independence of their three battalions. By the logic of revolutions the disciplined force that had done this should have been the kernel of the new German Wehrmacht, the conscript citizen army that was created within a few months of the executions. But the SS did not become the kernel of the Wehrmacht, nor did it get any footing in the High Command and General Staff. Scattered on many fronts and under many field commands, all the armed SS could retain was an internal independence, a nuisance to the professional High Command but never a threat to its conduct of the war.

By the logic of revolutions this is not what should have happened. Napoleon's armies were led to victory not by descendants of Condé and Turenne but by the sons of small tradesmen, who had been NCOs or subalterns at the time of the Revolution. But in the story of the SS this logic of revolutions did not apply—simply because there was no revolution. There never was a less revolutionary person than Adolf Hitler, who sacked Social Credit theorists and appointed bank managers in their place and who murdered a Roehm only to establish a Blomberg. Nor was Hitler's personal background revolutionary. He rose to notoriety by appealing to the nation's mood which was created by the so-called 'Dictate' of Versailles, a mood of pure frustration with nothing constructive behind it but the tearing up of a humiliating treaty and the removal of foreign armies of occupation. It was a mood that expressed itself in the hatred of all that was liberal and conciliatory, and which welcomed any goal so long as it was reached by violence.

As the government of Germany came within Hitler's grasp, this primitive nihilism of his mind was modified. The well-entrenched social positions, the army, the diplomatic service, the law, big business, and the Church still caused him bitterness, but, so long as they worked for him, they must not be changed. They might be humbled, shouted at and punished like children, but they must remain at their posts. The trained expert was the best man at the job. He need not be a member of the party, so long as there were party members to keep an eye on him. Hence Hitler's passion for retaining party organisations, only half executive in their functions. The civil and military ramifications of the huge SS were never meant in his eyes to supplant ministries and armies. They were meant to watch them.

We are concerned with the history of an organisation whose origins are so obscure that it is not even known how it acquired its name, an organisation whose numbers in the first eight years of its life hardly exceeded two hundred men. The SS, the Schutzstaffeln or protection squads, began as a small group within Hitler's political fighting force, the force which went by the name of Sturmabteilungen, assault sections or SA. These SA men performed the task of stewards at Hitler's earliest political meetings, and they were sent to heckle the political meetings of Communists and others, to create scenes of violence, to shout and by any means possible to command attention; for the disturbance of the life of the bourgeois was desired, the dislocation of the taut quiet strings of German administration and the disruption of the work of a government which put internal order before international esteem. It was the mood of the displaced demobilised soldier and of Hitler who had been displaced from birth.

It was a mood which was never quite forgotten even during the drab, hedged-in existence of Germany at war in 1939-45. The huge, purposeless, over-administered SS was wholly its child. SS leaders—and Himmler in particular—still talked its vulgar, bitter, and brutal language. The key to it was the word Freikorps, the name given to the little, privately raised, but officially tolerated armies which sprang up at the end of 1918 after the capitulation of the High Command and the humiliation of German arms. It is not possible within the scope of this book to describe either the historical origins of National Socialism or the infinitely complex manœuvres behind its rise to power; but the Freikorps movement and the conditions which produced it must be grasped, for there is no border-line where the Freikorps ends and Hitler's SA and SS begin.

The conditions which produced the Freikorps bore no resemblance to those which have prevailed in Germany since the Rheims and Karlshorst armistices of May 1945. In the past eleven years, from 1945 to 1956, there has been no Freikorps movement, still less an SA or an SS deriving from it. Fear of Russia, even greater than that which was felt in 1918, has not resulted in the Western Allies tolerating any free arming of the German forces of anti-Bolshevism. That this is so is mainly due to the formula of 'unconditional surrender', which was agreed between the Allies at Casablanca in January 1943. In November 1918, however, when Marshal Foch wanted to hold out for the unconditional surrender of Germany, the Allied statesmen failed to support him. In the fear that Germany would be provoked to a desperate resistance, they agreed to armistice terms that left Germany inviolate beyond the Rhine, her General Staff intact and her arms dumps unsupervised. The fear that Germany was still strong was followed by the realisation that she was much weaker than had been thought. More terrible than the previous prospect of a Germany fighting in the last ditch was the present prospect of a German army in the hands of Soldiers' and Workers' Councils, a capital menaced by the extreme left-wing German Spartacists and large danger-spots in the east of Europe where the Red Army waited to step into the place of German troops. So, almost overnight, Germany was allowed a new army as hordes of disbanded men drifted into the Freikorps.

On 24 December 1918, six weeks after the armistice, it was sharply realised that the High Command no longer possessed the confidence of the German public and of their own troops in dealing with the forces of extreme revolution. On that day the Social Democrat leader Friedrich Ebert, who was to become the first President of the Weimar Republic, authorised General Lequis, commanding the Berlin Horse Guards, to attack a force of rebel sailors, Dorrenbach's Volksmarine division. The sailors had for some weeks occupied the Berlin buildings known as the Schloss and Marstall in the heart of the business quarter. The attack was a public and ludicrous failure, and on the same day General Groener, the Chief of Staff, authorised the formation of volunteer units composed of loyal anti-revolutionary soldiers. Ebert had already discovered qualities of military ruthlessness, unsuspected in a Socialist, in the person of Gustav Noske, the Mayor of Kiel, whom he at once made Minister for Defence. Three days later Groener and Noske reviewed the first Freikorps volunteers at Zossen.

By 10 March order had been restored in Berlin after the murder of the revolutionary leaders, Carl Liebknecht and Rosa Luxemburg, and a massacre of part of the Volksmarine force. The Freikorps were free to deal with the South. The Bavarian Socialist Republic had been formed in Munich three days before the armistice, but it foundered at the beginning of March 1919 when the leaders Eisner and Auer were shot by members of a reactionary body called the Thule Society. A Socialist-Communist coalition followed under Adolf Hoffmann and Ernst Toller, but this in turn was menaced by a Communist revolt, inspired by Russian emissaries. At first Hoffmann refused Noske's offer of Freikorps troops from the North. As a result the Bavarian Freikorps of General Franz Ritter von Epp suffered defeat at Dachau and the Communists gained possession of Munich, where they established the German equivalent of a Soviet, the Raeterepublik. After the shooting of twenty hostages by the Communists, the Munich middle classes organised themselves into self-defence units. In one of these, the Freischar of Lieutenant Lauterbacher, there may have served a nineteen-year-old agricultural student with large spectacles. His name was Heinrich Himmler.[1]

[1] Robert Waite, *Vanguard of Nazism: The Free Corps Movement in Post-War Germany*, 1918-1923 (Cambridge, Mass., 1952), footnote, p. 87.

The Communist Raeterepublik came to an end late in April, when a combination of Freikorps and regular forces under General von Oven mastered the city. Hundreds of alleged Communists were murdered after this ludicrous interlude, which left a legacy of hysteria and violence that was to colour political thought in Bavaria as long as political thought was permitted, that is to say till 1933. It had a profound effect on the development of National Socialism, for Hitler, Himmler, Hess, and Rosenberg were all in Munich under the Raeterepublik.

By a law of the Ebert government, dated 6 March, the Freikorps units had been embodied in the regular army or Reichswehr in flagrant disregard of the Allies' armistice terms; but, after the Raeterepublik and Spartacist affairs, the activities of the Freikorps were unwisely welcomed by the Allied powers. In Riga the newly created Latvian Republic appealed for the aid of the Freikorps against the Russians. Until the true intentions of the Freikorps leader, General Rudiger von der Goltz, became evident, the British military mission gave him their blessing. Finally, in the summer of 1919 the Latvians had to be armed by the British in order to get rid of the Freikorps, who made their way back to Germany in October, plundering as they went, an earlier and less spectacular crusade than Hitler's against 'the Marxist hordes of Asia'.

Some time before the return of the Baltic Freikorps from Riga, the German government had been compelled to declare their activities illegal. As a result the Freikorps rebelled against the government that had called them into being and between 13 and 17 March 1920 the government was actually driven out of Berlin by an allegedly disbanded Freikorps. This was the 'Naval Brigade' of Captain Ehrhardt, acting on behalf of Wolfgang Kapp, a Prussian civil servant who tried to form a government of his own. This absurd incident, the Kapp Putsch, which was only made possible by the neutrality of the Commander-in-Chief of the German Army, General von Seeckt, ended in a general deflating of reputations. The Cromwellian Noske was driven from Berlin to live a life of total insignificance. Kapp and his partner, General Luettwitz, gave in on the threat of a general strike, and Ehrhardt obligingly put down the strike on behalf of the returning Ebert government.

The incident typified the Weimar Republic's relations with the Freikorps, which at one moment would be declared illegal under Allied pressure and at another moment invoked to restore internal order. In April 1920, Freikorps units were used by the Prussian Minister of the Interior, Carl Severing, to put down the 'Red rising' in the Ruhr. In May 1921 they repelled Polish freebooter attacks in the disputed regions of Upper Silesia. Early in 1923 they operated in small groups in organising sabotage against the French occupying forces in the Ruhr. The Weimar Republic never really suppressed them. The Freikorps maintained their solidarity in secret and only ceased to count when there was no one left to fight. They were not supplanted by the Nazis but slowly fused into the movement. Their essential anarchy and love of brawling was silently canalised into a political crusade, though politics, other than an extreme hatred of liberalism, they had none.[1]

The appeal of the Freikorps to middle-class Germans was so universal that, during Hitler's Third Reich, former Freikorps members were to be found as much in the Resistance movement as in the Nazi hierarchy or in the higher ranks of the fighting SS. Between 1918 and 1923 it had been impossible for a young German of good family, unless he chose the extreme left in politics, to avoid joining either a Freikorps unit or one of the civilian guard corps which sprang into being. Hitler himself joined no Freikorps, but he used these disbanded warriors and their thirst for a further dose of war just as he used the modest party programme of the railway foreman toolmaker, Anton Drexler—only to discard them when they became an embarrassment. In their day the Freikorps leaders had attracted him. Their restless destructive psyche appealed to the former Vienna doss-house waif. Though their fate under Hitler's final dictatorship was largely banishment or obscurity or in some cases death during the blood purge of June 1934, Hitler never stopped being sentimental about the Freikorps movement. Particularly was this so during the war years, in the small hours of the morning before the log fire of his military headquarters. It was then that Hitler would regale a yawning audience of women stenographers with the feats of long-forgotten SA men who had come to him from the ranks of the Freikorps in the days before the Munich Putsch of 1923. After Hitler's body had been scorched by the Generals' plot of July 1944 he praised the Freikorps leaders still more. Hitler's hatred of the German officer class was no longer balanced by reliance on the slavish Himmler and the loyal colourless SS. They too were

[1] For an outstanding example of this canalisation, see the case of Rudolf Hoess (see *infra*, p. 283-4).

embraced in his suspicion of all that was disciplined and that possessed a service mentality. What were wanted were improvisers and
amateurs, lone wolves like himself, the old Freikorps fighters and
not their disciplined successors. But at the end of 1944 most of the
surviving Freikorps chiefs had been out of military employment too
long to replace Hitler's General Staff for him. Hitler had to be
content with the knowledge that a former chief of the SA, Franz
von Pfeffer, commanded a Volkssturm or Home Guard division
near the quiet Swiss border and that Wilhelm Scheppmann, the last
chief of the SA, was now training the Volkssturm in rifle drill.[1]

Outward signs of Hitler's debt to the Freikorps movement were
the swastika, the brown shirt and the Hitler salute, all of which had
been previously adopted by Freikorps units. And even as part of
the armed forces in the Second World War the SS retained the
clumsy substitutes for military titles which the SA had inherited
from the Freikorps—the Obergruppenfuehrers, Obersturmbann-
fuehrers, and the rest of them. They dated from a time when the
failure of the Kapp Putsch had concentrated in Munich most of the
Freikorps leaders who had turned against the Weimar Republic.
Here, after March 1920, the separatist Bavarian ministry of von
Kahr protected them from the official ban on their activities. Two
of these Freikorps leaders perceived at this time the value of the
obscure German Workers' Party of Anton Drexler and of its orator,
Adolf Hitler. The leaders were Captain Ernst Roehm of the army
and Captain Ehrhardt of the navy.

In 1920 Roehm was ADC to the military area commander in
Munich, General Franz Ritter von Epp. Roehm's particular interest
was the Einwohnerwehr—an armed civic guard which had been
formed in Munich to fight the Communists in the weeks following
the 1918 armistice. After 12 October 1920, when the Allies demanded
the disarming of the remaining Freikorps units in Germany, Roehm
enabled the Einwohnerwehr to hide their arms. Hitler had just
formed his 'Strong-Arm Squads' (the future SA), and Roehm, who
had joined Drexler's German Workers' Party earlier than Hitler,
saw to it that the Strong-Arm Squads received some of the hidden
arms.[2] But on 29 June 1921 the government of Josef Wirth and

[1] Felix Gilbert, *Hitler Directs His War*, pp. 134, 136; Institute for International
Affairs, *Hitler's Europe* (London, 1954), p. 44.
[2] Waite, *Vanguard of Nazism*, p. 199.

Walter Rathenau was forced to capitulate to the Allies' demands for a more drastic and genuine disarmament of the Freikorps units. It was on account of this that Hitler changed the name of his Strong-Arm Squads to Sportsabteilung, or Sports Section, a typical Freikorps disguise. In October this name in turn was changed to Sturmabteilung.[1] It was not till another eight years had passed that Hitler first used the abbreviation SA, when giving evidence in a trial at Schwednitz.[2]

It is probable that some of the membership of the banned Einwohnerwehr were concealed in the innocently named Sports Section of the German Workers' Party. Yet the first commander, Josef Klintsch, was a member not of the Einwohnerwehr but of Ehrhardt's Naval Brigade. Klintsch had been in prison for his part in the murder of Matthias Erzberger, who had signed the Versailles Treaty, and in this way the SA was linked with the Vehmgericht, the secret murder tribunal which was Ehrhardt's speciality. Ehrhardt had taken part in the Kapp Putsch and had been allowed to retire to Munich, where he wanted to unite all the Bavarian separatist parties into one Fatherland bloc—and this Hitler was willing to join, even though he hated Bavarian separatism. But there was nothing in common between Hitler and this aggressive romantic. In August 1922, when Ehrhardt was arrested and imprisoned for a short time in connection with the Rathenau murder, he and Hitler drifted apart. The real split occurred during the French occupation of the Ruhr in January 1923, when Hitler refused to subscribe to the typical Freikorps idiocy of demanding war with France, preferring to get rid of the Weimar Republic first. As a result Erhhardt refused to lend his Naval Brigade for Hitler's Munich Putsch in the following November.[3]

The real influence over the training and indoctrination of the SA was not Ehrhardt but Roehm. In later years Hitler was reluctant to admit that Roehm had created his first party army. He pretended that the origin of the SA had been quite haphazard.

[1] Konrad Heiden, *Der Fuehrer* (Boston, 1944), p. 106.
[2] Hans Frank, *Im Angesicht des Galgens* (Graefelfing, 1952), p. 103.
[3] After the seizure of power, Hitler incorporated Ehrhardt's Naval Brigade into the SS, but Ehrhardt himself remained outside the party and was marked down for execution in June 1934. He escaped to Switzerland, but was pardoned and returned to live obscurely in Germany, a typical figure of the Freikorps past. *The Answers of Ernst von Salomon* (London, 1953), pp. 30-2, 260-2.

It was in 1921 that I first heard Fascism mentioned. The SA was born in 1920 without my having the least idea what was going on in Italy. Italy developed in a manner at which I was the first to be surprised. I could see fairly clearly the orientation that it would be proper to give the party but I had no idea concerning paramilitary organisations. I began by creating a service to keep order and it was only after the bloody brawls of 1920 that I gave these troops the name of Sturmabteilung as a reward for their behaviour.[1]

Thus Hitler avoided any reference to the use of firearms or to the man who had provided them, a man whose career has a singular quality of loneliness. Although Ernst Roehm was a professional soldier, he did not belong to the officer caste, being the son of a Bavarian railway clerk. In appearance he was gross and plebeian with a strong suggestion of perversion. He only succeeded in reaching the rank of captain at the end of the First World War after twelve years' service. Roehm was attracted to the Freikorps movement because he was a misfit anywhere else. He was what Konrad Heiden has so aptly called an armed Bohemian,[2] the kind of rootless, aimless, ruthless being whom the Freikorps movement attracted like a magnet. There is nevertheless a tendency in Germany today to regard Roehm as a man who took the Socialist side of the Nazi programme seriously, an old-fashioned revolutionary who believed in barricades and who did not understand Hitler's sham legality and camouflaged terrorism.[3] But it was not Socialism that ruined Roehm with Hitler. From the very beginning Roehm was too ambitious for Hitler, though his capacity for keeping freebooter armies together made him indispensable to Hitler for most of twelve years.

The difference in policy, which was to prove Roehm's destruction in June 1934, was apparent already in February 1923. Under the 'Seeckt-Severing pact' which followed the French occupation of the Ruhr, the Berlin government secretly permitted arms to the banned Freikorps units as part of an illegal national army known as the 'Black Reichswehr'. In getting the SA treated as part of the Black Reichswehr Roehm hoped to become himself head of this national army. Hitler, however, wanted his SA kept completely separate. He did not wish to fight the battles of the Weimar Republic as part of a Black Reichswehr which the Weimar Republic could then disown.

---

[1] *Hitler's Table Talk* (London, 1953), p. 266, 31 January 1942.

[2] Heiden, op. cit., p. 210.

[3] Hermann Mau in *Vierteljahreshefte fuer Zeitgeschichte* (Stuttgart, April 1953): *Die Zweite Revolution*, pp. 125-6.

Hitler had no intention of becoming another Freikorps leader. In 1923 he perceived better prospects, for the almost dictatorial Minister-President of Bavaria, von Kahr, was planning a monarchist and separatist Putsch. Hitler's plan was to force him on, make him burn his boats and march on Berlin. Then, and only then, with the Weimar Constitution abolished, might the question of a national army be considered.

The story of Hitler's Munich Buergerbraeukeller Putsch of 8-9 November 1923 needs no retelling. The plan to force von Kahr, together with General von Lossow and Colonel Seisser, to march on Berlin failed. Hitler and his SA found themselves on the wrong side of the Isar river with Roehm blockaded in the Military Area Head-quarters in the centre of the town. Without the least prospect of success, Hitler and the old mad Field-Marshal Ludendorff marched with their men to relieve Roehm, a march that was pre-eminently meant to save face. For twenty-one years and throughout the war the morning of 9 November was celebrated as a day of heroism and martyrdom, the day of the 'Blood order' of the party. And so, at a time when thousands of anonymous acts of heroism went unrecorded every day, honour was done to a few hundred bullies who had not distinguished themselves in the least and who had not even vindicated their honour, unless turning back from a much smaller force of policemen could be so counted.

For more than a year after this Hitler was in prison, but Roehm, without whom the arming of the SA and the allied Kampfbund could not have happened, was allowed by the protection of General von Epp to go free. This widened the breach with Hitler still more. Moreover, in Landsberg prison, in the intervals of dictating *Mein Kampf*, Hitler had leisure to meditate; and in these meditations the role of his professional rowdies underwent a change. The road was to be the slow one of legality. Brute force was to be camouflaged. If in practice Hitler was henceforward to use the might of his SA to blackmail a succession of Chancellors of the Reich—Bruening, Schleicher, and von Papen—in theory he bargained with them in all correctness for Reichstag majorities. These new conditions demanded a break with the Freikorps background, the desperate and anarchical aftermath of defeat. The marching young men in brown shirts must be made to impress the prosperous and the conventional.

It is said that just before the Munich Putsch Hitler was warned by his adjutant, Wilhelm Brueckner, that soon it would be too late.

The mass of unemployed men in the SA would desert unless a successful revolution converted their position into that of a paid professional armed force.[1] But it was already too late before Brueckner spoke. In September 1923 passive resistance to the French in the Ruhr had ended. Reconciliation with the Allies, the Dawes plan for German recovery and the end of inflation were round the corner and with them six years of fallacious prosperity. The German public was already sick of military adventurers who wouldn't be demobilised, of enemies of authority who had no alternative authority to offer, of the sentimental murders and beerhouse brawlings of heartsick youth. Neither Hitler's Putsch nor his subsequent trial was anything more than a nine days' wonder. It was the era of the Bright Young People. What was wanted was not romantic chauvinism but Fascism on the Italian model, which removed the touts from the streets, made the trains run to time, and put running water in the hotel bedrooms.

Such was Germany on 20 December 1924 when Hitler came out of Landsberg prison. Everything had to be started from the beginning. The SA had been banned, Hitler himself barely escaped deportation and Goering had fled to Sweden. Roehm still struggled to re-create the Kampfbund of illegal organisations which had marched with the SA at Munich, but in the following April he gave it up and for a time resigned from the party. Within the party itself there was an open split between the old beer-mug pushers of the Anton Drexler days and the cleverer adherents who had got themselves into the Reichstag, defying the orders of the imprisoned Fuehrer. 'I shall need five years', Hitler declared with inspired accuracy, 'before the movement is on top again'.[2]

In April 1925, when Roehm resigned, Hitler was left with two typical legacies of the Freikorps period to take Roehm's place. On the one hand there was Edmund Heines, the reputed lover of Roehm, turbulent and hysterical and a perpetual menace. On the other there was Captain Franz von Pfeffer, whom Hitler made chief of staff of the SA eighteen months later. Pfeffer was a typical military man, fiery and obstinate, intent only on moulding the SA into another 'Black Reichswehr' which he could one day turn over to the army as a corps of his own creation, after having made a Putsch in the interest of a military government. Pfeffer was a greater menace than

[1] Heiden, op. cit., p. 182.
[2] Alan Bullock, *Hitler, a Study in Tyranny*, p. 114.

the scandalous Heines. He tried to infiltrate the regular army with his SA men, who drilled with army units[1]; and in September 1930 he got three young officers of the Ulm garrison involved in a treason trial before the Leipzig Federal Supreme Court, at which Hitler was forced to affirm his intention of keeping the army out of politics.

It was now that Hitler began to feel seriously the need for a loyal inner bodyguard, remote from politics, whose one duty was to rally to his own person. The Schutzstaffeln had survived Hitler's imprisonment in spite of their small numbers and disreputable leadership, perhaps because the authorities had forgotten to ban them. At Weimar in July 1926, when Hitler was permitted for the first time to hold a public demonstration, these two hundred men of the original SS joined in the march past and Himmler presented them with a 'blood flag' for their part in the Munich Putsch.[2]

Originally the Schutzstaffeln had been known as the 'Adolf Hitler Shock Troops'. At some time in 1922 this small group of men had grown together round the persons of Hitler's professional strong men, Maurice, Schreck, and Erhard Heiden, who sometimes also drove his car for him when he could afford to have one. Of this remote period in the history of the SS Hitler himself is the best witness.

Being convinced that there are always circumstances in which élite troops are called for, I created in 1922-3 the 'Adolf Hitler Shock Troops'. They were made up of men who were ready for revolution and knew that some day things would come to hard knocks. When I came out of Landsberg everything was broken up and scattered in sometimes rival bands. I told myself then that I needed a bodyguard, even a very restricted one, but made up of men who would be enlisted without conditions, even to march against their own brothers, only twenty men to a city (on condition that one count on them absolutely) rather than a dubious mass. It was Maurice, Schreck, and Heiden who formed in Munich the first group of toughs, and were thus the origin of the SS; but it was with Himmler that the SS became an extraordinary body of men, devoted to an ideal, loyal to death.[3]

The figures should be noticed—only twenty men to a city. In another specimen of table talk Hitler recalled that an average Schutzstaffel in 1922-3 had not exceeded seven or eight men.[4] Yet there was already a link with the highly regimented SS of Heinrich Himmler; that link was the name first given to them, for the name Stosstruppe or Shock Troop had been invented in 1914 for specially

[1] Heiden, op. cit., p. 217.   [2] Bullock, op. cit., p. 124.
[3] *Hitler's Table Talk*, p. 167, 3 January 1942.   [4] *Ibid.*, p. 266.

trained assault units. After the Battle of the Somme every division was expected to train a battalion of them. They had a harder discipline than other units and a more arduous training, but they also had privileges and were only sent to the trenches when there was a 'push' on. There was also a relaxation of the rigid etiquette of the Imperial army. The Shock Troops were sometimes heard addressing their officers as 'Du'. In all this one might well be reading about the Waffen SS in the Second World War.[1]

While the SA grew, the Stosstruppe or Schutzstaffeln remained static. It is said that at Elberfeld in May 1923, 70,000 SA men marched past the bier of the Nazi protomartyr, Leo Schlageter, who had been shot by the French for sabotage in the Ruhr. It is said that in the following September 15,000 SA men possessed arms as part of the Black Reichswehr.[2] But in those days the Stosstruppe were too small to be noticed. They are not mentioned at that noisy early triumph, the banned march to Coburg in October 1922, while in the Munich Putsch a year later their part was limited to wrecking the presses of the Social Democrat newspaper *Muenchener Post*. Five more years were to pass before the Stosstruppe or Schutzstaffeln became identified with the name of Heinrich Himmler—five years of almost total obscurity. Himmler then took over a force whose numbers had grown little beyond the two hundred who had marched past at Weimar.

2. HIMMLER

The man who became Reichsfuehrer of the SS on 6 January 1929 was twenty-eight years old. He was the only top-flight Nazi leader who came from Bavaria, though it was in Bavaria that the movement was born. Heinrich Himmler, the son of a schoolmaster, was by no means unique in belonging to the middle-class intelligentsia; for of all the founders of this so-called revolution only Hitler, Goebbels, Ley, and Sauckel could claim to represent the working man and the peasant. Himmler shared with Goebbels the distinction of having had a Catholic religious upbringing and of only breaking with the Church when well past adolescence—in Himmler's case perhaps not till he was past the age of thirty-five. More than one contemporary, including Hitler himself, compared Himmler with Ignatius Loyola,[3]

[1] Waite, *Vanguard of Nazism*, p. 27.   [2] *Ibid.*, p. 237.
[3] *Hitler's Table Talk*, p. 168; Rudolf Diels, *Lucifer ante Portas* (Zurich, 1947), p. 5.

linking the intensive inner discipline which Himmler tried to enforce on his flock with that of the Jesuit order. There appears, however, to be equally little ground for supposing either that Himmler was inspired by the Jesuits or that his attacks on Christianity were a revolt against an education that had been too rigidly orthodox.

Mr. Frischauer, in the only attempt that has yet been made at a biography of Heinrich Himmler,[1] has devoted a great deal of necessarily difficult inquiry into Himmler's family background. The results are extremely negative. None of Frischauer's interrogations of Himmler's family elicited anything which suggests strong repression in the home. He publishes, however, a revealing photograph of Himmler's schoolmaster father[2] taken in 1935 at the age of seventy. With his neat goatee beard, kind humorous eyes and humanistic profile, Gebhard Himmler seems the embodiment of the contemplative philosophic Bavarian—a race that has been carted away with the Munich rubble and which the new city, rising like some São Paolo or Stalingrad, will never know again.

Karl Gebhardt, the murderous medical experimenter of later years, who was Himmler's companion at the school kept by his father at Landshut, spoke at his own trial of 'the family of a strict schoolmaster who brought his son up with severity'.[3] Yet one would have thought that if Himmler's childhood had been repressed, he would have been less prone in later years to imitate his father. Himmler was constantly relapsing into a Bavarian schoolmaster. To vindicate his theories he dug up the past. In 1935 he conducted excavations in East Prussia to prove that the eastern expansion of the Germanic races was older than the Teutonic knights. At this time the Reichsfuehrer SS was particularly interested in Henry the Fowler and Henry the Lion—Dukes of Bavaria and Saxony in the early Middle Ages—whom he regarded as forerunners of a purely Germanic Reich, rather than Charlemagne who was a hated foreigner. Henry the Fowler was particularly sympathetic to Himmler. He had resisted the Holy Roman Empire, had had himself crowned without the offices of the Church and had advanced eastwards against the Slavs and Hungarians. Hitler, who found this cult of Himmler's particularly funny, thought that he got it from a book by Walter Darré, *Um Blut und Boden*.[4] But Darré's education was by no means German. He was born in the Argentine Republic and he went to

[1] Willi Frischauer, *Himmler, the Evil Genius of the Third Reich* (London, 1953).
[2] *Ibid.*, p. 64.   [3] See p. 21.   [4] *Hitler's Table Talk*, p. 347.

school at King's College School, Wimbledon. The Saxon Henrys are more likely to be Himmler's discovery than Darré's, fruits of Gebhard Himmler's Realschule in Landshut rather than of Wimbledon.

On 2 July 1936 Himmler, surrounded by the SS higher leadership, attended a ceremony for the thousandth anniversary of Henry the Fowler's death. Himmler's speech was published as a pamphlet by the SS journalist Gunter d'Alquen, editor of the official SS journal *Das Schwarze Korps*. It is indeed a schoolmasterlike performance with its recitation of names of ancient Slav tribes, Hevellians, Notarians, Obotrites, Dalaminzians, and the rest. It may just have been honour to the ancestors of the Wittelsbach House, Gebhard Himmler's royal patrons. Some, however, saw in it Himmler's belief that he was a personal reincarnation of Henry the Fowler, destined to colonise the old German lands that had been wrested by the Slavs.[1]

There is little here to suggest that Himmler revolted from his father's background. Were not his rigidity of mind and inaccessibility to horror and pity more likely due to a lack of motherly love? Himmler's marriage at the age of twenty-seven to a hospital nurse six years older than himself suggests that motherly love was something he was still seeking to replace. Himmler's mother, however, remains a shadowy figure, a conventional matriarch revered and respected. Gebhard Himmler junior told Mr. Frischauer that in 1941, at the summit of his career, Himmler allowed himself to appear at her strictly Catholic funeral.[2]

In short the background of one who ranks so high in the company of historic monsters sounds depressingly normal. His easily identifiable physical appearance was also not unusual, though unsuitable for the head of an organisation which was to preserve the blonde, blue-eyed, true Nordic species. Gottlob Berger, who had been one of Himmler's foremost experts on racial selection for the SS, declared at Nuremberg after the war that Himmler was 'an unassimilated half-breed and unfit for the SS'.[3] To those less obsessed with the Nordic mania than Gottlob Berger, Himmler will appear very German. In civilian dress—in which he was hardly every photographed—Himmler looked like a humble bank clerk, absolutely inconspicuous. But when he marched in procession, tripping over

[1] Himmler, *Rede der RFSS im Dom zu Quedlinberg*, 1936.
[2] Frischauer, op. cit.
[3] Berger's evidence in the Wilhelmstrasse case, *Tagesspiegel*, 22 May 1948.

the skirts of his SS general's overcoat, Himmler had all the glamour and dignity of a self-conscious gander.

At times the camera made Himmler appear Mongolian, almost Chinese. It may have been for this reason that Himmler made a cult of the historic personage of Jenghiz Khan, referring to him often in his speeches and presenting his friends with a German book on the subject for their birthdays. It may have been for this reason that after the entry of Japan into the war Himmler made the Mongolians honorary Aryans, declaring that they had furnished Russia with the only element 'apart from our own blood' which was not of inferior race. To this Asiatic element the Russians owed not only Attila and Jenghiz Khan, but also Lenin and Stalin.[1] When making such speeches, Himmler may have been specially conscious of his own Mongolian appearance; but he was not, as some of his staff later suggested, a Mongolian idiot, nor was he a throwback to the passage of the Huns through Bavaria. Being short-sighted, Himmler tended to contract his eyes and his huge spectacles exaggerated the effect. A flat nose and a withdrawn forehead did the rest.

Himmler could be genial enough and even rather childish on occasions, but the official face which he assumed when being photographed was not very human. It is never, however, positively diabolical like the first of the two death masks which were taken at Lueneburg, a face which grins like a gargoyle. But this mask, which was published by the magazine *Time*, was taken during rigor mortis. The second mask is so composed in the peace of death that one would say it was the face of a kind man . . . but such is man's nature.[2]

The strangest thing about the background of Heinrich Himmler was its normality and its security. It is true that Hitler rescued Himmler from the ranks of failure, and that at the age of twenty-eight he was an unsuccessful poultry farmer without university education and unhappily married. But it was a physically comfortable failure. Himmler never had to peddle water-colours painted on the backs of postcards, or live in a doss-house. He had not quarrelled with his parents, who were reasonably affluent. He was not an out-and-out social misfit. Fastidious persons like Count Ciano and

---

[1] Himmler's first Posen speech, Nuremberg Document PS 1990, and François Bayle, *Psychologie et ethique du national-socialisme* (Paris, 1953), p. 429. See also *infra*, p. 202.

[2] Photograph in Bayle, op. cit.

Ulrich von Hassell could converse with Himmler without observing any Caliban-like characteristics.

Himmler's father had been tutor to the Crown Prince Heinrich of Bavaria, who was killed in action in 1917. This prince had stood god-father to his tutor's child in 1900 and the infant was named Heinrich after him. The elder generation of Himmlers were royal house-pets and there was an uncle who served as court chaplain.[1] Himmler could never quite rid himself of his monarchist affections and his snobbery. It was not only that he strove to make his SS a new aristocracy, but he welcomed good aristocratic blood into it and at one moment it was a nursery of princes. Hitler took strong repressive measures concerning the German princes after the mon-archist plot against Mussolini in July 1943, and after the plot against himself in July 1944. Himmler had to co-operate in these measures, but he did so with reluctance.[2]

On the other hand it is clear that Himmler had never been at home in the august circles where his father was patronised. He was incapable of practising the art that men learn at courts, the art of 'producing' oneself. Goebbels noticed Himmler's short fat fingers and dirty nails,[3] while Hitler himself described him as 'an inartistic man'. Himmler was vulgar but he had no swagger. His cloak was one of embarrassing modesty and timidity. Moreover, as he accu-mulated responsibilities, Himmler lost his astonishing capacity for work and became a professional invalid, constantly retiring into nursing homes and fussing about his food and hours of sleep. When he visited the Bormanns, Magda Bormann had to provide 'Uncle Heini' with rice.[4] Himmler probably copied his vegetarianism from Hitler, from whom he also derived a habit of spinning far-fetched theories on commonplace subjects, such as the merits of porridge and mineral water for the SS man's breakfast, raw garlic for women slave workers[5] and the universal virtues of the milk of the wild mare of the steppes.[6]

These and similar fantasies were registered in Himmler's mind like blurred prints from discarded negatives. He was not an ordinary crank, he was a universal crank. He resembled Flaubert's two

---

[1] Walter Hagen (Hoettl), *Die geheime Front* (Linz, 1950), p. 90.

[2] See *infra*, p. 248.

[3] Rudolf Semmler, *Goebbels, the Man next to Hitler* (London, 1947), p. 178.

[4] *The Bormann Letters* (London, 1954) p. 31.

[5] See *infra*, p. 355.   [6] Hagen, op. cit., p. 92.

retired bank clerks, Bouvard and Pécuchet, who inherited a fortune and became obsessed with the wonders of science and progress and tried to interest themselves in everything constructive, but always with the worst consequences. This side of Himmler's nature was as much responsible for his destruction of human life—in which respect he far surpassed his hero, Jenghiz Khan—as was his blind obedience to a dæmon. The concentration camp underworld of half a million human beings suffered from it and also from Himmler's intense parsimony. In this respect he was the very reverse of Hitler, who had scarcely ever possessed more than the price of his next meal till he was past the age of thirty, who had no feeling for money, and was incapable of apportioning expenditure. Himmler went to the other extreme. He never tried to grab anything for himself and was almost the only Nazi leader who was never accused of acquiring riches. To Himmler, economy was an end in itself. It never occurred to him to ask for more. Felix Kersten believed that his salary did not exceed 24,000 Reichsmarks a year, which was equivalent during the war years to less than £1,000.[1] In September 1939 Himmler complained to Schellenberg that he had two families to keep and could not allot more than 300 Reichsmarks a month to each.[2] And when Kersten bought a Swedish watch for him, Himmler apologised because he could not lay hands on 160 Reichsmarks till his next month's salary came in. Equally, Himmler's officials were underpaid. During his first three years as Himmler's adjutant Karl Wolff received only the equivalent of £270 a year.[3] The result of this parsimony was corruption all the way down the ladder, corruption of which Himmler was constantly informed.

Of Himmler in his Jenghiz Khan aspect, much was heard before and during the war. Since the war a different picture has emerged. SS leaders who were very close to Himmler such as Walter Schellenberg, Karl Wolff, Gottlob Berger, Oswald Pohl, Karl Gebhardt, and Erich von dem Bach-Zelewski have been called to give evidence. As implicated men, they have mostly told the same story, namely that Himmler's utterances had appeared to them too crazy to be believed and that his manner was so insignificant and silly that he fooled them, so that they never grasped the horror of what he was doing without their knowledge. The effect of these testimonies is as

[1] Felix Kersten, *Totenkopf und Treue* (Hamburg, 1953), p. 401.
[2] *Quick*, Munich, 18 October 1953.
[3] *Trial of Major War Criminals, V*, 770.

misleading as the Jenghiz Khan picture; for the transcripts of several speeches, which Himmler delivered to a select circle and which were not intended for publication, show that his language could be blunt enough and that there was nothing that he hid from the higher SS leadership.

One study of Himmler, which appeared in 1950, has been particularly favourable to the case presented by the incriminated SS leaders. It is the work of Colonel Willi Hoettl of the SS, the Gestapo's Chief of Intelligence in South-east Europe and Italy. Hoettl, an Austrian who joined the Gestapo after the Anschluss, had personal dealings only once on the telephone with Himmler and only records what he picked up from his colleagues. In Hoettl's view, Himmler was no more than a rubber-stamp man who owed his position to the intrigues of Heydrich, who meant to supplant him. In June 1942, when Heydrich was killed, Hitler decided that a rubber-stamp man was all that he needed to take the too ambitious Heydrich's place. Hitler therefore let Himmler carry on Heydrich's functions as well as his own. Thus Himmler, who ended up as Minister for the Interior, Chief of Police, Head of the armed SS, Commander-in-Chief of the Replacement Army and of an Army Group in the field, was one of those who have greatness thrust upon them.

This view is not borne out by the facts. Heydrich could not have been responsible for Himmler's insatiable greed for new offices and his restless interference with every government department long after Heydrich's own death. Himmler's successful bid to control the development of 'secret weapons' towards the end of the war shows the extent of his power-lust. Major-General Walter Dornberger, who describes this, can hardly be regarded as a defence witness on Himmler's character. Yet he has drawn a picture of Himmler at work which is as different from Himmler's prattlings to his father-confessor, Felix Kersten, as it is different from Himmler showing off to his police chiefs at Posen.

Himmler possessed the rare gift of attentive listening. Sitting back with his legs crossed, he wore throughout the same amiable and interested expression. His questions showed that he unerringly grasped what the technicians told him out of the wealth of their knowledge. The talk turned to the war and the important questions in their minds. He answered without hesitation, calmly and candidly. It was only at rare moments that, sitting with his elbows resting on the arms of the chair, he emphasised his words by tapping the tips of his fingers together. He was a man of quiet unemotional gestures, a man without nerves.[1]

[1] Walter Dornberger, "V2" (London, 1953), p. 179.

This impression of candour and lack of nerves will be found in most honestly recorded accounts of interviews with Himmler. The impression of hysteria created by Kersten's narrative is understandable. Himmler was then in the hands of his father-confessor. Himmler was quite a practical man when he was in contact with realities—but that was seldom in the incredible position that he came to occupy. Himmler was not a great man nor even a man of much value, but he could be all things to all men. While to Hoettl he was a mere clerk in office, to Wolff Helldorf he was the greatest actor of all time.[1] To Konrad Heiden he was silent and fishlike,[2] to Friedrich Hossbach expressionless and inscrutable,[3] to Oswald Pohl, a schoolmaster with a passion for economising,[4] clever without being extremely intelligent. Martin Bormann found him chilly and critical,[5] Goebbels found him a political realist behind all his fantasies.[6] To Karl Gebhardt Himmler was not interesting, not a split personality, without originality but very industrious,[7] while to Felix Kersten he was a man who knew only gods and devils.[8] Himmler became Chief of Police in a land which had already submitted to police government —not a position that brings out virtues in a man. He seems almost to have been chosen on account of what he lacked.

One may wonder how this mediocre personality would have developed without the guiding star of Adolf Hitler. Even in 1927, after at least five years' association with the party, Himmler's life on the poultry farm at Waldtrudering seems innocent and rather cranky. He had just married Marge Conzersowo, a nurse in a fashionable Berlin clinic who had seen through the science of medicine as practised by the orthodox faculty.[9] She interested Himmler in mesmerism, homœopathy, and herbal remedies. Himmler with his agricultural diploma particularly liked herbs. Years later he

---

[1] Hans Gisevius, *To the Bitter End* (London, 1948), p. 149.

[2] Heiden, op. cit., p. 720.

[3] Friedrich Hossbach, *Zwischen Wehrmacht und Hitler* (Wolfenbuettel, 1949), p. 33.

[4] Evidence Oswald Pohl, Nuremberg, Case IV, transcript pp. 1265, 1275.

[5] *The Bormann Letters* (London, 1954), p. 1.

[6] Wilfrid von Oven, *Mit Goebbels bis zum ende* (Buenos Ayres, 1949), vol. II, p. 208.

[7] Excerpt from Gebhardt's evidence in François Bayle, *Croix gammée ou caducée* (Freiburg, 1950), p. 218.

[8] Felix Kersten, *Totenkopf und Treue*, p. 78.

[9] Evidence of Karl Gebhardt, in Bayle, *Croix gammée ou caducée*, p. 222.

established herbal gardens in all the concentration camps,[1] and one of them at Dachau was run by his mother's physician, Dr. Fahrenkamp.[2] If Himmler had not chosen Hitler as the dæmon of his career, he might have stayed a herbalist. And if Himmler had not grown up in Germany, the tortured Germany of the early 'twenties, he might have projected that dimly artistic, speculative side of his nature. Buried in the Cotswolds, Heinrich Himmler and his Marge could have cultivated their herbs, clothed in homespun wool and nurtured on wholemeal bread, occasionally throwing peasant pottery or playing duets on reconstructed mediæval instruments. At the worst there might have been a brief period of attachment to the British Union of Fascists and a short confinement in the Isle of Man.

But Himmler had lived through the hysteria of the Munich Raeterepublik, that damp squib of Communist rule in the winter of 1918-19. He may have served in one of the anti-Communist bands, the Freischar of Lieutenant Lauterbacher.[3] He may have encountered some of the heady poison that was distilled in Munich by the White Russian refugees and by the Thule Society.[4] If so, Himmler could have acquired a racialism as crazily intolerant as that preached by the man he was yet to meet; but in fact nothing is known of the political views of the young Himmler. He printed nothing till he was past the age of thirty-five, and even in that turgid pamphlet there is little beyond veneration of the German race and execration of Bolshevism,[5] larded with a fantastic historical survey of the world conspiracy of Jewry and Freemasonry beginning with Esther and Ahasueras. The politics in this pamphlet and in most of Himmler's speeches are simply the common stock of the Nazi movement, a combination of anti-Semitism, anti-liberalism, and anti-clericalism. They are perfunctory politics. It became Himmler's duty to destroy Jews, liberals, and priests. But his dizziest flights of oratory were reserved for a castle of the Teutonic Order in the Urals, or for a polygamous SS stud farm which would banish the dark strains from Europe.

These things may well have germinated in Himmler's mind in the period from November 1918 to May 1919, when Socialism, Communism, and extreme reaction succeeded each other in the light-

---

[1] See *infra*, p. 235.   [2] Frischauer, op. cit., p. 175.
[3] Waite, op. cit., p. 87.   [4] Hagen, op. cit.
[5] Himmler, *Die Schutzstaffel als antibolschewistische Kampforganisation* (Munich, 1936).

headed city of Munich. A pink and doe-eyed Himmler walked the streets. He was eighteen years old, an agricultural student at the Hochschule, having become a civilian again after less than a year's war service of the most sheltered sort. Through his father's influence at court he had entered the 11th Bavarian Regiment as a Fahnen-junker or officer-cadet, serving on probation as an NCO. This would seem to be the most reliable version of Himmler's military career,[1] though Karl Gebhardt said that Himmler's father kept him away from the army on a farm, while Himmler himself told Count Berna-dotte twenty-seven years later that he had led men into action as a sergeant-major of the Bavarian Guards at the age of sixteen.[2]

After the episode of the Raeterepublik, Himmler continued his agricultural studies and in 1922 he obtained his diploma and his first employment as a salesman for the fertiliser factory, Stickstoff GmbH of Schleissheim. It was from Schleissheim that Himmler and his younger brother Gebhard marched to Munich in Hitler's Putsch of 8 November 1923. The brothers served in a Freikorps contingent, the Reichskriegsflagge of Captain Heiss. It was a small group, very closely associated with Ernst Roehm whose acquaintance Himmler must have made, for a photograph exists which shows the young Himmler carrying a banner by Roehm's side during the occupation of the Military Area Headquarters in the Schoenbergstrasse.[3] After this foolish adventure the Himmler brothers left Munich, unmo-lested. Nine-tenths of the men who had taken part in Hitler's Putsch had nothing else in view than the restoration of Prince Rupprecht to the throne of Bavaria, of which Himmler's parents presumably approved. There is no evidence that Himmler had met Hitler or that he had studied the programme of National Socialism. Himmler nevertheless became a bearer of the 'blood order' of the party.

A year later Himmler was out of work and, after failing to re-enlist in the army, he became secretary to Gregor Strasser.[4] In spite

[1] Frischauer, op. cit.

[2] Bayle, *Croix gammée ou caducée*, p. 218; Bernadotte, *The Curtain Falls* (New York, 1946), p. 51.

[3] Frischauer, op. cit.

[4] Himmler may have known Gregor Strasser much earlier. Writing of the SA rally on the Oberwiesenfeld parade ground on 1 May 1923, Mr. Alan Bullock says: 'The Landshut detachment led by Gregor Strasser and Himmler brought 140 rifles and a number of light machine-guns with them' (op. cit., p. 87). Mr. Bullock does not quote the source of this statement, which is inconsistent with Himmler's very modest role on 9 November

of Himmler's part in the murder of Gregor Strasser in June 1934, it
is natural that he should have sought his patronage ten years earlier.
Himmler came from Landshut, the home town of the Strasser
brothers, and as a salesman for a firm of fertiliser manufacturers
Himmler may have formed a link with Gregor Strasser's pharmacy
business. With Hitler still in prison, Gregor Strasser was the leading
man in the party. But he was a sincere Socialist and already at
loggerheads with Hitler. Strasser would not have kept Himmler under
his protection in 1924-9 if he had not found him politically sympathetic. Like Goebbels, Koch, Ley and many other future Nazi
bearers of office, Himmler had come under the spell of Hitler's
rival; but he had little in common with this company of radical
demagogues. It may be that since Himmler was unpolitical, apart
from his theories of 'blood and soil', he was all the more useful to
Gregor Strasser. Himmler was ready to like anything that was un-
compromising and authoritarian. They were common enough in the
1920s, these young men with large spectacles who wanted to take
life seriously and to be uncomfortable.

During the war one sometimes met the inaccurate statement that
Himmler, the chief of the Gestapo, the extermination squads, and
the concentration camps, had been a Communist. This no doubt
was a memory of the period when Himmler had enjoyed Gregor
Strasser's confidence. Konrad Heiden tells a story that, in 1930,
Himmler discussed the autobiography of Leon Trotsky with Hitler.
Himmler then declared that, in addition to reading this, he had made
a thorough study of the Russian secret police system, which he
thought he could run better than the Russians did.[1] If the story is
true, Himmler had been boasting; for he remained till the end wil-
fully ignorant of Russia and Marxism. Himmler could never have
wooed the Left with any seriousness. His attachment to Gregor
Strasser must have been unpolitical and uncritical. Strasser probably
found Himmler an absolutely obedient employee, just as Roehm and
Hitler were to find him later.

3. THE SS IN 1927-33

Between 1925 and 1927 Himmler was Gregor Strasser's deputy
Gaufuehrer in Bavaria, Swabia, and the Palatinate.[2] Strasser's duties

---

[1] Heiden, op. cit.
[2] Notes prepared by Wiener Library, London.

were mainly concerned with propaganda because as a Reichstag deputy he could travel throughout Germany free of charge. The deputy's duties did not amount to much. Himmler could conduct them from his poultry farm at Waldtrudering after 1927, as well as his modest duties as second-in-command of the Schutz-staffeln. In 1925 the 200 SS men were commanded by Josef Berchtold, who, as editor of *Voelkische Beobachter*, used to send the part-time warriors out to canvass advertisement space.[1]

It was renewed trouble in the SA which ended this idyll. In 1928 Hitler resisted very strong pressure to get Edmund Heines, the most notorious of Roehm's lovers, reinstated as head of the Munich SA. Roehm had left the SA in 1925, but, as ADC to the Military Area Commander, Franz Ritter von Epp, whom he had persuaded to finance the first Nazi newspaper, *Voelkische Beobachter*, Roehm still carried a great deal of weight at the newly embellished party headquarters, the Braunehaus in the Briennerstrasse. Disgusted with Hitler's treatment of Heines, Roehm accepted an appointment as colonel on the staff of General Kundts' military mission in Bolivia. It was very shortly before Roehm's unpredicted departure, on 6 January 1929, that Hitler promoted Himmler to be 'Reichsfuehrer of the SS'. Some eight years later Himmler explained that he had been told to transform the SS into 'a corps d'élite'. Could it be that Himmler was chosen to keep an eye on the activities at the Braunehaus of the Epp-Roehm-Heines faction?[2] In January 1929, however, the greatest danger to Hitler was not the Munich SA but the still more radical SA in Berlin, where the influence of the Strasser brothers was paramount. To deal with this Hitler appointed Kurt Daluege to command the Berlin SS. Daluege, the engineer of the city refuse dump and a former Freikorps man, had been commissioned originally by Hitler to found the first SA troop in Berlin, but in 1926 Daluege had fallen foul of Gregor Strasser.[3] It seems that Daluege's appointment to the SS in 1929 as an enemy of the Strassers had nothing to do with Himmler, whose authority he did not begin to acknowledge till early in 1934. The actions of the SS against the Berlin SA in September 1930 and April 1931 must be regarded as something independent of Himmler, who scarcely left Munich and who was

[1] Heiden, op. cit.
[2] Nuremberg Document PS 1992: Himmler's address to Wehrmacht officers, January 1937.
[3] Heiden, op. cit., p. 293.

preoccupied with creating his system of racial selection and his elaborate methods of SS training. Nor did these actions cause Hitler to have much confidence in the new role of the SS. In both cases the aid of the civil police had to be invoked to clear the rebels out of Goebbels's headquarters. After the first revolt Pfeffer, the supreme SA leader, was replaced by Roehm of all people, Roehm, who had returned from Bolivia and rejoined the SA in January 1931 after nearly six years' absence, two of them abroad. Hitler even permitted the scandalous Edmund Heines to have command of the Berlin contingent. Roehm and his clique were now stronger in the party than ever before, and this at a time when the party was in sight of its ultimate goal. Moreover, if there had ever been any question of the Berlin SS taking orders direct from Himmler, it was now Roehm who gave the orders in person; and after the second rebellion he appointed his own man, Friedrich Krueger,[1] to be director of training for the SS.

Himmler, who had been called in to protect the Fuehrer from Freikorps leaders who would not come to heel, was ready enough to take orders from the same Freikorps leaders when Hitler had come to terms with them; and Roehm had no reason to want to get rid of Himmler, who appeared on the same public platforms with him, deferentially endorsing his speeches almost till the moment when he was required to kill him, just as he was to kill his earlier master Gregor Strasser.

During the next twenty months, the record of the SS was squarely compounded in that of the SA, banned from wearing uniform when the SA uniform was banned and participating in all the SA's excesses. But there was a vast increase in recruiting. In January 1929 the SS had numbered 280 men.[2] In April 1932, when Bruening's decree officially disbanded both the SA and the SS, there were 30,000. Most of this recruitment dated only from 1931, when Himmler in Munich received the moral support of Heydrich. It had been necessitated by the weak role of the SS in suppressing the two SA rebellions, but years were to pass before the SS again performed a party police function; and throughout the complex political manœuvres which finally brought Hitler to power in January 1933 the SS played no part as distinct from the SA. Only in the discreet

[1] See *infra*, p. 133.
[2] Nuremberg Document PS 1992; Himmler's address to army officers, January 1937. At the end of 1930 there were still only 400 permanently enrolled SS men and 1,500 part-timers.

building up of an information service under Heydrich could there be traced the future role of the SS as a secret police force. The intrigues that brought this about did not begin till after the seizure of power, and will be studied in the next chapter. In the meantime Himmler established himself as a member of Hitler's court, not as a potential police chief but as a diplomatist. It was a modest achievement and it did not bring Himmler very close to the source of power. Himmler in fact never became intimate with Hitler.

The background of Himmler's diplomatic mission was as follows: The lifting of the ban on the SA and SS on 15 July 1932, after von Schleicher had become Reich Chancellor, had produced a wave of terrorism of which the Altona riots and the Potempa murder were the worst examples. The conservative business circles who had supported Hitler began to feel alarm. On the eve of his triumph Hitler was menaced with the withdrawal of his sources of finance and it is said that towards the end of the year SA men were out on the streets begging passers-by 'to give something to the wicked Nazis'.[1] More perhaps than the public outrages, the party's unrepentant economic policy, as announced by Gottfried Feder and Otto Wagener, had contributed to the falling off of financial support. In August 1932 Hitler got rid of Gottfried Feder after Schacht and Walter Funk, Hitler's future ministers for economic affairs, had warned him against Feder's Social Credit schemes.[2] But Feder's disciple, Otto Wagener, continued to advise on economic policy and was in fact not dismissed till three months after Hitler had become Chancellor. Wagener's successor, Wilhelm Keppler, was not a politician but a business man. Moreover, Keppler, who represented Germany at the World Economic Congress in London in June 1933, had been introduced to Hitler by Himmler.

This was the closest link with Hitler that Himmler had yet achieved and Keppler's ascendancy at court did not end till 1936, when Goering became Hitler's economic genius with the creation of the four-year economic recovery plan. Keppler continued to serve Himmler, who employed him during the war to administer confiscated industries for the SS in Poland and Russia. It was Keppler who founded the circle of potential financial backers, known as 'The Friends of the Reichsfuehrer SS'.[3]

In 1931 or 1932, when Hitler made the acquaintance of Keppler,

[1] Bullock, op. cit., 218.   [2] *Ibid.*, p. 198.
[3] Nuremberg, Case XI, transcript of judgment 28,440-7, 28,599, and 28,794.

Himmler was engrossed in the creation of the SS code of racial selection and eugenic marriage, and was earning the reputation of an intellectual crank who need not be taken seriously. That Keppler, who made himself the liaison man of the business world with the party, should have sought out Himmler of all people appears on the face of it curious. But Himmler's views on racial selection had begun to appeal to the sons of the aristocracy who wanted a place in the coming political party. It was these years which saw an incursion of princes, barons, and counts into the SS. Through Himmler Keppler was introduced to Hitler, and on 9 December 1932 Hitler sent Keppler to the house of the Cologne banker, Kurt von Schroeder, to arrange a meeting with Franz von Papen.[2] Both Himmler and Keppler attended the meeting, where, though von Papen protests the contrary, it seems probable that a joint Chancellorship was proposed to Hitler in order to bring about the overthrow of von Schleicher.[1] In any case through Keppler's introduction to von Schroeder funds were made available and it was no longer necessary for the SA to beg for 'the wicked Nazis'.

After the negotiations had been embarrassed by a leakage in the press, it was Himmler who got them resumed through a second intermediary whose career Himmler thereby assisted, though he was to regret it for the rest of his life. Joachim Ribbentrop was a man to commend himself to von Papen, because he had only joined the party in the last few months and because as a wine salesman he frequented impeccable monarchist and anti-Bolshevik circles. Himmler and Keppler knew—and as yet this knowledge was not very general—that Hitler had got beyond the stage of using Ribbentrop simply to read foreign newspapers to him. Hitler had begun to attend the dinner parties of Anneliese Ribbentrop, née Henkel, the champagne heiress. The Ribbentrops' Dahlem villa on the Lenze Allee was therefore the ideal spot for secret conferences, and of these there were several in January 1933. At all these meetings between Hitler and von Papen Himmler and Keppler were present. Anneliese Ribbentrop carefully recorded the dates and they are published in her edition of her husband's papers.[2]

The significance of the meetings was that here was concocted

---

[1] Bullock, op. cit., p. 220; Heiden, op. cit., p. 520; Von Papen, *Memoirs* (London, 1952), p. 227; IMT,XVI, pp. 329-35.
[2] Paul Seabury, *The Wilhelmstrasse* (Berkeley, 1954), pp. 48-9; *Ribbentrop Memoirs*, pp. 22, 29.

the plot through which the aged Hindenburg was induced to give his presidential sanction to a Hitler-Papen government. On 18 January Ribbentrop proposed bringing Oskar von Hindenburg, the President's son, and he duly arrived on the 22nd. Oskar von Hindenburg persuaded his father six days later to dismiss von Schleicher.[1] On the strength of this meeting both Ribbentrop and Goering were to boast that they had achieved the impossible in obtaining Hindenburg's support for the despised Austrian or Czech corporal. Perhaps Himmler, too, could claim his share in this feat,[2] though he never mentioned it in his recorded speeches.

Keppler was not the only link between Himmler and Hitler in his complex manœuvres for power in 1930-33. Walter Darré, the future Minister of Agriculture, had figured as early as 1928 in a shadow Nazi cabinet and in March 1930 he had published as part of the party's official policy a scheme for alleviating the burdens of small farmers. Darré's views, like Gottfried Feder's, were too Socialist for Hitler, and before his final dismissal from the Ministry of Agriculture in May 1942 he was more than once in trouble. But in 1930-31 he helped Hitler to capture the agricultural vote, having impressed him with his book *Um Blud und Boden*, which came out in 1929.

Some of the theories which Darré expressed in his book have a strong affinity with Himmler's, such as the view that certain soils produce natural peasant aristocracies. Mr. Frischauer thinks that Himmler made Darré's acquaintance as early as 1927 when he was still a poultry farmer.[3] In 1931 Darré joined the SS in order to found for Himmler a queer little office called 'Race and Settlement', Rassen und Siedlungshauptamt, or RUSHA. This office was devoted to research into German racial survivals in Europe. Under the Nazi system it expanded into a bureau which decided the claims of alleged racial Germans abroad to German citizenship. In October 1939 Darré used this office for a totally different purpose, the dispossession

[1] Blackmail pressure was denied by Oskar von Hindenburg at his denazification trial in March 1949 (Bullock, p. 224). The story goes that Hindenburg had evaded tax payments on the estate given him by the German nation at Neudeck, and that Hitler offered to stop an inquiry (Heiden, p. 533; Wheeler-Bennett, *The Nemesis of Power* (London, 1953), pp. 275, 279).

[2] There may be an oblique reference in the remark Gregor Strasser made to Hans Frank in November 1932: 'Hitler seems to me now to be entirely in the hands of his Himmlers and Anhimmlers' (Hans Frank, *Im Angesicht des Galgens*, p. 108).　　　[3] Frischauer, *Himmler, the Evil Genius of the Third Reich*.

of Polish farmers. Later, when it had passed out of Darré's hands, RUSHA was exploited to even worse purposes in the name of selecting and resettling alleged Germanic stock.[1]

Thus Darré developed into a sort of lesser Himmler, but in 1931 he was a major influence on the Reichsfuehrer of the SS, who was six years younger than himself. The peculiar marriage code which was rigorously enforced throughout the history of the SS from its publication in January 1932 derived from Darré's passion for blood categories and the grading of women. These were Himmler's great preoccupations in the days when there were only a few SS men, who had to pay for their own boots and black trousers.[2] Darré may well be regarded as Himmler's evil genius, who taught him how tribal prejudice could be turned into a cult which killed millions of people in concentration camps and deportation marches. But on 8 August 1953, when Darré died in a Munich clinic, *The Times* preferred to treat the charge lightly. *The Times* touched lightly, too, on Darré's five years in prison after the war, while devoting only gentle irony to his books and theories. He was once again *Herr* Darré.

[1] See *infra*, pp. 129, 131, etc.

[2] See *infra*, p. 72. The marriage code was known as the *Heiratsgenehmigung* or SS order, No. 65, and the full text is contained in the Organization Book of the National Socialist party. Presented at Nuremberg as document PS 2640, the German text will be found in the American (Nuremberg) edition of the proceedings, Vol. XXX, page 134. All requests to marry by members of the SS had to be approved by the Racial Office which then formed part of Darré's RUSHA. Both parties to the marriage were expected to show proof of Aryan ancestry as far back as 1750 and proof of hereditary soundness of constitution. The SS man's bride had to submit to a medical examination and provide testimonials as to her philosophy of life.

2

The SS as a Political Police

1. HEYDRICH AND THE SD

The year 1931 was not only the year of the codification of the SS rules, it was also the year that Heydrich came to Munich to organise Himmler's secret political police, the future Gestapo.

Reinhard Heydrich was born in March 1904, the son of Bruno Heydrich, a well-known teacher of music from the Dresden Conservatoire who had settled in Halle. Thus Heydrich came from social surroundings identical with those of Himmler, but the two boys could scarcely have grown up more diversely. Heydrich was theatrically and almost effeminately handsome. He was slick and showy whereas Himmler was awkward and over-modest. Heydrich was one of those gifted beings who can do perfectly whatever they set out to accomplish. A restless ambition to excel at any price dogged him through his short life, so that he could not only play the violin, ski, fence, and pilot an aeroplane to perfection but he was also prepared to undertake any office.

Yet this slick quality was not the key to Heydrich's personality. He was—far more than Himmler—a misfit. Even among the unexacting company of Himmler's staff the sociable Felix Kersten found Heydrich a lonely figure[1] who was forced to spend his evenings with a few chosen toadies in the Berlin *boîtes de nuit* which had survived the Nazi revolution through his good offices. Among these heavy tasteless delights Himmler's Intelligence Chief seemed by nature to belong, a night-club king in politics. Sometimes Heydrich's sullen figure in menacing black SS uniform and varnished boots would be pointed out fearfully to foreign journalists as they sipped their bad brandy at inconspicuous tables. They would be told that they had just seen the most dangerous man in Germany.[2]

Heydrich did not like official gatherings and he was rarely seen in public in the light of day except at SS rallies and at the picnics and outings which Himmler's staff were expected to attend. To find his

[1] Kersten, *Totenkopf und Treue*, p. 119.
[2] Howard Daniel in *Who*, February 1942.

photograph during the prewar years it is necessary to consult the
files of *Das Schwarze Korps*, an illustrated weekly paper for SS men
which from April 1935 onwards Heydrich largely directed himself.
Thus Heydrich received next to no international publicity and was
no doubt grateful for it. A life, closely partitioned between the office
desk and the companions of night, was an asset to a Secret Police
chief. British Military Intelligence knew well whom they were killing
in May 1942, but the British public only knew that the Protector of
Bohemia-Moravia, the hangman of Prague, had died. They did not
know that a British bomb had extinguished the creator of the
Gestapo and the extermination squads, the appointed executioner
of the Jewish race.

Heydrich, whom men were reluctant to meet, is an elusive personality to reconstruct. If such a person is capable of happiness, he
came nearest to it in his evening pleasures. He was ill at ease in the
company of prominent persons and inclined to show off. At Ribbentrop's dinner to Molotov and Dekanazov on 12 November 1939 he
found himself seated next to the fastidious von Papen, who believed
that Heydrich meant to murder him. Heydrich started a bright
conversation by observing that he felt nearer the Almighty in an
aeroplane than in a church.[1] In order to observe his reactions, he
described to Felix Kersten a plan for a homosexual brothel for
distinguished foreign visitors.[2] In such anecdotes one perceives the
high-pitched voice and anxious glance of the true exhibitionist.

Hans Gisevius, who had uncomfortable dealings with Heydrich
and who is at least a first-hand witness, does not share the general
view that Heydrich was a cynic. To him Heydrich was less of a
hypocrite than Himmler. In spite of his brutality, he was the real
idealist of the SS and the things that he practised were part of his
ideal of the good German.[3] It seems to be a common habit, not
confined to Germany, to regard any *idée fixe* as idealism, particularly if it is a brutal one. Heydrich loved power for its own sake and
he found that the herd instincts, which served it best, were envy,
intolerance, and sadism.

Externally Heydrich had to conform to Himmler's SS code, pagan
but in its own way moral. He had to marry and sire from an approved
piece of pedigree German livestock the requisite number of biologic-
ally adequate children. In 1932, within a few months of joining the

[1] Von Papen, *Memoirs*, p. 467.   [2] *Totenkopf und Treue*, p. 125.
[3] Hans Gisevius, *To the Bitter End* (London, 1948), p. 149.

SS, he married the daughter of a schoolmaster on the Baltic island of Fehmarn. In this way he became the owner of a pleasant holiday home. According to Walter Schellenberg, Lina Heydrich, who bore him two sons, led a miserable frightened life.[1] Willi Hoettl, who knew less about it, says that Heydrich's wife 'belonged to the type of evil, ambition-ridden women who are described in German legends'.[2] In July 1953 Lina Heydrich was still living with her two sons on Fehmarn, having won after some protest in the Bonn parliament a pension from the Schleswig insurance office. As the widow of an SS general 'killed in action', Lina Heydrich receives £10 a month. She was also awarded £1,000 in respect of eight years' arrears.[3]

Not only von Papen but almost everyone who held office in Hitler's government believed that Heydrich planned to murder him. Since the war it is as important in Germany to show that one's name was on Heydrich's list as it is to show that one belonged to the Resistance movement. Undoubtedly Heydrich inspired a great deal of fear, a fear not so much of his person as of the position which the guardians of German law had permitted him to occupy. Men like Frick, the Minister of the Interior, Guertner, the Minister of Justice, and Hans Frank, the party adviser on law, knew very well what were the safeguards of the subject's liberty and security. Heydrich was a Frankenstein's monster, produced negatively by their craven passivity. Those who crossed Heydrich's path found an unimpressive figure, a coarse-mouthed blusterer, unadroit and unsure of himself. Captain Payne-Best, interrogated by Heydrich shortly after his abduction from the Dutch border,[4] saw him 'literally foam at the mouth. At all events he sprayed me liberally with his saliva'.[5] And Captain Payne-Best remembered the dry comment of Mueller, the head of the Gestapo: 'Soup is never eaten as hot as it is cooked'.

It seems to have been common gossip that Heydrich was half a Jew. If it was true, there was little in Heydrich's physical appearance to betray it. He had straight and abundant blond hair, a smooth razor-edged face with a nose particularly straight and vertical, and

---

[1] Extract from Schellenberg's memoirs published as *Die grosse Moerder GmbH. Aus den Aufzeichnungen des Oberst Z vom SD:* magazine *Quick*, Munich, 13 September 1953.

[2] Hagen (Hoettl), *Die geheime Front*, p. 28.   [3] *The Times*, 9 July 1953.

[4] See *infra*, p. 14.

[5] Payne-Best, *The Venlo Incident* (London, 1950), p. 42.

sensual bluish lips. His small pale eyes were rather hooded and his ears heavy-lobed, degenerate characteristics but not un-Germanic. As a boy in Halle his looks had been no bar to his joining a violently anti-Semitic Freikorps association, known as the Deutschvoelkische Jugendschar,[1] the German racial league of youth. Yet the legend of Heydrich's Jewish origin was so persistent that, if one may credit Willi Hoettl, he had to fight three libel actions in 1934, 1935 and 1937. The first action was against a Halle baker who had declared that Bruno Heydrich had married a half Jewess. When Heydrich won, the baker deposed that Heydrich's birth certificate had been forged. It was then discovered that Heydrich had used his position as head of the Security service to abstract from the Halle registry all the entries for March 1904. After the third libel action Heydrich had a new tombstone made for his grandmother's grave in Leipzig which omitted the name Sarah.[2]

No such publicity surrounded Heydrich when he came to Himmler in Munich in 1931. But later it was to be one of Himmler's habits to pick men who could be blackmailed or easily eliminated, when it came to choosing the personnel for the appalling tasks demanded by his and Hitler's Rassenpolitik. Heydrich was possibly the first of a long line which included Eichmann, Globocnik and Hoess of Auschwitz concentration camp. Thus Hoettl provided a sequel to the story of Heydrich's first libel action, according to which Himmler rescued from Heydrich's clutches the lawyer who had defended the Halle baker. But at the beginning of the war this lawyer joined the Abwehr, or Military Intelligence service, and delivered all his material on Heydrich's case to his chief, Heydrich's bitterest rival, Admiral Canaris. Thus Canaris was able to blackmail Himmler as well as Heydrich.[3]

Such stories are not all fantasy, for under Hitler's system of government it was practically impossible to attain office and to remain in office without using blackmail. Hitler's own electioneering tactics set the standard which his followers adopted. And in dealing with Heydrich Himmler himself showed the way. In August 1942, soon after Heydrich's death, Felix Kersten learnt from his patient Himmler that Hitler had known the whole story. 'He told me that the rumour was true and that he had reported it to Hitler when he first became chief of the Bavarian Political Police [that is in January

---

[1] Waite, op. cit., p. 286. [2] Hagen, *Die geheime Front*, p. 20.
[3] *Ibid.*, pp. 111-12, and see *infra*, p. 237.

1933]. Hitler, however, had regarded this fact as an advantage since Heydrich's gifts were of so dangerous a kind that they could only be used if one had a handle over him. Hitler had considered that Heydrich's vulnerability made him specially suitable for the action against the Jews, the task that no one would accept'.[1]

Here then we have the second clue to Heydrich's career. The first was his ambition as an Intelligence officer, forced to leave the navy, his ambition to command all the Intelligence services of the Reich, both within the country and without; to pull the strings of international politics through his secret agents, to make wars and to unmake kings. The appalling act which will be for ever linked with Heydrich's name, the destruction of the Jewish people, though he accepted it without reluctance, was only a fatigue duty. To carry it out efficiently gave Heydrich some satisfaction for the fact that Hitler had trapped him. Just as Heydrich, a part Jew or a reputed one, had been made to assume this guilt, so he made the Jews their own executioners. Hitler, so Himmler went on to tell Kersten in that memorable conversation, knew of Heydrich's hatred for his own Jewish blood.[2] And Heydrich knew of others who had this pathological Jewish self-hate. He ferreted them out with his infallible scent, the Globocniks, Eichmanns, Knochens, Danneckers, and Brunners, those doubtful Aryan types who had got themselves enmeshed in the SS and its Security service.

But while Heydrich permitted himself a cynical enjoyment of the plight of underlings who were made to share his position, he had a genuine enthusiasm for his foreign secret service. It was a religion to him, and if he had survived the war he would no doubt have written a pedantic treatise on the subject, for the blackmailer and night-club king had literary ambitions. In addition to an introduction to Artur Nebe's treatise on the criminal police, Heydrich published in 1935 a pamphlet called *Wandlungen unseres Kampfes*, which Franz Eher, the party publisher, and Max Mueller, Hitler's printer, brought out for the price of twenty pfennigs. It is only twenty pages in length and small enough to go into a trouser pocket, but none the less unreadable. Still, it offers some insight into Heydrich's one idealism. In terms almost of pathos he begs the German public to sympathise with the SD man's eavesdropping role, quite the reverse of Himmler's recurring theme, 'we do not expect to be loved'.[3]

[1] *Totenkopf und Treue*, p. 128.   [2] *Ibid.*, p. 131.
[3] Karl Paetel in *Vierteljahreshefte fuer Zeitgeschichte* (Stuttgart, 1954), II, 1, p. 10.

Otto Ohlendorf, who had run Heydrich's Information service for many years, told Felix Kersten that Heydrich's great exemplar was England, where the secret service was an affair not of paid agents but of patriots.[1]

'Every decent Englishman is in the employment of the secret service without any need to be specially sworn in and he considers it his natural duty to report to it, inasmuch as the power of England depends basically on the secret service, since the victor is he who is best informed. . . . .

'The English system of Information service as a gentlemanly career is the ideal of the SS. Himmler knows that in this matter he has to combat many prejudices such as Germans are inclined to oppose to any Information service. The Germans see in an Information service an organised system of denunciation. Heydrich made it his business to overcome this prejudice. He made the Information service a service of honour (Ehrendienst)'.

It is possible that Heydrich really believed that spying for a party political police in peacetime was regarded in England as just as honourable as spying for the nation in time of war. At any rate the basis of his system was not to separate the two functions. Nice-mannered young embassy attachés abroad during the Second World War were as likely as not to be members of the Gestapo. Conversely, the cream of the Intelligence service, who should have been following the intricacies of the Resistance movement in Germany, wasted their time reporting the names of people who presented illicit bread coupons or who remarked that the Fuehrer never went near the bombs. Thus the whole conception of a universal and united secret service was muddle-headed from the start.

But in 1931 Himmler must have taken very strongly to Heydrich's theories. Anything that called itself an Ehrendienst must have been very heady wine to him. As a naval officer Heydrich had already had experience of the kind of Intelligence service Himmler wanted. Heydrich had been Intelligence officer to the Baltic command. When Captain Canaris had held this post, he had used it as a former member of the Freikorps to continue the work of Ehrhardt's Vehmgericht, ferreting out the names of those who had revealed hidden arms to gain favour with the Allied Control Commission. Canaris, who was later to be Heydrich's commander on the training ship *Niobe*, influenced him a great deal, and there can be little doubt that Canaris formed Heydrich's taste for this sort of thing. But Heydrich's career as a naval Intelligence officer ended with his

[1] Kersten, op. cit., p. 266.

mysterious resignation at the age of twenty-seven, and, when he next encountered Canaris, it was as a too successful rival for Hitler's favour.[1]

Heydrich resigned his commission in the summer of 1931. The popular Gestapo legend on the subject, as recounted by Willi Hoettl,[2] was that Admiral Raeder had forced him to do so when he refused to marry the daughter of a shipbuilder whom he had compromised. It was easy to turn this into the victimisation of a National Socialist officer and a post was found for Heydrich in Hamburg and then at Koenigsberg, where Koch was Gauleiter. There are several versions as to why Heydrich left Koch for Himmler. According to one of them, Koch discovered an intrigue with his wife. According to another, Heydrich made Koch recommend him to Himmler by threatening to disclose his correspondence with Gregor Strasser.[3]

At this time, the autumn of 1931, the party was ravaged with spy mania. Since the Berlin SA revolt in April many SA leaders were suspected of contacts in Prague with Otto Strasser's Black Front. As to Gregor Strasser, who stayed in Berlin, he had not completely broken with Hitler, but he opposed Hitler's union with Hugenberg and the German National Conservative bloc as well as Hitler's candidature for the presidency. The followers of both Strassers had therefore to be watched. Heydrich persuaded Himmler that he needed an Intelligence service and he proposed to begin by detaching the Information officers—in plainer words, informers—from their respective SS units and forming them into a new arm to be known as the Sicherheitsdienst, the Security service or SD.

The Security service official Willi Hoettl, who follows the tradition of his office in never betraying his sources, asserts that in 1931 Heydrich already intended to get the SD established as the unique information service of the party, that he had persuaded Himmler to use the SD as soon as Hitler acquired power, in order to screen the Bavarian political police and that he meant Himmler to take over this force as the nucleus of a secret political police for all Germany. It is Hoettl's thesis that Heydrich was able to use Himmler

---

[1] The evidence for any continuity in naval Intelligence work between Canaris and Heydrich derives from an interview between Mr. Ian Colvin and a former member of Canaris's staff, Richard Protze. Ian Colvin, *Chief of Intelligence* (London, 1952), p. 15 (see *infra*, p. 93).

[2] Hagen, op. cit., p. 13.

[3] *Ibid.*, and Howard Daniel in *Who*, February 1942.

throughout as a puppet, but this is not borne out by the order of
events, for while Himmler acquired the Bavarian political police as
soon as Hitler came to power, Heydrich's SD was only recognised
as the unique party Intelligence service on 6 June 1934.[1]

The significance of this story is that there existed a purely political
police both in Munich and Berlin in the days of the Weimar Republic.
The Gestapo, which was the direct successor of the political police,
was in fact a product of the Weimar Constitution of 1919, conceived
in the double fear of Bolshevism and Freikorps anarchy. The Weimar
political police was an instrument waiting for a dictator to come
along and use it. Most of the permanent officials of the political
police, both in Berlin and in Munich, stayed at their posts in spite
of Himmler's and Heydrich's purges—and they included Heinrich
Mueller, who remained chief of the Gestapo throughout the war.

The continuity of the political police and the Gestapo should be
remembered against the very faulty current assessments of Weimar
democracy. Deprived of the finely evolved balance of a two-party
system, the Weimar Republic had constantly to resort to force in
internal affairs. The case of Karl Severing, Social Democrat Minister
of the Interior in the Prussian cabinet, is eloquent enough. In April
1920 he authorised the Freikorps to march against the Communists
in the Ruhr.[2] In October 1923 he sent the Prussian Black Reichswehr
into the 'Bolshevik' state of Thuringia. Finally, on 20 July 1932, he
was accused of seeking Communist support and thrown out of his
office by a police captain and five constables, acting under the orders
of that idol of military men, General Gerd von Rundstedt, commander of Military Area III. And this too was done quite legally
under article 48 of the Weimar Constitution, which permitted the
President to govern by emergency decree.[3] Against this background,
so unlike that of any true parliamentary country, political policemen
take their natural place.

Heydrich used the SD to screen the Bavarian political police in
February 1933, as soon as Hitler was made Chancellor. Some indeed
of the officials of this office, Amt VI in the Munich Police Praesidium,
lost their jobs, but the Gestapo witnesses at Nuremberg were agreed
that the staffs selected for the Gestapo, both in Munich and Berlin,
consisted exclusively of members of the former Political, Criminal

---

[1] Frischauer, op. cit., p. 64.   [2] Waite, op. cit., p. 178.
[3] Von Papen, *Memoirs*, p. 255; IMT, XIV, p. 265.

and State police.[1] As late as 1938 it was found that all but ten or fifteen out of a hundred Gestapo men in Coblenz had joined the police under the Weimar Republic.[2] Thus was demolished the myth that the inquisitors of the Gestapo were a new race of men, a scum brought to the surface by revolution. A policeman is the last sort of being to reject totalitarian rule, and rare indeed are the policemen who have sacrificed their careers for freedom of speech and opinion. Nor was it a good moment to quit the police when the uniform and red trousers of a colonel-general were to be won in its more profitable ramifications. Though it was not centralised, the pre-Hitler German police was run on military lines. It was armed and its ranks were named after those of the army. After 1918 many demobilised officers who later commanded fighting divisions of the Waffen SS, joined the Schutzpolizei, a riot police which operated in military formations—particularly when they failed to remain in the disbanded Freikorps or to return to the hundred thousand strong 'Versailles' army. Thus in the early 'twenties the German police were built up into what was virtually a second Reichswehr, doubling the size of the standing army which was permitted by the Allies.

Naturally such a police force as this had little to fear from the screening of Himmler and Heydrich. The Security service official, Colonel Willi Hoettl, thinks that Heydrich deliberately chose non-Nazis for the political police, preferring practised police spies to party idealists. And Hoettl contrasts Heydrich's suspicion of the Hitler-intoxicated Werner Best, one of the first adherents of the SD, with his fondness for Heinrich Mueller, a member of the anti-Nazi Bavarian Volkspartei.[3] When war broke out, all Gestapo officials had to have an SS rank. It was then discovered that Mueller, the head of the Gestapo, had never joined the party and that the party office were not anxious to admit him.

Who was this Heinrich Mueller who remained for ten years the embodiment of the cold, dispassionate, ever-ready police chief? It seems almost as if his life's study was to avoid being known. One personal impression is interesting because it comes from an Englishman, Captain Payne-Best.[4]

Mueller was a dapper, exceptionally good-looking little man, dressed in imitation of Adolf Hitler in a grey uniform jacket, black riding breeches and

[1] IMT, XXI, pp. 267-9.   [2] IMT, XXI, p. 165.
[3] Hagen, op. cit., p. 161.   [4] The Venlo Incident, pp. 26-7.

top-boots . . . he had rather funny eyes which he could flicker from side to side
with the greatest rapidity and I suppose that this was supposed to strike terror
into the beholder.

Other accounts of interviews, notably those of Erwin Lahousen and
Walter Dornberger,[1] suggest a dull unreasoning obstinacy, bordering
on stupidity, while the edited fragment of Schellenberg's memoirs
conveys only cold murderous hatred. In all probability Mueller was
a mediocrity. Since Heinrich Mueller was last seen in Hitler's bunker
on 29 April 1945, fantastic rumours of his survival have been current,
including several to the effect that he is employed by the Russian
secret police, whose methods he once studied.[2]

For a year after it had been screened by the SD, the Munich
political police retained its old name of Amt VI as part of a police
Praesidium, controlled by Himmler. But as Himmler acquired
control of the political police office in one federal state after another,
so they were handed over to Heydrich, the Berlin office not till April
1934 and others as late as 1935. On 26 June 1936 the executive force,
serving the amalgamated offices, became known as the Sicherheitspolizei, the Security Police or SIPO. Heydrich's title was henceforward Chief of the Security Police and SD. Subordinate chiefs were
either Befehlshaber or Kommandeure, known in official correspondence as BdS and KdS. 'SIPO and SD' became a single term, but it
retained the fiction that the SD had an individual existence.

There was a twofold reason for this mystification. Firstly officials
from the original SD liked to protest that they were an Information
Service, unconnected with arrests, and secondly Heydrich tried to
keep this group of officials removed from Himmler's authority since
the SD was not a government department but a party 'Gliederung'.[3]
This situation, however, came to an end at the beginning of the war,
when the SD became Amt III of the newly formed Reich Main
Security Office.[4]

Even after this the SD tried to maintain that it was separate from
the executive, and never so strongly as in the Nuremberg witness-
box. Otto Ohlendorf was able to show that under his rule Amt III
was capable of independent behaviour. As late as 1943 Ohlendorf
came into collision with Heydrich's successor, Kaltenbrunner, as
well as with Himmler on account of the objective quality of the

[1] IMT, I, p. 279; Major-General Walter Dornberger, "V2", London 1954.
[2] Walter Hagen (Hoettl), *The Secret Front* (London, 1954), pp. 5, 310-15.
[3] IMT, XX, p. 171.   [4] See *infra*, p. 138.

daily 'SD reports'. Goebbels, too, tried to stop these reports, but they went on till the end of the war,[1] probably because they were useful to Mueller, and to Martin Bormann of whom everyone was afraid. Ohlendorf did not like to hear his SD or Amt III office confused with the Gestapo,[2] but his own career as a leader of an extermination group of the SIPO and SD in Russia shows that the separation was a myth. Some of the SD defendants went so far as to declare at Nuremberg that they had joined these expeditions to Russia out of scientific curiosity, but by this time the Tribunal had already ruled that as a criminal organisation the SD ranked with the Gestapo.[3]

The great 'Einsatzgruppen' trial of 1947-8, perhaps the most dramatic of the twelve later Nuremberg war trials, dragged into the daylight a queer assortment of the membership of Heydrich's SD. Among the twenty-one defendants the only common denominator was that nearly all had been to a university and the majority had achieved the doctorate so dear to the German middle class. 'Displaced intellectual' is their best description, for what else could Heydrich's shifty and muddle-headed system have attracted?[4] An architect who took to drink, an unfrocked parson, a fallen opera singer, and an unemployed dentist, all were typical of the Gestapo's Information service. The true revelation of the trial, however, was not these bankrupt lives, but those of two men who had done the work of massacre behind the lines of the front in the middle of careers of exceptional academic brilliance.

The don who becomes an Intelligence officer or Secret Service agent is, after two world wars, a familiar figure. The don who becomes a copper's nark for a political police in peacetime is less so. We have already seen that Heydrich was determined to make no distinction between the two roles. It would nevertheless be difficult to understand how men like Otto Ohlendorf and Franz Six could have so prostituted their talents, were it not that their story is so essentially German. At all times and in all countries university professors have meddled in politics, but nowhere in such a sinister way as in Germany since the later nineteenth century. The formulation of philosophical or economic theories, gratifying to the power groups of the day, was a *sine qua non* of office long before the Nazis. Under

---

[1] *The Goebbels Diaries*, pp. 4, 158, 258, 293.
[2] Kersten, op. cit., pp. 255-60, 264.   [3] See *infra*, p. 116.
[4] See *infra*, p. 181.

National Socialism the ill paid lecturer, rewarded as a sound party man with a professorship and a handsome extra-mural appointment, was in a position from which it was very untempting to retire. Such in particular was the case of Professor Six of Heydrich's SD. He came to Heidelberg University in 1930 at the age of nineteen, and for the next four years lived there on twenty shillings a month—as sound a reason as any for joining a revolutionary party. In 1935 Himmler's economic adviser, Professor Hoehn, persuaded the young Doctor of Philosophy to enter the SD as a 'reporter on scientific matters'.[1] Promotion now came swiftly. By 1938 Six was not only head of the SD's 'Cultural Activities' section, but at the age of twenty-seven a full-fledged professor and dean of a new faculty in Berlin University, devoted to foreign affairs. Till October 1941, as a professor and Sturmbannfuehrer or major of the SS, he taught his pupils to distinguish between decadent states, which were governed by the majority and doomed to perish, and 'Fuehrer principle' states which were destined to rejuvenate themselves with new strength.[2] Then the SD claimed him for greater things. Heydrich promised Six that he would not have to shoot anyone, but only sort archives in the Kremlin. Neither the German army nor Professor Six reached the Kremlin and his research team was kept in Smolensk identifying captured commissars for execution.[3] Then back to the Cultural Activities section in Berlin. In April 1943 Ribbentrop wanted an SS man who was also a professor of foreign affairs, and Six's section was transferred to the Foreign Office,[4] where he helped to plan a gigantic pan-European anti-Semitic congress which was cancelled after the Allied landings in Normandy. The Americans released the professor from Landsberg at the end of 1951. How strange that he should be only forty-five years old now.

Both Six and Ohlendorf were brought into the SD by Himmler's court economist, Professor Hoehn. To judge from their Nuremberg evidence, both men found the SD of the middle 'thirties a quaint little backwater of research and a haven of rest for unwanted economists. It had been Ohlendorf's ambition to found, in conjunction with his friend Professor Peter Jessen, an institute for the

[1] Trial evidence of Franz Six in François Bayle, *Psychologie et ethique du National-Socialisme* (Paris, 1953), p.102.

[2] Rainer Hildebrandt, *Wir sind die Letzten* (Berlin, 1947), p. 138.

[3] Affidavit Franz Six, *Nuremberg Document* NO. 4546.

[4] See *infra*, p. 236.

scientific study of National Socialism and Fascism. They had tried unsuccessfully to introduce this curriculum both at Jessen's university, Kiel, and at Berlin. Finally Jessen passed Ohlendorf on to Hoehn.[1] Eventually Heydrich threw off the influence of the academic minds of Hoehn and Jessen, but he held on tight to Ohlendorf. Behind the man's pedantic mania for regarding everything as an object of scientific analysis he scented the Grand Inquisitor.

This air of an institute for learned research disguised a huge expansion of the spheres of activity of the SD which had taken place since the blood-purge of 30 June 1934. Even at the critical time of Hitler's struggle for the Chancellorship, twenty or thirty members of the SD had been sufficient to report on 'political rivals', that is to say Roehm and the Strassers.[2] After the blood-purge the SD was reserved for a wider range of state enemies, the Church, the Jews, the Freemasons, and the hidden Marxists. Yet the SD had still to compete with other agencies and its growth was slow. In May 1936, said Ohlendorf, 'the whole central organisation consisted of about twenty young people without any office building'.[3] At the beginning of the war the SD was incorporated into the newly-formed Reich Main Security Office (RSHA), an amalgamation of all Heydrich's offices, including the Gestapo and Criminal Police. As 'Amt III' the SD became a typical overgrown wartime government department, a grave of the intelligentsia, sheltering hundreds and even thousands of shady *embusqué* characters.

2. THE BIRTH OF THE GESTAPO

On 31 January 1933, the day of the seizure of power, Heydrich's twenty or thirty SD men and his newly acquired Bavarian political police did not amount to very much. How came it then that within seventeen months Heydrich's organisation was strong enough to set the SS against their blood brothers of the SA, who were ten times as numerous, and with decisive results? In brief it was because of the support of Hermann Goering, but the story cannot be told in very precise and crisp terms, since Himmler and Heydrich built up the striking arm of their political police in secret and, after more than twenty years, little of the secret has leaked out.

In the distribution of offices on 31 January 1933, Himmler became

[1] Private interrogation of Ohlendorf in Bayle, p. 38.
[2] IMT, XX, p. 183.   [3] Ohlendorf's evidence, Case IX, transcript, p. 491.

police president for Bavaria. It was a minor appointment, but Himmler, except for his role in reviving the von Papen negotiations, was not a member of Hitler's inner council nor had the post of Reichsfuehrer SS any significance as yet. The Berlin SS men had not greatly distinguished themselves in dealing with the SA rebellions of September 1930 and April 1931. They were not relied on to meet the perils of the eventful day of the seizure of power when Hitler expected the doomed Chancellor, Kurt von Schleicher, to organise a military Putsch. Hitler relied on Major Wecke's six military-trained battalions of Prussian state police, who had been won over to his side, as well as on the Berlin SA under Roehm's close friend, Wolff Helldorf. Never had Roehm's stock stood higher than at the time of the seizure of power. Even in Munich it was Roehm's close associate Ritter von Epp and not Himmler who was called in to remove the Catholic conservative government of Heinrich Held. This operation, which took place on 8 March, completely ignored Himmler as the new police president of Bavaria. It was a noisy triumph for the SA clique of the Munich Braunehaus, whom Himmler was expected to keep in check.[1]

If this was the situation in Munich, Himmler and Heydrich held still fewer cards in Berlin. It is true that Kurt Daluege, the Berlin SS leader, had been appointed ministerial director of the Prussian police department, but even as an SS leader Daluege did not recognise that Himmler had any authority over him at this time, while as a police chief in the Prussian Ministry of the Interior he came under Goering's direct authority. In Berlin there was deadly rivalry between Goering and Roehm, the latter controlling the streets through his huge 'armband' army of SA men. Although Goering had command of the regular police forces, they were for the time useless, and only in the political police, the so-called Bureau IA, could Goering expect to create a rival terror to Roehm's terror bands. Goering was careful that no Heydrich should get hold of this weapon. He kept it for himself, picking from the permanent political police officials a man on whom he could rely.

The chosen head of the Berlin Police Bureau IA, the future Gestapo, was Rudolf Diels, who had married Goering's cousin and sister-in-law, Ilse Goering. Diels, although he had been employed in the Police Praesidium under the Social Democrat minister, Karl Severing, was a conservative. In July 1932 he had won the approval

[1] Heiden, op. cit., p. 587.

of von Papen by denouncing Severing's negotiations with the Communists.[1] Diel's strong anti-Communist line won him credit at the same time with Goering, to whom he reported a similar conspiracy by the Berlin SA leaders. Thus the future head of the Gestapo, family connections apart, was in every respect a man to appeal to Goering and the anti-revolutionary wing of the Nazi party. In the tussle which culminated in Hitler's blood-purge of June 1934, Diels was cast for a very difficult role. He has described it in his book *Lucifer ante Portas*, a book which is hardly his best testimonial. The best that can be said for Diels is that he was a humane man, but as muddle-headed as his writing and capable of very insincere conduct where his own ambition and his frantic fear of Communism were at stake. He was all too typical of the fumbling grave-diggers of constitutional government in Germany.

Goering's first appearance in the office of the Berlin political police in February 1933 was accompanied by a tirade against the underlings of the hated Karl Severing, but he concluded with the words, 'Naturally I am not going to work like a bull in a china shop'.[2] As a result, most of the eighty Berlin and three hundred provincial officials stayed on, willing as such persons always are to detect subversive activity for any masters. And at least they were united with Goering in resisting both the inquisitions of the by-passed SS man, Daluege, and the riotous incursions of the SA. But it was Goering himself who weakened the position of the office through the hysterical emergency decrees which he issued after the discovery of the so-called Reichstag fire plot.

The purpose of the decrees was to force a working majority for the Nazis in the March elections by creating the shadow of a Communist uprising. The Goering decrees authorised some 25,000 SA men, 15,000 SS men and 10,000 members of the ex-servicemen's Stahlhelm organisation to take over the policing of Berlin at their own discretion, with complete indemnity for the use of their firearms.

The armband army which was protected by the decree of 27 February created a reign of terror such as the German public had not previously witnessed. There were beatings-up in the cellars everywhere and private prisons and concentration camps appeared overnight. During March and April the deliberately provoked orgy

[1] Heiden, p. 473.
[2] Rudolf Diels, *Lucifer ante Portas* (Zurich, 1949), p. 128.

of violence enabled Hitler's cabinet to enforce emergency police rule on the eighteen German 'Laender', where the Gauleiters received special powers and new ministries were hand picked by police presidents. On 23 March a Reichstag, which was deprived of its Communist members by the simple expedient of locking them up, passed the enabling Bill which permitted Hitler to govern indefinitely by emergency decree. All this was done without even a majority vote of the nation for the Nazi party.

Goering, the hero of the Reichstag fire plot and of the emergency decrees, was rewarded. He became Prime Minister of Prussia and Hitler's personal deputy. Yet no one had more cause to be nervous of the new situation than Goering, who had done so much to create it. Hitler favoured a unification of the German police, and Himmler in Munich was already casting his eye on additional police presidencies. At any moment the Prussian Ministry for Police, which was in the hands of the SS man, Daluege, might pass under Himmler's control. Goering hoped to meet this danger by detaching the political police office from the Police Praesidium building in the Alexanderplatz and taking it to a building close to his own headquarters in the Leipzigerplatz. Geographically and politically it was equivalent to moving from the Mansion House to Whitehall. The place chosen for this transplantation was the notorious No. 8 Prinz Albrechtstrasse, the future home of the Gestapo and the Reich Main Security Office. The building, which was destined to be blockaded by insurgents in July 1944 and destroyed by Allied bombs in February 1945, was extremely rambling. It had been a school of arts and crafts, an exhibition centre, and a place of reunion for persons of advanced ideas. It had been denounced as a Communist meeting place, and after the Reichstag fire it was closed by the police.

It remained for Goering, who had just adopted the title of Chief of the Political Police and Chief of the Secret Police, to give this splendid establishment a name. The Secret Political Office, Geheimes Polizei Amt, was suggested. But the initials GPA sounded suspiciously like the Russian GPU. A Post Office official who was asked to design a franking stamp came to the rescue. Why not Geheime Staatspolizei, the Secret State Police or Gestapo—and this was the name under which in June 1933 the Berlin political police, or Bureau IA, was reconstituted. A postman had enriched the common vocabulary of the entire world.[1]

[1] Diels, op. cit., p. 169.

Before its detachment by Goering from the Police Praesidium there had already been a head-on conflict between Diels's office and Himmler. Among the many unofficial concentration camps which sprang up in March 1933 was one run by the SS at Papenburg near Osnabrueck. Diels, as the official responsible for political detentions, tried to discover the position in this camp. At the end of April he sought entry in the company of Guenther Joel, a junior public prosecutor and state secretary in the Ministry of Justice, who was tried as a war criminal in 1947. Diels declares that the SS guards actually opened fire on the Prussian state police who had been sent by Goering. Hitler at once supported Goering and authorised him to blockade the camp till Himmler sent an emissary to negotiate. Hitler even told Diels to borrow artillery from the army to blow the place to pieces.[1] Himmler was thus stirred into action and Papenburg camp capitulated.

This fracas must have been repugnant to the orderly soul of Heinrich Himmler, who prided himself on having created the model concentration camp for political opponents at Dachau, near Munich.[2] The SS lacked central authority and the incident was a warning that Himmler must manœuvre his way into Berlin and there make his peace with Goering. There was, moreover, already a strong SS element, supported by Daluege, in Diels's Gestapo. Its leader was the former chief of the Berlin criminal investigation department, Artur Nebe. Diels regarded Nebe not only as a spy against himself but also as a party to the atrocities which took place in the private SS prison in General Papestrasse, known as 'Colombia House' or 'The Colombia Bar'. On the other hand, Nebe was equally unpopular with Diels's and Goering's opponent, the Chief of Staff of the Berlin SA, the café waiter Karl Ernst.

This complication makes Diels's narrative difficult to follow. Diels would have us believe that his own chief concern was to stop the SA reign of terror in the streets and in the improvised prisons and camps. In fact Diels had been put where he was to establish Goering's position against both the SA and the SS. In neither case was he successful. At the end of August Karl Ernst invaded the office in person, shouted at Nebe and manhandled one of his officials.[3] Diels himself had thereupon to hide from the danger of murder by Ernst's 'Special Service' SA group.

At this despairing moment the conflict between Diels and Ernst

[1] Diels, pp. 193-5.　　　[2] See *infra*, p. 255.　　　[3] Diels, p. 231.

came to an abrupt end. Roehm had decided to make peace with the police as a price for eliminating the growing rivalry of the SS, 'since it was recognised that the future of the police lay in open conflict between Goering and his Diels and Heydrich-Himmler'.[1] In September Karl Ernst offered to make Diels an SA Gruppenfuehrer, but Roehm warned Diels that, since he would attract the enmity of Himmler and Heydrich, he had better 'put on the black uniform of the SS'.[2]

The situation was now changing completely and to Goering's disadvantage. Between October and December 1933 Himmler obtained control of the political police offices in Mecklenburg, Luebeck, Baden, Hesse-Anhalt, and Bremen'[3] Furthermore, Heydrich established an SD office under Hermann Behrends in Berlin, a direct defiance of Goering's authority.

Diels forbade the SD to exercise its activities—at this time they were directed chiefly against Jews and Freemasons—and Goering ordered him to arrest Heydrich if he set foot in Berlin. Diels protested that if he arrested Heydrich Himmler would have him back within an hour. And what would happen to Diels when Heydrich got control of the Berlin political police, as he must do in due course?[4] Heydrich did not in fact come to Berlin for another six months, but the mortal fear which he had created was already deep in the breasts of Diels and other Prussian bureaucrats.

Goering, moreover, failed to support Diels any longer in his fight against SS encroachments. In October Diels kept an SS man, who had directed a raid on the office, under arrest in the Police Praesidium. Goering tamely surrendered the man to Himmler on the ground that he was to be tried by an SS court. Himmler tried to appease the disgruntled Diels with a mere SS lieutenant's uniform, but a few days later Diels found that Goering himself had ordered the SS to arrest him in his own office. For the next five weeks Diels hid in Karlsbad, across the Czechoslovak border, and the office was directed by an SA man, the police president of Altona.

Our second witness on the early history of the Gestapo, Hans Gisevius, admits in his book quite freely that he conspired with the SS interest among the office staff to get Diels removed. Gisevius is a more colourful personality than Diels. A giant in physical stature,

[1] Diels, p. 231.   [2] *Ibid*, p. 236.
[3] Frischauer, op cit., p. 58.   [4] Diels, p. 236.

Gisevius worked in Switzerland in the spring of 1944 for the American Office of Strategic Services, although he was then a member of the German Abwehr or Military Intelligence, which had been taken over by the SS. He returned to Germany to play a disputed role in the July plot, escaped, and returned to Germany again after the war as a witness at the Nuremberg trial, ostensibly on behalf of Hjalmar Schacht and Wilhelm Frick but actually as a prosecution witness against Goering. Gisevius kept the court spellbound with his story of the German Resistance Circle and, furthermore, wrote a book about it which is more exciting than any novel.[1]

No wonder then that Gisevius, who now lives in the USA, was a privileged witness. Mr. Justice Jackson called him 'the one representative of democratic forces in Germany to take this stand to tell his story'. Mr. Allen Dulles, formerly of the US Office of Strategic Services in Switzerland, wrote an introduction to the English translation of Gisevius's book, praising him even more highly. Since those days the story has had to face the light of rival chroniclers. Every line must be sifted with care, since a man who played so many roles does not command unqualified confidence. And if there is one subject on which Gisevius is reticent it is that of his own motives. Why did this staunch conservative, a member of the Stahlhelm and follower of Hugenberg, join the Gestapo in August 1933? Gisevius tells us[2] that it was customary for young men, who had just passed their Bar examination and had become 'assessors', to begin their career as assistants to the political police. It was a remarkable custom, if it is true, but as Professor Rothfels observes, this statement discredits the narrative from the beginning.[3] And if it were true, why should Gisevius have had to smuggle himself past the sentries, as he tells us, in order to get into the building at all?

A still more pertinent question can be asked. Why was Gisevius, who spent four months in the Gestapo office, officially thanked on behalf of Heydrich and Himmler, so that even Daluege, who came down on Himmler's side in the end, told him that he was 'using Beelzebub to drive out the devil'?[4] Gisevius claims that he was thanked for disclosing the profound wickedness of Diels. It seems that in February 1934 Gisevius and Nebe were summoned to

---

[1] Gisevius, *To the Bitter End*, London 1948.   [2] *Ibid*, op. cit., p. 49.
[3] Hans Rothfels, *German Opposition to Hitler* (Chicago, 1948), p. 30.
[4] Gisevius, pp. 146-8.

Lichterfelde barracks by Sepp Dietrich, who commanded the SS Leibstandarte, Hitler's bodyguard. Dietrich thanked them for their fight against corruption in the Gestapo, and invited them to write a report for the benefit of Himmler and Heydrich. They were to disclose all that they knew of excesses committed by the Gestapo and SA. 'What amazing naïve good faith we had!' Gisevius writes. The reader, who has got thus far in Gisevius's book, may think that a man, who planned to throw the Chief of the Gestapo out of the window, was capable of sending reports about him to Himmler and Heydrich for motives other than 'naïve good faith' in their idealism. It may well be, as Werner Schaeffer deposed at Nuremberg,[1] that Diels in his desire to remain friendly with Roehm and Ernst made no effort to interfere with the notorious concentration camp at Oranienburg. But would Gisevius's friends Nebe and Daluege have acted any better? The one was certainly concerned in the creation of the gas chambers[2] and the other in the extermination commandos in Poland. Diels attributed Gisevius's enmity to an ambition to control the Gestapo himself. Willi Hoettl goes even further, suggesting that if Gisevius had succeeded in opposing Heydrich's bid to control the political police throughout Germany, he would have had to stand trial at Nuremberg in place of Heydrich's successor, Kaltenbrunner.[3]

This is putting too high a valuation on the part played by Gisevius in history. He was ambitious and he was jealous of Diels, whom he had known in his student days at Marburg, but this jealousy served other masters. Diels's efforts on behalf of the arrested political opponents, such as these efforts were, brought him up against the party office in the persons of Rudolf Hess, Martin Bormann, and Erich Koch. In the end Goering was persuaded by this group to sacrifice Diels, but he refused their blandishments to hand over the office to the SS and in a very short time he recalled Diels and turned out Gisevius. On 1 December, however, Hitler made Roehm a Reich Minister. This news, intensely alarming to Goering, decided him finally to throw in his lot with Himmler, even at the price of letting him become police chief of Germany.

Gisevius thinks that Goering's hatred of Roehm dated from October 1933 when Roehm stole Goering's thunder at the opening of the Council of State.[4] In reality Goering's jealousy of Roehm, whom he had preceded in time as head of the SA, was much older.

---

[1] IMT, XXI, pp. 122-3.   [2] See *infra*, p. 279.
[3] Hagen, op. cit., p. 20.   [4] Gisevius, op. cit., p. 117.

Goering shared Roehm's ambition to be Commander-in-Chief of a rearmed Germany. Hitler's action in recognising Roehm's position with an award of cabinet rank frightened Goering, who saw in Roehm a rival so unscrupulous that he was capable of overturning the capitalist system to obtain his own ends.

The time had not yet come for Goering to grasp the nettle and hand over the precious Gestapo office to Himmler and Heydrich, but he warned Diels on his return from Karlsbad that he must assist the SS in their search for evidence against Roehm. And Goering advised Diels to accept Himmler's improved offer of an SS colonel's uniform. It was the advice that Roehm had given Diels in the previous September, for Himmler had followed the very cunning SA practice of creating 'Ehrenfuehrer' or bearers of honorary rank.[1] It was based on sound knowledge of the German love of uniform. The German Beamter or civil servant has no hereditary sense of dignity derived from his black coat and white collar. On the contrary, among shiny peaked caps and varnished boots he feels positively naked. The extremely civilian figure of Hjalmar Schacht, president of the Reichsbank, was photographed in the uniform of the customs service and the insignia of a colonel-general.[2] Even Ulrich von Hassell, the Tacitus of the aristocratic Resistance Circle, wore an SA uniform in those strenuous days,[3] while Prince Schaumburg-Lippe, when Goebbels forbade him to do the same, designed a uniform of his own.[4]

The value of the Ehrenfuehrer to Himmler was considerable. A person like Ribbentrop, head of the Foreign Office, did not become an SS man under Himmler's order by accepting a uniform. But the fact that he, like so many others, had been seen in this fancy dress made it impossible for him to criticise the 'racial' policies of the SS, even if he had wanted to do so. Many German bureaucrats, less débrouillard than Diels, succumbed to the joys of the black uniform and silver SS runes, not realising that they were like the Arab who has eaten bread and salt with his enemy. Henceforward they could object to nothing with which the initials SS became associated.

[1] Rosenberg, *Memoirs* (New York, 1949), p. 179. Diels is named in SS lists as a colonel.

[2] Friedrich Hossbach, *Zwischen Wehrmacht und Hitler*, p. 30.

[3] Rudolf Pechel, *Deutscher Widerstand* (Zurich, 1947), p. 258. Photograph in Erich Kordt, *Nicht aus den Akten*, Stuttgart 1950.

[4] Prince Schaumburg-Lippe, *Zwischen Krone und Kerker* (Wiesbaden, 1952), p. 137.

With Diels, the offer was a prelude to becoming virtually an assistant of Himmler, though the latter did not take over the Gestapo officially as Goering's deputy till 20 April 1934. But Hitler was not altogether satisfied with Goering's pact with Himmler, for in the middle of March he made a very illuminating remark to Diels:[1] 'Through Roehm and his companions I have enough lice under my skin. If Goering thinks he can involve me with Himmler and Heydrich too, he is mistaken. Himmler shall run his SS and you, who are a civil servant, will stay at your post'.

This seems to show that, at a time when Hitler was already having Roehm closely watched and when perhaps he had already decided to liquidate Gregor Strasser and von Schleicher, he was still suspicious of the Goering-Himmler set-up. Nevertheless the surrender of the Gestapo to Himmler and Heydrich proceeded. The two men were introduced personally to the Berlin office on 10 April, some days after Diels had resigned. Henceforward the Prinz Albrecht-strasse was Himmler's headquarters and his home too was transferred to Berlin, to the villa 'Am Donnerstag', close to Ribbentrop's house in Dahlem where Himmler had arranged the Hitler-Papen conferences. Heydrich established himself at No. 103 Wilhelmstrasse, in what was known as the Security Head Office of the Reichsfuehrer SS.

Thus Himmler came at long last to Berlin. Except in Bavaria Himmler had no control over the ordinary police. As Reichsfuehrer of the SS, he was still subordinate to Roehm. His strength lay, as the fateful day of 30 June was to demonstrate, in a string of political police offices, three battalions of relatively well disciplined and equipped whole-time SS men and in the peculiar talents of Heydrich's SD. The stage was set for the turning point in Himmler's career.

As to Rudolf Diels, he had already concealed himself in the local government presidency of Cologne. Three days before the blood-purge Goering came to Cologne and warned his protégé that he was on Heydrich's proscription list. So Diels found it prudent to spend the next six years in private employment in the inland shipping administration of the Hermann Goering Werke. In 1940 he returned to local government and became Regierungspraesident in Hanover. Goering saved Diels from arrest several times, and also rescued him

[1] Diels, op. cit., p. 296.

from prison after the July 1944 plot.[1] After the war Diels was employed for a time in the provincial administration of Lower Saxony, a notorious centre of Nazi revival, but questions were raised in the Bonn parliament and the first Chief of the Gestapo now describes himself as 'Regierungspraesident Retired'.

[1] Diels, p. 308; Hagen, op. cit., p. 17.

3

The Second Revolution

30 JUNE 1934

'All revolutions eat their own children'. These were the words used by Roehm to Hans Frank, the then Bavarian Minister of Justice, on the eve of his execution in Stadelheim prison,[1] and with these words Roehm recognised the historic inevitability of what had happened to him. Goering's jealousy, Hitler's treachery and the pitiless obedience of Himmler and his SS leaders were part of a biological process which Roehm could perceive when facing his death. But he could not have perceived the successive changes in Hitler as the processes of history took charge, nor is it any easier to do so today.

Hitler had needed Roehm's help so badly that he had at one time openly condoned the homosexual practices which formed the greater part of the charges he levelled against Roehm after his execution. In 1934 Hitler did not accept easily a situation in which he had to support a playboy-adventurer like Goering with shady business friends against a man who spoke his own revolutionary language. The doubtful evidence that Hitler hated Roehm comes chiefly from Alfred Rosenberg, who claims that on 14 June 1934 Hitler discussed the question of Roehm's successor with him. Hitler then divulged to Rosenberg that he had never in his life asked Roehm to eat with him.[2]

Why, then, had Hitler pressed the reluctant Hindenburg in December 1933 to make Roehm a Cabinet Minister? The answer is that he had to do so. The SA had grown from 300,000 men in the previous January to a figure approaching three millions. They had ceased to be an auxiliary police, for in August Goering had terminated the rule of the Berlin street gangs, and now the SA did not

[1] Frank, *Im Angesicht des Galgens*, p. 149.

[2] Rosenberg, *Memoirs*, p. 288. Prince Schaumburg-Lippe, however, says that he saw Roehm make a speech at Hitler's New Year's dinner at the end of 1933. *Zwischen Krone und Kerker*, p. 167.

quite know what they were, except that after twelve months of revolution they were still for the most part without jobs. Roehm's threats were unmistakable. On 6 August he declared 'Anyone who thinks that the tasks of the SA have been accomplished will have to get used to the idea that we are here and that we intend to stay here, come what may'.[1] On 5 November at the Berlin Sportpalast he was still more menacing:[2] 'One often hears voices in the bourgeois camp to the effect that the SA have lost any reason for existence, but I will tell these gentlemen that the old bureaucratic spirit must yet be changed in a gentle or, if need be, an ungentle manner'.

While Hitler's speeches in 1933 mainly emphasised that the social revolution had gone as far as he wanted, Roehm preached that the revolution had not been fulfilled. It may, then, appear surprising that on 5 November Roehm shared the platform with Himmler and that Himmler copied the language of his chief. 'Revolutions only triumph if every man who is sent to a post considers himself an official not of the state but of the revolution'.

Why did Himmler have to present himself on this platform? It must be concluded that, however fine a nose he possessed, Himmler did not believe that Hitler viewed this sort of talk with disfavour. Himmler's rival at the beginning of November was still Goering, who stood in the way of his police ambitions. But with Roehm as Minister of Defence, Himmler might well fulfil these ambitions. Whether he achieved them by helping Roehm to put Goering out of the way or vice versa was immaterial to him. It was probably not till February 1934 that Himmler perceived which way the tide was setting. Roehm's plan for a Ministry for Defence to control all the 'Para-military organisations' as well as the regular forces was put before the cabinet that month.[3] Clearly such a ministry could only be run by Roehm, who commanded nearly three million men. It was impossible for Hitler to support such a proposal. Hindenburg still had sole competence in military affairs, and Hindenburg by altering his will could still spoil Hitler's chances of combining the offices of Chancellor and President. Moreover the Ministry for Defence was in the hands of a man whom Hitler had still to treat diplomatically, the enthusiastically Nazi general Werner von Blomberg. Furthermore the disarming of the SA was to be Hitler's title to respectability in international politics. On 21 February he told Mr. Anthony Eden,

[1] Heiden, *Der Fuehrer*, p. 723.   [2] *Ibid.*, p. 735.
[3] Bullock, *Hitler, a Study in Tyranny*, p. 262.

then Minister of State, that he was willing to demobilise two-thirds of the SA and permit the Allied Disarmament Commission to inspect the remainder.[1]

There is not the slightest doubt that after the failure of his proposals Roehm had an interest in making a Putsch and that the army leaders knew in the following June that they stood to gain by Hitler's murders. But there is no real evidence that the army leaders made a contract with Hitler to recognise his succession if he removed Roehm. The story that Hitler made such a contract with Blomberg, Fritsch, and Admiral Raeder on 11 April, when reviewing the fleet from the battleship *Deutschland*, is accepted by Mr. Bullock and Mr. Wheeler-Bennett. Yet it is a hearsay story, published by refugees in Paris.[2] Another version, neither more nor less creditable, puts the meeting on board the 'Strength through Joy' ship *Robert Ley* and as late as June.[3]

Looked at in the light of their natures, neither Hitler nor the three service chiefs were likely to trust the outcome of such a bargain. Hitler did not expect to have to proceed against the Roehm group either so soon or so far. The goad that stirred him into action may have been the imminence of Hindenburg's death, but it was the Himmler-Goering alliance that made the act possible and that precipitated it.

The alliance must have been apparent to all in February 1934, for in that month Goering installed Himmler's élite force, the Leibstandarte Adolf Hitler, in the suburbs of Berlin. Actually the Leibstandarte formed part of the 'Prussian State Police Group General Goering', and together with Major Wecke's picked State Police, it occupied the chief cadet school at Gross-Lichterfelde. The Leibstandarte was not yet a name to conjure with, since till 27 March it had been simply the staff guard of the Munich Braunehaus, consisting of 120 men whose incorporation dated from 1928.[4] It was commanded by one of Hitler's old party fighters of the days before November 1923. Josef (Sepp) Dietrich, born at Hawangen in Bavaria, had been intended for the trade of butcher, but in 1911 at the age of nineteen he had enlisted in the imperial army and he survived the First World War as a sergeant-major. Major Milton

---

[1] Wheeler-Bennett, *The Nemesis of Power*, p. 311.
[2] *Weissbuch ueber die Erschiessungen des 30 Juni* (Paris, 1935), pp. 52-3.
[3] Wheeler-Bennett, op. cit., p. 312.
[4] Himmler's address to Wehrmacht officers, January 1937, *Nuremberg Document* PS 2640, IMT III, p. 134.

Shulman, who interrogated Sepp Dietrich after the Second World War when he was a captive general, found him 'a rather battered bartender' in appearance and crude, conceited, and garrulous in conversation. He thought that Sepp Dietrich had become a colonel-general more through his ruthless energy than through any military ability—and he endorsed von Rundstedt's description of the man who had commanded an army under him in Normandy and the Ardennes: 'He is decent but stupid'.[1]

Yet Sepp Dietrich, though he had been a butcher's assistant and had achieved his first step on the ladder in June 1934 as a butcher of men, could not have been all that stupid. As an NCO in 1917 he had taken a technical course and had served with one of the first armoured units of the Bavarian army. In spite of his peasant appearance he belonged to the mechanical age. During the Second World War his successive promotions were achieved against strong opposition from the General Staff. Though the record of Colonel-General Sepp Dietrich as a strategist from June 1944 to April 1945 showed the opposition to have been justified, there is no doubt of his part in creating the high fighting morale of the better SS divisions. Physically without dignity—his general's uniform made him look undersized and pig-like—his powers of leadership were all the more remarkable. Hitler's praises of Sepp Dietrich[2] were not wholly unmerited. The man had personal magnetism.

The low strength battalion of SS bodyguards which Sepp Dietrich brought to Berlin in February 1934 consisted of Bavarians. This could only increase the tension between SA and SS which had existed in Berlin since 1930. The arrival of Himmler at the beginning of April increased it even more, for Himmler's ambition and ruthlessness were already known to the Berliners. Soon after Himmler's installation in the Prinz Albrechtstrasse, Karl Ernst, the commander of the Berlin SA, declared that Himmler had laid a plot to murder him and that he was 'going to get even with that black Jesuit'.[3] Himmler returned the accusation. On 20 June he arrived in great

[1] Milton Shulman, *Defeat in the West* (London, 1947), p. 104.

[2] See p. 190.

[3] Diels, op. cit., p. 54; Gisevius, op. cit., p. 136. A hand grenade had been thrown from a roof in Unter den Linden. Finally a charge was brought against one Erwin Schulze, a builder's labourer and a Communist, who as a result spent eleven years in prison. In September 1955 Schulze was declared exonerated on the ground that he had admitted under torture a crime to which another man had since confessed. (*The Times*, 17 September 1955).

excitement at the pompous reburial ceremony at Schorfheide which
Goering was holding in honour of his first wife, Karin von Kanzow.
On the way Himmler's car windscreen was shattered by a stone and
he declared that SA men had fired a shot at him.[1]

On 5 June, a fortnight before this incident, Hitler opened his final
gambit against Roehm. He summoned Roehm to a long private
conference, during which he reproached him with the accusations of
homosexuality that had again been made by the Party office. Hitler
claimed that he also begged Roehm to stop a development in the
National Socialist revolution which could only lead to catastrophe.[2]

Some understanding was reached, because two days later it was
officially announced that the entire SA would spend the month of
July on furlough. Roehm himself left at once for Bad Wiessee, south
of Munich, to take a cure in a sanatorium. This part of the plan was
almost certainly Hitler's own and owed nothing to Himmler and
Goering. It may even have been a sincere *rapprochement* between
Hitler and Roehm, but it offered an opportunity which neither
Goering, Himmler, nor the chiefs of the army ignored.

The real political wire-puller at the War Office at this time was
not Werner von Blomberg, the Minister of War, an extremely tall,
white-haired general with a face of almost indecent adolescence, but
Walter von Reichenau, who headed the Truppenamt or Army
Administration section. Reichenau was younger, not more than
fifty years old, a menacing figure with the air of a grand inquisitor.
He had met Himmler through Hans von Friedeburg, a naval
captain, who as an admiral was to negotiate the Rheims capitulation of May 1945.[3] Both Blomberg and Reichenau had opposed
Hitler's recent appointment of Werner von Fritsch to be Commander-
in-Chief of the 100,000 strong 'Versailles Army'. According to a
memorandum, which he composed later, Fritsch had no part in the
combination against Roehm and he believed that on the day of the
blood-purge the party leaders published his own name as one of
the victims. That at least is what Fritsch wrote at the time of his
final fall from grace in February 1938, but a rather different light on
his conduct is thrown in an affidavit by Field-Marshal Ewald von

---

[1] Diels, p. 54. Mr. Frischauer accepts a version according to which Himmler
was fired at while in Hitler's car and actually wounded while receiving a bouquet.

[2] Norman Baynes, *The speeches of Adolf Hitler*, 1922-1939. Oxford, 1942, Vol.
I, p. 316.

[3] Hossbach, op. cit., p. 70.

Kleist, who died in a Russian prison camp in 1954. This affidavit was only published years after the Nuremberg trials had ceased.[1]

On 24 June 1934 Kleist, who was then military area commander in Silesia, learnt suddenly from Fritsch that the SA were about to attack his troops. After hearing other reports of the same kind, Kleist sent for Edmund Heines, the lover of Roehm and his deputy as SA leader in Silesia. Heines denied the reports. Five days later Heines asked Kleist why military preparations were on foot throughout Germany. Failing to obtain an explanation, Heines decided to fly to Roehm at Wiessee and there he was shot on 30 June.

In the meantime Kleist reported in person to Fritsch that he believed that Himmler had been inciting the army and the SA against each other. Fritsch refused to make any comment but referred Kleist to von Reichenau. Eleven years later Kleist still remembered Reichenau's words: 'That may be correct, but it is too late now'.

Later, Fritsch told von Papen that on 30 June he had been unable to assume the duties of a Commander-in-Chief because he could not oppose Blomberg. But Reichenau could not have arranged for army units to co-operate with the SS unless he had Fritsch's authority. And the orders were certainly given. Freiherr von Eberstein, commander of the SS 'Higher Section' for Dresden, was ordered by Himmler to muster his men in an army barracks and keep contact with the Military Area Command.[2] Karl Wolff and Werner Best, who were in Himmler's immediate entourage, have described Heydrich's orders to the 'Higher Section' commanders following after a conference between Himmler and Reichenau. Sepp Dietrich's Leibstandarte detachment which accompanied Hitler to Wiessee had been brought from Berlin partly in army transport, while at Dachau concentration camp Theodor Eicke's SS battalion, the future 'Totenkopf', was told to report for duty at an army barracks.[3]

Behind these preparations the individual manœuvres of Goering, Himmler, and von Reichenau are not distinguishable, whereas Hitler's movements can be followed closely. A speech made by von Papen at Marburg on 17 June set the ball rolling. Von Papen said what Hitler himself had been saying for months: 'Have we gone through an anti-Marxist revolution in order to carry out a Marxist

---

[1] Hermann Mau in *Vierteljahreshefte fuer Zeitgeschichte*, No. 2 (Stuttgart, April 1953), p. 131.

[2] IMT, XX, pp. 249, 265.   [3] Mau, op. cit.

programme?'[1] But instead of tacitly approving the language of the Vice-Chancellor, Hitler launched a violent attack on this speech, declaring that von Papen was 'a pygmy attacking the gigantic renewal of German life'.

Hitler's attack was accepted as a cue by Goebbels, who followed up at Essen with one of his rabble-rousing speeches in the old vein, attacking the upper classes as the enemies of National Socialism. Papen and the right wing of Hitler's cabinet offered to resign. With Hindenburg's death so obviously near, this presented a dangerous situation. On 21 June Hitler flew to Neudeck, ostensibly to report to Hindenburg concerning his visit to Mussolini, but in fact to find out how far Hindenburg would go in support of von Papen. It has been said that at Neudeck Hitler was virtually blackmailed by Hindenburg, who threatened to let Blomberg govern in the name of the army unless the split in the Cabinet was healed[2]; that the army claimed the fulfilment of the bargain, allegedly made on board the *Deutschland*, and that Hitler's blood-purge of Roehm, Gregor Strasser, von Schleicher and their followers was forced upon him by the difficult situation he was in.

In practice, Hitler's subsequent action was approved both by Blomberg and Hindenburg. But to suppose that they forced Hitler to carry out the blood-purge is reading far too much into the characters of these two men, Blomberg, the Hitlerjunge or 'rubber lion', and the truly moribund Hindenburg. Had Hitler chosen to support Roehm's aspirations, Hindenburg could hardly have asserted his authority against the entire SA, using only the hundred thousand army of the Versailles Treaty. It does seem likely, however, that Hitler made some form of amends for his burst of bad temper against von Papen, and that he did so to make sure of Blomberg's support in the liquidation of the Roehm-Schleicher-Strasser group.

Proof of this support came soon after the Neudeck visit. Fritsch's warning to Ewald von Kleist was sent on 24 June, and on the 25th Blomberg issued a standing order. All army establishments must remain at the 'Lesser Alert'. This meant the suspension of all leave and night passes. The SA leaders seem to have been singularly unsuspecting. Roehm remained in the Hanslbauer sanatorium at Wiessee, and Karl Ernst continued his preparations to spend his

---

[1] Bullock, op. cit., p. 272.
[2] Wheeler-Bennett, op. cit., p. 320; Bullock, op. cit., p. 273.

furlough in Madeira. He was arrested after a car chase on the road to joining his ship at Bremerhaven.

The next move was a telephone call from Hitler to Roehm on 28 June. Roehm told his guests, Ritter von Epp among them, that Hitler would arrive at the weekend to participate in the SA staff conference which was to precede the general month's furlough. Roehm was in high spirits, declaring that 'all outstanding differences and misunderstandings were to be settled'.[1] So, without attaching any importance to the emergency orders to the army, Roehm proceeded to book the tables for a reunion dinner with Hitler at the Munich Vierjahreszeiten Hotel.[2]

But to Hitler the telephone call had been part of a tortured promenade of his nerves. He had just flown in from a two-day tour of the Austrian border and he left Berlin at once to attend Gauleiter Terboven's wedding in Essen. Here Hitler received a personal report from Himmler which caused him to send Goering back to Berlin.[3] The following day was spent visiting camps of the Labour Service, east of the Rhine, and in the evening Hitler put up at the Dreesen Hotel in Godesberg. During the night a number of party officials reported to him. Among them were Goebbels, the Gauleiter for Berlin and Minister for Propaganda, Otto Dietrich, Hitler's Press Minister, and Viktor Lutze, a Gruppenfuehrer from the SA who had brought Hitler intelligence before. Goebbels is said by Konrad Heiden to have inflamed Hitler's fears by telling him that the Berlin SA had returned to their posts against orders.[4]

This was possibly an enlargement of Himmler's original report which had caused Hitler to send Goering to Berlin. Goebbels's real motive in going to Godesberg was to avoid Goering's proscription list by sticking close to Hitler, but Alfred Rosenberg believed that Hitler sent for Goebbels to make the trip to Wiessee with him 'in order to give him an object-lesson'.[5] It was known at Wiessee already on the 28th that Goebbels was coming, because Prince Isenburg heard Roehm announce Hitler's impending visit with the mysterious words, 'Will Goebbels tear the mask from his face this time?'[6]

Goebbels's position was equivocal because he was certainly in correspondence with Otto Strasser in Prague[7] and he acted as liaison

---

[1] Mau, op. cit., p. 128.   [2] Heiden, op. cit., p. 757.
[3] Evidence of Paul Koerner, IMT IX, p. 10.   [4] Heiden, p. 757.
[5] Rosenberg, *Memoirs*, p. 164.   [6] Mau, op. cit., p. 128, footnote 9.
[7] Louis Lochner in introduction to *The Goebbels Diaries*, English edition, p. 33.

officer between Hitler and Roehm. He undoubtedly favoured a really radical revolution, headed by Hitler, Roehm, and Gregor Strasser, and this he may even have expected when he made his Essen speech on the 19th. Prince Schaumburg-Lippe, who stood very close to Goebbels at this period, is convinced that Goebbels would not have survived 30 June if he had not been sly enough to take with him on his journey to Godesberg a well-known SS leader, Gauleiter Hanke of Breslau.[1]

A year later, during a dinner party in this same Hotel Dreesen, Hitler recalled that Goering had telephoned him from Berlin during the night with news so momentous that he took off from Bonn airport for Munich at two o'clock in the morning.[2] As the aeroplane landed at Schleissheim, Hitler had been relieved to see not the uniforms of the SA but the steel helmets of the army. What, then, was this mischievous telephone call? Nearly twenty years later Ernst von Salomon published a story which he had heard from Roehm's legal adviser, Dr. Lutgebruene. The commander of the Munich military area, presumably General Wilhelm Adam, had been to the Wiessee sanatorium. He had come to recover the weapons which Roehm had issued to the SA from the illegal army stores in the old Freikorps days. It was these weapons, the general said, which lay at the root of Hitler's troubles with the army. And so Roehm agreed to give them up to the local police. Himmler, as Chief of the Bavarian police, was informed, but he allowed his SS men to investigate the loading of the arms on to lorries as 'an unusual military activity'. As such it was reported to Hitler at Godesberg.[3]

This may be the explanation of the arrest of the Munich SA leaders before Hitler's arrival. Obergruppenfuehrer Schneidhuber, Roehm's deputy in Bavaria, was brought to the airport, and at four in the morning Hitler tore off his insignia as soon as he was out of the aeroplane which had brought him from Bonn. Schneidhuber, who could have explained the movement of the arms, was not allowed to speak. He had been arrested with Schmidt, his adjutant, before midnight on the initiative of the Munich Gauleiter, Ludwig Wagner. According to the version put out by Goebbels over the wireless, Wagner had discovered an alert signal for the SA, 'The Fuehrer is against us, the Reichswehr is against us! Into the streets!'[4]

[1] Schaumburg-Lippe, op. cit., pp. 173, 176.   [2] Hossbach, op. cit., p. 57.
[3] *The Answers of Ernst von Salomon* (London, 1953), p. 274.
[4] Gisevius, p. 176.

It was an even cleverer notion to send to the airport, together with the prisoners, Hitler's old companions of the beermug-throwing days, Christian Weber the Munich jockey and publican, Emil Maurice the chauffeur and Josef Berchtold, perhaps the first commander of the embryonic SS. Hitler was inflamed by their weeping loyalty. The pages of his table talk, which reveal this sentimental side of Hitler's nature, show how effective such a demonstration could be; but the artist behind it is unknown, unless, as Heiden suggests, it was Major Walter Buch, the president of the Party Tribunal and father-in-law of Martin Bormann.[1] It must be borne in mind that Goering, Himmler, and Heydrich were all in Berlin.

Towards six o'clock on the morning of 30 June, Hitler left Schleissheim airport in a column of cars and motor lorries. He was in the hands of the SS. All the old companions of the inner bodyguard were there, Wilhelm Brueckner, Julius Schaub, and Sepp Dietrich, besides Weber, Maurice, and Berchtold. Schaub was destined to stay with Hitler to the end, the rest to sink into disgrace or obscurity, except Dietrich, who was to command an army. The column headed east and soon it was on the new Munich-Salzburg autobahn, which stretched before them, colourless and inhuman, as if it were not part of the landscape. To right and left spread Tacitean —forests, black and low. The column turned southward and at Gmund it reached the shores of the Tegernsee, the Nazi Valhalla where many Party leaders had their weekend villas. Here Hitler's nerves became so bad that, when the driver of a car twice tried to overtake him, he questioned the man personally. The car was Hans Frank's and the driver was Frank's chauffeur who had come to fetch him from Fischhausen to investigate the trouble in Munich. 'Go quietly on your way', Hitler told him, 'give Dr. Frank my compliments and tell him that at the very last moment I have been able to avert a catastrophe from the Reich'.[2]

Another car, which was forced to halt, contained a group of SA leaders on their way to Roehm's conference. Among them was Hans Ludin, the young officer whose intrigue with the SA in 1930 had forced Hitler publicly to renounce revolution.[3] Hitler gazed at the captives lining the road and muttered the one word 'Ludin'. The man who had been sacrificed, when Hitler chose 'power through legality', was not sacrificed again. Seven years later he became

[1] Heiden, p. 760. [2] Frank, *Im Angesicht des Galgens*, p. 147.
[3] *The Answers of Ernst von Salamon*, p. 540.

Hitler's ambassador in Slovakia and in 1948 he was sentenced to death by a Bratislava court.

A mile or two farther on lay Bad Wiessee with its nursing homes and boarding houses, a place without patina or charm, incredibly white, neat and German. Appropriately, it was to be the theatre of the great drama of the mid-twentieth century, but of this drama only hearsay accounts are available. It is said that Edmund Heines was surprised in bed with his favourite and that he was taken into one of the waiting cars, where Emil Maurice and Christian Weber shot him. A year later the fastidious military attaché, Geyer von Schweppenburg, had to escort the second of these privileged murderers to Newmarket.[1] It seems that Hitler attacked Count Spreti, the friend of Roehm, with a whip and that he dared Roehm, as he lay in bed, to commit suicide.[2] It seems that an SA leader took aim at Hitler and was disarmed by Sepp Dietrich.[3] But, except for the case of Edmund Heines, there was no summary execution. On the contrary, there was much hesitation, for nearly two hours elapsed before the Roehm circle were packed into cars and driven to Stadelheim prison. In the meantime Hitler left for the Munich Braunehaus.

Hans Frank reached the prison at two o'clock in the afternoon, having failed to telephone to Guertner, the Minister of Justice in Berlin. He found that forty men from Sepp Dietrich's Leibstandarte were guarding two hundred arrested SA leaders. Frank thought that he had averted a massacre by replacing the SS men with green-uniformed Bavarian Landespolizei. But in the evening Sepp Dietrich arrived in person, bringing with him the first of Himmler's blue-blooded converts. This was Prince Josias of Waldeck-Pyrmont, who was to receive a life sentence at the American Buchenwald trial in 1947. These two persons showed Frank a list in which 110 names were underlined with Hitler's pencil. When Frank declared that he could not carry out any executions without a legal warrant, Sepp Dietrich telephoned Hitler at the Braunehaus and Frank was summoned to the receiver. Hitler bawled at him, 'I am Reich Chancellor and this is a Reich matter which in no way comes under your authority . . . they are only your guests; I and the Reich decide about them, not Bavaria'.[4]

---

[1] Geyr von Schweppenburg, *The Critical Years* (London 1952), p. 55.
[2] Heiden, p. 762.
[3] *The Goebbels Diaries*, p. 12, footnote by Louis Lochner.
[4] Frank, op. cit., p. 149.

Frank now telephoned Rudolf Hess, the head of the Party office, who possessed Hitler's ear more than anyone at this time. Frank protested that the SA leaders had been caught in no conspiracy but had been dragged from their beds or taken off trains. Hess agreed to speak with Hitler again but in the meantime Frank was reminded by Sepp Dietrich's NCOs that soon it would be too dark for the men to shoot straight. At last Hess rang back to say that Hitler had just obtained full emergency powers from Hindenburg. Nevertheless the new list which Hess dictated contained only nineteen names and Roehm's was not among them because further information was awaited. Hitler cut short a further remonstrance from Frank and the nineteen men, including Schneidhuber and two famous Freikorps leaders Hans Heyn and Peter Heydebreck, were shot on the spot.

Many more men were shot in Stadelheim prison in the next three days, but Roehm was left in his cell till the morning of 2 July. As to Frank, he received a severe rocket from Hitler and then resigned from the post of Bavarian Minister of Justice. But resignation, though a Christian virtue, was never a National Socialist one and Frank was persuaded to return. Hitler cited his own case in November 1923 to show that treason could not be dealt with effectively by process of law. Frank, who had himself diffidently handled a pistol at the Museumsbruecke on that occasion, could not help seeing the logic.[1] However, at the next anniversary of the Munich Putsch Hitler was heard to mutter about 'a Minister who demanded paragraphs when I was going to be murdered', and at the end of the year 1934 he abolished the Bavarian Ministry of Justice.

Hitler flew to Berlin immediately after the telephone conversations and Gisevius has described his arrival at Tempelhof airport. Hitler, who had certainly not taken any sleep for forty hours, was pale, dishevelled, and utterly exhausted. Nevertheless, as Himmler presented him with the list of Berlin executions, he insisted on reading it on the runway.[2]

The day in Berlin had been Wagnerian. Goering had appeared at the morning conference in the Ministry of Propaganda in place of Goebbels to announce that Roehm had been prevented from marching on Berlin. Even as Goering spoke, the place swarmed with SA leaders, including Count Helldorf the protégé of Roehm, Prince

---

[1] Frank, op. cit., pp. 154, 61   [2] Gisevius, p. 168.

August Wilhelm of Prussia, Prince Schaumburg-Lippe and an unfortunate Press reporter, employed by Karl Ernst, who was shot in the course of the day.[1] In the Police Praesidium the consternation was even greater. Daluege learnt that Goering had alerted his special police garrison at Gross-Lichterfelde without informing him. As the morning advanced, it became apparent that the entire Ministry had been by-passed. Goering was conducting a police action of which neither Daluege nor Wilhelm Frick, the Minister of the Interior, knew anything.[2] The proscription lists, the arrests, the judgments and the executions were all apparently in the hands of Heydrich's Gestapo.

In fact even this was an over-simplification and there still remains much doubt today as to who composed the lists as they were given to the murder squads at Gross-Lichterfelde. For instance von Papen is sure that they were prepared by Hermann Behrends, who ran Heydrich's SD service for him in the Wilhelmstrasse, while Walter Pechel writes that Erich Gritzbach, one of Goering's secretaries, had the lists drawn up by Theodor Eicke, the commander of the Totenkopf guards at Dachau.[3]

In any case, Hitler never saw the complete lists till after the event. If on the one hand Hitler had demanded the heads of men like Roehm, von Schleicher and Gregor Strasser, others were arrested or unostentatiously murdered simply because they had incurred the jealously of the two triumvirates, Goering, Himmler and Heydrich, or Hess, Walter Buch, and Bormann. Moreover, members of Hitler's old bodyguard conducted vendettas of their own, such as Emil Maurice's murder of Father Stempfle, a priest who had once helped Hitler by proof-reading *Mein Kampf*.[4]

The headquarters of the Berlin proscription was Goering's combined residence and office in the Leipzigerplatz. Here Goering sat in a study, opening into an anteroom which was full of victims under guard, petitioners and other interested people, and which smelt of panic. Goering was accompanied throughout the day by

[1] Schaumburg-Lippe, pp. 173-5.   [2] Gisevius, p. 155.

[3] Pechel, *Die deutscher Widerstand*, p. 77.

[4] Heiden, p. 389. But was Father Stempfle murdered by Maurice? Hitler told his photographer, Heinrich Hoffmann, that 'the swine have also murdered my good Father Stempfle'. Yet Hitler took no steps against Maurice, who survived the war, although Hitler owed him a double grudge as the reputed lover of Geli Raubal in 1925. Heinrich Hoffmann, *Hitler was my Friend* (London, 1955), p. 76.

his private secretary Paul Koerner, by Himmler and by Heydrich. These four men decided the fate of the listed victims as they were brought in. Koerner, the future head of the Four-Year-Plan Office and the Hermann Goering Werke, was an out-and-out bureaucrat and his presence on such an occasion is rather surprising, but then, as he admitted at Nuremberg in 1938, 'Pilli' Koerner had joined the SS in 1931 because he had supposed it respectable.[1] So respectable, in fact, that by 1942 he was able to wear the uniform of a lieutenant-general.

Gisevius and von Papen have both described the scene in the Leipzigerplatz, its intense horror heightened by liveried footmen serving sandwiches. Gisevius's presence was as unaccountable as his presence in the Bendlerstrasse on that somewhat parallel occasion, 20 July 1944. Papen had come to urge Goering to call on Hindenburg to use the army, but Goering assured him that 'with the help of the SS he was completely in command of the situation'. The SS in fact were not disposed to let Papen go, but Goering, mindful of the uses of Papen's Marburg speech in the fight against Roehm, had Papen piloted out by his adjutant, Karl Bodenschatz.[2] This does not mean that there were any misunderstandings between Goering and Himmler. Goering was in command of a situation that he had himself created. Little was heard from him through the open door of the study except shouts of 'Shoot him! Shoot him!',[3] yet the men he wanted to shoot were those to whom he had given unlimited licence in March 1933. Students of revolution might reflect that the arrival of Thermidor had beaten the book and that Robespierre had changed sides.

The victims were rushed off to the cadet school at Gross-Lichterfelde, where the executions were carried out by the Leibstandarte companies attached to Goering's Landespolizei force. Stories that Goering, Himmler and Heydrich were present that afternoon among the executioners are all false. Their function was in the Leipzigerplatz and at the Tempelhof airport.[4] It is equally untrue that von Fritsch sent the Berlin Military Area Commanders, Rundstedt and von Witzleben, to hold a watching brief by the shooting wall.[5] It is not even known what officer was in charge of the executions, which

---

[1] Case XI, transcript, p. 28802.   [2] Von Papen, *Memoirs*, p. 315.
[3] Gisevius, p. 160.   [4] For such stories, see Frischauer, op. cit., p. 65.
[5] Rosenberg, *Memoirs*, p. 233.

were said to have been horribly amateurish.[1] The number of victims is also obscure. Hitler admitted in his Reichstag speech that fifty-eight had been executed and that nineteen others lost their lives. But the basic figure of fifty-eight seems to take no account of executions outside Stadelheim and Gross-Lichterfelde. In the provinces, particularly in Silesia, there were bigger mass-killings. Walter Pechel gives a figure of 922, including twenty-eight women. It is at least certain that the number ran into hundreds.[2]

A concrete plot could not have existed at the moment of the blood-purge, as Hitler pretended in his Reichstag address of 13 July. It was nevertheless true that the forces of Roehm, Schleicher and Gregor Strasser and perhaps Goebbels too, were drawing together. If given the chance, they would have altered the character of Hitler's revolution. Hitler's explanation of 13 July, although a half-truth, is therefore worthy of some examination.[3]

According to Hitler, Kurt von Schleicher, the politician soldier wanted to get back as Vice-Chancellor in place of von Papen, and for this he was prepared to accept the Socialist Strasser as a colleague and even to support Roehm's 'people's army'. Schleicher used the same intermediary to approach Roehm as he had used to approach the army for a coup against Hitler in January 1933, a certain Werner von Alvensleben, whom Hitler referred to as 'Herr von A'. This 'Herr von A' was to put the terms to Hitler and, if he did not accept them, the Stabswache, an SA élite force resembling the Leibstandarte of the SS, was to kidnap him in Berlin. This ultimatum was to have reached Hitler on the day that he surprised Roehm in the sanatorium

[1] The whole strength of the Leibstandarte at this time was eight hundred men. Forty took part in the Munich executions and perhaps the same number at Gross-Lichterfelde. It would be interesting to know how many future high commanders of the Waffen SS besides Sepp Dietrich were concerned in these murders. At least three future divisional commanders were serving in the ranks of the Leibstandarte at this time, Fritz Witt, Theodor Wisch and Juergen Wagner. An early issue of the SS weekly magazine *Das Schwarze Korps*, dated 27 March 1935, gives the names of Sepp Dietrich's Leibstandarte officers as follows: Colonel Johannsen, Lieutenant-Colonel Kohlrose, Major Deitsch and Captain Collani. Only the last named, who was killed commanding a regiment of Dutch volunteers at Narva in 1944, achieved any distinction. See Ernst Kraetschmer, *Die Ritterkreuztraeger der Waffen SS* (Goettingen, 1955), for the various biographies.

[2] Pechel, op. cit., p. 77.

[3] Norman H. Baynes, *The Speeches of Adolf Hitler*, Vol. I, pp. 300-2.

at Wiessee. It was to have been brought to him by a certain Colonel Uhl of the SA.[1] So Hitler said and, since Uhl had been shot, who could deny it?

This simple story hardly fitted with the surprise arrest of so many SA leaders in their beds, so Hitler in his address embroidered on it. He had learnt that the triumvirate, Schleicher, Roehm and Strasser, had been guilty of treason not only to the Head of the State but to the nation too. There had been attempts to make contact with a foreign power.

When three traitors meet with an ambassador of a foreign power and conceal the fact from me, then I give orders to have these men shot, even should it be true that at such a meeting only the weather, ancient coins, and similar subjects were discussed.[2]

This was thought to be an allusion to meetings between the three men and the French ambassador, M. François Poncet. The French government went so far as to deny the report, which was probably Heydrich's first incursion in the field of international Intelligence. Hitler believed it because he believed everything wholeheartedly that fitted in with his own plans. A year later he told Hossbach how he treasured the dossier he had received on the treason of the military victims of the blood-purge, Schleicher and von Bredow.[3] Heydrich, however, was not destined on this account to become first Chief of Intelligence for the new armed forces of the Third Reich. In 1934 it was not yet politic to reward the services of the SS in the blood-purge too noisily. The heroes were the army—as Himmler recalled with great bitterness ten years later.

The exultations of the old Officer Corps were indeed far more indecent than Hitler's apologia before the Reichstag. Blomberg's subservient Order of the Day, justifying the killings, was capped by Hindenburg's alleged telegram of congratulations to Hitler[4] and his

---

[1] *Weissbuch ueber die Erschiessungen*, p. 96.   [2] Speech quoted in Heiden, p. 748.
[3] Hossbach, op. cit., p. 57.

[4] The Hindenburg telegram is as dubious as most of the great sayings of history. In von Papen's memoirs there is a story that Otto Meissner, the former head of the President's Chancellery, asked Goering in Nuremberg prison 'how he had liked HIS telegram'. (pp. 317, 320). Hindenburg is alleged also to have said: 'Anyone who tries like Hitler to make history must be prepared to shed guilty blood and not to be weak'. It is odd that this remark is always traced to Hitler himself. According to Hossbach, Hitler repeated it at the Godesberg dinner party where the first anniversary of the purge was celebrated (*Zwischen Wehrmacht und Hitler*, p. 57). Hans Frank heard the same sentence from Walter Funk, who got it from Hitler. (*Im Angesicht des Galgens*, p. 152).

legalisation of murder. Compared with these, the memorandum which is said to have been sent to Hindenburg on 18 July by thirty staff officers did less than vindicate the integrity of the old German officer corps. Headed by August von Mackensen, an eighty-five-year-old field-marshal, and by Kurt Hammerstein, a commander-in-chief in retirement, they demanded the vindication of Schleicher and von Bredow. Mr. Wheeler-Bennett puts his trust in a private communication, declaring that this induced Hitler to absolve the two generals but only in a letter to the General Staff, which was intended to be secret. This was in February 1935, yet several months later Hitler told Hossbach of the SD dossier on Schleicher's treason,[1] which he particularly treasured. And for all his protest, the aged Mackensen sat beaming at Hitler's side during the ceremony for the birth of the conscript Wehrmacht a month later.

Hitler with the aid of the SS had saved the old officer corps, and on 2 August 1934, when Hindenburg died, Hitler's succession seemed a small price to pay for this. Mr. Alan Bullock has delivered a weighty judgment of the situation.[2]

What the army leaders did not foresee was that within less than ten years of Roehm's murder the SS would have succeeded where the SA failed in establishing a party army in rivalry with the generals' army, daily encroaching still further on their once proud but now sadly reduced position. No group of men was to suffer so sharp a reversal of their calculations as the army officers, who in the summer of 1934 ostentatiously held aloof from what happened in Germany and expressed an arrogant satisfaction at the Chancellor's quickness in seeing where the real power in Germany lay.

What the army leaders did not foresee in June 1934 was unforeseeable, but in any case the hamstrung position of the old High Command in 1942, after Hitler had lost his respect for them, was blissful compared with what would have awaited them after a

---

[1] Wheeler-Bennett, *Nemesis of Power*, p. 329. But the latest German study of this subject treats the story of the thirty high-ranking officers who signed 'the Blue Book of the Reichswehr' as a foreign Press canard which was seized upon by the Gestapo as an attempt to create discord between the party and the army. Mackensen was not prepared to go anything like as far and it was only an 28 February 1935 that he demanded the rehabilitation of Schleicher and Von Bredow as men who had died honourably. Then, too, this was only said in the privacy of the Von Schlieffen Association, a staff officer's club, and, after Reichenau had reported it to Blomberg, Goering forbade the Press to print anything about it. (Helmuth Krausnick, *Wehrmacht und Nationalsozialismus*, second instalment. Supplement to *Das Parlament*, 9 November 1955, pp. 666-7). *Weissbuch, etc.*, page 139.   [2] Bullock, p. 280.

successful coup by Roehm and Gregor Strasser. Only in internal matters of discipline and administration did the Waffen SS become in any sense a rival army. The Wehrmacht generals retained complete control of the SS divisions in the field. Only two political soldiers who sought a career in the SS reached the rank of colonel-general, Sepp Dietrich and Paul Hausser—apart from Himmler, who was never a soldier at all. And after Sepp Dietrich's failure in Hungary at the beginning of 1945 Hitler mistrusted the SS as much as he mistrusted the army.

Had 30 June 1934 turned out, even ten years later, to have been a victory of the SS over the old officer corps, Himmler at least should have appreciated it. Yet, since the discovery of his speech to the Gauleiters on 3 August, 1944, we know that Himmler still regretted profoundly that the army leaders had cashed in on their loyalty to Hitler during the blood-purge. Himmler even regretted the fate of Roehm, the chief at whose side he had once preached 'duty to the revolution'.[1]

In 1934 Roehm had an opportunity to win much influence over the army with his SA—were it not for his miscalculations and his treachery, all of them unfortunate. The 30 June destroyed that opportunity. On that occasion the army stayed wonderfully well as the loyal, true, brave army.

---

[1] *Die Rede Himmler's vor den Gauleitern am 3 August 1944* in *Vierteljahreshefte fuer Zeitgeschichte* (Stuttgart, October 1953), p. 566.

4

Himmler's Fight for Army and Police Control

JUNE 1934 – FEBRUARY 1938

1. THE ARMED SS

The disarming of the SA, which had begun before the blood-purge, proceeded peacefully. Almost overnight the three million enrolled SA men found themselves members of an organisation as innocuous as the Women's Institute movement. Within four weeks of the murders, on 26 July 1934, Hitler issued a decree freeing the SS from the supervision of the Chief of Staff of the SA and making Himmler directly responsible to himself.[1] Yet Himmler proceeded extremely slowly with his plans to annex the police forces of the Reich and, as to the encroachment of the SS into the army, he achieved nothing till the following year when the shadow of a vast conscript army in violation of the Versailles Treaty loomed before him. Still stranger, Himmler proclaimed himself reluctant to increase the force with which he had triumphed. He remained content to observe the ratio which had been decreed by Roehm, the ratio of one SS man to every ten SA men. Himmler was so intent on the perfect racial selection of his recruits that he kept well below his quota and on January 1937 he declared:[1]

I insist on a height of 1.70 metres. I personally select a hundred or two a year and insist on photographs which reveal if there are any Slav or Mongolian characteristics. I particularly want to avoid such types as the members of the 'Soldiers' Councils' of 1918-19, people who looked somewhat comic in our German eyes and often gave the impression of being foreigners. To ensure the right spirit of sacrifice I insist on their paying for their own black trousers and boots, which cost forty marks. . . . Between 1933 and 1935, while other party organisations increased their membership, I closed the SS. I pushed out about 60,000 of them, even though the actual number today is 210,000. We still choose only fifteen out of every hundred candidates who present themselves.

---

[1] PS 1992a; IMT III, pp. 129-31.

Thus, according to Himmler, the closing of the ranks of the SS was dictated by his own physical fastidiousness. We now know that it was nothing of the kind. In the autumn of 1934 even Blomberg was opposed to increasing the three-battalion strength of the armed SS. Hitler himself abstained from expressing his gratitude to the SS after the blood-purge, realising that this would not be popular with many sections of the party. The murders were always mentioned with embarrassment. Himmler in his Posen speech of 4 October 1943 seemed to find a natural comparison between the blood-purge and the extermination of the Jews. It was, he said, 'a matter we have never spoken about and we will never speak of it'.[1] Furthermore, in the weeks following the murders Himmler must have felt extremely uneasy concerning his own future. Many of the generals felt that Himmler had tricked them over the affair of the 'Lesser Alert'. If on Hindenburg's death the generals should refuse to accept Hitler as President as well as Chancellor, Himmler's career must end.

On 2 August, when Hindenburg died, the state of tension was almost as great as it had been on 30 June. Blomberg endorsed Hitler's succession to Hindenburg, but Fritsch, the Commander-in-Chief, and Beck, the Chief of Staff, were believed to be opposed to it. It was not expected that the army would pledge its oath to Hitler as sole Head of the State as readily as it did. Ludwig Beck explained his passive conduct to Gisevius by declaring that the 'oath of perpetual loyalty' was obtained by a trick.[2] The officers thought they had sworn the customary oath to the Chancellor as temporary Head of the State till the appointment of a new President. A decree, dated 20 August, told them however that the oath they had sworn was permanently binding.

This decree, von Papen believed, had been inspired by Blomberg, the Minister of War, who supported Hitler's charges against the generals, Schleicher and von Bredow.[3] There was now an open rift between Blomberg on the one hand, Fritsch and Beck on the other. Himmler began to exploit his position by a whispering campaign against Fritsch, suggesting that this leader, though he had been, to say the least, accommodating during the action against Roehm, was planning an army Putsch on his own. By Christmas 1934 rumours were current everywhere of SS or army Putsches. Himmler, it seems,

---

[1] Nuremberg Document PS 1919; see *infra*, p. 278.
[2] Gisevius, op. cit., p. 280.   [3] Von Papen, *Memoirs*, p. 335.

persuaded Goering that the Putsch was to be timed for 10 January 1935. On that day, says Fritsch, Himmler and Goering performed a tactical exercise, strongly reminiscent of the blood-purge. On the invitation of Blomberg they addressed an informal gathering of the High Command during a beer evening at the Kaiser Wilhelm Academy. Both Himmler and Goering told the 'same story. Fritsch, they said, had arranged for a legal expert to lecture to the War Office in order to prove that under present conditions a military Putsch was legal.[1]

This vindictive action might be explained by the jealousy of Himmler and Goering after Hitler's Opera House address to the party leaders in the previous week, in which he had reaffirmed his confidence in Fritsch. It must be remembered, however, that Goering had made peace with Himmler not only to destroy Roehm but also to get control of the armed forces for himself. Even as late as April 1934, when he had surrendered the Gestapo tamely to Heydrich, Goering had been to Fritsch to enlist his support against Heydrich 'who had been expelled from the navy and hated the officer corps'. Fritsch believed that, because he would not intrigue with Goering, he was himself the victim of Goering's intrigues.[2]

The background to the squalid cabal of January 1935 was the imminence of Hitler's announcement on the reintroduction of conscription, which was actually published on 16 March. Goering expected to profit by Fritsch's known opposition to step into Fritsch's shoes and Himmler expected to fare no worse under Goering than he would have done had his old chief, Roehm, fulfilled his ambitions. Thus the creation of the new conscript Wehrmacht began with vilifications of its officers by the disgruntled SS; vilifications from which even Blomberg was not excluded, for, since the first discussions with Hitler on the composition of the new conscript army, Blomberg had insisted that the SS should remain limited to their three trained and equipped battalions. Himmler had had to accept Hitler's decision and on 13 January, the day of the Saar plebiscite, a reconciliation between army and SS was arranged by Blomberg at one of his beer evenings. In the following month Blomberg was trusting enough to invite Himmler to lecture to army officers in the Hotel Vierjahreszeiten in Hamburg. The astonished officers learnt that Himmler

[1] Fritsch's memorandum of February 1938, quoted in Hossbach, op, cit., p. 71,
[2] *The von Hassell Diaries* (London, 1948), p. 29. Conversation with Fritsch on 18 December, 1938.

expected to arm new SS formations as a home defence army to protect Germany from a second 'stab in the back' during the next war.[1]

It may be that Himmler had exceeded his brief, for from now on Blomberg regarded Himmler's ambitions with more diffidence. If Hitler in his conscription scheme of 16 March 1935 allotted one of the proposed thirty-six divisions to the permanent establishment of the SS, Blomberg saw to it that this was not fulfilled. Blomberg's immediate instructions were only for the military training of the SS force, known as the Verfuegungstruppen, and this was equivalent to less than an infantry regiment. The complete SS division, promised by Hitler, had not come into existence even during the Polish campaign of September 1939.[2]

Hitler, it seems, had turned against the original plan of March 1935, for even the dismissal of Blomberg and Fritsch three years later did not cause him to revise the programme of arming the SS. In 1935 Himmler was not yet 'Treuer Heinrich', the man who could be trusted with anything. To Hitler he was another party intriguer 'to add to the lice under his skin'. Furthermore, the Austrian crisis which had followed the Dollfuss murder must have partly destroyed Hitler's confidence in the SS, coming as soon as it did after the blood-purge.

On 25 July 1934 a group of Austrian National Socialists, all of them SS men, murdered the Federal Chancellor, Dr. Engelbert Dollfuss and attempted to create a union of Austria with Germany. Mussolini at once mobilised his forces on the Italian-Austrian frontier and was apparently prepared to protect Austrian independence. Hitler had to simulate a repudiation of the movement which he had provoked, even though he allowed most of the active Austrian Nazis to find refuge in an Austrian SS camp at Lechfeld on the German side of the border. But the failure of the Austrian conspiracy left Hitler with a serious setback to his diplomatic preparations for German rearmament and probably, too, with a hunger for scapegoats. Since the murderers of Dr. Dollfuss belonged to the Austrian SS, the complicity of Himmler and Heydrich was in question.

Like the blood-purge, the Dollfuss murder was not as yet regarded by the SS as a title to publicity, but it certainly became one after the Austrian Anschluss. On 25 July 1938 the fourth anniversary was

[1] Wheeler-Bennett, op. cit., pp. 341-2.
[2] Paul Hausser, *Waffen SS im Einsatz* (Goettingen 1952), pp. 11, 14; Hossbach, op. cit., p. 38,

celebrated as an heroic act comparable with the Rathenau and Erzberger murders. The survivors of 'SS Standarte 89' marched to the federal Austrian Chancellery, which had been renamed the Reichstatthalterei. Here the bereaved families of thirteen men were addressed by Rudolf Hess. A tablet was unveiled which proclaimed that:

154 German men of the 89th SS Standarte stood up here for Germany on 25 July, 1934. Seven found death at the hands of the hangman.[1]

There had been no addresses by Rudolf Hess four years earlier. Discreet silence was then the order of the day, under cover of which Himmler was no doubt told to limit the functions of his SS to those of a party bodyguard. Possibly a stricter military discipline was ordered, for in the following November Himmler took an unusual step. He accepted a lieutenant-general from the army into his SS.

The position of Paul Hausser, the father of the Waffen SS or field SS, was unique. Many regular officers had joined the SS in the year or two preceding the seizure of power, but, as in the cases of the future generals, Karl Wolff and Erich von dem Bach-Zelewski, they were officers of junior rank for whom the hundred thousand army offered no career. Retired officers of general rank, although they were numerous in the early 'thirties, were not similarly tempted. Hausser was not a party member. He had left the army in 1932 at the age of fifty-one, believing that the Stahlhelm organisation offered him the prospects of a successful conservative revolution. After the blood-purge he was left high and dry in what was euphemistically called the SA reserve. He was therefore available to the only party organisation that retained its arms.

Thus it came about that Hausser joined the staff of the SS Verfuegungstruppen. This force comprised three battalions, only one of which, Sepp Dietrich's Leibstandarte, possessed any motor transport. Hausser did not retain his army rank and Sepp Dietrich, the ex-chauffeur, was actually his superior, having been made a major-general on the day of the blood-purge. In May 1935, when Hitler ordered the Verfuegungstruppen to be trained as military units, Hausser was instructed to form an officer cadet school. In fact he re-formed the SS leadership school which Heydrich had founded in 1932 at Bad Toelz in the Bavarian Alps.[2] In June, Hausser was appointed to supervise a second school in the Welfenschloss at Brunswick.

Hausser, who had been a staff officer all through the First World

[1] IMT, I, p. 219, and Document L, 273.   [2] IMT XXI, pp. 293-4.

War and who was old by the standards of the Second World War, might well have remained a director of training, but in the invasion of France he revealed unexpected qualities as a tank commander and in February 1943 he won the last German victory on the Russian front in the Battle of Kharkov. In Normandy he had the thankless task of opposing Patton's break-through, when commanding the 7th Army. In 1945 he even commanded an army group for some ten weeks. Paul Hausser was a more than usually competent general, but in his own writings he regards his record in the field as of less importance than his achievement in creating the ideological training system of the SS. Bad Toelz remained Hausser's darling till the end, a school of chivalry which he has praised in his book *Waffen SS im Einsatz* and in his Nuremberg depositions and which he still praises as a seventy-five-year-old boy scout when he attends the SS old comrades' reunions of today. Hausser is responsible for a creed, not altogether popular in the newly armed Federal Republic, that the Waffen SS was the first 'European Army', the forerunner of NATO. But one may search in vain in Hausser's book, his depositions and his speeches, for any acknowledgment that he entered the SS in November 1934 to lick into shape the killers of Stadelheim and Gross-Lichterfelde.

Under the influence of Hausser's cadet schools the Waffen SS was to develop the most efficient of all the military training systems of the Second World War, a cross between the Spartan Hoplites and the Guards Depot at Caterham. It was in fact a joint product of Himmler's dreamy studies of ancient military orders and of Hausser's hard, practical experience of the Prussian army.

For the SS recruit the day began normally enough with reveille at six and an hour's physical training before breakfast, for which, however, Himmler favoured mineral water and porridge after the SS economic administration had acquired a monopoly by swallowing the Apollinaris and Mattoni concerns.[1] After breakfast there was weapon training, but three times a week this was interrupted for a lecture on the inspiring life of the Fuehrer, the ideology of National Socialism or the philosophy of racial selection, the principal textbooks used being Alfred Rosenberg's *Myth of the Twentieth Century* and Walter Darré's *Um Blud und Boden*. This was a complete military innovation and it started many years before our junior subalterns were burdened with such matters as 'The British Way and Purpose'.

[1] Nuremberg, Case IV, transcript, p. 1535.

After his dinner the SS recruit spent a prodigious time on the square. The SS never encouraged the theory that warfare had passed into the hands of tradesmen and specialists who could whistle with their hands in their denim pockets. The drill was worthy of a detention barracks or of Gibbon's description of Roman discipline: 'The effusion of blood was the only circumstance which distinguished a field of battle from a field of exercise'.

Drill was followed by an orgy of scrubbing, plank scouring, pipe-claying and polishing, all of which was subjected to a clinical inspection, after which the recruit could leave barracks if he was still capable of standing on his feet. But he had to look as if he had just been unpacked to hang on a Christmas tree, incredibly pink, fresh and Teutonic, his well-flattened pockets containing only a modest supply of paper currency which did not bulge, his paybook, his handkerchief creased according to regulation, and one prophylactic. On Sundays there was no church parade, for the SS had no chaplains, and Hitler liked to think that they were godless.[1] But it was worse than a church parade, because the going-out inspection was so tough that one out of three recruits failed to pass the gates.

In accordance with a practice, which Himmler had introduced in 1931 and which still figured in the 1942 edition of the SS man's 'Soldier's Friend',[2] the recruit remained a novice until he had completed the first course and passed the physical and ideological SS tests. Only then was he permitted to take the SS oath and in theory he was still entitled to withdraw. A worse ordeal lay ahead—a spell in the SS infantry or armoured warfare schools. Here he might be called on to dig himself into the ground, knowing that within a prescribed time the tanks would drive over his head, whether the hole was completed or not. If he was an officer candidate, he might be required to pull the pin out of a grenade, balance it on his helmet and stand to attention while it exploded.[3] These courage tests were inspired by Heydrich, who was said to have declared that the Waffen SS ought to practise on each other with live rounds. Goering guyed Himmler about it, telling him that the Luftwaffe did even better: a

[1] See *infra*, p. 147.

[2] Nuremberg Document, PS 2825, and IMT III, p. 136.

[3] For this and other details of SS training I have followed the interrogations reported in Georges Blond's *L'agonie de Allemagne*, 1944-5 (Paris, 1952), pp. 102-6.

small correction in the parachute drill, twice with the parachute and the third time without.[1]

For the crack SS armoured divisions this training remained unchanged almost till the end of the war. Till 1943, even the foreign and 'racial German' SS recruits went through the entire mill. There was no abridgement of the training till an enormous expansion of the Waffen SS was begun, shortly after the Kharkov victory. At the end of the war new ragtag and bobtail SS divisions were formed, receiving scarcely more training than the Volksgrenadiere divisions and the Home Guard or Volkssturm levies. Even then, however, the political instruction and the ceremony of the SS oath continued.

From the beginning these methods filled German professional officers with deep misgiving. Lieutenant-General Siegfried Westphal believes to this day that Himmler had the Waffen SS taught 'to oppose the point of view of the army alongside of whom they were to fight'.[2] In the early days of 1934 it would not have been difficult to encourage friction which undoubtedly existed. War had not yet taught the German soldier to recognise the SS man as in any sort a companion in arms. Moreover, the scales were weighted. While the regular soldier despised the untrained SS man, the latter was out of reach of army discipline and had the advantage in answering back. Blomberg and Reichenau, when they arranged for the Verfuegungstruppen to train with the regulars, did not appreciate the resentment they would cause.

The first fruits of the army's consent to the blood-purge, the obligation to send contingents to the Nuremberg party rally of September 1934 and the introduction of the Nazi form of greeting (though not yet the Nazi salute), were very bitter to the old officer corps. But Himmler took particular pleasure in any occasion which advanced the assimilation of army and party. The early issues of his new magazine for SS men, Das Schwarze Korps, printed proud notices every time the SS put in an appearance with the army. In July 1935 Sepp Dietrich marched with his execution squads at the manœuvres at Leopoldshain and Greiffenwehr; in September Himmler received Reichenau in his marquee at the Nuremberg rally. And in the previous June Heydrich had had himself photographed leading a route march with a soldier's pack on his shoulders in unmistakable emulation of Reichenau, the unconventional general who

[1] Kersten, Totenkopf und Treue, p. 121.
[2] Westphal, Heer im Fesseln (Bonn, 1950), 0p. 92.

had just left his desk in the Bendlerstrasse for a field command at the age of fifty-two and who was credited with this bizarre practice. In the Polish campaign of 1939 Reichenau was to set an example to the new race of athletic generals in gold braid and running shorts by swimming the Vistula at the head of an entire division.

But Friedrich Hossbach, Hitler's liaison officer with the High Command, found the harmony that was portrayed in *Das Schwarze Korps* very thin. When the SS battalions held a review of their own on the army's parade ground at Altengrabow that summer, the men were addressed with speeches openly attacking Fritsch.[1] The Commander-in-Chief himself declared that the full-time SS men rarely saluted an army officer and that the part-time SS men, when they were called up for the army, sent political reports on their officers to the SS head office in spite of a strict prohibition by Hitler's deputy, Rudolf Hess.

Blomberg, in spite of his doubts of the SS, failed to support such complaints. He was now in the strongest favour with Hitler, who in May 1935 issued a decree permitting him to retain his field rank while serving as a minister. Hitler was even said to have intended the rank of Reichsmarschall for Blomberg.[2] Why then should Blomberg worry about a few amateur battalions of Verfuegungs-truppen and a few thousand Death's Head Guards from the concentration camps who might become one day quite respectable under the guidance of Paul Hausser? The main thing was that the SS was not expanding and that in the hands of such a choosy crank as Himmler it was not likely to expand.

But the weakness of Blomberg's situation and the strength of Himmler's lay not in the irresponsibility of SS officers but in the purpose which underlay Hitler's blood-purge. Hitler only preferred Blomberg to Roehm as his Minister of Defence because he meant his new Wehrmacht to fight and because he needed the professional experience and organisation of the old High Command. It was when Hitler realised that the High Command lacked confidence in his policies, and when he realised that their fears had spread even to Blomberg and Reichenau, that he listened again to Goering and Himmler.

Blomberg had opposed the introduction of conscription from the beginning and seven years later Hitler in one of his fireside talks

[1] Hossbach, op. cit., p. 84.   [2] Hossbach, op. cit., p. 64.

blamed Blomberg more than 'good old Fritsch', with whom he had had a 'battle royal' on the day that he decreed conscription.[1] But in March 1935 neither Blomberg nor Fritsch thought fit to resign. Throughout 1936 they remained tepidly in opposition to Hitler's two challenges to the Versailles powers, the remilitarisation of the Rhineland and the Four-Year Plan for rearmament and economic self-sufficiency. It was a form of opposition with which Hitler could cope, and there was no real question of replacing the Defence Minister and the Commander-in-Chief until Hitler was ready to use his armies in earnest. In the meantime the Goering-Himmler alliance gained prestige at Hitler's court. To Hitler the value of the SS was not that of an adjunct to the Wehrmacht or that of an additional back-bone to the party. Rather it was an instrument to prevent the pessi-mism of the High Command spreading to the population. Hitler was well aware that his favourite legend of the 'November criminals' and the Dolchstoss or 'stab in the back' was a perversion of facts. The Kaiser's armies had thrown in the sponge before the Kaiser's ministers had done so and the army, not the cabinet, had demanded his abdication.[2] A strong police force, centralised and military in its organisation and with a highly efficient listening service, could in Hitler's view have halted the rot in the armies in 1918 at the frontiers of the homeland. And this was precisely the role Hitler intended for the SS.

Himmler was authorised to tell this to the officers of the new Wehrmacht. He spoke to them during a one-week 'political-instruc-tion' course in January 1937, and his lecture, shorn of some of its more macabre warnings, was printed in a services manual.[3] A fuller version, which fell into the hands of the opposition, was published by the exiled Social Democrat newspaper *Neuer Vorwaerts* in Karls-bad in the following September, and Himmler's unmistakable style shows this to have been no mere pirated version.[4] The speech con-tains a great deal of information on the build-up of the armed SS, the methods of selecting recruits, the regime of the concentration camps, the uses of the SD, the survival of Communism in Germany

---

[1] *Hitler's Table Talk*, p. 632.

[2] This was admitted with extreme frankness by Himmler in his anti-Wehr-macht speech to the Gauleiters at Posen on 3 August 1944; see *infra*, pp. 335-6.

[3] Extracts in Nuremberg Document PS 1992 and in IMT, I pp. 129-33.

[4] *Neuer Vorwaerts*, 26 September 1936. Mr. Frischauer in quoting this seems to be unaware of the earlier printed version.

and some of Himmler's archæological fads. Much of it will be found quoted in this book. Here we are concerned with the passage on Himmler's plans in the event of 'total war':

'The next ten years will see an annihilation war conducted by the sub-human enemies of the entire world against Germany as the kernel of the Teutonic race, against Germany as the guardian of the culture of the human race. They will mean the existence or non-existence of the white race of whom we are the leading nation'.

For this war of annihilation Himmler, like a far-seeing German governess, outlined his arrangements. The war would mean in the first place the internment in concentration camps of a much-increased number of 'uncertain cantonists'. The concentration camp guards, the Totenkopfverbaende, would be increased in strength from 3,500 men to 25,000 men, organised in thirty special battalions which would guarantee the safety of the interior, because a war would leave the regular police much reduced in strength. The armed forces would claim 15,000 to 20,000 out of the 90,000 German uniformed policemen. 'Civil troubles will have to be met by the Death's Head units. Saboteurs and terrorists cannot be opposed by old reservists. My aim is to convert the police into a force equal to any army formation'.

This was to be the role of the SS in a war that Himmler envisaged as so unpopular that Germany would be the prey of terrorists. As to the role of the SS as a force serving in the field, there was never a word in January 1937. Himmler gave statistics of the growth of the Verfuegungstruppen, who were to become the Waffen SS, but he said nothing of their future. Yet already the three original Standarte, the Leibstandarte Adolf Hitler and the Standarten known as Germania and Deutschland, had been expanded since the conscription decree of March 1935 to the strength of infantry regiments or field brigades, and in addition there were two pioneer battalions and a battalion of scouts. The whole force of thirteen battalions required an annual recruitment of 2,200 men, who were enlisted for four years. Here were the makings of a promising infantry division, yet in September 1939 when the field strength of the SS Verfuegungstruppen had increased from 9,000 to 18,000 men,[1] there was only one SS artillery regiment and the SS were brigaded haphazard with Wehrmacht units. Hitler went to war still resisting the idea of a 'parallel army'.

Uncertainty concerning the future of the armed field SS in the

[1] Hausser, op. cit., p. 10.

years 1935-9 gave it a confused organisation. From the very beginning of the war, field units were muddled with police companies,
sabotage groups and outright murder squads. For this reason many
thousands of ordinary conscripts, many of them not even Germans,
had to wait in confinement after the war until their past was eluci-
dated. There was a striking instance of this confusion of purpose in
November 1935 when Himmler and Heydrich, accompanied by the
now much-deflated figure of General Ritter von Epp, opened a new
training barracks for the SS Standarte Deutschland, a fighting unit.
Yet the barracks were sited in Dachau concentration camp[1] and
henceforward the battalion garrisoned the place jointly with the SS
riding school and two battalions of Death's Head Guards. In the
Nuremberg witness-box Hausser insisted that there had never been
any personal or official contacts between them. Such thugs never
contaminated the future Waffen SS. But this was an untenable plea.
As soon as war was declared, the younger members of the Death's
Head Guards were drafted indiscriminately into line units of the SS.
Himmler did it to stop their being drafted into the Wehrmacht,
thereby losing their SS status.[2]

Hausser regarded this as a malicious deception, practised by
Himmler on his men, but in fact the deception was Hitler's. On
17 August 1938 he issued a decree which, according to Hausser, was
kept secret from the men it concerned. The SS Verfuegungstruppen
(Hitler only used the expression Waffen SS after July 1940) were to
be part neither of the armed forces nor of the police,[3] but a 'unit
of the party, to be exclusively at my disposal'. If employed by the
supreme commander of the armed forces, they would come completely under military law and regulations, while remaining politically a party unit. If used in an emergency in the interior of Germany,
they would be entirely at Himmler's orders. In case of mobilisation
for war, Hitler alone would decide whether and how the Verfuegungstruppen would be incorporated in the wartime army.

Hitler gave a different ruling for the concentration camp guards
or Totenkopfverbaende, who were under the orders of civilian authorities. The decree of 17 August 1938 ended the anomaly by which
they could be conscripted out of the SS into the Wehrmacht. On the
outbreak of war they were to become a replacement force for the

---

[1] *Das Schwarze Korps*, 14 November 1935.

[2] Hausser, op. cit., pp. 14 and 24, and Hausser's evidence in IMT XX, p. 300.

[3] Nuremberg Document PS 647; IMT, III, p. 134.

Verfuegungstruppen, and their concentration camp duties would be gradually taken over by older men. This accounts for the preservation of the name Totenkopf, or Death's Head, to denote one of the most famous SS field divisions.

When Hitler issued this decree, he did not visualise a situation in which the mass of trained SS men would have to serve in the field. Nor had he in mind a war long enough for the SS units serving with the army to grow into divisions, army corps and even armies. Himmler, the Reichsfuehrer SS, was to command a unit of the party as a party disciplinarian and not as a soldier. Those who had destroyed Roehm and 'Roehmism' were not to step into Roehm's shoes. The decree of August 1938 was meant, however, to allay some of the suspicions of the army and it marked a relaxation of tension, one symptom of which was that young SS officers who had been trained at Bad Toelz and Brunswick were now seconded to the army for periods of six to twelve months.[1] But Hitler continued till well into the war to remind the SS that they were not intended to be regular soldiers. In August 1940 he told them that they were intended to be an élite police force not exceeding five to ten per cent of the peacetime strength of the army;[2] while in a fireside musing for Himmler's benefit in January 1942 he declared that it had been necessary to send the SS to the front, simply in order to maintain their prestige. In peacetime the SS must lose their military status.[3]

By the same reasoning Hitler never allowed the SS to infiltrate the High Command. The High Command staffs of the combined armed forces (OKW) and of the army (OKH) never contained a single SS man, nor did Hitler ever appoint an SS man either as his own chief of staff or as his personal adjutant to the High Command. Apart from Paul Hausser, who had been a general before he joined the SS and who in the end commanded an army group, only two SS men, Sepp Dietrich and Felix Steiner, commanded armies and that only in the last five months of the war. Yet by that time Hitler had created at least thirty-six colonel-generals and eighteen field-marshals, many of whom had had very little experience prior to the rearmament of 1935.

Paul Hausser publishes the names of sixty-eight SS men who commanded divisions, army corps or armies, and the biographies of

[1] Hausser, op. cit., p. 12.   [2] See *infra*, p. 151.
[3] See *infra*, p. 190

most of them will be found in Ernst Kraetschmer's book.[1] They fall into four very distinct categories. The first comprises the police leaders whom Himmler turned into field commanders with a stroke of the pen. The second contains former regular officers of the Reichswehr who entered the full-time SS after the conscription decree of March 1935. The third contains high-ranking officers who transferred to the Waffen SS during the war, while the last category comprises the young divisional commanders of 1944-5 who had made their whole career since adolescence in the full-time SS.

The first category is the least comprehensible. Butchers like Theodor Eicke, Franz Jaeckeln, von Gottberg, Friedrich Krueger, Heinz Reinefarth, von dem Bach Zelewski and Oskar Dirlewanger, as well as Heydrich's office deputy Bruno Streckenbach, received field commands, whole army corps in the case of Bach-Zelewski and Heinz Reinefarth. It is true that Bach-Zelewski had been a regular officer. Reinefarth, however, whom Hitler disgraced in the end, was only a sergeant in the summer of 1940. In the more profitable ranks of the police he became a full general within four years.[2] It seems that Himmler preferred policemen, whose warlike activities had been under his own strategic direction, to Waffen SS commanders whose merits had been discovered by the hated Wehrmacht generals.[3]

The second category includes all the senior SS generals and nearly all the divisional commanders before the invasion of Normandy. These were the men who had been attracted into the SS by Paul Hausser, elderly men born in the eighties and nineties with good records in the First World War. All had served in the Freikorps, some had got back to the hundred thousand Versailles army, others had found posts in the militarised police or in the secret air force which was trained in Russia. Among them were the SS army corps commanders, Felix Steiner, Herbert Gille, Wilhelm Bittrich, and Georg Keppler and perhaps a dozen others Military experience counted more than politics. Felix Steiner for instance can almost be reckoned a Wehrmacht general. In 1935, when he joined the SS, he was director of education at the War Office[4] and twice he held Wehrmacht commands in the field, in 1942 as commander of the IIIrd Armoured Corps and in March 1945 as Commander-in-Chief of the improvised 11th Army.

---

[1] Ernst Kraetschmer, *Die Ritterkreuztraeger der Waffen SS.*
[2] Kraetschmer, op. cit., p. 361.   [3] See *infra*, p. 372.
[4] Kraetschmer, op. cit., pp. 16-18.

The third category, comprising the high-ranking officers whom the SS took over during the war, was indeed remote from the pot-house background of the old Leibstandarte and Verfuegungstruppen and still more so from the party army ambitions of Roehm and Himmler. In this category were the commanders of the foreign SS divisions: Artur Phleps, a general of the Rumanian army; Wolde-maras Veiss, a former Latvian prime minister; Leon Degrelle, the Belgian Fascist leader, and the old Austrian professional officers Fritz Freitag and von Pfeffer-Wildenbruch, who created divisions of Ukrainians and Hungarians.

The SS generals of legend, starry-eyed, youthful and fanatical, made a late appearance. The first seems to have been Fritz Witt, a member of the 120-strong Leibstandarte of 1933, but so young that, when he was chosen to form the new Hitlerjugend SS division ten years later, he was unique in becoming a major-general at thirty-four.[1] Wounded in the Normandy fighting, Witt was succeeded by an even younger divisional commander, Kurt Meyer, who is chiefly known on account of his massacre of Canadian prisoners,[2] but in the last months of the war there was a whole crop of SS men who commanded divisions in their thirties, Theodor Wisch, Karl Ullrich, Joachim Rumohr, Otto Kulm, Fritz Klingenberg, Georg Bochmann, Hugo Kraas, and Heinz Harmel.

Hitherto the better SS generals, such as Paul Hausser, Georg Keppler and Herbert Gille, had tended to look like benign and bespectacled university professors, for even in the SS young generals offended the German militarist tradition, though they were no phenomenon among the enemy. It was, in fact, the English public-school system that the new commanders tried to emulate, joining their men in football and community singing. They were all intensely popular and known by nicknames, whether they were embittered, class-conscious and brutal like Kurt Meyer, the miner's son, or skilfully gentle like Fritz Harmel, 'Der Alte Frundsberg'. Incident-ally, when his men called him 'old Frundsberg', Harmel was a very young thirty-seven and looked like an athletic curate.[3]

At the end of the war there were hundreds of SS commanders at the regimental and battalion level who had led this cloistered and indoctrinated life since early adolescence. These were the men who, wherever they might be, tried to organise 'the fight to a finish',

[1] Kraetschmer, pp. 27-8.   [2] See *infra*, p.196.
[3] Kraetschmer, op. cit., pp. 163-6.

intimidating and very frequently hanging or shooting reluctant local authorities or wilting Volksstuermers. They were an added terror to the terrors of German life in dissolution. But their backs had been broken by Hitler's ingratitude and Himmler's cowardice. SS men were not lacking among the officers who disobeyed callous and ridiculous orders. Such were Colonel Gonnell, who let the Brunswick officer cadets escape from beleaguered Posen, and Major-General Georg Bochmann, who led his SS division from doomed Oberglogau and was cashiered for it by Field-Marshal Schoerner.[1]

In spite of the intensified training of the rank-and-file, in spite of the allegedly revolutionary methods of Bad Toelz and Brunswick, the SS leadership failed to produce anything at all spectacular. Hausser, the professional, was a better than average army commander; Sepp Dietrich, the amateur, was a bad one. Their pupils were at best good leaders of men, never good strategists. Nothing came out of the SS training comparable with Napoleon's self-made marshals. Twelve years were not enough and the genuine revolutionary background was lacking. More important still in creating the negative balance sheet of SS leadership was Hitler's own attitude. Only a small military establishment was the reward of the SS for their part in the blood-purge of June 1934. Even during the victorious campaigns of 1939-42 Hitler kept the establishment small and well dispersed. Only after defeat—when the SS armoured divisions had given proof of superior morale—was Hitler prepared to allow the armed SS unlimited expansion and unlimited responsibility. The decision dated from March 1943.[2] It was then too late to find the right leadership within the SS's own ranks. Ten years had been spent playing at Janissaries and Samurai with never a thought of an SS with thirty-five divisions and half a million combatants. Himmler had not been chosen for such a private army. It was something unintended and unpredicted. It was not implicit in Hitler's action of 30 June 1934. It was not the outcome of the army's bid for protection against the forces of revolution, but a by-product of the war itself and even then only in its later stages.

2. HIMMLER AS CHIEF OF POLICE

The military revolution of February 1938 by which Hitler secured personal control of the armed forces was largely the work of Himmler, because he had engineered the 'Fritsch-Blomberg' crisis.

[1] Kraetschmer, p. 110.   [2] See *infra*, p. 194.

In this affair Himmler was the first German police official to succeed in breaking the hollow square of the German officer corps. Himmler could not have done this, had he not also been the first official to command the police forces of all Germany.

At the time of the blood-purge Himmler had been chief of police only in Bavaria. Outside Bavaria he was head of the Prussian Political Police Office, which Goering had turned into the Gestapo, but he did not command the Prussian police as a whole, nor had he any authority over the police in the federal states. Here the chief was Wilhelm Frick, the first German bureaucrat to become a Nazi, and Frick's authority was weak. The decree of March 1933, which gave formidable powers to the police presidents in the Laender or federal provinces, in a sense strengthened federalism against the central authority. But if the police forces in the Laender still eluded Himmler, he had in several cases acquired control of the IA bureaux or political police. In 1934-6 Himmler was able to complete this net-work. Whether or not the urge behind Himmler's elbow was his Gestapo chief, Heydrich, the tactics were Himmler's own. They were not the tactics of such a vain impractical dreamy person as his adjutants tried to depict when they were facing trial after the war, but they suggest a distinct capacity for painstaking slyness.

Most of the evidence for Himmler's manœuvres in 1934-6 comes from Hans Gisevius, who, having left the Gestapo, stayed on in the police branch of Frick's Ministry of the Interior till Heydrich forced him out. Gisevius's post of observation was, one must concede, unique; but when he describes the resistance of himself and his colleagues to the further encroachments of the Gestapo, his story must be accepted with reservations. Resistance of a sort there un-doubtedly was. The blood-purge forced party leaders, who had watched the arbitrary confinements in concentration camps with in-difference, to think otherwise of an organisation that had liquidated so many of their old colleagues. Even Wilhelm Frick forbade the political police in the Laender to join Himmler's network without his authority. But Himmler's encroachments were tacitly supported by Hitler and actively supported by Blomberg. In the many prob-lems presented by the introduction of conscription Blomberg used Himmler to sidetrack Wilhelm Frick's bureaucratic methods.[1] Thus, in 1934 Himmler already had a footing in the Ministry of the

[1] Gisevius, pp. 188-92.

Interior, though another nine years were to pass before it fell completely in his hands.

Frick tried to impose limitations on the power of the Gestapo as early as April 1934 in a directive to the federal provinces concerning concentration camp commitments. It was a weak directive and the Statthaelters ignored it.[1] After a meeting with Hitler both Frick and Guertner dropped it. However, at the end of that month Goering's Prussian Ministry for the Interior was subordinated to Frick's office nd Frick should now have been much better placed to oppose the encroachments of the Gestapo. Yet he did nothing. Nearly a year later Guertner, the Minister of Justice, supplied Frick with a considerable dossier on concentration camp practices. Heydrich, having obtained a copy, contested Guertner's right to interfere, but Frick got so far as to draft the terms of a law which would give prisoners in 'protective custody' access to the courts and it was placed on the agenda of the Prussian Ministerial Council.[2] Quite unconstitutionally Himmler attended the meeting, where he was able to get the motion quashed.[3] On 2 May 1935 the Prussian Court of Administration announced that the Gestapo was outside its jurisdiction. The only redress available against a Gestapo arrest or act of violence was an appeal to the next authority within the Gestapo itself.[4]

This contemptible grovelling by Prussian bureaucracy showed that the fear inspired by Heydrich and Himmler gave these two men a strength far beyond their nominal offices. Himmler followed up his success on the Prussian Ministerial Council by removing the conservative Admiral von Lewetzow from the Berlin Police Praesidium. Himmler had him replaced by the man who had come over from Roehm to the SS, Wolff Helldorf. Gisevius was removed at the same time from his proximity to Wilhelm Frick.[5] And on 10 February 1936 Himmler completed his control of the political police offices in the Laender. A decree of Hitler's recognised the Gestapo as a special police organisation, competent for the entire Reich.[6]

There had long ceased to be any question of rival police chiefs, like Helldorf, Daluege and Nebe, playing off Himmler and Goering as they had done before the blood-purge. The failure of Frick and Guertner to get the powers of the Gestapo defined had made

[1] Nuremberg Document PS 774; IMT XII, p. 204; Frank, op. cit., p. 160.
[2] Nuremberg Document PS 3751; IMT XII, p. 266.   [3] Gisevius, p. 192.
[4] Nuremberg Document PS 2437; IMT III, p. 189.   [5] Gisevius, p. 202.
[6] IMT XXII, p. 258.

Himmler a power above the police, so that the ratification of this position by Hitler on 17 June 1936 was a mere formality, even though it created a unified German police for the first time in history. Himmler's new title was 'Reichsfuehrer SS and Chief of the German Police in the Ministry of the Interior'.[1] But so long as the Reich Ministry of the Interior remained in the hands of such a rubber stamp of a man as Wilhelm Frick, Himmler's subordination to the Ministry was a fiction. Hitler's decree gave Himmler access to the Reich cabinet in all matters of concern to the police and by the beginning of 1937 Frick was no longer able to obtain access to Himmler.[2]

The period between 30 June 1934 and 17 June 1936 was the most critical in Himmler's career. He was a young man, thirty-four years old at the beginning of these two years, and generally despised for his part in a sordid political massacre. Yet in these two years he became the most powerful person in the internal administration of Germany. Little of the inner history of Himmler's advancement is known. More is heard of him during these two years in connection with his racial and archæological fads, the attacks on the Church, which he encouraged after the death of his father, and the curious new offices which he created to gratify his passion for expert information. These were the years of the libellous attacks on the Church leaders in *Das Schwarze Korps*, of Himmler's fantastic 'Henry the Lion' speech at Quedlinburg,[3] of the castle of the SS order of knighthood, the Wewelsburg near Paderborn, of the old Germanic excavations at Nauen and Altkristenberg conducted by the Ahnenerbe, an SS institute for 'research into German ancestral heritage'.

At the end of the two years Himmler was the first Chief of German Police in history, yet his intrigues to force his way into the leadership of Germany in war had failed. In July 1936 Himmler's private army as Reichsfuehrer SS consisted of barely a dozen battalions, inadequately armed by modern standards and of dubious function. If the control of three million SA men had not won Roehm the Ministry of Defence, how much less did the armed SS qualify Himmler for a say in the High Command. But there was another road open and this lay through Heydrich's Security Service or SD. Fundamentally this was an intelligence service to 'combat ideological enemies

---

[1] Nuremberg Document PS 647; IMT III, p. 146.
[2] IMT XXII, p. 311.   [3] See *supra*, p. 16.

within the state', but how could these enemies be separated from the agents of foreign powers and how could such agents be fought on German soil alone? From its first recognition as an official party information service, the SD was a challenge to the army's right to provide its own information services, a challenge to the established conception of 'Military Intelligence'.

Furthermore, any agency which was permitted to investigate complicity with foreign powers could be a handle against the High Command, which had had—like most modern professions from bishops to folk-dancers—their honeymoon with the Soviet Union. In the days before it became treasonable to criticise Hitler's anti-Comintern hysterics, most Germans had been proud of their General von Seeckt, who had signed the protocols of 1926 with Marshal Tuchachewski. Had not Seeckt hoodwinked the Allied Control Commission by signing an agreement which permitted an illicit Luftwaffe to train on Russian soil in the guise of instructing the Russians? It had been a long honeymoon and in the main a harmonious one. The old officer corps had been delighted with a country where the army retained so many privileges and where rank was so much respected. The Soviet Union was an old love of that starry-eyed boy scout Blomberg, before he became bewitched by Hitler. Having stayed in Russia in 1927-9 in the days when he served in the 'Truppenamt' at the War Office, Blomberg had come home 'almost a Bolshevik'.[1] As to Hammerstein, who succeeded Seeckt as Commander-in-Chief in 1931, he had signed the Tuchachewski protocols after many meetings with the 'Old Guard Bolshevik' Karl Radek, and it was believed by Hammerstein's friends in the Resistance Circle that Hitler had dismissed him in January 1934 because he was a 'Red general' who was too friendly with trade union leaders.[2] It was a fact that Hitler, even at the moment when he was most fervently wooing the High Command, fought shy of the protocol signatories. At Seeckt's funeral on 30 December, 1936 Hitler most pointedly left before the oration.[3]

In the days before they had the good luck to exploit Fritsch's homosexual friendships and Blomberg's scandalous marriage, the protocols were the point of Himmler's and Heydrich's attacks. Very soon after the blood-purge of June 1934 Heydrich found out that the

---

[1] Wheeler-Bennett, p. 296.
[2] Fabian von Schlabrendorff, *Offiziere gegen Hitler*, (Zurich, 1946), p. 49.
[3] Hossbach, op. cit., p. 53.

Chief of Military Intelligence, the naval captain Konrad Patzig, had used an aeroplane for photographic reconnaissance over Poland, with whom a ten-year non-aggression pact had been signed as the gravestone of the Seeckt-Tuchachewski protocol. Blomberg was induced to dismiss Patzig, who went to see him on 31 December, reproaching him bitterly for his blindness towards the intrigues of the SS. Blomberg defended Hitler's faith in the SS and Patzig shouted 'Then I regret that the Fuehrer does not know what a dungheap he has under him'.[1] Somewhat shaken, Blomberg went off to appoint in Patzig's place not the informer Heydrich but yet another naval officer, Heydrich's old instructor on board the training ship *Niobe*, Captain Canaris. And Patzig lived to be an admiral.

The appointment was a blow to the influence of the SS at court, yet on 1 January 1935 Blomberg had no reason to suppose that this was an appointment which would displease party purists. A man like Canaris, who had helped to acquit the murderers of Rosa Luxemburg and Karl Liebknecht in 1919,[2] might at least be presumed ideologically sound. In principle Himmler could not complain, though in August 1944 he was to talk of Canaris as Heydrich's bugbear 'whom we had always known to be a swine'.[3] In April 1945 moreover Himmler had Canaris murdered, but one must not read history backwards. In 1935 Canaris had the reputation of an unorthodox sailor with all a sailor's dislike of the professional military caste. Canaris's admirers portray him as a fastidious man, yet he remained intimate with Heydrich till Heydrich's death. And as late as February 1943 a group of young staff officers at Smolensk refused to shake hands with Canaris when they learnt that this apparently civilised being was on his way to a private talk with Himmler.[4] The quality of Canaris's opposition to the SS was never very certain and in this respect it resembled his alleged opposition to Hitler's annexations. Canaris was typical of the irresponsible Freikorps leaders who had supported secret rearmament and open political reaction under the Weimar Republic, believing that they could share that devil's supper with a teaspoon.

[1] Helmut Krausnick, *Wehrmacht und Nationalsozialismus*. Supplement to *Das Parlament*, 9 November 1955.
[2] Karl Abshagen, *Canaris, Patriot und Weltbuerger* (Stuttgart, 1949), pp. 69-74, 95.
[3] *Vierteljahreshefte fuer Zeitgeschichte* (Stuttgart, October 1953), p. 566.
[4] Fabian von Schlabrendorff, op. cit., p. 78.

Apart from the obvious reason that Heydrich coveted his post, there were two factors that were to alienate Canaris from the SS. The first was his fear in 1935-9 that an irresponsible use of Military Intelligence by Himmler and Heydrich might drive Hitler into war. The second factor was the awareness of Himmler and Heydrich that Canaris knew too much about them. The Berlin police chiefs Helldorf and Nebe had had to accept the incursion of the SS into their offices in 1934, but they played a double game and by 1937 they were supplying information on Himmler and Heydrich to Major Hans Oster in Canaris's office.[1] Outwardly, however, there was harmony between the Abwehr and the SS and a deliberately cultivated friendship between the former naval instructor Canaris and his former pupil Heydrich. They were neighbours till August 1936 in the Berlin suburb of Sudende and when Canaris moved to Schlachtensee Heydrich followed him.[2] Even after Heydrich's death Canaris gave this mass-murderer a rousing funeral oration.[3]

The two men were in fact obliged to work together. Under the Weimar Republic the Abwehr had no police force of their own. When police help was needed, they had to apply to the IA groups at the various state Police Praesidia. But in January 1945 practically all the IA groups had been merged in the Gestapo. Military Intelligence could take no action except through the Gestapo's own squads, the SIPO or security police. Heydrich might therefore refuse the aid of his men if he were not allowed a considerable share in Military Intelligence himself. In fact, so far from exploiting this situation, Heydrich in 1935 subscribed to the so-called 'ten commandments' by which his SD services were to refrain from military activity and pass on to the Abwehr any military information they possessed.[4]

Since Heydrich gave way so easily and since he never apparently tried to ruin or murder Canaris, the Gestapo chronicler Willi Hoettl concludes that Canaris blackmailed him with the secret of his non-Aryan origin.[5] But Heydrich did not observe the Abwehr's ten commandments and Canaris knew that he did not intend to do so. Accordingly Canaris persuaded the War Office to allow the Abwehr

[1] Abshagen, op. cit., p. 144; and see *infra*, p. 102.
[2] Abshagen, op. cit., p. 147.   [3] See *infra*, p. 217.
[4] Paul Leverkuehn, *The German Secret Service* (London, 1953), p. 34.
[5] See *supra*, p. 34.

to recruit a 'Secret Field Gendarmerie', should war break out,[1] in order to preserve some executive power of their own in a position which might turn out immeasurably to Heydrich's advantage. On the other side, Heydrich indicated in the mysterious Tuchachewski affair that he had no intention of keeping his SD services out of the domain of Military Intelligence.

Early in 1937 Heydrich asked Canaris for the services of his Abwehr in order to obtain examples of the handwriting of the signatories of the Seeckt-Tuchachewski protocol. The purpose was to supply the Russian secret police with forged evidence against the Russian High Command.[2] Canaris is alleged to have refused because he thought that Heydrich's real plan was to ruin not the Russian but the German signatories. And in fact Ernst Niekisch, who had been the adviser of Seeckt and the friend of Radek, was arrested by the Gestapo on 22 March. However, after the notorious Moscow generals' trial and the execution on 12 June 1937 of the generals Tuchachewski, Uborewitch, Eideman, Primakov, and Putna, Heydrich boasted that, acting on Hitler's own instructions, he had destroyed the Russian High Command.

Willi Hoettl has tried to fill in some of the gaps in the obscure story of Heydrich's first incursion into Military Intelligence in the light of Gestapo gossip picked up during the war. It seems that Heydrich had learnt before Christmas 1936, from Russian refugees in Berlin of Tuchachewski's plans for a Russian military Putsch, and had received Hitler's permission to supply faked evidence. The specimen signatures of the generals were obtained by Hermann Behrends of the SD without Canaris's co-operation and Behrends was to have conveyed the forged documents to Stalin via the Czech General Staff.[3] The plan was then changed and the evidence was sold by the SD to Russian secret agents in Berlin.

The interesting thing about this story, which Hoettl got from Behrends himself, is that something like the original plan was carried out too; but not, it would seem, by Heydrich. In the autumn of 1936 the German Foreign Office, then directed by Constantin von Neurath, put pressure on President Beneš to abandon his Russian alliance, warning him that he might find himself isolated after a 'high military conspiracy' in the Soviet Union. Dr. Beneš has

<hr />

[1] Leverkuehn, op. cit., p. 37.

[2] Abshagen, op. cit., pp. 168-71; Ian Colvin, *Chief of Intelligence* (London, 1952), p. 41. [3] Hagen, op. cit., pp. 83-7.

recorded that he at once warned the Russian legation in Prague of this conspiracy.[1]

Most of the condemned Russian generals confessed to a treasonable correspondence with the German General Staff and one of them is said to have admitted corresponding with the Gestapo, but such confessions, which are essential to Soviet state trials, are scarcely proof that Heydrich's claim was genuine. If there really was a plot of which the German Foreign Office had information, one would have thought that Hitler would have been only too pleased for Tuchachewski to get on with it rather than help Stalin re-form his High Command. Peter Kleist, an expert on Russian affairs in the Foreign Office at this time, had heard a story that Canaris did in fact supply Heydrich with the handwriting specimens, but Kleist thinks that Heydrich's intrigue had no effect in bringing about the trials.[2] It seems far more probable that Heydrich tried to forge material in order to start a treason trial in the Bendlerstrasse. Behrends believed that it was the GPU which used Heydrich, rather than the other way round;[3] and Himmler may have thought so too, for at Posen in October 1943 he said:[4] 'During the Moscow trials of 1937-8 we were persuaded in Europe and also in the SS that Stalin had made his greatest blunder. That was an out-and-out error on our part'.

One outcome of this unelucidated mystery was that Canaris became so alarmed by the combination with whom he had to work that he began to seek contacts with the Resistance Circle—in the summer of 1937 according to his friend Abshagen.[5] This did not prevent Canaris dutifully fulfilling the functions of the Abwehr. It was he who camouflaged the mobilisation against Austria as a field exercise;[6] nor was Canaris found wanting in expedients of this sort during Hitler's subsequent annexations. It is therefore very difficult to accept Canaris's part in the Resistance movement as more than a prudent bet the other way. Romantic theories that he was a friend of Britain, an ally of the British secret service or a passionate fighter for world peace can be discounted altogether. Canaris was a

---

[1] Peter Kleist, *Zwischen Hitler und Stalin* (Bonn, 1950), pp. 210-13.

[2] *Ibid.*, p. 213.   [3] Hagen, op. cit., p. 87.

[4] Nuremberg Document PS 1990.   [5] Abshagen, op. cit., p. 171.

[6] IMT X, p. 331, where Keitel states that Canaris came to his flat in order to discuss the matter with him and Goebbels.

pessimist and after some experience of Heydrich's methods he saw the future of his office as a dim one.

From the very beginning, in January 1935, there had been no clarity in Canaris's position. Hitler ruled like a Byzantine emperor, having a court but neither parliament nor co-ordinating cabinet. In the general scramble of the rival palace cliques no office of state could get its own way except by fighting other offices. At the end of 1936 SS agencies were able to meddle in the Tuchachewski affair, and yet this was a high matter of state in which Himmler had no competence as head either of the party bodyguard or of the German police. This SS meddling was possible because there were no less than seven rival Intelligence services in Hitler's Germany. Besides the Foreign Office there was the unofficial Bureau Ribbentrop which doubled its functions. There was Ernst Bohle's Auslandsorganization and Rosenberg's Foreign Political Office. There was Goering's Air Force Research Office, busy tapping telephone calls, and finally there were the Abwehr and the SD playing hide and seek with each other.

At the time of the Tuchachewski plot the SD was still only a party office. It was small, and officially it possessed no foreign intelligence or military section. On 17 January 1937, when Himmler explained the SD to his army officer audience, there was no hint of such ambitions.[1] 'Detailed problems of execution do not concern the SD, but only ideological problems'. One would think from this description of the three or four thousand members of the SD that they were a summer school for moral rearmament. But by this time the army officers may have known something of the ambitions of Reinhard Heydrich, director not only of the SD but of the armed Security Police Force as well; ambitions which he could pursue in the face of six competing agencies with the most comfortable of all reflections:

> Whatever happens we have got
> The Maxim gun and they have not.

---

[1] Nuremberg Document PS 1992A.

5

Conspiracy and War

NOVEMBER 1937 – SEPTEMBER 1939

1. THE FRITSCH-BLOMBERG CRISIS

It was 5 November 1937. The first of the great Russian state trials
had persuaded Europe (and, as Himmler observed years later, also
the SS) that this was indeed the idol with the feet of clay. Italy was
about to enter the anti-Comintern pact and the Poland of Colonel
Beck had just concluded an agreement with Hitler on the treatment
of minorities. So, when Hitler summoned the service chiefs—Blomberg, Fritsch, Admiral Raeder, and Goering, together with the
Foreign Minister, Constantin von Neurath—to a specially secret meeting in the Reich Chancellery, it was probably expected that Hitler
would talk of the coming trial of strength with Russia. But although
he scarcely stopped talking for four and a quarter hours, Hitler
hardly mentioned Russia at all.[1] To the amazement of his auditors
he spoke much of the inevitability of war with the Western powers.
Only a new living-space in Europe could solve Germany's problems,
since the aim of economic self-sufficiency had proved unattainable.
Austria and Czechoslovakia must be absorbed at latest in 1943-5,
when the present weapons with which Germany was rearming would
be getting obsolete. But, if need be, Hitler was prepared to absorb
both countries in 1938, since he did not think that Britain would
assist France on behalf of the Czechs.

With the exception of Admiral Raeder, all Hitler's auditors criticised this underestimate of the West, but there were no protests or
resignations. Blomberg reported to his first counsellor, Wilhelm
Keitel, that he thought Hitler had been bluffing.[2] Fritsch, when
egged on by Neurath and Ludwig Beck, had a second interview with
Hitler. Neurath made several attempts to do the same, suffered
several heart attacks between 5 November and Christmas and, when

---

[1] 'The Hossbach Protocol'; Nuremberg Document PS 386; Documents on
German Foreign Policy, Series D, Vol. 1, pp. 29-39; Hossbach, op. cit., p. 217.
[2] IMT XIV, p. 112.

at last he got an interview, was told that his services were no longer needed.[1]

It was suggested to Admiral Raeder at Nuremberg that the dismissals of Fritsch and Blomberg were really due to their attitude on 5 November 1937. To this the Admiral replied that, if Hitler had needed to get rid of them, he could have done it long ago,[2] an argument which seems convincing when it is considered that the service chiefs only voiced the same sort of flabby criticism which they had voiced ever since the introduction of conscription, and that Hitler really knew very well where he stood with Fritsch and Blomberg. The plot to ruin Fritsch and Blomberg in all probability did not originate with Hitler at all. In Fritsch's case the accusations were three years old. It may be believed, however, that Hitler was more receptive to Himmler's and Goering's denunciations after 5 November than he was before.

Two months before Hitler's conference there had already been a rumour that the SS were planning a Putsch against the army. Two members of the future Resistance Circle, Hjalmar Schacht the recently dismissed Minister for Economic Affairs, and Karl Goerdeler, the former Reich Price Commissioner, tried in vain to warn Fritsch of this. Fritsch left for a holiday in Egypt five days after Hitler's disclosure of his war plans, unaware that Heydrich was dogging him with two Gestapo agents.[3] When Heydrich was confronted with this evidence during the Fritsch inquiry, he deposed that he had been acting on Goering's instructions. It is nevertheless possible that the evidence, which Heydrich was accumulating against Fritsch, would not have been released anything like so soon if it had not been for the coincidence of Blomberg's scandalous marriage.

In Munich on 22 December, when Hitler attended Ludendorff's funeral at the Feldherrnhalle, Blomberg was observed to take Hitler aside. It was to impart the news that he, a German field-marshal, was about to marry 'a person of humble origin'.[4] To this Hitler made not the least objection, and Blomberg's marriage to Erna Gruen, the masseuse of Neukoelln, took place on 12 January 1938 with Hitler and Goering as witnesses. But on the 20th Blomberg returned hurriedly from his honeymoon and one of Fritsch's adjutants received an anonymous telephone call which was believed to have

[1] IMT XVII, p. 128.   [2] IMT XIV, p. 199.
[3] IMT XII, p. 226; Gisevius, op. cit., pp. 243, 251; Hossbach, op. cit., p. 139.
[4] Hossbach, p. 123.

come from the Gestapo—'Your field-marshal has married a whore'.

It seems that only that morning a lengthy dossier concerning Erna Gruen and her mother had been placed by a zealous police officer on the desk of the Berlin police president, Wolff Helldorf. The papers showed Blomberg's bride to have been a persistent prostitute with at least one criminal conviction for posing for indecent photographs. Helldorf was not the man to resist ruining a field-marshal if it should be to his advantage. But he had to be on his guard. Quite recently he had been in trouble for passing on a report concerning a homosexual lapse by Walter Funk, Schacht's successor in office. He decided that Blomberg, as a darling of Hitler's, would need still more delicate handling. So, instead of taking the papers to Himmler, he showed them first to Blomberg's own counsellor at the Bendlerstrasse, Artillery-General Wilhelm Keitel.[1]

Keitel had been on the General Staff in the First World War. At fifty-one years of age he was an arrogant, good-looking man with, so Hitler declared, 'the brains of a cinema commissionaire'.[2] Unfortunately Keitel had just enough brains to see that he was in the succession. Unfortunately, too, one of his three sons had just married Blomberg's daughter. The field-marshal's distasteful cavortings had intruded behind the lace curtains of Keitel's family life, but, as part of the game of military musical chairs, they had their uses. So Keitel did not share Helldorf's unusual delicacy. Instead of passing the papers on to Fritsch, who would doubtless have appointed a discreet court of honour to examine the affair, he bounced them back to Helldorf—which meant that they must now go to Himmler, the enemy of the High Command.

Helldorf himself did not go to Himmler, but on 22 January he saw Goering, which amounted to the same thing. On the 24th Goering had a long audience with Hitler and next day Hossbach learnt that Blomberg, 'who alone of the officer corps understands me', would have to go. He had made a fool of his Fuehrer. It seems, however, that Blomberg had not made a fool of Goering. When Helldorf brought him those explosive papers, Goering admitted that he had known everything about Erna Gruen even before escorting Hitler to Blomberg's wedding. He had been Blomberg's confidant for months and he had helped him by shipping overseas an awkward former lover of Erna Gruen's.[3] Goering had let Hitler go to the wedding deliberately and so had brought about Blomberg's ruin.

[1] Gisevius, p. 225.　　　[2] *Von Hassell Diaries*, p. 214.　　　[3] Gisevius, p. 247.

This is the story Helldorf told Gisevius, though not till February, when the hue and cry against Blomberg had died down. But, if it was true, why did Goering make this admission to so unreliable a character as Helldorf? Why should he admit it to anyone? Gisevius had already printed this story on 24 April 1946, when he gave evidence at Nuremberg, but Blomberg, who could have said something of Goering's role in his marriage, had died in the witness wing of the court prison in the previous month, a pathetic bedridden old man. On his way to give evidence, Gisevius heard Goering's counsel, Dr. Stahmer, threaten Schacht's counsel, Dr. Dix, that, if Gisevius mentioned the name of dear honoured Blomberg, Goering would give evidence against his co-defendant, Schacht. The court was scandalised and Gisevius resumed his evidence, wearing the halo of a man for whom Goering was gunning even then.[1]

Thus the third-hand story of Goering's role in the Blomberg marriage was repeated at Nuremberg without a challenge and became an historic legend, but there is at least one contradictory version current. Oberfuehrer Meisinger, who prepared the case for the Gestapo against Fritsch, is said to have admitted that he faked the Erna Gruen dossier himself, that he inserted and altered documents which concerned not Erna Gruen but her mother. Meisinger, who was sentenced to death in Poland in 1947 for his part in directing the Warsaw Gestapo office, also declared that neither Goering nor Hitler knew that Heydrich possessed this material when they attended Blomberg's wedding.[2]

On 25 January 1938 Hitler sent for Blomberg and asked him to name a successor as Minister of Defence. Blomberg at once proposed Goering, but was told that Goering was too complacent and too lazy. Blomberg carefully omitted to suggest Fritsch, who was said to have demanded Blomberg's resignation as soon as the scandal broke. In fact, Blomberg recollected in Nuremberg prison having hinted to Hitler that 'Fritsch was not a man for women'.[3] Neither did Blomberg propose the names of Beck, Leeb, or Brauchitsch. He knew that they had all been in the witch-hunt against him. The Minister of Defence whom Blomberg proposed was Hitler himself.

Next day Friedrich Hossbach, in his capacity as personal adjutant with the High Command, spent no less than ten hours in Hitler's company. He was delighted to find that Hitler had not the least

---

[1] IMT XII, p. 214.   [2] Hagen, op. cit., p. 52.
[3] Bullock, p. 379; Hossbach, p. 131.

intention of allowing Goering to step into Blomberg's shoes, but he was horrified to learn that Hitler was going to get rid of Fritsch as well, using a charge of homosexuality that dated back to the beginning of 1935, the days of the Saar plebiscite and the plans for the new conscript army, when Goering and Himmler had launched their campaign agaínst Fritsch.

Hossbach disobeyed an order from Hitler that he was not to repeat anything to Fritsch. He sought him out the same night in his flat in the Bendlerstrasse building, so ill prepared for the shock that he was actually waiting to hear of his succession to Blomberg. Fritsch at once realised that Goering and Himmler had planted a spy on him and his suspicions turned to 'a needy Hitlerjunge' whom he had once taken into his house and expelled for theft.[1]

Hossbach should have persuaded Fritsch to keep this damaging admission to himself, for Gisevius learnt that Fritsch actually admitted it later to Hitler.[2] Next day Hossbach broke the news to Hitler of his disobedience without provoking any of the usual emotional disturbances, but Hitler was very hard on Fritsch. He absolutely opposed Fritsch's demand for a public inquiry. Instead he proposed confronting Fritsch that very evening with his denouncer.

Once again Hossbach could not dissuade Fritsch, who cried 'I will see the swine unconditionally', though Canaris had tipped off Hossbach that the denouncer was a convicted criminal. And now at last Himmler, who had been waiting for Fritsch since the aftermath of the blood-purge, appeared openly on the scene. As Hossbach accompanied Fritsch through the vestibule to the Chancellery library, Himmler 'advanced towards him like the incarnation of ill-will'. During the confrontation of Fritsch with his denouncer, Hossbach had to sit next door to the library. Suddenly Goering rushed out, just as he had rushed out of his office during the signing of the execution warrants on 30 June 1934, shouting 'It was he, it was he'. The blackmailer Schmidt had identified the Commander-in-Chief.

Hitler, however, was not so precipitate. For the moment he decided only that 'good old Fritsch' had better go on indefinite leave. He sent for Keitel, Blomberg's First Counsellor, and told him that he still hoped to make Fritsch Minister of Defence, but first Himmler's accusations must be cleared up. Keitel was then sent to Heinrich Rosenberger, head of the Justice Department of the Wehrmacht, to convey Hitler's proposals for a special court. Rosenberger advised

---

[1] Hossbach, p. 127.   [2] Gisevius, pp. 233-4.

that it must be a military court of the highest order, and he quoted
the guttural French of Frederick the Great, 'Les lois doivent parler
et le souverain doit se taire'. Hitler expressed due admiration for the
sentiment and sent Rosenberger off to Guertner, where for the
moment everything was hung up—as was inevitable with Guertner
—by long arguments over procedure.[1]

On 27 January, the day following Fritsch's confrontation, Blomberg left the Chancellery for the last time, wearing civilian dress and
without military salutes. Before leaving Hitler, he had added another
faggot to the blaze by agreeing with Hitler that Fritsch might have
'succumbed to weakness'.[2] Then, having abandoned all for love, the
field-marshal resumed an interrupted honeymoon in Rome and
Capri like a middle-class Antony in his golden galley. He was never
recalled, but Hitler more than once sighed for his memory and even
Himmler was to declare that Blomberg was decent, loyal and true,
though as a man he had behaved tragically.[3]

On the 28th it was Hossbach's turn. While he was lunching at
Hitler's table in the Chancellery a telephone call from the Bendlerstrasse informed him that he had been superseded by Colonel
Schmundt, who was destined to remain Hitler's military adjutant
till the bomb of 20 July 1944 mortally injured him. Hossbach did
not leave without a defiant scene with his Fuehrer, for which, however, he did not suffer. He rose during the war to the rank of
colonel-general and in 1945 was dismissed by Hitler for disobedience
on a second occasion, when he ordered a retreat on his own initiative while commanding an army in East Prussia.

For a few more days Fritsch remained a Commander-in-Chief on
indefinite leave. His friends Beck and Rundstedt tried to persuade
Hitler to establish a military court,[4] while the Schacht-Goerdeler
faction tried for their part to interest Fritsch in a military Putsch
against Hitler. Through Artur Nebe, of the criminal police and
Admiral Canaris, the conspirators had obtained an inkling of Heydrich's methods. They knew that Fritsch had been saddled with the
dossier of another man.[5] But Fritsch was the last person on earth to
stage a Putsch against Hitler, although it was said that Himmler had
persuaded Hitler to believe this and that Hitler postponed his usual

---

[1] Narrative of Heinrich Rosenberger in *Deutsche Rundschau*, 8 November 1946.
[2] Hossbach, p. 131.
[3] *Vierteljahreshefte fuer Zeitgeschichte*, October 1952, p. 566.
[4] Bullock, p. 381.   [5] Gisevius, p. 243.

anniversary speech to the Reichstag, which he was to have delivered on 31 January, because he had learnt from Himmler that some of the troops might show their loyalty to Fritsch by surrounding the building.[1]

This story, which comes from Dr. Otto John, illustrates the state of hysteria of the time rather than the workings of Hitler's mind. Hitler had good reason to postpone his Reichstag speech, because he was expected to announce the new military appointments on which he could not make up his mind.[2] And one would have thought that even Himmler could hardly make Hitler's flesh creep about poor Fritsch, who had been idiotic enough to present himself at the Prinz Albrechtstrasse in order to be interrogated by the Gestapo. And when Hitler finally announced the new appointments, Fritsch actually consented—against his lawyer's advice—to resign till such time as the court should have cleared his name. Because of the resignation, the impossibly pedantic Guertner now ruled that Fritsch was no longer a soldier and therefore could not be tried by a military court.[3]

Thus, in one short week from his confrontation with the black-mailer Schmidt, the position of the Commander-in-Chief had completely deteriorated. But a change was taking place, too, on the side of the enemy. While Himmler wanted to ruin Fritsch altogether, Goering had second thoughts. He had already grasped the fact that, if Hitler was prevented from replacing his faithful Blomberg with his trusted Fritsch, then he would abolish the post of Minister of War altogether. That might suit Himmler, but it revived in Goering's breast the fear of 'National Bolshevism' which had set him against Roehm in 1933. During these critical days Goering not only saw his ambition thwarted, but also his present position as Chief of the Luftwaffe menaced by a Heydrich-inspired purge of the High Command on the lines of Stalin's recent state trials. Goering was swinging round to the side of the 'Generalitaet'. He was ready to see Fritsch's honour vindicated, provided that Fritsch could be kept out of Hitler's way till the seizure of Austria had been accomplished.

When Hitler delivered his delayed Reichstag speech on 3 February 1938, the resignations of Blomberg and Fritsch were bedded in a formidable mass of ministerial, military and diplomatic resignations

---

[1] Dr. Otto John, quoted by Wheeler-Bennett, op. cit., p. 371.

[2] According to Gisevius Hitler had to wait for a courier to bring him Blomberg's official resignation from Capri. Gisevius, p. 244.

[3] *Deutsche Rundschau*, 8 November 1946.

and appointments. At the Foreign Office Neurath was superseded by
the Ambassador to London, Joachim Ribbentrop. At the War Office
Hitler himself was to reign supreme, while Fritsch's place as Commander-in-Chief was to be taken by Walter von Brauchitsch, a
general who had never been considered as a successor. As commander of the 1st Army Corps and East Prussian military area,
Brauchitsch had quarrelled in 1935 with the Gauleiter, Erich Koch,
thereby incurring Hitler's disapproval.[1] Nevertheless, in February
1938 he was preferred to von Reichenau, the friend of Himmler and
Goering. Hitler's preference for Brauchitsch was the more singular
in that Brauchitsch was to be a constant nuisance to him, even
though he was never seriously a member of the Resistance Circle.
Hitler's failure to appoint Reichenau may partly have been due to
Reichenau's attack on Julius Streicher, the Gauleiter of Franconia,
who had come into conflict with the local garrison commander in
July 1934. In these circumstances Hitler listened to the observa-
tions of his generals, who regarded Reichenau as a desk general
without field experience. Hitler, moreover, was already engaged in
the political conversion of Brauchitsch. It had come to his ears before
the general post of February 1938 that Brauchitsch was seeking a
divorce from his wife in order to marry an ardent Nazi, Charlotte
Schmidt. It was Hitler himself who finally persuaded Brauchitsch's
first wife to agree to a divorce.[2]

As already mentioned, Hitler himself took over the War Office—
or, rather, he abolished it, together with Blomberg's post. In its place
he created the institution known as OKW, the High Command of
the Armed Forces, but the High Commander was Hitler himself.
Wilhelm Keitel was to be only Hitler's representative and he did not
succeed to Blomberg's cabinet rank. Goering, who had succeeded
neither to Blomberg nor to Fritsch, received an empty scabbard, the
rank of General Field Marshal and Senior Officer of the Reich.
Himmler received no reward and needed none. He had smashed the
privileged citadel of the High Command, and he could survey his
handiwork—a dozen army corps commanders dismissed, including
Rundstedt, the senior general. The commander of the XVIth Panzer
Corps, General Luetz, only heard of his dismissal through the Press.[3]

And now, with the attention of the German public and of the

[1] Hossbach, p. 43.
[2] Milton Shulman, op. cit., pp. 11 and 322 (Interrogation of Helmuth Greiner).
[3] Von Schweppenburg, op. cit., p. 174.

world focused on the crisis that Hitler had provoked in Austria, the judicial inquiry into the accusations against Fritsch was pursued. It had become a duel between the Gestapo and the army with Goering and the Minister of Justice, Guertner, hovering between the two sides. The four assessors at the inquiry, Karl Sack and Hans Oster for the army, von der Goltz and Hans von Dohnanyi for the Ministry of Justice, were a safe team as far as Fritsch was concerned, and they did their best for him. On the eighth day of the inquiry they discovered the true identity of the man with whom the black-mailer Schmidt had consorted at Wannsee railway station in January 1935. Schmidt mentioned an address in Lichterfelde where he had gone to collect his money. And Schmidt's client was still living there, not Field-Marshal von Fritsch but Rittmeister von Frisch, an almost bedridden retired cavalry officer. Schmidt's error had been genuine, for both personages had been decorated in the Continental Baronial style—a green hat, a jacket with a fur collar, a silver-handled cane, and a monocle.[1]

But before the four assessors had a chance to take the dying depositions of Rittmeister von Frisch, he was whisked off by the Gestapo. The army had now to rescue both Schmidt and Frisch from the Prinz Albrechtstrasse so that they could be produced at the court martial. They were fished out with some difficulty by the Ministry of Justice, but Schmidt had been primed and he now de-posed that he had known both Frisch and Fritsch. Probability was not on the Commander-in-Chief's side. There was the 'needy Hitler-junge' he had mentioned to Hitler. General Alfred Jodl noted in his diary on 26 February that both Guertner and Admiral Raeder be-lieved Fritsch guilty. The desperate Fritsch tried to challenge Himmler to a duel with pistols. Hossbach says that he still has the challenge, which was drawn up by Ludwig Beck. Rundstedt was to have delivered it at Himmler's office, but he never dared to and carried it about for weeks.[2] It is inconceivable that Hitler would have allowed Himmler, who was short-sighted, to fight and one can only speculate on the memorable scene the world was spared. Himmler, who signed orders that were the death-warrants of millions of people, was probably never under fire in his life, not even from aerial bombardment or long-range artillery.

Hitler's announcement of the composition of the 'Reich Court Martial' which was to try Fritsch must have relieved the defence of

[1] Gisevius, p. 249.   [2] Wheeler-Bennett, p. 375.

their worst anxieties. It could hardly have been more respectable, consisting as it did of the supreme heads of the army, navy and air force and of two blameless Senate Presidents of the Leipzig Supreme Court. The chief anxiety of the defence lawyers was Fritsch. Would he hit back, denounce the intrigues of Goering and Himmler and perhaps hamstring the Gestapo for ever? But on 11 March, when the court was to meet, Hitler suspended the proceedings. The heads of the services were needed elsewhere. That night German troops were on the march to Vienna.

On 17 March, when the court sat again, Hitler was once more a public hero; there had been no Allied ultimatum to Germany ordering her forces out of Austria and the Anschluss was about to be acclaimed in yet another German plebiscite. Stupefied by the massed brass bands, Fritsch and the service chiefs Raeder and Brauchitsch, who were more his co-defendants than his judges, refrained from attacking the Gestapo. Yet the occasion was unique. The blackmailer Schmidt broke down and admitted that he had been threatened with death by Meisinger unless he stuck to his story—and the total disappearance of Schmidt from history seems to imply that Meisinger was as good as his word. To judge from Gisevius's secondhand description of the trial, the initiative against Schmidt was taken not by Fritsch's counsel but by Goering, who personally bullied Schmidt into making his retraction in open court.[1]

With the dramatic appearance of Goering challenging the Gestapo, the four-year-old Himmler-Goering alliance ended abruptly. Henceforward Goering recognised in Heydrich a new enemy, a man who possessed evidence against everybody, who had no friends and who, as chosen Private Security Officer, could see Hitler when he pleased. Heydrich had not withdrawn a scrap of the doctored evidence against Fritsch, because he believed that the least display of weakness would finish his career, and he told Nebe that the appointment of a Reich Court Martial would be the end of him.[2]

It was not the end of Heydrich, nor was it even a loss of face, since the trial had been held *in camera*. But from now on Goering was on the look-out for a chance to get this dangerous and resentful person put away. Five days before the verdict, von Papen learnt in Vienna from Goering's Luftwaffe Chief of Staff, Karl Bodenschatz, that Goering was going to denounce Heydrich to Hitler for the murder of von Ketteler, a member of von Papen's embassy staff in Vienna.

[1] Gisevius, pp. 256-7.   [2] IMT XII, p. 232.

Heydrich counter-attacked with very dubious evidence that Ketteler had planned to shoot at Hitler from a balcony of the Kaiserhof Hotel.[1] Years later, Felix Kersten learnt that Heydrich had demonstrated to Hitler with the aid of a telescope how it could be done.

After 18 March 1938, when Fritsch was acquitted, the telescope[2] demonstration may have saved Heydrich from being thrown to the lions. In any case Hitler did not want any sensational repercussions from Fritsch's acquittal. A week afterwards he congratulated Fritsch on 'recovering his health'. Five months later, Fritsch was made honorary commander of his old regiment, the 12th Artillery, among whom he was formally welcomed—but that was all. Fritsch received no appointment worthy of a colonel-general. He lived without employment at a country house which the army presented to him at Achterburg, near Soltau. In September 1939 he accompanied his regiment to Poland as a supernumerary officer in his own car and on the 18th he walked into the enemy's field of fire near Praga on the Warsaw front. It was like most of Fritsch's gestures—a useless one. Hitler hauled Brauchitsch over the coals because he had issued an Order of the Day extolling the heroism of Fritsch's death.[3] And Ulrich von Hassell wrote in his diary that everyone assumed that Fritsch had been murdered by the SS.[4]

2. THE ANSCHLUSS. HIMMLER AND THE FOREIGN OFFICE

With the removal of Blomberg and Fritsch and with the beginning of Hitler's control of the armed forces, Europe passed into the era of naked aggression. Only nineteen months separated Hitler's Reichstag address of 3 February 1938 from the Second World War. For the purposes in view Hitler had not selected his new team badly. As each successive challenge was flung to the foreign powers, Hitler received from his service chiefs murmurs but not protests, though Goering as economic dictator showed misgivings at the prospect of an early war and Brauchitsch listened with apparent sympathy to the nebulous Putsch proposals put to him by the Schacht-Goerdeler group. In the Foreign Office Hitler enjoyed the services of Ribbentrop, who not only took his orders blindly but concealed them from his own Ministry, as well as from the Ministries with whom he was

---

[1] Von Papen, *Memoirs*.   [2] Kersten, *Totenkopf und Treue*.
[3] Helmuth Greiner, *Die Oberste Wehrmachtfuehrung*, 1939-45 (Wiesbaden, 1951), p. 61.   [4] *Von Hassell Diaries*, p. 74. Erich Kondt, *Nichtaus den Akten*.

supposed to maintain contact. These were passive agents. In Himmler and Heydrich he had something equally essential, men who could watch and arrest the flow of public gossip each time the threat of war appeared; men who had fought in no wars themselves, who had no share in the generals' fear of responsibility and who saw in war only a greater demand for their services.

The Austrian Anschluss brought Himmler and Heydrich to Vienna when they were still in their thirties. For the first time they exercised their office in a foreign capital and behind them was an unbounded sense of authority. It is strange that there had to be so much repression in a city which put out flags to celebrate its return to the Germanic community. The scale of arrests could not have been greater had their been armed assault and bitter resistance. But from the first there was a state of panic among the officials, German and Austrian, who took over the government. It was due to the fact that no one knew what Hitler was doing. His decisions had been made suddenly; and on 9 March, when Hitler learnt of Schuschnigg's plebiscite, which was the excuse for his intervention, Reichenau, who was to lead the troops, was attending an international Olympic Games conference in Cairo. On the evening of the 11th, when the first German troops crossed the frontier, it was by no means clear to the commanders what action they were covering. They had to believe that all this was being done in order that one Austrian Minister, Seyss-Inquart, should take over the duties of Chancellor from another Austrian Minister, Schuschnigg, who had already accepted the situation. It was not till 13 March that Hitler overcame his hesitations about annexing Austria to the Reich, having acquired confidence after the reception accorded to him by his boyhood town of Linz.

Hitler did not venture to set foot in Vienna till the night of 14 March. Himmler preceded him by three days, arriving at Aspern, the airport of Vienna, at three in the morning on 12 March. Himmler brought with him Karl Wolff, Gottlob Berger, and most of his Adjutantur. He was received by Ernst Kaltenbrunner, a turbulent small-town lawyer and chief of the Austrian SS. Kaltenbrunner was accompanied by Odilo Globocnik, who had been the go-between of the Austrian National Socialists with Hitler. Globocnik, who was probably of mixed blood, came from Trieste and represented perhaps the very worst of what the SS had to offer. In 1942-3 he became the organiser of the massacre of the Jews of Poland,[1] employing many members of the Austrian SS of pre-Anschluss days.

A third member of the reception committee must have caused Himmler embarrassment, for he was Michael Skubl, the Austrian Chief of Police. Skubl had been appointed by Dollfuss on 24 July 1934, the day of his murder, and Himmler was accompanied by one of the murderers' accomplices, the naval lieutenant Meissner. Skubl left in silence and by noon Himmler had demanded his resignation. Kaltenbrunner, who was to succeed Skubl, was put temporarily in charge of the 'executive force', and within a few days Skubl was under arrest.[2]

Himmler went on almost at once to Linz in the company of the Austrian Ministers, Seyss-Inquart and General Edmund Glaise-Horstenau, in order to arrange a reception for Hitler. The streets were filled with the tanks and armoured cars of Guderian's XVIth Army Corps. Before they advanced any further, Guderian proposed that the vehicles should be beflagged and decorated in Austrian colours. Ludwig Beck, still hanging on uneasily as Chief of Staff, objected. As it happened, Sepp Dietrich was present, for, as parade troops, the Leibstandarte had attended every ceremonial entry since the return of the Saar territory in 1935. Sepp Dietrich, though no more than a battalion commander in Guderian's corps, could still use his friendship with Hitler to get the Chief of Staff of the German army overruled.[3] It was to be history's irony that, when Sepp Dietrich himself became an army commander, Hitler refused to see him, mistrusting his own sentimentality too much to listen to the 'old party fighter's' objections to the Ardennes offensive of December 1944.

Next day Himmler was installed in the Imperial Hotel in Vienna and the first mass arrests began that night. Dr. Steinbauer, counsel for Seyss-Inquart at Nuremberg, declared that they included communists and monarchists, priests and freemasons, and even boy scouts.[4] Three weeks later a special train conveyed 165 former Austrian government officials to Dachau, where they either died or spent the next seven years in captivity. Among the latter were Dr. Figl, the present Austrian Chancellor, and Dr. Geroe, who was to become Minister of Justice. By the end of May 1938 the trains from

[1] See *infra*, p.p. 133, 173, 217.   [2] IMT XVI, p. 220.
[3] Heinz Guderian, *Erinnerungen eines Soldaten* (Heidelberg, 1951), p. 43.
[4] IMT XIX, p. 165.

Vienna to Dachau and Buchenwald provided a weekly service and the victims numbered thousands, a large proportion being Jews.

One of Himmler's activities during the few weeks that he spent in Vienna was to look for a site for a concentration camp. He chose the neighbourhood of the Wienergraben, a huge quarry near Mauthausen, from which Vienna had obtained paving-stones since late imperial times. Mauthausen is a pretty village on the north bank of the Danube a few miles from Enns, but the massive fortress which was to spring up on the wooded heights above the quarries might have been in Siberia for all that the villagers can tell you about it today. It seems that, a few months after the Anschluss, Himmler had the Wienergraben quarries transferred to DEST, one of two industrial undertakings which he had just founded for the SS.[1] A party of convicted felons were brought over from Dachau to start work and by the end of 1938 Mauthausen concentration camp was ready for its first inmates. But construction was slow. The place must have been meant to outlast the 'Thousand Years Reich' and it is possible that it will perpetuate for the next thousand years the memory of its first six years of infamy. A space on the wooded hillside was levelled and enclosed with huge sloping granite walls. On the walls were wooden guardhouses with curling roofs, deliberately imitated, according to some nebulous historic concept of Himmler's, from the guardhouses on the Great Wall of China. Inside these walls one may inspect a rectangular camp with a finely paved parade ground and broad alleyways. It is now a martyrs' memorial, but it is impossible to visualise behind the geometric military and Teutonic neatness of Mauthausen the filth, overcrowding, hunger, corpses, and tortures which were the characteristics of the place till May 1945.

Thus within a few months of the Anschluss, Austria acquired the most essential feature of a part of the greater Reich. No longer was it necessary to send subjects of protective-custody orders more than a hundred miles from Vienna. Gradually, however, Mauthausen lost its Austrian character. Frenchmen, Czechs, Russians, Spanish Republicans and Jews from all countries were sent there, but throughout the six and a half years of its existence Mauthausen never lost the reputation of the most murderous of all concentration camps.[2] More than 33,000 people were done to death there and in the dependent labour camps.

[1] See *infra*, pp. 258-9.   [2] See *infra*, p. 269.

The more illustrious prisoners of the Gestapo, which in Vienna as in Germany retained its monopoly of political arrests, were kept in the Metropole Hotel, among them Chancellor Schuschnigg and Baron Louis de Rothschild. The former was destined to spend seven years in German concentration camps; the latter was released a year later and allowed to emigrate after handing over his steel rolling-mills to the Hermann Goering Werke.[1] It was neither the first nor the last deal between Nazi leaders and the 'arch-enemies' who figured in Hitler's speeches. But the Rothschild case had little in common with the doom of some 180,000 Vienna Jews who were handed over to Heydrich, henceforward to be the arch-enemy of their race.

The Austrian Anschluss marked a new stage in Heydrich's career, with the birth of an organisation that was in the end to encompass the death of more than four million people. It began in occupied Vienna as the 'Office for Jewish Emigration'. For the first time the Gestapo became the sole agency that could issue exit permits for Jews. It was a lucrative monopoly. The hundred thousand Jews who were able to get out of Austria before the outbreak of the Second World War left the country mostly destitute. Soon the 'Office for Jewish Emigration' extended its monopoly to the Old Reich and from March 1939 to annexed Czechoslovakia. Later in that year it handled forced deportations to Poland, and by the autumn of 1941 outright extermination. The Director of this organisation remained the same till the collapse of Germany. He was an Austrian and a native of Hitler's home town of Linz, and his name was Karl Adolf Eichmann. He had been sent to Vienna by the Gestapo to prepare the ground shortly before the Anschluss.[2]

It was in Vienna that Hitler had first imbibed political anti-Semitism from the Christian Socialist Fritz Lueger in the early years of the twentieth century. The establishment of Eichmann's office in Vienna was therefore more significant than any other part of Himmler's reign of terror. But to Hitler the Vienna Jews were of as little interest as Vienna itself, a place which had created an ineffaceable bitterness in his soul and which he quitted after spending only a night there.[3] The destruction of the Jewish race was not the main purpose of Hitler's urge for dictatorship and conquest, but only one

[1] Case XI, transcript, 28, 677.
[2] Nuremberg Document No. 2259; Reitlinger, *The Final Solution* (London, 1953), pp. 25-6.　　　[3] Bullock, p. 395.

of the ultimate consequences of pan-Germanism. In March 1938 Hitler probably regarded the expulsion of the Vienna Jews as little more than a job for Heydrich and a means of stopping him from dragging up further dirt against the army and his party colleagues.

Eight weeks after the Anschluss Hitler and the whole of his court were in Rome. Mussolini had accepted the situation with southern fatalism and was believed to be indifferent to the treatment of the next victims, the Czechs. It was the moment to cement the Rome-Berlin alliance in the eyes of the world with a well-publicised state visit, but it was neither Hitler's nor Himmler's first visit to Mussolini. Himmler had paid a purely complimentary visit in 1937 and had been received by Ambassador von Hassell, for whom he retained what seems to have been more than a formal acquaintanceship. At the end of that year, when von Hassell was recalled, Himmler took over the Embassy chauffeur and in April 1939 he told von Hassell that he had refused to listen to the man when he had 'talked out of school'.[1]

It was natural enough that Himmler should accompany Hitler's court to Rome, but unusual that a chief of police should have to stay with Hitler at the Quirinal. It could hardly have been because Himmler was the godson of a Prince of Bavaria or because Hitler needed protection. Nor did Himmler stay in the palace for pleasure. In spite of a royal-tutor father and a royal-chaplain uncle, Himmler felt as uncomfortable among the starchy ceremonies of the House of Savoy as did Hitler. 'Here one breathes the air of the catacombs', he remarked, and this was repeated to the king.[2]

In reality Hitler took Himmler with him because, since the days of the secret meetings with von Papen, he regarded him as a diplomatist. After the state visit to the Quirinal, Hitler considered Himmler as particularly acceptable to Italians. In December 1939, when he needed to convince Mussolini that the Russian alliance was neither ideological nor permanent, he sent Himmler on a personal mission. Himmler could be trusted to talk about the sub-human enemy as if nothing had happened. Himmler was habitually polite and could undo some of the harm caused by the previous missionary, the foul-mouthed Robert Ley. It was Count Ciano's belief that Himmler was successful at this secret interview. He had persuaded

[1] *Von Hassell Diaries*, p. 43.
[2] Filippo Anfuso, *Du palais de Venise au lac de Garde* (Paris, 1949).

Mussolini to promise to enter the war and Ciano noted in his diary 'The fewer Germans Mussolini sees the better'.[1]

After his mission to Italy in December 1939, Ciano developed an exaggerated respect for Himmler's astuteness and understanding. In one particular he was not far wrong. Himmler learnt to mistrust the Italian Fascists far more than did any other member of Hitler's entourage. He was not deceived by the events of July 1943 and in the middle of a great deal of hysteria Himmler showed sense. Yet of all the affairs of state in which Himmler tried to meddle, foreign policy, for which alone he had some aptitude, was the one in which he was destined to succeed least.

And yet at the time of the Anschluss Himmler's foreign political ambitions seemed promising. Ribbentrop had not been present at Linz on 13 March when Hitler signed the law for the reunion of Germany and Austria. He was in London and there seems to be some reason to believe his plea that he had denied the Anschluss in all ignorance.[2] Himmler, on the other hand, was personally in charge of the arrangements for the Linz ceremony, which took place in an hotel bedroom. Himmler knew that Ribbentrop's recent appointment had pleased no one in the party but Hitler; from now on he began to infringe more openly on the Foreign Office's competence.

The accession of Ribbentrop as Foreign Minister during the Fritsch-Blomberg crisis had not meant any immediate influx of old party members into this caste-bound service. Most of Ribbentrop's amateur diplomatist friends of the 'Bureau Ribbentrop' were jettisoned, and, apart from his own inner office, the bureau RAM, Ribbentrop himself was content to support the older permanent officials whom the party ridiculed. But the lack of party affiliations frightened Ribbentrop, and soon after the Anschluss he asked Himmler to accord SS rank to his new State Secretary and Under-State Secretary, Weizsaecker and Woermann. Himmler's alacrity in consenting showed that he would have liked more of such pledges of Foreign Office loyalty,[3] but there were no more requests, perhaps because Ribbentrop felt that he had weakened his position. At any rate, it was only after the fall of France that, in a letter of excessive fulsomeness, Ribbentrop accepted from Himmler his promotion from Gruppenfuehrer to Obergruppenfuehrer or general in the SS.

[1] *Ciano's Diary*, 1939-42 (London, 1947), pp. 185-6, 195.
[2] Ribbentrop memoirs; Fritz Hesse, *Hitler and the English* (London, 1954).
[3] Paul Seabury, *The Wilhelmstrasse*, pp. 64-5.

With the outbreak of war, when Ribbentrop was pleased to travel to Poland in Himmler's own train, his enthusiasm led him into far more dangerous concessions. Ribbentrop's embassies, legations, and consulates abroad became flooded with robust military material who, it seems, were 'police attachés' from the Gestapo.[1] When he realised that the reports of these men completely sidetracked the Foreign Office, Ribbentrop started a feud with the RSHA. Thus, after the annexation of the Balkans in April 1941, he chose five new ambassadors, who as SA leaders close to Roehm had barely escaped Himmler's execution squads in June 1934. But this was only a gesture of pique, a permanent state of mind with Ribbentrop. His quarrels with the SS were not ideological but concerned only with fields of competence. The idea of a party élite army of strong-muscled young men appealed to Ribbentrop. His own son served as a captain in the Leibstandarte, winning the Knight's Cross in 1943 as the only Old Westminster boy in the Waffen SS.[2] Ribbentrop was by no means the only person of his class to find in the selectivism of Himmler's SS laws a substitute for snobbery. Sometimes he would urge the admission of SS men in the Foreign Office or the introduction of SS methods of training. In June 1942 he proposed to Himmler that ten young SS men should be provided for the Foreign Office in return for every ten thousand recruits who should be procured for the Waffen SS by embassies and legations abroad.[3]

There were moments when Ribbentrop felt nearer to Himmler than to his professional diplomats. Ribbentrop's experience as a temporary military attaché in Istanbul at the end of the First World War had only exacerbated his class-consciousness. Himmler's contempt for Ribbentrop's efficiency was therefore tempered by some sympathy in regard to his position.

But in the essential point, the struggle against the old diplomacy, I am absolutely at one with Ribbentrop. For the past century or two it has been practically a monopoly of some twenty to thirty noble families.[4]

In reality the protocol-ridden mentality of the professional diplomats served Himmler well. There was no thuggery from the deportation of Jews for the gas chambers to the crimping of alleged Germanic stock to serve in the Waffen SS, in which the German diplomats

[1] See *infra*, p. 144-5.
[2] Kraetschmer, *Die Ritterkreuztraeger der Waffen SS*, pp. 208-9.
[3] NG 3649, quoted in Seabury, op. cit., p. 197.   [4] Kersten, op. cit., p. 115.

abroad did not assist Himmler's offices. It was only the jackbooted former SA men like Ambassador Killinger in Rumania who occasionally spluttered with outraged dignity.[1] As to the persecution of Jewry, it had been an interest of the Foreign Office even before Ribbentrop's day under the rule of Constantin von Neurath. In 1937, for instance, there was an onslaught by every party body in the Reich against a Finance Ministry agreement with the Jewish Haavara economic agency in Palestine, by which Jews emigrating from Germany to Palestine might still be permitted to retain a fraction of their possessions. In the Foreign Office contact with the party was maintained by Vicco von Buelow-Schwante of the department 'Deutschland', who joined most effectively in the hue and cry against the Haavara agreement. Yet this was before that department had become an outpost of Heydrich's Security Office, and it was precisely at this time that Buelow-Schwante was supposed to be helping Gisevius to collect material on SS atrocities.[2]

In September 1938 there arrived under the rule of Ribbentrop a successor to Buelow-Schwante in the Deutschland department. Martin Luther (not the religious gentleman, as the American prosecutor remarked at Nuremberg) was a furniture removals contractor and collector of party funds for the suburb of Dahlem. Luther had been useful to Ribbentrop in 1932 in getting him a low party-membership number. In 1936 Luther entered the 'Bureau Ribbentrop', having been employed shipping furniture to the German embassy in Carlton House Terrace. When two years later Luther took over the Deutschland department, he created a separate establishment with its own building in the Rauchstrasse. During the war it became to all intents the protocol branch of Eichmann's 'Jewish Emigration Office'. Luther was completely devoted to Himmler and this was perhaps Himmler's biggest encroachment on Foreign Office terrain. But Himmler's ambitions could not be satisfied through this financially shady stool-pigeon. In 1943, when Luther used his access to Himmler in order to plot Ribbentrop's downfall, Himmler sacrificed him.[3]

It was not Himmler's nature to proceed openly against a fellow

[1] See *infra*, p. 145.
[2] *Documents on German Foreign Policy*, D, V, p. 749. IMT XVII, p. 219.
[3] Peter Kleist, *Zwischen Hitler und Stalin*, p. 12; Rudolf Rahn, *Ruheloses Leben* (Duesseldorf, 1949); Seabury, op. cit., p. 73; see *infra*, pp. 234-6.

satrap, particularly one like Ribbentrop for whom Hitler had an objective admiration that surpassed even his personal dislike. To the very end of the war Hitler regarded the arrogant ass as a second Bismarck and well Himmler knew it. During the war years Himmler extended his attempts to usurp the functions of the Foreign Office but through fear of Hitler they were furtive attempts. They resembled his former assaults on the army and police, not direct assaults but progressive undermining. Against the Foreign Office Himmler's best weapon was the position he enjoyed after October 1939 as pleni-potentiary for resettlement questions in occupied Europe. At the time of the Munich crisis Himmler had not advanced so far, but Heydrich's military intelligence activities had already invaded Foreign Office terrain. It had been evident, as early as the Austrian Anschluss that the fifth column, which preceded Hitler's armies of occupation, had slipped out of the hands of Canaris's Abwehr and of the Foreign Office alike.

3. MUNICH AND AFTER. THE SS FIFTH COLUMN

Between the Anschluss and the Munich agreement, Himmler and Heydrich were concerned with the creation of a fifth column in Sudetenland, the border districts of Czechoslovakia. Some light—but not enough—was shed on this very secret episode in a file of documents which the Soviet prosecution produced very late in the first Nuremberg trial.[1] The first document in this remarkable file is an instruction from the head office of the SD, issued in June 1938, the month in which Hitler briefed his generals at Jueterbog for an invasion of Czechoslovakia. The document speaks of the recruiting of eleven 'Action Commandos' of the SD to follow close on the fighting troops. They were to fulfil functions similar to those of the SD in Germany, in particular 'to secure political life and national economy' more specifically to prevent sabotage, to keep a watch on Czech industrial plant and to make arrests. At Nuremberg this docu-ment finally destroyed the alibi of the SD as a harmless non-executive information service, for in the competent hands of Colonel Smirnov it was used to floor a very muddled Gestapo witness, the SS colonel Rolf Hoeppner. Smirnov showed that the organisation of these eleven Action Commandos was identical with that of the notorious Special Commandos which were to serve in Russia. In the chart of

[1] Nuremberg Document USSR 509.

1938 there even appeared the names of the same officers. For instance, Major Heinz Jost, the head of SD's Foreign Section (later Amt VI), to whom the chart was sent on 13 September 1938, was destined to command an Extermination Group in Russia in 1942.[1] Names on the chart included the later Extermination Group commanders, Schulz, Biermann, and Stahlecker, all of whom in 1938 were 'Information officers' of the SD. The transport officer of the commandos in Czechoslovakia was to be Captain Rauff who was destined later to organise the gassing-vans both in Russia and Serbia, while other officers nominated by the SD for the invasion of Czechoslovakia included Fritz Seidl who was to command the Jewish camps Theresienstadt and Bergen-Belsen, and Hans Guenther, who was to be Heydrich's agent for the extermination of Czech Jewry.

Although the Munich agreement rendered it unnecessary to use the 'Einsatzkommandos of the SIPO and SD', their cadre was retained. The peaceful annexation of Bohemia-Moravia and the creation of a satellite state in Slovakia in March 1939 averted their second mobilisation, but they took the field in earnest in Poland in the following September. These commandos, however, had been only part of the army which Himmler had hoped to direct in the invasion of Czechoslovakia, for he was also fighting for the control of the Freikorps Henlein, a fifth column of 40,000 Sudeten Germans, whose operations were directed from Hitler's side of the border.

The struggle between Himmler and Brauchitsch over the Freikorps Henlein is revealed in another file of Nuremberg documents.[2] Originally Henlein was to have run his Freikorps with the help only of an advisory officer from the army. On 19 September, four days after Neville Chamberlain's visit to Berchtesgaden, when Hitler had ordered the mobilisation of thirty-six divisions, the instructions were altered. The High Command was to take over Henlein and all his works.[3] But Henlein in his headquarters at Schloss Dorndorff was in touch simultaneously with Canaris, the army's Intelligence Chief, and with Gottlob Berger, Himmler's agent for Czechoslovakia. On 26th September, four days before Munich, Himmler was stimulated by Berger's reports to inform Henlein that he would come under his exclusive orders in the event of war.[4] This was flatly

---

[1] See *infra*, footnote to p. 145. [2] Document PS 998; IMT II, p. 35.
[3] Document PS 1780.
[4] IMT III, p. 124, and II, p. 38; Document PS 3036.

contradicted by Keitel on the 28th. Not only would the Freikorps come under the High Command and the competent General Staff, but its sector 'would be fitted in the scheme of army boundaries'. And so, too, would two battalions of Death's Head Guards from Dachau whom Himmler had moved secretly into the Czechoslovak enclave at Eich. As to the four other Death's Head battalions whom Himmler had moved up towards the frontier, they would come under army orders forthwith. The order, which Alfred Jodl of OKH distributed to no fewer than forty-five command posts, ended with the pointed words: 'It is requested that all further arrangements be made between the Commander-in-Chief Army and the Reichsfuehrer SS'.[1]

Two days later the outcome of the Munich meeting of Hitler, Chamberlain, and Daladier solved this dispute, leaving only the simpler problem of policing an annexed frontier. It was now possible to offer a sop to Himmler's vanity. The High Command laid down that the Freikorps Henlein could be withdrawn from the line 'in agreement with the Reichsfuehrer SS'. This ended another flare-up of the old SS-army feud. Hitler supported the High Command against the SS, but only so far as the field army was concerned. Hitler never interfered in the muddle by which the SD operated its own commandos in a front-line area, and the Sudetenland crisis established a mischievous principle which was to prevail on every front and throughout the war.

To judge from this file of documents, Brauchitsch, the Commander-in-Chief, and Halder, his Chief of Staff, had little to do at the time of the Munich crisis but maintain their precedence over the latest encroachments by Himmler and Heydrich in their war area. Resistance Circle writers, however, give the squabble with Himmler a different interpretation. Brauchitsch and Halder were expected by the Resistance Circle to depose Hitler. The army was to attack the SS under the pretext that it was securing Hitler's person against a plot which Himmler and Heydrich were preparing against him. The SS garrisons round Berlin were to be disarmed by the troops of General Erwin Witzleben, supported by a division which was to march from Potsdam under Graf Brockdorff-Rantzau, while the police chiefs, Wolff Helldorf and Fritz von der Schulenburg, were to provide the help of the Berlin state police. In the meantime Erich Hoeppner's XVIth Panzer Corps in Thuringia was to prevent the

[1] Document PS 386, No. 36.

possibility of a march of Himmler's Leibstandarte from Munich to Berlin. All this was to happen the moment Hitler invaded Czechoslovakia, and an outline of the plan was conveyed to the British government. It was, according to Hans Gisevius, a plot which failed only because Chamberlain gave way at Munich: 'Let us put it more drastically. Chamberlain saved Hitler'.[1]

This sinister legend threatens to become hard currency even outside Germany, together with its well-worn corollary that the Generals' Plot of July 1944 was frustrated by the Allies' 'unconditional surrender' formula. But, if Chamberlain was the villain of this piece, were the heroes really Brauchitsch and Halder? One may believe or not believe than von Brauchitsch intended to present Hitler with an ultimatum in September 1938, but one can at least be certain that Brauchitsch had been preparing the plans for the invasion of Czechoslovakia since May. One may believe that 'tears of indignation' ran down Franz Halder's cheeks when Hitler refused Chamberlain's offer of mediation,[2] but one can at least be sure that he never resigned his position as Chief of Staff. One would have thought that a very much more certain way of avoiding world war than disarming the SS would have been the resignation of the High Command, but in fact not a single general followed the example of Ludwig Beck. And if disarming the SS would have ensured the arrest of Hitler, why did Witzleben, Brockdorff-Rantzau and Hoeppner have to wait to see what Mr. Chamberlain was going to do first? As commander of the IIIrd Military Area, Witzleben disposed of an entire armoured division,[3] whereas the SS garrisons within access of Berlin did not possess a single tank and they must have been seriously denuded by Himmler's dispatch of six Death's Head battalions to the Czech border.

But need these failures seem odd at all if the patriots whom the British government failed to trust in September 1938 are examined on their record? Canaris made no objection, when asked to camouflage the invasion of Austria as a field exercise, and he competed with Himmler for the direction of Henlein's Freikorps. Helldorf, who clung to office under Himmler after Himmler had killed his friend Roehm, took part, six weeks after Munich, in the Jewish

---

[1] Gisevius, *To the Bitter End*, p. 327.   [2] *Ibid.*, p. 325.
[3] Rudolf Pechel, *Deutscher Widerstand*, p. 151.

pogrom in Berlin with a gusto that angered even Goebbels.[1] As to Helldorf's deputy, Fritz von der Schulenburg, he had once sided with the strikers in Recklinghausen and had been labelled the Red Count. His entry to the National Socialist party had been via the radical Gregor Strasser, yet Strasser's murder in 1934 had not deterred Schulenburg from accepting high office in a Himmler-controlled police force three years later. Schulenburg is said to have explained that he did this 'in order to become Hitler's Fouché'.[2] Failure to recognise a traitor at a dictator's court is scarcely a reproach to foreign statesmen. If the plotters missed their last true opportunity in September 1938, it was certainly not because of Mr. Chamberlain's umbrella and the apprehensive trenches in Hyde Park.

The truth was that the generals mistrusted the will of their men to attack the SS. Jealousy there might be between army and SS, but the soldiers could not be persuaded to accept that rather silly canard of the Resistance Circle, recurrent right up to the bomb plot of 20 July 1944, which credited Himmler with the intention of replacing Hitler. Since 1935 and the introduction of conscription, the squabbles between the army and the armed SS had been confined to officers. To the soldiers the SS had become a symbol of loyalty to the Fuehrer. Brauchitsch had perhaps a better idea when he thought of reviving the SA as an adjunct to the army, for in January 1939 he told von Hassell that he planned to get the SA under army control as a training and reserve force[3] and that 'Himmler was in a rage about it'. On 3 February the magazine *Der SA Mann* printed a photograph of Brauchitsch reviewing an SA unit in the company of the insignificant Viktor Lutze, under the caption 'We will be the bridge between the party and the Wehrmacht'.[4]

Nothing much came of this Roehm movement in reverse, except that Hitler allowed his army to wear their old SA sports insignia as a military decoration. Brauchitsch was not permitted to upset the fine balance, which Hitler maintained between his generals and his

---

[1] Prince Schaumburg-Lippe, *Zwischen Krone und Kerker*, p. 256. A wartime report that this hero of the Resistance organised the massacre of the Jews of Kharkov in October 1941 calls for some investigation. Helldorf's friend and colleague, Artur Nebe, accepted a similar assignment in White Russia at precisely this time and it was Himmler's and Heydrich's practice to give their police chiefs a spell of this sort of experience. Boris Shub in *Hitler's Ten Year War on the Jews* (New York, 1943), p. 196.

[2] Annedore Leber, *Das Gewisser steht auf* (Berlin, 1953), p. 218.

[3] *Von Hassell Diaries*, p. 38.   [4] IMT III, p. 123.

Reichsfuehrer SS, by acquiring a territorial army of three million men. This fine balance was perhaps misinterpreted in the Resistance Circle, where it was thought that Himmler had gained an enormous ascendancy at Hitler's court. In August 1939 Karl Goerdeler told von Hassell that 'Goering no longer has much to say; Himmler, Ribbentrop, and Goebbels are now managing Hitler'.[1] Nevertheless, a week later, when Hitler announced at a momentous military conference his plans for the invasion of Poland, Himmler was not present. Three years were to elapse before Himmler could play the part of a military or diplomatic adviser.[2] Himmler kept close by Hitler's side in the last weeks before the invasion of Poland, but he was not engaged in policy-making. The roles that Himmler was expected to play had already been created during the Sudeten crisis: namely the provocation of border incidents and the founding of police rule in occupied territory through the existing organisation of Heydrich's 'Einsatzgruppen of the security police and SD'.

The most famous of the border incidents, the faked attack on the German radio station at Gleiwitz, actually bore the name 'Operation Himmler', yet even here Himmler had no free hand. In the course of August 1939 Canaris had created a force which doubled the function of Heydrich's Einsatzkommandos. This 'K force' was intended to secure industrial installations before the Poles could blow them up. It was recruited from racial Germans living in Poland and operating in civilian dress, and on 17 August it was decided that the 'K force' should be employed to secure the frontier bridge at Dirschau.[3] But Canaris, too, was concerned in the Himmler operation. Canaris had been to the High Command to ask for Polish uniforms on Heydrich's behalf as early as 10 August, when not even the beginnings of a Polish crisis had been cooked up by Hitler.[4] That Canaris should aid his rival, Heydrich, to pin the guilt of the war on an innocent government may be a proof of the subtlety and the Greek character of his

---

[1] *Von Hassell Diaries*, p. 60.

[2] One may speculate on Himmler's visit to Ambassador Oshima on 31 January 1939. For the benefit of his staff office Himmler recorded that he had discussed with Oshima a treaty to consolidate the Tripartite Pact. Why should the Chief of Police discuss a treaty with Japan? It is possible that Himmler came to spy on Admiral Canaris, for he learnt that Oshima was planning sabotage in the Caucasus and Ukraine as well as attempts on the life of Stalin 'in conjunction with the Abwehr'. Document PS 2195, IMT II, pp. 262-3.

[3] Karl Abshagen, *Canaris, Weltbuerger und Patriot*, p. 234.

[4] *Ibid.*, p. 191; Ian Colvin, *Chief of Intelligence*, p. 81; IMT III, p. 191.

mind, but was this really the 'little admiral' of legend who fought so hard in the cause of peace that he wanted to kill Hitler and that he warned menaced governments of their impending peril?

Walter Schellenberg, the future head of the military intelligence service of the SS, who had discovered the existence of 'Operation Himmler', was gratified to learn from Heydrich, who apparently had no high opinion of it, that he was not to be implicated.[1] The faked Polish attacks were to be in the hands of Heinrich Mueller of the Gestapo. The most important of them, the attack on the Gleiwitz radio station was to be managed by Alfred Naujocks, a typical amateur Gestapo investigator, half ruffian and half intellectual. Naujocks had been an engineering student at Kiel, where his nose had been smashed in a party brawl with the Communists. He was chosen by Heydrich as a professional tough man, a forerunner of the much better known Skorzeny. Thus Naujocks also managed the knuckle-duster work in 'action Venlo'[2] and was involved in the plan to use Dutch and Belgian frontier guard uniforms in the invasion of May 1940. This was worked in connection with a forged-passport factory, which Naujocks ran for a section of the SD's intelligence service known as VIF. While thus employed, Naujocks made the first proposals for bombarding England with forged bank-notes, the future 'Action Bernhard'.[3]

This garrulous bully was not the sort of man for high policies—not that the Gestapo ever found one—and the reign of Alfred Naujocks was brief. With the invasion of Russia Heydrich turned his Intelligence Service inside out, and Naujocks was compelled to serve in the ranks of the Leibstandarte. Even there Naujocks was pursued by Heydrich's hatred, against which he was protected by his commander, Sepp Dietrich. Hoettl, a friend of Naujocks and a man of much the same kidney, declares that Naujocks at the time of the bomb attack on Heydrich was hoping to murder him on his own account. After being wounded in the field, Naujocks returned to Amt VI, and early in 1944, while nominally employed in the economic administration of Belgium, he conducted a series of murders of members of the Danish Resistance movement.

In November of that year, Naujocks deserted to the Americans

[1] *Quick*, Munich, 18 October, 1953 (anonymous memoirs of Schellenberg).
[2] See *infra*, p. 141.
[3] W. Hoettl, *Hitler's Paper Weapon* (London, 1955), pp. 20-1, 31, 38.

and while in captivity confessed to some of these activities.[1] In 1946 he avoided trial by escaping from a war criminals' camp[2] and has not been heard of since. He is a more picturesque figure than Skorzeny and his memoirs, published perhaps in Buenos Aires, would be a gift to history.

According the Naujocks affidavit, Mueller, the Chief of the Gestapo, supervised the faked Polish attacks in person from the Silesian town of Oppeln.[3] On 31 August 1939, at the last moment, Naujocks was provided with a casualty, a dying man in Polish uniform who was in fact a concentration camp inmate, one of a dozen delivered at the border under the name of 'canned goods'. After Naujocks and his disguised Security policemen had seized the radio station, a short broadcast was delivered in Polish, some shots were fired and the casualty was photographed for the Press.[4]

Thus the war began with one of the most horrible of the SS atrocities; but, like many others, it was the work of several agencies and for these the SS provided the first of its extremely convenient alibis.

[1] Nuremberg Document PS 2751.

[2] The escape is described in Schaumburg-Lippe, *Zwischen Krone und Kerker*, p. 382.

[3] IMT III, pp. 191-2.

[4] The number of faked attacks is not known. Naujocks declared that another faked attack was directed by Criminal Commissar Mehlhorn, the future Gestapo chief of the city of Lodz. Emanuel Schaeffer, who was then head of the Staatspolizei in Upper Silesia, described at his own trial in Cologne in 1952 a similar incident at a German customs shed which also involved the use of 'canned goods' (*The Times*, 7 October 1952).

6

The SS goes to war

SEPTEMBER 1939 – MAY 1940

1. THE SS IN POLAND

On 22 August 1939 Hitler summoned Brauchitsch, Goering, and Admiral Raeder, as well as all his army commanders, to his mountain villa on the Obersalzberg. There these eminently patient men listened to two long speeches with only a short luncheon interval between them. Hitler's purpose was to announce the dispatch of Ribbentrop to sign a non-aggression pact in Moscow. Poland, he declared, was isolated and would be attacked within four days.

No one was allowed to take notes, but at least four memoranda, which were taken down with varying accuracy, have been preserved, and they are agreed on one point:[1] Poland would not merely be occupied; it would be destroyed. There would be a new German eastern frontier 'according to a healthy principle', and possibly a protectorate state as a buffer against Russia. But the story that Hitler spoke of Death's Head units of the SS, 'who were to kill without mercy the entire Polish race', was rejected by the Nuremberg prosecution, because it was no more than a contemporary American newspaperman's 'scoop'.[2] Yet Hitler certainly made some allusion to special tasks of the SS and more than a year later Field-Marshal Fedor von Bock told Fabian von Schlabrendorff of his recollection:[3]

At the same time Hitler informed the generals that he would proceed against the Poles after the end of the campaign with relentless vigour. Things would then

---

[1] The unsigned versions, PS 798 and 1014, which were produced at the Nuremberg trial, were discovered in the captured OKW files in the Tyrol. They were made from shorthand notes taken surreptitiously by Admiral Canaris. Helmuth Greiner, *Die Oberste Wehrmachtfuehrung*, 1939-45 (Wiesbaden, 1952), p. 38; IMT I, p. 171.

[2] Nuremberg Document L3. This was the version which reached Sir George Ogilvie-Forbes only three days after the Obersalzberg meeting. It was given him by the American journalist Louis Lochner, whom it had reached in a roundabout way through Ludwig Beck, *Documents on British Foreign Policy*, Vol. VIII, 1954, p. 257.   [3] Fabian von Schlabrendorff, *Offiziere gegen Hitler*, p. 34.

happen which would not be to the taste of German generals. By this Hitler meant to warn the army not of the notorious liquidations but of the destruction of the Polish intelligentsia, in particular the priesthood, by the SS. He required of the army that the generals should not interfere in these matters but restrict themselves to their military duties.

Canaris raised this matter of the destruction of 'the Polish nobility, intelligentsia, and priesthood, and, of course, the Jews' at a staff conference in Hitler's train at Illnau on 12 September. Keitel then told Canaris that, if the armed forces dissociated themselves from such things,[1] 'they would have to accept the fact that the SS, the Security Police and such organisations would be employed together to carry out these very measures. Thus at the side of each military commander a corresponding civilian official would be appointed'. Hitler had confronted the generals with the dose that Roehm was alleged to have prepared for them in 1934, a political commissar at every desk, and they had yielded to the blackmail. Provided the generals were spared that nightmare, the SS might do what it liked with the Poles and the Jews.

The army's compact was illustrated by a case which occurred two days later. A sergeant-major in the military police, assisted by a gunner from the only SS artillery regiment which served in Poland, had collected fifty Jews in a synagogue and then shot them for no other reason than the fact that, having worked them all day repairing a bridge, they did not know what to do with them. After a lot of references to and fro, the two men were entirely acquitted under the terms of a general amnesty. But, before this was even published, Brauchitsch had personally set aside a very light court-martial sentence of imprisonment.[2]

Such incidents were common during the eighteen days' war but the organised reign of terror began after the fighting was over, when Himmler had installed his higher SS police leaders chiefly to supervise the planned exchanges of population. Von Hassell called it the 'SS reign of terror in Poland', but many German agencies were involved in the resettlements and the number of SS men in Poland was small; so small that their numbers must be compared very critically indeed with the magnitude of the performance before a famous alibi is once again accepted.

[1] IMT XX, p. 351; Document D 421.
[2] *Von Hassell Diaries*, p. 76, referring to 19 October 1939.

There were only 18,000 fighting men of the SS in Poland, distributed between the Leibstandarte, Totenkopf, and Verfuegungstruppen. The greater part were withdrawn to be re-formed into divisions immediately after the cease-fire. Himmler, however, still kept in Poland, besides a handful of Heydrich's Einsatzgruppen, three regiments of Theodor Eicke's Totenkopfverbaende, numbering 7,400 men. Some of these were used to conduct the despoliation operation known as the 'Jewish resettlement' at Nisko,[1] but within a few weeks they too were sent away to be incorporated in the 2nd SS Field Division, the famous Totenkopf. They were replaced by ordinary German policemen of the Ordnungspolizei who were too old to be conscripted for the army. These policemen had been trained at Wandern by Major-General Muelverstedt of the SS as the SS Police Division or 4th SS Division. They were the quota of men whom Himmler obtained when new divisions of over-age men were planned for the fortress duties of the Siegfried Line.[2] Thus the men who carried out the forcible deportations and resettlements in Poland, though passed off as SS, were in fact pre-Nazi German policemen. And they carried out the worst part of the work, for it was only in the summer of 1940 that the police division was withdrawn from Poland to be retrained for service in the front line in Russia.

At first this division's place was taken in Poland by a further recruitment of Death's Head battalions, but after July 1941 a new terror was used. As the German police and Death's Head battalions were drafted into field divisions, their place was taken by battalions of what Himmler called 'savage peoples' from the Baltic states, chiefly Lithuanians who were not considered reliable enough for the field SS. In 1943, battalions of Russian deserters known as 'Askaris' were added. The smallness of the actual German police formations which were at Himmler's disposal remained remarkable throughout the war in view of what was accomplished over immense areas of Eastern Europe, but other agencies were always at their disposal. In Russia the police troops were destined to co-operate with the Rear Area Commands of the army.[3] In Poland there was collaboration from the very beginning in the country itself. In actions against the Polish intelligentsia there was the 'Blue Police', recruited from racial Germans in Poland. In actions against the Jews the SS could

[1] Reitlinger, *The Final Solution*, p. 43.
[2] Paul Hausser, *Waffen SS im Einsatz*, pp. 14-15; Helmuth Greiner, *Die Oberste Wehrmacht Fuehrung* p. 57.   [3] See *infra*, p. 177.

use most sections of the Polish population, and in the Ukrainian areas one might say the entire population.

All, however, came under the direction of the German security police and regular police units, of whom Himmler was particularly proud. Far more than the Waffen SS, the police units represented the aims for which the SS was intended, though it was not easy to explain this to SS men who had fought as front-line soldiers. 'The activities of the man in the green jacket are as important as your own', Himmler told the Leibstandarte after their triumphs in Holland and France;[1] and he then explained to them the strain of organising the deportation of women and children in the depths of winter. Hans Gisevius, too, found the lot of drafted elderly German policemen a hard one. It was not their fault that their task turned out to be one of racial extermination.[2] Gisevius does not suggest that it was the fault of his friends, Daluege, Nebe, and Helldorf, all of whom had won the red trousers of a general in Himmler's police.

Himmler himself left for Poland on 3 September 1939 and established his headquarters in a special train called 'Heinrich' which was drawn up at various places in the Danzig region—Gogolin, Illnau, and Zoppot—alongside the two trains of Hitler and the High Command. At this stage in history Ribbentrop did not object to going to war in the company of Himmler. Thus the train also housed the staffs of Lammer's Reich Chancellery and Ribbentrop's inner office, the bureau RAM.[3]

It seems that Himmler was present at the victory celebrations in Warsaw on 25 September, but he certainly never went near the front, nor is it at all clear what his activities were, since he exercised no tactical authority over the dispersed SS field units. These were not specially commended for their part in the campaign and after the conquest of France Himmler complained bitterly about it:[4] 'After the war in Poland they said that the SS had huge casualties because they were not trained to the job. Now that we have very small losses, they say we have not fought'.

Himmler was particularly incensed with the treatment of an illicit local defence battalion of the SS, recruited in the Free City of Danzig. Together with the Death's Head battalions it had taken part on 8 September in the storming of the spit of coastland known as the

---

[1] Nuremberg Document PS 1991; and see *infra*, pp. 129-30.
[2] Gisevius, op. cit., p. 491.   [3] Seabury, op. cit., p. 104.
[4] Nuremberg Document PS 1918.

Oxhoefter Kempe, but because this battalion, which subsequently became part of the Totenkopf division, had been attached to a Pomeranian local defence division under Colonel Graf Rittberg, it had been mentioned in orders as the Rittberg battalion. The injustice still rankled with Himmler in August 1944.[1]

Hitler moved his headquarters back from Zoppot to Berlin on 26 September and Himmler went with him, but he was to make many more journeys to Poland, since he regarded that unhappy land as the ideal experimenting ground for his theories. In the following January, Paul Schmidt of the Foreign Office told von Hassell that he had heard Himmler 'with wobbling pince-nez and a cruel expression on his vulgar face say that the Fuehrer had given him the task of seeing that Poland should never rise again'.[2]

Himmler had received this commission three months earlier, on 6 October 1939 when the first hint of the importance of population redistribution in Poland had occurred in an incredibly long and rambling speech which Hitler made to the Reichstag. This was the same speech in which he claimed to be offering generous peace terms to the Western powers. Hitler spoke of population exchanges mainly in connection with the Jews of Poland, but he also declared that 'the whole problem of Lebensraum was to be organised in conformity with the principle of nationalities, which meant the solution of the minorities problem'.[3] On the day following his speech, Hitler published a decree appointing Himmler to be head of a new co-ordinating office called the Reich Commissariat for the Strengthening of German Nationhood (Volkstum) or 'RKFDV'. Germany, according to the decree, had achieved part of her Lebensraum and could now accept within it Germans who had been compelled to inhabit foreign lands. Himmler's duties were to bring back such racial Germans as were eligible, to weed out of Germany foreign elements who were not eligible, and to use the new subjects and the new space to create German colonies.[4]

The office RKFDV was to co-ordinate the actions of the police in Poland with the two old agencies of the SS known as Volksdeutsche-Mittelstelle (VOMI) and Rasse und Siedlungshauptamt (RUSHA). The office VOMI had been taken over by Himmler from Hess's party office at a time when it was a harmless affair, concerned

---

[1] *Vierteljahreshefte fuer Zeitgeschichte*, October 1953, p. 568.
[2] *Von Hassell Diaries*, p. 100.   [3] Quoted in *Black Book of Polish Jewry*, p. 15.
[4] Nuremberg Document PS. 686.

with the welfare of German-speaking groups who lived abroad. That VOMI had a political future became apparent as early as January 1937 when Himmler appointed Werner Lorenz to it, for Werner Lorenz was a wealthy early adherent of the SS who had large industrial interests in the Danzig Free State. During the Sudeten crisis VOMI provided a medium for aiding Henlein's adherents.[1] After the occupation of Poland it became a welfare organisation for the racial Germans who were due to be brought back to the Reich. Like a great many welfare organisations in the most over-governed era in the history of man, it grew into a tyranny and VOMI ended up as a press-gang for any Germanic-looking individuals in any occupied country. Those who came under the protection of VOMI were made to fight in the ranks of the Waffen SS for a Reich that had never been theirs and never would be.[2]

RUSHA had been the SS marriage bureau since 1931. Under Walter Darré, who ruled it till 1938, it was also concerned with research on racial Germans living abroad. Darré was followed by a series of typical SS leaders, Guenther Pancke, Otto Hoffmann and Richard Hildebrandt, who gave the researches of RUSHA a different orientation. In the name of racial selection and the detection of Nordic blood, RUSHA kidnapped children to be brought up as Germans, decided who should be deported from desirable resettlement areas, who should be conscripted for slave labour in the Reich, who should lose their property and who should be executed for miscegenation with Germans, in all of which matters RUSHA was at the disposition of the executive police of the SS.

The schemes concocted in the RKFDV office ran their riotous course, particularly during the seven months of the 'phoney war'. Carried out largely in the depths of winter, the resettlements brought a harvest of death many times greater than Hitler's promised persecution of the Polish intelligentsia and governing classes. Himmler, when he addressed the Leibstandarte after the fall of France, was not at all oblique about it.[3]

[1] IMT III, p. 170.

[2] Werner Lorenz was sentenced at Nuremberg in March 1948 to twenty years' imprisonment, but the sentence was later revised and he was released early in 1955. He was possibly the least inhuman of the SS Gruppenfuehrers, in spite of the gravity of the charges. The worst excesses of VOMI were committed in Slovenia, where the first head of the Berlin SD, Hermann Behrends, acted without always consulting his authority.

[3] Nuremberg Document PS 1918; IMT XIX, p. 98.

Exactly the same thing happened in Poland in weather forty degrees below zero, where we had to drag away thousands, tens of thousands, hundred thousands; where we had to have the toughness—you should listen to this but also forget it immediately—to shoot thousands of leading Poles, where we had to have the toughness, otherwise it would have taken revenge on us later.

In many cases it is much easier to go into battle with a company of infantry than it is to suppress an obstructive population of low cultural level or to carry out executions or to haul away people or to evict crying and hysterical women.

Thus Himmler made no secret of the fact that the deportations were completely callous, but the wastefulness and stupidity of the resettlements were increased by the realisation that the whole conception was premature. The wretched racial Germans were brought back to a Reich that could not absorb them, except as cannon fodder. Yet within a year or two Himmler was to plan more German colonies abroad and in 1942-3 racial Germans from countries as far away as Slovenia and Bosnia were transplanted to a part of Poland, the Zamosc region, from which other racial Germans had been 'repatriated' in 1939-40.[1]

Again, the failure of the resettlements sprang from the falsity of the premises on which Himmler's brief of October 1939 rested. The racial Germans were collected into the Reich, not because the Lebensraum of the German race had been achieved, but because the position of the racial Germans had been made unsafe by Hitler's deal with Russia. Under the original Moscow pact 134,000 Volhynian Germans, living in what was then Eastern Poland, passed under Russian rule. Through the secret protocols, signed by Ribbentrop on 27 September on his second visit to Moscow, another 100,000 Baltic Germans came into the future Russian sphere of influence. Since Hitler had no intention of honouring his treaties and meant to have a show-down with Russia sooner or later, these German hostages had to be got out of the way. The Russians were obliged by the protocols to facilitate the emigration of the racial Germans, even to the extent of admitting German supervisors who were appointed by Ribbentrop's Foreign Office. These supervisors and their German staffs met with little obstruction, since the emigrations were so agreeable to Russian policy that they became in practice evictions.[2]

The racial Germans changed their ancient homes and farms for the aimless camp life of the displaced person. Yet their fate was mild

[1] Reitlinger, op. cit., pp. 45, 75, 296.
[2] *Nazi Soviet Relations* (Washington, 1948), p. 106.

compared with that of the ineligible elements, Jewish or Slav, whom they were intended to replace and who were mostly sent to no address, taking with them nothing. It was expected that nearly all the incoming racial Germans could be accommodated in the regained eastern German provinces that had been lost to Poland in 1919. So on 9 October 1939 Himmler announced that 550,000 of the 650,000 Jews who lived in these provinces, together with all Poles whom Himmler's offices should reject as unfit for assimilation, should be moved east of the Vistula. This meant the bulk of the population and bordered on the impossible.[1] In January, Hans Frank, who was now Governor-General of the unincorporated part of Poland, declared that an immigration of a million and a half people into an area of twelve million inhabitants would produce intolerable rural overcrowding.[2] Yet by the winter of 1941 precisely these numbers had been expelled, that is to say, 1,200,000 Poles and 300,000 Jews. In their place only 497,000 racial Germans had arrived. In August 1943 there were 566,000 racial Germans from the Baltic states, Volhynia, Bessarabia, Bukovina, Bosnia, and the Dobrudja, occupying the space of three times as many Poles and Jews. Yet 99,500 were still unabsorbed in industry and 22,000 were still living in camps.[3]

Thus the German refugee problem began not in 1945 but in 1939, and its begetters were not the vengeful Slav peoples but Himmler and Darré and their theorising German experts. Darré, who had kept a complete survey of Polish farms in the territories to be annexed, complained bitterly to Himmler in October 1939 that he had to surrender the task of redistributing the farms to the SS. In the end Himmler took pity on the man who had inspired him with theories of blood and soil, so on 24 November the RUSHA office restored to Darré as Minister for Agriculture the right to appoint German managers to the confiscated Polish estates. It was an unfortunate victory, because in 1949 it earned Darré a sentence of seven years' imprisonment.[4]

But at the time of his temporary reconciliation with Darré, Himmler had even more extreme advisers who put Darré's woolly ideas to more extreme practice. Two officials of Rosenberg's Racial Political Office, Wetzel and Hecht, sent Himmler a memorandum on

[1] Case VIII, NO. 4059. [2] IMT II, p. 425. [3] Reitlinger, op. cit., p. 40.
[4] Case XI, judgment, transcript, pp. 28, 417-24. Darré, however, was released in November, 1950.

25 November 1939.[1] According to this document it was impossible to remove all at once the Poles in the new Reich territories who were unsuitable for Germanisation. For the present these Poles would have to stay on as Helots, forbidden to own a business or exercise an independent trade, or to send their children to school beyond the kindergarten stage unless they were found eligible to be brought up as Germans. They must be taught that it is a divine law to obey the Germans and to be neat and industrious. Reading would not be required or counting beyond five hundred. Even religious services must be in German, and Polish cafés, restaurants, theatres, and places of assembly must close down.

For some reason Himmler waited four months before presenting the Wetzel-Hecht report to Hitler as the recommendation of his RKFDV office. Hitler then declared that it was 'very good and correct', but he decided that it should have the force of a Fuehrer Order, that is to say, a secret decree communicated only to a few persons.[2] In some respects the German achievements in the new Silesian territory, in Danzig-Westpreussen and in the Warthegau, the domains of the Gauleiters Hanke, Greiser, and Foerster, fell short of the recommendations, but perhaps five years were not enough to carry out the Wetzel-Hecht plan.

By December 1939 the whole machinery of spoliation and eviction was in full swing. Jews and Poles were pouring eastward into the newly created General Government, while racial Germans from Volhynia were heading westward towards the Reich. Apart from these two cross-currents, there was in the General Government itself a huge upheaval of Jewish life which involved nearly two million people. The Jews were concentrated into a number of large towns as a prelude to the creation of ghettoes and also into a rural area south of Lublin. The directors of this movement, Himmler's higher SS police leaders and Heydrich's commanders of the security police and SD, were in many respects independent of Hans Frank's civil administration and absolutely independent of General Blaskowitz, the military governor. The result was a weird bureaucratic chaos which explains why Frank found 40,000 German civil servants insufficient to run a country 'half the size of Italy'.[3]

This complete cleavage of authority was later copied in occupied Russia and in all areas that had no sovereign native administration,

---

[1] NO. 1830. Law reports, XIII, pp. 7-9; Case XI, page 28, 421.
[2] Case XI, transcript, page 28. 422.   [3] IMT XII, p. 108.

simply because the same cleavage existed in Germany. It was not Hitler's intention to make Himmler the power behind the scenes wherever Germans ruled, but rather to prevent any individual Germans, Himmler included, from exercising too much authority on their own. While Hans Frank complained of the interference of the higher SS police leader, Friedrich Krueger, the latter often complained against Frank with an equal lack of success. In April 1943, for instance, Krueger, backed by Himmler and Lammers, got a long report against Hans Frank through to Hitler without the slightest result, though for the past nine months Frank was said to have been in the deepest disgrace.[1] In the end Frank outstayed Krueger in the General Government of Poland. The fact was that Himmler, in spite of his extraordinary position, was not well served by his higher SS and police leaders, not one of whom was an outstanding personality. Krueger had once been Goebbels's expert in street fighting,[2] and under the Gestapo had done a good deal of gun-running across the Czech border for the Freikorps Henlein, but he was past forty-five in 1939 and getting extremely fat. He was removed in September 1943, when the General Government had become a partisan warfare area. For a few months Krueger commanded the SS division 'Nord' in Finland, and he died obscurely in Austria at the end of the war.[3]

The second-ranking SS police leader in Poland, Odilo Globocnik, was even less satisfactory. He owed his position to his success as a liaison man between the Austrian National Socialists and Hitler, but he had, even in pre-Anschluss days, been involved in a murderous jewel robbery in the Vienna suburb of Favoriten, and in January 1939, when he was Gauleiter for Vienna, he was dismissed for illegal speculations in foreign exchange. In November Globocnik was pardoned by Himmler and appointed higher SS and police leader for Lublin.[4] Globocnik was chosen for this area of the General Government because it was intended as a 'reserve' for expelled Jews. In 1942, when the Lublin province was to be the last stage in the journey of European Jewry to extermination, Globocnik became, by natural evolution, head of the death camp organisation 'Abteilung Reinhard'.[5] Globocnik was one of those men whom Himmler and Heydrich picked for the worst assignments because at any moment their past could be brought against them. Himmler failed to see,

---

[1] IMT XII, p. 108.   [2] Case XI, transcript, page 28. 460-1.
[3] See *infra*, p. 403, footnote 2.   [4] Reitlinger, op. cit., pp. 245-6.
[5] See *infra*, pp. 173, 217.

however, that even in such actions as the resettlements of 1939-40 and the massacres of 1942-3, honesty and efficiency were as important as ruthlessness. Finally, after Frank's civil administration had put up with this drunken Austrian sadist for four years, Himmler himself was moved by Globocnik's peculations to transfer him.[1]

Compared with the 'Reinhard action' of 1942-3 the resettlements of 1939-40 were of a less inconceivable savagery. That was because the U.S.A. still had eyes in Poland. Ribbentrop's Foreign Office officials were so sensitive to American reactions that, under Ribbentrop's nose, they established a 'Referat' to collect evidence in Poland of actions that might prejudice Germany's good name.[2] The Foreign Office also enabled a number of American relief organisations to maintain correspondents in this sealed kingdom of Dr. Hans Frank.

There was a second brake on the wheel. The German generals who had served in Poland were all opposed to a campaign in the West in which they had no confidence. Anything which might inflame a warlike spirit in France and Britain, such as atrocity stories, they regarded as dangerous. Yet they would not risk their careers by interfering with Himmler's agents in Poland, because they had accepted the surrender of their rights which had been made by Keitel and Brauchitsch. The generals did no more than grumble, yet their grumbles carried some weight.

The most serious complainant was the Commander-in-Chief of the 3rd Army Group, and for a time the military governor of Poland, Colonel-General Johannes Blaskowitz. He was an old adversary of the SS and soon after the end of the fighting he tried to prosecute Sepp Dietrich, the party pet, for looting.[3] In December Blaskowitz drew up an elaborate memorandum on the conduct of the higher SS and police leaders in Poland, over whom, as he complained, he had no authority except in cases of mutiny and revolt. He believed that if the SS were to be permitted to live outside the law they would turn against their own people.[4]

Blaskowitz carried the memorandum around in his pocket for more than a month, intending to send it to Hitler. Finally, on 15 February 1940, he submitted his memorandum to Brauchitsch, who saw that it went no farther; and soon afterwards Blaskowitz, who had become the white hope of the Resistance Circle, resigned his

[1] Reitlinger, op. cit., pp. 295-6.
[2] Peter Kleist, *Zwischen Hitler und Stalin*, p. 106.
[3] *Von Hassell Diaries*, p. 77.   [4] *Ibid.*, p. 95; Nuremberg Document NO. 3011.

post.[1] A general who served later on many fronts and who surrendered Holland to the British, Blaskowitz never again questioned Hitler's policies; but his dislike of the SS remained and when in 1947 he committed suicide in Nuremberg prison, his fellow prisoners believed that Blaskowitz had been murdered by SS men.[2]

To the name of Blaskowitz there must be added, strange to say, the name of Field-Marshal Walter von Reichenau, who had remained friendly with Himmler after his own sinister role in the events of 30 June 1934 and who had approved the training of the SS as a military formation a year later. As a critic of SS atrocities Reichenau's career was brief and opportunist, for during the Russian campaign of 1941 he was to issue a notorious order of the day condoning a stupendous massacre of Jews which the SS conducted at Kiev.[3] Why then did Reichenau, who had not the least connection with the generals' Resistance Circle, align himself with the protesters? Just before the invasion of Poland he had returned from an Olympic Games committee in London, declaring truculently that the British would not fight.[4] It seems, however, that on 10 October, when he heard Hitler outline his plans for a surprise attack on the Low Countries, it was the Germans whom Reichenau doubted and not the British.

In the course of October Reichenau and his Chief of Staff, the then Lieutenant-General Friedrich Paulus, received the Abwehr chiefs, Canaris and Lahousen, at Duesseldorf. Canaris found Reichenau pessimistic and he worked on his fears with a portfolio on the SS police measures in Poland. Paulus (it is worth recalling that the Field-Marshal whom the Russians have preserved with such loving care was once described in *Pravda* as 'the butcher of Kharkov') retorted with a warm defence of these measures.[5] Reichenau, however, was inspired to compose a memorandum which he entitled *Die Sicherung des Deutsches Sieges*[6] and in which he inserted his complaints on the SS. Like Blaskowitz he carried it about in his pocket and failed to send it to Hitler, but the news got round and on 30 October von Hassell wrote:[7] 'The conduct of a man like Reichenau

[1] *Von Hassell Diaries*, p. 103; Wheeler-Bennett, op. cit., p. 462.

[2] Schaumburg-Lippe, op. cit., p. 323.

[3] IMT IV, p. 14; Document D 411; Reitlinger, op. cit., p. 197.

[4] Geyr von Schweppenburg, op. cit., pp. 150-6.

[5] When Paulus broadcast from Moscow for the Free Germany Committee, it was said that 'Saulus had become Paulus'.

[6] Karl Abshagen, *Canaris*, pp. 224-5.   [7] *Von Hassell Diaries*, p. 81.

is significant. He always hears the grass grow. For some time now he is said to have been critical and even to have risked a word against the SS bestialities in Poland'.

Hitler got to know about it and on 23 November, when Brauchitsch offered to resign and a successor was under consideration, he told Guderian abruptly, 'Reichenau doesn't come into the question'.[1]

In Poland the evictions, death marches, and mass shootings continued. On 30 January 1940 Heydrich held a conference of all the SS agencies who were concerned in the resettlement, including the chiefs of RUSHA and Eichmann of the Jewish Emigration Office. New deportations were pending. The 30,000 gipsies living in the Reich, as well as the Jews of Stettin and Schneidemuehl, were the first German subjects to be affected by the plan.[2] On 12 February Himmler suggested to Goering that 30,000 racial Germans in Lublin province could be moved out in order to make room for Jews. Goering advised postponement till the movement from Volhynia was over, but Jews continued to pour into 'Lubinland' in appalling conditions. Reports reached Switzerland that the deportation trains were full of the frozen corpses of children and that the reception villages were riddled with typhus.[3]

It was now that the proposal to move Jews from Germany proper created trouble. On 15 February von Weizsaecker of the Foreign Office was in a panic because the Swiss paper *Neuer Zuercher Zeitung* had got wind of the plan. At the beginning of March some 1,200 old people and children left Stettin for Piaski, near Lublin, and by the 12th 230 of them had died of exposure.[4] A report of the Stettin death march reached a member of Frank's bureaucracy from the American Society of Friends, acting with the Polish Jewish Relief Committee, TOZ. This was forwarded to Lammers at the Reich Chancellery and thence to Himmler. Rumours were now flying round the Corps Diplomatique in Berlin that the whole Jewish population of Germany was to be deported.[5] So Goering ruled the suspension of all deportations into the General Government. Heydrich had to bow to Goering's authority because his brief to direct Jewish emigration came not from Himmler but from Goering as President of

---

[1] Guderian, *Erinnerungen eines Soldaten* (Heidelberg, 1951), p. 75.
[2] *Trials of War Criminals*, IV, p. 55; Document NG 5322.
[3] Reitlinger, op. cit., p. 44; *Nuremberg Document* EC 305.
[4] Document NO. 2480, Case XI, transcript, page 28. 469.
[5] Case XI, Document NG 3175.

the Defence Council. It may be that two years after the Fritsch court martial Goering was still ganging after Heydrich.

Goering, however, was challenged from another quarter. Artur Greiser, the former president of the Danzig Senate and an SS man of long standing, governed the Warthegau, which included the old Posen province and the annexed Polish city of Lodz.[1] He claimed that at the meeting of 12 February Goering had clearly promised Himmler the expulsion of the 200,000 Jews of this city, the second largest Jewish community in Europe. This complication delayed the final ruling and it was only at the beginning of May that Goering issued a decree, forbidding all deportations into the General Government till the completion of the 'Volhynia' action.[2] By this time half the Jews had left the incorporated Polish territories, as well as ten per cent of the Poles. A few days later Hitler began the invasion of the Western countries and by July there was another plan for the solution of the Jewish problem through deportation to the island of Madagascar. It was not quite the end of the plan to dump unwanted blood on to the poor soil of Poland east of the Vistula. For another year there were occasional expulsions of Jews and Poles into the General Government, but by the end of 1941 Jewish emigration was directed to the death camps and Polish emigration to the labour camps and farms of Germany.

2. THE SS AND THE 'PHONEY WAR'

In January 1937 Himmler had explained to officers of the army his plans in the event of a world war: the increase in the size of the concentration camps, the expansion of the Death's Head battalions, the direction of the struggle against terrorists and saboteurs.[3] Himmler did not, however, mention a corresponding expansion of the Gestapo and its allied SD services. And it is by no means certain that this expansion, as decreed on 27 September 1939 in a form so favourable to Heydrich, was what Himmler himself had in mind.

The Reichssicherheitshauptamt, RSHA or Reich Main Security Office, which emerged from this decree, was an amalgamation of three things: the security police or executive arm of the Gestapo, the criminal police or KRIPO, and the security service or SD. The head of the amalgamation was Reinhard Heydrich. As the war dragged on, RSHA spread outwards beyond the original premises of

[1] See *infra*, pp. 408-9.   [2] *Dokumenty i Materialy* (Lodz, 1946), III, pp. 167-8.

the Gestapo in the Prinz Albrechtstrasse and of the SD in the Wilhelmstrasse. It became a typical overblown bureaucracy, sheltering thousands of wartime rejects and *embusqués*, desk-mandarins and dug-outs of every description, not visibly different from those of any other ministry. The complexity of RSHA was unequalled even in Germany. 'It was practically impossible for an outsider', declared Lieutenant-Colonel Dieter Wisliceny, 'to find his way about in this maze of offices'.[1] Wisliceny himself belonged to bureau IVA, 4b, one of at least a hundred similarly labelled sub-sub-sections, a modest camouflage of the fact that it handled the progressive extermination which Hitler planned for the ten million Jews of Europe.

RSHA had seven basic divisions. AMT 1, the personnel office under Heydrich's deputy, Bruno Streckenbach, selected personnel for the various executive units of the security police and SD and was responsible for their discipline. Amt II was the legal section, while Amt III was the original SD, now classed as the 'German sphere of life' office, but generally known as the Information Service, the creation of Otto Ohlendorf. Amt IV was the Gestapo itself under Heinrich Mueller, who now for the first time received an SS rank and became a Major-General; Amt V was the criminal police, still under the rule of Artur Nebe and Amt VI the foreign department under Heinz Jost, responsible for investigations abroad, which included Heydrich's Military Intelligence service. Lastly, there was Amt VII, which was devoted to 'ideological research', the domain of the cranks and professors who were so easily to turn themselves into executioners when the Einsatzgruppen were created for Russia.[2]

To Heydrich the most interesting part of his greatly enlarged kingdom was the section VIA, the Military Intelligence branch. He had acquired his astonishing position by the manufacture of plots and scandals, and without the manufacture of still more plots and scandals Heydrich was threatened with extinction through an outbreak of peace. Canaris, with his pathological fear of Russia and Communism, wanted peace with the West at all costs and his Abwehr forces had their ears to the ground to detect the least signs of it. But Heydrich's Military Intelligence was devoted to detecting signs of bellicosity among the apparently torpid Allies. The failure of the Western powers to attack Germany, when her frontier was almost undefended, was to Hitler a proof of the soundness of his own

[1] IMT III, p. 289, address to Wehrmacht officers (PS 1992).
[2] IMT III, p. 184; Document L 185.

intuition. But to the German public it was something sinister, hiding factors which could not be weighed. What if Hitler with his famous intuition sensed this mood of depression and offered genuine peace? It might be the end of all that Himmler and Heydrich had built up. But if the gulf between Hitler and his generals widened, if their attitude forced him to get rid of the whole structure of the High Command, then who could tell what prospects an aggressive war with the West might offer the SS?

Hitler's plan, composed soon after his return from Poland, was for an attack against the Low Countries to take place between 15 and 20 November. The whole of the High Command opposed this plan. On 5 November Brauchitsch was stirred into reading Hitler a memorandum in which he declared that the infantry in the Polish campaign had not been up to the standard of the First World War. There had been cases of indiscipline as bad as any in 1918. Hitler challenged Brauchitsch to produce the commanders of the units the same night and Brauchitsch could not even give their names. Hitler went off in a rage and gave the final orders for invasion to the most Nazi of the generals available at OKW, Walter Warlimont.[1] The date was to be 12 November, but on the 7th Hitler cancelled the order on account of a bad-weather forecast from the Air Ministry.[2]

The bewilderment, created by this postponement, was increased by the fact that after the dispute of 5 November Hitler did not send for his High Command again till the 23rd, and then, though he still insisted on the importance of getting into the Low Countries before the Allies, he no longer named a fixed date for the invasion. Two mysterious events could have accounted for this. Between 5 and 23 November there had been the kidnapping at Venlo and the Buergerbraeukeller bomb plot. It might be inferred that these incidents, which were later manufactured into a case against the Dutch government, were meant to give Hitler the *legality* for which he was waiting, as he had waited during his political struggles. It might also be inferred that on 7 November Hitler countermanded the invasion order out of genuine pessimism and for good; that the two incidents, Venlo and the Buergerbraeukeller, were created on account of Hitler's pessimism as a form of pressure by Heydrich and Himmler, not only to frighten the dissident generals into submission but also to force

---

[1] Helmuth Greiner, *Die Oberste Wehrmachtfuehrung*, p. 167.
[2] Evidence of Brauchitsch, IMT XX, p. 28; Evidence of Warlimont in Milton Shulman, op. cit., p. 37.

Hitler to change his mind about the cancellation of the invasion. The Venlo incident was an involved one and it is impossible to make it anything else. Towards the middle of October 1939 a Gestapo agent made contact with two British Intelligence officers who were attached to the Embassy at The Hague. These officers were trying to discover the existence of opposition elements in Germany. Impressed with the report, Himmler ordered Walter Schellenberg, who served in the newly created Amt VI, to impersonate a fictitious member of the military Resistance Circle. Schellenberg therefore assumed the papers of a serving major who lived in Duesseldorf and whose name was Schaemmel. Under this name Schellenberg had several interviews with the British officers, Captain S. Payne-Best and Major R. H. Stevens. They met at a house at Venlo a few hundred yards inside the Dutch border.

On 30 October, at the very first interview,[1] Schellenberg spoke of the generals' plot to kidnap Hitler, his purpose being probably to trap the two officers into revealing any knowledge they possessed. Mr. Wheeler-Bennett thinks that Schellenberg knew nothing about the real plotters and that Himmler failed to pick up any clues till well into 1942.[2] Yet Captain Payne-Best attributed the deception that had been practised on him to the fact that Schellenberg, 'a conceited, self-opinionated and distinctly stupid man', had been well briefed.[3] Heydrich's Intelligence service surely knew something about military conspiracies, for at this moment the position of Brauchitsch himself was compromised by the indiscreet conduct of Franz Halder, his Chief of Staff, Heinrich von Stuelpnagel, his Quartermaster-General, and Erwin von Witzleben, who commanded the Rhine army. It seems that these generals had talked about another attempt to seize Hitler, and they had talked about it to the Schacht-Goerdeler circle, not the most reliable of partners. The story, told by Gisevius that Brauchitsch informed Witzleben that Heydrich was after him[4], suggests that Himmler had been influenced in sending

---

[1] Payne-Best, *The Venlo Incident*, p. 12.   [2] Wheeler-Bennett, op. cit., p. 478.
[3] Payne-Best, op. cit., p. 43.

[4] Gisevius p. 389. At Nuremberg Brauchitsch denied any connection with these plans (IMT XXI, p. 33). A Panzer corps was to have dealt with the most urgent tasks of the plot in Berlin, but this corps would certainly not have acted. The commander, Geyr von Schweppenburg, told Stuelpnagel that he could not rely on the 3rd Panzer Division, which had been addressed by Hitler in Poland. 'There would have been a battle between the two Panzer regiments in the Wilhelmstrasse if they had been required to take part in a Putsch' (Schweppenburg, op. cit., p. 20).

Schellenberg to the Dutch border by the possession of a certain amount of genuine information.

On 7 November the two British officers gave 'Schaemmel' a cautious message from London for the chiefs of the Resistance movement. 'Schaemmel' thereupon proposed to bring one of these chiefs to the frontier on the following day, but this visit was postponed to the 9th. On the night of the 8th-9th a cunningly concealed time-bomb exploded in the Munich Buergerbraeukeller on the spot where Hitler had just concluded his annual speech commemorating the 1923 Putsch. Himmler at once telephoned Schellenberg at his Duesseldorf flat. It was, he said, Hitler's wish that the two British officers should be kidnapped and brought to Germany.[1]

On the following day Alfred Naujocks of 'Amt VIF' waited at the frontier barrier with a special commando of sixteen tough security policemen. The victims arrived at the usual rendezvous and, after a brief scrimmage in which a Dutch lieutenant was killed on Dutch soil, they were dragged across the border and driven first to Duesseldorf and then to the Prinz Albrechtstrasse. But the news was not released in Germany till a fortnight had passed. A story was then told that the officers had directed the Munich bomb plot. The presence of the British officers on the Dutch border had been turned into a new 'Reichstag fire' story. Just as the Reichstag fire had been the excuse for the Enabling Act of dictatorship in 1933, the Venlo incident was to be the excuse for violating the Low Countries. But in Germany a still more colourful version of the affair had already gained currency. It was that Himmler, who had sent Schellenberg to the border, had also planted the bomb in the Buergerbraeukeller.

Hitler himself used to boast that he had been preserved by Providence.[2] Yet every circumstance suggests that the attempt was a concocted affair. First there was the ease with which the assassin, the carpenter Elser, was able to conceal inside a hollow column of the cellar enough explosives to bring down the entire roof of the gaudy place and to kill seven and injure sixty people. Then there was the studied absence of Himmler and Goering from the meeting and Hitler's own abrupt departure after cutting short his speech only a matter of minutes before the explosion. Then there was the simplicity with which Elser, the engineer of this affair, allowed himself to be picked up next day at the Swiss border, carrying a marked postcard of the scene of his crime. Finally there was the careful preservation

[1] *Quick*, Munich, No. 45, October 1953.   [2] *Table Talk*, 3 May 1942, p. 451.

of Elser in Sachsenhausen and Dachau camps throughout the war for a state trial which never took place.[1] Elser was not tried. He was murdered.

The dissident generals and the opposition circle who believed in Himmler's plot saw in it a second '30 June', to be directed this time against themselves. Their only chance of survival was to persuade the loyal generals that Himmler had planned to blow up the Fuehrer and so get them to make the first arrests. It could indeed be made to look as if Himmler and Heydrich had thought nothing of risking Hitler's life. A fuse, made from an ordinary alarm clock and set ten days ahead, could not be trusted to go off within so small a margin of accuracy as five to ten minutes.

It was in fact nothing but a revival of the 'SS Putsch' canard of September 1938 and again its author was the strangely unrealistic Colonel (later Major-General) Hans Oster. He wanted Franz Halder to arrange the arrest of Himmler and Heydrich and the 'protection' of Hitler. The apparent cancellation of the invasion orders had, however, relieved Halder of the worst troublings of his conscience, so he gave Canaris's man a back answer. Why, asked prim little Halder, should not Canaris kill Hitler himself?[2] But Canaris, who was reputed by his followers to be playing with the idea, did something more prudent. While the dissident generals waited for the new '30 June', he went to Heydrich. He was told that the two British officers had not incriminated any members of the Abwehr and Resistance circles. Heydrich had learnt little from them, but, he warned Canaris, he already knew of 'a number of uncertain cantonists in higher Wehrmacht circles'.[3]

In the upshot there was neither a 30 June for the generals nor a 20 July for Hitler. Hitler probably restrained Himmler and Heydrich as firmly as Halder restrained the counter-plotters. But Himmler

---

[1] The version which Elser wrote for Captain Payne-Best in the Sachsenhausen 'Bunker' sounds too fantastic. Elser said that he went daily to work on his bomb in the Bierbraeukeller while a prisoner in Dachau. That he had been promised his life on these terms by two men in the Dachau Kommandantur. They had told him that the bomb was not meant for Hitler but for a band of conspirators who intended to shoot him at the end of his speech (Payne-Best, op. cit., pp. 130-2).

[2] Abshagen, op. cit., pp. 227-8; Gisevius, pp. 402-4. In the 'answers of Ernst von Salomon' it is suggested that Canaris had planned in March 1939 to get Hitler murdered by one of his old Freikorps associates, Helmut Plaas (see infra, p. 303).

[3] Abshagen, op. cit., p. 360, quoting the Huppenkothen trial.

had to contradict the rumours that he had prepared a Putsch. So the great Canaris legend was set in motion by the admiral's adversaries, who declared that he had been training parachute troops to kidnap the Fuehrer.[1]

These troops, recruited by Admiral Canaris, had been known unemotionally on their first formation on 15 October 1939 as 'Lehr und Baukompagnie zV 800', and were merely an expansion of the original K troops who had been used as a fifth column against the Poles six weeks previously. They were built up to form the Brandenburg battalion, which became in 1942 a division and which inspired the creation of the British combined operation troops, though the Brandenburg war record was by no means equal to that of the Commandos. Some colour was lent to Heydrich's accusation of November 1939 during the trials of the Communist 'Rote Kapelle' conspirators in 1942-3, when it transpired that the chief organiser of Rote Kapelle, Schulze-Boysen of the Air Ministry, had provided a parachute expert for the original Lehr und Baukompagnie, but it turned out that the parachutist had no connection with Rote Kapelle. In November 1939, however, the Brandenburg unit merited suspicion. Karl Abshagen, the apologist-in-chief for Admiral Canaris, agrees with Gisevius that the commander of the unit, Lieutenant-Colonel Heinz, was aware of the plans which had been concocted by his chief, Colonel Oster of the Abwehr, to kidnap Hitler, but Heinz's men were all fanatical Nazis, as indeed they had need to be.[2]

Nothing came of Himmler's visit to the unit's 'laboratory' at Tegel, where he showed great curiosity in a stock of camouflaged saboteurs' bombs.[3] Unable to make any arrests in this quarter, Himmler turned his attention to his own officials. If one is to believe the earlier, more dramatic and much less reliable version of Kersten's memoirs, Himmler told his masseur that he had been obliged to arrest some dissident elements in the SS.[4] Thus we see Himmler hunting in circles, not to find victims, but to conceal the failure of his own plans.

Officially, Himmler proposed to arrest forty Bavarian nationalists for lack of more plausible culprits, while Goebbels's Propaganda Ministry thundered against Otto Strasser, who, from his hide-out in

[1] Paul Leverkuehn, *German Military Intelligence* (London, 1954), p. 116.
[2] Abshagen, op. cit., p. 237.   [3] Leverkuehn, op. cit., p. 54.
[4] *The Memoirs of Dr. Felix Kersten* (New York, 1947), p. 58.

Switzerland, had united the efforts of the British War Office and a German Communist.[1] Hitler was not satisfied with this explanation. According to Gisevius he was so irritated by its stupidity that he took the inquiry out of the hands of Mueller and the Gestapo, and handed it over to Nebe's professional criminal investigators.[2] One may believe, however, that Hitler was not greatly interested in a genuine inquiry. The two affairs had given him what he required. The conversations with "Schaemmel" at Venlo and the so aptly timed bomb had given him his 'legalitaet' wherewith to answer the generals who opposed the invasion of the Netherlands.

Nevertheless, the kidnapping incident had no consequences that were worthy of so dangerous a game. Schellenberg was promoted to become an SS Major-General at the age of thirty. Mueller put the leading Gestapo and Kripo experts on to interrogating Best and Stevens about the German Resistance Movement, but there was nothing to be learnt in this quarter. So Himmler made the best he could out of the connivance that had gone on between the British and Dutch Intelligence services. A note of protest, naming the Dutch Major-General von Oorschot, was officially presented to the Dutch Minister in Berlin on the day of the invasion of the Netherlands,[3] but so little was this official protest followed up by German propaganda that it is impossible to believe that it was the sole purpose of the Venlo incident.

Once again the actions of Himmler and Heydrich reveal nothing concrete. Yet, poor though the results of the Venlo kidnapping were, they advanced the position of the 'Foreign SD' tremendously. From this time dates the practice of sending SD men or Gestapists to the legations and embassies abroad in the guise of commercial or cultural attachés.[4] Although nominally subordinated to the Foreign Office, they reported direct to the Reich main Security Office or to Luther's Deutschland department, which had now become virtually a branch of the SS.[5]

Why did the paranoiac Ribbentrop, who could work himself into a frenzy over the finest distinctions of precedent, submit to this most serious of Himmler's encroachments? It may well have been the result of a momentary impulse. It may have been the baleful influence of Martin Luther; the suspicion of Canaris, which Ribbentrop

---

[1] Von Hassell, p. 87.   [2] Gisevius, p. 403.
[3] Nuremberg Document NG 4672, case XI.   [4] See *supra*, p. 115.
[5] Nuremberg Document NG 4588.

shared with all Hitler's entourage, also played a part. In any case Ribbentrop was to regret it. On 7 August 1941 he at last exacted an undertaking from Himmler that Schellenberg's SD attachés should not intervene in the internal politics of the state in which they operated, and that henceforward they should keep their Foreign Office mission chiefs informed of all their activities.[1] Soon this became a dead letter, too, and a year later Manfred von Killinger, the ambassador to Rumania, complained that Luther had completely by-passed him in transmitting to Richter, the SD attaché in Bucharest, Himmler's instructions for a renewed deportation of Jews.[1]

In February 1944, when Himmler absorbed the Canaris organisation, the hamstringing of the embassies was completed. The attaché Moyzisch, who negotiated for the secrets of the famous spy 'Cicero', worked entirely outside the authority of the ambassador in Ankara, von Papen. As a Gestapo man he reported to his chief, Kaltenbrunner. When Moyzisch tried to take his precious documents to Ribbentrop, he was kidnapped by Kaltenbrunner on the way to Berlin and Ribbentrop refused to recognise the importance of the Gestapo's discoveries so that this remarkable counter-espionage coup was largely nullified.[2] All Ribbentrop chose to do about it was to send von Papen a tremendous rap on the knuckles for allowing Moyzisch's report to go to Schellenberg and Kaltenbrunner.[3] Such was the ultimate disastrous harvest of the Venlo kidnapping and the promotion of Schellenberg.[4]

After the kidnapping of the British officers, open opposition by the High Command to Hitler's plans for the invasion of the Low Countries ceased. From Brauchitsch downwards no one knew how far he had been compromised by the Resistance Circle and their supposed contact with the British. The Resistance Circle, however, continued to plot, and the hope of taking Hitler into protective

[1] Nuremberg Document NG 2195; Reitlinger, op. cit., pp. 403-4.
[2] I. C. Moyzisch, *Operation Cicero* (London, 1950), pp. 81-97.
[3] Nuremberg Document NG 4852, quoted by Paul Seabury, op. cit., p. 131.
[4] Schellenberg remained deputy to Heinz Jost, the actual head of Amt VI, till the beginning of 1942, when Heydrich got rid of Jost. Like his assistant Stahlecker and the troublesome Ohlendorf, Jost was given the disgraceful command of an Einsatzgruppe in Russia, which it seems he dared not refuse. Jost got out of it pretty soon and entered the Ostministerium under Alfred Rosenberg as liaison man at Ewald von Kleist's headquarters in South Russia. Himmler did not discover him till May 1944 when he succeeded in getting this police Major General called up in the Waffen SS as a second lieutenant (Reitlinger, op. cit., p. 192; Nuremberg Document NO. 5884.)

custody was not abandoned. In December 1939 Witzleben was involved in a crackpot scheme to use divisions, which had to pass through Berlin on their way from Poland to the Western Front, for a Putsch on the usual lines.[1] Furthermore, the Canaris circle now began to use their unique position to sabotage the secret plans for a surprise invasion of the Low Countries, preparations in which they themselves were as deeply involved as they had been in the attack on Poland. Once more it was to be a joint action of the Abwehr and SD. The 'ten commandments' were abrogated, and the SD were to have their own disguised saboteurs on the lines of Canaris's Brandenburg battalion. Canaris, who had procured Polish uniforms for 'Operation Himmler', had to procure the uniforms of Dutch and Belgian frontier guards. The uniforms had to be stolen and it was not done skilfully. On 20 November, in the presence of Canaris, the ultra-Nazi General Reinhardt told Hitler that the Dutch Press had published a cartoon of Goering, dressed as a Dutch tram conductor.[2] Hitler had a brainstorm in front of his generals, but it was Canaris who soothed him and it seems that soon after this incident Canaris succeeded in getting the responsibility for using the foreign uniforms pinned on to Keitel. A few days before the invasion of the Low Countries, word was conveyed to the Dutch military attaché Colonel Sas that the same Gestapo experts who had operated on the Polish border, Naujocks and his associates, had applied for Dutch visas.[3]

On the day of the invasion a group of SS men in Dutch frontier-guard uniform was duly parachuted across the Meuse at Maastricht, but the company from the Brandenburg regiment, which had the duty of securing the three bridges behind them, failed to find the fuses, so that the Dutch, who had perhaps profited by some of the warnings Oster had sent Colonel Sas, blew them up. But another Brandenburg company secured the bridge lower down at Gennep, and Reichenau had only to divert his armoured columns in this direction.[4]

Canaris's warnings to the Dutch, if warnings they were, had not achieved much; but then, in the state of the Western allies in May 1940, there was not much that could have been achieved. The second act in the drama of 1939-45 had opened. The phoney war had been succeeded by the victory-parade war, in which the dissensions of Hitler's experts were things of little consequence.

[1] *Von Hassell*, pp. 113, 120.   [2] Abshagen, p. 239.
[3] Allen Dulles, *Germany's Underground* (New York, 1947), p. 60, quoting Gisevius.   [4] Abshagen, p. 244; Leverkuehn, pp. 99-100; Helmuth Greiner, p. 101.

7

The High Tide of Conquest

SPRING 1940 – WINTER 1941

1. TOWARDS A EUROPEAN SS

In the six weeks' Blitz campaign in the West the SS fought for the first time in divisional formations which acquired the new name of Waffen SS and also the high, perhaps exaggerated, reputation which they were to retain among friends and foes for the next five years. Yet Himmler's military contribution to victory in the West was not spectacular, two SS divisions—the Totenkopf and the SS Verfuegungs division and a partly armoured regiment, the Leibstandarte Adolf Hitler—out of a total of eighty-nine divisions deployed in the line. But it was a completely motorised force, and the Totenkopf division was able to remain in touch with the enemy the whole way from the German-Belgian border to the Pyrenees. The Leibstandarte Adolf Hitler, moreover, was equipped at Hitler's personal instructions with the latest Mark IV armoured vehicles, because he believed that the mandarins of the High Command had spurned them.[1]

In this campaign the Leibstandarte became a show force who were switched to the more spectacular sectors of the front at Hitler's wish. They took Rotterdam on the first day of the invasion in combination with General Student's parachute troops, they marched to the sea at Boulogne, and finally they figured in a victory parade in Paris after an awkward moment on 25 May, when Sepp Dietrich narrowly escaped spending the next five years in a British prisoners' camp. The incident typified the new Waffen SS, unorthodox and amateurish and not good enough in Hitler's eyes to justify a big increase in their strength.[2] In the winter of 1940 Germany had seven million men under arms but only eighty thousand Waffen SS men. Even a year later the SS could barely scrape up six divisions for Russia. 'I have six divisions of SS composed of men absolutely indifferent in matters of religion. It doesn't prevent them from going to their deaths with serenity in their souls'.[3]

---

[1] *Hitler's Table Talk*, p. 634.

[2] Paul Hausser, *Waffen SS in Einsatz*, p. 31.   [3] *Hitler's Table Talk*, p. 143.

It also enabled the armed SS to bring to the West the standards of ruthlessness which they had acquired in Poland, particularly the Totenkopf division with its 7,400 former concentration camp guards and its commander, the former head of the concentration camp service, Theodor Eicke. On 27 May 1940 the division received its baptism of fire, when, after an unopposed march through Belgium, the XVIth Army Corps found the British Expeditionary Force defending the La Bassée canal in front of Bailleul. Eicke declared the readiness of his raw division to force the canal, regardless of casualties, and was reproved by his corps commander, the future Resistance general, Erich Hoeppner: 'You are a butcher and no soldier'.[1] And, as it turned out, the casualties were heavy. Lieutenant Fritz Knoechlein, commanding the fourth company of the 1st Battalion of the 2nd Totenkopf Regiment, seeing his men fall in such numbers, lost his head. In Le Paradis farm a hundred men of the 2nd Royal Norfolks kept up the fire long after they had been surrounded. A white flag was run up and the defenders marched out to what they believed was honourable capitulation. But Knoechlein shouted at them that they had fired after the hoisting of the flag and they were all machine-gunned in front of a barn wall, the dead and the wounded being left together in a sprawling heap. Even after the massacre, Knoechlein, twenty-eight years old and a product of Hausser's cadet school at Brunswick, still ran round like a man demented, looking for wounded English soldiers who might be in hiding.

Knoechlein was not liked by his fellow SS officers, who wanted to challenge him to a duel after this exhibition, which caused a considerable stir. From Hoeppner's staff office came demands for an inquiry. As it happened, Colonel Gunter d'Alquen, who had edited *Das Schwarze Korps* for Heydrich, arrived in Le Paradis next day as a war correspondent of the Wehrmacht propaganda section.[2] He saw the bodies and was told the very lame story that dum-dum bullets had been used by the massacred men. But Eicke delayed the

[1] Quoted in Gerhard Ritter, *Karl Goerdeler und die deutsche Widerstandsbewegung* (Bonn, 1954).

[2] Gunter d'Alquen wrote for Himmler an official pamphlet *Die SS*. At the end of the war he became head of the Wehrmacht propaganda section in succession to General Wedel, a particular bugbear of Goebbels who declared that Wedel had increased the propaganda section to the size of a division. D'Alquen was also an assistant to Hans Pruetzmann in the creation of the 'Werwulf' organisation (IMT XVII, pp. 277, 297). In July 1955 he was fined 60,000 marks by a Berlin denazification court (*The Times*, 26 July 1955).

investigation, in which 6th Army Headquarters were interested, till he had moved his troops out of the XVIth Corps area to take over from the Leibstandarte at Boulogne. There was no court martial for Fritz Knoechlein. He commanded a regiment of Norwegian volunteer SS men in Courland in December 1944 and received the Knight's Cross as a Lieutenant-Colonel.[1]

But from under the sprawled heap of dead there had crept two badly wounded privates of the Royal Norfolks. They had surrendered to another German unit and had been sent to hospital and on 25 October 1948 their evidence convicted Fritz Knoechlein before a British military court at Altona. Three months later Knoechlein was hanged. Private Pooley, who rose from the dead, had been repatriated to England before the end of the war as a severely disabled soldier, but no one in British military circles believed his story even in 1943. Atrocities were something that happened only in Russia and Poland.[2]

Had this story come out sooner, the world might have been prepared for many things that were yet to be. As it happened, it was only after the murder of eighty-three American prisoners at the Malmédy cross-roads in December 1944 that a peculiar illusion died. This was the illusion that the special standards of warfare of the Waffen SS were only intended for the races whom Himmler did not recognise as fellow Herrenvolk. Colonel-General Paul Hausser, who has described the plan for a British and American SS, fighting for the common ideals of Europe, and who has published a photograph of the Ukrainian SS celebrating mass, has nothing to say about Le Paradis.

The most remarkable thing about the participation of the SS in the conquest of Western Europe is the absence of Himmler. He made no appearance at Hitler's field headquarters either at the Felsennest in the Eiffel mountains or at Brûly la Pêche in Belgium. He was absent from the capitulation ceremony in the Forest of Compiègne on 22 June and he was absent from the victory parade in Paris a week later. The most probable explanation is that he was ill. Felix Kersten, the Baltic German masseur, had first attended him for nervous stomach cramps in March 1939. Within a few days of the

---

[1] Kraetschmer, *Die Ritterkreuztraeger der Waffen SS*, pp. 396, 401.

[2] *History of the Second World War: The war in France and Flanders*, 1939-40, p. 192, official narrative by Major L. F. Ellis. *The Vengeance of Private Pooley*, by Cyril Jolly (London, 1956), pp. 162-3, 203-6, etc. This book contains a good précis of the Altona trial.

occupation of Holland in May 1940 Himmler sent for Kersten, who was living at Scheveningen and had him 'interned' on Kersten's own property at Harzwalde, near Berlin, in order to keep him on hand.[1] Thus there began the long and somewhat ambiguous relationship between the Reichsfuehrer and his father confessor, to which we owe so much picturesque and revealing detail.

When at last Himmler was able or willing to inspect his victorious divisions in the West, he was in a poisonous mood. In spite of all they had achieved, Himmler was no better disposed after the fall of France towards the men of the Wehrmacht alongside of whom the SS had fought. He told the Leibstandarte officers when he addressed them at Metz on 7 September:

> Then there is the complaint from the Wehrmacht that we have heard ever since 1933. Every SS man is a potential NCO but it is a pity that their commanders are so bad. After the war in Poland they said that the SS had huge casualties because they were not trained to the job. Now that we have very small losses, they suppose that we have not fought.[2]

This was a language which Himmler never ceased to use and which he used still more violently after the July 1944 plot when he became a war lord. On 3 August 1944, for instance, he complained at the Posen Gauleiters' conference that his SS men were attached to other divisions, where they were used as maids-of-all-work and frequently annihilated. Huge casualties were caused to the Waffen SS because Manstein, whom Himmler called Herr Marshal von Lewitzki, deliberately starved them of armour and equipment. It was, he said, just like the time when it was 'unmodern' to get on well with the SS or with himself. And he recalled an incident of that time —to wit, the occasion of his visit to France after the capitulation:

> Schoerner was a lieutenant-colonel beyond the age of forty and did not obtain command of a mountain division till 1940 when he was forty-four. On that account Schoerner had to explain his conduct before his Commander-in-Chief, Herr von Brauchitsch, because I once visited him at Pontarlier in the Jura. For that he was ordered to Berlin and had to explain why he had received this irregular and unlawful visit from a suspicious Nazi.[3]

It was an odd recollection of the most startling victory in German history and one which implies that Himmler's visit to the front had not been a success. Many reasons for Himmler's disgruntlement

---

[1] *Memoirs of Felix Kersten*, p. 19.

[2] Nuremburg Document PS 1918; IMT XIX, p. 98.

[3] *Vierteljahreshefte fuer Zeitgeschichte*, Stuttgart, No. 4, p. 565. Schoerner was actually three years older.

suggest themselves. On the day of the Compiègne armistice, 22 June, Hitler had impetuously ordered the demobilisation of thirty-five divisions. A fortnight later, when he was flirting with the 'Sea Lion' plan for an invasion of England, Hitler altered his instructions to the extent of keeping half these divisions in cadre.[1] The Waffen SS were not included in the demobilisation plan, but on 6 August Hitler addressed his SS commanders, making it plain what their task would be after demobilisation.[2] Only a snippet of the armed SS would be retained, equivalent to five per cent of the standing army. It would be a volunteer élite force for political police duty in Germany. It would be composed of men 'above fraternisation with the proletariat and the underworld'.[3] It was no random utterance. The speech was committed to writing and, curiously late in the day, on 21 March 1941 it was distributed by OKH to all officers of general rank.[4]

'Meanwhile Hitler sent the following edict to Keitel:
"After the war we shall have many rebellious peoples to rule; in order to manage them he wishes to put into control not the army but the combat units of the SS. He therefore wants the SS transformed into a special service branch, equipped with all arms including air weapons and under his personal command".'

On top of this, it was the turn of the generals to be favoured by their Fuehrer. Not one of the 'uncertain cantonists', whom Himmler and Heydrich had watched for signs of a military Putsch in November 1939, resigned their commands in May 1940 in protest at the naked aggression they were called on to serve; and among the twelve new field marshals named in Hitler's Reichstag speech on 19 July were Brauchitsch and Witzleben. Nobody, not even Napoleon, had ever before created twelve field marshals in one day. It was not an atmosphere in which the Gestapo and SD could discover new generals' plots and Himmler may well have feared that he was about to lose his vocation.

In a Germany, slightly relaxed and looking slightly less like a police state, Hitler examined the plans which had been put before him for the invasion of England. But his own intuition appeared to be telling him that England would accept any terms he cared to put,

---

[1] Helmuth Greiner, op. cit., p. 112.   [2] See *supra*, p. 84.
[3] Nuremberg Document D664; IMT XX, pp. 313, 321.
[4] The version of this secret speech which reached von Hassell is near enough to the mark (22.9.40, page 139).

once he was fully master of the continent of Europe. At length, on 29 July, hardly more than five weeks from the capitulation of France, he sent Jodl to the War Office with the intimation that Russia would be attacked in the spring. It was now clear to the initiated that the continued instructions concerning 'Operation Sea Lion' were a mere bluff. So relieved were the generals, or rather field marshals as many of them had become, that they forgot to conspire. Only Admiral Raeder regretted the definite abandonment of 'Sea Lion' and only General Thomas of the Armament Office, an expert on Russian military resources, came out firmly against the belief in a Blitzkrieg in the East. Many Germans have testified at Nuremberg how they had been outraged by this most unnecessary and illogical of all Hitler's military adventures, yet nothing seems to have united the bickering Nazi leaders so much as the expectation of 'Plan Barbarossa'.

In December 1940 it was decided to raise the strength of the field forces from 146 to 186 divisions, but even now Hitler seemed determined to restrict the Waffen SS, which was allotted a single new motorised infantry division. Himmler could obtain no more than 1·1 per cent of the numbers recruited for the army.[1] There seems to have been a change of mind about this, for the 1920 class alone provided the Waffen SS with 17,719 volunteers and 113 conscripts, a much bigger percentage than 1·1. No doubt the Waffen SS had by this time enough glamour to attract the better sort of volunteer, but it was only after July 1944 that Himmler could use his position as head of the Replacement Army to ensure, as General Westphal complains, that the best drafts went to his Waffen SS.[2]

Under the wholesale conditions of total war it was becoming particularly difficult for Himmler to keep up the choosiness on which he had preened himself in his Wehrmacht address of 1937. Enough divisions in the field to give him a say in the military councils of the war and nothing but the élite of Nordic youth were incompatible aims, but here the theories of Walter Darré gave him a loop-hole. These pure Nordic peasant aristocracies need not be German. Germanic types could be unearthed almost everywhere. The first hint of a new policy came in the Metz speech of 7 September: 'We must attract all the Nordic blood of the world to us and deprive our adversaries of it'.[3]

---

[1] Helmuth Greiner, op. cit., p. 312.
[2] Westphal, *Heer im Fesseln*, p. 89.   [3] Nuremberg Document PS 1918.

The idea may have occurred to Himmler as early as April 1940 when two ancient Nordic lands, Denmark and Norway, came under the German heel. Heydrich, who lived on a Baltic island and was as fond of this sort of *mystique* as Himmler, is said to have flown over Norway with the Luftwaffe on the day of the invasion. Himmler himself dispatched two police battalions of the SS from Prague. They were sent to assist Gauleiter Terboven of Duesseldorf, who was intended to establish a civil government, but Himmler with his love of runes and pagan gods may also have thought of staking his own claim to one of the lands of Northern twilight. Soon after his Metz speech he visited Norway himself, and in the same October he named his new SS division 'Viking'.

In a conversation with Felix Kersten, Berger claimed that it was he and not Himmler who had persuaded Hitler to make the SS[1] an international army. Berger told Kersten, 'As a soldier I feel with the soldiers of Europe. French volunteers wear the Iron Cross next to the *Légion d'Honneur* even when they have won it in fighting Germans. Two proud decorations of the two nations on the same breast —there you have the New Europe'.

Berger, whom we last saw directing the Henlein Freikorps movement across the Czechoslovak border in 1938, had been made by Himmler in April 1940 chief of the Fuehrungshauptamt, that is, Himmler's Chief of Staff for the military SS. He was forty-four years old and he had been a gymnastic instructor and sports champion. He was passionately fond of nature, painted landscapes, and took films of eagles and bustards in flight. A man with bushy eyebrows and a puzzled, rather tortured face, just the man for the other Himmler who cultivated herbs and believed in porridge. Berger, moreover, was a Swabian with a large number of turbulent Germanic relatives living in south-eastern Europe. On that account Himmler regarded him as a man of wide international outlook, particularly as he sometimes broke into French when writing to the Reichsfuehrer. Berger was clearly the right choice for a European crusade. A romantic and usually kind man, he had much influence over Himmler—benign if we are to credit Kersten, but some other aspects of Berger's mind will be studied later.

It was not, however, Berger's congenial woolly thinking that converted Himmler in October 1940 to the idea of the European SS. Whether Himmler's or Berger's, it was in fact a brilliant stroke.

[1] Kersten, *Totenkopf und Treue*, p. 318.

Hitler had forbidden Himmler to exceed his quota of recruits and he had doomed the Waffen SS to a strength barely exceeding four divisions. But what if Himmler offered him a trained army of foreigners, of young men who might otherwise be messing about with Resistance movements in France, the Netherlands and Scandinavia, merely for lack of employment? Hitler, who, as his table talk often reveals, had not the slightest idealism about a united Europe other than as an economic expansion ground for Germany, did in fact fall for this argument, though only very slowly. He was not completely converted till March 1943 and thus it was that at the end of the war there were thirty-five Waffen SS divisions, whereas in September 1939 there had not been one.

October 1940 was a critical moment in Himmler's life, for on 7 October he celebrated his fortieth birthday and a portentous volume called a Festgabe was dedicated to him by his pet experts, among them Professor Hoehn, his court economist, and his legal and constitutional experts, Werner Best and Wilhelm Stuckart. The theme was Grossraum—expansion—and Himmler was recognised as the true architect of the new order in Europe.[1] October 1940 was also the precise psychological moment for recognised Nordic blood to join a crusade. The occupied countries from the North Cape to the Pyrenees were still numbed from their experience. No organised opposition to the Germans had crystallised at any point. Even the Communists in the occupied countries supported Ribbentrop's Moscow pact in conformity with the party doctrine and this had a paradoxical result, for the absence of any revolutionary crusading spirit made it easier to appeal to anti-Communist sentiment. The wrongs of Finland, invaded and deprived of her strategic bases by the armistice of 12 March, and of Rumania, forced in August 1940 to give up to the Russians Bessarabia and Bukovina, were a useful red herring to stimulate the dreams of adventurous youth who did not speculate too much on the diplomatic background of these wrongs. It was freely given out that the German troops, massing in northern Norway, would seek justice for the Finns in place of the British and French help which never came.

Thus it turned out that the fourth SS motorised division, the only division Himmler was allowed to recruit as part of the huge programme for the winter of 1940, was partly foreign, though it was

[1] *Festgabe zum* 40 *Geburtstage des Reichsfuehrers SS, Heinrich Himmler* (Darmstadt, Wittlich Verlag).

based on the regiment, 'Germania SS', which had been raised in Hamburg after the seizure of power. After the fall of France the Germania regiment was detached from the Verfuegungs division, which had been renamed 'Das Reich', and it was sent to the army training area at Heuberg. On 11 November 1940 the Germania regiment was expanded into the Viking division, SS, and Felix Steiner of the Germania regiment became a divisional commander. This was the Steiner whom Hitler, at the time of his death, expected to lead an army into Berlin. A figure who will recur more than once in this book, he is still to be found at SS public reunions when they take place in different parts of Germany.[1]

To the 'Germania' regiment were added the regiments 'Nordland' and 'Westland', half of whose recruits were volunteers from Holland, Denmark, Norway, and Finland. In 1940 no occupied country contributed an SS unit above battalion strength and the first complete national regiment or brigade to be recruited abroad was not ready for action till November 1943. This was the SS storm brigade, 'Wallonia', originally a Wehrmacht volunteer battalion recruited in the Walloon districts of Belgium. The other 'national legions' from Norway, Denmark, Holland, France, and Flanders did not reach regimental strength till 1944. In fact the largest expansion of the 'European volunteer' or 'Germanic SS' took place in September of that year after Himmler had become Commander-in-Chief of the Replacement Army.[2] Fifteen new SS divisions had to be found at a time when the best sources of German man-power had been drained, and also at a time when numerous collaborators and their families had fled to Germany from France and Belgium. The national legions were therefore raised to divisional strength. France contributed the 'Charlemagne' division, Belgium the divisions 'Flandern' and 'Wallonia', Holland the division 'Nederland', and Scandinavia the division 'Nordland'. These divisions were never brought up to strength and the last actions of the war decimated them. At Stettin in March 1945 Léon Degrelle's Wallonia division numbered barely 700 men,[3] while in the Battle of Berlin the divisions 'Nordland' and 'Charlemagne' were reduced to similar contingents.

The moral value of the European volunteer SS, Berger's creation of 1940, did, however, become considerable at the end of the war,

---

[1] See pages 432-4.   [2] See *infra*, p. 387.

[3] Léon Degrelle, *Die verlorene Legion* (Stuttgart, 1955), p. 444; Paul Hausser, pp. 105, 116, 185.

in spite of their small numbers. In the Russian campaigns their field record had been unsurpassed, though many of the volunteers must have had other reasons besides pan-European idealism for seeking the protection of a German uniform. After the Liberation of France circumstances made them fanatics. To the German soldier, surrender meant a prisoner-of-war camp, but to the foreign collaborator it might well mean the firing squad. To the very last their position was never clarified. The legend of the fanatical SS, who fought on after the twelfth hour, reposes largely on the feats of these foreigners, who believed that the loss of their arms meant the loss of their lives. In the end, Hitler, raving in his Chancellery bunker, could only rely on enemy subjects to carry out his orders to the full. Thus, on 19 April 1945, 650 men of the Wallonia division were completely immolated in attacking the main Russian assault force, which had crossed the Oder south of Stettin. Hitler's orders were carried out to the letter. They reached the edge of the water and thirty-five men survived.[1]

Léon Degrelle, the Belgian Fascist leader whom Hitler intended to be the head of a Belgian state had the Ardennes offensive of December 1944 succeeded, made some confused efforts to save the French, Belgian and Dutch volunteers from the last holocaust. He even released the men who did not want to fight on, but he suffered from the fantastic delusion that his men might win some sort of terms by continuing the fight in Norway after[2] the capitulation. Many of them had to serve prison sentences in their own country. Degrelle himself escaped from Norway to Spain.

In this matter of fanaticism and 'last-ditch' fighting morale the western and northern European volunteers must be distinguished carefully from the racial Germans who were conscripted in 1941-4 in Hungary, South-east Europe, the Baltic States, and former Russian territories. Many of these were turned into Germans by Himmler's VOMI and RUSHA bureaux, merely in order to press-gang them into the SS. Their morale was of the lowest. Not even Hausser and Berger can pretend that, like the original Viking division of Felix Steiner, these men represented the spirit of the New Europe, vowed to the destruction of godless Bolshevism. Their peculiar features will be studied in the next chapter.

Today the name of the first foreign volunteer SS division is perpetuated in the journal of the former Waffen SS, *Viking Ruf*, an

[1] Léon Degrelle, op. cit., p. 462.   [2] *Ibid.*, p. 498.

innocuous parish magazine devoted to old comrades' rallies. The original Vikings achieved their first battle honours at Tarnopol in Galicia on 29 June 1941. Was it the idealism of the Pan-Europeans that caused Heydrich's extermination commanders to be so grateful to the Viking men for what they did in their sector? The Einsatzgruppen report for 11 July records that 'six hundred Jews were executed at Zborow between Tarnopol and Lwow by the Waffen SS as a reprisal for Soviet cruelties'.[1]

The collaborationists from the Western countries need not have been so zealous, for gratitude was the last thing they could expect. Early in 1942 Himmler refused to allow Mussert, the Dutch puppet Premier, to recall his legion, which was fighting in Russia with the Viking division, in order to reinforce his own precarious position in Holland. He was told that the Dutch army after the war would be based precisely on the number of men they sent to Russia. Hitler commented on this[2]:

When speaking to the Germanic races of the north-west and north one must always make it plain that what we are building is the Germanic Reich, or rather the Reich with Germany constituting her most powerful source of strength, as much from the ideological as from the military point of view.

And then he went on to discuss with Keitel the annexation of Dutch Friesland.

The foreign collaborationists were not told as much. It was concealed from them that they were to belong, not to a Bund or federation but to a Reich or empire. Only a fortnight after his conversation with Hitler, Himmler attended a swearing-in ceremony of the Dutch SS, at which Mussert again put Quisling's case for a German Bund. Himmler was careful never to commit himself on the subject, but by May 1943, when he had established a 'Germanic House' in Hanover for the purpose of bringing about the union of the Germanic peoples as a Germanic Reich, it must have been realised that, whatever Reich meant, Germanic could only mean German. It must have been realised that the real purpose of all the friendly froth distilled from

[1] Hans Fanslau, who had been Hausser's adjutant at Bad Toelz, served with the division and was tried in connection with this charge in 1947. He was acquitted however, on the ground that, as divisional supply officer, he had nothing to do with the massacre order. Fanslau was sentenced to twenty-five years' imprisonment, being concerned with concentration camps later in the war. He was released in 1955 (Case IV, Judgment 8104).

[2] *Hitler's Table Talk*, 5 April 1942, pp. 402-3.

the lips of the Reichskommissars, Terboven in Norway and Seyss-Inquart in Holland, was recruitment for the SS.[1]

In 1943 the foreigners began to outnumber the Reich Germans in the training centres and cadet schools of the Waffen SS, and there at least more effort was made to disguise the stark truth of annexation. The old emphasis, dictated by Himmler, on German racial purity and on strict party indoctrination, had to be modified if not changed. Absolute obedience to the Fuehrer, the basis of the SS man's oath, was invested with a new significance. The cadets at Bad Toelz were now commanded by a young colonel, Fritz Klingenberg, the hero of Belgrade, who was killed at the end of the war leading the last nominally German division of the SS. Klingenberg taught them that foremost of all they were Europeans, champions of the historic values of civilisation against Asiatic Bolshevism. They learnt that Himmler was prepared to nominate a member of any European nation as his own successor. They were allowed to study Marxian dialectic and the works of banned German authors and to criticise National Socialism in their discussion classes. In 1944 there was even a plan to select American and British prisoners of war to attend fortnightly courses at Bad Toelz. It was abandoned when the entire school had to be sent to the front.[2]

Naïvely the former Colonel-General Paul Hausser has stated these things in a book which is an object lesson on the German mind, a perpetual flight from the thorny problems of living with people into the shadowy realm of theories and systems, of substitute faiths and fictitious brotherhoods. Of these there is a humbler and therefore more striking witness than Paul Hausser—the Swedish volunteer Wiking Jerk, who served with the forces of Finland in 1939 and with the Viking and Nordland divisions of the SS throughout the Russian campaigns and during the Battle of Berlin. Jerk's little book is a record of unspeakable sufferings, told with pity for his stricken companions but with a weird bloodless lack of sensibility and a total inability or unwillingness to question their necessity. This seems to be a characteristic of the writings of SS men and it is far more revealing than the apologetics of their chiefs.

Sergeant Jerk venerated his chiefs and believed what they told him. With pious wonder he records an address by his hero Felix Steiner, who created the Viking division, and it is an address which

[1] Institute for International Affairs, *Hitler's Europe*, 1954, pp. 76-7.

[2] Paul Hausser, *Waffen SS im Einsatz*, pp. 233-4.

typifies the extreme latter-day teaching of the SS in decline. It was made at Schwedt on the Oder front in March 1945.[1]

He awoke the memories of the fortunate days when we had advanced singing through Russia and when we had conquered the Bolshevik wherever he had met us in battle. He described the circumstances which had brought us here to the last breakwater of the German nation and also of the Western world against the savage flood from the East, the Oder line. The greatest danger that had ever threatened the Western peoples and their culture since Jenghiz Khan and Attila, had found them more divided than ever before. Instead of opposing the new invasion of Huns with united weapons, the West had whittled down its own strength in internal conflict. This had the result that only a part of the fighting power of greater Germany, the chief weapon against world Bolshevism, could be brought against the Barbarians.

After the address the great Obergruppenfuehrer himself shook hands with his SS men.

As he approached me, his stern features brightened into a beaming smile. He had recognised me. And yet it was almost a year since I had taken part in a deputation from all ranks of the division which had greeted him at Narva on his birthday. Since then he had seen innumerable new faces and yet he recognised mine. He called me by my name. I stood no longer on the ground but swam in a rosy cloud of happiness.

Sergeant Jerk escaped from Berlin to Sweden, ignorant of the fate of 'der Alte' with his clear blue eyes, and there he indulged in a reverie.

Felix Steiner, brave soldier, leader and friend! We forget you not. Maybe today you lie in some mass grave, savagely mutilated by the Red *Soldateska;* maybe you are in prison as a war criminal among other soldiers who did their duty; maybe you are in hiding from the triumphing enemy.[2]

But none of these things happened to Felix Steiner, one-time Education Officer in the old War Office of the Weimar Republic. Resisting alike Hitler's furious orders to immolate his skeleton army in Berlin and the appeals of disgruntled SS Gruppenfuehrers that he should dethrone Hitler in favour of Himmler, the crusader for a united Western civilisation quietly marched his men to the British lines.[3]

The response to the appeals for a European crusade had never been strong, and the figures for recruitment in the occupied Western and Northern countries in the days of German conquest are not really impressive. In 1943 the situation became critical. With the mounting evidence of Germany's inevitable defeat Himmler began

[1] Wiking Jerk, *Endkampf um Berlin* (Buenos Aires, 1947), p. 77 (translated from the Swedish *Ragnaroek*, Stockholm, 1946).
[2] Wiking Jerk, op. cit., p. 79.   [3] See *infra*, pp. 432-4.

to see that mere starvation and frustration under German rule was not driving Western European youth into the SS, though this might do for the helpless racial Germans in the East. He began to see his own inconsistency, and in December 1943 he reprimanded his higher SS and police leader for Norway, who had made a mass arrest of Oslo students. It was just when Himmler wanted to recruit 40,000 to 60,000 Norwegian SS men for the new police troops and the new Nordland SS division.[1] But no real gesture of conciliation to Norway was made till it was too late to matter. In the summer of 1944 one of Hausser's instructors from Bad Toelz became Hitler's personal SS adjutant. This man, Lieutenant-Colonel Richard Schulze, persuaded Hitler to send a telegram on 28 September to the puppet Premier, Vidkun Quisling, promising Norway an 'independent national and socialist existence' after the war. 'The news of this achievement by one of their staff filled the Bad Toelz school with great rejoicing', writes Paul Hausser. What on earth had the good Europeans to rejoice about in September 1944?[2]

2. HIMMLER'S FIRST PEACE FEELER

Italy's involvement with Greece and the oscillations of Jugoslav policy delayed the great adventure in the East from spring to summer 1941. The newly reconstituted SS divisions found themselves called on to serve in an unexpected quarter. In February 1941, when it was learned that British troops were to be sent to the aid of Greece, Bulgaria was hustled into the Tripartite Pact. So the Leibstandarte Adolf Hitler were suddenly moved from Metz to Sofia. On 6 April they invaded Southern Jugoslavia, engaged the Greeks on the Albanian border and in Thessaly, crossed the Gulf of Corinth and fought round through the Peloponnese to end up in Athens.

Early in 1941 the division Das Reich was ordered suddenly to move by road from Vesoul in Burgundy to Temesvar in Roumania, one of those immense marches which were only possible for divisions as well provided with motor transport as Das Reich and quite impracticable at the end of the war. On 13 April Captain Klingenberg, Hausser's former ADC and a future divisional commander, entered

[1] *The Goebbels Diaries*, 5 December 1943, p. 444.

[2] The Nordland division, which included a Danish regiment, went into the line in Estonia in the summer of 1944 and took part in the retreat to the Courland pocket. Remnants under Major-General Joachim Ziegler were among the last defenders of Berlin. Kraetschmer, op. cit., p. 394; Paul Hausser, p. 231.

THE HIGH TIDE OF CONQUEST

Belgrade in a motor boat and received the surrender of the city
after it had been exposed to a week's heavy bombing without warning or declaration of war. Of this occasion the much-publicised Otto
Skorzeny, who served with the division as a subaltern, remarks with
the disarming simplicity that is his only charm, 'It was seldom that
a friendly smile greeted us'.[1]

The dramatic use of his SS divisions was not what Himmler had
expected. He had built them up for the reckoning with 'The World
Enemy', and from this he had been diverted by unnecessary complication in the south-east. Viewed from this angle, the short-lived
British intervention in Greece had a moral value far greater than
its military achievement. Not only did it delay the attack on Russia,
but it also woke the Nazi leaders, if not Hitler himself, from the
favourite Hitler illusion that the Russian campaign would be fought
with both hands free. Besides inspiring Rudolph Hess's peace journey
to England, which was so damaging to German prestige and morale,
the intervention in Greece created numerous pessimists in high
places, and among them Heinrich Himmler.

Himmler did not shrink from the Russian venture. It was the
dream of his life, a legacy of the 'Raeterepublik' days in Munich,
when he went to the agricultural technical school. Himmler was deep
in the inner secrets of the Barbarossa plan. In February 1941 he made
a second journey to Norway, accompanying Terboven to the far
north—to Kirkenes, Vardoe and Vadsoe—where he visited his Totenkopf and police units, chiefly with an eye to the winter equipment
needed in a Russian campaign. 'Obergruppenfuehrer Pohl and his
men had now to obtain the currency to buy necessary furs and
stoves'.[2] Moreover in March Himmler assembled the men whom he
intended to act as higher SS and police leaders in Russia at the
Wewelsberg, a sort of castle of the SS Order which he had had built
in 1934. Here he told them that the Slav population of Europe would
have to be reduced by thirty millions.[3] A man who talked like that
was not half-hearted about the forthcoming Russian adventure. It
was only that he wanted peace with England first.

Himmler may have been in the secret of Hess's flight to Scotland
on 10 May 1941. He was certainly sympathetic towards it. If this
view seems inconsistent with Himmler's role, it must be borne in

[1] *Memoirs of Otto Skorzeny*, p. 37.
[2] *Vierteljahreshefte fuer Zeitgeschichte*, No. 4, p. 570; and see *infra*, page 191.
[3] IMT IV, p. 36, evidence von dem Bach-Zelewski.

mind that Hitler himself would not have disowned Hess, had the British government permitted him to return to Germany as a negotiator. Hitler still believed that England would sign a treaty with him in person as head of the German state. It was only after the unconditional surrender pronouncement of January 1943 that Hitler came to regard the very mention of negotiation as treachery, because the word postulated the sacrifice of his own person. After the bomb attempt of 20 July 1944 it was enough to have been the friend of a peace advocate to merit death in the strangler's noose. Yet after 10 May 1941 Hitler demanded no victims at all. Even the true architect of Hess's flight, who had planned it in detail, was not detained long by the Gestapo. Professor Albrecht Haushofer was released at Hitler's command in order that his foreign contacts might be observed and perhaps utilised on a future occasion.

This Albrecht Haushofer was the son of a still more famous professor, Karl Haushofer the geopolitician, whose career recalled the legendary German professors in whom the British Press believed during the First World War—professors who prepared the youth of Germany for the Kaiser's military machine and who could become generals with the ease of German housemaids in seaside boarding houses, spotting gun emplacements for the German Secret Service. Karl Haushofer really did become a General or, at any rate, a Major General commanding a reserve division, but his more important activities began after the 1918 Armistice when he directed the Munich Geopolitical Institute. From this place there emanated an enormous amount of frothy matter in which the theme of German living-space came foremost. The theorists of National Socialism drank from this fountain, Hess, Darré, and Rosenberg and, via Hess, Hitler himself. In 1920, when he was twenty-four years old, Hess became Haushofer's class assistant, and it was Haushofer who hid him from the police after the failure of Hitler's Munich Putsch three years later.

Karl Haushofer's long honeymoon with the Nazis ended in 1938, when, as German delegate to the Africa Congress at Convegno Volta, he ran gleefully to Hitler, declaring that he could negotiate the return of Germany's colonies against the renunciation of all claims in Eastern Europe. This, in Hitler's eyes, so contradicted all the work of the Geopolitical Institute that he had a brainstorm. Karl Haushofer retired to private life, but Rudolf Hess protected the Haushofer family from the wolves of the party. In 1933 Hess had been forced to get rid of Albrecht Haushofer as an official adviser because of accusations of non-Aryan ancestry. Now Hess cultivated him more than ever. In March 1938 Albrecht Haushofer had quitted a brief appointment in the Foreign Office after quarrelling with Ribbentrop, but within eighteen months Hess, who loathed Ribbentrop, got Haushofer reinstated as head of an Information section.[1]

The strangest aspect of this strange man was his resiliency. Not only did he survive the Hess scandal, he survived the arrest of one of his pupils in the Rote Kapelle case,[2] he survived the trials of his friends of the Resistance Circle and his final murder during the Battle of Berlin was unofficial. Himmler at least had meant him to survive. The reason seems to be that the Nazis found Haushofer plausible and likeable. He was one of those good-looking, sympathetic dons who know when to provide muffins and who teach not only pupils but disciples. He wrote classical tragedies in blank verse which were performed in Berlin theatres with some success. He was a cosmopolitan with an affection for England and with the aid of a guardsman moustache he managed to look very like an Englishman.

It seems that Haushofer had the confidence of the Goerdeler-Hassell circle as early as the Munich crisis. Moreover, by the summer of 1940 he was already discussing with a trusted disciple the prospects of murdering Hitler.[3] Yet Haushofer's scheme to send Hess to visit the Duke of Hamilton shows a certain ambivalence, for Hess's peace offer involved neither the sacrifice of Hitler nor of Hitler's territorial ambitions in the East. If the terms which the poor dizzy-headed creature put to Lord Simon and Sir Ivone Kirkpatrick were in Haushofer's brief, it was the brief of the geopolitician's son and not of the member of the Resistance Circle. Hess knew that 'Plan Barbarossa' had already been delayed beyond the original zero hour, yet he stoutly denied that Hitler would attack Russia in the near future. Instead of offering the British a share in a European anti-Bolshevik crusade, he offered a free hand in the British Empire against a German free hand in Europe. This was clearly a dose of early Haushofer senior.[4]

The tortuous mind of Albrecht Haushofer will not be found in the pious tract of a hero-worshipping disciple. Haushofer went to Geneva at the end of April 1941 to play a double if not a treble game.

---

[1] Rainer Hildebrandt, *Wir sind die Letzten* (Berlin, 1947), pp. 27, 35, 38, 51.
[2] See p. 230.   [3] Hildebrandt, op. cit., p. 27.
[4] IMT VI, pp. 159-62; XIX, p. 377.

Through his friendship with Professor Karl Burckhardt, the President of the International Red Cross, Haushofer tried to prepare the Duke of Hamilton for Hess's reception. At the same time he asked Burckhardt to take letters to England for members of the Resistance Circle. But, as Haushofer told Frau von Hassell, Burckhardt also received an agent who represented Himmler. This agent wanted to know whether the British would consent to discuss peace terms with Himmler in place of Hitler. Three months later, when he met this agent of Himmler's in person, von Hassell noted that he too was a member of Haushofer's intimate circle.[1]

On Sunday afternoon, 17 August, I received a visit from Langbehn the attorney, whom I knew by name as a friend of Popitz's and as an associate of Albrecht Haushofer. He reported that Karl Burckhardt, who was spending some time in Germany on Red Cross matters, would soon be going to England on a mission and that it might be profitable, therefore, to have a talk with him.

This Karl Langbehn was a lawyer whose international practice took him to many countries. Haushofer met him on board ship returning from Japan in 1937, while Himmler made his acquaintance a year or two later. Himmler made friends with difficulty and his meeting was an accident. The Langbehns had a villa close to the Himmlers at Gmund on the Tegernsee. Gudrun, the daughter who was born to Himmler in 1929, went to school with the Langbehns' daughter and so the parents were introduced to each other.[2] Langbehn, the son of a German planter, had been born in Sumatra. Of Himmler's own age, Langbehn's portrait reveals a rubicund prematurely bald blond with rather sly eyes. He seems to have been one of those genial Bohemians who live on the extreme frontiers of probability, a sort of second Felix Kersten and the kind of extrovertive marvel for whom Himmler's lonely nature most craved.

Early in 1940 Langbehn's collector's instinct acquired him the friendship of an even more retiring character than Himmler, the acting Prussian Finance Minister, Professor Johannes Popitz, who was in the very centre of the Resistance Circle.[3] In this way Langbehn obtained entry into the exclusive wartime club of the German intelligentsia, Canaris's Abwehr, for which his journeys abroad particularly commended him. Nothing could have suited Himmler better. A man in the Abwehr could work for him abroad in secret and over the heads of Heydrich and his SD Intelligence officers, but

[1] *Von Hassell Diaries* (London 1947), pp. 183, 448.
[2] Allen Dulles, op. cit., p. 147.   [3] See *infra*, pp. 296-7.

in the end, as we shall see, the SD caught up with Langbehn in spite of Himmler.[1]

It is a matter of conjecture whether Langbehn really had Himmler's instructions at the end of April 1941, when he visited Professor Burckhardt. Langbehn may have sounded Himmler on behalf of Haushofer and his almost hypnotic instrument, Rudolf Hess. On the other hand, Langbehn used to exploit his relations with the Abwehr circle in order to build up a Himmler legend in that quarter, a legend of a 'Resistance' Himmler which may have had no other purpose than to obtain information for Himmler himself. Langbehn seems, for instance, to have persuaded that eminently persuadable person, Dr. Otto John, who was then an Abwehr colleague, that during the first great reverse on the Russian front in the winter of 1941 Himmler thought of an SS Putsch against Hitler.[2] That at least is what Dr. Otto John wrote for Mr. Wheeler-Bennett. Langbehn dropped the same hint to von Hassell in March 1942. 'Langbehn still suspects that all sorts of things are being planned round Himmler. A person in that corner is in a better position to act than one in Beck's entourage'.[3]

Echoes of Langbehn's stories concerning Himmler got even further for, a few weeks later on 9 April, Count Ciano wrote: 'Himmler himself, who was an extremist in the past but who now feels the pulse of the country, wants a compromise peace'.[4]

It is not justifiable to build up very much from the role of Karl Langbehn. Himmler allowed all sorts of individuals to find things out for him. He could always disavow them afterwards, as the plausible Langbehn was to learn. But at least one can say this: in his fear of a war on two fronts Himmler remained absolutely consistent. His dreams of German colonisation in the east were firmly based on peace in the west. Heydrich, however, had no such realism. He was too much of a megalomaniac to weigh alternatives and, if he found anyone else weighing them, he saw only an opportunity to gain credit with Hitler by denouncing a doubter.

One may contrast Heydrich's and Himmler's parts after the Hess escapade. Felix Kersten, who had treated Hess as a patient, was grilled by Heydrich and only released on Himmler's instructions.[5] On the other hand, Fritz Hesse, Hitler's Foreign Office expert on

---

[1] See p. 299.   [2] Wheeler-Bennett, op. cit., p. 577.
[3] *Von Hassell Diaries*, p. 221.
[4] *Memoirs of Count Ciano*, p. 455.   [5] *Totenkopf und Treue*, p. 125.

English affairs, was interrogated by Himmler in person because he had known Hess in his student days. Himmler was all blandness during the interview and, turning to Ribbentrop, said, 'It is established that Dr. Hesse is in no way implicated in this affair. The Fuehrer only wants to ask him what prospects Hess's peace mission may have'.[1]

3. THE SS IN RUSSIA

It was against this undecided background that Himmler entered his life's great adventure in Russia. His realism, on the one hand, saw a second front in the West as a future menace; his incredible mental mushiness, on the other hand, could see England as a party to SS rule in Europe. It was under such a vacillating chief as this that in the summer and autumn of 1941 the SS divisions became engaged in the vastest land battles in human history. Their role was limited by their numbers, for, apart from an improvised and poorly equipped police division, the 4th SS, and the mountain division 'Nord', which was isolated in the Arctic Circle, only four SS divisions served on the main Russian front. The invasion of Russia will, however, always be associated with the SS, not for the part that they played in the fighting, but for their part in policing the country, in the massacres of Jews, in the hunt for political commissars and partisans, in the reprisals on villages, and in the round-ups of slave labour.

After July 1941 Himmler spent much of his time in Russia. For two years he had a permanent headquarters in the former Soviet Military Academy at Zhitomir in the Ukraine, about a hundred miles north of Hitler's headquarters, 'Werwulf' in Vinnitsa. Here Himmler passed part of each summer, occasionally visiting his higher SS police leaders and his divisional commanders in the field. Himmler's main interest was in the former. His interest in the Waffen SS, though fatherly, was always secondary. Till 1943 there was no SS Field Command above the level of a division. Though two SS Departments firmly controlled the staff and supply problems of these divisions, the SS commanders took their orders in the field from Army Corps Commanders of the despised Wehrmacht. The Waffen SS could well be left their own hospitals, their own courts martial, and their own prisons, so long as SS divisional commanders carried

[1] Fritz Hesse, *Hitler and the English*, p. 126.

out the orders of the higher army commands as well as any other. There was no friction save in Himmler's imagination. But in the rear areas it was the military commanders who were at the disposition of Himmler's police leaders. That was his own kingdom.

The record of the Waffen SS in the first Russian campaign was more brilliant than ever. The Leibstandarte, which was now called the Adolf Hitler division, fought its way from Poland to the Black Sea at Kherson, then in November 1941 along the Sea of Azov to the short-lived occupation of Rostov. But in the fighting around Rostov and the retirement to the Mius River the Leibstandarte ceased to fight a victory-parade war. It was their first experience of the defensive. Accused in previous campaigns of wasting his men, Sepp Dietrich now saw them decimated. Reichenau, who had succeeded Rundstedt as Commander-in-Chief of the Southern Army Group,[1] broke the news gently to Hitler, but Hitler needed no gentleness. 'Losses can never be too high, they sow the seeds of future greatness'.[2]

The Adolf Hitler division had been too mauled to face a second Russian campaign. In June 1942 it was withdrawn to Paris to be re-formed as an armoured division. The Viking division, a neighbour in the line, stayed on with von Kleist's armoured group and in September 1942, before the great retreat from Stalingrad, the division reached the Caucasus, some two thousand miles from the old borders of Germany.

The SS division Das Reich fought on the central front. In August 1941 it achieved distinction at the Battle of Yalnya, east of Smolensk, but in September it was switched south to the battle for Kiev, where it fought as part of Guderian's armoured group. It was then moved back north to take part in the fatally delayed assault on Moscow. The division emerged badly battered after fighting during the winter as part of Model's 9th Army north-west of Moscow.[3]

The division Das Reich was taken out of the line in March 1942 and re-formed in the south-west of France as an armoured division. In the following November it provided a unit for a force which tried to prevent the scuttling of the French Toulon fleet. After fighting again in Russia in 1943, 'Das Reich' was stationed on the Atlantic

---

[1] He died a few weeks later, on 17 January 1942, of a mysterious infection at the age of fifty-eight. He had just been made a field marshal.

[2] Trevor-Roper, *Last Days of Hitler*, p. 79.   [3] Hausser, p. 57.

coast of France and during the retreat of August 1944 it figured in the massacre of Oradour-sur-Glane.[1]

The third Waffen SS division, the Totenkopf, fought on the Leningrad front together with Himmler's regular police battalions, which had been organised as the fourth division, a very improvised affair of over-age men and horse-drawn transport. The Totenkopf, including a small Danish legion, was one of the divisions which were cut off for several months on end in the so-called 'Demiansk Kessel' in the Valdai Hills. Like the Das Reich division, it was withdrawn from Russia in the autumn of 1942 and was re-formed in France in a quiet part of the invasion front.

In this way the four classical SS divisions—Adolf Hitler, Totenkopf, Das Reich, and Viking—were all converted into armoured divisions. They had entered Russia with a small proportion of foreigners on their strength, but they were still overwhelmingly German. The position changed in the second Russian campaign. Most of the original strength had been worn away and the new drafts began to show a foreign preponderance. Moreover, by the summer of 1942 the SS divisions had lost the character of an élite corps. The permanent SS had started with a clear distinction between Totenkopf units and Verfuegungstruppen, a distinction which Hitler himself had drawn in his decree of August 1938.[2] Now there was both a Totenkopf division and a force of Totenkopf guards, for ten more regiments of these were recruited for their original purpose in 1940. They were formed, according to Hausser, to serve as police troops in the event of Himmler's governing the occupied territories, 'but it turned out otherwise. The Governors General and General Commissars undertook this task.' This meant that the Totenkopf regiments with their dubious experience and training became available in the field, and in the winter of 1941 they began to fill the gaps in the SS divisions.[3]

Hausser's explanation of this change of role is not quite accurate. Though it is true that the occupied territories were governed not by Himmler but by civil commissioners, Himmler still controlled the police. In February 1941, for instance, he was able to send a new Totenkopf battalion to put down a general strike in Amsterdam. If Himmler indeed failed to keep these battalions in France, Norway and the Netherlands, it was not for lack of authority but because the Waffen SS constantly needed new drafts and Himmler had not yet

[1] See *infra*, p. 170.   [2] See *supra*, pp. 83-4.   [3] Hausser, p. 69.

achieved the first choice in recruiting. 'I have sent to the front,' he declared at Posen in August 1944, 'police regiments with an average age of forty-six years'.[1]

Clearly, this was material different from the young men who had gone through Himmler's elaborate testing in order to enter the prewar SS. Himmler himself felt that he had to apologise for them, and this is how he described his ten new Totenkopf regiments in his speech to the Leibstandarte in September 1940:[2]

In some parts of Poland there have been sometimes real guerrilla affairs which have been much more painful than the war itself. It is then that we need troops, formations, and men who have received an ideological training for the occupation of these countries, exactly as in Czechoslovakia and Poland. I used the occasion to reinforce our troops and to form new regiments—ten. It is evident, gentlemen, that the commanders of these battalions and companies have not the advantage of your training, nor your qualities as soldiers who have been five or six years in the service.

Then, after a well-known passage, concerning the deportations from Poland,[3] Himmler went on to tell his chosen Leibstandarte,'we must begin to do with the Waffen SS what we have already done with the SS and police, and we must understand that the activity of the man in the green jacket is as important as your own'.

With the mixing up that followed of Totenkopf men, of security policemen of the Gestapo and of drafted regular police with fighting SS, the claim that the fighting divisions had no connection with the extermination measures becomes hollow indeed. Himmler's police leaders in Russia could call on the Rear Area Commands of the army to supply *any* units available for the war against partisans, and these operations, conducted by regular troops, were often nothing else than mass executions of the Jewish population. The Wehrmacht were no more exempt from such calls than the Waffen SS; but the material of the Waffen SS, particularly the reserve units in rear areas, was chosen by preference as the best trained for the task. During the great march south of the division Das Reich after the Battle of Yalnya, a rear-area company of the division as far back as the neighbourhood of the old Polish border assisted Heydrich's extermination squads to massacre 920 Jews at Lachoisk, near Minsk, and this duly figured in one of Heydrich's operation reports.[4]

[1] *Vierteljahreshefte fuer Zeitgeschichte*, No. 4, p. 571.
[2] Nuremberg Document PS 1980.   [3] See *supra*, p. 130.
[4] Nuremberg Document NO. 3143, Case IX; Reitlinger, op. cit., p. 211.

Just as significant as the admixture of police and fighting men in the individual SS units was the training which taught them not to criticise such activities. The company which carried out the massacre at Oradour-sur-Glane in August 1944 was a typical latter-day SS infantry company. It consisted partly of redundant ground staff of the Luftwaffe, drafted piecemeal into the SS, and partly of conscripted Alsatians who had been brought up as French subjects.[1] They were very raw SS men, yet they carried out their massacre without protest and with remarkable dispatch. Similarly, the smoking out of 56,000 Jews who survived in the Warsaw ghetto in April-May 1943, was performed in a thirty days' witches' sabbath by two SS training reserve battalions, cavalry and Panzer grenadiers, most of whom had not worn uniform for more than three or four weeks and had only just taken their SS oath.[2] Even Paul Hausser, when he gave his muddle-headed Nuremberg testimony, could not pretend that these were Russian deserters like the SS Kaminski brigade, or drafted German criminals like the Dirlewanger regiment, wearing the SS uniform only by a dirty subterfuge of Himmler's.[3]

Cases like Oradour and the Warsaw ghetto have in fact led some witnesses for the SS to draw the opposite moral: it was not the fanatical 'Old Party Fighters' who committed the excesses but the ragtag and bobtail SS who were racial Germans or foreigners. Sometimes, however, the champions of the old volunteer SS can be very revealing. Thus Erich Kern, a Vienna journalist who fought in the ranks of the Adolf Hitler division in the first Russian campaign, describes the very correct behaviour of the division towards the Jews of Kherson, who were all killed by Heydrich's men two months afterwards. He is sympathetic towards the Russians he meets, understands their problems and even uses his connections with party notables to compose a memorial on their treatment and to obtain an interview with Goebbels. Yet it is the same Kern who tells the story of the affair of Gejgowa. A number of bodies of German prisoners had been discovered who had been horribly tortured to death. During the Leibstandarte's advance to Kherson Sepp Dietrich, so genial and tolerant in later records, so violently opposed to Hitler at the end, was the divisional commander. He ordered that all prisoners taken in the next three days should be shot in reprisal. 'It was a question of the lives of 4,000 men, for that was the number

---

[1] See pp. 400-1.   [2] Nuremberg Document PS 1016; Reitlinger, op. cit., p. 277.
[3] IMT XX, p. 231.

that fell into our hands during those three days that were so fatal to them'. And Kern goes on to describe the execution in groups of eight in what had already become the standard SS mass grave, an anti-tank ditch. He has not the slightest comment to offer on the ethics of murdering 4,000 men for a crime with which very few, if indeed any, of them, were concerned.[1]

The distinction between the specialised extermination units and the fighting SS becomes even vaguer when it is realised that posting to the former was a recognised part of Waffen SS discipline. Georg Keppler, a benign-looking elderly regular officer and police official, who led the SS division Das Reich on its return to Russia, admitted this to Felix Kersten in a remarkable conversation at Himmler's Headquarters at Zhitomir in the summer of 1943:[2]

They are late or they fall asleep on duty. They are court-martialled but are told they can escape punishment by volunteering for Special Commandos. For fear of punishment and in the belief that their career is ruined anyway, these young men ask to be transferred to the Special Commandos. Well, these commandos, where they are first put through special training, are murder commandos. When the young men realise what they are being asked to do and refuse to take part in mass-murder, they are told the orders are given them as a form of punishment. Either they can obey and take that punishment or they can disobey and be shot. In any case their career is over and done with. By such methods decent young men are frequently turned into criminals.

Normally the practice in the Waffen SS as in the Wehrmacht was to send men convicted by courts martial to probation units, generally parachute battalions, but there was also the Dirlewanger regiment. We can accept Himmler's own description of this, as he gave it in August 1944:[3]

Dirlewanger, a brave Swabian ten times wounded, is an original. Only 400 of his original 2,000 convicted poachers are still alive. The gaps have been filled with probation people from the Waffen SS, since in the SS we have a terribly hard justice. They get years of imprisonment for even two days' absence without leave, and it is good when justice is severe. For instance, in the entire battalion that surprised Tito in his headquarters there were only probation troops. All 800 of them were men who had to redeem their honour. After that affair I told Dirlewanger to choose men from the concentration camps and habitual criminals. The tone in the regiment is, I may say, in many cases a medieval one with cudgels and such things. If anyone expresses doubts about winning the war he is likely to fall dead from the table. It cannot be otherwise with such people.

---

[1] Erich Kern, *Der Grosse Rausch*, pp. 41, 52, 86.
[2] *Memoirs of Felix Kersten*, p. 153.
[3] *Vierteljahreshefte fuer Zeitgeschichte*, No. 4, p. 563.

The text of Himmler's second Posen speech was only discovered in 1953, and it casts a dubious light on the testimony, given years previously at Nuremberg, by Gottlob Berger, chief of Himmler's staff office, and by Erich von dem Bach-Zelewski, his chief of partisan warfare. Both had fought hard to maintain that the Dirlewanger regiment was not part of the SS at all. Yet Himmler regarded it as an essential part of Waffen SS discipline, linking it with the 501st SS Parachute Battalion, which had descended on Marshal Tito at Dvor, as just another probation unit for SS delinquents.[1]

The nucleus of the Dirlewanger regiment had been formed in June 1940 when Himmler was raising his ten new Totenkopf regiments. It was something extra special even among that illustrious company. Oskar Dirlewanger was indeed, as Himmler observed, an original. He was one of the decidedly less fortunate military companions whom the innocent and rather dog-like Gottlob Berger had collected in the First World War. In 1935 Dirlewanger, who was then aged forty, was sentenced to two years' imprisonment for offences on a minor. When he was released, Berger used his influence to get poor old Oskar into the Condor Legion, who were serving in Spain under General Franco. In 1939, when Dirlewanger had to return to Germany, Berger, as head of the SS Staff Office, got him reinstated as a colonel of the general SS Reserve. It was still not easy to use Dirlewanger's services and it was not till June 1940 that he was commissioned as a lieutenant in the Waffen SS. He was then training his first draft of German convicted poachers at the headquarters of the Totenkopf units, the former Oranienburg concentration camp.

In September Dirlewanger's company was sent to Poland. For the next year they dug trenches in the so-called Otto Line and guarded a camp for Jewish labour at Dzikow. Then they moved into White Russia and in April 1942 were engaged in suppressing a 'partisan republic' in the Usakine region.[2] In May they moved to Cracow, a whole battalion in strength. At Cracow an immense number of convictions for looting and assault attracted the attention of Conrad Morgen, a judge advocate of the SS police branch. Morgen's

---

[1] The practice was opposed by Colonel Bender, Chief Judge Advocate of the SS. In March 1944, when Berger wanted to transfer all the SS men in detention at Marienwerder to the Dirlewanger regiment, Bender advised Himmler only to send men convicted of criminal offences who would not be accepted by parachute units (Case IX, NO. 2723 and NO. 2061).

[2] Nuremberg Document NO. 2920-1, Case XI.

inquiries led him to Lublin, where Globocnik had permitted Dirlewanger to terrorise and blackmail the ghetto. One of the stories was
that he had entertained the officers of his mess with the death
struggles of Jewish girls to whom he gave strychnine injections.[1]
Morgen applied for a warrant for Dirlewanger's arrest, but was
surprised to learn that Friedrich Krueger, the highest police leader in
Poland, had no competence, since Dirlewanger was subject only to
Gottlob Berger at the SS Staff Office. All Berger would do was to
move the Dirlewanger battalion back to White Russia, promoting
Dirlewanger to lieutenant-colonel on the way.

Having done this to oblige Krueger, Berger, the champion of
European chivalry, regretted his treatment of an old friend. So he
wrote to Himmler in June 1942 that surprise attacks by Polish
partisans had started as soon as Dirlewanger's special commando
had left the Cracow area, 'having been removed by more or less
fair means'. It was a warning that the special commando's policy
had been quite right. 'Better shoot two Poles too many than two too
few. A savage country cannot be governed in a decent manner'.
And as to Dirlewanger's men, the trouble was there were not enough
of them. Would the Reichsfuehrer allow him, with the help of
Mueller of the Gestapo, to comb the prisons for some more
convicted poachers so as to form a second battalion? Hitler himself
thought it a splendid idea. 'As it is, a poacher kills a hare and
goes to prison for three months. Personally, I would take the fellow
and put him in one of the guerrilla companies of the SS'. So a
second battalion was formed and next year Dirlewanger commanded a brigade.[2]

In August 1943 Dirlewanger received the German Cross of Gold
in recognition of his part in 'Operation Kottbus', the reduction of
the Russian 'Partisan Republic of Lake Pelik'—15,000 partisans
wiped out for the loss of 92 Germans killed, 218 wounded, and 8
missing. The strange thing about those 15,000 dead partisans is that

[1] Case XI, Transcript, p. 28393.

[2] *Hitler's Table Talk*, 20 August 1942, p. 640. It is probable that Himmler
disguised his convict units as mere poachers in order to appeal to Hitler's sympathies. Hitler had a romantic affection for poachers and liked to extol their
natural virtues to the detriment of party leaders like Goering who organised
elaborate shooting syndicates. It may have been a throwback to Hitler's vagabond
grandfather. In a specimen of table talk preserved by the photographer, Heinrich
Hoffmann, Hitler proposes that Himmler should form the convicted poachers
into a corps of gamekeepers (*Hitler was My Friend* (London, 1955), p. 205).

only 1,100 rifles and 326 pistols were found on them.[1] A horrified civilian propaganda officer, touring the partisan area, complained that some of the partisans had been burnt alive in a barn and their half-roasted bodies had been devoured by pigs. Wilhelm Kube, the Reichskommissar for White Russia, forwarded a protest through the Rosenberg Ministry to Himmler and the reply came from Berger that it was all nonsense. The Dirlewanger Brigade were quite decent, 'just former party members who were punished for poaching or some stupid action'.[2]

And so it went on. In July 1944, when the Central Army Group vanished into spray, 4,000 Dirlewanger men found their way back to turn up in Poland as birds of ill omen in operation against the Warsaw rebels.[3] At the end of the war, when everything that could walk went into the line of battle, more convicts, concentration camp inmates, and SS men in detention were sent to serve under Dirlewanger. He became a major general and his command grew to a division. At the break-up of the Reich, Dirlewanger disappeared. At one moment there was a rumour that he was employed training the Egyptian army. It is probable that he is still alive.[4]

I have followed the history of this single unit because it sums up a case which the witnesses for the SS never answered. Why was an outright extermination unit so peculiarly honoured? It was not habitual for the commanders of 'special commandos' to be mentioned by name in Himmler's speeches and Hitler's table talk, to receive the German Cross of Gold, or to be championed by Gottlob Berger, the revivalist of European knighthood and chivalry. Nor were extermination units in general regarded as the right nursery for young SS men who had overstayed their leave. The Dirlewanger regiment achieved all these distinctions because it was wholly German and it was under Gottlob Berger's protection. Berger was sentenced to twenty-five years' imprisonment, but was released after six and a half years' detention. He is quite a personality again and his articles may be read in *Nation Europa*, a glossy monthly magazine published in Coburg.

---

[1] Case XI, transcript, p. 28394 and document NO. 2608.
[2] Case XI, transcript, p. 28394 and document NO. 3020.   [3] See pp. 375-7.
[4] After the Warsaw affair in October 1944 Dirlewanger received the Knight's Cross. This proved very destructive of the alibi that the Dirlewanger regiment formed no part of the Waffen SS, for in *Die Ritterkreuztraeger der Waffen SS* Ernst Kraetschmer has enrolled him in the company of heroes (pp. 361-2).

4. HIMMLER'S POLITICAL ROLE IN RUSSIA

It will already have been perceived that Himmler's position in Russia was one of virtual independence. For all that went on behind the immediate battle line he had no authority over him but Hitler. It must have been clear that this would happen the moment Hitler decided to attack in the East. The brief of October 1939, appointing Himmler in charge of all racial re-settlement arrangements, had already split the authority of the Governor-General in Poland and deprived the Military Area Commanders of any say in matters concerning the civilian population. Furthermore, as the time approached when detailed preparations and positive dates could be worked out for 'Fall Barbarossa', Hitler made it quite clear to his generals what Himmler was expected to do and what was meant by the ominous words, 'political tasks'.

The earliest intimation seems to be a memorandum which was circulated by Keitel after an interview with Hitler on 3 March, 1941. At this period, before he knew the intoxication of military success which is such a bad thing for the German psyche, Hitler did not think of Russia only as a space for colonial enterprise and mass emigration, but as a country with some tradition of government where order could not be maintained merely by an alien sword. There would have to be a number of separatist Russian states, of necessity unarmed; and, since the Russians knew no other way of life, they must be Socialist. Who were to run these states? The White Russian *emigrés* in Germany seemed to Hitler just as bad as the 'Jewish Bolshevist intelligentsia'. No German military man, acting as a temporary governor, could in Hitler's view be entrusted with the task of creating entirely new states. Reichskommissars would therefore have to be appointed. Yet normal civilian powers would not be sufficient to eliminate the traces of the Bolshevik commissars and headmen. For this purpose it might be necessary 'to establish organs of the Reichsfuehrer SS alongside the army's Secret Field Police, even in the operation areas, in order to prepare a political administration'. It would mean not merely a political purging of Russian candidates for the administration but 'the extermination of entire grades of society'.[1]

Here is the first mention of what was to be the notorious 'Commissar Order' and of those Special Action Groups or Einsatzgruppen

[1] Helmuth Greiner, *Die Oberste Wehrmachtfuehrung*, p. 369.

who were to carry them out. As a result of this interview Keitel sent a circular on 13 March, of which a copy survives, reminding the High Command that in his 'special tasks' Himmler would act independently and on his own responsibility.[1]

It seems that Hitler then decided that somehow the army must be got into the business too, for on the 30th he spoke to his Chief of Staff, Franz Halder.

> The new Russian states must be Socialist but without any intelligentsia. The creation of a new intellectual caste must be prevented. A primitive socialistic intelligence is all that is necessary. We must struggle against the poison of dissolution. This is not a task for military courts. The individual commanders must be fully conversant with this matter. They must be leaders in this struggle. The troops must strike towards the rear with the same methods that they would use in attack. Commissars and GPU men are criminals who must be treated as such. This need not mean that the troops must get out of hand. Rather should the commander give orders that appeal to the general impulse of his people.[2]

On the same day Keitel broke the news to the generals that, if the troops captured political commissars (it was never established how low in the administrative scale this definition went), they must either execute them themselves or hand them over to the nearest Gestapo unit.[3]

After the conference Brauchitsch was very earnestly approached by the three Army Group Commanders, Leeb, von Bock and Rundstedt, none of whom could be described as dissident generals, and begged to make a protest to Hitler. This Brauchitsch absolutely refused to do. He undertook, however, to issue a general order threatening dire penalties for excesses against civilians and prisoners of war. This, Brauchitsch maintained at Nuremberg, was sufficient to nullify the Commissar Order. Up to the time of his own dismissal as Commander-in-Chief (7 December 1941) Brauchitsch did not know of the execution of a single commissar.[4]

It is hard to decide who were the bigger hypocrites, Brauchitsch or the three generals who chose to believe him. All of them knew that Keitel would sign any agreement with Hitler and that Brauchitsch's general orders to troops could have no significance in the rear areas. There was the merest pretence of an argument between Himmler and OKW on the extent of these new powers. The first fortnight of June was occupied with negotiations between Eduard Wagner, the Quarter-master-General of the Army, and Heydrich in person. Wagner, who

---

[1] IMT VI, p. 179.   [2] Case XII, NO. 3140; extract from *Halder Diary*.
[3] IMT XXI, p. 32.   [4] IMT XXI, pp. 32, 40.

was to end up as a hero and martyr of the Resistance, did not like to deal with Heydrich and in the following year he came into outright conflict with him when Heydrich demanded powers in France and Belgium similar to those he exercised in Russia. But in June 1941 Wagner had not become a dissident general and though he was distrusted by party leaders, he did not struggle unduly to make the best of terms. In any case Wagner's hands were tied by Keitel and Jodl. The minutes of the Heydrich-Wagner conferences were taken down by Ohlendorf and Schellenberg, two men with the same ambition. Though they lost the minutes, they are the only subject on which these two loving characters were agreed.

The discussions were concerned only with the definition of Himmler's area of competence. It was agreed that in the fighting area the special units of the security police and SD should come entirely under army control, but in the operations area and in the rear areas the army's authority would not extend beyond tactical matters.[1]

In brief, Heydrich's commandos could commit every crime known to God or man, so long as they were a mile or two from the firing line; but in fact the army's bargain was something even worse. In the rear areas, which were not operational, army units could be called on to assist Himmler's SS police leaders. Heydrich, who had the dispatches from his special commandos carefully edited by a criminal police official and distributed to all the ministries, drew attention affectionately every time a rear-area commander lent his services. But in cases of large-scale partisan outbreaks, such as began during the first Russian winter, it was not quite so simple. Major-General Ernst Rohde, who had been chief of Himmler's Command Staff, complained at Nuremberg that on such occasions he had to go cap in hand to Quartermaster-General Wagner, but 'he realised today' that, by means of their standing agreements with OKW and OKH, the security police used partisan warfare as an excuse for the annihilation of Jewry and Slavism.

> I am of the firm conviction that an energetic and unified protest by all field marshals would have resulted in a change in these missions and methods. If they should ever declare that in that case they would have been succeeded by even more ruthless commanders-in-chief, this in my opinion would be a foolish and even cowardly evasion.[2]

After the signature of the Heydrich-Wagner agreements, both OKW and OKH gave up their interest in the fate of prisoners who,

[1] IMT III, pp. 246, 290.   [2] IMT, IV, pp. 223, affidavits 17-18.

trusting to the common rules of honour, had surrendered to the German army. Admiral Canaris, however, made one of his characteristically furtive and fatuous attempts to intervene. Some of the complications of Hitler's Commissar Order had been brought to his attention by Helmuth von Moltke, who was employed in the Abwehr as an expert on international law.[1] It struck Canaris as hopeless to enlist Russian Intelligence agents, when any Russian who came near a security police unit could be shot either as a Jew or as a bearer of Bolshevism. But Canaris did not want to put his point of view in person. He sent instead the Austrian Brigadier-General Erwin von Lahousen on the Gilbert-and-Sullivan grounds that Lahousen would be able to use much stronger language because of his subordinate position.[2] So Lahousen met Heinrich Mueller, the head of the Gestapo, a week or two after the invasion of Russia, when something had already been seen of Heydrich's men in action. Keitel was represented by General Hermann Reinecke, head of the General Wehrmacht Office or Army Chancellery (AWA), a perfectly loathsome little man who was regarded as the party's chief indoctrination officer and was known as the 'little Keitel', or 'Oberpolitruk'. The army was represented by Colonel Breuer of the Prisoners of War Department. Reinecke began with a lecture, declaring that every Russian soldier was an enemy to death of National Socialism, that Russians must be treated accordingly and that in these matters the officer corps of the German Army was still 'in the Ice Age'. Lahousen was then allowed to say his piece, only to find that Reinecke supported Mueller at every point. 'Tell me', said Lahousen to Mueller, 'according to what principles does this selection take place? Do you determine it by the height of a person or by the

[1] See pp. 303-4.

[2] Canaris did not abandon the matter. In the following September Keitel consented to pass on a memorial from Canaris to Hitler. In this Canaris complained that the execution of commissars by the Special Commandos could not be checked by Wehrmacht establishments and that the directives were not communicated to them. In his marginal notes Keitel wrote that the Wehrmacht knew all about it, that the Special Commandos were highly efficient and that the secrecy of the actions was 'highly expedient'. And then, most damning for Keitel, who looked so correct, so soldierly and so honourable in the dock, he appended this note for his Fuehrer.

'These objections arise from the military conception of chivalrous warfare. We are dealing here with the destruction of a world philosophy and therefore I approve such measures and sanction them.—Keitel' (Document USSR 356 and IMT XI, pp. 73, 104; see also IMT I, p. 279).

size of his shoes?' Only one concession was to be gained; Mueller would see that the executions took place in secret places and not in front of the troops.[1]

On 17 July Mueller issued instructions to the Special Commandos working in the prisoner-of-war camps. Lahousen's point about attracting Russian agents to work for Germany had been very nicely met by Mueller. The commandos were to look for agents—it did not matter if they were Communists—in order that the agents could tell them who in their camp had been commissars, Jews, or bearers of Bolshevism. As to rewards, the Gestapo had their own system. The obliging prisoners of war who had spotted the commissars were now 'Geheimnissetraeger', repositories of secrets, or men who knew too much. In time, they were taken from their camps and got rid of in lonely farmhouses. Later on, both the suspected commissars and their denouncers were executed in German concentration camps, because to the eye of the German civil servant this looked more orderly. Mueller signed the warrants in person and in the autumn and winter of 1941 about two hundred Russian prisoners of war met their end against the cork wall outside 'Block Eleven' in Auschwitz camp.[2]

Most German army witnesses from Russia have either denied all knowledge of the existence of the Commissar Order or, if sufficiently highly placed, they have described their refusal to co-operate. In spite of such pleas Heydrich's reports show that the bag in the first few months was not negligible, and that army units did not always withold their aid. But it will never be known how many fell victim to the Commissar Order. After the great encirclement battles of 1941 it was impossible to sift the vast anonymity of the German cages. Since most of the millions who entered the cages died of neglect, the question is academic.

[1] IMT I, p. 281. Reinecke was acquitted of complicity in crimes committed by the Einsatzgruppen, but he was found guilty of the wilful neglect of Russian prisoners of war who remained under his office till July 1944, when Gottlob Berger took it over. Some of Reinecke's orders concerning the treatment of these Russians come under the heading of wilful murder rather than neglect. Had Reinecke been tried in 1945 by any Allied Court, a noose would have been round his neck with the greatest dispatch. But Reinecke was not sentenced till 8 October 1948, when the era of death sentences was past. He is, at the moment of writing, the only German general besides Warlimont in American custody, but his release from Landsberg is not likely to be delayed. The 'Oberpolitruk' may expect on his release the usual German bouquets of flowers and the public praises due to a martyr.

[2] IMT III, p. 204; Case XI, transcript, pp. 28565-8.

But the Commissar Order in the end was the undoing of that sleek man Walter Schellenberg. Ohlendorf gave it as his opinion that Schellenberg would not have refused to command an Einsatzgruppe if he could have pleased Himmler this way.[1] Perhaps the hero of Venlo was a bit too sly for that. The court accepted his plea that, when he drafted the terms with Ohlendorf and Wagner, he knew nothing about forthcoming murders of Jews and commissars. They listened sympathetically to Schellenberg's claim that he had been 'only an information service'. Then it was found that the liquidation of the Russian spies was handled by one of those pleasant little one-room offices of the RSHA and that this office came under Schellenberg's own foreign Intelligence service, Amt VI. So Schellenberg, the man who had arranged Himmler's peace talks with Count Bernadotte, had after all to go to prison. His sentence was for six years but he was released in December 1950. Schellenberg died in Italy in the summer of 1952, aged only forty-two.

In these conferences and talks there was apparently no mention of the order by which every Jew in the invaded territory—man, woman or child—was to be killed. It is possible that the army commanders knew nothing about it until it happened. There was, indeed, no reason why Heydrich or Mueller should disclose such things, when the High Command were ready to sign away all their responsibility, washing their hands in advance of something they did not know. Even the men who were to carry out the massacres were approached cautiously and nothing was put on paper. A few of the higher commanders of the Einsatzgruppen have stated that Heydrich addressed them in person, others that they were never told at all.[2]

Most of the Einsatzgruppen officers were instructed by Heydrich's deputy and head of the RSHA Staff Office, Bruno Streckenbach. This man was the son of a customs official and in the very earliest days of the SS he had commanded the first 'Stuerm' in Hamburg. In October 1933, when the Gestapo absorbed the Hamburg political police, Streckenbach was appointed to run it. After the conquest of Poland he was made commander of the security police for the General Government and in May 1940 he directed the mass arrests of Polish intelligentsia, known as 'Action AB'.[3] This achievement was the cause of Streckenbach's promotion in January 1941.

Streckenbach kept his position after Heydrich's death, but early in

---

[1] Case IX, transcript, p. 639.   [2] Case IX, NO. 4145, affidavit Walther Blome.
[3] IMT XII, pp. 116, 125.

1944 he left RSHA to take over the command of a second Latvian SS division, the 19th Panzergrenadier. The division was one of those cut off in Courland in July 1944. At the capitulation Streckenbach, who had deputised for Heydrich and who had organised the Einsatz-gruppen, passed into Russian captivity. He was not surrendered to the Nuremberg Tribunal to face the charges which were brought against Ohlendorf and his associates, nor was he hanged in Russia. The unpredictability of Russian policy reserved for him a fate no worse than that of Seydlitz, who worked for the Moscow Free Germany Committee, or of the man who pressed Hitler's trousers. Streckenbach is due for repatriation to his Fatherland (July 1956).

Towards the end of May 1941 Streckenbach instituted a three weeks' course. It was held near Leipzig at the Frontier Police School at Pretzsch on the Elbe. Apart from lectures on the sub-human enemy, which would have been commonplace to the hundred or so candidates, all of them from the Gestapo or the SD, there were 'terrain exercises'. One of the indicted officers described them as games of hide-and-seek.[1] In spite of all that had been associated in the past seven years with the word Gestapo, the candidates must have looked a funny collection doing their 'terrain exercises'. Of those who survived to stand trial in 1948, one had been an old man even in 1941, one was an opera singer and grossly fat, one an unfrocked parson and one a dipsomaniac architect. The careers of the twenty-one men who faced trial in 1948 had all the charm of the slightly abnormal and the slightly dishonest, but on the whole they emerged as drab men from the common rut. On the other hand the four leaders, who became colonels and even brigadiers in order to command them, had rather more to show, but only one of them, the most startling personality of all, lived to stand trial.

Most of the rank-and-file officers of the Einsatzgruppen were 'Racial Germans', combed out of the temporary wartime bureaucracy for their knowledge of Russian. They were down-at-heel individuals who expected more from their change of job than they actually got. Their commanders, however, were men who accepted unattractive assignments for motives of placation, or because they dared not refuse. Ohlendorf thought he had been sent to Russia as a punishment because he had criticised the persecution of the Jews, which he was nevertheless unique in defending from the dock.[2] But he supplied the

[1] Case IX, transcript, page 4374
[2] François Bayle, *Psychologie et éthique de national-socialisme*, p. 39.

real clue himself. He had been quarrelling with Himmler since 1936, and Kersten's memoirs show him still quarrelling in 1943.[1] Himmler had actually dismissed Ohlendorf in 1940 after a journey to Warsaw, but Heydrich had him reinstated, not because he liked him but in order to oppose Himmler, who described Ohlendorf as 'an unbearable Prussian, without humour, defeatist and anti-militarist and a professional de-bunker'.

So Ohlendorf went to South Russia in order to stay in the good graces of his protector, Heydrich, and managed it so well that after arranging, as he admitted, some 90,000 murders, he returned in March 1942 to his old office in the Wilhelmstrasse, from which he continued to pour out till the last days of Hitler's Reich the pessimistic daily internal intelligence reports that so infuriated the party leaders. Ohlendorf also returned to a comfortable job in the Department of Overseas Trade. In April 1948 a photograph was taken in court at Nuremberg while Ohlendorf was reading his last horrifying self-justification. He still looked like an oncoming parliamentary secretary or some Oxford don who had done absolute wonders in a wartime government department.

With Artur Nebe the motive was again placation. We have seen him in 1933-4 ganging for Himmler against Goering over the question of Gestapo control, and we shall find him a very questionable member of the Resistance Circle at the time of the great bomb plot. But, first and foremost, Nebe was an old police official. Since 1934 he had seen his Criminal Police Department invaded by amateur Gestapo men, and in September 1939 he had seen it taken over by Heydrich. After his capture at Venlo, Captain Payne-Best had a unique opportunity of studying the Criminal Police in their headquarters, and he observed how the new criminal commissars of the Gestapo swaggered over the old criminal secretaries who had been born and bred in the police.[2] If Nebe did in fact retain his office till 1944, it was because of the five months he spent in Russia. His friend, Gisevius, says very politely that Nebe spent a few months *at the front*.[3]

The headquarters of Nebe's extermination group were at Minsk and then at Smolensk, where he was in touch with another old friend, Colonel Hans Oster, who was attached to Central Army Group headquarters. Nebe is said to have fought against Heydrich's

[1] *Totenkopf und Treue*, pp. 255-6.   [2] Payne-Best, op. cit., p. 45.
[3] Gisevius, p. 456.

orders and to have disclosed them to the Oster circle, who had used him as an information post for the past four years. No doubt that is why Heydrich's reports credit Nebe's stewardship with the quite modest score of 46,000 executions as against Stahlecker's 221,000.[1]

Himmler himself paid two visits to the Einsatzgruppen commanders in 1941, though they were not under his immediate command but under that of Heydrich as Chief of the security police and SD. Heydrich, however, was absent from his duties during the first six weeks of the Russian campaign, flying with the Luftwaffe, and after 23 September he was mainly in Prague. Himmler's first visit was to Nebe in Minsk in July or August. Here at his own request the Reichsfuehrer watched a mass execution. It was a small affair but it upset Himmler very much. He nearly fainted and he shouted hysterically and showed every appearance of being deeply shocked. He would even have liked to save a young Jew because he was fair-haired and looked Aryan. Himmler demanded that Nebe should use his high police authority in Germany to discover more humane methods of mass killing than the firing squad. The gassing vans, which made their appearance in Russia before the year was out and which were the forerunners of the standard German extermination system of 1942-4, were the result of this incident. After the war an amateur film, showing a gas chamber worked by the exhaust gas of a lorry, was found in Nebe's former Berlin flat.[2]

Three months later Himmler visited Ohlendorf at Nikolaiev and lunched in the Einsatzgruppe mess, taking with him Quisling's chief of police from Norway.[3] Here Himmler's inveterate dislike of Ohlendorf was rekindled when he learnt that the man had spared the workers on the collective farms in the Jewish settlement area between Krivoi Rog and Kherson in order not to lose the harvest. So the matter was put right.

Himmler was not destined to see what a real mass execution looked like, something like the massacre of 33,700 Jews which was conducted at Kiev over a period of three days in September 1941 within earshot and almost within sight of the fine city squares overlooking the Dnieper. Eye-witness accounts of such affairs, even the reminiscences of men who took part in them, are not lacking; and many tasteful products of the German soldiers' *Leicas* have survived,

---

[1] Fabian von Schlabrendorff, *Offiziere gegen Hitler*, p. 49.

[2] Reitlinger, op. cit., p. 130, footnote; and see *infra*, pp. 278-9, quoting an affidavit of von dem Bach-Zelewski.   [3] Case IX, transcript, p. 536.

though army orders were issued forbidding such snapshot-hunting.[1] But neither in these nor in the dreary officialese compilations of the Einsatzgruppen commanders, nor in their long-drawn evasions when they were on trial, can one grasp the true Dantesque horror. One report, however, deserves a lengthy quotation because it is the work of an unlettered man, whose profound and shattering experience gave his words the quality of true literature, even when read in an English translation at the Nuremberg trial. The author was one Hermann Graebe, a civilian works engineer employed by the Whermacht in the Ukraine, and the incident took place on a disused flying ground at Dubno on 5 October 1942.[2]

. . . An old woman with snow-white hair was holding this one-year-old child in her arms and singing and tickling it. The child was cooing with delight. The parents were looking on with tears in their eyes. The father was holding the hand of a boy about ten years old and speaking to him softly; the boy was fighting his tears. The father pointed towards the sky, stroked the boy's head and seemed to explain something to him. At that moment the SS man at the pit shouted something to his comrade. The latter counted off about twenty persons and instructed them to go behind the earth mound. The family I have described was among them. I well remember the girl, slim and with black hair, who, as she passed me, pointed to herself and said: 'Twenty-three years old'.

I walked round the mound and found myself confronted by a tremendous grave. People were closely wedged together and lying on top of each other so that only their heads were visible. Nearly all had blood running over their shoulders from their heads. Some of the people who had been shot were still moving. Some lifted their arms and turned their heads to show that they were alive. The pit was already two-thirds full. I estimated that it held a thousand people. I looked for the man who did the shooting. He was an SS man who sat at the edge of the narrow end of the pit, his feet dangling into it. He had a tommy gun on his knees and was smoking a cigarette. The people—they were completely naked—went down some steps which were cut in the clay wall of the pit and clambered over the heads of those who were lying there to the place to which the SS man directed them. They lay down in front of the dead and wounded. Some caressed the living and spoke to them in a low voice. Then I heard a series of shots. I looked into the pit and saw that in some cases their bodies still twitched, in others that their heads lay motionless on top of the other bodies before them. Blood ran from their necks.

I was surprised that I was not ordered away, but I saw that there were two or three civilian postmen in uniform standing near me. Already the next batch was approaching. They went down in the pit, lined themselves up against the previous victims and were shot. When I walked back round the mound, I noticed that another truckload of people had arrived. This time it included sick and feeble people. An old, terribly thin woman was being undressed by some other women,

---

[1] Reitlinger, op. cit., pp. 205, 233-4.

[2] Nuremberg Document PS 2992; IMT XIX, p. 457. I have made a number of alterations to the official printed translation.

who were already naked, while two people held her up. The woman appeared to be paralysed. The naked people carried her round the mound. I left with my foreman and drove in my car back to Dubno.

On the morning of the next day, when I visited the site, I saw about thirty naked people lying near the pit—about thirty to fifty metres away from it. Some of them were still alive; they looked straight in front of them with a fixed stare and seemed to notice neither the chilliness of the morning nor the workers of my firm who stood round. A girl of about twenty spoke to me and asked me to give her clothes and help her escape. At that moment we heard a fast car approach and I noticed that it was an SS detail. I moved away to my site. Ten minutes later we heard shots from the vicinity of the pit. Those Jews who were still alive had been ordered to throw the corpses into the pit, then they themselves had to lie down in the pit to be shot in the neck.

And after all this it is a fact that many high-ranking German witnesses had never heard of the Einsatzgruppen. It was certainly not a household word; but then this force, which had been designed to cover the entire rear area of occupied Russia, numbered less than three thousand men and a few women. That such a force should have executed, according to Heydrich's statistics, close on half a million Jews and gipsies in six months and hundreds of so-called commissars is pretty extraordinary, but unlike pavement artists, the Einsatzgruppen could not claim it as 'all their own work'.[1] Almost the first task of these Gestapo agents was to recruit local volunteer units. In half-Germanised Latvia, Lithuania, and Estonia they were very successful and nearly as successful in the Ukraine, but much less so in White Russia. Latvia, in particular, supplied entire regiments which were sent later to liquidate the ghettos of Poland. This was all part of the picture. The Einsatzgruppen, as Brauchitsch and Manstein were able to recall from Keitel's lectures, had been sent to prepare the political administration,[2] that is to say, to get rid of everything that might stand in the way of an administration to German liking.

In fact the civil administration arrived in their thousands, long before the extermination groups had finished the job. With their advent the function of the Einsatzgruppen changed. Only a small

[1] It is possible, however, that such figures as the 221,000 executions which Stahlecker claimed in the Baltic states were reached carelessly and that some totals were added several times over. On the other hand, the statisticians were never able to include the huge death-roll among Jewish fugitives. At the end of 1942 Himmler's actuary, Dr. Korherr, made the figure of Jews 're-settled' from Russia and the Baltic states 650,000. For a full discussion of these figures see *The Final Solution*, pp. 499-500. Very much higher figures than these are currently accepted.

[2] IMT XXI, pp. 39, 56.

proportion stayed behind in the civil administration area, mostly in the administrative capitals. There, under the eyes of a prolific German wartime bureaucracy in Riga, Kovno, Wilna and Minsk, they carried out the most systematic and prolonged of all the massacres. In the newly created ghetto of Wilna close on 40,000 were killed in a pogrom occupying several weeks. Everyone knew about it, some deplored it and at least two of the Reichskommissars eventually stirred themselves to the point of sending memoranda to Alfred Rosenberg, the Minister for Eastern Affairs. One of these was Heinrich Lohse at Riga, who now draws a pension from the Bonn government, and the other Wilhelm Kube at Minsk, who was murdered in 1943. But neither Lohse, Kube, nor any other commissar risked dismissal by openly challenging the authority of Himmler's police.[1]

After the disasters of the first winter in Russia there was a hunt in Germany for scapegoats. Why had the Russian population, even in the places where they had trodden on minefields in order to welcome the Germans with flowers, allowed themselves to be engulfed in Stalin's patriotic war, a war which extended hundreds of miles behind the German lines? Was it the fear that the murderous methods used by Heydrich's police against the Jews would be extended to themselves? Was it the Reichskommissars with their battening armies of amateur bureaucrats, the corrupt Erich Koch in the Ukraine in particular? Was it Fritz Sauckel, the plenipotentiary for labour, with his press-gangs, a new menace in 1942? And why had the Wehrmacht not done better? Was it the generals who had failed to provide winter equipment for their men? As it was impossible to be in Russia without belonging to the army, the SS, the

[1] On 15 November Lohse asked for a ruling from Rosenberg's office whether all Jews in the Eastern territories were to be killed 'regardless of economic considerations'. The reply, signed by Otto Braeutigam, assistant to Georg Leibbrandt, the head of Rosenberg's 'Political Section', was that economic considerations were not to apply at all. 'Such matters should in any case be settled with the higher SS and police leaders'. The Political Section had charge of all directives to the civil commissars concerning the Jewish question, and it was Leibbrandt who forwarded to Lohse the first proposal for a permanent gas chamber near Riga. (See p. 280; Nuremberg Document PS 3666; IMT XII, p. 66; *Trials of War Criminals*, Vol. I, pp. 803, 870, 888.) In January 1950 the Nuremberg Landgericht preferred charges against Leibbrandt and Braeutigam, but they were never proceeded with. Braeutigam is now in the West German Foreign Office, and his name was actually considered for the list of experts who were to accompany Dr. Adenauer to Moscow in the summer of 1955.

civil administration or the Sauckel organisation, each of these blamed and fought the other. Every German leader believed that someone had thwarted his liberal ideas. The soldiers thought that they understood 'Der Iwan', who was a fighting man and a good fellow. The Reichskommissars had all sorts of bright plans for organising Russian youth in non-Marxist bands, like Wilhelm Kube's 'Jugendhilfe' in Minsk.[1] Even Himmler did not carry out massacres of Jews from personal choice,.and he would sooner have been engaged selecting wonderfully corn-haired Russian boys for the SS than opposing grim partisans with over-age convicts. The real scapegoat was cloistered in East Prussia, in the dripping woods of the Wolfsschanze, a cross between a wholly stationary Napoleon and a Chinese emperor, ready enough to admire the iron authority of Stalin or the strange genius of the Russian infantryman, who could attack across a swamp or a snowdrift, but never ready to recognise his enemy as a human being. Had Hitler been able to do so, this was a war that need never have been lost.

[1] Kleist, *Zwischen Hitler und Stalin*, p. 174.

8

Recession

OCTOBER 1941 TO MARCH 1943

1. THE WAFFEN SS IN 1942-3

The defeat of Germany began neither with Alamein and the North African landings of November 1942, nor with Stalingrad in the following February. It began in 1941 on the Moscow front. It was Hitler's first and greatest military blunder and it sprang from his knowledge of history, which was little but dangerous. Napoleon, he reasoned, had done wrong in taking Moscow in 1812. Von Kluck had been wrong in advancing on Paris in 1914. Capitals could always wait; what was needed was a brilliant flanking battle.[1] Of course the General Staff, who never understood economic matters, could not see that before attacking Moscow one must deprive the Russians of the Ukrainian harvest and the Donetz minerals. So Hitler had fought the greatest land battle of all time, had captured a Russian Army Group, had taken Kiev and advanced to the Sea of Azov. Unfortunately this meant an unnecessarily exposed right flank and Moscow still remained the centre of all Russia's communications. Then, too, the Russian winter was not supposed to begin in November and the Siberian divisions were not supposed to be any good. The Germans on the Moscow front got bogged down in their positions and soon the positions became untenable. The generals wanted to withdraw to a shortened winter line but Hitler forbade it. By December 1941 heads were beginning to fall.

Hitler's Reichstag speech of 11 December 1941 denounced the very generals whom he had made field marshals in his speech after the surrender of France. No one in history had ever dismissed so many generals at once, not even Napoleon. In the course of the month Brauchitsch, Halder, von Bock and Rundstedt were dismissed, and among corps commanders Guderian and Hoeppner, the leading exponents of armoured warfare, besides thirty-five divisional

[1] *Hitler's Table Talk*, 10 October 1941, p. 52.

commanders.[1] Hitler was to command the armies in Russia in person. It meant that from now on he refused to lunch with the General Staff. He became the recluse of Rastenburg, 'pacing to and fro in the empty card-room at nights to get ideas',[2] or throwing oblique hints in the small hours of the morning to a drooping secretariat concerning the true destination of the deported Jews.

The state of defeatism and depression in Germany, which is noticeable at this time even in so bouncing a diary as Goebbels's, would have amazed us in England had we known it. At the end of January 1942 Goebbels compared notes with Hitler's military adjutant, Colonel Schmundt, concerning defeatist staff officers. Nothing could equal their gloom, yet in London this was a blacker hour than Dunkirk; Singapore was falling, the Japanese had almost reached Australia, the toll of submarines on our shipping was the highest ever recorded and air raids on London were expected to return. How hard it was at that time to believe in Russian victories when the Kremlin guns roared a salute every time twenty miles were gained—as if a retreat of twelve hundred miles had meant nothing. Even so, though the German crisis did not show on the map, it remained a crisis till the March rains. Only then did the army commanders know that they had retained the jumping-off bases for a second campaign.

At the end of December Himmler had been present with Goering, Goebbels, and Ley when Hitler announced that he would be his own Commander-in-Chief. At this inner party conclave not even the ultra yes-man Keitel was admitted. It was the occasion when Hitler made the grateful remark that Keitel had the brains of a cinema commissionaire.[3] But the presence of Himmler, who was not usually consulted on military affairs, was significant. A whispering campaign had begun, which advanced the claims of the SS to direct the war.[4] It was mildly supported by Goering, who once more needed Himmler's friendship; Goering, for whom the failure of the bombing attacks on England and the abandonment of 'Operation Sea-Lion' had meant the beginning of political eclipse. At Goering's extravagant birthday reception on 12 January, Sepp Dietrich, the founder of the Leibstandarte, was introduced by his host as the 'pillar of the Eastern Front'—and this when he was a mere divisional

---

[1] Von Bock, Rundstedt, and Guderian were reinstated by 1943.
[2] *Hitler's Table Talk*, 26 February 1942, p. 340.   [3] See *supra*, p. 99.
[4] *Von Hassell Diaries*, p. 2134.

commander. Hitler had praised Sepp Dietrich in the same spirit on 3 January:[1]

The role of Sepp Dietrich is unique. I have always given him the opportunity to intervene at sore spots. He is a man who is simultaneously cunning, energetic, and brutal. Under his swashbuckling appearance Dietrich is a serious, conscientious, and scrupulous character. And what care he takes of his troops! He is a phenomenon in the class of people like Frundsberg, Ziethen and Seidlitz. He is a Bavarian Wrangel, someone irreplaceable. For the German people Sepp Dietrich is a national institution. For me personally there is also the fact that he is one of my oldest companions in the struggle.

In reality, the time was not yet ripe for so political an appointment to the High Command as Hitler's old chauffeur and strong-arm man, the Hawangen butcher's boy who could not speak German properly, in spite of the fact that as an old companion of the early party days Sepp Dietrich could still demand private audiences with Hitler. At one of these he tried to persuade Hitler to refuse the resignation of his army chief, Guderian, surely an unusual privilege for a divisional commander.[2] Yet these things did not speed Sepp Dietrich's promotion. A year later, when it was decided to group the three newly armoured SS divisions into an army corps, it was not Sepp Dietrich who was appointed to command them, but the former regular army general, Paul Hausser, who had served under Sepp Dietrich in November 1934.[3]

Between Hitler's spiteful Reichstag attack on the High Command in December 1941 and his long delay in promoting any of the SS divisional commanders on the Russian front there appears to be a contradiction, but the explanation is simple. Even now Hitler had not withdrawn the view of the SS which he had stated after the surrender of France.[4] Almost a literal repetition occurs in *Hitler's Table Talk* for 3 January 1942, when he made his eulogy of Sepp Dietrich. It is not clear in what company Hitler praised so generously Himmler, Sepp Dietrich and the old SS of the days of the struggle for power, but Hitler chose his words with care and Martin Bormann saw to it that they were recorded.[5] The SS, Hitler declared, should not recruit too much. Young men who only wanted to show off must be deterred from joining it by the knowledge that the SS had to pay the butcher's bill. As soon as peace returned the SS would have to regain its complete independence from the Wehrmacht and

---

[1] *Hitler's Table Talk*, p. 168.
[2] Heinz Guderian, *Erinnerungen eines Soldaten*, p. 247.
[3] Hausser, op. cit., p. 89. [4] See *supra*, p. 151. [5] *Hitler's Table Talk*, p. 166.

its intended role of an élite police. In the meantime the SS had to go to the front so that its prestige might not be lowered.

With all their politeness, these words must have damped Himmler's hopes of a private army. The check on SS recruiting was not removed until March 1943. For the present, Hitler, with his memories of Roehm and von Pfeffer, did not trust Himmler sufficiently to allow him a complete army corps or to manufacture arms on his own account in the concentration camps.[1] It was no coincidence that, in all the generals' plots that were ever discussed, a corps of three armoured divisions was regarded as the best weapon for making a Putsch. Nor is it a coincidence that Hitler's change of mind in March 1943 followed soon after the Allies' declaration of their 'unconditional surrender' policy. That declaration, if it was to be believed, must destroy the possible value of any German private armies as bargaining counters in negotiations.

Nevertheless, in January 1942 Himmler's ascendancy at the Rastenburg court was very strong. Goebbels's propaganda maintained that Himmler looked after his men in Russia far better than did the professional officer corps. There had been and there continued to be a fantastic casualty list from frostbite, and much of it was due to the wrong clothing. Goebbels, who had organised a winter relief collection in Berlin when it was already too late, was the army's bitterest critic next to Hitler. As late in the day as October 1941 Keitel had refused to admit to Goebbels that there would be any winter fighting. 'We shall be sitting in our warm quarters in Leningrad and Moscow. You can let that be our trouble.' And then there was Quartermaster-General Eduard Wagner, who had shown Goebbels over an exhibition in Smolensk, an exhibition of winter equipment that had not even been ordered.

In reality it had been Hitler who had forbidden Keitel to make any arrangements for the winter and who had banned public collections of clothing because he had not wanted the population even to think of the prospects of a second campaign. Himmler, on the other hand, had been a realist. He had studied the whole question four months before the invasion of Russia, when he visited his Totenkopf units in northern Norway.[2] Oswald Pohl of the SS Economic Administration had had to find foreign exchange in order to buy the furs. In fact Himmler had been more realistic still.

[1] See *infra*, pp. 262-3.
[2] *Vierteljahreshefte fuer Zeitgeschichte*, No. 4, Himmler's second Posen speech.

Oswald Pohl had simply confiscated the furs from the Polish ghettos, a private preserve which was denied to the Wehrmacht. Old people had died in many thousands in unheated sheds and attics to clothe the Waffen SS in Himmler's peculiar Mr. Squeers war.

The opening of a second campaigning season in Russia found Himmler still a realist. On 19 May 1942 Count Ciano learnt from Eugen Dollmann, Himmler's cultured police attaché in Rome, that Himmler considered the offensive would be brilliant but not decisive and that a winter lay ahead which would be both materially and psychologically hard.[1] Another summer passed; the Germans were in the Caucasus and on the Caspian coast, penetrating farther than any European army since Pompey, and Rommel's tanks were a day's drive from Cairo. But Himmler was still a realist. Professor Popitz of the Prussian Ministry of Finance heard that Dr. Langbehn had returned from another visit to Switzerland on Himmler's behalf.[2] In the following December von Hassell wrote that the SD had approved of conversations which Dr. Langbehn had had with a British official in Zurich and an American official in Stockholm.[3]

The Reichsfuehrer's commissions to Dr. Langbehn were as good as a rheumatic toe in indicating heavy weather ahead for the Third Reich. Allusions to a permanent German frontier in the Urals were even better, but they only began to appear in Himmler's recorded speeches and conversations from the autumn of 1943, when there was no longer the least question of territorial acquisitions in the East. Himmler copied these fantasies from the language of Hitler's table talk, which he had occasionally to suffer. It is more likely that it was his own morale rather than that of the German people which he stimulated in this way.

Yet the campaigning season of 1942 opened magnificently for Hitler. In May a Russian effort to take Kharkov had petered out within a few weeks and the real offensive was launched by the Germans at Kursk on 28 June. Within a month they had crossed the Don and at the end of August they held the entire Don bend and most of the northern slope of the Caucasus, together with the Maikop oilfield. Hardy Alpine athletes planted a flag on Mount Elburz and looked down on Asia. On 16 September the Germans were on the lower Volga in the outskirts of Stalingrad. If a Russian

---

[1] *Memoirs of Count Ciano*, English edition, p. 472.   [2] Dulles, op. cit., p. 156.
[3] *Von Hassell Diaries*, p. 251.

army could be encircled in this unique focal point, surrounded by hundreds of miles of lonely steppe, the whole front would roll up and peace could be dictated somewhere between Moscow and the Urals.

It was an unreal hypothesis, for the Germans had already far outdistanced their effective supply lines. Hitler insisted that the footing in Stalingrad must be maintained, even when the great Russian advance which began on the Don front in November had completely isolated it. So it was the Sixth Army of General Paulus that was encircled and not the Russians. By 2 February 1942 all that was left of 300,000 German and Roumanian troops had surrendered.

There were still enough reserves to mitigate the disaster. As the Russians poured into the industrial Donetz basin, fresh German divisions were already on their way from the West. At the end of January Paul Hausser arrived at Poltava with a new command staff which he had brought from France. On 11 February Hausser's Adolf Hitler and Das Reich divisions were in action defending Kharkov—in vain, for on the 16th the Das Reich division had to evacuate this huge industrial city. The situation was so serious that next day the recluse of Rastenburg made a furious appearance at Manstein's headquarters. Hausser's corps was built up to strength by the arrival of the newly armoured Totenkopf division, but on the 28th the divisional commander, Adolf Eicke, was shot down and killed while visiting a forward unit in his aeroplane. He was the first head of Dachau and the founder of the concentration camp system, but Hausser comments on Eicke only as a soldier; how he was the life and soul of the division and how he particularly inspired the foreign volunteers.[1]

A complicated but successful battle was fought far to the west of Kharkov and on 11 March the Adolf Hitler division was back in the city, though it took three days to clear the last of the Russians out. The great Russian Stalingrad offensive had been completely stemmed, but this was the last time such a thing happened on the Eastern Front. Henceforward the German army was never capable of anything more than a delaying action or a local counter-attack. The next Russian offensive, which began four months later, very soon retook Kharkov and breached the Dnieper line and then there

[1] A Stosstruppe risked their lives in bringing back Eicke's body from behind the Russian lines. Kraetschmer, op. cit., p. 61; Hausser, op. cit., p. 81.

began an orderly but depressing German retreat across Russia, evading encirclements or disastrous sieges. Some of these battles of extrication—Tcherkassy, Uman and Skalat—may be destined to become staff college models, but they only served to show that retreat was now the one wisdom. By the end of 1943 Russian patrols had already reached the old borders of Poland, Roumania and the Baltic states.

The six weeks that followed Stalingrad were the greatest crisis Germany had yet had to face. Far more drastic steps towards a total war economy were taken than during the first Russian winter. Heavy Allied bombing, an innovation of the last few months, increased the sense of urgency. Kharkov was indeed the last grand-scale victory of the German army and within two months of it disaster, comparable with the fall of Stalingrad, followed in Tunis. But in the war between Himmler and the General Staff Kharkov had a far greater significance. No one could now say a word against the methods of training of the SS and the quality of their leadership. Hitler's own objections to the creation of more SS divisions, his fear of private armies, his anxiety not to provoke the General Staff too far, both disappeared. A large and immediate increase of the strength of the Waffen SS was sanctioned soon after the happy termination of the battle.

In all the twenty-one months since the invasion of Russia only three new divisions had been added to the Waffen SS and two of these were improvised from existing brigades of mountain troops and cavalry. After Kharkov the three classic SS divisions became Germany's crack armoured corps and Sepp Dietrich was able to achieve the promotion that the party had so long desired for him. He was recalled to Berlin to form a second SS armoured corps. Before the year was out a third armoured corps was created under the command of Felix Steiner of the Viking division. Four completely new armoured divisions were recruited with a large component of Western European volunteers. They were named Hohenstaufen, Frundsberg, Nordland and Hitlerjugend, the last being recruited from former members of that organisation who were particularly welcomed in the SS. Goebbels, however, thought the choice of names most injudicious. It would give other nations the idea, he said, that Germany was forced to call up schoolboys, and so it did.[1]

The difficulties, that arose in the creation of these new SS armoured

---

[1] *The Goebbels Diary*, p. 262.

divisions, showed that Hitler's instinct had been sound in opposing
the expansion of the Waffen SS. During the battle for Kharkov,
Heinz Guderian, the dismissed Armoured Group Commander, was
fished out of retirement and invited by Hitler to become Chief
Inspector for Panzer troops. Guderian soon knew what this meant.
On 9 March, at Hitler's field headquarters at Winnitsa, he found
the obstructions of the disunited commands so insuperable that
after four hours' discussion he fell insensible to the ground without
being noticed among the gesticulating brass hats. Among other
things, the artillery would not allow the Inspectorate of Armoured
Warfare to take over their self-propelled guns because it was the
only weapon with which an artilleryman could win the Knight's
Cross.[1] Nor was it any better on 11 April when Guderian saw
Himmler in person at Berchtesgaden. Himmler was resolutely
opposed to his new armoured divisions becoming administratively
any part of the Wehrmacht, even though he pretended to accept
Hitler's orders for the unification of training. Guderian came away
from his interview with the impression, which perhaps he had
formed in advance, that Himmler wanted a private army and a
Pretorian Guard.

If it was a private army, it bore an astonishing resemblance to
the Wehrmacht. The immense proportion of non-combatants, which
was as noticeable in the armies of Germany fighting for her existence, as it was among the Allies who took their own time, extended
even to the revolutionary SS. One of the elaborate balance-sheets,
prepared by Himmler's private statistical office[2] which was run for
him by Dr. Korherr, is a Waffen SS roster for 30 June 1944. At that
time there were fifteen Waffen SS divisions, a matter perhaps of
150,000 combatants, but the men in these divisions numbered
actually 368,654. The real strength of the Waffen SS, however, was
close on 600,000. Not less than 39,415 of these were employed by
the 'SS Leadership Main Office'. Dr. Korherr himself told Himmler
that he could create three new divisions out of the desk-borne SS.
It was not an idle boast, for the figure of 39,415 did not include the
gigantic bureaucracy of the Reich Main Security Office, which
probably accounted for most of the 64,614 men of the General SS
who were classed as 'not called up'. These conditions remained till
the end of the war. The expansion of the Waffen SS in 1945 to a

[1] Guderian, op. cit., p. 272.
[2] For Dr. Korherr's office, see pp. 221, *et sequitur*.

nominal thirty-five divisions was done not by drawing on its own fat but by conscripting more foreigners.[1]

2. THE EASTERN EUROPEAN SS

On April 23rd 1943, twelve days after his interview with Guderian and long enough after its recapture to make sure that the place was safe, Himmler paid a visit to Kharkov. The occasion called for a speech to the officers of his three victorious SS divisions and Himmler addressed them in the university of the much-battered city. As was generally the case on the few occasions when Himmler spoke to the Waffen SS, he did his men no service by his utterances. In a passage destined to become very notorious, Himmler declared:[2] 'We will never let that excellent weapon, the dread and terrible reputation which preceded us in the battle for Kharkov, fade, but will constantly add new meaning to it.'

Hausser, who made one of the worst of Nuremberg witnesses, recalled that he had remonstrated with Himmler for his choice of expressions. But what had Himmler meant by a dread and terrible reputation? During the retreat from Kharkov, according to the Russian prosecution, the second regiment of Sepp Dietrich's Leibstandarte had burnt down three towns and this Hausser did not remember at all. Why then should he have objected so strongly to Himmler's figure of speech? It was not a coincidence that the most esteemed of the battle-group commanders in the Leibstandarte at the capture of Kharkov later massacred Canadian prisoners on the Normandy front. This was Kurt Meyer, a labourer's son who had been in his time a miner and a policeman. Soon after the recapture of Kharkov, Kurt Meyer was sent by Sepp Dietrich to the new Hitlerjugend armoured division. 'Schnellermeyer', or 'Panzermeyer', was now a leading figure in SS circles. Loaded with every sort of decoration, a brigadier general and regimental commander at the age of thirty-three, Meyer helped to build up the new division in its training ground at Beverloo in Belgium. A few days after the Allied invasion he became the divisional commander, the youngest in the

[1] Nuremberg Document D 878; IMT XX, pp. 366-7, 371. The witness Guenther Reinecke, head of the SS courts, could not make up his mind whether the 24,000 men of Oswald Pohl's WVHA office were concentration camp guards or personnel of Himmler's many business enterprises. The Staff Office of the Waffen SS employed a further 9,349 men.

[2] Nuremberg Document PS 1919b; IMT XX, p. 302.

German forces. At his trial at Aurich in December 1945, this dark little man surrounded by upstanding Canadians, looked like a pathetic small boy, a cross between a jockey and a melancholy boy scout. He was nevertheless the man who had exhorted his regiment to take no prisoners, who had watched the butchery at the Ancienne Abbaye Ardenne repeated before his eyes.[1]

Himmler's speech at Kharkov had another purpose in view. It was to remind his commanders that they must expect a greater proportion of foreign recruits. Himmler did not tell them that within a few months the SS would be recruiting foreigners who were not even of Aryan blood, and that of eight new SS divisions, to be formed during the year 1943, four would consist of East Europeans. But he did tell them that all Roumanians of German origin would be conscripted into the SS. Even men serving with the Roumanian army would be taken over, but the SS commanders must see to it that they did not leave for the front until they had been 'indoctrinated with our spirit'. And then Himmler broke into one of his famous fantasies: 'One day we shall incorporate the millions of Germans living in America'.[2]

The enlistment of Roumanian racial Germans was not new in April 1943. In October 1940, when he began recruiting for the SS from the Western European countries, Gottlob Berger had planned to make the Waffen SS an instrument for forging together all the scattered racial Germans of Axis Europe. The racial German SS division, the 7th Mountain Division or 'Prince Eugen', was not formed, however, till a year later. It was commanded by Artur Phleps, an old Austrian soldier who had raised a national guard in 1918 in his native Transylvania to fight Bela Kun's Hungarian Communists. Finding that he could do this better in the company of the Roumanians who had advanced on Budapest, he took service in the Roumanian army, where with the versatility of some hero of the thirty years war he commanded the Mountain Corps till 1941. The Prince Eugen division was trained in Carinthia, but the first recruits were Germans from the Serbian Banat to whom Roumanian Germans were added later. The numbers were impressive: conscripting the racial Germans in former Jugoslavia yielded 42,000 Waffen

[1] B. J. S. MacDonald, *The Trial of Kurt Meyer* (Toronto, 1954), *passim*. Kurt Meyer's death sentence of 28 December 1945 was twice commuted. He was released from Werl prison on 7 September 1954, exactly ten years after his capture by the Americans.   [2] Nuremberg Document PS 1919b.

SS and police troops. In Roumania no less than 54,000 racial Germans were conscripted and they overflowed into the volunteer divisions of Scandinavians and Western Europeans, where they were looked on as untidy Orientals. The current expression was *Mussul-maenner*, a word which had been coined by the concentration camp guards to describe the living wrecks who had been written off.[1]

The conscription of racial Germans in Roumania was a particular concern of Gottlob Berger, because his son-in-law Andreas Schmidt was the political group-leader of the Transylvanian racial Germans, who were mainly of Swabian origin. The Transylvanian Germans became the subject of one of those wartime struggles for personal influence which should dispel for ever the myth that the Nazi state was an efficient machine. In Roumania Hitler supported the dictatorship of Ion Antonescu, who had become premier in 1939 with the blessing of Ribbentrop's Foreign Office. Most of the Nazi party however and the SS in particular favoured the strongly anti-Monarchical and Fascist Iron Guard movement, led by Horia Sima. Himmler interfered in Transylvania through Gottlob Berger and his twenty-eight-year-old son-in-law, Andreas Schmidt, and also through Werner Lorenz and his VOMI office. The interferences were odious both to the German embassy in Roumania and to Antonescu. On top of this, the conscription of the racial Germans, above all those already serving in the Roumanian army, was an affront to all Roumanian parties. As a result the Roumanians as a military ally dragged their feet.

After an unsuccessful Iron Guard *coup d'état* in January 1941, which was put down with the aid of German regular troops under General Reinhardt, Horia Sima was hidden by Andreas Schmidt and many of his adherents were smuggled into Germany by the Abwehr section of Heydrich's SD. For a time Himmler resisted Ribbentrop's demands and only used his police powers in December 1942 to require the extradition of Horia Sima when the latter had set up an opposition bureau in Italy. The Horia Sima group were kept as privileged internees in Dachau till August 1944, when Roumania surrendered to Russia and Antonescu was taken prisoner. Henceforward Himmler amused himself with a shadow Iron Guard Cabinet under Horia Sima which was intended for the reconquest of Roumania.[2]

---

[1] Wiking Jerk, *Endkampf um Berlin*, page 26.
[2] Wilhelm Hoettl, *The Secret Front* (London, 1954), pp. 178-82.

The curious case of Horia Sima is typical of the interferences of the SS, not only in Roumania but also in Hungary, Slovakia and Jugoslavia. That Himmler was able to oppose the official Foreign Office policy so openly was due to his position as sole arbiter on resettlement questions. Himmler used his position to intrigue against cabinets which were recognised by Ribbentrop, but this activity was secondary to gaining possession of the bodies of the racial Germans in these countries. Many more SS divisions were provided by the Germanic stock of Roumania, Hungary, Slovakia and Jugoslavia. The Prince Eugen or 7th SS mountain division was only the first of them, it was by no means a crack division and like the rest it was badly equipped. The chief value of these divisions lay in the racial Germans' notorious hatred of the Slavs. They were therefore sent to the places where this could best be exploited. Armed with captured weapons, the Prince Eugen division was sent early in 1942 to the Banat,[1] then to Montenegro and then to the areas of Croatia where partisan outbreaks had occurred. In the summer of 1943 Phleps was given a corps command, the 5th SS Mountain Corps, and in October a second SS division appeared in Jugoslavia, the 13th Division 'Handschar'. It consisted of 20,000 Bosnian Moslems, the so-called 'Mujos'. A further Moslem SS division, recruited in the Balkan countries in 1944 and known as the 23rd SS division 'Kama', was never brought to completion. These Moslems were traditional enemies of the Christian Serbs, and in 1941 their religious zeal had urged them to join in the massacres of Serbs, which were carried out by the 'Ustashe', the militia of the Croat leader Ante Pavelic. As pillage was followed by discipline, the energy of the Mujos was canalised into the Waffen SS. The Mujos were organised on the lines of the Bosnian regiments of the old imperial Austrian army, with officers and even N.C.O.s of German race, but they wore the Turkish fez with their SS runes and, in contrast with the 'six godless SS divisions' of 1941, each battalion had a chaplain or Imam. While training in France, the division received the spiritual ministrations of the Mufti of Jerusalem.

The Mufti Hajji Imam had fled to Berlin after the failure of the pro-German Iraq rebellion of May 1941. A shabby fraud with an impressive record of failure, he was treated by Ribbentrop's Foreign Office as a plenipotentiary of the Arab peoples. Himmler made the Mufti an SS Gruppenfuehrer and in May 1943, when the Handschar

[1] Hausser, op. cit., p. 106.

division was still in the paper stage, he wanted to move him to the SS leadership main office in order that he might direct the recruiting.[1] A few months later the good offices of the Mufti quelled a mutiny of these dubious mercenaries while training in France. They were not a very good investment. Although the Handschar division spent only a few months in the Partisan area before moving to Hungary in March 1944, it rivalled the bad reputation of the Prince Eugen division. Thirty-eight of the division's German officers and N.C.O.s were extradited for trial in Jugoslavia after the war.[2]

The end of Artur Phleps, who entered the SS as a Roumanian general, was as ambiguous as his career. In September 1944, when most of the Hungarian army commanders were on the point of surrendering to Russia, he was flown from Montenegro to form a front in Transylvania, the home of his boyhood. Two days after Phleps had left Budapest, Himmler ordered his arrest. He had been accused by Ohlendorf's SD of defeatism, but he was never found. It is alleged that he was shot down in a reconnaissance plane, that he committed suicide and also that he was shot by a Russian tank commander to prevent his escape. Finally, in April 1945 it was announced by Radio Moscow that Phleps was directing a Resistance movement in Roumania.[3]

Within a week of the occupation of Kharkov, Himmler was to give his crack divisions even shadier bed-companions. On 24 March 1943 there was a German radio report that a Ukrainian War Committee had been formed in this 'liberated' city. The purpose was to recruit a Ukrainian army for the fight against Bolshevism. In May it was reported that recruiting had begun in Lwow for a new SS division.[4] It was called the 14th SS Grenadier Division Galicia.

The formation of Russian units, even of divisional strength, to fight for the German army was no novelty in May 1943. At the very beginning of the campaign individual army commanders had formed battalions of auxiliary volunteers or 'Hiwis' (*Hilfsfreiwillige*) from the prisoner-of-war cages and sometimes these battalions served in the line. But Hitler was not supposed to know about them, and they were not entered on the strength. Only late in 1943 were the 'Hiwis' made into a command.[5] Much larger Russian formations were

---

[1] Nuremberg Document, Case XI, NG 3334.
[2] Hausser, op. cit., p. 108.
[3] Kern, *Der grosse Rausch*, pp. 160-1; Kraetschmer, op. cit., pp. 204-5.
[4] *Wiener Library Bulletin*, IV, 1950, pp. 5-6.   [5] Kleist, op. cit., p. 205.

created in the summer of 1942, for no less than 70,000 Don Cossacks
had deserted during the great German advance. Fifty-two thousand
of these Cossacks were formed into General von Pannwitz's Cossack
corps of two divisions, while 18,000 served as a militia under Ataman
Domanow.[1] When it was found that the Cossacks drifted back to
the Russians, they were transferred to Jugoslavia and to the Atlantic
Wall. Major von Rinteln told von Hassell at Dax, near Bordeaux,
that he sometimes heard from his former soldiers, who were 'getting
along famously on the other side'.[2]

The Cossacks were a huge joke. The generals told Hitler that they
wore red fur caps and red trousers with silver stripes. 'They fight
Voelkerwanderung style, taking everything with them', Jodl added.[3]
It was necessary to find a settlement area for their women and cattle,
and a vast nomad encampment grew up at Tolmezzo in Friuli. In
1944 the liberated and impotent Mussolini made diplomatic protests
about it, and in 1945 the problem was left to confront Allied Military
Government officials.[4]

With the occupation of the North Caucasus and the Kuban in
the autumn of 1942, still more Russian racial minorities could be
used as German troops. 110,000 Turkomen were enrolled, including
the 162nd Turkoman Division, which served on the Italian front and
at one moment fought an American Japanese regiment. There were
also 110,000 Georgians, Armenians and other Caucasians, 35,000
Tartars of the Crimea and twenty-three squadrons of Kalmuk light
cavalry, mounted on ponies. In all, there were 650,000 former subjects
of the Soviet Union wearing German uniform.[5]

In the winter of 1942, when this mass of men followed the retreating German armies to avoid the reprisals that awaited them
from the Russians, Himmler would probably not have objected to
procuring them for the SS. He could always pretend that he had
chosen those who were 'nearest to our blood' in order to make
Germanics of them, an elastic conception which stretched with the
mounting demands of war. 'It is irrevocable', Himmler declared at
Posen in August 1944, 'that we shall add thirty million people of
Germanic origin to our ninety millions so that we can extend our
blood basis to a hundred and twenty million Germanics'.[6] It was

[1] Kleist, op. cit., p. 270.   [2] *Von Hassell Diaries*, p. 290.
[3] Felix Gilbert, *Hitler Directs his Armies*, p. 123.
[4] Filippo Anfuso, *Du palais de Venise au lac de Garde* (Paris, 1949), p. 378.
[5] Kleist, op. cit., p. 205.   [6] *Vierteljahreshefte fuer Zeitgeschichte*, No. 4, p. 594.

inevitable, but it was not to be done in a hurry. In October 1943 Himmler had defended death sentences against Poles and Russians who had consorted with German women. He even urged caution in granting German nationality to soldiers who were 'of the third Volkslist and had won the Iron Cross, second class'.[1]

Himmler had decided, however, that it was only the Slav and the Jew in the Russian stock who were sub-human. There was a superior element in the Russian nation which had come from Asia and which had produced Attila, Jenghiz Khan, Tamerlane, Lenin and Stalin. In October 1943, when Himmler reached this conclusion, plenty of good Turanian stock had just been drafted into the SS division Handschar. If there had not been a scheme afoot at that moment for an autonomous Russian Liberation Army, Himmler would have had his theory ready to justify the recruitment of Russian divisions for the SS. But, because the High Command and the Foreign Office backed the Liberation Army, Himmler ignored 650,000 ex-Red Army volunteers and restricted himself to a single Galician division. Yet this was after Stalingrad, when Hitler had lifted the ban on the recruitment for the SS of 'national legions'.[2] Hitler had relented so far that on 18 May Himmler told Goebbels of plans for an anti-Bolshevik Legion for service on the Russian front, to be formed of British prisoners of war.[3]

And so, late in June 1943, Himmler formed his first Slav SS division under the elderly and professorial-looking Austrian Major-General Fritz Freitag. It was the very reverse of a nationalist Russian legion. At this moment Himmler was still bitterly hostile to the former Bolshevik general, Andrej Vlassov, who had been encouraged by the army and the Foreign Office to recruit such a legion.[4] It was only late in 1944, when Himmler commanded an immense foreign army, that he could find a use for Vlassov. Himmler restricted the recruiting of his 14th SS Division to the former Austrian part of Poland, a mere fraction of the ethnic Ukraine. Most of the officers and NCOs of the division were ex-service men of the First World War who had fought in the Austrian army. They had come under Russian rule only after the Moscow pact of September 1939.

Nevertheless, the material of this SS division was Slav, that is to say, in Himmler's view it was sub-human. The Ukrainian SS, therefore, was not a project on which he expatiated in his Kharkov

---

[1] Himmler's first Posen speech, Nuremberg Document PS 1919.
[2] Kleist, op. cit., p. 178.   [3] *The Goebbels Diary*, p. 302.   [4] See *infra*, p. 389.

speech. So little boasting was done about it that at the end of the war, when a second division, part Ukrainian and part White Russian, had been formed, Hitler did not know of its existence.[1] His only comments on it were that the Austrian Ruthenians had been pacifists even under the old empire, and the best thing to do with them was to give their weapons to a German division.

Born in a furtive and confused atmosphere, the Ukrainian SS were not fated to distinguish themselves. The 30th Division was used only against partisans in Poland and Slovakia. The 14th was not sent to the front till July 1944, when 14,000 men of the division were cut off as part of Lindemann's XIVth Army Corps in the Brody-Tarnow 'Kessel'. Only 3,000 succeeded in crossing the passes into Hungary.[2] Hitler was told in March 1945 that the division had not been employed since that debâcle. This should not have surprised him.[3] The German dealings with Ukrainian nationalism, a prickly plant at best, were of such blatant stupidity that the failure of the Ukrainian SS was inevitable from the beginning.

It began with the meddlesome Admiral Canaris and his love of everything that smelt of reaction. From his appointment as Chief of the Abwehr in January 1935 the Admiral had maintained contacts with the exiled Ukrainian leaders of the Petliura faction, who had lived in Germany since the Russian civil war. They possessed an organisation, known as OUN, which Ribbentrop tried to steal from Admiral Canaris and which he wanted to use in September 1939 in order to terrorise Jews and Polish farmers in the anticipated Valhalla of the German occupation of Galicia.[4] As it turned out, Eastern Galicia, including Lwow, had to be surrendered to M. Molotov, who demanded the disbandment of OUN and its leader, Colonel Melynik.

Canaris continued to keep in touch with OUN. A number of Ukrainians were taken out of the interned Polish army and drafted into the Abwehr Sabotage Regiment, Brandenburg 800.[5] They were briefed for sabotage duties in the forthcoming attack on Russia. At the same time Melynik and a certain Stepan Bandera were to

[1] Gilbert, op. cit., p. 149.

[2] Erich Kern, *Der grosse Rausch, Russlandfeldzug* 1941-1945 (Zurich, 1948), p. 150; Kraetschmer, op. cit., pp. 360-1.

[3] In fact the division put up an unexpectedly tough resistance at Graz in Austria at the end of the war.

[4] Evidence of Erwin Lahousen in IMT I, p. 275.

[5] Evidence of Erwin Stolze, IMT VI, p. 252.

incite the Galician population. Bandera had been picked up by the
Germans in September 1939 in a Warsaw prison, where he was
serving a sentence for his part in a political murder.[1] During the
occupation of Lwow in July 1941 these Ukrainian leaders co-
operated with Heydrich's Einsatzgruppen, who were good enough
to help them organise a pogrom which they dedicated to their dead
hero as 'Action Petliura'.[2] But more than pogroms were needed to
keep Ukrainians happy. The Ukrainians, who were attached to the
Brandenburg regiment, seized the Lwow wireless station and proclaimed an independent West Ukrainian state. After some scrim-
mages with German troops, Melynik, Bandera and other Ukrainian
leaders were interned in Sachsenhausen concentration camp. Shortly
afterwards Lwow and Eastern Galicia were handed over to the
tender care of Hans Frank as part of the General Government of
Poland. Some of Melynik's followers set up a partisan movement in
Galicia and the Western Ukraine, called UPA. It was not pro-
Stalin, but it was very anti-German.[3]

In April 1943 the Ukrainian nationalists were released from
Sachsenhausen and some of them entered the 14th SS Division.
There is nothing in Himmler's writings and speeches to suggest that
his visit to Kharkov had converted him to Ukrainian nationalism.
Probably he was realist enough to see that a year of Sauckel's press-
gangs and eighteen months of Erich Koch's extortions had lost the
Germans in the Ukraine any respect they had ever earned. Poor-
quality mercenaries who would join anything to save their skins
were all he could expect. Most of the released Ukrainian nationalists
boycotted the 14th SS Division and some were hauled back to Sachsenhausen,[4] but Bandera was allowed to recruit his own militia.
In July 1944, when the 14th SS Division retreated into Slovakia,
the Benderovce collected their weapons from them as they crossed
the passes, determined to defend Galicia from a second Russian
occupation even if the Germans were no longer able to do so.[5]

Bandera himself remained with the Germans, and he represented
the Ukraine at Vlassov's Prague conference in November 1944.
After the war he was interned by the Americans but not extradited
to Russia and in 1950 he still ran a Ukrainian committee in Munich.
In the postwar years the Benderovce in Galicia were joined by

---

[1] *Wiener Library Bulletin*, IV, 1950., pp. 5-6,   [2] Reitlinger, op. cit., p. 229.
[3] Kleist, op. cit., pp.186-90; Leverkuehn, op. cit., p. 164-6; Abshagen, *Canaris*,
pp. 213-17.   [4] Abshagen, op. cit., p. 215.   [5] Kern, op. cit., p. 148

numerous former members of the two Ukrainian SS divisions[1] and the Vlassov army. At one time they controlled entire areas on both sides of the Polish-Russian demarcation line. They may be the only part of the Waffen SS who are still at war.

During the breathing space after the Kharkov victory, recruitment also began for the first of three Lettish and Estonian SS divisions. Himmler could afford to be enthusiastic over people who, even if they did not speak an Aryan language, were mainly blond and blue-eyed with strong admixtures of Scandinavian and German blood, and who rejoiced in such suggestively European names as Adamson and Ansons. But neither Alfred Rosenberg, the Minister for Eastern Affairs, nor Heinrich Lohse, the Reichkommissar for the Baltic states and White Russia, favoured autonomy for these former sovereign states. Rosenberg, though ineffectual as an administrator and woolly-headed as a philosopher, had all the Baltic German's brutal colonial mentality. Nevertheless, in February 1943 an autonomy statute for the three Baltic states was drawn up by one of Rosenberg's officials. It had Himmler's approval because he hoped that such promises would secure a good recruitment for the SS.[2]

Rosenberg would not back the Baltic autonomy plan. He was more interested in autonomy for the Ukraine. In the following June this led to a crisis with Erich Koch. Georg Leibbrandt, the head of Rosenberg's Political Department, had drawn up another memorandum on a Ukrainian state. Koch succeeded in getting Leibbrandt called up for the army. In despair of making any headway against Koch and his protector, Martin Bormann, Rosenberg had at last to make peace with the SS. The successor to Leibbrandt was none other than Gottlob Berger, who proceeded to set up a sort of rival Eastern Ministry in the SS head office.[3]

Gottlob Berger was expected to introduce a more tolerant note in the handling of Russian affairs. He had the reputation of being a critic. On 9 March 1943 he had written Himmler a letter, attacking certain SS leaders who had fallen on the Baltic states and the Ukraine 'like a famished army of have-nots'.[4] But Berger was no more able than Rosenberg to break down the Martin Bormann barrier to Hitler. It was not till November 1944 that the leaders of

---

[1] The bulk of the Ukrainian SS, numbering 15,000, surrendered to the British in Austria and were interned at Rimini.   [2] Kleist, op. cit., p. 167.

[3] *Ibid.*, pp. 151, 181. For Leibbrandt see footnote, page 186.

[4] François Bayle, *Psychologie et éthique de national socialisme*, pp. 458-62.

the Latvian and Estonian SS had an opportunity to voice their national aspirations at Vlassov's Prague Parliament. It was then three years too late.

The story of the Latvian and Estonian SS illustrates how weak even the SS could be in the face of a palace dictatorship. In June 1943, when so much could still have been done in recruiting an army from the Baltic states, Himmler had no personal access to Hitler at Rastenburg. And Hitler listened continually to the brutal blinkered wisdom of Martin Bormann, who had declared 'There are no independent nations in the East, but only the Sovietised mass of Slavs, who must and will be mastered'.[1]

Thus Himmler's recruiting campaign in Latvia and Estonia resolved itself into a conscription of racial Germans, or rather of everyone whom VOMI and RUSHA could whip up as 'Germanic types'. Even in September 1944, when the German occupation of the Baltic states was to be numbered in days, Hitler could do nothing better for a friendly population than to send them the almost crazy Erich Koch, who needed a kingdom and who wanted to exterminate those 'Ostidiote' who thought of negotiating with Latvians, Lithuanians and Estonians. That, and not the useless defence of Estonian Narva by an all-European SS, was the true meaning of a New Order in Europe.[2]

3. RESISTANCE IN THE WEST

On these lines Himmler could well claim that the New Order in Europe was his own creation—as the authors of the 'Festgabe' of 1940 had declared.[3] Through his resettlement agencies he could create 'Germanics' wherever he pleased, and through his foreign Waffen SS he could obtain hostages to German fortune from every constituent country. Above all, Himmler was the acknowledged leader of the struggle of the New Order against Bolshevism. But it was a crusade which Himmler could keep as his own monopoly only so long as the Communists under the New Order lay dormant. With the physical invasion of Russia this changed, and in every occupied and satellite country the Communists became identified with Resistance movements. The struggle against Bolshevism was no longer a propaganda device but an armed warfare, over which direction was claimed by the Wehrmacht, in particular by the Wehrmacht's

[1] Kleist, op. cit., p. 187.   [2] Kleist, op. cit., p. 192.   [3] See *supra*, p. 154.

counter-espionage and counter-sabotage branch, the Abwehr. It was therefore with the invasion of Russia that Heydrich approached his trial of strength with Admiral Canaris.

Heydrich's position in occupied France and the Netherlands was far weaker than in Eastern Europe. There were no protocols making his security police commanders independent of the civil and military occupying powers. Hitler had not abrogated the authority of his generals. It may be that he did not expect to be confronted with an occupation problem so soon. He may have considered that Western Man was not fanatical and that he could deal with Communists in France and the Netherlands as easily as he had dealt with them in Germany, even if his trial of strength with Russia should bring the Communists over to the side of the Resistance.

Hitler did not expect the liberal groups in the Western countries to co-operate with the more drastic and direct methods of Communism. He believed that anti-Semitism and anti-Marxism had a universal appeal. Consequently the alliance between the French patriotic groups and the Communists, uneasy though it was, astonished him and aggravated the incredible brutality of his nature. In spite of the presence of de Gaullist agents, there had been barely the shadow of a Resistance movement in France before the invasion of Russia. In the occupied zone the military government of Otto von Stuelpnagel[1] had been able to rely on the French police, for the Gestapo organisation in France, though large, had very little police of its own. But the growth of a Resistance movement in France demanded the same German system as in Russia and the military governor was to lose his competence in police matters. But here the victory of Himmler and Heydrich was slow and in the meantime the Abwehr and the SD conducted the fight against saboteurs in rivalry and often in open conflict.

The first assassination in France took place on the Paris Métro on 21 August 1941, the victim being a German naval officer. Stuelpnagel demanded the surrender of fifty hostages for execution, but the German Foreign Office found a more cunning way of exerting pressure than this. The French might be let off with only six victims, but they must be killed by the French in accordance with French law. Instead of surrendering fifty hostages, the Vichy Government agreed to publish a retrospective law, backdated to the time of the

[1] To be distinguished from the better-known Heinrich von Stuelpnagel who succeeded him in March 1942.

murder, by which six Communists, who were already in prison, could
be executed for activities that had nothing to do with it. The French
judges tried to bargain for mitigated sentences, but by the end of
September all six Communists had been executed *by the French*.[1]

In the same month Heydrich's security police began the direct
shooting of hostages, but without deterrent effect. On 20 October
the Town Commandant of Nantes, Colonel Holz, was shot and in
the next two days forty-eight hostages were executed by Stuelpnagel's order, most of them in Chateaubriand prison. On 5 December
Stuelpnagel, who needed no prompting in such matters, proposed
to Keitel the execution of a further hundred hostages as a reprisal
for three recent murders, and this was carried out within the next
ten days. Stuelpnagel also proposed to Hitler that the Jews of Paris
should pay a fine of a thousand million francs and that a thousand
Jews and five hundred Communists should be deported to Eastern
Europe. Otto Abetz, the so-called ambassador in Paris, had it all
put on a legal footing. The deportees were to be described as 'Soviet
and secret service agents of Judeo-Communist and de Gaullist
origin'. On 12 December the first of the great Jewish round-ups took
place in Paris with the collaboration of the French police, but
Heydrich discovered that the Wehrmacht had banned deportation
trains to Poland and Russia during the troops' Christmas leave.
So the first trainload of 1,100 Jews did not reach Auschwitz from
Paris till 30 March 1942, even though in the next two years more
than 60,000 were to travel the same road.[2]

Thus, at the end of 1941 a German reign of terror had reached
France, but it did not prevent the acts of sabotage increasing. The
Gestapo, which carried out the executions, had to rely on other
agencies to make the arrests and French and British saboteurs
could profit from the rivalry of Gestapo and Abwehr. In 1939 the
Abwehr had been permitted their own police troops by the High
Command. These were the Secret Field Gendarmerie, corresponding
to the British Field Security Police.[3] Whereas in Russia this force
co-operated in carrying out the Wagner-Heydrich protocol, it was
quite outside Heydrich's authority in France. It was therefore
Heydrich's aim on the one hand to absorb the Secret Field Gendarmerie, on the other to stop the army and Abwehr from interfering
in Gestapo affairs. The methods of the Gestapo in France were

[1] Robert Aron, *Histoire de Vichy* (Paris, 1954), p. 416.
[2] Reitlinger, op. cit., pp. 309-10.   [3] See *supra*, p. 175.

probably neither less clever nor more brutal than those of the Abwehr, but in this matter Heydrich wanted to dictate his own procedure. Above all he wanted to see no secret police but his own in any part of Europe, for the Abwehr's police had been an affront to him from the beginning.

Heydrich's new campaign found an opening in a ludicrous incident. On the night of 2 October 1941 an amateurish attempt was made to blow up two Paris synagogues. The commander of the security police and SD, Colonel Helmuth Knochen,[1] reported to Stuelpnagel that the French police suspected Eugéne Deloncle, the former leader of the ultra-Fascist 'Cagoulards', who had come to life under the name of 'Mouvement Sociale Revolutionnaire'. Knochen forgot to say that he had arrested a member of his own staff, Lieutenant Sommer of the SS. Stuelpnagel discovered quite by accident that Sommer had admitted to a court of inquiry that he had provided the explosives under Knochen's orders. Stuelpnagel complained to Keitel that the Gestapo were increasing his difficulties with the French, which the 'necessary shooting of hostages had already made bad enough'. On 22 October Keitel wrote to Heydrich, requesting the recall from France of Max Thomas, the higher SS police leader, and Knochen, the security police leader. Heydrich answered Keitel from Prague with a letter to Quartermaster-General Wagner which he worded in the most insulting terms.

My director of services in Paris did not think it necessary to tell Stuelpnagel because our experience gave little hope of his comprehension. I was well aware of the political consequences of these measures, the more so since I have been entrusted for years with the final solution of the Jewish problem.[2]

Major-General Max Thomas had already been transferred to Russia, where Heydrich saddled him with an Einsatzgruppe, but Heydrich refused to recall Knochen. Wagner reminded Heydrich that, by the terms of the agreement, covering the Western countries, the special commandos of the RSHA had to accept the orders of General Stuelpnagel. On 5 February Stuelpnagel withdrew his complaint, because Knochen had expressed his willingness to co-operate. For the moment the honours were with the Wehrmacht, but on 7 May, when the new higher SS police leader, Lieutenant-General Karl Oberg, arrived in Paris, the German police in France came

[1] Condemned to death by a Paris court in October 1954 but still in prison.
[2] Henri Monneray, *Les Persecutions des juifs en France* (Paris, 1947), Documents 65-8.

under the control of a man who took his orders only from Himmler.

On 3 March Otto von Stuelpnagel had been succeeded as military governor in France by the Chief of the Armistice Commission, a distant kinsman called Heinrich von Stuelpnagel. This second Stuelpnagel was an active member of the Halder-Beck circle, and he had been deep in the Putsch plans of 1939. His staff of hand-picked intellectual young men prided themselves on their hostility to the SS.[1] Yet the second Stuelpnagel had to submit to a far worse bargain with Himmler than the first. What had happened between 5 February and 7 May 1942? It was simply that Keitel had been hauled over the coals for one of his few gestures of independence in complaining of Heydrich. No doubt the ante-room king, Martin Bormann, had been at work. Keitel's surrender involved that of Admiral Canaris and a humiliating end to his negotiations with Heydrich, which had dragged on since August 1941, when the first assassination had occurred in France.

On 23 May, soon after Oberg's appointment, Canaris was form-ally reconciled with his old pupil in the presence of Keitel and Himmler at Heydrich's new royal residence in Prague, the Hradcin Palace. This conference gave the SS and its police forces in France the same status as they enjoyed in Russia. Canaris's Secret Field Gendarmerie was now an arm of the Gestapo. Canaris could no longer interfere with Gestapo practices in France, but he thought he could do some good by retaining his hamstrung position as an observation post. It was not the view of his humbler employees and the opinion, expressed by a rather remarkable sergeant of the Secret Field Gendarmerie, is worth recording.

Admiral Canaris knew better than anyone else in Germany what the crimes of the Gestapo were. Yet this influential and astute Chief of Intelligence did not prevent the Gestapo and SD from out-manœuvring his service. If he had resigned at an appropriate time, it would have excited tremendous attention in Germany and abroad. Instead of that he let his subordinates carry on a guerrilla war with the SD and obliged them finally to co-operate with the rival service, which was a task not easy to reconcile with a clear conscience.[2]

---

[1] Otto von Stuelpnagel was charged in December 1946 with ordering the Chateaubriand massacre, but committed suicide in the Cherche-Midi prison in February 1948 rather than stand trial. Heinrich von Stuelpnagel was executed after the July 1944 plot (see *infra*, page 345). Oberg and Knochen were not tried till September-October 1954. It is unlikely that the death sentences will be carried out (August 1956).

[2] Hugo Bleicher, *Colonel Henri's Story*, edited by Ian Colvin (London, 1954), p. 54.

4. THE LAST OF REINHARD HEYDRICH

Six days after the meeting in the Hradcin Palace Heydrich received the wounds from which he died. With this, the end of the Heydrich-Himmler rivalry, the unification of the SS Police State was complete. The death of the most ruthless man in the SS organisation had the paradoxical result of making it still more ruthless. Heydrich was too disordered and rebellious a personality to fit in with an organisation which was only one of several at the disposition of a dictator. During the last year of his life he was thwarted of his real ambition and driven to undertake activities which could not help him. Heydrich wanted to be not merely a police spy working in the shadows, a night-club king in politics, but a minister of the Reich with the police in his control, the ambition which Himmler was to realise in August 1943. Himmler fought this ambition of Heydrich's but nevertheless proposed a ministerial status for him. After 22 January 1941, when Guertner, the Minister for Justice, died, Himmler wanted the administration of civil law to be handled by Frick's Ministry of the Interior, which he virtually controlled himself through the State Secretary, Wilhelm Stuckart, a loyal SS man. Criminal law, Himmler told Hitler, could be handled by Heydrich, who held the Security Police Department in the Ministry.[1]

At this stage Hans Lammers, Head of the Reich Chancellery, whose sense of protocol often overcame his own natural brutality, made his objections. Forced to choose between Guertner's State Secretaries, Roland Freisler and Franz Schlegelberger, Hitler chose Schlegelberger, but so reluctantly that he gave him only an acting status. 'Freisler was nothing but a Bolshevik. As for the other, his face could not deceive me. It was enough to have seen him once'.[2] Probably Hitler needed no prompting from Lammers to reject Heydrich. Even a year later, when Hitler was permitted the complete abrogation of German law, he did not consider Heydrich for a Department of Justice whose main purpose was to assist the Gestapo. Hitler found that the best way to prevent Himmler giving him trouble was to multiply his offices. The best way with Heydrich was to divide them. Balked of a dictatorship over the criminal courts, which would have completed the power of the Gestapo, Heydrich had to look elsewhere. He must have wanted the party

[1] *Von Hassell Diary*, 16 March 1941, p. 260.
[2] *Hitler's Table Talk*, 29 March 1942, p. 376.

office, which became vacant in May 1941 after the flight of Rudolf Hess, but Martin Bormann, who had virtually run it since the outbreak of war, stepped into his chief's shoes without needing any special decree. And Bormann used the position to become a far more powerful person than Heydrich could ever have been.

Without control of the criminal courts the RSHA and the Gestapo were nothing like as omnipotent as is generally supposed. The best refuge from the Gestapo was to be in the custody of the court. It is true that the Gestapo might keep a man out of the court's reach, and it could pounce on him after the court had freed him, but such is German protocol that, once a man possessed a judicial record, it was no longer possible for the Gestapo merely to spirit him away. His legal existence continued even in a concentration camp. And if he happened to be a Jew, he was not whisked into the gas chamber along with old people, mothers and their children on reaching Auschwitz camp. His court record travelled with him; he was given a registration number in the camp files and, protected by his criminal record, he had a chance of survival. This Erewhonian justice prevailed till the end of the war, a monument to the incompleteness of the Gestapo system.[1]

Soon after Guertner's death Heydrich became aware of the limits of his powers. On 31 July 1941 he received his commission from Goering to extend the 'Final Solution of the Jewish Problem' to the entire German field of influence in Europe.[2] Other agencies were to participate if the matter touched on their competence, but Heydrich complained that these agencies would not co-operate at all.[3] By 20 January 1942 Heydrich was compelled to call an intra-ministerial conference in the "Interpol" office at Wannsee in order to listen to objections. He was forced to place his cards on the table and to disclose the true nature of the 'Final Solution', and he had to give way to the demands of Goering's Four-Year Plan office, which protected its Jewish armament workers. The deportation of all the Jews of Berlin had been promised by Hitler to Goebbels in August 1941, but as a result of this conference the deportation was not completed till March 1943.[4]

At the beginning of the Russian campaign Heydrich had again

[1] Ella Lingens-Reiner, *Prisoners of Fear* (London, 1948), p. 74.
[2] Nuremberg Document PS 710, Reitlinger, op. cit., p. 82.
[3] Case XI, Document NO. 1020.
[4] *The Final Solution*, page 84, quoting an unpublished fragment of the *Goebbels Diary*.

flown for six weeks as a pilot officer with the Luftwaffe. It was no escapist flight from his own careerism, for almost immediately an opening presented itself, an opening which offered, as Heydrich thought, better prospects than murdering Jews and suspected commissars. Since April 1939 Bohemia and Moravia had been a protectorate. The Czechs retained their own parliament and president, but there was a Reich Protector in the person of Constantin von Neurath, who had been Foreign Minister for Germany between 1932 and 1938. At the time of his appointment Neurath was sixty-three years old and completely discredited in party circles. He was given the post in order to make Hitler's annexation look respectable. The real subjection of the country was carried out by Karl Hermann Frank, the fanatical Sudeten German Freikorps leader and close associate of Himmler during the Munich crisis. As higher SS and police leader, Frank was directly subordinate to Himmler and he was also a state secretary in the Ministry of the Interior.[1]

In spite of the strength of Frank's position, Neurath kept certain powers of intervention and the period of his protectorship was marked by student demonstrations which might not have taken place had Frank been omnipotent. Hitler's fury that such things could happen in the very heart of a Reich at war gave Himmler an opportunity to advance the position of the SS police state and at the same time to remove the uncomfortable presence of Heydrich from his court for at any rate half the year. On 3 September 1941 Hitler made Heydrich Deputy Protector, while von Neurath retained only a nominal office. At the same time Heydrich was to continue to rule the RSHA and to command the security police in all occupied territories.

Had Heydrich been a more intelligent person he would not have gone to Prague, for almost immediately he weakened his position in Berlin. As early as December 1939 Himmler had removed the economic administration of the concentration camps out of Heydrich's hands. He had given it to a former naval paymaster-captain called Oswald Pohl.[2] In February 1942 Himmler profited by the new drive for man-power for German industry to put the entire concentration-camp system under Oswald Pohl's economic office, WVHA, excluding Heydrich altogether. Thus Heydrich, the cashiered naval officer who had lost the Abwehr to a naval captain in 1935, lost the concentration camps to another naval captain seven years later.

[1] IMT XVII, p. 138.   [2] Case IV, Transcript 8081.

But Heydrich showed no signs of fretting at an appointment which gave Himmler so much chance to harm him. He took on the task in Prague with enthusiasm. Responsibility for mass exterminations in Russia was not uncongenial to Heydrich's temperament, but he resented that this should be thought a piece of dirty work which no one but he would undertake. One way of showing his resentment was to blackmail the more intellectual and uppish members of his RSHA office such as Ohlendorf, Stahlecker, Nebe and Jost into sharing his guilt. But in Prague Heydrich had an assignment which he could carry out with all the limelight directed on him. After a few months of this new sort of life everyone (except the Czechs) agreed that Heydrich had made himself popular with the honest working population of Bohemia and Moravia. Goebbels, who saw Heydrich on 15 February, reported that, though the Czech intelligentsia might still be hostile, the threat to German security had been overcome.[1] Heydrich had mastered the crisis with ease; the protectorate was in the best of spirits. Later Hitler is said to have declared that the British Secret Service had had to kill Heydrich because his statesmanship was winning over the Czech people.[2] Heydrich had believed this himself, for in this most violated of capitals he dropped all the Nazi ceremonial of armour-plated cars with police escorts on motor-bicycles and behaved instead like a film star, driving daily from his country villa to the Hradcin Palace alone in an open sports car, conspicuously dressed in his SS Obergruppenfuehrer's uniform.

No doubt the female vanity which lay behind most of Heydrich's actions made him spurn the security methods which were in vogue among his colleagues. Hitler remarked 'that a man as irreplaceable as Heydrich should expose himself to unnecessary danger I can only condemn as stupid and idiotic'.[3] But Hitler's words were wise after the event, because Heydrich had persuaded everyone, including Hitler himself, that the Czechs liked him for it. Heydrich possessed the eminently German characteristic of not noticing that a man dislikes you until he has hit you on the jaw. The Czechs did not shake their fists at Heydrich nor shout 'Schweinehund'. That meant that the sub-humans were friendly.

This figure in his film-star uniform, arrogantly driving his open sports car, seems the very embodiment of the Eternal German, a

---

[1] *The Goebbels Diary*, p. 51.   [2] Felix Kersten, *Totenkopf und Treue*, p. 127.
[3] *Hitler's Table Talk*, p. 512.

believer in methods and disciplines, in national cults and historic destinies, an inmate of a world inhabited by neatly pigeon-holed racial categories, certainly not by human beings who are unpredictable alike in their glory and in their squalor. The driver of the sports car is as clearly destined to be betrayed and murdered as the state which he serves, betrayed and murdered through crass inability to see that the other man has had enough.

So it came about that on 29 May 1942 two men waited for Heydrich's car at one of the Moldau Bridges, where the road takes so sudden a bend that drivers must change into low gear. These men, Jan Kubis and Josef Gabcik, were members of the Free Czechoslovak Forces who had parachuted from a British plane. Heydrich's car was almost blown to pieces by a British-manufactured bomb, but Heydrich survived with a shattered spine.

Himmler's efforts to save Heydrich's life seem to have been genuine. He was surprisingly loyal to the man who wanted to supplant him. A remarkable story was told by Albrecht Haushofer to his disciple, Rainer Hildebrandt. Since Hess's flight to Scotland in May 1941 Haushofer had been under close observation and Hitler had twice personally questioned the woman Gestapo reporter whose business it was to find out Haushofer's English contacts. This reporter was in reality on Haushofer's side and, a few days before the attack in Prague, she told him some gossip, which she had picked up concerning Heydrich's plans to step into Himmler's shoes. Haushofer decided that a friendly warning to Himmler might dispose him to throw in his lot with the Resistance Circle. So the essential Dr. Langbehn was sent to Himmler. But, though he thanked Langbehn for the tip about Heydrich, the only action Himmler took was to arrest the woman reporter for spreading false rumours.[1]

So, soon after the explosion of the bomb, Himmler arrived in Prague, having flown from his headquarters in East Prussia in the company of three doctors. These were his own favourites, the murderers Karl Gebhardt and Karl Brandt, and Hitler's court quack, Theodor Morell. Despite them all, Heydrich lived till 6 June. Because Heydrich's wounds had become gangrenous and Gebhardt was blamed for it, hundreds of women inmates of concentration camps were later to die from Gebhardt's experiments in the use of sulphanilamide.[2] Since death rarely points a moral, opinions differ as to whether

[1] Rainer Hildebrandt, *Wir sind die Letzten*, pp. 135-6.
[2] See *infra*, pp. 262-3.

Heydrich died with a sneer on his lips or in deep contrition.[1]

Kubis and Gabcik, who had escaped behind a smoke-cloud, were picked up in Prague, but not till 20 June when they fought till death, barricaded in the Karl Borromeus Church. In the long interval there had been other victims to atone for the killing of the Reich Protector. Himmler seems to have been determined on a hecatomb to avenge the hero's death in accordance with ancient German mythology. It was discovered that the Mayor of Lidice, a small village near Kladno, had a son in the Free Czechoslovak forces and, besides, possessed an illegal wireless set; but the official version handed out by Goebbels's ministry to the Press spoke of arms dumps and a transmitter.[2]

On 9 June ten trucks of German security police under Colonel Max Rostock[3] surrounded the village. The entire male population were locked in the Mayor's barn and next day they were taken into the garden in batches of ten and shot. The village was then burnt and levelled to the ground. Those who had been away on 9 June were picked up later and executed in Prague. In all, 199 men and boys were shot, 195 women were taken to Ravensbrueck concentration camp, where fifty-two of them died before the end of the war. Ninety children were removed to Gneisenau in German-incorporated Poland and out of these seven were selected to be brought up as Germans by Lebensborn, an organisation which ran maternity homes and orphanages for the SS.[4] This was the result of a suggestion which Himmler made to Max Sollmann, the director of Lebensborn, more than a year later. Since the children were orphans, a charge of abduction made against Sollmann at Nuremberg in 1947 was dropped.[5]

The world has remembered Lidice, perhaps on account of the beauty of its name, but this village only provided a small fraction of the ultimate hecatomb. Reckless executions were carried out by military courts in Prague and Bruenn of everyone suspected of the smallest breach of regulations. One of the reports which was sent to Kurt Daluege, who succeeded Heydrich as Reich Protector, gave the figure as 1,331, including 201 women.[6] But the chief victims were

---

[1] Frischauer, op. cit., p. 195.   [2] IMT VI, p. 172.
[3] Extradited from Russia and hanged in Prague, August 1951.
[4] IMT VII, p. 87, Czech Government Report.
[5] Law Reports of Trials of War Criminals, XIII, p. 34.
[6] *Wiener Library Bulletin*, 1951, V, pp. 1-2.

the Jews. On 29 May, the day of Heydrich's mishap, Goebbels recorded in his diary that he had arrested five hundred Berlin Jews and that he would kill a hundred to a hundred and fifty for every 'Jewish plot'. On the day Heydrich died the Gestapo notified the Berlin Finance President that 152 Jews had been killed in prison in a 'special action' and that as a consequence their property was forfeited to the state.[1]

Between 10 and 12 June three trains took more than three thousand Czech Jews from the so-called privileged ghetto of Theresienstadt in the Protectorate 'to the East'. The trains were routed to the transfer stations of Ujasdow and Trawniki in the General Government of Poland, but not a single Jew has survived and the trains went certainly to one of the extermination camps, probably Malo Trostinec in White Russia.[2] Furthermore, the organisation, which had carried out the massacre of the Jews of Poland for Heydrich during the last two months, was now dedicated to the hero's shade under the name of 'Einsatz Reinhard'.[3]

Hitler delivered a funeral oration at the memorial service for Heydrich at the Reich Chancellery and so did Heydrich's rival, Admiral Canaris. The pious Karl Abshagen writes that Canaris 'thought it proper in the presence of Heydrich's colleagues to declaim in a hollow voice choked with tears that he had specially treasured and honoured Heydrich as a great man and that he had lost a true friend in him'.[4] After the service Hitler told President Hacha and his Czech delegation that if he had any more of it, he would deport the entire population. Thereupon dear old Otto Meissner, head of the Presidential Chancellery since the early Weimar Republic, who never had anything to do but arrange the seating at dinner, took Dr. Hacha for a walk in the garden and told him that the Fuehrer meant it. The result was a mass rally in Prague, declaring the loyalty of the Czech nation. Hitler was deeply impressed.[5]

Yet there is nothing in Hitler's table talk, such as Martin Bormann thought worthy of recording, to suggest that the loss of Heydrich had upset him. Hitler was indignant that the Catholic Church in

---

[1] *The Final Solution*, p. 101, footnote, quoting an unpublished fragment of Goebbels's Diary.

[2] Zdenek Lederer, *Ghetto Theresienstadt* (London, 1953), p. 216.

[3] See *infra*, p. 281.   [4] Abshagen, op. cit., p. 149.

[5] *Hitler's Table Talk*, 4 July 1942, p. 558.

Bohemia should have sheltered the murderers and yet offered to pray for the murdered man.[1] But that was the limit of his indignation; perhaps he, too, shared the general relief. Himmler told Felix Kersten that Heydrich's death meant more to him than the loss of a battle. Hitler had intended Heydrich for great tasks and Himmler himself did not know whom to appoint as his successor in the police.[2]

Himmler's relief was expressed by the fact that he did not appoint a successor for nearly eight months and that, sooner than have any more geniuses about the place, he gave himself the impossible task of running RSHA on top of his other commitments. And this suited Hitler too, for he preferred this dull, unspectacular man. It is inconceivable that Himmler could have become at the same moment Minister of the Interior, Chief of Police, Reichsfuehrer of the SS, Commander-in-Chief of an army group, Commander of the Replacement Army and of all foreign armies in the Reich, if Kubis and Gabcik had not been waiting at that awkward bend in the road.

[1] *Hitler's Table Talk*, p. 554.   [2] Felix Kersten, *Totenkopf und Treue*, p. 127.

9

Himmler and the Rival Satraps

JUNE 1942 – OCTOBER 1943

1. HIMMLER AS HEYDRICH'S SUCCESSOR

With Heydrich's death all the offices of the SS came under Himmler's direct control. It was a personal dictatorship, based on that of Adolf Hitler and a replica of all its most bizarre features. The Fuehrer could not dictate from day to day the policy for each of his Ministries, since that was a physical impossibility. Nor could the Ministers make their own policy for long without risking Hitler's displeasure. The only way these parts of the mechanism of state could work together efficiently was through a co-ordinating body or War Cabinet, but this Hitler refused to have. Even if a Cabinet could be relied on to take his orders on all occasions, it sounded too much like democratic practice. A committee or War Cabinet, if it met too often, might turn into a Parliament. And so the Reich Defence Committee existed only in name. Co-ordination in defence could result only from privately engineered personal agreements.

So too with Himmler. He could not personally attend to the daily business of the SS, which was scattered in twelve separate office buildings in Berlin and its suburbs, some of them as far away as Oranienburg and Lichterfelde. He could not attend to the six vast departments of RSHA, as well as the staff and leadership offices of the Waffen SS, the Economic Administration Office WVHA, the RUSHA and VOMI offices, the Office for the Strengthening of German Nationhood, the regular police, the lunatic fringe offices Ahnenerbe and Lebensborn, the Mattoni mineral water factory, the Allach porcelain works and the publishing firm Nordland Verlag. But he would have nothing so simple as a committee of chiefs. They might get together to oppose him; they might denounce him to the Fuehrer. When Oswald Pohl suggested that a representative of each office might be included on Himmler's personal staff, he answered with a sly smile, 'I think we will leave it as it is. Let each one work on his own and no groups can then be formed'. Oswald Pohl added that he had never seen two heads of main departments in Himmler's office at the same time.[1]

Himmler had to get his information from his adjutants, who formed a sort of court, and here too the practice was based on that of Hitler's. As Felix Kersten puts it, 'The adjutants played a specially curious role in the National Socialist state. When they got together, they could almost run the Third Reich'.[2]

Himmler's general adjutant for all departments was Rudi Brandt, a perfect secretary, intent only that everything his master said was passed on, a sort of feebler Martin Bormann. At the time of the blood-purge of June 1934 Rudi Brandt had been Himmler's typist, a youth of twenty-five. By August 1943 he was Personal Referent to the Reichsfuehrer SS and 'Head of the Minister's Office in the Ministry for Interior', with the SS rank of lieutenant-general. He was the commissioner who was entrusted by Himmler with everything that was most secret, a man who might arrive in your office with an order to kill all albino babies or perhaps the warrant for your own arrest. Yet when he was tried for his life in 1947, in the jovial company of murderous experimenting doctors, Rudi Brandt still looked like Himmler's typist, absurdly doe-eyed and baby-faced and blinking through huge spectacles.

In condemning Brandt to death the court took account of his lack of personal initiative, but remarked that no Himmler could exist without a Brandt to see his orders carried out. Himmler was lucky to find him, for Brandt was the ideal product of the Hitler state, offering no criticisms, passing no judgments, seeing to the best of his ability that a dictatorship remained strictly a dictatorship. But Brandt was far from typical of the men on whom Himmler depended. A survey of the SS leaders produces an impression, not of ruthlessness nor of sadism but of amateurishness. The type figures are Karl Wolff, Gottlob Berger, Werner Lorenz and Walter Schellenberg, muddled men, not without repulsion for their task, more typical than the coldly brutal Heinrich Mueller and Oswald Pohl or the savagely brutal Reinhard Heydrich and Ernst Kaltenbrunner. They are slightly cranks and slightly misfits, ambitious, idealist in a perverted sense, and not efficient. Alfred Rosenberg, who spoke from some experience, summed it up in his death cell memoirs as

[1] Case IV, transcript, p. 1273: Evidence of Oswald Pohl.
[2] *Totenkopf und Treue*, p. 119.

follows:[1] 'When I saw the queer people who were among Himmler's protégés, I remembered the crackpots who between 1920 and 1923 had appeared on the political scene in Munich only to disappear again'.

Himmler was from the first aware of the lack of competent professional men in the big bureaucracy which grew up behind his army of strong-muscled uncritical Lieder-singing youths. He tried constantly to recruit intellectuals, but in the main he was not successful with them. His economic experts, the professors Hoehn and Six and even the economist Otto Ohlendorf, a willing mass-murderer, tried to contract out of their assignments, since the fate of the intellectuals in the SS bureaucracy was not a happy one. The jack-booted office heads regarded these men as spies—and not without reason, since even Himmler preferred the confidential reports of genuine professionals to the stuff sent him by his own officials.

As we have seen, in October 1939 Himmler became omnipotent in all matters concerning racial selection and resettlement.[2] After a few months he began to mistrust the statistical returns sent him by the RKFDV, RUSHA and VOMI departments, and in July 1940 he was on the look-out for a professional actuary with experience in population returns. In 1927, when Himmler was still a poultry farmer in Waldtrudering, an essay had appeared in a Bavarian periodical on population shrinkage and its causes. Although the author, Dr. Richard Korherr, wrote from a Roman Catholic stand-point, the article had impressed Himmler so much that in 1935 he had republished it himself with his own introduction. And so at the end of 1940 Korherr left a post in the local government administration in Wuerzburg to become 'Inspector for Statistics to the Reichs-fuehrer SS'. Working outside the SS and reporting direct to Himmler's personal office, he soon came up against the higher SS Fuehrers. Korherr discovered that the recruitment figures of the Waffen SS had been falsified by the SS leadership office, while the RUSHA and VOMI offices had exaggerated the figures of racial resettlement and 'Germanisation'. Korherr's criticisms did not end there. He commented adversely on the distribution of field decorations to the desk-borne bureaucrats of the General SS, on a project of Himmler's own for bigamous SS marriages and on a Munich art exhibition in homage to German motherhood. He wrote to Himmler that he could create three new field divisions from the office staffs of the SS

[1] Rosenberg, *Memoirs*, p. 187.   [2] See *supra*, pp. 127-8.

without in the least diminishing their efficiency. He even went out of his way to tell him that there was evidence that his favourite Nordic hero, King Henry the Lion, had black hair and dark eyes. As a result Himmler was bombarded with demands from his office chiefs for the internment of Dr. Korherr in a concentration camp. By this time Himmler had little cause to love his statistician, but, like Ohlendorf, whom he disliked still more, he protected him on account of the fear that his office chiefs might obtain absolute power without some countercheck.[1]

Matters came to a head in August 1943 when Dr. Korherr was summoned to the office of Richard Hildebrandt, the head of RUSHA, and severely manhandled in the presence of several SS Fuehrers who were prepared to use their pistols in the event of any resistance. Fortunately for Dr. Korherr, he had already arranged to evacuate his office, a modest one, from Berlin to his home town of Regensburg. From a room in the Tiergarten palace he continued to write letters, demanding satisfaction for his injuries and begging Himmler to dismiss him. It was not till January 1944 that Korherr obtained an interview with Himmler at Birkenwald, his East Prussian 'field headquarters'. Himmler apologised for the manhandling of Dr. Korherr but exacted silence henceforward on this subject. He agreed, however, to transform the 'Statistical Inspectorate of the Reichsfuehrer SS' into a purely academic 'Statistical Scientific Institute', where Korherr was enabled to study the Downfall of Ancient Civilisations till Regensburg itself fell into the hands of the American forces. Thus, having been thrust into the most unpleasant of assignments, Dr. Korherr survived the hazards of Hitler's Reich, a living tribute to the innate toughness of the academic mind. But his troubles did not end with the war. One of his statistical reports[2] had been concerned with the numbers of Jews who had died, emigrated, or suffered deportation 'to the East'—that is to say, had been murdered—till the beginning of 1943. The report fell into the hands of the Nuremberg prosecution, but a letter from Himmler to Kaltenbrunner showed clearly that the reason for incorporating the RSHA figures in the work of a reputable statistician had been 'concealment'. Dr. Korherr himself, now happily denazified and employed by the West German Finance Ministry, claims that he was never

[1] See *supra*, p. 182.
[2] Nuremberg Documents NO. 5192-4, not available in print, but see Reitlinger, op. cit., pp. 490-1.

permitted to know the truly murderous significance of his own balance-sheet.[1]

Dr. Korherr's description of life with the SS office-holders, their animosities and protections and their internecine vendettas, conveys no impression of efficiency, yet this was the 'state within a state' that had been built up since the blood-purge of 1934. Himmler and the SS Fuehrers could hardly have been any more efficient than this in their alleged domination over the legitimate organs of government. Could such a nest of scheming rowdies truly have controlled so many sources of power and encroached on so many competences? If the SS was able either to control or encroach, it was only through the latent threat of the Gestapo's powers of arrest. These the SS seldom used, however, except on the helpless and the pre-condemned. Apart from this background threat of Gestapo arrest, Himmler's SS offices only encroached on ministerial competence in the way that every German ministry encroached on every other. Their alleged terrorisation by the SS, the alibi of so many Nuremberg defendants, had been no more than a symptom of the overlapping of functions and the absence of clearly defined boundaries, which were the deliberately created weaknesses by which Hitler hoped to govern.

Himmler knew the undefined boundaries and how to exploit them. He was often skilful and cunning. Witness his successful efforts in 1942-3 to obtain control of research and production in V-weapons. General Dornberger's picture of the Himmler whom he met in this capacity is far different from Kersten's picture of his amiable lunatic patient.[2] But why should Himmler or the SS control such matters at all? And what help was it to Germany's war to push men out of their jobs simply to gain another office for the SS? Once more Rosenberg finds the right description for these activities.[3]

Whether it might be publishing houses, art institutes, medical journals, popular quizzes, the manufacture of porcelain, concentration camps, the planting of Kok Sagys (rubber roots), or the strengthening of the SS, all this was merely, as I put it later, a collecting of points to prevent others doing their duty and eventually to take their jobs.

So in the fleeting wartime years Himmler bored away at trifles, figuring very little in the wars of the *Diadochi*, the struggle for precedence between Goebbels, Goering, Bormann, Lammers, Speer

---

[1] For the experiences of Dr. Korherr I am indebted to a memoir which he kindly compiled for me in 1955.

[2] See *supra*, p. 21.   [3] Rosenberg, op. cit., p. 186.

and Ley; fighting, it would almost seem, a losing battle until Stauffenberg's bomb blew all the trump cards in the pack into his hands—
but even then Himmler did not know how to use them, and in any
case the value of the stakes in the game had been destroyed.

In June 1942, when Himmler took over RSHA, he acquired
tremendous advantages in the struggle for power. Not only was
Heydrich disposed of, but the powers over criminal law which
Himmler had desired for himself and for Heydrich at the time of
Guertner's death, were almost in his hands. Yet the personal influence at work behind Hitler's abrogation of German law in April
1942 had been not Himmler at all but Goebbels, who recorded it
proudly in his diary without a thought of the weapon he might be
giving to two men who had once sought his own life.[1] During a
visit to Rastenburg on 19 March Goebbels had begged Hitler to
get rid of Schlegelberger, his acting Minister of Justice, who always
stuck to the letter of the law, and to appoint the 'People's Court'
judge, Otto Thierack, to be permanent Reich Minister of Justice.
Through Thierack's offices and a special Enabling Act passed by the
Reichstag, Hitler, so Goebbels explained, could imprison or execute
without trial officers or officials who failed to do their duty. Hitler
was enchanted with the idea, which was not the first of this sort to
come from Goebbels, who in Himmler's opinion had persuaded
Hitler to use the SS for the extermination of the Jews and so put
the blame on himself.[2]

Schlegelberger now tried to save his miserable office and succeeded
in doing so for another five months. On 10 March, with the aid of
Hans Lammers of the Reich Chancellery, he drafted a decree em-
powering the public prosecutor to intervene and quash the verdicts
in cases of special importance to the national community. Hitler
signed it with Lammers's amendments on the 21st, but Lammers
and Bormann, the two monumental pillars of despotism, added
their weight to Goebbels's arguments and Hitler agreed to address
the Reichstag on 26 April.[3] The wording of the resolution, which
the Reichstag approved unanimously without debate, was almost
precisely that used by Goebbels as recorded in his diary on 19
March.[4]

---

[1] *The Goebbels Diary*, p. 90.
[2] *Memoirs of Felix Kersten*, p. 168; *Totenkopf und Treue*, p. 199.
[3] Case XI, transcript, 28475.
[4] Nuremberg Document PS 1961; IMT III, p. 35.

The SS at the time of the Munich *putsch*, 1923.

Himmler with Roehm (centre), 1934.

HEINRICH HIMMLER IN 1930

Left to right: General von Leeb, General von Fritsch, Himmler, General von Blomberg, Secretary of State Koerner, Admiral Raeder, General von Rundstedt, 1935.

Left to right: Heydrich, Himmler, Frank, Best, Daluege, Helldorf.

Above, Sepp Dietrich.

Right, Reinhard Heydrich.

GENERAL VON BLOMBERG   GENERAL WILHELM KEITEL

GENERAL BLASKOWICZ

GENERAL VON REICHENAU

ERNST KALTENBRUNNER

GOTTLOB BERGER

OTTO SKORZENY

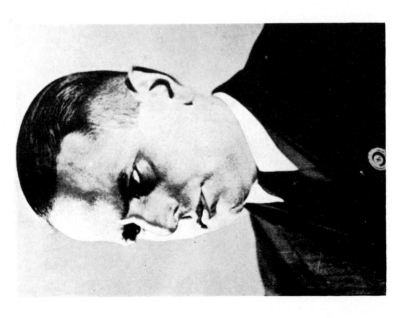

OTTO OHLENDORF

PROFESSOR JOHANNES POPITZ

KARL GOERDELER

Above, below and on facing page, a massacre of Jews in Russia or Poland
(see pages 184-5).

Above, deported Jews arriving at Auschwitz siding. Below, the deportees, sorted into two files; on the right, for work; on the left, for the gas chamber. A German doctor (carrying a stick), makes the selection.

Goering examining damage at Rastenburg after the 20 July bomb plot.

KARL WOLFF

HEINRICH MUELLER
(extreme right, front row) head of the Gestapo 1935-45.

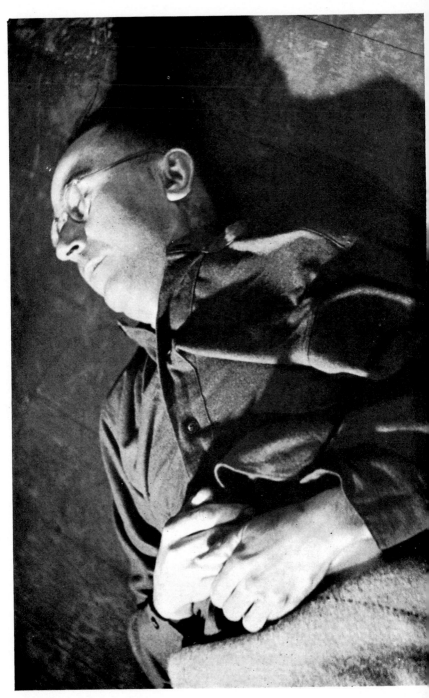

The body of Heinrich Himmler.

Goebbels had recommended making one severe example and Hitler with appropriate malice chose a lawyer. Dr. Carl Lasch, the first president of the German Academy of Law, had been made by Hans Frank, who was his friend and protector, Governor of the Lwow Commissariat in the General Government. He had been arrested at the beginning of the year 1942 on charges of embezzlement and thefts of works of art. In June he was delivered to the Gestapo at Breslau, where he was shot without trial.

Frank engineered an effective protest. He asked Hitler's permission to make a speech in praise of the German legal system. He then used his position as Reichskommissar for Law to give a course of lectures at German universities, advocating a return to the constitution.[1] Retribution, however, was rather slow in coming, for Hitler did not remove Frank and Schlegelberger from their legal offices till 20 August. And Frank was allowed to stay on as governor-general in Poland because Hitler regarded this as the most unpleasant task he could give anyone.

Thierack was made Minister of Justice at last and yet the reign of terror, long threatened by Dr. Goebbels for German officials, never came into being, for in fact the case of Governor Lasch was unique. No German civil servant or officer was executed without trial even during the proscription which followed the July 1944 plot. Within a few weeks of Dr. Lasch's execution, the 'Rote Kapelle' conspiracy came to light, implicating a half-dozen German civil servants and wartime bureaucrats in high treason, but not one of them was summarily executed under Hitler's special powers in spite of a great number of death sentences. Even Himmler never used Hitler's enabling decree to get rid of any of his own bêtes noires. To be sure, the shadow of protective custody continued to hang over the bureaucratic small fry, as it had done since 1933, but rarely had a big man anything to fear from it. The only state secretary to become the subject of a protective custody order was Martin Luther of the Foreign Office, and Himmler would certainly have saved this useful SS agent if he had been less afraid of Ribbentrop's influence with Hitler.[2]

The appointment of Otto Thierack served Himmler in a different fashion. Thierack's brief from Hitler of 20 August 1942 empowered him to deviate from any existing law in order to establish a 'National

---

[1] *Von Hassell Diaries*, pp. 219, 235; IMT XII, p. 117; evidence of Hans Frank.
[2] See *infra*, p. 235.

Socialist administration of justice'.[1] But it was to be a National Socialist justice for foreigners. Goebbels saw Thierack on 14 September and suggested to him that quite a large range of people, in addition to Jews and gipsies, to whom this treatment had been applied for the past year, could be 'exterminated by work'.[2]

It may seem incredible that any person calling himself a Minister of Justice should have worked (and worked hard) to make such a proposal legally practicable. Thierack unfortunately was able to commit suicide in Nuremberg prison in 1946 before the trial of the German judges, so we shall not have his explanation. These things, however, happened in the mid-twentieth century, not an age of exceptional frivolity but, as we are sometimes reminded, the century of the common man.

With the approval of Martin Bormann, Thierack and his state secretary Rothenberger flew, four days after this meeting with Goebbels, to Himmler's field command post at Zhitomir, where they interviewed Himmler in the presence of Bruno Streckenbach, the Deputy Chief of RSHA, and of Lieutenant-Colonel Bender, the Waffen SS Judge Advocate.[3] The agreement, which took, according to Thierack's minutes, five hours and a half to reach, was entitled 'The Delivery of A-social Elements to the Reichsfuehrer SS to be Worked to Death'.

Goebbels had suggested to Thierack that extermination by working to death should be applied to all Jews and gipsies, to Poles serving sentences of three years' imprisonment and more and to Czechs and Germans serving life sentences. Himmler improved on this, and in Thierack's new draft the candidates for working to death included all Germans, serving sentences of eight years and over, and all persons who were already in protective custody. In his letter to Bormann, Thierack commented that the administration of justice could only make a small contribution to the extermination of members of these peoples, and that no useful purpose could be served in keeping them for years on end in German prisons. The best way was to surrender them to the police 'who can take the necessary measures unhampered by any legal criminal evidence'.[4]

The terms of the outrageous and insane agreement were carried out and they affected all conscripted Eastern workers who were

[1] Law Reports of Trials of War Criminals, VI, p. 7.
[2] IMT IV, p. 389; Document PS 682.   [3] IMT III, p. 43; PS 654.
[4] Nuremberg Document NG 558, Case III.

employed in the greater Reich, including the newly incorporated parts of Poland, but there was never any written decree. On 4 December Streckenbach circularised the higher SS police leaders, who were told to inform the Gauleiters of their procedure in the usual way.[1] Before the end of the year there was a mass commitment of Eastern workers to the concentration camps, roped in under any conceivable pretence by the new 'simplified procedure'.[2] The appalling powers invested in Thierack and Himmler had been brought to bear not on suspected Resistance leaders or Communist agents, not on dissidents in the High Command, nor on Himmler's critics, but on the submerged millions of the disfranchised and dispossessed, over whom alone Himmler exercised the authority of a state within a state.

Some questions remain to be answered. Why did the suggestion for extermination by working to death come from Goebbels in the first place and not from Himmler? Why did Bormann, whom Goebbels hated at this period, prove so accommodating to his plans? It may be inferred that both were seeking Himmler's favour and this was an inexpensive way of getting it. In September 1942 Goering had lost much of his ascendancy at court, and it was generally believed that Himmler was next in the succession to Hitler. But the decline of Goering was not yet so catastrophic as it became after the Luftwaffe's failure to supply Stalingrad. For instance, in November Goering succeeded in retaining as his own private army the new infantry divisions, formed from the huge redundant ground staffs of the now largely inactive bomber command. According to General Walter Warlimont, who handled recruiting and man-power questions at OKW headquarters, Goering still interfered with everything at this period without scruple or responsibility.[3] Goebbels could not achieve his ambition to become a war lord, handling great masses of men, simply by ganging with Himmler against Bormann. He must take Goering into account and if possible revive the old Goering-Himmler alliance.

Goebbels's plan was to re-create the 'Ministerial Council for the Defence of the Reich', the name of a War Cabinet which had been planned at the beginning of the Polish campaign. The council had not met for a very long time, because Goering could not get on with the smug old-time bureaucratic figure of Hans Lammers. At

---

[1] Nuremberg Document L 32; IMT III, p. 44.   [2] See *infra*, p. 263.
[3] Shulman, op. cit., p. 86.

Goebbels's own suggestion Hitler had replaced the Ministerial Council with a committee of three. But Goebbels had failed to get on the committee himself and the 'Three Wise Men' now consisted of Keitel, Lammers and Bormann. Since these Three Wise Men enjoyed their strength only as the literal and authentic mouthpieces of Hitler, they met seldom and took no decisions. It was Goebbels's plan to increase the size of the Committee of Three by the inclusion of himself, Himmler, and Goering, and later by others, so that the original project of an Inner War Cabinet might be fulfilled.[1]

But Himmler did not like committees at which he could not dictate his wishes or read off three-hour speeches about the Watch on the Ural Mountains and the Orders of Germanic Blood. And he certainly did not like Goebbels's private conversations with Hitler. In the Goebbels diary 'Friendly contacts and understanding with the Reichsfuehrer SS' are not mentioned before November 1943.[2] A year earlier, at the time of Goebbels's conferences with Thierack which were intended to give Himmler so much power, Himmler was no more inclined to welcome friendly contacts with Goering than he was with Goebbels. Since March 1938, when he had changed his mind and fished General von Fritsch out of the clutches of Heydrich and the Gestapo, Goering had been at loggerheads with the SS and it had been believed at one time that he was trying to destroy Heydrich.[3] The death of Heydrich had not drawn Himmler nearer to Goering. It had made Himmler more ambitious and it is possible that from this time dates Himmler's illusion that he was intended to replace Goering in the succession to Hitler. This may explain the failure of an act of placation which Goering reluctantly made towards his former partner in the conspiracy against Roehm and Fritsch.

It may be that Himmler's puritan nature was outraged by the extravagance of Goering's birthday celebrations in January 1942, or that he was jealous of Goering's praises of Sepp Dietrich, but soon afterwards Himmler started probing into the affairs both of Goering's Air Ministry and of Goering's Adjutantur, where the ostentatious living and air of corruption which always accompanied Goering was most prominent. In July 1942 von Hassell learnt that Hitler had stopped Himmler's inquiry in order to avoid public scandal and

---

[1] *The Goebbels Diary*, pp. 202, 236.
[2] *Goebbels Diaries*, p. 354; see *infra*, p. 381.
[3] Von Papen, *Memoirs*, p. 433; and see *supra*, p. 74.

that Goering had presented Himmler with a Luftwaffe uniform with flyer's wings to keep him sweet.[1] But the matter did not end there, for within a week or two the far greater scandal of the Rote Kapelle burst under the Air Ministry roof.

2. ROTE KAPELLE AND AFTER, KALTENBRUNNER

Short-wave transmitters supplying information to Russia were the trouble. They had been observed almost as soon as Russia was invaded and had existed long before. The transmissions came from every part of occupied Europe and even from Berlin. When the Abwehr had established that the transmissions were co-ordinated and were distinct from the Polish Resistance transmissions, they invented the words 'musicians' to describe the operators and 'red orchestra' or Rote Kapelle to describe the organisation.[2] By the spring of 1942 a hundred transmitters had been observed. One transmission from Brussels had been traced to its source in December 1941, and as a result a Russian-parachuted army officer was arrested together with his contact, a refugee Jewess. Through the latter there were revealed the broad outlines of a network which was directed by two persons known as 'Grand Chef' and 'Petit Chef'.[3] In May 1942 a second Brussels transmitter was traced. It led to the arrest of Wilhelm Schwarz, a German Communist from Koenigsberg who had emigrated to Russia in 1934. Among the addresses in code which were found on Schwarz was that of Harro Schulze-Boysen, a lieutenant in the Luftwaffe and a member of one of Goering's cherished departments, his own Intelligence Service, known as the Luftwaffe Research Office, which had a monopoly in tapping telephones.

Here the matter went very deep indeed. Schulze-Boysen had got into the Research Office through family influence. His wife, Libertas Haas-Heye, was the daughter of Countess Eulenberg, a friend of Goering's. Schulze-Boysen himself came from the same circles and was the grandson of Admiral Tirpitz. In 1931 he had started an extremely left-wing paper called *Der Gegner*. He had gone round in a black sweater and a mop of gold hair, concerting with surrealists and artistic revolutionaries and generally behaving like a displaced

---

[1] *Von Hassell Diary*, p. 235.
[2] Manfred Roeder, *Rote Kapelle* (Hamburg, 1952), p. 8.
[3] Paul Leverkuehn, *The German Secret Service*, p. 178.

boy scout.[1] In 1933 he was rescued from the clutches of the SA while they were torturing him in a cellar. Later, when Schulze-Boysen tried to get into the Luftwaffe, his past pursued him. But at the outbreak of war Goering accepted him in the Civil Aviation Ministry, from which he gravitated to the Research Office through the attaché section of the Luftwaffe.[2]

It might have been the background of a quite harmless drawing-room Red, but the Rote Kapelle yielded other clues and they all led to Schulze-Boysen. He had contacts with the Abwehr, who warned him, and he kept away from the office, but in August 1942 he was picked up and with him over a hundred people were held for trial.

Schulze-Boysen's name lifted the conspiracy from the ordinary international ragtag and bobtail of espionage into the ranks of Prussian Junker aristocracy, and into the defeatist Berlin intelligentsia, which even at the best of times drew out the class-conscious paranoiac in Adolf Hitler. Had the Abwehr only landed in their nets Russian parachutists, German Communist emigrés, cabaret artistes and paid agents from the criminal underworld, it is possible that no one would have bothered to tell Hitler. But as the clues closed in round Schulze-Boysen and his circle, opportunities arose to pay off old scores. The affair of Burgess and Maclean will give some idea what capital can be made when someone with a leftish record enters and betrays a position of trust. The emotions roused are out of all proportion to the things that have been betrayed. Canaris declared that the conspiracy had cost the lives of 200,000 German soldiers. His nose was not of the best and he read in 'Rote Kapelle' the hand of the 'Brown Bolshevik', Martin Bormann, in whose fishlike nature he saw the Professor Moriarty of crime.[3]

Canaris's reaction was shared by most of the Resistance Circle who were still a long way from Stauffenberg's disastrous wooing of the German Communists. Von Hassell's diary, for instance, dismisses the Rote Kapelle trials in a few lines. And yet the conspirators had been encouraged by the darkest horse of the Resistance Circle, Albrecht Haushofer. One of Haushofer's pupils, Horst Heilmann, introduced him to Schulze-Boysen and in the spring of 1942 Schulze-Boysen told Haushofer in detail of his plans for nation-wide sabotage

---

[1] Dulles, op. cit., p. 100; *Answers of Ernst von Salomon*, p. 300.
[2] Roeder, *Rote Kapelle* (Hamburg, 1952), p. 12.
[3] Roeder, op. cit., p. 27; Leverkuehn, *The German Secret Service*, p. 197.

by independently acting cells. Haushofer thought that the force of this example might stimulate the hesitating Resistance generals, but he was frightened of it and kept his knowledge secret.[1]

The extent of Schulze-Boysen's influence was astonishing. Bormann's Party Chancellery, which had been picked on by Canaris, was perhaps the only Ministry not to be involved in the network. Schulze-Boysen worked in Goering's Air Ministry, but his closest associate was Arvid Harnack, another young man with a revolutionary past who was in the Ministry for Economics. Harnack was employed in the U.S.A. Section of the Ministry because he had studied at Wisconsin University, where he married an American student, Mildred Fish. Harnack had had years of official contacts with the Soviet Trade Delegation in Berlin. Then there were the contributions to Rote Kapelle from the Foreign Office—Franz Scheliha, who had been a Legation Counsellor in Warsaw and who sold information to pay his debts, and Horst Heilmann of the Foreign Broadcasts Monitoring Service, which Goebbels had suspected since the beginning of the year. In the Ministry for Labour there was Countess Brockdorff and Frau Schumacher.

The detection of the members of the Rote Kapelle conspiracy was done by Section II of Canaris's Abwehr. It was by no means complete. 'Grand Chef' and 'Petit Chef' were never found and a number of the German conspirators are in office today in the East German People's Republic. Nevertheless, it was the most considerable success the Abwehr ever achieved and one can scarcely fail to notice Canaris's zeal against the Bolsheviks as compared with his consideration for the enemies of Fascism in Italy, whom he imagined to be monarchists. As to the rival Abwehr of Schellenberg and the SD, it could claim no credit, though under the terms of the Canaris-Heydrich accord, as signed in May 1942, the actual arrests had been made by Canaris's Secret Field Police in conjunction with the Gestapo.[2]

Although Mueller and Schellenberg had played a minor part in detecting the conspiracy, Hitler allowed the Gestapo the conduct of the cases, that is to say, the instructions to the judge which are the most important part of German criminal proceedings. These were at first prepared by Mueller's deputy, Lieutenant-Colonel Panzinger, the head of Section A or Internal Affairs Department of the

---

[1] Rainer Hildebrandt, *Wir sind die Letzten* (Berlin, 1947), p. 155.

[2] Roeder, op. cit., p. 8.

Gestapo.[1] But it was not for this that Goering had just given Himmler his flyer's wings. He ran protesting to Hitler and, according to Ribbentrop's death-cell memoir, tried to pin the blame on 'an entirely unimplicated man from the Foreign Office'.[2] Hitler, according to Ribbentrop, was still frightened of Goering. He agreed that a Luftwaffe judge, the Oberstgerichtsrat Manfred Roeder, should be the special commissioner with the Reich court martial.

But in spite of his reputation as a 'bloodhound', Roeder was too lenient for Hitler. Only fifty of the seventy-five defendants were condemned to death. Hitler demanded death sentences for the remainder, mainly the wives of the convicted men, but Roeder dissented[3] and was dismissed from the case. Even in the second trial Mildred Harnack, the American, and Erika von Brockdorff received only prison sentences. These, too, Hitler personally altered to the death penalty. Furthermore, as a mark of special indignity, the sentences were to be carried out not by the axe or guillotine but by hanging, which was not part of the Prussian criminal system. There were neither gallows nor mechanical drop in Ploetzensee prison and the victims were strangled by a rope, hanging from an ordinary hook. It was a precedent for the dreadful Ploetzensee executions which were filmed at Hitler's orders after the July 1944 plot.[4]

To Himmler the greatest mortification had been neither the dismal failure of his immense Gestapo organisation to get in before the Abwehr, nor the bold cavortings under his very nose of high-placed German Communists who were supposed to have been extinguished nine years before. The greatest mortification had been his failure to manage the penal proceedings himself. Only after the July plot, when he had become Minister of the Interior and Chief of the Reserve army, was Himmler in a position to put that right. 'In consequence of the folly of separate courts for civilians, airmen, sailors, soldiers and police I have proposed to the High Command a court of honour which will release the implicated servicemen to the Volksgericht'.[5]

On 4 October 1942, half-way between the two Rote Kapelle sets of trials, Goering delivered a harvest thanksgiving speech before an immense Berlin audience in the Sportpalast. Von Hassell thought

[1] Guenther Weisenborn, *Der lautloses Aufstand* (Hamburg, 1953), p. 204.
[2] *Ribbentrop Memoirs*, p. 49.   [3] Gisevius, op. cit., p. 426.
[4] Weisenborn, op. cit., p. 213.
[5] *Vierteljahreshefte fuer Zeitgeschichte*, No. 4, p. 583.

that Goering's position was unassailable and that the 'black rats of the SS' had retreated into their holes.[1] Yet it was almost Goering's last public oration. He became crushed beneath the weight of the Luftwaffe's failure and retired to his hunting and to his art treasures at Karinhall. In December the Luftwaffe failed miserably to supply beleaguered Stalingrad and the Inspector-General of the Luftwaffe, Ernst Udet, took his own life. In March 1943 Hitler made a tremendous scene with Goering's adjutant, Bodenschatz, in the middle of the night, because Goering was in Rome during the great British air raid on Nuremberg. In the following month Hitler openly abused Goering at his military conference at Winnitsa[2] and by July 1943 Goering was so much in retirement that his suicide was rumoured.

From now on, Goering had only a nuisance value. He still retained a private army, comparable with the Waffen SS, the twenty-two infantry divisions known as the Luftwaffe replacement army, which consisted of the now redundant ground staffs of the former bombing force. It was only at the time of the July 1944 plot that these men were surrendered to the Wehrmacht or to the Waffen SS. On the other hand Goering retained the parachute divisions, mostly parachutists only in name, till the surrender of Germany, thus perpetuating another of those overlapping fields of competence that lost Hitler's war.[3]

Goebbels himself dropped any genuine interest in a Goering alliance against Bormann and the 'three-man board' after March 1943, when he had a squalid row with Goering over his protection of Horscher's black market Berlin restaurant.[4] There were now three men of all the old party leaders who believed themselves capable of directing a total war, classless, rigorous, and unprivileged. They were Himmler, Goebbels and Bormann, but the time for effective action was long past before Goebbels and Himmler succeeded in making a common front against the man whose one aim in life was to ruin everyone else. Partly this was because Himmler mistrusted Goebbels's advances and resented his *tête-à-têtes* with Hitler more than he resented the ante-room dictatorship of Martin Bormann. Partly it was because Himmler gave himself no time for cabals. Obsessed with being a true dictator over his many departments, he took too much work on himself, a great deal of it trivial in relation

[1] *Von Hassell Diary*, p. 242.   [2] *The Goebbels Diary*, pp. 221, 247.
[3] Westphal, op. cit., pp. 90, 92.
[4] Rudolf Sammler, *Goebbels: The Man Next to Hitler* (London, 1947), p. 77.

to the tasks of war besides being horrible. In particular, the Final Solution to the Jewish Problem, the task taken over from the dead Heydrich, spurred him to incredible energy. It is strange that a man who ran the Waffen SS, the entire police, and all the anti-partisan measures in occupied countries, could find time in January 1943 to make a surprise personal visit to Warsaw to find out why the ghetto had not been evacuated,[1] or that he could undertake in July 1942 a mission to Finland in order to demand the deportation of a few hundred more Jews.

This absorption in details, at a time when he was expected to handle broad questions of policy, is characteristic of Himmler. Occasionally the struggle between the rival satraps would reach Hitler's ears and provoke either a scene of fury or a quick trenchant decision. Only momentarily shaken by the intervention of the All-Highest, the satraps quickly resumed their battle. Not so Himmler; his life was dictated by his terror of a carpeting by Hitler. He dared not figure in a scandal involving the highest leadership of the Reich. He would not be a bad example to the docile disciplined German nation at war, so he glued himself to his desk and allowed the cabals to pass over his head. This is perhaps the explanation of his failure to use an opportunity which was sent him in February 1943, as if by Providence, to oust Ribbentrop from the Foreign Office.

By the end of 1942, Martin Luther, head of the much-bloated 'Deutschland' section of the Foreign Office, had turned on his creator. Rudolf Rahn thinks it was a domestic quarrel. Anneliese Ribbentrop, who had first discovered the practical uses of the man who came round with the party subscription list, was tired of entertaining this gross fellow with a Vorstaedter accent.[2] This, however, was probably a secondary cause, for Ribbentrop himself had long had reason to regret the advancement of Martin Luther. The man had ceased to uphold Ribbentrop's position in his 'precedence squabbles' with Himmler and his financial lapses had again been brought to Ribbentrop's attention, this time in connection with the funds of the Personnel Division.[3] Towards Christmas it began to be known in the Foreign Office that Luther had written a long memo-

---

[1] 'I did not know I was going to Warsaw and I did not inform you!' Himmler to Major-General Friedrich Krueger of the SS and police, 14 January 1943; Nuremberg Document NO. 1811; and Reitlinger, op. cit., pp. 272-3.

[2] Rudolf Rahn, *Ruheloses Leben*, p. 142.

[3] Nuremberg Document, Steengracht I, Doc. 6.

randum on Ribbentrop's mental disabilities. A second complication in Luther's life forced him to use the memorandum forthwith. Two private individuals, a bookseller and a lawyer, got a complaint to Ribbentrop that Luther had threatened them with the Gestapo for purposes of blackmail and into this, too, Ribbentrop ordered an inquiry.[1] So Luther sent his memorandum to Schellenberg and in February it reached Himmler. Steengracht von Moyland, who stepped into Weizsaecker's shoes as a result of the Luther scandal, thinks that Karl Wolff passed the memorandum straight on to Ribbentrop, but Rudolf Rahn declares that it actually reached Himmler, who thought of using it. But Wolff told Himmler of Luther's past peculations and Himmler, who disliked the unrespectable even though he failed to recognise them, reluctantly sacrificed his man.[2]

In the web of neo-Byzantine intrigue which surrounded Hitler's court, the disclosures produced paradoxical effects. Because he had been the first to write that Ribbentrop was crazy, the hateful Luther won what Hassell called 'belated sympathy',[3] Ribbentrop, who was forced to overhaul Department Deutschland, raved about replacing the professional Foreign Office staff with 'forty SS men, forty SA men and forty Hitler Youth Leaders', the most certain recipe, it might be said, for creating further Martin Luthers. As to Hitler, he wanted to hang Luther, but at the end of March Ribbentrop persuaded him to send Luther to the Sachsenhausen 'political bunker', the most privileged section of the least lethal of the concentration camps.[4] There Luther was put to work, cultivating medicinal herbs, a concentration-camp activity which was the fruit of Himmler's oldest and least noxious passion. Luther was in the first circle of the damned, which Himmler reserved for recalcitrant bishops and professors, and there Captain Payne-Best saw him in the autumn of 1944, plunged in melancholy after two attempts at suicide and looking eighty years old though in fact forty-eight.[5]

When Captain Payne-Best left Sachsenhausen, he did not know what had happened to Luther and for many years it was believed that Luther had died in the camp, the only State Secretary to meet

[1] Case XI, transcript, 9760-8; evidence of Steengracht.
[2] Rudolf Rahn, op. cit., p. 14. Von Hassell thought that the Gestapo were not interested in Luther but arrested him in order to get more information about Ribbentrop (*Von Hassell*, op. cit., p. 261).   [3] *Von Hassell Diary*, pp. 263, 270.
[4] Case XI, transcript, 9760, evidence Steengracht.   [5] Payne-Best, op. cit., p. 126.

with such a fate. But in 1951 Mr. Paul Seabury discovered Luther's widow, from whom he learnt that Luther was released early in 1945 and sent to hospital, and that he died of heart failure soon after the capitulation.[1]

After the fall of Martin Luther there was a wild general post in the Foreign Office. The leading permanent officials, Weizsaecker, Friedrich Gaus, and Woermann, departed with such ability as they possessed for distant exile. Still more colourless persons, chosen from the old Bureau Ribbentrop, took their place. Luther was replaced by Horst Wagner, an instructor of gymnastics whom Ribbentrop had met at the Olympic Games festival in 1936.[2] Under Wagner the Department Deutschland lost none of its business. The protocol arrangements for the deportation and gassing of the Jews were carried on from a new office, Bureau Inland II, as they had been under Luther. Eberhard von Thadden, a bad representative of a distinguished family, did the work if anything more thoroughly than Franz Rademacher before him, but unlike Franz Rademacher, von Thadden has never had to face a trial.[3]

Ribbentrop did not carry out his threat of filling the Foreign Office with SS and SA men. Only one appointment was made from the SS, Professor Franz Six, who was seconded from the 'Cultural Activities Section' of RSHA to the Cultural Division of the Foreign Office.

When Himmler so lightly passed off the Luther revelations he was an exhausted and overburdened man. The Rote Kapelle trial must have shown him that he could no longer handle in person all the huge organisation of RSHA. It was rumoured in September that Heydrich was to have a successor, either Wilhelm Stuckart or Walter Schellenberg.[4] Probably Himmler thought the former too much of a lawyer, although he liked wearing an SS general's uniform, and the latter too useful for his contacts in neutral countries and in the fight to acquire the Abwehr. In the end Himmler chose someone relatively obscure, Ernst Kaltenbrunner, the higher SS police leader for Vienna.

[1] Seabury, op. cit., p. 196.   [2] *Ibid.*, p. 134.

[3] For the documents relating to von Thadden's relentless activities in pressing on the deportation arrangements for the Jews of Hungary and the occupied countries, see Reitlinger, op. cit., *passim.* Several charges were brought against him after the Nuremberg trials at the instance of German courts, and in June 1952 he was arrested by order of the Cologne Schwurgericht. I can find no evidence that these charges have been proceeded with.

[4] *Von Hassell Diary,* p. 252.

The choice is inexplicable. If Himmler needed an administrator to relieve him of his own burdens, Kaltenbrunner, during his five years in office, had given no proofs of capacity. If he needed a yes-man like Rudi Brandt, he could not expect to find one in this low intriguer, an excitable, self-indulgent, deceitful and slightly daft Austrian, a man with a scar-face and criminal's ears. It may be that Himmler chose Kaltenbrunner just because he knew him so little, but it is even more likely that he did so because Kaltenbrunner, who had scarcely left Vienna since the Anschluss, knew no one 'in the office'. Whether Himmler intended this deliberately or not, the position of Kaltenbrunner as a stranger proved very uncomfortable. He had to supervise six office chiefs, each of whom had reported to Himmler for the past eight months separately and in secret. Kalten-brunner told Otto Skorzeny that Mueller and Schellenberg persist-ently side-tracked him;[1] that Mueller and Nebe both did what they liked but pinned on him the responsibility for what they did. One thing at least the newcomer shared with them all and that was a profound conviction that after Stalingrad the war was already lost. Like Kaltenbrunner, the RSHA chiefs believed that the SS, as dis-posers of an army within an army, held the only cards for bargaining with the Allies, Eastern or Western.

Kaltenbrunner was tried at Nuremberg and hanged in October 1946 for the exterminations and murders carried out by the Gestapo and SD. The man seems to have signed everything, though he did not always recognise his own signature, but, as an amateurish lawyer and professional conspirator, Kaltenbrunner's real interests lay, like Heydrich's, in military intelligence and counter-espionage. He started in office on 30 January 1943 with the firm intention of acquiring the overgrown and largely hamstrung Abwehr organisation of Admiral Canaris. Three weeks later Kaltenbrunner had a hostile personal interview with Canaris in Munich. Canaris's nerves were upset by Kaltenbrunner's cold-blooded conversation, his figure like an Alpine tree-feller and his 'murderer's paws'.[2] But Canaris won the round. Himmler warned Kaltenbrunner that he would not tolerate any inter-ference in the Abwehr. So Kaltenbrunner told Willi Hoettl, one of his few office friends, that Himmler was being blackmailed by Canaris and Hoettl, like a faithful Gestapist, ferreted out the story of Heydrich's Jewish blood and how Himmler had tried to cover it up.[3]

[1] Walter Hagen, *Die Geheime Front*, pp. 84-5. [2] Abshagen, op. cit., p. 354.
[3] Hagen, op. cit., p. 111; and see *supra*, p. 34.

But in order to keep out of the clutches of Kaltenbrunner and Mueller, there was no need for Canaris to blackmail Himmler. Canaris in Himmler's view was better where he was, because, *au fond*, they were two men pursuing the same aims. Like Himmler's discreet inquiries in the same direction, Canaris's leakages of information had been directed towards avoiding a conflict with the Western powers and, when the Western powers were out of the ring, to avoiding a war on two fronts. Not even the wildest exponents of the Canaris legend have suggested that he ever sent information to Poland or Russia. Canaris may have looked the other way when members of the Abwehr supplied Stauffenberg with bombs, but he had nothing to do with Stauffenberg's latter-day Resistance Circle who wanted *rapprochement* with Russia. The Russian Press hailed the conspirators of 20 July 1944 as martyrs, but the Western Press rejoiced in the undoubted fact that there were now several German generals the less, even if Hitler had not been killed. In view of this contrast, it is illuminating to read the sour comments of the Russian Nuremberg prosecution after Canaris had been built up into a hero in the evidence of Lahousen and Hans Gisevius. The Russians knew Canaris as an implacable anti-Bolshevik and so did Himmler.

After 18 February 1944, when Kaltenbrunner achieved his ambition and the Abwehr had become a branch of his RSHA office, Kaltenbrunner stepped into Canaris's shoes as a persistent seeker of contacts with the West. Sometimes he would contrive to work in with Schellenberg, sometimes he would employ his Austrian protégé, Willi Hoettl, who had contacts with Mr. Allen Dulles; but even in this game, in which Kaltenbrunner's purposes were identical with Himmler's, he was at loggerheads with him and in one case deliberately wrecked Himmler's negotiations in order to start one of his own.[1] The antagonism dated from the very beginning, when Kaltenbrunner discovered his own subordinates' secret access to Himmler. Kaltenbrunner's handling of Himmler seems to have been very stupid, but then he was, even for a leader of the Austrian Anschluss movement, an exceptionally stupid and brutal man.

Kaltenbrunner made his first appearance at Himmler's court at Zhitomir in February 1943, together with a second important stranger. This was the newly appointed director of cavalry remounts in the SS Leadership Office, the then Major-General Hermann Fegelein. This Fegelein was a little jockey of a man, who at the time of the

[1] See *infra*, p. 417.

seizure of power had been a show-rider in Munich, where he had made friends with another former jockey, the publican Christian Weber, who had been one of the founders of the Stosstruppe or original SS. Through Weber Fegelein met Himmler and also Sepp Dietrich, who took him into the first Leibstandarte. Soon after the seizure of power Fegelein founded a riding school for the SS. In 1941 he led an SS cavalry brigade on the Moscow front and in the following year a cavalry division, the 8th SS or 'Florian Geyer', which reached the Caucasus and earned him the Knight's Cross.[1]

When Fegelein obtained the staff appointment which kept him at court, he had had the good sense to marry Grettl Braun, the sister of Hitler's inconspicuous mistress, Eva Braun. It may be that Fegelein's later career provides the only case of this lady's playing the Frau Pompadour of the Third Reich, or it may have been just happy coincidence. At any rate, in this month of February 1943 when Fegelein and Kaltenbrunner took up their new functions, it happened that Karl Wolff, Himmler's liaison officer with the Fuehrer, fell ill and that a long if not permanent absence was ensured when he went to Karl Gebhardt for an operation for cancer of the kidneys. It seems that Himmler's chief of the Adjutantur had collapsed because he had had to fit his hours of duty to suit the habits both of Hitler, who went to bed in the early morning, and of Himmler who started work at about the same time.[2] In April, when it seemed that Wolff would not recover quickly in the hands of Karl Gebhardt, Hitler persuaded Himmler to appoint Fegelein temporarily in his place and the appointment was made permanent in September when Wolff was transferred to Italy.

The replacement of Wolff by Fegelein marked an important change in the character of Himmler's court. Wolff was a relic of the days when the SS was considered the respectable section of the party, suitable for the sons of princes. Wolff himself had been an adjutant of Ritter von Epp and Himmler respected him as a man of the world who understood etiquette. Wolff was the very reverse in appearance of the typical higher SS leaders with their bullet heads and well brushed back hair, their powerful build and insolent demeanour. Wolff's face was sick, sensitive and aristocratic with a huge hooked nose; his body was long and ungainly and engaged in a permanent struggle with his general's uniform, if the photographs

[1] Kraetschmer, op. cit., p. 89.
[2] François Bayle, *Psychologie et ethique du national-socialisme*, p. 265.

of SS public occasions are a true guide. Wolff possessed sufficient exhibitionism to desire an SS Fuehrer's uniform, an exhibitionism which has caused him to appear as a defence witness at numerous postwar trials of SS men. But he was also a confirmed leg-puller who liked telling malicious stories which were by no means welcome with the elderly schoolboys and night-club thugs who combined to run the SS state. Fegelein, on the other hand, had spent his life making up to everybody and had a gift for warming the vitals of the most cheerless personalities at court. Kersten thinks that Kaltenbrunner was so quick to cultivate Fegelein because he wanted to obtain access to the kittenish charms of Eva Braun,[1] but it was really just common sense. Till the advent of a rival in the person of Hitler's last military adjutant, Wilhelm Burgdorf, Fegelein had the advantage of being the only person who could be jolly in the company of the quite inhuman Martin Bormann. In April 1943 Bormann had reached the zenith of his power,[2] having made a War Cabinet impossible two months earlier by inveigling himself on to the 'three-man board'. It was in April, too, that Bormann became Hitler's special personal secretary and the man who held all the tricks. Through Bormann, who was at least friendly enough with Kaltenbrunner not to try to ruin him, Kaltenbrunner could by-pass Himmler in his approaches to Hitler. Soon Kaltenbrunner made Himmler's position as uncomfortable as it had been when his post was occupied by Heydrich.

3. HIMMLER AND THE FALL OF MUSSOLINI

Himmler's next advancement, his long-delayed appointment as Minister of the Interior to succeed Frick, was certainly hurried by the arrest of Mussolini and the impact of this event on Hitler. Ever since his state visit to Rome in May 1938 Hitler had come to rely on Himmler for missions to Mussolini. Himmler had used his eloquence on Mussolini in December 1939 when the dictator still hesitated to come into the war. Himmler's visit undid some of the harm caused by the mission of Robert Ley of the Labour Front, who had got drunk in public.[3] Himmler was not a bad choice for such embassies since he never offended anybody, a gift made all the more valuable by the fact that no one wanted to offend Himmler.

[1] *Memoirs of Felix Kersten*, p. 200.
[2] *The Bormann Letters*, p. 150. For the 'three-man board', see *supra*, pp. 228, 233.
[3] *Count Ciano's Diary*, English edition, p. 187.

On 10 October 1942 Himmler paid Mussolini a second visit, the purpose of which is obscure though it had been planned as early as May.[1] Mussolini, who was not looking forward to it, told Count Ciano that he was going to read Himmler a lecture on German behaviour in occupied territories. It is not recorded whether Mussolini did so, but after the interview Himmler pumped Ciano about the Italian Monarchy and the Vatican.[2]

Probably Himmler learnt more about these matters from his own agents in Rome. In 1941, when German troops began to use Italy as a base for North Africa, Heydrich had been allowed to appoint a Security Police Commander in Rome, a typical Gestapo man ready to do anything. He was Colonel Hubert Kappler, who was destined to carry out the sickening Ardeatine Tunnels massacre of March 1944. Kappler was expected to be an Intelligence Office as well as a butcher, since this was the normal combination under Heydrich's system. But Hitler forbade the use of secret agents on the friendly soil of Italy and the two Abwehrs, Canaris's and Schellenberg's, were only allowed to seek information through their Italian opposite numbers. Such co-operation was obviously beyond the capacity of a Gestapo bully, even though Hoettl describes his colleague Kappler as 'an intelligent Swabian'.[3] Partly for this reason and partly to be free of Heydrich's interference, Himmler appointed his own police attaché to the Rome embassy, choosing a man who should be acceptable at all three Roman courts. It is not clear how Captain Eugen Dollmann, another of Himmler's intellectuals, was attracted into the SS. He was an art historian who had been brought up in Rome and who spoke fluent Italian. Besides having an *entrée* into the best houses, he was tolerated by Mussolini and friendly with Count Ciano. Dollmann may have been, as Hoettl says, a 'drawing-room hero', but he had his nose well to the ground and he was perfectly placed to keep Himmler informed of the rumours that blew through the Roman warren of defeatism and discontent.[4] But if Himmler learnt much of this during his visit of October 1942, he did not show it. To Felix Kersten, whom he saw a week later, Himmler reserved his indignation for twenty robust Germans whom he had observed in Rome, wearing the red robes of the German Collegium.[5]

---

[1] *Count Ciano's Diary*, p. 471.   [2] *Ibid.*, pp. 508, 510.

[3] W. Hoettl, *Hitler's Paper Weapon* (London, 1955), p. 62.

[4] W. Hoettl, *The Secret Front*, p. 228.   [5] Kersten, *Totenkopf und Treue*, p. 194.

These journeys to Italy may have appealed to Himmler as much as Count Ciano thought they did, but they never failed to stimulate his distrust of an ally, who had delayed Hitler's Anschluss plans for four years and whose ridiculous Abyssinian victories had been mocked in *Das Schwarze Korps*. Himmler did not share Hitler's touching faith in Mussolini. He made a study of him. On the day following Mussolini's arrest, Otto Skorzeny heard Himmler rattle off a lot of secret police information on Italian leaders and their affiliations as if he had the whole thing at his finger-tips. Himmler knew of the negotiations, conducted by Badoglio with the Allies in Portugal, and he was certain of Italy's defection.[1] Hitler too must have got this information from Himmler on the morning of 25 July 1943, when he most astutely observed that the calling of the Fascist Grand Council by Farinacci had put Mussolini in great danger.[2] Even Goebbels had no such information, and he reacted, to judge from Wilfrid von Ovens' description, like a German governess who has discovered an apple-pie bed.[3]

Himmler was informed through Eugen Dollmann and perhaps to some extent through Schellenberg's agent, Willi Hoettl. But by contrast the Foreign Office and the military Abwehr were grossly incompetent. Ribbentrop, for instance, instructed Ambassador Rahn to demand Badoglio's arrest and Mussolini's liberation, unaware that there were absolutely no German troops in Rome.[4] Canaris's actions were as usual vague and inexplicable. He warned his opposite number, Colonel Amé of the Italian Intelligence, that Himmler was going to remove the Pope to Germany. This was a project from which Ribbentrop, Goebbels and Rudolf Rahn had some difficulty in dissuading Hitler. But whether Himmler really undertook to kidnap the Pope is very uncertain. Since his final breach with the Church in 1935 it was a subject on which Himmler was unrealistic. It is much more likely, however, that it was a form of camouflage, when one recalls that the SS force which was intended for the rescue of Mussolini was disguised as a parachute unit intended for the capture of the King of Italy.[5]

Delicatesse pour delicatesse, in return for the information Colonel Amé confided in Canaris that Badoglio was going to capitulate. Canaris did not divulge this to Keitel, because, as he told his friends,

---

[1] *Memoirs of Otto Skorzeny*, p. 103.   [2] Gilbert, *Hitler Directs His War*, p. 44.
[3] Wilfrid von Oven, *Mit Goebbels bis zum Ende*, I, p. 68.
[4] W. Hoettl, op. cit., p. 231.   [5] Hoettl, op. cit., p. 234.

he wanted Italy out of the war and he wanted to spare the country the attentions of Himmler's Einsatzgruppen.[1] Since Keitel had authorised Canaris's dubious visit to Amé in Venice, Kaltenbrunner could not interfere, but Skorzeny believed that his difficulties in locating the captive Mussolini were due to the help Canaris gave to Badoglio's secret service.[2]

Himmler's reliable information, followed by Skorzeny's success in rescuing Mussolini, convinced Hitler of the superiority of the SD's Intelligence and contributed to Himmler's conquest of the Abwehr in the following February. Yet Himmler's personal feelings were probably against the rescue. He forwarded to Hitler soon after Mussolini's arrest a report, in which Schellenberg's Bureau VI recommended that Badoglio be kept neutral and that the German troops be moved back to a strategic defence line, running from the Swiss border to the mouth of the Po. Hitler thought this the rankest treachery to Mussolini and Kaltenbrunner had to shelter Schellenberg from his rage.[3] But at the end of the war Hitler told Kaltenbrunner that Schellenberg's services had judged correctly and that his own loyalty to Mussolini had caused him to make a mistake. Hitler had resisted his own first intuition. After sleeping over Mussolini's arrest, he told his morning staff conference that he had every confidence in the Italian Fascist loyalists. All they needed was the bolstering of two SS divisions.[4]

And that is exactly what Hitler gave them. Hausser's Second SS Armoured Corps was withdrawn from the hard-pressed South Russian front and attached to Rommel's reserve army in North Italy, together with part of the Adolf Hitler division. These divisions remained till the end of the year with the assignment of disarming the Badoglio Italians.[5] In October even Sepp Dietrich was spared from the imminent counter-offensive of his 1st Armoured Corps towards Melitopol in order to inspect the Leibstandarte who guarded the re-enthroned but practically imprisoned Mussolini at Rocca delle Caminate. A shocked Bavarian peasant, Sepp Dietrich told

[1] Abshagen, op. cit., pp. 357-8.   [2] Skorzeny, op. cit., p. 127.
[3] Hoettl, op. cit., p. 233.
[4] Gilbert, op. cit., p. 60. It is possible that Hitler again changed his mind, for, when interrogated in captivity, General Vietinghoff declared that the instructions were to evacuate Italy gradually in the event of an Allied landing. It was only when the Allied landing was held up at Salerno that Kesselring (against the opinion of Rommel) recommended the holding of a defence line south of Rome, Milton Shulman, *Defeat in the West*, p. 85.   [5] Paul Hausser, op. cit., p. 102.

Goebbels that it had been the duty of the Leibstandarte to escort the notorious Clara Petacci to her true love on the shores of Lake Garda.[1]

Hitler's afterthought on 25 July had momentous consequences. It was not only the British and Americans who wasted a year of the war and their best field divisions in an attack on the 'soft underbelly of the Axis', which turned out to be not soft at all but as prickly as the Apeninnes. Hitler made an even bigger mistake in trying to defend it and Himmler, whose offices had given good advice, had to bustle round looking for the absolutely valueless person of the kidnapped dictator. On 15 August Hoettl reported to Kaltenbrunner and Karl Wolff on his recent discovery that Mussolini was on the island of Maddalena. He was told that Hitler would not credit the information of a mere Italian and that the news would have to come via Skorzeny. Wolff then hit upon a subterfuge. Himmler had pinned his faith in astrology and, though most of the German astrologers were in concentration camps, he had had them moved to the guest house which was run by Ohlendorf's SD at Wannsee, in order to work on the problem. Hoettl contrived that a pendulum-swinger should point his pendulum, as it swung over a map of Italy, on to Maddalena. Himmler told Kaltenbrunner that he had watched the performance. 'This Dr. Hoettl is quite right after all about Maddalena'.[2] So Hitler too was persuaded.

The rescue of Mussolini was one of those cloak-and-dagger affairs, like Lawrence's organisation of the Arab revolt in the First World War, which acquired a prestige beyond its practical value. With the terrific increase in Allied bombing and the universal smell of betrayal in August 1943, the German people and the SS in particular badly needed a success story. The build-up of Skorzeny by Goebbels's Propaganda Ministry was so successful that even now English newspapers publish flesh-creeping articles from time to time on the most dangerous man in Germany, the toughest man in Europe and so on. As to Skorzeny's commercial-traveller activities in Brazil and Egypt, they have become the deepest of conspiracies.

Skorzeny, the man chosen for Hitler's symbolic act of devotion to a friend who was in the hands of traitors, was a very new star in the SS firmament. He was a protégé of Kaltenbrunner, whom he had known in Vienna at the time of the Anschluss, when Skorzeny had offered the use of a large sports car to the Austrian SS. In February 1940 Skorzeny was rejected by the Luftwaffe because at thirty-one he was deemed too old to fly, and so he joined the Leibstandarte as an engineer-cadet. Early in 1942 he was invalided from Russia with gallstones. Willi Hoettl, an embittered colleague of Skorzeny's both in the Leibstandarte and in Schellenberg's Amt VI, says that Skorzeny failed to pass his examination for company commander and was posted to Berlin as a driving instructor.[1] Through Kaltenbrunner's influence he was transferred to the Special Purposes Regiment Oranienburg, the rival and now the successor to the Brandenburg division, which had become an ordinary unit since Canaris's surrender to Heydrich in May 1942.

Chosen from commando officers of greater experience, Skorzeny was summoned to Hitler's presence at Rastenburg on the day following Mussolini's arrest. In keeping with the picturesque practice of the Third Reich, where co-operation between the services was equivalent to sedition, Skorzeny was told by Hitler that both Ambassador Rahn and Field-Marshal Kesselring had a false view of the situation and would handle the matter wrongly if they knew the true nature of his mission.[2] In Rome, therefore, Skorzeny could confide only in Kappler and Dollmann.

But the conspiracy could not be restricted to so privileged a circle. The original plan to rescue Mussolini from Maddalena, which is near the northern tip of Sardinia, failed when Skorzeny's aeroplane was shot down into the sea. The Waffen SS had to be drawn into the affair. Mussolini was to be captured by a new brigade called 'Guernica', the nucleus of a raw SS division, the 'Reichsfuehrer SS', which was stationed on the island of Corsica.[3] But by this time

---

[1] Skorzeny, op. cit., pp. 7-19; Hoettl, op. cit., p. 318.

[2] Skorzeny, op. cit., p. 101.

[3] Formed from the remains of the 1st Totenkopf Regiment, this division, the 16th SS, was soon afterwards sent to Laibach and was one of the divisions which entered Hungary in March 1944. In the following July it fought the British on the Arno front. 'Reichsfuehrer SS' was soon afterwards involved in a massacre of 2,700 Italian civilians in reprisal for the activities of a partisan brigade in the Apennines. Max Simon, the divisional commander, was condemned to death by a British court in Padua, but the sentence was commuted and he was freed in 1954. Major Walter Reder was sentenced to life imprisonment by a Milan court as late as October 1951 in connection with this massacre, and is in prison at Gaeta (Kraetschmer, op. cit., pp. 64-6, 180-2). For Max Simon's later adventures see *infra*, p. 450.

Mussolini had been spirited away to an hotel on the top of the Gran Sasso, the highest point in the Apennines, a ski-ing resort accessible only by a rope railway. Then came 8 September and Eisenhower's announcement of Italy's capitulation. A reconnaissance was made which showed that a landing on the mountain by glider-borne troops was just possible. General Student of the Luftwaffe supplied pilots and gliders and on the 13th the attempt took place. The gliders landed a party from the SS special unit Oranienburg close to the Campo Imperatore Hotel. It was Skorzeny himself who carried Mussolini off in a Fieseler-Storch, a tiny aeroplane which was almost immobilised by the addition of his own vast bulk to Mussolini and the pilot. Mussolini was taken as far as Vienna the same night, while Skorzeny's men remained unmolested on the Gran Sasso till a German unit relieved them.

Hitler had recovered an ally who was far from proving the rallying point that he expected and whose family intrigues made him regret the whole affair within a fortnight. On the other hand the most valuable hostages had eluded him, for the Italian Royal Family had passed safely across the Allied lines.[1] It was now Himmler who wanted the re-establishment of Mussolini. On 10 September, even before the rescue, he told Goebbels that there would have to be some sort of Italian Fascist government in North Italy because he just did not have enough police troops to govern by force.[2] North Italy remained, nevertheless, a sort of SS preserve. At the end of that month Mussolini was allowed to leave his temporary retreat in Bavaria. He moved to an Italian residence on the shores of Lake Garda, chosen for his security by Karl Wolff, the Villa des Ursulins at Rocca delle Caminate, near Garignano. Mussolini's palace was guarded by a strong SS detachment and Karl Wolff in the guise of a special police attaché was practically his gaoler.

At Rastenburg Wolff's place had been definitely filled by Fegelein and Wolff believed that he had fallen out of Himmler's favour. But if Wolff was in disgrace he lost nothing by it, for after the July 1944 plot he became military governor of the Italian combat zone, a unique position for an SS man. This position enabled Wolff, with Rahn and the indispensable Eugen Dollmann, to start surrender negotiations for the army in Italy in March 1945. It enabled Wolff to be received by Mr. Allen Dulles in Zurich and to gain so much credit with the victors that he gave his evidence at Nuremberg

[1] Skorzeny, op. cit., p. 131.   [2] The Goebbels Diary, p. 350.

wearing the insignia of a general of the armed forces, a thing that he never was. In fact the turn of events, which sent Wolff packing to Italy in September 1943, served him even better than that for the Allied Courts refused to try him. For Wolff's complicity in procuring one of Himmler's most disgusting medical experiments he received a derisory and nominal sentence from a German denazification court.[1]

4. HIMMLER AND BORMANN

Himmler's own advancement to Minister of the Interior had taken place on 24 August, three weeks before the rescue of Mussolini. Hitler feared the possibilities of a German *coup d'état* on Badoglio lines, and therefore tried to strengthen the hand of his police chief. Outwardly Hitler concealed these fears. On 23 September he discussed his High Command with Goebbels, but could find nothing very spiteful to say about any of them. 'Taken as a whole, our generals bear no resemblance to the Italians. Treason such as the Italian generals committed against Mussolini is impossible considering the mentality of the German and especially the Prussian generals'. Goebbels's answer implied that if parachutes and gliders could rescue one dictator, they could kidnap another. Hitler reassured Goebbels. He told him that he had strengthened the security measures at Rastenburg. In fact, he had begun the construction of the famous bunker, where Stauffenberg's bomb was intended to explode and in which he practically lived from January 1944.[2]

Hitler had taken other precautions. The Princess Mafalda, daughter of King Victor Emmanuel, was married to Prince Philip of Hesse, an ardent Nazi and associate of Goering whom Hitler used for diplomatic missions to Italy. Both were now in concentration camps, the prince in Sachsenhausen and the princess in Buchenwald, where later she was killed in an Allied air raid while occupying a flat in the camp brothel. On 11 September Hitler ordered all German princes of the old reigning houses to be discharged from the Wehrmacht. In 1940, after the ostentatious military funeral of the Kaiser's fifth son, Prince Wilhelm, he had already forbidden them to serve at the front.[3] Prince Schaumburg-Lippe even found that his

---

[1] See *infra*, pp. 419-422.
[2] *The Goebbels Diary*, p. 383; Wilfrid von Oven, op. cit., I, p. 177.
[3] Wheeler-Bennett, op. cit., p. 505.

promotion to corporal was revoked.[1] But Himmler, the godson of a Bavarian crown prince, had a soft spot for German royal houses and continued to keep them in the SS.

To be in line with the Fuehrer, Himmler made appropriate attacks on royalty in his speeches, but his heart was not in it.[2] Prince Josias of Waldeck-Pyrmont, who had joined the SS in 1929 and had attended the execution of Roehm's followers in Munich, remained in office till the end of the war as higher SS police leader in Kassel-Mainfranken with jurisdiction over Buchenwald camp and the rank of a lieutenant-general.[3] Among the princes who had joined the SS in 1933 were Mecklenburg, Hohenzollern-Sigmaringen and Lippe-Biesterfeld. Himmler was therefore in no position to start a proscription. On the petition of von Papen a few months later, he showed enough independence to release from Dachau Prince Hohenberg, a grandson of the Emperor Franz Josef.[4]

Hitler's attack on the German princes was a fair indication of a state of panic to which he did not own in his conversation with Goebbels. It might be thought that Himmler's promotion was a still more panicking measure, but in fact the dismissal of old Wilhelm Frick and his appointment to Neurath's shadow post of titular Protector of Bohemia-Moravia was a mere formality. Himmler had virtually run the Ministry of the Interior in all its ramifications since 1935. Frick's chief state secretary, Hans Pfundtner, another Weimar Republic official, was replaced by Wilhelm Stuckart who had drawn up the Nuremberg laws in 1935. This, too, was a formality, for in all matters except the police Stuckart had run the office since 1939. Far from giving Himmler any power which he had not possessed before, the new appointment increased the hostility of the clique which had grown up in the previous January round Martin Bormann after the appointment of Kaltenbrunner. Himmler wanted to strengthen the authority of his higher SS police leaders, who, though omnipotent in occupied Europe, had become shadow figures in Germany. Albert Speer has deposed that after August 1943 some of these HSPFF tried to use their position as representatives of the new Minister of

[1] Schaumburg-Lippe, op. cit., p. 296.

[2] Kersten's story that after the escape of the King of Italy Himmler wanted to execute all the German princes occurs only in the earlier and edited version of his memoirs and is difficult to take seriously (pp. 164-8).

[3] See *supra* page 64. He was sentenced to life imprisonment by the American Dachau court on 18 August 1947.

[4] IMT XX, p. 247; Von Papen, *Memoirs*, p. 394.

the Interior to trespass on the preserves of the Gauleiters. 'Bormann immediately reported such cases to Hitler, and exploited them to fortify his own position. To our surprise it did not take Bormann long to stalemate Himmler as Minister of the Interior'.[1]

This is undoubtedly the truth. In his efforts to suppress the provincial parliaments in 1933, Hitler had given intolerable powers to the promoted Gauleiters or Reichsstatthalters and these men came under only one authority, not the Minister of the Interior but the Head of the Party Office, which was known also as the Party Chancellery, or Office of the Fuehrer's Deputy. It was an office of which Rudolf Hess, its creator, had made nothing, but of which Bormann made everything. The measures which were taken against invasion in 1944 were to make Bormann far stronger than any of the other competing satraps, Himmler included. During the last days of the Reich, if there was any government in Germany it was Bormann.

In Speer's view it was Bormann himself who arranged Himmler's successive promotions in 1943-4 in order to carry him away from the centre of power. Thus in December 1944 Bormann got Himmler made Commander-in-Chief of an army group in the field in order to keep him out of Berlin, and Hausser ag ees with Speer though he does not altogether acquit Himmler of some ambition in the matter. This may sound like another of those far-fetched theories which Germans liked to spin concerning Hitler's Byzantine wartime court, but it does not lack probability, for where Himmler and Heydrich failed to obtain Hitler's confidence, Bormann had succeeded. In the days before the seizure of power, Bormann had bought the Berghof property at Berchtesgaden for Hitler, who with a Bohemian's detestation of housekeeping had allowed him to run it for him. From this it was a small step to becoming financial manager for the party, then Hess's deputy as Head of the Party Office and, after Hess's flight in May 1941, his successor with greater powers than Hess had ever possessed. Finally, in April 1943 Bormann, the son of a Prussian trumpet-major often seen in the bandstands of Edwardian English seaside towns, became Hitler's personal secretary and the unique arbiter of access to the All-Highest.

It was Bormann who transformed the humble 'Haus Wachenfeld', which Hitler rented from Frau Winter in 1928 for £5 a month, into the super-Kremlin of the later war years.[2] Even after heavy bombing

[1] Private interrogation of Albert Speer in Trevor-Roper, *The Last Days of Hitler*, p. 41.   [2] *Hitler's Table Talk*, p. 216.

and two successive demolitions by the Allies, one may still obtain some idea of the satellite villas, the strategically placed groups of guard barracks and the galleries in the rock connecting them. One may contemplate the still intact monument of Bormann's megalo-maniac devotion to his Fuehrer, the massive pavilion at the top of the Kehlstein, reached by a road that disregards the hazards of Nature together with a two-hundred-foot lift in the heart of the mountain. If one may trust an older and much soured favourite, the court photographer Heinrich Hoffmann, Hitler hardly ever visited it and found it a bore.[1]

During the war years the whole Obersalzberg mountainside was enclosed with barbed wire and not less than two whole precious Leibstandarte battalions of the SS were kept away from the front to guard the Fuehrer's person. Hitler once remarked that since their arrival the countryside abounded with jolly and healthy children.[2] The SS dominated this barbaric kingdom and yet the head of the SS had no place in it. No villa was built for Himmler and in 1942, when he found it necessary to move his personal office from Berlin to Berchtesgaden during the migrations of the court, he could find quarters no nearer than Schloss Aigen in the suburbs of Salzburg, seventeen miles away.

It is a remarkable fact that except in Berlin, which Hitler seldom visited till the last six months, Himmler during the war never poss-essed an office close to the seat of power. In East Prussia his head-quarters were nearly thirty miles from the Wolfsschanze. In the Ukraine in 1942-3 and in Western Germany during the Ardennes offensive, Himmler's headquarters were more than a hundred miles from Hitler's and when Hitler finally moved into the Reich Chan-cellery Himmler had to remain with his field command. Himmler was probably not too anxious to be where Hitler could have him at his beck and call and Bormann profited by this shyness to see that Himmler, no more and no less than other department heads, could only communicate with Hitler through his own office.

After April 1943 Bormann must have caused Himmler far more frustration than ever the dynamic and ambitious Heydrich had done, but it must not be supposed that Bormann disliked Himmler, even if he wanted to ruin him. With such an impersonal Prussian bureau-crat's passion for power as Bormann's, dislikes did not enter into it.

---

[1] Heinrich Hoffmann, *Hitler was my Friend*, translated by Lieutenant-Colonel R. H. Stevens (London, 1955), p. 192.   [2] *Hitler's Table Talk*, 3 April 1942, p. 434.

The man was hardly human enough to have any dislikes. So in Bormann's dreary letters to his credulous wife, piously edited by a round-eyed Swiss, Himmler is always Uncle Heini and the military operation that was to destroy the last vestige of Himmler's credit was 'Uncle Heini's Offensive'.[1]

One immediate effect Himmler's promotion was intended to have and did have in that sombre autumn of 1943. Hitler wanted a sharp curb to the wave of German defeatism that followed the fall of Fascism in Italy. Himmler, who was induced by his friend Langbehn to discuss treason on the very day of his own nomination as Minister of the Interior, was to give a lesson, not to the 'uncertain cantonists' in high places but to the people who gossiped in trams, listened to the BBC or bought an illegal pat of butter. For these inadequate Germans even Thierack, who had drafted decrees for working whole populations to death in concentration camps, was no longer thought a tough judge by Hitler: 'In the end he keeps sticking to his legalistic egg-shells'.[2] It was an unfair comment on the man who had just hit on the idea of cutting down the time-limit for appeals on the ground that another bomb on Ploetzensee prison might release all the inmates of the condemned cells.[3] But Hitler did not want any appeals at all and in the following January Thierack's State Secretary, Kurt Rothenberger, was dismissed on account of the complaints against unsatisfactory court decisions.[4]

Frick, who in his day had put up a dim bureaucratic sort of fight against concentration-camp commitments, was still capable of using the Home Secretary's prerogative of mercy in People's Court cases. There was no question of it when Himmler was in his place. Himmler dismissed an appeal on the day of his nomination, a *Regierungsrat* condemned to death for defeatist talk.[5] Several other members of the professional classes were executed during the next few weeks and their cases were given special prominence in the Press. Following close on these events, on 4 October, Himmler gave his famous Posen address to the higher SS police leaders:[6]

The German people has indeed shown some signs of weakness and we have had to shoot a certain number. . . . The cowards are to be found in particular

[1] Hausser, op. cit., p. 207.   [1] *The Bormann Letters*, p. 189; and see *infra*, p. 407.
[2] *The Goebbels Diary*, p. 394.   [3] *Ibid.*, p. 362.
[4] Case III, transcript, 10796 (Judgment).
[5] Institute for International Affairs, *Hitler's Europe*, p. 33.
[6] Nuremberg Document PS 1919. The best version will be found in François Bayle, *Psychologie et ethique du national-socialisme*, p. 30.

among the ruling classes because intellect rots the character. But it will be enough to shoot one defeatist in a hundred. We have forbidden listening-in to enemy stations, but we have not been able to punish all who have listened. Today we punish a little more, since at the moment of Badoglio's *Schweinerei* there was a wave of defeatism in Germany. You may learn today that the Regierungsrat X, the manufacturer Y, the café waiter Z, the chauffeur M or employee K have had their heads cut off for defeatism. We have had to shoot a lot of people. We have had to do it and I too have had to do it, but it becomes more and more painful to sign a sentence of death.

This display of crocodile tears occurs in the most notorious of Himmler's recorded speeches, a speech delivered to the select inner circle of his executioners, which has been much quoted in this book. It contains Himmler's most vivid account of the extermination of the Jews and his vision of the SS as an élite order of the future, spending every second winter guarding the Urals from the hordes of Asia.[1] Nothing will be found in it concerning Himmler's troubles with the Abwehr and Admiral Canaris, or concerning the dossier which he had acquired on the Resistance Circle. Himmler was fond of broad hints, but of these there are none, Only the second Posen speech, delivered nearly a year later, reveals how much Himmler must already have known. If there were no hidden threats directed at the Canaris-Oster, Halder-Beck, Goerdeler-Popitz and other circles, it was because for the present Himmler wanted neither to warn them nor to interfere with activities which ran in some respects parallel with his own and which he hoped one day to exploit.

[1] Part of this speech, which lasted over three hours, is to be found in Himmler's own handwriting and part of it in a gramophone recording of his voice. According to Oswald Pohl a hundred and fifty people heard it, including twelve SS Gruppenfuehrers (Case IV, transcript, 1795). The only leaders of consequence who were absent were Karl Wolff, Kaltenbrunner, Daluege and Globocnik. Comments have differed widely. Berger had forgotten about the extermination part and had to be reminded by the playing of a record (Case XI, transcript 28388). Pohl remembered it but said it came as a surprise to him, while Richard Hildebrandt and Werner Lorenz said that, after listening to Himmler at Posen, nothing could surprise them any more.

I O

The SS State

1. THE CONCENTRATION CAMPS

When Himmler became Minister of the Interior, he had ruled for ten years a private and secondary kingdom of his own, a kingdom where no party struggles for power and precedence could interfere. This kingdom had probably been at its height in October 1941 on the eve of the battle for Moscow. Himmler's subjects then numbered about five millions. Overwhelmingly they were Jews, close on three millions in Poland, three-quarters of a million in occupied Russia, nearly a million in the Greater Reich and the remaining occupied countries. In addition to the Jews, there were four hundred thousand inmates of German concentration camps besides an immense number of hostages, suspects and others, awaiting deportation to Germany.

Even after the murder or slow extinction of most of the Jews, it was still a sizable kingdom. In the autumn of 1944 the concentration-camp population exceeded six hundred thousand.[1] It was a source of vexation to the Reichsfuehrer that his subjects gave him no voting strength. He could not use their presence behind wires as a threat to anyone else. He never succeeded in making his SS self-supporting by the labour of their muscles. He never dared make the SS rich by bargaining wholesale for their release. Even the Jews who were destined for the slaughter-house could not be sold in significant numbers. The concentration-camp system was too small an empire to bargain with, yet too big a one for Himmler to understand its workings. By the end of 1942 Himmler had come to regard the system as a death factory pure and simple, but this had not always been so. To Himmler the concentration camps had hitherto been model though severe reformatory schools, filled with well-scrubbed though bitter faces, resounding with patriotic though compulsory songs.

Basically the system was inevitable in Hitler's Reich. Though Hitler came to power constitutionally, he had no independent

[1] Nuremberg Document PS 1166.

majority in the Reichstag. The Enabling Act, that made it possible to govern without the constitution, was passed by the simple expedient of locking up the Opposition deputies first. To continue for the next twelve years to govern the country by dictatorship and war, when few Germans sincerely wanted either, was not possible without terrorism. Thus, though the greater part of the concentration-camp inmates were foreigners, the hard core was always German. From 1938 to 1945 there were seldom less than a hundred thousand German-speaking internees at any given moment.

And yet, when the first year of power had passed, Hitler had been nearly prepared to abolish the concentration camps. The sense of insecurity which culminated in the blood-purge of June 1934 held him back. Nor did the blood-purge alter the situation. Between June 1934 and the Austrian Anschluss of March 1938, there was not the shadow of any resistance to Hitler's authority. Nevertheless in these four years the population of the concentration camps seldom fell below twenty thousand. The sledge-hammer diplomacy, which created the triumphs of the régime and which gave Germans a sense of greatness, created still more tenseness and insecurity. And so, a year before the Austrian Anschluss, new concentration camps were ordered at Sachsenhausen and Buchenwald.

With the first defeats in the field the increase in the camp population became immense. At the end of 1942 there were sixteen main camps and the subsidiary labour camps in the Greater Reich alone exceeded a hundred. In addition there were dozens more of such camps in Russia and Poland under the control of local security police commanders. By this time arrests for acts of resistance and sabotage had ceased to be the main sources of recruitment. Henceforward Himmler's ambition to have his own share in war production had to be fulfilled by kidnapping foreign conscript workers.

The first concentration camps of the year 1933 were no monopoly of the SS. They were created at random by local Gauleiters and SA leaders, largely for blackmail. Of these only Oranienburg, an SA camp near Berlin, and Dachau, an SS camp near Munich, were destined to survive for the next twelve years. Dachau was a personal creation of Himmler's, but this kernel of the concentration-camp system was authorised by a Minister who had been eight years in office under the Weimar Republic, Heinrich Held, Minister-President of Bavaria.[1] Held was the staunchly Catholic leader of the

[1] Diels, *Lucifer ante Portas*, p. 33.

Bavarian People's Party who had removed the ban on the Nazis after Hitler's release from prison in 1925. Only a few days after the founding of Dachau, Held was himself expelled from office in an SA coup which was organised for Hitler by Ritter von Epp.[1]

In the following October Theodor Eicke[2] the commandant of Dachau, issued regulations which became the basis for the whole future ramifications of the camps. These regulations were the result of many judicial complaints. There had been four murders in Dachau at the end of May alone.[3] But the new regulations did little more than give legal authority to some of the causes of murder, such as the practice of shooting at prisoners who approached the barbed wire.[4] After the Christmas Armistice of 1933 there was some hope of a mitigation of the lot of the internees, but, in spite of a change of heart among certain Nazi Ministers concerning Gestapo arrests, there was no change in the position of the detainees.

The amnesty was of disputed origin. Rudolf Diels, then head of the Gestapo, says that he got permission from Hitler to release the twenty-seven thousand internees at his own discretion, but that Goering refused to free the ten thousand who were alleged to be Communists. Later Hitler told Goering that he should have put all the internees on board hulks and sunk them at sea, a change of mind which Diels attributed to Himmler's influence,[5] since on Christmas day Hitler had consented to be present at a party given by Goebbels to the freed internees of the Communist belt of north Berlin.[6] In the end only a fraction of the twenty-seven thousand internees was released, and everyone claimed the credit for it except Himmler.[7]

With Himmler it was far otherwise, for he boasted later that he had got Dachau excluded from the amnesty.[8] Soon after the blood-purge of June 1934 Hitler had the entire concentration-camp system transferred to the control of the SS and the command of Theodor Eicke and the mass releases ceased altogether. Hitler became

---

[1] Bullock, *Hitler, A Study in Tyranny*, pp. 116, 246.

[2] Eicke was then forty-one years of age. He was the son of a railway clerk and after the First World War had entered the Schutzpolizei, the goal of many unemployed soldiers. His career in the police was not sensational. After passing an examination he became a Kriminalbeamte, equivalent to a CID sergeant (Kraetschmer, op. cit., p. 61).

[3] IMT III, p. 150.   [4] Nuremberg Document PS 778.

[5] Diels, op. cit., p.254.   [6] Schaumburg-Lippe, op. cit., 165-6.   [7] IMT IX, p. 79.

[8] *Neuer Vorwaerts*, Karlsbad, 26 September 1937.

convinced of the necessity of retaining the concentration camps. At the same time he told Hans Frank that, if he had a Siberia at his disposal like Stalin, he would not have to endure the reproaches of the foreign Press for keeping a couple of thousand people behind barbed wire, 'living better than our own soldiers frequently have to do'.[1]

Less than five years later, on 10 April 1939, it was no longer a question of keeping two thousand people behind barbed wire. There were no less than 279,168, more than half of whom were Schutzhaeftlinge or protection internees who were not charged with any offence but were kept in the camps to prevent their committing one.[2] The number was a tribute to Heydrich's round-up of Jews after the November 1938 pogrom, to Himmler's police measures after the Austrian Anschluss and to the two rapes of Czechoslovakia, for early in 1937 Himmler had himself given the number of protection internees as only eight thousand.

Probably the population of the camps had kept little more than level till the mass arrests in incorporated territories. Of the camps enumerated by Himmler in January 1937, only Dachau and Sachsenhausen were retained permanently. Sachsenhausen, the concentration camp for Berlin, was the successor to Oranienburg, whose inmates had been removed in 1934 to Esterwege in connection with the Emsland reclamation plan, and then moved back to within a few miles of Oranienburg early in 1937. A few months later, on 17 July 1937, the third great SS camp was established at Buchenwald under the notorious Captain Koch. A fourth camp at Mauthausen followed soon after the Austrian Anschluss.[3] By the outbreak of war Neuengamme, Gross Rosen, Ravensbrueck, and Flossenbuerg had been added to the list of parent camps. In 1940-2 there followed Lublin, Auschwitz, Theresienstadt, Strutthof, Dora, StuetthofNatzweiler and Herzogensbosch; while in 1943 there were added Plaszow in Poland, Kaiserswald in Latvia and Bergen-Belsen, an 'exchange camp', for Jews in Germany. By this time the average combined population of the concentration camps had increased from three hundred thousand at the outbreak of war to the neighbourhood of half a million. Himmler had prophesied correctly in January 1937 that war would fill the concentration camps with 'a much increased number of uncertain cantonists'.[4]

Before the Austrian Anschluss, when the camp population averaged

[1] Frank, op. cit., p. 154. [2] Weisenborn, op. cit., p. 38. [3] See *supra*, p. 110.
[4] See *supra*, p. 82.

twenty thousand or less, the problem of exploitation was not taken seriously. Himmler removed the camp at Esterwege when Constantin Hierl, the Minister of Labour, objected to land reclamation as too honourable a service for protection internees.[1] The inmates of the camps were kept occupied extending the accommodation in the camps themselves, for the influx of newcomers was not unexpected. After the Anschluss, however, Himmler considered making the camps a source of finance for the SS. During the hectic weeks preceding the Munich agreement Albert Speer had presented Hitler with a plan for rebuilding Berlin and Nuremberg, a plan which was to include some of the largest buildings in the world.[2] Even at this innocent stage in his career Speer was already involved in slave-labour proposals. Himmler proposed to quarry stone and gravel and to supply bricks and cement from Sachsenhausen, Dachau and Buchenwald camps. For this purpose he formed in the winter of 1938-9 two companies, Deutsche Ausrustungswerke (DAW) and Deutsche Erd- und Steinwerke (DEST). The SS was to go into business as a commercial company and the administration was to be in the hands of the Verwaltungsamt, the business management office of the SS which had been run since 1934 by Oswald Pohl, a working-man's son who had reached the rank of paymaster-captain in the Weimar Republic navy.[3]

The proposal was by no means popular with the heads of the service. Heydrich regarded the camps only as places for liquidating the kind of people he disliked. He was not interested in commerce and furthermore he saw in Himmler's plans an attack on his position. In July 1936, when he became head of the unified German police, Himmler refused to ratify a decree which gave Heydrich, as head of the Gestapo, entire control of the camps.[4] Himmler retained the camp inspectorate as a branch of his own SS staff office. The intrusion of Oswald Pohl, therefore, upset not only Heydrich but also Theodor Eicke, who was then head of the inspectorate.[5]

The views of the Verwaltungsamt conflicted with those of the inspectorate till the very end, causing chaos and confusion. The horrors of Belsen were its final expression. The Verwaltungsamt had to fight on the one hand corruption among the camp officials, on the other the belief that the feeding and welfare of the internees did

[1] *Neuer Vorwaerts*, 26 September 1937.   [2] IMT XVI, pp. 385-6.
[3] Case IV, transcript, 1537.   [4] IMT XX, p. 147; evidence of Werner Best.
[5] Case IV, transcript, 1335.

not matter, because the sooner they died the better. Himmler never realised that by encouraging ruthlessness he encouraged corruption and bad management. How could it be wrong for a camp guard or an official to sell the prisoners' food and stores if the prisoners were not meant to survive? Sometimes Himmler issued instructions ordering better food and incentive bonuses for internees doing skilled labour. And yet he perpetuated the fantastic 'green triangle' system by which authority remained vested in habitual criminals whom the courts had delivered to the concentration camps for life.

The founder-members of Dachau had been combed by Himmler from the gaols in 1933-4. These were the 'Prominente', who, though they were never embodied in the SS, were to run the camps for the next twelve years. They were intended frankly for the part of medieval fiends in a Last Judgment painting, stoking up the fires of hell. After five years' practice at this, the Prominente were seriously expected to boost production in the name of the patriotic war effort. Naturally, these citizens amused themselves during the boring idle days at the quarries by murdering anyone whose starved body broke down at the task. At every concentration camp such murders were tolerated at one time or another. At Mauthausen, the Austrian camp, they were regularised and they were part of the commandant's system even during the stay of a Swiss Red Cross delegate in April 1945.[1]

Under the role of corrupt camp commandants and murderous Prominente or 'Kapos' there was little progress in the plans for DEST and DAW after the outbreak of war. The building programme had been shelved and, since the shortage of labour in the armaments industry had not begun, the labour of concentration-camp inmates was not taken seriously. But with the capitulation of France Hitler became so confident that the war would end that the Speer building plan was revived. In conjunction with this plan, Himmler wanted a housing programme for the demobilised SS. 'No one is going to give me the money. It must be earned by forcing the scum of mankind, the prisoners, the professional criminals, to do positive work'.[2] And then Himmler explained to his Leibstandarte officers that it would be their peacetime duty to provide guards for the concentration camps whose inmates would build the houses for the SS.

[1] International Red Cross, *Documents sur l'activité de la Croix Rouge* (Geneva, 1946), p. 134.   [2] Nuremberg Document PS 1918, VII, p. 159; XX, p. 98.

It was not till February 1942, when the Russian winter campaign had produced an armaments crisis, that Speer protested to Hitler at this continued wasteful use of concentration-camp labour. The resources of DEST and DAW were still being diverted to a purely civilian constructional programme. In June 1941, when DEST controlled eight quarries and brickworks, the labour exchanges were instructed to direct freed internees back to these works as overseers.[1] The first Russian winter created no interference, and on 5 December 1941 Himmler again reminded Heydrich and Oswald Pohl that the concentration camps were expected to train five thousand bricklayers and ten thousand stonemasons for the Fuehrer's building projects. Hitler, he said, had ordered from DEST a hundred thousand cubic feet of granite. The bricklayers and stonemasons were to be treated as a camp élite with extra food and clothing and there was to be only such discipline for them as training required. Himmler added for Heydrich's benefit, 'for years leading SS experts prophesied that prisoners could not be turned into skilled workers. Since then these gentlemen have had to convince themselves that the opposite is true'.[2]

Yet the proportion of internees who did productive work was ludicrously low. In November 1941 Hitler exclaimed, 'I have a hundred and fifty thousand convicts making felt slippers'.[3] A roster of the male camp at Birkenau, or Auschwitz II, dated as late as 11 May 1944, shows 6,269 at work out of a camp roll of 17,589, and even then the majority were employed on camp fatigues.[4] At Sachsenhausen, which supplied the labour for the largest DEST brickworks, the commandant, Loehritz, built himself a yacht with camp labour. There was a court of inquiry and in July 1941 Himmler transferred Loehritz to Norway, replacing him with Lieutenant-Colonel Kaindl. With the departure of the corrupt Loehritz, Captain Payne-Best noticed some improvement in the appearance of the internees.[5]

Although in 1941 the economic situation of Germany seemed so sound that the potentialities of 350,000 camp inmates were overlooked in the war-production programme, Himmler found other uses for them. Among the definitely cranky circle of Marge Himmler,

[1] Case IV, Document NO. 2309.
[2] Case IV, Document NO. 385; Reitlinger, op. cit., p. 103.
[3] *Hitler's Table Talk*, p. 128.
[4] *Dokumenty i Materialy*, Vol. I, pp. 100-5   [5] Payne-Best, op. cit., p. 111

née Conzersowo, was a lady who had married a man fifteen years younger than herself and who was to become a credit to German motherhood by producing three children after passing the age of forty-eight. Since mother-worship formed an essential part of his folklore, Himmler became interested in the young man who had contributed to this prodigy. Sigmund Rascher was urged to join the General SS, where he showed the right spirit by denouncing his own father.[1] On 15 May 1941 Rascher, who was undergoing a very boring medical course with the Luftwaffe in Munich, wrote to Himmler asking him if he would oblige with human guinea-pigs for high-altitude experiments in a pressure chamber which involved the death of the victims. Himmler agreed and Rascher was allowed to experiment in Dachau camp with an apparatus borrowed from the Luftwaffe.

A year later, Field-Marshal Milch had some misgivings about this and wrote to Karl Wolff, asking him to send the apparatus back to the Luftwaffe and suggesting that Rascher be employed on freezing experiments.[2] In August Rascher started on his new researches and in November he received a visit at Dachau from Himmler in person. Rascher had mentioned the use of 'animal heat' in reviving frozen airmen and, though Rascher's report showed that this had been useless, Himmler found the idea fascinating. He was so struck that he ordered Oswald Pohl to have four prostitutes sent to Dachau for further experiments in reviving the frozen human guinea-pigs. Later he protested primly that Pohl should not have selected girls of German blood.[3]

Himmler now got Rascher transferred to the Waffen SS and permanently installed at Dachau. At the end of 1942 there began an orgy of experiments throughout the concentration camps which continued well into 1944. At Ravensbrueck Polish girls were given gas-gangrened wounds by Himmler's dearly loved Dr. Karl Gebhardt. At Ravensbrueck and Auschwitz Horst Schumann and Hans Clauberg performed sterilisation experiments on Jewesses. At Buchenwald victims were infected with typhus; at Dachau and Buchenwald gipsies were made to live on sea water. Professor Joachim Mugrowski of the SS Health Institute observed the effect of poisoned bullets. There seems no end to the grisly catalogue, which can best be

---

[1] Bayle, *Psychologie et ethique du national-socialisme*, pp. 305-8; *Croix gammée ou caducée*, p. 21.   [2] IMT III, pp. 160-1.
[3] Nuremberg Document PS 1583; IMT III, p. 163.

studied in the massive record of the 'Doctors' Trial' and in the excellent résumés of Dr. Bayle.

In all these experiments Himmler took a sober interest and also some pride because he had been able to produce from his incomparable organisation doctors who were not 'inhibited by any Christian prejudices'.[1] In this respect the SS doctors were by no means alone. In May 1943 Karl Gebhardt and his assistant Fritz Fischer lectured publicly at the Berlin Military Medical Academy on their gas-gangrene experiments. Among the audience sat a surgeon of international repute, Ferdinand Sauerbruch, whose connections with the Resistance Circle did not prevent him from seeking the company of Leonardo Conti, Karl Brandt and others of the same murderous tribe. The audience, Fischer declared, understood perfectly how the subjects had been procured and how the SS Health Institute had supplied the virus, yet Sauerbruch rose to his feet only to vindicate surgery as against the use of sulphanilamide.[2]

Rascher remained at work in Dachau camp till May 1944, when the Freiherr von Eberstein, higher SS and police leader for Munich, came to arrest him—but not for his experiments. It had been discovered that the children whom Frau Rascher had borne after the age of forty-eight had in reality been kidnapped from orphanages.[3] The camp commandant and the chief medical officer at Dachau thereupon discharged a flood of complaints against Rascher, whom they described as a dangerous, incredible person who had been under Himmler's personal protection for years, performing unspeakable horrors. Himmler naturally refused to have the Raschers tried, but they were confined in the political bunkers of Dachau and Ravensbrueck, the fate under the Third Reich of people who knew too much. Captain Payne-Best met Sigmund Rascher during the southward evacuation of the Dachau political bunker at the beginning of May 1945. He found Rascher garrulous and sympathetic. One of Rascher's boasts to Captain Payne-Best was that he had invented the gas chamber. Perhaps that was why Sigmund Rascher disappeared soon afterwards, and likewise Frau Rascher who was last seen in Ravensbrueck.[4]

---

[1] Nuremberg Document PS 1617, Himmler to Milch.
[2] Nuremberg Document NO. 472; Bayle, Croix gammée ou caducée, p. 370.
[3] IMT XX, p. 258.   [4] Payne-Best, op. cit., p. 227.

2. THE CONCENTRATION CAMPS, EXTERMINATION
THROUGH WORK

From September 1941, when Heydrich was compelled to spend most of his time in Prague, Himmler felt free to interfere more in concentration-camp affairs. Hitherto Oswald Pohl had handled only the business side of the camp administration. On 2 March 1942 Himmler sent for Pohl and told him that Richard Gluecks, the inspector and successor to Theodor Eicke since 1939, was too soft to work in with Fritz Sauckel, the new Reich plenipotentiary for labour, nor could Heydrich, now that he was enthroned in Prague, put the required pressure on Gluecks. It would have to be Pohl's affair. Pohl maintained at his trial that this was a trick played on Heydrich by Himmler through the jealousy of Theodor Eicke, who intrigued against his old chief even while commanding the Totenkopf division in Russia.[1] But it was Pohl who benefited from it and not Eicke. Under the new name of WVHA Pohl's bureaucracy became enormous. At the newly requisitioned offices in the Berlin suburb of Lichterfelde he had fifteen hundred employees, quite apart from the inspectorate, which, under the new name of Department C, stayed at Oranienburg. There was perhaps no office of Hitler's Reich which gave worse value than this Ministry of Misery.

After the formation of WVHA Himmler turned at once to the question of armament production. The new appointments of Albert Speer as Minister for Armaments and War Production and of Fritz Sauckel as Minister for Labour Recruitment, foreshadowed a tremendous shifting round of man-power. Himmler asked to be allowed to make munitions of war with his own labour force in his own camps. With the assistance of General Fritz Fromm, who was then in charge of the armaments section of OKW, Speer dissuaded Hitler. He pointed out that uncontrolled production of arms by the SS was a menace to the state.[2] In February 1942 such persuasion was not difficult. Himmler was still rationed to his eight Waffen SS divisions and Hitler had just expressed himself forcibly against further expansion. But Himmler persisted, and in September Speer, who had no scruples whatever against using all the slave labour he could lay hands on, proposed a compromise. Himmler was to provide

[1] Case IV, transcript, pp. 1263, 1280, 1330.
[2] IMT XVII, p. 17.   Himmler did not forget Fromm (see page 330).

concentration-camp inmates to work in private-enterprise factories, and from five to eight per cent of their output was to be allotted to the equipment of the Waffen SS.[1]

Himmler believed that if he could find the equipment himself, Hitler would permit him to recruit an unlimited private army. So Speer's proposal to Hitler was followed by Goebbels's suggestion to Thierack which gave Himmler as many concentration-camp inmates as he liked without any pretence of political crime or protective custody.[2] Under the new agreement between the Ministry of Justice and RSHA, thirty-five thousand Eastern workers—Ukrainians, Russians, and Poles—were to be surrendered to the Gestapo in the course of December 1942 and January 1943. By 31 December some twelve thousand had been delivered to the camps, but, as Kaltenbrunner complained to Oswald Pohl, the concentration-camp inmates were dying quicker than the rate of replacement.[3]

A report was sent to Himmler which showed that between June and November 1942 there had been 136,700 commitments to the concentration camps, but during these six months 70,610 had died, 9,267 had been executed, 28,846 had been transferred out—a euphemism for the gas chamber—and only 4,711 had been released, a wastage rate of nineteen thousand a month.[4] On 28 December Himmler circulated an order headed, 'The Reichsfuehrer has ordered that the death-rate absolutely must be reduced'. Monthly reports of progress were demanded and a severe rocket was delivered to the SS medical service, who had concealed the typhus epidemics.[5] But it was not till July 1943 that Himmler sent a judge advocate of the SS, Conrad Morgen, to institute prosecutions at the main camps. As a result some officials were shot, including Koch of Buchenwald, while the ex-convict Hoess was transferred from Auschwitz.[6] To no purpose. With the deterioration of Germany the concentration camps were allotted less food and stores by the provincial administrations and the death-rate went up in 1944 almost to the 1942 level. During the last few months of Hitler's Germany this was far exceeded.

In the meantime the Thierack-Himmler agreement filled the camps with kidnapped Eastern conscript labourers. By the spring of 1944 Himmler had made serious inroads on Speer's labour force. In the

[1] IMT II, p. 335; Document R 124.   [2] See *supra*, pp. 225-7.
[3] Trials of War Criminals, V, p. 273; Documents PS 1063d and NO. 1523.
[4] Nuremberg Document PS 2171.   [5] PS 2171, Annexe II.
[6] IMT XX, p. 303.

first six months of the year there were 310,668 arrests, more than double the number recorded in the second half of 1942.[1] Not less than 193,000 were foreigners who had been arrested nominally for abandoning work. But, in fact, any Eastern worker, who faced a small police court charge, was sent to the camps under the 'simplified procedure' and he was not released after the expiry of his court sentence. Men who were murdered by the 'Green Triangles' in the quarries or who rotted to death in superimposed shelves in the infirmaries, were often only expiating an illicit purchase of unrationed food or a day off from work or a conversation with a German woman. In 1944 Speer complained to Hitler that Himmler was bagging his labour force at the rate of 30,000-40,000 a month. Himmler denied this, but the weekly party statistics show that Speer was accurately informed. In the end Himmler had to promise the release of short-sentence offenders after the expiry of their term.[2]

Speer's anxiety to recover these workers showed that he regarded the concentration camps as a dead loss. The inmates were leased to German industrialists for negligible sums, but they were feeble and they died at their work and, even if there was not the least scruple against using them, there was not much competition for their services. The great firm of I.G. Farben found it worth while giving the slaves a midday bowl of soup. Krupps, on the other hand, showed no interest at all and allowed the Hungarian Jewesses, who were sent to their works in Essen and other West German towns in the last months of the war, to exist under absolutely murderous conditions.[3]

The worst exploiters of Jewish slave labour were the smaller German firms who administered requisitioned factories in Poland. A number of these factories fell into the hands of the notorious Walter Toebbens, who got his labour from the Warsaw ghetto. When the ghetto was to be liquidated, he enticed his workers into the labour camps of the SS under a false promise of protection and, until they were murdered, he shared his profits with the SS police leader Odilo Globocnik.[4]

In other Polish factories the German civilian overseers lent their

<hr>

[1] Weisenborn, op. cit., p. 149, quoting *Die Lage*.   [2] IMT XVII, p. 47.

[3] IMT XII, pp. 322-3; Law Reports of Trials of War Criminals, 1949, Vol. X, pp. 100-2.

[4] Reitlinger, op. cit., pp. 68, 273-9, 294-9; *Begruendung* of the Bremen Schwurgericht, May 1950,

assistance to the 'resettlement commissioners' of the Gestapo in selecting the less-productive workers for the gas chamber or in disclosing the places where children or aged parents were hidden. One such case was tried by the Bremen Schwurgericht as late as May 1953. The defendant, Fritz Hildebrand, had been an officer in the Waffen SS and in 1943-4 directed slave labour at the great oilfield and refinery of Borislav-Drohobicz, where Himmler permitted a nucleus of Jewish labour to survive almost till the arrival of the Russians. Hildebrand, who was in one case so helpful to the murder squads as to order a woman worker to choose which of her children was to be gassed, got a sentence of eight years' imprisonment.[1]

But, cheap though concentration-camp labour might be, it was a wasteful use of man-power, since every twenty inmates of a concentration camp required an armed sentry whose services were lost to the armed forces or to industry.[2] Moreover, liability to serve as concentration-camp guards gave the Waffen SS a bad name, of which Himmler was sensitive in spite of the inconsistent way he acted over it. He told Felix Kersten in August 1942 that he would not allow officers and men of the Waffen SS to be burdened with matters 'which they could not understand or judge', and he went on to describe how carefully he had separated the concentration-camp service from the Waffen SS. And Oswald Pohl explained that, though the camp guards were recruited from the Waffen SS, they were mostly volunteers who had been found unfit for war service and who were not likely, therefore, to be transferred to the field divisions.[3]

Gottlob Berger always opposed the employment of the Waffen SS on such duties and particularly objected to the concentration-camp guards wearing a uniform which was indistinguishable from that of the field divisions except for a sleeve stripe. But Gottlob Berger's trial evidence differed from Pohl's. He claimed that by 1942 the greater part of the concentration-camp guards, who wore the Waffen SS uniform, were men drafted into home defence battalions from all three services.[4] Furthermore, towards the end of the war great

---

[1] *Begruendung* of the Bremen Schwurgericht, May 1953. Wilhelm Krell a witness, in *Demokratischer Bund*, No. 8-9, Vienna 1953.

[2] Guenther Reinecke, head of the SS judicial section, declared that in June 1944 there were 25,000 concentration camp guards. At this time the number of internees was just under half a million (IMT XX, p. 371).

[3] Kersten, *Totenkopf und Treue*, 1953, pp. 311-2.

[4] Kersten, *Totenkopf und Treue*, p. 202; Case XI, transcript, 28399.

numbers of former concentration-camp guards were re-drafted into the field divisions of the Waffen SS, whose bad reputation they certainly did not diminish. For instance the guards, who were observed by Brigadier-General Glyn-Hughes in April 1945 shooting indiscriminately among the mob of gibbering skeletons at Belsen, were racial German recruits for the Waffen SS from Hungary, who were in training at the neighbouring armoured warfare school.[1]

Between the tens of thousands of men who guarded concentration camps at one time or another and the even larger number of civilians who worked alongside concentration-camp inmates in the factories, a large portion of the German public knew the conditions under which the inmates lived. At the end of 1944, when the great evacuation of the camps began, appalling trainloads were on public view, steaming slowly through the crowded railway stations of Eastern and Central Germany, long chains of open trucks filled with ragged skeletons, milling for scraps of bread or crying for water. Descriptions of this sort could be quoted by the dozen. No more ineffective conspiracy to commit perjury has ever been seen than that of the twenty-one highest Nazi defendants, who agreed together not to admit knowledge of more than two or three concentration camps and not to admit knowledge of anything that went on inside them.

By June 1944, when Speer obtained from Himmler a promise to release the short-sentence prisoners, the camps were threatened with the arrival of more inmates than they could hold. For, with the adoption of Speer's 'Jaeger Plan' in April 1944, Hitler reversed his policy and brought Jews back to the Reich. The plan was to construct underground fighter-aircraft factories, inaccessible to Allied bombing attacks. They were to be built by a hundred thousand able-bodied Jews whom Hungary was expected to surrender.[2] But that was not all. On 2 August 1944 it appears that there were 524,286 inmates in the camps. An additional ninety thousand Hungarian Jews were expected from Budapest; four hundred thousand Poles were expected from Warsaw, that is to say practically the whole adult population which was in the throes of rebellion; sixty thousand Jews were expected from the Lodz ghetto, fifteen thousand members of the French Resistance movement who had been rounded up since D-day, and seventeen thousand Polish officer prisoners who must

[1] *The Belsen Trial* (London, 1949), edited Raymond Philipps, p. 34.
[2] See *infra*, p. 355.

be moved because of the Russian invasion of Poland. Thus a concentration-camp population of 1,100,000 could be anticipated in the
near future.[1]

In actual fact only thirty thousand additional Jews came from
Hungary, while a large part of the sixty thousand Jews of Lodz were
gassed; from Warsaw only a few thousand men and women who
had acted as troop leaders in the rebellion were sent to Germany.
Even so, the camp population soared that autumn well past the
six hundred thousand mark, though barely a quarter of a million
could be employed in war industry.[2] But the space narrowed too.
After the Russian break-through in June 1944 and the collapse of
the Central Army Group, several camps had to be evacuated westwards: Lublin or Majdanek in July, Kaiserswald, near Riga, in
August and Plaszow, near Cracow, in October, besides numerous
Jewish labour camps in Poland and Estonia. In September the
Allied advance in the West forced the evacuation of Herzogensbosch
in Holland and Stuetthof-Natzweiler in Alsace. In the following
January, after the collapse of the Vistula line, the evacuation of the
huge complex of camps known as Auschwitz I, II and III, which
still contained approximately fifty-eight thousand people, had to be
completed within sound of the Russian guns. By February 1945
there had already developed the conditions which the Allies found
at Belsen and Buchenwald, for the deportees from Poland and
Hungary had brought typhus with them to western Germany.

The last stage in the history of the concentration camps reveals
the utmost confusion of purpose. At Lublin the Polish and German
prisoners formed an illegal committee which resisted the final
evacuation of the camp.[3] On 24 July 1944 they arrested the SS
guards and handed them over to the Red Army. Russian propaganda was thereby enabled to make a great deal out of an intact
gas chamber and crematorium. After these disclosures the Germans
took great pains to evacuate the Auschwitz group of camps, but in
January 1945, when the shadow of retribution loomed so clearly,
not even Himmler and Kaltenbrunner dared to give the order to
murder three thousand immovable invalids in their beds. These remnants of Auschwitz fell into Russian hands alive and told all they knew
concerning the thirty months of the crematorium fires and the four

---

[1] Nuremberg Document PS 1166, Return of Clothing from WVHA, Amt D.
[2] Case IV, transcript, 1338; evidence of Oswald Pohl.
[3] Eugen Kogon, *The Theory and Practice of Hell* (London, 1953), p. 247.

huge gas chambers which the Germans had recently blown up.

Several Ministries of the Reich were now interested in seeing that no more inhabited camps fell into Russian hands. The inmates of Strutthof, Gross Rosen, Dora, most of Sachsenhausen and Ravensbrueck, besides the camps attached to the naval armament factories on the Baltic coast, had to join the westward trek to Buchenwald and Belsen. But in February Hitler ordered that no camp inmates were to be surrendered to the Western Allies either. There resulted an utterly chaotic movement mainly from Buchenwald and Dachau towards the 'mountain redoubt'. This was gradually stopped by Himmler, Kaltenbrunner and Gottlob Berger, each acting on his own initiative, and eventually rather more than 250,000 internees were liberated by the Western Allies.

This part of the story will be resumed in Chapter 15, since it is bound up with Himmler's negotiations with the Red Cross and his final resolution to seek peace over Hitler's head. But it may be wondered why the last great holocaust of concentration-camp victims was necessary at all. The largest single element among the six hundred thousand camp inmates in Germany in the winter of 1944, larger even than the survivors of the Jews, were the Eastern workers, who might just as well have been allowed to join their compatriots, who worked in a form of semi-confinement and in conditions that at least were not murderous. This, however, was the one thing Himmler dared not do. He expected the Eastern workers to turn on their masters, the moment vigilance was relaxed, and the accession of the starved, ill-treated *Haeftlinge* to their numbers would be a disaster.[1] In commenting upon the plans of the Stauffenberg circle to free the concentration-camp inmates within a few days of Hitler's death, Himmler revealed how great were his fears on this score. Addressing the Gauleiters at Posen on 3 August 1944, he said:[2]

We have five hundred and fifty thousand detainees, of whom about four hundred and fifty thousand are foreigners. It meant therefore that a half-million of the most embittered political and criminal enemies, political enemies of the Reich and criminal enemies of every human and social order, would be poured out over Germany. It meant that in the next two or three weeks crime would blossom and the Commune would reign over our streets.

This genuinely represented the state of mind of the Nazi hierarchy, both after the July plot and on 21 January 1945 when there

---

[1] See *infra*, p. 423.   [2] *Vierteljahreshefte fuer Zeitgeschichte*, NO. 4, p. 593.

was a false alarm that the Russians had crossed the Oder. Goebbels ordered the alarm signal, 'Gneisenau', to be given and the Berlin Home Guard to be turned out in case of a rising by the Eastern workers.[1] Fear, which is the basis of totalitarian rule, works downwards as much as upwards and the explanation for the last and worst of the war atrocities can be traced to plain fear alone.

Himmler had detailed statistics drawn up for him by a professional actuary, Dr. Richard Korherr,[2] giving the totals of resettled, that is to say, murdered, Jews in the various territories. Possibly he did this not for his own pleasure but in order to show Hitler that he was carrying out his task. No such balance-sheet was prepared for the concentration camps. Working to death had been named in private correspondence, but it was not mentioned in any decree and in theory the concentration-camp inmates were put there not to die but to be educated or to be made to work harder. The real state of affairs in the camps only emerges piecemeal from figures which served other purposes, and it may never be possible to reach an exact total of the number of people who died in German concentration camps and their dependencies. In the Auschwitz group of camps it is said that 363,000 people were registered on the books from February 1940 to January 1945. Allowing for the evacuations westward at the end, something like 280,000 people must have died in this group. But nine-tenths of the number were Jews and their death was a delayed form of planned extermination.[3] By comparison, the official death registries show 33,462 at Buchenwald and 35,318 at Mauthausen, but these may omit a few transports which were directed to Euthanasia and other extermination camps.[4] Belsen, a privileged camp with a low death-rate, may have accounted for close on forty thousand victims in its last two months alone. Deaths of Aryan internees in concentration camps, properly so called, may well have exceeded a quarter of a million between 1933 and 1945. This massacre by ill-treatment was only fractional, as compared with the deliberate extermination of Jews and with the callous abandonment of the Russian prisoners of war in 1941. Nevertheless, it stands comparison with the entire German civilian losses from Allied bombing. It was not a deliberate ideological policy like the extermination of the Jews, nor was it an inevitable part of total war like the air

[1] Von Oven, op. cit., II, p. 212.   [2] See *supra*, pp. 221-3.
[3] Reitlinger, op. cit., p. 460; Filip Friedman, *This was Oswiecim* (London, 1946).   [4] Eugen Kogon, *Die SS Staat* (Berlin, 1947), p. 165; IMT II, p. 376.

raids on civilians. It was not in the budget and it was admitted to
be a mistake. It came from a combination of bureaucratic incompetence, dishonesty among subordinates and muddled thinking with
massed panic fear at the top. It was Himmler's most personal
monument.

3. DEATH CAMPS : EUTHANASIA

Alongside the concentration camps there existed the out-and-out
death camps which were intended for the 'Final Solution of the
Jewish Problem'. The greatest was at Auschwitz in the heart of
industrial Upper Silesia, which had been made part of Germany
in 1939. The Auschwitz gas chambers, which were in use from
March 1942 to October 1944, were, however, in an enclosure distinct
from the concentration camp. In Poland there were the death camps,
Belsec, Sibibor, Treblinka and Chelmno, each of which was in use
for about eighteen months. For much shorter periods the Germans
ran death camps at Ponary near Vilna, at Malo Trostinec near
Minsk, at Bikernek near Riga, at Fort Number Nine near Kovno
and at Piaski near Lwow, all these being shooting and not gassing
establishments. These camps were run by the SS and in them
perished perhaps half of the four million Jews who disappeared
from Europe.

It was only at the very end of the great international Nuremberg
trial, on 7 August 1946, that a clue was dropped by the SS witness
Conrad Morgen, which led to the true source of the greatest murder
organisation in history.[1] In the subsequent 'Doctors' Trial' this clue
was followed up and it showed that the whole thing had started, in
the name of social hygiene, with the elimination of the incurably
insane. This had been carried out in Germany on an enormous scale
between October 1939 and August 1941. Later the organisation
which carried this out was transferred to Poland for the mass
murder of Jews.

The earlier extermination plan, restricted to the insane, seems to
have been firmly linked in the German mind with the name of the
SS. And well it might have been, for that well-tried alibi was never
used to better purpose by German officials than in the case of the
euthanasia killings; but in reality neither Himmler nor any member
of his leadership staff had any part in formulating Hitler's euthanasia

[1] IMT XX, p. 380.

programme. The SS provided medical officers and warders when called upon to do so. And so, for that matter, did the health departments of several German local authorities. Undoubtedly the running of a dozen extermination establishments in Germany and Austria was facilitated by the existence of Death's Head units with concentration-camp experience. It is possible, too, that there would not have been enough doctors to carry out these murderous selections if there had been no SS medical service, but there were plenty of euthanasia doctors outside the SS and some of them may be in practice today.

The programme, which accounted for the death of some fifty to sixty thousand German citizens in the first two years of war, is still largely a mystery. Hitler never advocated euthanasia in his public speeches and writings, nor is it clear when he decided on it. Racial purity was generally associated in party oratory with sterilisation, which was made compulsory in certain extreme cases by a decree dated July 1933. In September 1935, when the first anti-Jewish code of laws was published, a speech was made at the Nuremberg party rally by the Nazi medical leader for Franconia, Gerhardt Wagner. The orator, a protégé of Hess, who was destined to become medical leader for the entire party, advocated sterilisation for Jews as well as for defectives.[1] After the meeting Hitler was believed to declare that he would see that this was done in the event of war, but it was also said that what Hitler promised was not sterilisation but euthanasia, and that he had remarked that the war would make this step easier because then the Church would not be able to oppose it.[2]

Euthanasia was not welcomed by the party leaders, who saw in it something not in the book and difficult to fit in with their own popularity. But Hitler had achieved a system by which he could ignore his leaders whenever he liked through making a new authority, and there were plenty of ambitious officials in the Department of Health to serve such an authority. And here, more than in any other case, Hitler could rely on the cold zeal of Martin Bormann, then working patiently to supplant Rudolf Hess as head of the party office and Deputy Fuehrer. It is a curious commentary on the psychology of the German nation that the scheme was carried out under the noses of seventy million people for nearly two years on end without the publication of a decree, and that none of the officials concerned could have quoted his ultimate authority if summoned

[1] Alice Platten-Hallermund, *Die Toetung Geisteskranker im Deutschland* (Frankfurt, 1948), p. 35. [2] Case I, transcript, 2413.

before a court. Himmler himself disapproved of the euthanasia plan, at any rate in the case of Aryan German subjects, but such was the position his Gestapo had acquired that no court would intervene with what was legally irresponsible mass murder, carried out by local government officials.

Even Guertner, the Minister of Justice, had to make repeated attempts to obtain the text of Hitler's secret decree from Hans Lammers at the Reich Chancellery and he only got a copy in the winter of 1940. What Guertner in fact received from Lammers was a photo-copy of a handwritten note which had been sent by Hitler to Philip Bouhler, the head of the Fuehrer's Chancellery. It had been sent in October 1939, but back-dated to the first day of the war.[1] It seems that on receiving this contemptible thing Guertner abandoned all direct legal interference.

The photo-copied note charged Philip Bouhler and Karl Brandt with 'expanding the authority of duly appointed physicians so that they can order mercy killing for incurables'.[2] Of these two men, Brandt and Bouhler, the first was ruined by Bormann's intrigues and, when he was captured at Kiel at the end of the war, he was awaiting a death sentence from a court appointed by Hitler.[3] The second of them, Philip Bouhler, degenerated into a mere messenger boy for the all-powerful Martin Bormann. At the end of the war he sought Goering's protection and together with his wife followed Goering's last peregrinations, which ended near Zell am See in Austria. Here the Bouhler couple committed suicide shortly before the arrival of the Americans.

At the beginning of the war Bouhler ranked higher in Hitler's estimation. His 'Fuehrer's Chancellery' had been transformed from a simple private secretariat to an executive organisation for secret decrees. The euthanasia institutes and later the gassing camps for the Jews in Poland were the responsibility of this organisation and the role of the SS in providing staff for them was secondary.

As director of the programme, Hitler at first chose Leonardo Conti, an old party member and bearer of the Blood Order of 1923, who served as head of the Health Department under the Minister of the Interior, Wilhelm Frick.[4] Although not a reluctant collaborator, Conti went at once in great trepidation to Hans Lammers to

---

[1] Case I, transcript, 2690; evidence of Hans Lammers.
[2] Nuremberg Document PS 630.   [3] Trevor-Roper, op. cit., pp. 73, 186.
[4] IMT XI, p. 130.

get his position legalised, whereupon Hitler in a fury replaced him with Bouhler, a timid, soft-faced creature whose only qualification was that he had at one time edited *Voelkische Beobachter* and that he was interested in purging Nazi school-books. But another Nuremberg testimony, that of the heavily implicated Viktor Brack, suggests that Himmler, Frick and Goering, though not much allied in other respects, intrigued to get Bouhler appointed because Conti was too much Bormann's man.[1]

Conti, indeed, seems to have been the only official of Hitler's Reich to whom Bormann was consistently loyal. In September 1944, when Carl Brandt succeeded in getting Conti dismissed from the Health Department, Bormann not only made his arrangements to ruin Brandt but offered his own resignation to Hitler.[2] But even five years before this Bormann proved too strong for the supporters of Brandt and Bouhler. He saw to it that they acted in consultation with Conti, who certainly signed the first orders of the euthanasia department.[3]

Hitler chose Bouhler and Brandt because the former was in a position to side-track Lammers and Guertner, while Brandt, as Hitler's private physician since 1934 and party representative of the medical profession, was believed to know the right sort of doctors. In reality the selection of consultants proved too difficult under the handicaps of a secret and invisible decree and it became necessary for Bouhler's office to call on the SS for many of the medical men and for all of the rank and file.

Himmler already possessed a close link both with the Fuehrer's Chancellery and the Health Department. In 1929, at the birth of Himmler's daughter Gudrun, Frau Himmler, a former Berlin nurse, was attended by one of her own medical associates, a certain Dr. Brack; she also appears to have brought to Himmler's attention the doctor's twenty-four-year-old son, Viktor, who was then a Munich student of economics. The newly appointed Reichsfuehrer SS, emerging from the obscurity of Waldtrudering, needed a chauffeur.[4] Himmler seems to have been very friendly with Viktor Brack, who was five years younger than himself, but he could not keep him for ever as a chauffeur. It was not easy to place him and it was not till 1936 that Bouhler employed Brack as a sort of liaison officer with

[1] Case I, transcript, 7658.   [2] *The Bormann Letters*, p. 79.
[3] Platten-Hallermund, *Die Toetung Geisteskranker im Deutschland* (Frankfurt, 1948), p. 39.   [4] Trials of War Criminals, I, p. 842. Document NO. 846.

the Department of Health. Brack, who was surrounded in the dock in 1947 by German medical men, looked very like a dentist, but he had no medical experience and, though he learnt a lot in 1936-9 about Department of Health officials, it seems that as the son of a respectable practitioner he knew no one suitable for the work; nor could Dr. Linden find many such practitioners in the still relatively respectable Health Department. Brack had to apply to Himmler for medical officers from the Death's Head units, while others, like Mennecke and Gorgass, had to be withdrawn from active service in the field SS. One way and another, some twenty to thirty medical officers were briefed to select the wretched mental home inmates who were to be dispatched to the six principal extermination institutes, Hadamar, Graefeneck, Sonnenstein, Bernberg, Hartheim and Brandenburg. These, in turn, delegated some of their work to smaller and more obscure institutes.

A few of the SS doctors managed to quit their horrible task, while a few, like Thilo and Mengele, stayed on to conduct the enormous selections for the Auschwitz gas chambers. Others, like Horst Schumann, transferred their activities to human guinea-pig experiments in the concentration camps. Since the war their fate has been diverse. Conti, Bouhler and Linden committed suicide, Brandt and Brack were hanged and a few more were sent to prison by German courts, but most of the euthanasia doctors have gone underground. Still worse, many doctors, who gave so-called euthanasia injections to unknown foreigners in the secrecy of concentration camps, returned to civilian practice and may be there today. Karl Theiner of Mauthausen, Otto Heidl of Strutthof and Hermann Fischer of Flossenbuerg were not apprehended till late in 1954[1]

But basically this was a slaughter not of political enemies, disowned Jewish subjects or sub-humans from the unspeakable East, but of Germans, among them the aged parents, near relatives and even infant children of serving soldiers and loyal party members. And what makes it more extraordinary is the huge staff involved, not merely a few perverted doctors like Heyde and Mennecke and a few de-humanised bureaucrats like Brack and Blankenberg, but thousands of nurses, male and female, besides ambulance drivers, asylum guards and crematorium stokers.

Though the extermination institutes were secluded buildings, well wired and guarded, they were nevertheless in Germany and neigh-

[1] *The Times*, 5 January 1955 and 9 November 1955.

bouring villagers could not avoid knowing a great deal about them. The most notorious of them all, Hadamar, was only a few miles from Limburg on the Lahn in the tourist-frequented Westerwald. In May 1941 the Frankfurt Appeal Courts reported to Schlegelberger, the acting Minister of Justice, that the inhabitants of Hadamar village knew what went on at the asylum. They could see the smoke of the crematorium chimney every day. It was common knowledge that the patients were taken to the gassing room, wearing nothing but a paper shirt. The children would shout as the asylum vans passed, 'Here come some more to be gassed'. In the evenings the asylum staff were seen quite openly drinking at the local Gasthaus.[1]

Reports and protests from provincial courts grew in volume at the beginning of 1941, when the death of Franz Guertner, who had never in his life taken a strong line on anything, was thought to remove an impassable barrier. In the meantime there had been candid comment from the heads of the Churches, both Catholic and Protestant, notably Cardinal Faulhaber's letter to Guertner in October 1940.[2] There had even been a direct approach to Hitler that summer by Prince Philip of Hesse, the son-in-law of the King of Italy. At that time the Prince was still in Hitler's favour and was, moreover, Oberpraesident of Hesse-Nassau where Hadamar was situated. Prince Philip of Hesse, who survived his own internment in Sachsenhausen and who gave evidence at the Frankfurt 'Hadamar Trial' in March 1947, testified that he had offered his resignation but that he had been compelled by Hitler to continue in office and condone the euthanasia programme. It was a heavy responsibility, for in this former principality of his family a mad reign of terror was conducted from Wiesbaden by the Gauleiter Jakob Sprenger and the head of the Local Health Department, *Landesrat* Bernotat.[3]

But most important in the campaign to end euthanasia was the peculiar action of Heinrich Himmler. The largest number of cases was handled not at Hadamar but at the Graefeneck Institute in Wuerttemburg. A nursing sister, who tried to visit her old patients in Graefeneck in 1940, found it guarded by SS men who chased her away from the wire.[4] When it was known that the SS were associated with Graefeneck, a lady acquaintance of Himmler's wrote to him personally—he was strangely amenable to private correspondence—

[1] Case I, Document NO. 844.   [2] Case I, NO. 846.
[3] Platten-Hallermund, op. cit., pp. 24, 109.   [4] IMT I, p. 169.

and in December 1940 he informed his friend Brack that the Graefeneck Institute was causing grave disquiet.[1] He would do better to
close it and educate the Wuerttemburgers instead with films on
mental and infectious diseases. Brack did both. He closed Graefeneck in January and he commissioned a film about a professor who
performed euthanasia on his wife, called 'I Accuse'.[2]

Seven more months were to pass till 16 August 1941, when Hitler
ordered Brandt to telephone Bouhler that the action must be stopped
—again without decree or written authority. Fritz Mennecke believed that it was because Hitler had been jeered at by the crowd
when his train waited in a station while lunatics were being shipped
off.[3] Another reason was certainly provided by the famous von
Galen sermons, the last of which had been delivered in Muenster
Cathedral a fortnight previously. Of these sermons Hitler seems to
have been genuinely terrified, for, although he swore that he would
exact retribution from the bishop to the last farthing, he added that
it would be after the war.[4] After the third Muenster sermon Himmler
demanded von Galen's arrest,[5] and Bormann, whose office was responsible for relations with the Church, wanted him hanged. Yet
von Galen suffered nothing worse than confinement to his palace.
Goebbels, who had been educated at one time for the priesthood,
had urged moderation. 'The bishop's arrest', he said, 'would have
meant writing off Muenster and the whole of Westphalia for the
duration of the war'. Yet von Galen had not minced his words.

As I now reliably learn, lists have also been drawn up in the Health and
Nursing Institutes of the Province of Westphalia, showing the cases to be removed as unproductive subjects to be deprived of life within a short space of
time. The first transport left Mariental near Muenster in the course of this week.
. . . I am, moreover, assured that in the Reich Ministry of the Interior, as well
as in the office of the Reich medical leader, Dr. Conti, no concealment is made
of the fact that a great number of mental cases have been deliberately killed and
will continue to be killed in the future'.[6]

After the publication of these facts in a well-packed cathedral,
von Galen's immunity threatened to weaken the position of the
Ministry of the Interior's officials throughout the Laender. Moreover, on 28 August the detestable Leonardo Conti (incidentally
not a German but a Swiss from Lugano) received a letter from

---

[1] Case I, Document NO. 018.   [2] Bayle, *Croix gammée ou caducée*, p. 843.
[3] Case I, transcript, 2481.   [4] *Hitler's Table Talk*, p. 555.
[5] *Von Hassell Diary*, p. 191.
[6] Dulles, op. cit., p. 118; Weisenborn, op. cit., p. 48.

the aged dean of St. Hedwig's Cathedral in Berlin, Dr. Bernhard Lichtenberg.

If this statement were untrue, you, Herr Reichsaerztefuehrer, would have branded the episcopal preacher long ago as a libeller and you would have instituted judicial proceedings against him, or else the Gestapo would have concerned itself in the matter. That has not happened. You therefore acknowledge the justice of the assertion. . . . I am communicating the contents of this letter to the Reich Chancellery, the Reich Ministries and the Gestapo.[1]

The letter was sent when Hitler had already withdrawn his instructions to Brandt and Bouhler, but the fact that Lichtenberg was not at once arrested shows how seriously von Galen had shaken the Nazi leadership.[2] The euthanasia institutes were never again used for the murder of free German citizens. Their sporadic activities, which continued till the end of the war, were limited henceforward to the elimination of incurables among Eastern workers and their children, and to the execution of selected victims from concentration camps, who were dispatched in considerable numbers under the cover of bogus lunacy certificates, the notorious 'form 14f, 13'.

And so in August 1941 the euthanasia personnel were threatened with redundancy, but these were witnesses too awkward for release into the ordinary walks of life. Luckily, August 1941 was the month when the Einsatzgruppen in Russia began the first large-scale massacre of Jews. It was also the month in which Hitler told Goebbels that he intended to deport the Berlin Jews to the East.[3] The pressure of popular opinion against euthanasia showed Hitler that these useful servants could be employed to better advantage and with less danger to his popularity at home by utilising them in the 'Final Solution'.

4. DEATH CAMPS : RACIAL MURDER

The direction of the extermination of the Jews had been entrusted to Himmler and Heydrich certainly as far back as March 1941.[4]

[1] Weisenborn, op. cit., p. 59.

[2] Domprobst Lichtenberg was not arrested till 23 October. He was not charged with his letter to Conti, but with his notes for a projected sermon in which he was to intercede for the first Berlin Jews deported to Poland. He was sentenced to ten years' imprisonment, but was released two years later on the intercession of the Bishop of Berlin. Following their usual practice, the Gestapo picked him up at the prison gates. He died a fortnight later, when on the way to Dachau (Weisenborn, op. cit., p. 55; Case XI, NG 4447).

[3] Fragments, Goebbels diary quoted in Reitlinger, op. cit., p. 84.

[4] See *supra*, p. 180.

But there is no evidence that at that time Himmler was an embittered anti-Semite or indeed that he ever became one. It is a peculiar thing that Himmler's surviving speeches are largely free from the savagely anti-Jewish utterances which were fashionable even among the more moderate of Hitler's Ministers. Himmler's one and only public allusion to the extermination of Jewry, which he made at Posen on 4 October 1943, incredibly though it reads, is worded in a whining, apologetic style.[1]

I also want to talk to you quite frankly on a very grave matter. Among ourselves it should be mentioned quite frankly and yet we will never speak of it publicly. . . . I mean the evacuation of the Jews, the extermination [Ausrottung] of the Jewish race. It is one of the things it is easy to talk about. 'The Jewish race is being exterminated', says one party member, it is quite clear, it is in our programme—elimination of the Jews; and we are doing it, exterminating them. And then they come, eighty million worthy Germans, and each one has his decent Jews. Of course, the others are vermin, but this one is an 'A1' Jew. Not one of those who talk this way has witnessed it, not one of them has been through it. Most of you must know what it means when a hundred corpses are lying side by side or five hundred or a thousand. To have stuck it out and at the same time—apart from exceptions caused by human weakness—to have remained decent men, that is what has made us hard. This is a page of glory in our history which has never been written and is never to be written.

This open admission, made before a select audience of SS police Fuehrers, may be compared with Himmler's feeble evasions, when he wrote to Dr. Hilel Storsch in March 1945 of his efforts to enable Jews to emigrate from Germany. It may also be compared with his explanations of the ghettos and the crematoria which he gave Norbert Masur in the following month.[2] Himmler himself would have seen nothing inconsistent in this. It was 'a page of glory' for his staff to have stuck it out through millions of executions, but personally he had never wanted these executions. In the days before his orders he used to dissociate himself from the organised exaction of ransom by Heydrich's Jewish Emigration Office. Far from taking responsibility for Heydrich's policy, he used Heydrich's name as an alibi. On the night of 8 November 1939, when Heydrich circulated instructions to the Gestapo for a pogrom in revenge for the murder of the embassy attaché Ernst Vom Rath, Himmler pretended that he had not consented. Guenther Schmidt, the chief of Himmler's bodyguard, spread a story that Himmler did not know of Heydrich's instructions till the very last moment. Later Professor Popitz told

---

[1] Nuremberg Document PS 1918. See also pages 201 and 252.

[2] Kersten, *Totenkopf und Treue*, pp. 358-9.

von Hassell that Himmler at first refused to co-operate, but when Hitler failed to reply to his telegram, he changed his mind in a panic.[1]

In a discussion with Felix Kersten in March 1940 Himmler's language was astonishingly mild. In words which recall G. K. Chesterton, Himmler declared that, since he did not himself wear a caftan and ringlets, he did not see why a Jew should wear leather breeches in order to roam about Bavaria. 'The Jew is himself neither better nor worse than any other nation, but everyone must remain restricted to the forms of his own existence and culture'.[2] On 11 November 1941, when the extermination policy in Russia was about to be extended to the Jews deported from Germany, Himmler appeared to his father-confessor to be genuinely upset and at great pains to find philosophical arguments to justify his instructions. A year later, however, Himmler had convinced himself that he was a victim of the wicked counsels which Goebbels had imposed on Hitler.[3]

Having assuaged his conscience in the matter, Himmler's economic instincts were still outraged by the fact that Hitler wanted to exterminate able-bodied workers. This Himmler partly prevented by allowing the Jewish workers to survive, if only for a matter of months, in the murderous labour camps, a policy that he pursued more thoroughly after Heydrich's death. Himmler's orderly instincts, too, were outraged by the publicity given to the casual and unorganised mass shootings which were carried out by the Einsatzgruppen in July-October 1941. We have already seen how badly Himmler reacted to the small execution which he witnessed near Minsk during those months.[4]

Artur Nebe, the head of the Criminal Police, as well as the commander of an Einsatzgruppe, was well placed to carry out Himmler's instructions to look for a new method of mass killing. In 1939 he had lent a commissioner from his Criminal Investigation Department, one Christian Wirth of Stuttgart, to the euthanasia organisation. In 1939-40 victims of euthanasia were usually killed by barbiturates or phenol injections. Wirth, however, was given a disused sanatorium at Brandenburg an der Havel, twenty-five miles from Berlin, in which to experiment.[5] His first death chamber was operated

---

[1] *Von Hassell Diary*, pp. 22, 28.   [2] Kersten, *Totenkopf und Treue*, pp. 35-40.
[3] *Ibid.*, pp. 149, 201.   [4] See *supra*, p. 183.
[5] Nuremberg Document; Affidavit SS 67 (Morgen).

by coal gas and the inaugural gassing was watched by Brack and
Bouhler.[1] This was at the end of 1939, but it was not till the summer
of 1941, probably immediately after Himmler's visit to Minsk, that
Wirth was sent by Bouhler and Brack to found a new 'institute' near
Lublin. In reality Wirth was employed in Poland, adapting lorries
as gassing vehicles, and the first of them was used in Russia as early
as September.[2]

On 25 October Hinrich Lohse, the newly appointed Reichskommissar for the Baltic States, learnt from Ernst Wetzel, the 'racial
political expert' of Rosenberg's Ministry, that the first permanent
gassing camps would be near Riga and Minsk, where Jews would
shortly arrive from the Reich. The necessary installations would be
constructed on the spot by Viktor Brack's chemical expert, Dr.
Kallmeyer, who would work under the general instructions of Adolf
Eichmann, the head of the Jewish Resettlement Department in
Heydrich's RSHA. It was vitally important, Lohse learnt, that the
publicity of the recent mass shootings at Wilna should not be
repeated.[3]

Two days later there was a change of plan and the new gassing
camp was re-sited within short range of the Lodz ghetto whither the
first Reich deportees had been diverted. Wirth and Kallmeyer concealed their improvised gassing vans in an abandoned château known
as Chelmno and by the end of the year the first of the Polish death
camps had begun to function in this desolate place.[4]

By this time it had been decided, so Dr. Hans Frank informed his
cabinet in Cracow, to extend the 'Final Solution' to the three million
Jews of Poland.[5] For this more than one death camp was needed,
and on 10 January 1942 Brack headed in person a 'delegation' from
the euthanasia organisation which included some of the staff of
Hadamar and Sonnenstein. They were to 'help in saving our
wounded in the ice and snow on the battlefields of the East'.[6]
In reality the delegation provided assistance for Wirth and his
new Chief, Odilo Globocnik. Wirth acquired three death camps,
Belsec, Sobibor and Treblinka, which were opened between
March and July 1942. A letter from Brack to Himmler, dated

[1] Trials of War Criminals, I, pp. 876-9.   [2] *Ibid.*, p. 803; and Vol. IV, p. 212.
[3] See *supra*, p. 186; Trials of War Criminals, I, pp. 803, 870, 883; Nuremberg
Document NO. 365.   [4] Reitlinger, op. cit., p. 137.
[5] IMT II, p. 393; and Nuremberg Document PS 2233.
[6] Case I, Nuremberg Document NO. 907; evidence of Mennecke.

23 June 1942, speaks of a second loan of euthanasia staff to Globocnik.[1]

Although hundreds of thousands of Jews were killed in 1942-3 in the four Polish death camps, the contingents supplied by Brack were certainly not large. There were twenty to thirty in the first and the whole of Wirth's commando may not have exceeded a hundred men. More were not needed, since most of the work was done by able-bodied Jewish slaves who were picked out from the incoming trains, while the guards were provided from militia units which had been recruited by the Germans from the Latvians and Ukrainians. Brack's experts were concerned only with the last stages, but this was a very special assignment. The dismounted diesel engines taken from tanks and lorries, which operated the gas chambers, constantly broke down. When a transport, which had arrived with its passengers mostly half-dead, had to wait for days on end, it was the duty of the experts to go round braining the sick with any weapon that came to hand.[2] For this reason one of them, Hubert Gomerski, was always known as the Doctor.

These experts were rather peculiar citizens, who had been attracted into Theodor Eicke's Death's Head battalions in the early days and were thence selected for the euthanasia establishments, generally by Brack in person. Their dual role as mercy killers and race-exterminators has been difficult to trace and some of them, like Hirtreiter and Gomerski, both Totenkopf members, survived a trial for their Hadamar activities only to be picked up again years later for their parts at Treblinka and Sobibor.[3]

These men worked for Globocnik till the autumn of 1943, when the destruction of all but the physically toughest of the Jews of Poland and a series of rebellions by the slaves in the death camps put an end to a system which since Heydrich's death had earned the name 'Action Reinhard'. More than two million Jews had been killed in eighteen months and their property had been seized by the SS, even to their spectacles and the gold of their teeth, wrenched out on the way to the gas chamber. But Globocnik had helped himself too liberally and, after an unsatisfactory audit, Himmler discharged him and sent him to Trieste together with the Wirth commando. During its last days in Poland the commando was investigated by

[1] Trials of War Criminals, I, p. 711; Nuremberg Document NO. 205.
[2] *Frankfuerter Rundschau*, 24 August 1950; Reitlinger, op. cit., p. 140.
[3] Reitlinger, op. cit., p. 135; *Frankfuerter Rundschau*, 22 August 1950.

the SS judge advocate, Conrad Morgen. Himmler had not briefed
Morgen in this matter and the workings of the death camps were a
revelation to him. But perhaps Morgen's strangest discovery was that
the commando was still on the pay-books of the Fuehrer's Chancellery at No. 4 Tiergartenstrasse, and that Werner Blankenberg, who
had succeeded Brack, sent daily orders to Wirth from Berlin.[1]

Two years after the end of the euthanasia programme Bouhler
had not relinquished his men. He expected to recover them in order
to resume mercy killing after the war, and, according to Brack, he
protested to Globocnik because he had given them a task which
would make them unfit to carry on their high office. Bouhler was a
really silly man whom no one thought anything of.[2] He probably
believed it.

By the time of Morgen's discoveries, the death-camp machinery
had been applied to the Jews of the Greater Reich, the Western
countries and the Balkans. As early as October 1941 Jews had been
sent from Berlin and other Reich cities to the already hopelessly
overcrowded Lodz ghetto. Before the end of the year deportations
had followed to ghettos in the Baltic states and White Russia. In
the spring and early summer of 1942 there were much larger and
far more frequent deportations to the ghettos and transit camps
which Globocnik had established in the Lublin region, among them
many trainloads of Jews, dispatched by the compliant government
of Father Tiso in Slovakia.[3]

Usually three-quarters, but in many cases the entire transport,
were destined for execution. But there was no general rule. Jews
from the Reich, who had been entrained for Riga, Kovno or Minsk,
might be sent straight to the ghetto, where for another two years
they were permitted a life almost recognisably that of human beings.
Sometimes, however—and this was particularly true of Minsk transports—they never reached the ghettos at all. They were taken direct
to the extermination camps in the forests. Those who were sent to
places near Lublin mostly graduated towards the death camps,
Belsec and Sobibor.

Early in 1942 Himmler issued instructions through Eichmann and
Martin Luther of the Foreign Office for the first deportations from
Western countries and by July 1942 France, Belgium, and Holland
accounted between them for one deportation train of Jews a day,
running to a time-table. By this time the liquidation of the Polish

[1] IMT XX, p. 385.   [2] Trials of War Criminals, I, p. 733.   [3] See *infra*, p. 378.

ghettos alone, including Warsaw with its four hundred thousand Jews, had put too big a strain on the four camps at the disposal of Globocnik and Wirth. For some time Himmler had been trying to create a central clearing station and a unified procedure. As early as the summer of 1941 he had introduced Rudolf Hoess, the ex-convict and commandant of Auschwitz concentration camp, into the circle of the initiated. Hoess was to be in charge of the unified procedure. As a Nuremberg witness in 1946, aware that nothing waited him but the gallows, Hoess took a strange pleasure in recalling that Himmler entrusted him with the destruction of six million people and that two million and a half had actually died under his hands.[1]

With Hoess, the Nazi mass-murderer *par excellence*, we have completed the circle and returned to our first chapter, for Hoess was an out-and-out product of the Freikorps movement of 1918-23. Like Ernst von Salomon, the literary laureate of the Freikorps, Hoess as a young man had been picked by lot to play his part in murder and, like Ernst von Salomon, a dose of prison had not cured him of politics. If one is to believe von Salomon there was nothing more hateful to a true Freikorps man than Hitler's regimented treachery and cruelty, nothing more remote from that genial armed bohemianism than racial extermination—as if it meant nothing that every notorious SS Fuehrer who was old enough had been a Freikorps man. Surely in Crematoria Nos. 1-4 the spiritual anarchy of the men, who had not had enough war in November 1918, produced its long delayed harvest.

Rudolf Hoess came from a severe lower middle class Roman Catholic home in Baden Baden. During the First World War he was able to run away from a father as rigidly bigoted as himself and to serve on the Palestine and Mesopotamian fronts as a boy soldier, enlisted at sixteen. War was the only emancipation he knew from a horrible home life and so, after the armistice, the Freikorps swallowed him. Hoess was with the Freikorps Rossbach in all its campaigns, in the Ruhr, the Baltic states and Silesia. In January 1923 he was chosen by lot to take part in the ritual murder of a man who was supposed to have denounced Leo Schlageter, the Nazi protomartyr who was shot by the French in the Ruhr. And so this twenty-two-year-old clerk was sent to prison and, when he emerged under an amnesty in 1928, he rejoined the Rossbach corps, which survived in secret as an *Arbeitsgemeinschaft* on a Silesian farming estate.

[1] In fact considerably under a million. See Reitlinger, op. cit., pp. 460-1.

Married and with three children, too poor to buy a farm and leading a completely thwarted life, Hoess in 1930 made the acquaintance of Himmler who urged him to join the infant SS. Hoess was too dull and too lacking in social graces to excel even here, and we next hear of him at the end of 1934 as a newly-joined member of the Totenkopf, promoted to command a 'block' of detainees in Dachau. More than five years had still to pass before, with the rank of Lieutenant of the SS, Hoess was sent to command a small camp on his own, the former Austrian cavalry barracks at the tip of Silesia among the marshes of the Sola and Vistula near Auschwitz.

It is unlikely that in the summer of 1941 Hoess, who looked all his life like an unamiable and officious blue-eyed corporal, had attracted the attention of Himmler for any personal qualities.[1] He was the commandant of Auschwitz, and Auschwitz was the place where Himmler wanted his central death factory to be. Himmler approached Hoess, as he would have approached any other SS man who might have held the post, with the certainty that he would not refuse. If Hoess had enjoyed any protection in achieving his modest position in the service, it was probably, as Conrad Morgen was told, because Martin Bormann, who had gone to prison with Hoess in 1928 as a colleague in murder, kept an eye on him.[2] In November 1943, when Himmler made an example of some of the more corrupt of the concentration-camp commanders, Hoess was involved in a judicial inquiry concerning the smuggling of gold from the camp, gold torn from the mouths of corpses in the gas chambers, gold which should have been taken by a trusted SS courier to the strong-room of the Reichsbank. At this moment it was probably Martin Bormann who saved Hoess from the convenient disappearance which might have waited a *Geheimnissetraeger* or man who knew too much. Thus it was that Hoess ended the war as a lieutenant-colonel and deputy inspector of concentration camps, with all the shambles of Belsen beneath his glassy uncomprehending stare. In April 1947 the Poles hanged him like Haman from a high gibbet in his own camp.

Among the matters discussed during Hoess's first briefing in mass murder in the summer of 1941 was an improved apparatus for 'mercy killing'. Himmler had returned from his shattering visit to

---

[1] For Hoess's early life see G. M. Gilbert, *The Psychology of Dictatorship* (New York, 1951), pp. 240-5. Gilbert spent many hours in Hoess's company.

[2] Evidence of Conrad Morgen, in IMT XX, pp. 390-6.

Minsk, and Christian Wirth was already at work on his gassing vans, but Hoess, perhaps on Himmler's instructions, pursued a different line. Within a few weeks, on 15 September, Hoess conducted an experiment on invalid Russian prisoners of war in the sealed penal block of Auschwitz main camp. He used a commercial preparation, which was supplied to the camp as a disinfectant gas, the blue hydrogen-cyanide crystals, known as Zyklon B.[1] Hoess was ordered to adopt this system permanently in March 1942, when a small gas chamber was installed in a converted barn near the evacuated village of Birkenwald. Himmler was greatly impressed with Zyklon B because it offered no possibility of a mechanical breakdown, and in the following August he commissioned Professor Mugrowski (of the Health Department of the SS leadership office) to send a demonstrator to the Wirth commando in Poland. In 1945 this demonstrator, Kurt Gerstein, committed suicide in a French prison, having left behind him a confession which contains the only description of the death camps as seen through the eyes of a German official.[2]

The final choice of Auschwitz as the clearing-house for Jews, deported from Western Europe, was not made by Himmler till the early summer of 1942. He may have been influenced by the success which Hoess claimed for his installation, but he was influenced still more by the camouflage possibilities of a huge project to manufacture synthetic petrol in the Auschwitz neighbourhood. A second Auschwitz camp, which Himmler ordered Hoess to construct in November 1941, was intended to house the workers for this 'Buna' project, but in reality the camp was used for Jews who survived the selection for the gas chamber. A third camp had therefore to be constructed for the 'Buna' factory in 1942. This was the I. G. Farben or Monowitz camp and quite distinct from Auschwitz II.

---

[1] Nuremberg Document D 749, Affidavit Hoess; Friedman. op. cit., p. 18; Zenon Rozanski, '*Muetzen Ab*' (Hanover, 1948), p. 53 (an eye-witness account).

[2] Nuremberg Document PS 1553; Reitlinger, op. cit., pp. 152-4, 116-7. Originally the elimination of the sick at Auschwitz had been effected by phenol injections and it had been in practice, according to Zenon Rozanski, for some months before Hoess's Zyklon B experiment. Mass extermination of the sick in Auschwitz was generally restricted to Jews, who were only exempted from the 'Fuehrer Order' for their extermination so long as they were at work. It was, however, applied generally in Mauthausen and Flossenbuerg camps. Hermann Fischer, the Flossenbuerg M.O., deposed at his trial in November 1955 that there had been a secret Himmler order that all incurable sick in the concentration camps were to be killed by injections (*The Times*, 9 November 1955).

During the summer of 1942 a high proportion of the Jews arriving in the daily train from Western Europe were spared the gas chamber at Birkenwald and registered as inmates of the camp called Birkenau, or Auschwitz II. Soon, however, this proportion dropped to a third or a quarter and there were days when it did not exist. The influx into the camp of physically fit Jews, numbered, tattooed and officially registered as *Haeftlinge*, had grown out of hand. There was nothing for them to do, there was nowhere to put them. Death stalked the camp in the trail of the first of the typhus epidemics, which always followed the 'transport season' at Birkenau. On these occasions Hoess and his SS medical officers knew of only one solution to their difficulties. The camp infirmaries, piled to the roof, were emptied through further selections for the gas chamber. At first fictitious entries, naming a variety of natural-death causes, were entered in the camp books, but this exhausted a limited stock of imagination and the naked sick, dumped at the crematorium doors from a sort of rubbish tipper, were simply entered as 'released'.

Very early in the progress of the deportations from Western Europe, in the summer of 1942, there was a fall in the proportion of men under fifty and women under forty-five who could be spared from death. The original Birkenwald installation could no longer cope with a trainload a day, when the proportion of old people besides young children with their mothers, all of whom had to be gassed, remained so high. The four huge combined gas chamber-crematoria, which figure so much in the literature of Auschwitz, were therefore planned at this time, but the first was not ready till March 1943 and the four were not completed till the following autumn. The whole of Himmler's Auschwitz scheme was threatened by this delay, which was the result of wartime priorities in transport.[1] In March 1943, trains converged on Auschwitz from Holland, from Berlin, from Theresienstadt, from Poland, from Salonika and Macedonia. The Dutch trains had to be diverted to Sobibor, the Macedonian trains to Lublin and Treblinka. Only in the late summer, when the wave of deportations died down, could Auschwitz regain its monopoly as the only European clearing-centre for Jews.

The new crematoria were designed in the Auschwitz camp drawing office and some of the blue-prints have survived. The construction was in the hands of Heinz Kammler of Oswald Pohl's works department—Kammler, the king of the rocket-launching sites and the

[1] Trials of War Criminals, V, p. 619.

underground aircraft factories—a sort of concrete Pharaoh. The original euthanasia experts were also interested, for Oswald Pohl recalled that the orders for the new buildings came from Bouhler's office.[1]

Fabulous claims concerning the capacity of the crematoria have been made by witnesses before various judicial commissions, particularly by the not very statistically minded Rudolf Hoess at Nuremberg. But in November 1944, when they destroyed the crematoria, the SS left only the barest traces on the ground. Very few of the Auschwitz survivors of 1945 had seen even the outside of them and no photograph survives. In spite of their size, the installations could not cope with a death output of six thousand a day, such as occurred during the Hungarian deportations of May and June 1944. The bodies had to be burnt in trenches and many of the victims had to be shot.[2] Although German ingenuity had not been idle in the matter, the complete destruction of bodies so as to leave no trace could not be accelerated. At one time Heydrich had employed Paul Blobel, a Duesseldorf architect who had been an Einsatzgruppe leader in Russia, to make experiments in the death camps. An age that has produced the hydrogen bomb might in due course have done somewhat better than Paul Blobel, had not Himmler succeeded by October 1944 in contracting out of his most awkward assignment.[3]

Himmler visited Auschwitz more than once, but the story told by Hoess and others that Himmler witnessed the inauguration of the new crematorium in March 1943, peering coldly through the glass window of the gas chamber, need not be believed. Himmler was a moral coward and physically squeamish and his experience near Minsk had been enough for him. Himmler at Auschwitz was a remote-control killer, as he was elsewhere. The selections for the gas chamber, which occurred daily during the deportation seasons, were not a matter for his personal intervention nor were they of any interest to the makers of high policy. They followed an automatic routine prescribed by the Gestapo subsection for Jewish Affairs, Adolf Eichmann's bureau IVA4b in the Kurfuerstenstrasse. The returns of the selections were sometimes forwarded by Hoess to Eichmann's office and sometimes to a subsection of Pohl's camp administration in Berlin, but it does not seem that either was done

---

[1] *German Crimes in Poland* (Warsaw, 1946), I, p. 32. Nuremberg Document NO. 4472, Case IV, transcript, 1590.   [2] See *infra*, pp. 354-5.

[3] NO. 3197, Affidavit Blobel; Reitlinger, op. cit., p. 138.

as a matter of course or that the records were preserved. At the end of 1942 Himmler ordered his inspector for statistics, Dr. Richard Korherr, to draw up a balance-sheet from the figures sent him by RSHA. In this balance-sheet of 'resettlement' Dr. Korherr was not able to distinguish between the number of Jews who had been entrained for Auschwitz and the number registered on the camp roll.[1]

To this activity of one of his innumerable office staffs Himmler's attitude remained essentially impersonal. For remote-control killers, working from their office desks, are the shadow under which the present age lives. It was not for nothing that Ohlendorf justified his ninety thousand murders at Nuremberg by allusions to the 'press-button killers of the atom bomb'. The vaster the massacres, the more awful the weapons, the easier it becomes to arrange them. The little armies of office chiefs and stenographers are not nauseated by their work, because they do not see it. The historic massacres, carried out by Himmler's hero Jenghiz Khan, were exaggerated by hostile Moslem historians and were certainly far smaller than Himmler's. And perhaps the Mongol horsemen had their moments of doubt and repulsion. The men who stayed glued to their desks for fear of front-line service or the concentration camp had no such moments. Moreover, they lacked the imagination to see what happened at the end of the telegraph line. Himmler was mentally just such a small-office employee himself. These activities, the least important in his own eyes, provided a warning and a moral to which his life, dull and colourless in itself, must for ever point.

[1] NO. 5193-4, not in print, but see Reitlinger, op. cit., pp. 490-1. See also *supra*, p. 223.

11

Himmler and the Plotters

OCTOBER 1942 – JULY 1944

1. ARRESTS AND CLUES

One of the mysteries of the attempt on Hitler's life, which so nearly succeeded on 20 July 1944, is the inglorious role of Himmler's SS organisations. The security police of the Gestapo failed to prevent Stauffenberg's escape. Himmler took an unnecessarily long time following him to Berlin. Kaltenbrunner's agents, who investigated the rebel generals in the Bendlerstrasse, failed to bring an escort with them and were themselves arrested. Had the dissidents chosen to attack the Gestapo main office, they would have found it undefended and, had the troops who were detailed for 'Action Walkuere' truly carried out their orders, the Waffen SS garrisons would not have been able to withstand them.

Was this grouping of circumstances the result of mere carelessness and stupidity or was it, as the Gestapist Willi Hoettl suggests, a deliberate marking time by Himmler? Short of the discovery of very secret documents, which, if they ever existed, must surely have been destroyed, there will be no answer to this question. It can only be said that Himmler knew much about the Resistance Circle but that he did not know what they would do next, and that in all probability he would have welcomed the success of the plot. Constituted as they were, it is unlikely that the Resistance Circle, had they formed a government, would have made of Himmler the scapegoat and victim that Stauffenberg and some of his colleagues required. That the Allies would have demanded his head even as part of the terms of a negotiated peace was something Himmler was incapable of seeing.

It is not known how far Himmler went in his talks with the plotters, Langbehn and Popitz. It is not permissible to judge Himmler's meditated treachery in August 1943 by his peace negotiations in April 1945. But it can be said with certainty that no movement, which had a chance of negotiating with the Western Allies in 1943, would have been crushed by Himmler if he could have helped it. Himmler was reluctant to make any examples of the conspirators whom his agents discovered, because he feared that such examples would ruin the Resistance Circle as a whole. In the matter of these discoveries the ways of the Gestapo appear dilatory and amateurish to a point which has led writers like Abshagen perhaps to underrate the Gestapo's efficiency. Viewed, however, from the standpoint of Himmler's consistently dual personality they become explicable enough.

In considering the record of conspiracy between 1942 and 1944 a clear distinction must be made between the individual attempts of junior officers to murder Hitler, of which there were at least four, and the attempts of agents of the Resistance Circle to make treasonable contacts with the Allies. The former failed partly because Hitler's personal security measures were of almost inspirational cunning. But the officers themselves, if we are to trust their story, were extremely cunning too. No one was brought to trial for an attempt on Hitler between Elser's arrest in November 1939 and Stauffenberg's attempt in July 1944. By contrast, the efforts of the civilian conspirators to maintain contacts abroad were amateurish. The fact that only a few out of many such efforts were detected does not alter the truth that the discoveries which were made by the Gestapo would have been sufficient to ruin the entire circle, had the will existed to follow them up.

Three fascinating cases of detection will illustrate Himmler's perfect consistency and the true light in which he regarded the conspirators. They are the cases of Reichsgerichtsrat Dr. Hans Dohnany, of Ministerialrat Professor Johannes Popitz and thirdly of the circle of Frau Excellenz Hanna Solf.

In October 1942 the Bavarian frontier police pounced on a Munich business man named Schmidthuber, who had for some time been taking sums of money across the Swiss border on behalf of the Abwehr, for whom he acted as agent. It had been discovered that these sums of money had been paid over to fourteen Jewish refugees from Germany and that the requirements of the Abwehr were a pretence.[1] Canaris made no attempt to shield this doubtful agent and Schmidthuber proceeded to make revelations against his employers which he spun out in order to delay his own trial. It was learnt that Schmidthuber's services had been retained for the Abwehr by a prominent member of the Circle, none other than

[1] Gisevius, op. cit., pp. 469-70.

Dr. Hans Dohnanyi, the judge of the Supreme Court who had acted as Guertner's assistant at the time of the Fritsch investigation and who had sat as one of the assessors at Fritsch's trial.[1] Not long after the trial Guertner had got rid of Dohnanyi as not sufficiently Nazi. At the beginning of the war he had joined the Abwehr, that refuge of the displaced intellectual, and was employed under Colonel Hans Oster.

Dohnanyi was a Viennese. Considering the brilliance of his career he was young—only thirty-five at the time of the Fritsch affair—and, if we may trust his photograph, astonishingly callow-looking for his years.[2] Dohnanyi also seems to have been indiscreet even for an Austrian. According to Gisevius he had once been in contact with Karl Wolff in order to get Himmler into the conspiracy.[3] To Schmidthuber Dohnanyi seems to have let himself go. Schmidthuber had learnt of the mission of Dr. Josef Mueller to the Vatican in January 1940, when contact had been made via the Pope with the British Foreign Office and when peace offers from the Beck-Halder circle had been transmitted.[4] He had learnt of the meeting in May 1942 in Sweden between Pastor Bonhoeffer and the Bishop of Chichester. He had learnt that Oster had been interested in a plan made by a certain Josef Roemer to murder Hitler.

This was not the only plot against Hitler that Schmidthuber had heard of. He knew of another of the famous visionary schemes of Hans Oster. An armoured corps from Elbing was to occupy the sacred compound at Rastenburg and secure Hitler's person while the generals made a Putsch.[5] Hans Oster, as we have already seen, was not a realistic man.

Mueller of the Gestapo made no immediate use of these stories, which in any case would have needed a great deal of checking, but it is not at all clear why the arrests of Dohnanyi, his brother-in-law Pastor Dietrich Bonhoeffer and Josef Mueller were delayed nearly nine months, till 5 April 1943.[6] Gisevius has a story[7] that Himmler was afraid to proceed directly against an office like the Abwehr, which was protected by Keitel, and that to do this he had to enlist

[1] See *supra*, p. 105.   [2] Annedore Leber, *Das Gewissen steht auf*, p. 111.
[3] Gisevius, op. cit., p. 457.
[4] Abshagen, op. cit., pp. 248, 357; Weisenborn, op. cit., 133.
[5] Weisenborn, op. cit., p. 133.
[6] Dr. Rudolf Pechel thinks that the arrests were made at the instigation of Schellenberg. *Deutscher Widerstand* (Zuerich, 1947), p. 229.
[7] Gisevius, op. cit., p. 471.

Goering's support. The only way was to offer Goering a treason scandal in the Abwehr to compensate him for the scandal of Rote Kapelle, which had started in the Air Ministry. The explanation is inconsistent with the fall in Goering's prestige at this time. It seems more likely that Himmler hesitated because he did not want to spoil the foreign contacts of the Canaris circle—the motive of all Himmler's hesitations in this quarter.

It was perhaps for this reason that the arrest of Dohnanyi was not arranged directly through the Gestapo but through Goering's protégé, Manfred Roeder, the special commissioner with the Reich Military Tribunal in the Rote Kapelle case. To arrest Dohnanyi, Roeder, who was accompanied by the well-known criminal commissar of the Gestapo Sonderegger, had to proceed to the office of Hans Oster. It happened that Oster was caught signalling to Dohnanyi because Dohnanyi's desk contained incriminating papers. These papers were discovered. They showed that Oster had been in correspondence with Pastor Dietrich Bonhoeffer. This was the brother-in-law of Dohnanyi who had been to Stockholm and had conducted peace talks with the Bishop of Chichester. The papers were only concerned with exemptions from military service for clergymen of the Confessional Church, but some of Oster's goings-on had now become too exposed to be overlooked. He was placed under house arrest and suspended from his functions and henceforward became a man under observation, of no use to the Resistance Circle. Bonhoeffer and Josef Mueller were also arrested. Gisevius, who had a post with the Abwehr in Switzerland but who had come to Berlin in January in the hope of a generals' Putsch, was interrogated by Roeder, but managed to delay matters till Canaris had contacted Keitel. Canaris persuaded Keitel that the whole thing was an attempt by Himmler to attack OKW; so Keitel got Roeder transferred to the Luftwaffe in Greece.

The inquiry was now whittled down to the currency charges alone and the Schmidthuber revelations were allowed to sleep. Gisevius was not interrogated again, but he thought it best to return to his Abwehr post in Switzerland 'by a devious route'. Mr. Allen Dulles says that Gisevius was faced with a treason charge.[1] It is odd that a man who was threatened with a treason charge should retain his post even after February 1944, when Kaltenbrunner, the arch-enemy of Canaris, had taken over the Abwehr. One gets the impression

[1] Dulles, op. cit., p. 79.

that the last thing Himmler wanted to do was to deprive the Abwehr of the services of the Oster-Dohnanyi circle. Gisevius was not the only Abwehr member of the circle to survive the inquiry. Karl Guttenberg, a friend of Dohnanyi's who was probably even deeper in the circle than Gisevius, was recalled from Zagreb to be questioned, held in Berlin for months and still allowed to resume his post.[1]

The success of Admiral Canaris in duping Keitel seems an even worse explanation of the riddle, since, according to von Hassell, the Resistance Circle believed that with the Dohnanyi arrest Himmler was threatening them with another '30 June'. Fritz von der Schulenburg, formerly Wolff Helldorf's deputy in the Berlin Police Praesidium and now a staff officer at the Bendlerstrasse, had actually been under arrest for a few hours. Von Hassell too had been advised to hide in a nursing home.[2] Was Himmler really in such a weak position that he could not hit back against the Canaris circle? Could not Kaltenbrunner have got Bormann to put the whole thing up to Hitler? One would have thought so, yet how feeble was the sequel. The months went by and on 18 July von Hassell wrote that it was a scandal that the Dohnanyi inquiry was still proceeding without any legal warrant.[3] On 13 November he reported that Dohnanyi had now been indicted, but only for minor currency offences.[4] And in December this, too, was dropped and for a few months Dohnanyi was allowed to go free, though he was picked up again shortly before the July 1944 plot.

Dohnanyi was condemned as a member of the conspiracy in March 1945; he died mysteriously in Sachsenhausen concentration camp in the following month, the case against him having been prepared by the same criminal commissioner, Sonderegger, who had played second fiddle at his arrest nearly two years before.[5] Yet on Dohnanyi's release in December 1943 Himmler explained to Keitel that there were no grounds for proceeding with the charge, which had been unpolitical from the beginning. Himmler himself had no further interest in the matter.[6]

I find it unconvincing that the muddling, inconsequent Canaris should have been able to block all Himmler's special powers simply by a word to the colourless Keitel. If the whole of the long

[1] *Von Hassell Diary*, pp. 277, 285.   [2] *Von Hassell Diary*, p. 269.
[3] *Ibid.*, p. 279.   [4] *Ibid.*, p. 288.   [5] Von Schlabrendorff, op. cit., p. 166.
[6] Weisenborn, op. cit., p. 134; Abshagen, op. cit., p. 363.

devolution, Himmler-Kaltenbrunner-Mueller-Schellenberg, really wanted the truth about the Schmidthuber stories, nothing could have stopped their getting it. Having discovered Bonhoeffer's Stockholm visits and probably Goerdeler's too, it would have been a simple matter to trap them by sending bogus members of the Resistance to meet their Allied contacts. Schellenberg had done that before at Venlo in November 1939. But in those days Himmler had wanted to know something about the peace doves in the Abwehr circle. In 1942 he knew enough and he regarded the peace doves as something to be preserved at any cost. And preserved they were, even after February 1944 when Schellenberg stepped into Canaris's shoes and the Abwehr was part of Kaltenbrunner's RSHA office.

When we turn to the case of Popitz and Langbehn, we find a proposed treason of a different order. Himmler himself was intended to be in it and the clandestine game of the two Abwehrs, Canaris's and Schellenberg's, was to be interlocked. In this case the explosion burst while the Dohnanyi inquiry was still pending and nothing illustrates better than these two parallel events the complete consistency of Himmler's behaviour.

The story of the attempt to persuade Himmler to join the Resistance Circle must be followed back to November 1942, when Karl Goerdeler under the pretence of travelling for his firm, Messrs. Bosch, the electrical engineers of Stuttgart, visited Field-Marshal Guenther von Kluge at his headquarters in Smolensk. The meeting had been arranged by von Kluge's Chief of Staff, Henning von Tresckow, a member of the Canaris circle, while Goerdeler was introduced by Fabian von Schlabrendorff, a junior staff officer who had been in the Prussian Ministry of the Interior. Yet beyond the fact that von Kluge had cold feet concerning the next campaign in Russia, there was no reason to regard him as an anti-Nazi. Von Kluge was a terribly vacillating character and also incredibly subservient. In Guderian's view, von Kluge had deliberately ruined his best tank warfare general on the Russian front, Erich Hoeppner, in order to gain credit with Hitler.[1] Von Kluge was prepared for almost anything in order to please Hitler, who presented him with a gift of a quarter of a million marks.[2] In July 1943 Hitler expressed his gratitude when von Kluge burnt the farms and carried off the peasants in his retreat to the Dnieper.[3] Von Kluge had also proposed

---

[1] Guderian, op. cit., p. 248.   [2] Von Schlabrendorff, op. cit., p. 66.
[3] Felix Gilbert, op. cit., p. 65.

removing the peasants' children to Germany to work as slaves, and Himmler's police leaders had carried out his plan.[1]

Although von Kluge afterwards told Beck that Goerdeler had misunderstood him,[2] Goerdeler proceeded on the assumption that von Kluge would act. Goerdeler, therefore, with the aid of Henning von Tresckow, tried to ensure the capture of the Ministries by winning over part of the Replacement Army or Ersatzheer command in the Bendlerstrasse building, notably Friedrich Olbricht, the head of the Supply Office. Stalingrad was on the point of falling and Goerdeler believed that von Kluge would fly with Manstein to Hitler's headquarters to present him with an ultimatum, the moment von Paulus announced his surrender. Once again Goerdeler had misunderstood the generals. After the fateful 3 February, von Kluge and Manstein did indeed fly to Rastenburg, but they flew to reaffirm their loyalty.[3] The only German generals who declared themselves against Hitler did so from Moscow.

Two months later, at the time of the Dohnanyi arrest scare, Goerdeler began to act rather strangely. On 17 May he wrote to Olbricht, reproaching him for having shown no activity after Stalingrad and suggesting that after all there was a chance that Hitler might resign if the generals merely asked him. 'If such a talk can be brought about, there is no reason why it should end badly. Surprises are possible, not probable, but the risks must be taken'.[4] Surprises were indeed possible, but it would have been more than surprising if such a dim conspirator as Olbricht was to prove to be should go to his Fuehrer with such a proposition. Yet Goerdeler's friend and biographer, Professor Gerhard Ritter, finds this letter worthy of reproduction, all ten pages of it, in collotype facsimile.

Shortly afterwards the fertile mind of Karl Goerdeler moved on another tack. He had been visited in Berlin by the Swedish banker, Jacob Wallenberg, who told him that he had been approached on Himmler's behalf. The intermediary, Carl Rasche, was a fellow bank director and he had wanted to know whether Wallenberg would sound the British government on the prospects of peace with a Hitlerless but not Himmlerless Germany.[5] It was obvious that

---

[1] Rosenberg, *Memoirs*, p. 281; PS 031; IMT II, p. 291.

[2] Gisevius, op. cit., p. 458.   [3] Wheeler-Bennett, op. cit., p. 533.

[4] *Die Wandlung*, 1945-6, Heft 2; Wheeler-Bennett, op. cit., p. 568; Gerhard Ritter, *Goerdeler und die deutsche Widerstandsbewegung*, p. 352.

[5] Ritter, op. cit., pp. 422, 548.   See also *infra*, p. 340.

through the recent arrest of Hans Dohnanyi Himmler had tapped the Swedish contacts of the Resistance Circle. Goerdeler was emboldened to write in his next pastoral to von Kluge, which he sent off in July: 'I can also make Herr Goebbels and Herr Himmler your allies if you desire, for even these two men have long realised that with Hitler they are doomed'.[1]

It seems that von Kluge must have passed this light-hearted suggestion to at least one colleague. Henning von Tresckow had been transferred from Kluge's headquarters to Fedor von Bock's, and when he approached his new chief with plans for a Putsch, he was told abruptly that, to be successful, any military revolt must have the support of Himmler. So von Tresckow set about seeking a contact with Himmler. Normally the headquarters staff of an Army Group in Russia would have been the last place on earth wherein to find such a contact. But it happened that a close connection of Himmler's curious friend, Herr Langbehn, was right on the spot, employed as a civilian secretary. She was Marie Louise (Puppi) Sarre, a well-known Berlin sculptress and the daughter of the art historian, Friedrich Sarre. Puppi Sarre was sent to discuss with Langbehn the possibilities of a member of the Resistance Circle meeting Himmler. For this Puppi Sarre was later arrested, but she survived Ravensbrueck concentration camp and the war, an awkward witness on whom the saga-makers of the Resistance Circle are even more awkwardly silent.[2]

The man who consented to act as negotiator with Himmler was Professor Johannes Popitz, the acting Minister of Finance for Prussia, a name we have encountered more than once. Popitz was one of those Prussian officials who, like Rudolf Diels, had served under the Social Democrat government of Karl Severing and whom Goering chose to retain, because politically they had not been of the party of their chiefs. Popitz lived in a circle which had no contacts with Himmler. A Prussian bureaucrat since 1910, he had been Under-Secretary to the Finance Minister, Rudolf Hilferding, and in 1939 his successor at the age of fifty. A few months later, when the triumphant Nazis had driven Hilferding into hiding, Popitz was persuaded to use his influence to get him out of the country. But in 1941 Popitz felt no disgust at remaining in office when the former

---

[1] Wheeler-Bennett, op. cit., 573, quoting *Die Wandlung*, Heft 5; Gisevius, op. cit., p. 468, omits this portion of the letter.   [2] Dulles, op. cit., p. 151.

chief, for whom he expressed such admiration, was hounded to suicide in a Paris Gestapo prison.

In the later 'thirties, when Goering was still the next most powerful person to Hitler, Popitz enjoyed singular protection for a man from outside the party. His entry into the Resistance Circle on the eve of the Munich agreement was brought about by his belief that he could draw in Goering, who dreaded the prospect of a war with the West. Goering had told Popitz that he would not oppose a change of power provided he himself could live abroad and retain his fortune.[1] For a man of his principles, Popitz's record at this time was not very good. Although he had refused Gregor Strasser's inducements to join the National Socialist party in 1930, he accepted the golden party badge in 1937.[2] After the pogrom of 9 November 1938 he is said to have created some emotional impression on Goering by offering his resignation as acting Finance Minister. Nevertheless Popitz did not resign.[3] During the war Goering dropped his patronage of Popitz, who, however, continued for some time to regard Goering as indispensable in any government which should succeed Hitler. Popitz's lack of repulsion for Goering was dictated by the fact that he was a monarchist who wanted the return of the Crown Prince Wilhelm.[4] Liberalism concerned him little and he was prepared to support any basically capitalist régime which could secure peace.

In July 1943, at the time of the proposed meeting with Himmler, the Resistance Circle was still mostly of this character and on the military side entirely so, while the triumvirate Popitz-Goerdeler-Beck were still regarded as the movement's political leaders. Nevertheless the circle had grown; there were younger adherents and on the fringes Social Democrats and trade unionists and the movement was neatly split by Popitz's intention to approach Himmler. It may be said that this is still the case today, for in the latest album of martyrs, produced by the widow of Julius Leber, the portrait of Popitz will not be found, though Popitz was as well and truly hanged as the rest.[5]

According to the charges prepared against him by the People's Court late in 1944, Popitz was already out of the Resistance Circle at the time of the Stauffenberg bomb plot.[6] The People's Court were

[1] Rainer Hildebrandt, *Wir sind die Letzten* (Berlin, 1947), pp. 80, 87, 96.
[2] Dulles, op. cit., p. 148.   [3] *Von Hassell Diary*, p. 28.   [4] *Ibid.*, pp. 209-10.
[5] Leber, op. cit.,   [6] Dulles, op. cit., p. 156.

not concerned with establishing how many members of the circle had joined with Popitz in seeking an alliance with Himmler, but in Puppi Sarre's view there were quite a number, including Erwin Planck, Jens Jessen, Beck and even Goerdeler, because 'they did not object to anything which ex-Nazis like Popitz and Langbehn could do to create confusion in the Nazi ranks'.[1]

Langbehn, as we have seen, had been in a position to tell von Hassell the latest gossip about Himmler's peace plans as long ago as March 1942,[2] but in July 1943, at the time of von Tresckow's conversation with Field-Marshal von Bock, it was not so easy for Langbehn to approach Himmler. Early in the year he had received a warning from Himmler through Rudi Brandt to drop out of the Warsaw spying case, in which he represented the imprisoned Swedish directors of the Svenska Tandstick and Ericsson companies. The case had become a duel between Himmler and Ribbentrop and Langbehn was on the wrong side.[3] Nevertheless, Langbehn had been trying to arrange a Popitz-Himmler meeting since May through Karl Wolff, who, however, had had to go into hospital for his operation.[4] Having been approached again by Puppi Sarre in August, Langbehn had to assure Wolff that Himmler would be expected only to attempt personal persuasion and that Hitler would be given some honourable position in retirement.[5] Langbehn was also interviewed by von Tresckow, who counted on the co-operation of Field-Marshal von Bock. If Himmler would act, it should be possible to isolate Hitler in his headquarters at Rastenburg.[6]

Eventually Karl Wolff arranged an appointment with Himmler for 24 August. Langbehn told Karl Wolff that he would have to start the conversation, because Popitz was too timid, but actually the interview took place *a deux* in a room of the Ministry of the Interior, which Himmler had taken over only that day. Some days later Popitz told his friend Zahler that, though Himmler had interposed few remarks, he had not shown any disapproval even when

---

[1] Dulles, op. cit., p. 163.   [2] *Von Hassell Diaries*, p. 176.

[3] Kersten, *Totenkopf und Treue*, p. 275.   [4] See *supra*, p. 239.

[5] From this point onwards the source quoted is Allen Dulles, *Germany's Underground*, but Dulles's account is a résumé of the Volksgericht charges as drawn up by Roland Freisler and presented on 25 September 1944. The trial, which took place in October, was held in secret on Kaltenbrunner's personal intervention with Thierack. The documents were a chance discovery. They had been in a bombed and derailed truck and were found scattered on the tracks in Berlin (Dulles, op. cit., 147).   [6] Dulles, op. cit., p. 158.

Popitz had suggested negotiations without Hitler's consent.[1] After the interview Wolff told Popitz that Himmler would be prepared for a further discussion. It seems that Langbehn left almost at once to convey this momentous news to his contacts in Switzerland and that within a few days the Gestapo knew of Langbehn's instructions through a telegram, which had been decoded in Switzerland by one of Schellenberg's SD Abwehr agents.

It is unlikely that Himmler himself put the Gestapo on this dangerous track. Allen Dulles supposes that Mueller sent the decoded Swiss telegram to Martin Bormann without letting Himmler know. Yet Bormann proceeded cautiously. Langbehn was actually able to see Himmler again a few days after his return. Himmler appeared interested in Langbehn's contacts but did not try to find out names. Neither knew that the telegram had reached Bormann. Presumably Himmler was now threatened from that august quarter. If so, he could do nothing except arrest Langbehn and with him Puppi Sarre,[2] and this Himmler did.

But in spite of the powerful cabal against him, Himmler protected Popitz right up to the moment of the Stauffenberg plot. And this is all the more extraordinary since Bormann had evidently informed Hitler of the Langbehn disclosures. On 23 September 1943, that is to say only a very few days after Langbehn's arrest, Goebbels happened to criticise Popitz to Hitler for his behaviour on the Berlin air raid damage committee, and was told by Hitler that he was convinced that Popitz was an enemy. 'He is already having him watched so as to have incriminating material about him ready; the moment Popitz gives himself away he will close in on him'.[3]

In November Popitz himself plucked up courage to ask Himmler about Langbehn's case, but Himmler 'reacted sourly'.[4] By the end of the year the Resistance Circle, and the new star Stauffenberg in particular, were convinced that Popitz was being watched. Beck and Goerdeler had dropped Popitz as too dangerous, but Himmler was in fact shielding him, for on 8 November he told Goebbels that he was not certain whether Popitz belonged to the circle of the 'peace negotiators'.[5] In February both Popitz and Goerdeler were tipped off about their impending arrests, but nothing happened. In the political bunker at Sachsenhausen, Langbehn underwent endless

[1] Hildebrandt, op. cit., pp. 135-6.   [2] Dulles, op. cit., p. 164.
[3] *The Goebbels Diary*, pp. 383-4.   [4] *Von Hassell Diary*, p. 288.
[5] *The Goebbels Diaries*, p. 408.

interrogations by Leo Lange of the Gestapo, the prosecutor in the Rote Kapelle re-trials; but this was clearly one of those Gestapo inquiries which were meant to go on for ever in order to give some-one a job and to postpone making any decisions. Lange, who had to interrogate a member of Langbehn's circle in his own home, was said to have remarked to the man that strictly speaking Popitz ought to be examined, but that it was much too difficult.[1]

This was as late as 12 June, when the scandals of the Solf circle and of the Vermehren couple had passed Popitz by. It seems that he had been forgotten both by friend and foe. But with the mass proscription ordered by Hitler after 20 July, Himmler could no longer avoid arresting the acting Prussian Finance Minister. Furthermore, even though arrangements were soon made to hold the trials of Popitz and Langbehn in secret, Himmler had to find some version of this shady affair which would satisfy old party members. This is the explanation which Himmler made on 3 August at Posen in the presence of Bormann, Goebbels and all the Gauleiters in that mem-orable speech in which he summed up the antecedents of the July plot.[2]

Now there was another clue. An unusual man, a State Minister, Popitz, tried for some months to get into touch with me. He let it be known through a middle-man that he wanted an urgent interview with me. We let this middleman chatter, we let him talk, and this is more or less what he said. Yes, it was of course necessary that the war should end, we must come to peace terms with England—just as the opinion is today—and the first requisite was that the Fuehrer must be removed at once and relegated by the opposition to an honorary president's post. His group was quite certain about it that this could not very well be carried out against the SS. They therefore hoped, since I was an understanding and responsible German, that I would not interfere—only for Germany, of course, and in God's name no self-seeking matter.

The first time I heard it, I went at once to the Fuehrer and said, 'I will kill the rascal! Such an unblushing thing to put an idea like this into my head, of all people's'. But the Fuehrer laughed and said, 'Oh no, if that is the case you will not kill him, but you will listen to him. Let him come and see you. It might be interesting, and if he says the same thing at the first interview then you can arrest him'. I answered that I must have full powers, so that it will be possible to run him to ground, whether I arrest him in my room or later.

My first conversation with Herr Popitz was very interesting. It was my first interview as Minister of the Interior, on 24 August 1943, and quite unique. We had arranged to meet by telegram so that no time should be wasted. He came to me in the Ministry of the Interior, but he did not confide in me as much as I

---

[1] *Von Hassell Diary*, p. 312.
[2] *Vierteljahreshefte fuer Zeitgeschichte*, No. 4, p. 575.

had hoped. He begged for another interview very soon, but for my part the affair was still unripe. I told the Fuehrer, and he said, 'One day the time will be ripe for us to surprise a couple more of them. Popitz is only on the fringe; he works along with them; but the ones that matter are elsewhere; they are in the group behind Herr Halder'.

At last I pulled in the middleman. Since that time, nine months ago, Herr Popitz looks like a cheese. When you watch him, he is as white as a wall; I should call him the living image of a guilty conscience. He sends me telegrams, he telephones me, he asks what is the matter with Dr. X, what has happened to him; and I give him sphinx-like replies so that he does not know whether I had anything to do with what happened or not. I say to myself, the fellow is too cowardly to go on with it and for the moment he won't do anything because he is too scared. That, too, he has shown to be true.

Primarily this was for the ears of Martin Bormann. To most of the other auditors it must have been a strange and wonderful story, just a bit of the Reichsfuehrer's nonsense. A few, however, may have wondered why, after the Fuehrer's excellent advice, there was no second interview with Popitz and why the middleman had to be pulled in so soon. As a piece of historical explanation, it does not enhance the reputation of the grand inquisitor of the twentieth century, but then, as anyone who has had to wade through the Nuremberg trials will know, explaining away is not a German talent.

2. THE SOLF TEA-PARTY

The third of the Gestapo's discoveries for 1943, the Solf tea-party, followed the clues which had been dropped by Langbehn concerning the Abwehr peace circle. Himmler used Langbehn's clues to exploit the circle's activities rather than to circumvent them, but, like the two previous affairs, the tea-party made too much of a splash to remain a secret game of the Gestapo's. Moreover, two of the victims were tried before 20 July 1944, whereas in the other cases the arrested persons would have been kept alive as long as there was a war and a chance that further clues might be obtained from them.

The circle that met on 10 September 1943 at the house of Frau Hanna Solf, widow of a former governor of Samoa and ambassador to Japan, was decidedly Anglophil. Otto Kiep a Foreign Office representative in the Abwehr, was born in Scotland. He had been dismissed his post as Consul-General in New York for attending a public luncheon given in honour of Professor Einstein, but he had returned to favour and in 1937-9 he had served in London as Germany's representative on the Non-Intervention Committee.

Adolf von Bernstorff had likewise spent many years at the London Embassy, while Elisabeth von Thadden ran an evangelical school for girls on English lines. The Solfs, mother and daughter, had been cautioned by the Gestapo in the previous spring, when a Jewish family whom they had aided failed to cross the frontier.

Nevertheless, within a few months the Solfs offered the use of their house to Elisabeth von Thadden in order to introduce to their circle a courier who would take letters to Switzerland. This courier was a young Swiss doctor called Reckse, who practised at the Charité Hospital under Professor Ferdinand Sauerbruch, the friend of Beck and a man who, in spite of his ardent Nazi past, was in the confidence of the Resistance movement. Reckse was no Swiss student, but an agent of the Gestapo. Mr. Wheeler-Bennett thinks that he had been planted by Schellenberg, but according to the statements made by a Gestapo colleague, Walter Huppenkothen, at his trial in 1951, Reckse was an inspiration of Leo Lange—and it was Lange who was engaged in tracing the Langbehn episode.[1] Not only did Reckse take the letters, but he also undertook to interview the exiled former Chancellor of the Weimar Republic, Dr. Josef Wirth. And, indeed, Reckse returned from Switzerland with a message from Dr. Wirth for Franz Halder, the former Chief of Staff, who now lived in retirement at Aschau.

Reckse must have returned before 8 November, because on that day Himmler had a conversation with Goebbels, whom he was beginning to frequent. Himmler was unusually indiscreet.[2]

Himmler also told me about the existence of a group of enemies of the state, among whom are Halder and possibly also Popitz. This circle would like to contact England, by-passing the Fuehrer, and has already entered into negotiations in Switzerland with the former Reich Chancellor, Dr. Wirth. I regard these amateurish attempts as in themselves harmless, but naturally one must keep one's eye on them. Himmler will see to it that these gentlemen do no major damage with their cowardly defeatism. I certainly have the impression that the domestic security of the country is in good hands with Himmler.

The indiscretion may have been deliberate. Himmler may have reasoned that someone in RSHA was sure to inform Bormann and the only thing to do was to minimise the affair before it leaked out. In his Posen speech Himmler ridiculed the Solf tea-party, calling it

[1] Wheeler-Bennett, op. cit., p. 593; Weisenborn, op. cit., p. 114.
[2] *The Goebbels Diaries*, p. 408.

'a proper reactionary *Kluengel und Teequatsch*,[1] but he no longer pretended that the whole thing had been a joke.

We really knew about the present conspiracy for a very long time. . . . There was a Foreign Office man among them who has already been sentenced to death, Minister Otto Kiep. He, too, was mixed up in this. We had fallen absolutely on the right crowd. Herr Colonel-General Halder was mixed up in it. Since we have to have camouflaged names for everything nowadays, the whole thing formed part of a complex which we called Baroque, because baroque was just what it was. Herr Halder went under the name Reservist because he stayed in reserve in order to take over the German Army. There were others waiting to do that too.

The doings of Dr. Reckse had been in reality rather a disappointment. Before he even returned from Switzerland, the tea-party guests knew that they had been in a Gestapo trap. The exposure of Dr. Reckse is a queer illustration of the state of German morale in the shadow of doom. Dr. Goebbels's state enemies were neither Jews nor Communists, but frequently the same people whose hysterical lack of responsibility had brought Hitler to power. They were at work in the innermost key positions of the secret service, the so-called Air Ministry Research Office, just as had happened at the time of the Rote Kapelle arrests a year previously. The telephone-tapping section was now directed by Helmuth Plaas, a former naval lieutenant and a colleague of Ernst von Salomon in the Rathenau murder. Plaas recorded entire conversations between the SD and Dr. Reckse and passed them to Captain Gehre of Abwehr III.[2] Gehre passed them to Helmuth von Moltke of the legal section of the Abwehr. Von Moltke was a grandson of the famous field-marshal, a Christian Scientist, and half an Englishman. He was opposed to direct action against Hitler, but played an important part in the Resistance movement through a Socialist circle that frequented his Silesian estate. Von Moltke was largely responsible for bringing trade union and Socialist members into the Resistance movement.

Von Moltke's warnings could not save the circle who had been involved through the tea-party and the postman Reckse. In any case, Himmler became afraid of an international *détente*, should Reckse be arrested in Switzerland, and he forbade further journeys.[3]

[1] *Vierteljahreshefte fuer Zeitgeschichte*, No. 4, p. 576.

[2] Weisenborn, op. cit., p. 116.

[3] Weisenborn, p. 115. According to Ernst von Salomon, Plaas handed the news on not to Gehre but to Walther Muthmann and Fritz von der Schulenburg. Plaas was arrested at the same time as Moltke. He died mysteriously in the interrogation block in Ravensbrueck camp, his death being announced on the day before the Stauffenberg plot. *Answers of Ernst von Salomon* (London 1954) p. 299.

Strictly consistent again, Himmler delayed making an example of the tea-party. The two Solfs were arrested at Partenkirchen but not till 12 January 1944, months after Reckse's return from Switzerland.[1] It is possible that Himmler would not have pressed for the other arrests had not an international complication forced his hand. On 17 January *Pravda* published an article entitled 'Rumours from Cairo', which stated that Ribbentrop had met two British Cabinet Ministers in Spain in order to discuss peace terms.[2] Goebbels believed that this report had been published by Stalin as an alibi for his negotiations with Germany. Such an alibi, however, was no longer necessary, for Goebbels did not know that Stalin had withdrawn a real offer to negotiate after obtaining complete satisfaction from the Allies at Teheran.[3] For Ribbentrop, on the other hand, the *Pravda* canard produced a tricky situation. He had sponsored a genuine if tentative Russian negotiation in Stockholm which had produced such a burst of fury from Hitler that Ribbentrop's agent, Peter Kleist, had been arrested and Hitler had spoken of the offer of the Russian agents, Klaus and Alexandrov, as 'a third Jewish provocation'.[4] In August, however, Ribbentrop had persuaded Hitler to allow a resumption of the talks, but only for the purpose of obtaining information.

Confronted by Hitler with the *Pravda* story, Ribbentrop had to admit the truth, namely that a minor Foreign Office official had been seeking contact with the British through Dr. Wirth and that this was the cause of the Russian canard.[5] Neither Himmler nor Ribbentrop could afford to preserve Otto Kiep as a biological subject. Kiep and von Moltke were arrested almost on the day of the *Pravda* story, and with them some seventy-four persons who were implicated in Reckse's mailbag. Elisabeth von Thadden was traced, working for the Red Cross at Meaux, near Paris. She was tried with Otto Kiep on 1 July and executed in the following September. Halder was not arrested, but a watch was kept over him at his estate.

Even now Himmler tried to delay the moment when he must part with his valuable hostages from the party who wooed the West. To Himmler the officials of the Rosenberg Ministry or of OKW, who pressed for a moderate policy in the last shreds of occupied Russia, were traitors. There were traitors, too, in the Foreign Office who

---

[1] Pechel, op. cit., p. 91.   [2] *The Times*, 18 January 1944.
[3] Von Oven, op. cit., I, p. 180.   [4] Kleist, op. cit., pp. 252-3, 257.
[5] *Von Hassell Diary*, p. 302.

wanted to horse-trade these territories for Ribbentrop. But in the West it was another matter. Even though Himmler had been compelled to lock up Langbehn, even though Schellenburg and his Swiss contacts were being watched for Martin Bormann by the Kaltenbrunner-Fegelein circus, Himmler was still the head of the International SS, the true European army, and the leader of the anti-Bolshevik crusade. With the West Himmler believed he could play his trump card. And here Himmler had at least one supporter, Goebbels, who believed in the 'butterfly on the scales' theory; Goebbels, who thought that the slightest tremor—like the *Pravda* article on 17 January—would set the Western Allies negotiating on their own.[1]

A few weeks after the Solf tea-party arrests Himmler addressed a conference in the Goebbels Ministry. The frontier of German nationhood was, it seems, to be more than five hundred kilometres east of the Vistula and one day the farthest defences of the Reich would be in the Urals.[2] Goebbels explained to Wilfrid von Oven that Himmler did not really believe these things. He said them to raise people's confidence. Himmler was a political realist who was trying to reach an understanding with the West. Then, in order to show that he was a political realist, too, Goebbels added that he had tried in vain to make Himmler understand that the possibility of such an understanding no longer existed.

So Himmler preserved the former contact men of the Abwehr with loving care. On the day of the bomb plot only two trials had been completed, Otto Kiep's and Elisabeth von Thadden's. Gestapo interrogators, as Captain Payne-Best had noticed as long ago as November 1939, were adepts at spinning out a case,[3] and now a department was created which had no other purpose. It was a section of the Gestapo, known as IVA, 1b or 'Reichsopposition', and at the head of it was Leo Lange, who handled nothing but the cases of the arrested members of the Resistance Circle.[4] Dr. Rudolf Pechel has described how, with only a few days to go before the plot, he was still being interrogated by Lange in the Ravensbrueck bunker concerning conversations with Goerdeler which had taken place as long ago as December 1941.[5] One wonders whether Himmler had really got beyond 'the complex which we called Baroque', whether he had penetrated behind the figures of Beck, Goerdeler, Halder

---

[1] Von Oven, op. cit., I, p. 180.   [2] *Ibid.*, I, p. 208.
[3] Payne-Best, op. cit., p. 44.   [4] Weisenborn, op. cit., p. 117.
[5] Pechel, op. cit., p. 298.

and perhaps Witzleben, and whether he knew how much of the active serving staff of the Home Forces Army had become involved.

Little as Himmler must have desired the premature arrest of Otto Kiep, the sequel must have been still less welcome to him; of all the arrests made to date this caused the greatest stir. Kiep's close associates, Erich Vermehren and his wife, the Countess Plettenburg, were employed in the Abwehr in Istanbul, and both received a summons from the Gestapo to return to Berlin for interrogation. After considering the situation, the Vermehren couple put themselves at the disposal of the British secret service and were flown in a British air liner to Cairo. It was believed that they had taken with them the key to the Abwehr codes.[1]

Only a few weeks separated the Kiep and Vermehren scandals and the antics of the 'defeatist intelligentsia' in the Abwehr could no longer be hidden from Hitler. On 18 February 1944 he sent for Fegelein and gave instructions for the incorporation of the Abwehr in RSHA.[2] Hitler's language is said to have been intemperate, particularly towards Canaris and Paul Leverkuehn of Canaris's Near-Eastern Section. But Hitler did not send for Rattenhueber, his security officer, to whip off Canaris's head in the manner of Harun al Rashid and the Barmecides, a fate which had apparently been anticipated on one occasion by Hitler's favourite court entertainer, Walter Hewel.[3] Canaris was treated no differently from a minister or a general of a constitutional country who had done a little less than his best. He was made chief of the Office for Commercial and Economic Warfare.

The transfer of the huge staff of the Abwehr was handled with equal delicacy. Offices II and III of Canaris's organisation remained under their old chiefs, Freytag-Loringhoven and Georg Hansen. The only difference was that they were now part of the 'Military Office' in Section VI of the RSHA.[4] In the embassies and legations the cultivated young attachés from the military Abwehr worked henceforward with the cultivated young attachés from the Gestapo. Although there was not much left for them to do, it was the nearest thing to inter-departmental co-operation that was ever achieved in Hitler's Reich.

[1] Wheeler-Bennett, op. cit., p. 595; Moyzisch, Operation Cicero.

[2] Abshagen, op. cit., p. 369.

[3] On the occasion of Hewel's failure to share Goebbels's joy in the death of President Roosevelt (IMT X, p. 81).   [4] Abshagen, op. cit., p. 344.

During an interrogation by Mr. Trevor-Roper, Schellenberg described a meeting of the section leaders of the Abwehr which was addressed by Himmler in the Kursalon at Salzburg in May 1944. The speech seems to have followed the familiar lines of Himmler's surviving oratory. There was the same crescendo leading to his favourite fantasy about a permanent German frontier in the Urals. More to the point, Himmler told his audience that the very name 'Abwehr' or defence was un-German and that it was an offensive spirit which the organisation must now develop. But Himmler's auditors, Schellenberg among them, had little to fear. The name was not changed, nor was there any purge of the long of hair and lofty of brow, though some of their new colleagues were rather rough.[1]

In leaving the Canaris Garden of Eden some natural tears were shed, but not for long. Soon all the old listening posts and couriers were working again. It is true that Canaris was now inaccessible to his friends in the Office for Commercial and Economic Warfare at Eiche near Potsdam, while Oster was buried in a Leipzig suburb, where he walked about with two shadows.[2] Even so, and even though the Abwehr had fallen into the hands of the Gestapo, the U.S. Office of Strategic Services in Switzerland had no reason to complain that the Gestapo had cut off its sources of information.

3. THE SECOND RESISTANCE MOVEMENT

To understand the actions of Himmler, Kaltenbrunner, and Mueller on the day that Stauffenberg's bomb exploded, it must be shown how far the reality differed from the image of the Resistance Circle which they had obtained. Leo Lange's clients, who were in the Ravensbrueck bunker on 20 July, came from the outer fringe of the conspiracy. If they pointed to key figures, they pointed to Goerdeler, Beck, Witzleben and Halder. But a change in the movement had taken place as long ago as November 1942, after Goerdeler's visit to von Kluge. Before that time the civilian conspirators tried to approach Brauchitsch, the Commander-in-Chief, along with the highest-ranking generals, old gentlemen who talked treason but who were not prepared to act it. Now, after his failure with von Kluge, Henning von Tresckow drew the attention of the Goerdeler circle to

[1] Trevor Roper, op. cit., p. 30.

[2] Oster was arrested after 20 July on account of a telegram from the Bendlerstrasse, nominating him Military Governor of Saxony (Eberhard Zeller, *Geist der Freiheit* (Munich, 1952, p. 24).

the staff of the Replacement Army and to the commanders of home defence and training units who served under them. This vast staff were housed in the West End of Berlin in the former War Office building, Bendlerstrasse 11-13, which now became the centre of the conspiracy. Instead of relying on the support of field divisions, trained in battle and hopelessly loyal, the conspirators approached the half-raw troops who had to carry out the standing orders in the event of a civilian emergency.

It was through this significant change of tactics that, in the autumn of 1943, the Goerdeler circle made the acquaintance of a fresh personality, Olbricht's newly appointed Chief of Staff at the Army Supply Office (Allgemeine Heeresamt) in the Bendlerstrasse. Klaus Schenk, Graf von Stauffenberg, was, in spite of the many ramifications of his family in the higher ranks of the army, not a Prussian Junker but a Bavarian. He was thirty-five years of age and dramatically handsome. Until the previous April, when he had walked into an enemy minefield in Tunisia, losing the use of a hand and eye, a brilliant career in the field had been predicted for him. Stauffenberg was not a convert of Olbricht's or Henning von Tresckow's. He had been drawn into the opposition as early as 1942 when he had been a staff officer in Russia. It seems that Russia made him a Socialist.

In this respect Stauffenberg was entirely different from the heads of the military Resistance Circle who had no interest in politics, neither the figureheads, Beck and Witzleben, nor the real wire-pullers, Hans Oster and Henning von Tresckow, to whom Stauffenberg succeeded. Oster was at this time virtually under house arrest and von Tresckow unable to prolong his sick leave from the front any longer in order to plan the conspiracy in the Bendlerstrasse. When von Tresckow passed his plans on to Stauffenberg, he probably did not realise that Stauffenberg would seek civilian contacts outside 'the old firm', the circle of Goerdeler, Beck and Popitz. Since September 1938 that circle had been industriously drawing up its blamelessly monarchist cabinets and constitutions. In November 1943 Stauffenberg interfered to give the entire movement a leftish inclination.

In this task Stauffenberg found an ally in Graf Fritz von der Schulenburg. 'The Red Count' had fulfilled many offices since 1937, when he had become a police chief under Himmler in order to be 'Hitler's Fouché'.[1] In the summer of 1940 he had been dismissed from the post of deputy to Josef Wagner in Silesia, when the

[1] See *supra* p. 120.

'Christian Gauleiter' had fallen from grace. Schulenburg had thereupon enlisted in the army. In July 1944 he was working in the Bendlerstrasse building in the very heart of the conspiracy as an extremely junior staff officer.[1]

Stauffenberg employed 'the Red Count' to enlist the support of the 'Kreisau pinks'. This group had been without a leader since January 1944 when Helmuth von Moltke was arrested. At first the old hands of the Resistance Circle made no objection, but soon Goerdeler and von Hassell found themselves largely edged out of the plot and Popitz entirely so. The Cabinet-making had to be done all over again. At the time of the Stauffenberg bomb plot the new Chancellor of the Reich was to be not Goerdeler but Julius Leber, a former Social Democrat deputy. There were many strange names in the new Ministerial lists, names of men like Leuschner, Kaiser, Reichwein, Letterhaus and Haubach, who had suffered since 1933 for their political opinions and who now 'lived reservéd and austere', but nevertheless under the most careful observation.

In reality the plans of the Stauffenberg-Schulenburg group were neither so far from the ground as conservative-monarchist detractors pretended, nor were they essentially different from the plans of other Eastward-looking Nazis, Ribbentrop in particular. These plans were based on the Casablanca Declaration. The Allies would land in Europe, they would refuse to negotiate peace, they would force a total occupation of Germany and Russia would get the lion's share. But if the Russians were approached in time by penitent Germans of high rank and good family, Stalin would see the advantage of a German alliance which would keep the capitalist democracies out of Europe. The timing of the plot was dictated by this theory. So long as the retreat on the Eastern front was steady and methodical and so long as the Allies had not landed in the West, there was leisure to build up a pro-Russian position in Germany. For this Stauffenberg believed himself well qualified. As a staff officer in Russia in 1942 he had played a part in recruiting volunteers from the Russian prisoners of war. Sympathy for his recruits had generated a peculiar day-dream. It seems that Stauffenberg regarded the Russian volunteers with the German army and the Russian labourers in Germany not only as auxiliaries for a Putsch but as bargaining counters for a deal with Stalin.

For this reason there was a long lull in resistance activities.

[1] See p. 318.

Between February and July there were no attempts to assassinate Hitler because Stauffenberg thought it useless to kill him before the attitude of the Russians had been determined. It was better to make the Allies think that an understanding already existed between the Resistance Circle and Russia. In the Foreign Office Stauffenberg knew a very young legation councillor. Adam von Trott zu Solz had been a Rhodes scholar at Oxford and had represented the Resistance Circle in the U.S.A. as late as 1940. Through his Abwehr contacts in Switzerland, Trott zu Solz met Allied officials during 1943 and in April 1944 he made Mr. Allen Dulles's flesh creep with stories of the links of the Resistance movement with the foreign workers and with the Moscow Feee Germany Committee.[1]

This game of creating a Resistance movement among the Allies against 'unconditional surrender', a game essentially no different from that played by Ribbentrop and Goebbels, might have gone on as long as the war, but events conspired to hurry von Stauffenberg. The operative impulse was not the Allied invasion of France, which did not become a decisive victory till after the failure of the plot, but the Russian break-through at Bobruisk. In this affair the whole of the German Central Army Group dissolved uselessly into spray and over hundreds of miles there was no front at all. It was a far worse disaster than Stalingrad. Stauffenberg could no longer reckon on an eventual race into Germany between the Russians and the Allies, but a race which the Russians might win within a few weeks and on the Rhine. When Stauffenberg brought his bomb into the operations room at Rastenburg, Russian artillery fire could already be heard and Russian soldiers were inside the border at Augustowo. If Stauffenberg did not explode his bomb now, the whole of Germany might be devastated in a fight to a finish for Hitler.

While it is impossible to believe that Beck and Goerdeler could have overthrown Hitler without employing Stauffenberg, it could not have been the pure demoniac forces of destiny that ruined Stauffenberg's plot. It was the man himself. Some will protest that if Colonel Brant's leg had not itched, causing him to kick the dispatch case under the table, the Fuehrer would have been blown to pieces. It was a classical case of the horseshoe nail. But the horseshoe nail was lost through distraction of mind and it was surely distraction which put Stauffenberg at the mercy of an itching trouser-leg. He was not one man but two. Had Stauffenberg been only the

[1] Dulles, op. cit., p. 137; Gisevius op. cit., p. 480.

smart young staff officer who allotted the Bendlerstrasse brass hats their respective positions for 'Action Walkuere', he might have seized Berlin and the problem when and to whom to surrender could have been left to the politicians.

But Stauffenberg was a follower of Stephan Georg; he was a soldier, dark, bushy-eyebrowed and terribly handsome, who had views on the future at a time when the present alone was, goodness knows, hard enough to comprehend. Perhaps Stauffenberg's idealism was out of place among the cynical calculations necessary for a military Putsch, and yet it must have needed a great deal of idealism to convert the singularly stuffy collection of men in the Bendlerstrasse, and all within a few weeks of his arrival. Stauffenberg completely won over the six key-men; Helmuth Stieff of the Organisation Office, Eduard Wagner, the Quartermaster-General, Erich Fellgiebel, the Chief of Signals, Fritz Lindemann, head of the Ordnance Office, Paul von Hase, head of the Berlin Kommandatur and von Ronne of the Foreign Armies Section.[1]

Equally essential to the Plan Walkuere was Stauffenberg's ascendancy over the old hands of the Resistance group, the military governors of France and Belgium, Stuelpnagel and Falkenhausen. Progress was also made with the conversion of Fritz Fromm of the Replacement Army and Guderian, the Inspector of the Armoured Troops, but these, together with the field commanders, von Kluge and Rommel, were unpredictable quantities.

The key position was Stieff's 'Organisation Office', where Stauffenberg installed a cousin, Major Kuhn. This officer and his assistants smuggled saboteurs' bombs, which were supplied by the Abwehr, into the sacred compound at Rastenburg.[2] Previously bombs had been obtained from the Abwehr through Henning von Tresckow, but Stieff's office was a safer method of conveyance. Unfortunately Stieff's bombs, which were hidden in a woodpile at Rastenburg, exploded. Hitler ordered the Abwehr to carry out an inquiry, which revealed nothing, but this was before February 1944,[3] when the Abwehr was incorporated in the SS.

It is extraordinary that Himmler did not take over this inquiry himself, but it is clear that he had suspected Stieff. Himmler was

[1] Von Schlabrendorff, op. cit., p. 99. Gerhard Ritter thinks, however, that Stieff had been won over by Henning von Tresckow before 13 August 1943 (p. 357).

[2] Nuremberg Document PS 3881, Report of Volksgericht Proceedings.

[3] Pechel, op. cit., pp. 158-61; Von Schlabrendorff, op. cit., p. 12.

particularly bitter against Stieff in his second Posen speech, calling him 'a little poison dwarf, a bad edition of the King of Italy, whom I would not have near me as an ADC. Nine months ago Stieff stopped the overcoat assault-pack plots, because he feared he would have to be present and would be blown up'.[1]

The Gestapo made this discovery rather late in the day, for in February 1944 Stieff, who was of the same age as Stauffenberg and an impatient rival, decided not to wait for the high policies of Stauffenberg to mature but to make an attempt on his own. A lieutenant, Josef Hofmann, who was on duty at the Reich Chancellery, volunteered himself as living ammunition. He was to have paraded before Hitler in order to demonstrate a new type of assault pack. The bomb which it contained was set to go off five minutes after the inspection, which was timed for eleven o'clock, but Hitler, not so much through intuition as through a well thought out habit which he described himself in his Table Talk,[2] altered the time to nine o'clock.

It is by no means clear that Stieff changed his mind. Himmler's accusations that Stieff had been afraid of the explosion or alternatively that he planned to use an unsuspecting soldier need confirmation. Schlabrendorff says that an overnight air raid on Zossen had already destroyed the bomb, but Pechel states that it went off in the Reich Chancellery at the appointed time because there was no chance of removing it, and that this curious incident was remembered during the great proscription. The Hofmanns, father and son, were arrested on 27 July. The young lieutenant, incriminated by Stieff's evidence, survived the war, having been captured by the Russians while serving his sentence in a punishment battalion.[3]

The four attempts to blow up Hitler in 1943-4, Schlabrendorff's aeroplane bomb, the overcoats of Gersdorff and von dem Busch and Hofmann's assault pack, had this in common. They all misfired and they all escaped detection. Either Himmler was prepared to let Hitler be killed as an obstacle to peace, or the Gestapo was not clever enough to use the evidence, or the attempts never got as far as the authors claimed. Both the first and second assumptions are

---

[1] Vierteljahreshefte fuer Zeitgeschichte, No. 4, p. 579.   Stieff was nicknamed 'the poison dwarf' by reason of his malicious character.   Wilfrid von Oven, who saw him tried by the Volksgericht, said that Stieff looked like a Madrid shoe-shiner (Von Oven, op. cit., II, p. 110).

[2] Hitler's Table Talk, p. 553.   [3] Pechel, op. cit., pp. 164-6.

inviting. Fellgiebel of the Signals Section had been reported three times in 1942 and 1943 for defeatist utterances in front of Gestapo informers, yet Himmler, who had smashed the citadel of the War Office in February 1938, could not lay his hands on Fellgiebel. Early in November 1943, when Stauffenberg was winning his way into the OKH bureaucracy, Goebbels told Colonel von Bibra at what seems to have been a very un-jolly dinner party that the generals were well aware he had a fine ear when a knife was being sharpened somewhere. As a matter of fact he had heard that suspicious sound for some time. 'I cannot tell whether it is a conspiracy with a defined purpose and a defined organisation'. On the fifteenth of that month Goebbels noticed that the enemy Press was already naming likely generals, and on the 24th, with an almost inspirational premonition, he ordered the army's fire-fighting tanks from Potsdam to return to barracks after a Berlin air raid. 'Otherwise we would certainly have read in the enemy Press the following day that the Nazis had to call upon the Wehrmacht to protect themselves from the furious people'.[1]

But if doubts attend the Gestapo's readiness to interfere, they also attend the persistent failure of the plots. Dr. Rudolf Pechel thinks that Hitler's security precautions were so good that it was impossible for an officer to get near enough to shoot him,[2] while Schlabrendorff says that it was only possible to kill Hitler at a conference. And yet in July 1943 a junior officer still unknown to Hitler, Otto Skorzeny, was able to watch him at close quarters at Rastenburg, walking alone with his dog Blondi.[3] Hitler himself believed that ninety per cent of the assassination plots of history had been successful and that the only way to defeat the assassin was to come and go irregularly and unexpectedly. This method, which he had developed into a skilful technique, derived from his luck in leaving ten minutes before the explosion of the Buergerbraeukeller bomb in 1939. But the real reason why the assassins missed him in that year of plots, 1943, is supplied by a remark in *Hitler's Table Talk*.[4]

If some fanatic wishes to kill or shoot me with a bomb, I am no safer sitting down than standing up; and in any case the number of fanatics who seek my life is getting much smaller. Among the bourgeoisie and the Marxists alike it would be hard to find a would-be assassin ready to risk his own life if necessary.

---

[1] *The Goebbels Diaries*, pp. 412, 428-9; Von Oven, op. cit., I, p. 143.
[2] Pechel, op. cit., p. 167.   [3] Skorzeny, op. cit., p. 102.
[4] *Hitler's Table Talk*, 3 May 1942, p. 453.

The 20th July and After

1. 'ACTION WALKUERE'

When the Russians opened their summer attack of 1944, the Central Army Group was no longer commanded by von Kluge, who was fighting in Normandy. His place had been taken by Ernst Busch, a strictly Nazi general who enjoyed sitting on the People's Court Tribunals and to whom a Fuehrer order could not be anything but right. When the Fuehrer's orders proved impossible to fulfil, he took to drink. But Busch would not attempt a strategic withdrawal on his own responsibility. And so the huge bulge of his thinly scattered strong-points melted away as the Russians attacked. Between 22 June and 13 July the Russians advanced more than two hundred miles, reaching positions west of Minsk and Wilna. Of the forty and more divisions of the Central Army Group twenty-five ceased to exist as fighting forces. On the 15th the Red Army entered the Baltic states and one patrol actually got as far as the East Prussian border at Augustowo.[1] The situation was not underrated and as early as the 9th Goebbels warned an audience in Breslau that the invasion of the Fatherland could be expected. On 15 July Hitler left Berchtesgaden for Rastenburg to take over the defence of East Prussia in person.[2]

If events had overtaken Stauffenberg's plans, they had also played into his hands, for the crisis in Normandy and White Russia had created a demand for a reorganisation of the Replacement Army. During the critical days at the end of June Stauffenberg was promoted from Olbricht's office to Fromm's. He became Chief of Staff to the Commander-in-Chief of the Replacement Army and his duties took him daily to the Fuehrer's operations room.

At this moment Stauffenberg was trying to repair the results of an indiscretion for which the only remedy was to get on with the bomb plot. A small group whom Stauffenberg had taken over from the Kreisau circle had urged co-operation with the German Com-

---

[1] Von Schlabrendorff, op. cit., p. 130; Guderian, op. cit., p. 303.
[2] Von Oven, op. cit., II, p. 46; Guderian, op. cit., 305.

munists, such as were left of them. On 22 June, Stauffenberg, much against the advice of the original Resistance group, authorised Julius Leber, the former Reichstag deputy, and Professor Adolf Reichwein, author, schoolmaster and former Prussian bureaucrat, to meet a Communist group in East Berlin.[1] It seems that they saw two men called Anton Saefkow and Franz Jacob in the house of Dr. Rudolf Schmidt, a physician. Saefkow claimed to be the director of the Communist Underground in Brandenburg. He had been a companion of Ernst Thaelmann and like Thaelmann he had been arrested after the Reichstag fire, but had been released from a concentration camp during the war. Saefkow wanted a conference with the military leaders of the movement. For the moment a second meeting of the same persons was arranged for 4 July.[2]

The foolhardiness of this escapade is almost unimaginable. It was well known that Himmler deliberately kept a certain number of Communists at liberty in order to claim that 'Judeo-Bolshevist state enemies' still existed. The Rote Kapelle case had shown that the brief Ribbentrop-Molotov honeymoon of 1939-41 had added more strength to these people's elbows than Himmler supposed. The German Communists had become an Intelligence service for the enemy, but Himmler knew that it is not always good military policy to suppress an enemy Intelligence service altogether. The movement therefore continued to exist, but it was a nest of stool-pigeons. During the Moscow pact period, the NKVD had played the double game of planting agents in Germany, while in many matters co-operating with the Gestapo. The fact that they turned in to the Gestapo German Communist refugees in Russia is notorious. Heinrich Mueller of the Gestapo, a student of Russian police methods, had made good use of his contacts with the NKVD during this period and was credited with the creation of 'V-men', bogus Communists who got themselves accepted by the movement.[3]

It may have been one of these V-men who attended the meeting of 22 June. At any rate at the second meeting on 4 July Reichwein, Saefkow and Jacob were picked up. Leber was arrested in a round-up in the course of the next few days. There was now reason to fear that the Gestapo would find the clues leading to Stauffenberg and the Bendlerstrasse circle.[4]

[1] Von Schlabrendorff, op. cit., p. 135.   [2] Dulles, op. cit., p. 174.
[3] Hans Rothfels, *German Opposition*, p. 49.
[4] Emil Henk, quoted by Gisevius in *To the Bitter End*, p. 482.

According to the evidence obtained by the Gestapo and presented at the Witzleben trial, the decision to explode the bomb was taken on the day before Reichwein's arrest and was therefore not connected with it. It was taken at a meeting of Stauffenberg, Stieff, Lindemann and Fellgiebel at Wagner's house at Berchtesgadner Hof.[1] It was based on estimated military strengths and here it was evident that Himmler had not visualised a plot which would mobilise the regular troops in the capital. In 1937 he had designated 'Inner Germany' as the theatre of operations of his SS in the event of a European war.[2] But in 1937 Himmler had not dreamed of a huge Waffen SS serving on several fronts. Little effort had been made to place the training centres of the SS close to the capital. In July 1944 half a million men served in the SS, but the greater part had been recruited in occupied or satellite countries. The training schools and depots were far apart in France, Belgium, East Prussia, Carinthia, Slovenia, Bohemia and Poland. Round Berlin itself the SS could only muster the Panzer grenadier school at Saarow, the Officer Cadets at Lenkwitz and Gross Lichterfelde, the Totenkopf training centre at Oranienburg and Skorzeny's special service battalion at Friedental.

Against this, the Walkuere Order could be distributed to all the troops under the orders of the Bendlerstrasse and these included the army gunnery and weapon-training schools besides four home-service units, roughly of battalion strength, which were stationed in Berlin itself and were under the orders of a member of the Resistance, Major-General Paul von Hase. Within short call of Berlin, the Bendlerstrasse could issue orders to four more training schools, infantry at Doeberitz, mechanised cavalry at Krampnitz, tanks at Wuensdorf, artillery at Jueterbog and the Luftwaffe parachute school at Wannsee. On the other hand there was a big 'if'. The tanks at Krampnitz and Wuensdorf were at the disposal of Guderian, the Inspector of Armoured Troops. Guderian was known to favour the abrogation of Hitler's military powers, but in August 1943 he had turned down the overtures of Henning von Tresckow because they had come from his bitterest enemy, Guenther von Kluge.[3]

If the two tank schools could be relied on, the SS could be disarmed. The danger lay in the nature of the 'Walkuere' orders themselves. 'Walkuere' was the code name for a series of sealed

---

[1] Nuremberg Document PS 3881, p. 317.   [2] See *supra*, p. 82.
[3] Guderian, op. cit., p. 283.

instructions. They had been prepared by the 'General Wehrmacht Office' for the use of units under the orders of the Replacement Army. They were to be put into operation in the event of a revolt by the 'Eastern Workers' who were employed in Germany under slavery or semi-slavery conditions. Writers of the Resistance school assert, though without adducing evidence, that Hitler permitted this powerful instrument against his own person through the fear of the Eastern workers, which had been instilled in him by Admiral Canaris, himself of the Resistance Circle.[1]

Only when the signal 'Walkuere' was given could the military commanders open their packets of sealed orders, which reposed in the meantime in their office safes. The chances of their joining in a military Putsch against Hitler under the mistaken impression that they were restoring order depended upon the degree with which they observed the alleged code of the soldier, 'Their's not to reason why'. Stauffenberg overrated the potency of this code even among German officers. He overlooked the probability, not to say certainty, that German officers, when confronted with an order to burst into government buildings or to surround the establishments of the SS, would ask questions first and compare notes with others. Furthermore, a commander who secured his objective without opposition might still be diverted from it, unless he received strict and unmistakable follow-up instructions—as actually happened in the case of the commanders of the Krampnitz and Doeberitz training schools.

Worse still, it was impossible to foretell who would be the commanders who had to carry out these orders. The units were under the command of Olbricht and von Hase, but the postings were made by the Personnel Department of OKW at Rastenburg.[2] About this nothing could be done. In inner Berlin the action would be in the hands of the reliable Colonel Jaeger and his Grossdeutschland regiment, but only a week before the plot Count Helldorf discovered that there had been a new posting. A reputedly staunch party man, Major Otto Remer, had been chosen to command the guard battalion of the regiment. Beck wanted to transfer Remer to his home town, Koenigsberg. Stauffenberg objected that to pick out officers

[1] Zeller, op. cit., p. 177. Gerhard Ritter dates the Walkuere plan as far back as November 1942. *Karl Goerdeler und die deutsche Widerstandsbewegung* (Stuttgart, 1954), p. 343.

[2] Von Schlabrendorff, op. cit., p. 93.

for posting elsewhere would attract suspicion. So the dangerous Remer stayed with Jaeger's regiment.[1]

Whatever doubts existed on these counts, they must have been overcome at Stauffenberg's conference on 3 July, when the date was fixed. It was essential that both Himmler and Goering should be eliminated from the succession, Himmler in particular, since he could not be allowed to live to testify that he had never intended an SS Putsch and that the reason for the Walkuere Order was therefore a sham. This meant that the bomb would have to explode when Hitler, Goering and Himmler were in the room at the same moment. Such an opportunity was expected on 11 July. On that day Stauffenberg arrived in the operations room on the Obersalzberg. Hitler and Goering were present but not Himmler, so Stauffenberg left the conference room, taking his bomb with him.

On the 15th Stauffenberg again brought his bomb into the operations room on the Obersalzberg, but Himmler and Goering were absent and Stauffenberg went to the telephone to inform the Bendlerstrasse. In the meantime Hitler left the conference and Stieff removed the bomb, the time being about one o'clock.[2] At half past one Stauffenberg sent a signal cancelling Walkuere, but as early as eleven o'clock units in inner Berlin had received the order to cordon the Ministry quarter. This false alarm had to be explained to the troops as a tactical exercise. As a result Olbricht was hauled over the coals by Fromm for impeding the movement of tanks from the Krampnitz school, which were due to go to East Prussia. Fromm declared that Guderian would demand an explanation from him.[3] If a second alert were issued within a matter of days, it would excite the suspicion of Fromm, who, though a garrulous man in his complaints of the conduct of the war, never attacked Hitler. The Resistance Circle consoled themselves with the belief that Fromm himself was so much under suspicion that a Putsch must compel him to side with them. During the scare of the Dohnanyi-circle arrests in April 1943, Schulenburg had been detained for a few hours and Fromm received an admonishment from Keitel on account of a private conversation which he had held with this young staff officer. In the event of a Putsch, von Hassell thought that Fromm would readily accept a *fait accompli*. Very unwisely the conspirators seemed to

---

[1] Dulles, op. cit., p. 188; Gisevius, op. cit., pp. 417, 509.
[2] Gisevius, op. cit., pp. 518, 525; Zeller, op. cit., p. 213; Ritter, op. cit., p. 399.
[3] PS 3881, p. 397.

have reckoned that Fromm would be too lazy to take any action against them or otherwise.[1]

This uncertainty concerning Fromm meant that Stauffenberg would have to carry his next attempt through to the end, whatever obstacles he might meet and whether Himmler and Goering were present or not. So, on the day following the false alarm, he pledged his word to Beck, who was still the titular chief of the conspiracy, that he would act on the following Thursday, 20 July 1944.

2. 20 JULY

Through the false alert of 15 July, Stauffenberg was entirely at the mercy of circumstance—and circumstance was merciless. In the first place the morning conference of the 20th took place not in the Rastenburg bunker, where the ventilation system was out of order, but in the adjacent Speer Barracks, a long flimsy hut where an explosion must have less effect. In the second place neither Himmler nor Goering was there, and in the third place Stauffenberg's entry was conspicuous. He had flown from Berlin the same morning and he had to take his place at a conference which had started an hour ago. Stauffenberg, moreover, was expected to read a very important report on the state of the new Volksgrenadiere divisions which were being formed to replace the losses of the Central Army Group. This vital report lay cosily with the bomb in Stauffenberg's great shiny attaché case. It was such a prominent object that, since Stauffenberg's ADC, Werner von Haeften, had to stay outside the room, the great Keitel in person rushed to the disabled Stauffenberg. Being the sort of man who not only holds your overcoat for you but brushes it, Keitel offered to carry it for him.[2]

Stauffenberg, however, read his report without incident, left the attaché case under the table with the fuse of his bomb set and, with a mumbled excuse about a telephone call, quitted the room in such a nervous state that he left his cap and gloves. The handsome bare-headed officer, whom von Haeften had to drive through the three camp-barriers, was as conspicuous as if he had lost his trousers. Before they reached the third barrier, the Speer Barracks went up in a tremendous explosion, and still they had the luck to escape the hue-and-cry. The NCO in the guardroom would not let them through

[1] Zeller, op. cit., p. 343; *Von Hassell Diaries*, pp. 127, 248, 256-7.
[2] Von Oven, op. cit., II, p. 62.

without instructions from the staff office. Stauffenberg seized the
telephone from the man and, like the Hauptmann von Koepenick,
the magic of a colonel's voice did the rest. Still, a corporal took
careful note of the hatless officer at the telephone. They made him
a sergeant for it.[1]

For two hours and a half Stauffenberg and von Haeften were
removed from the world in a droning Heinkel which ten years later
would be as up to date as a hansom cab, and while they dozed
apprehensively history pursued its course, but not the course they
had expected. Shortly before the bomb went off, Hitler had changed
his position. A second-hand narrator, von Schlabrendorff, says that
Hitler was standing by one of the maps on the wall.[2] The stenographer, Heinz Bucholz, says that Hitler was leaning over a map on
the table.[3] In any case, Hitler's limbs were free and the blast blew
him with several others through the thin asbestos sheeting of the
walls to alight with his trousers half burnt off, bruised, scorched,
and deafened, but not out of action. Of the twenty-four men in the
Speer Barracks only four were wounded to death, while both Keitel
and Jodl escaped serious injury. The casualty rate illustrates Stauffenberg's chances of success. Only in the hermetically sealed bunker
could Hitler, Himmler and Goering have met a certain death even
if a moment could have been chosen when all three were there.

Human fallibility had gone astray. But Higher Party Circles believed that a still Higher Power had intervened. Hitler told Goebbels
that the Higher Power had caused a cavity in the floor to suck up
the blast. It was also said that Colonel Brant had pushed the dispatch case with his foot under the heavy transverse baulk of the
table-trestle.[4]

The time was eighteen minutes to one. From his office in Bunker
88, General Fritz Erich Fellgiebel saw his Fuehrer sail through the
air like a butterfly in the breeze and without hesitation telephoned
the code signal to the Bendlerstrasse. Then, as the shouting subsided
and the stretcher parties got to work, the Chief of Signals learnt that
Hitler was alive. Overwhelmed with fear, he ran to be among the
first to congratulate Hitler and of course he failed to carry out the
most essential part of the plot, namely the blowing-up of the Rastenburg telephone exchange. But it is doubtful whether Fellgiebel could
have done this in the best of circumstances, since there were several

[1] Von Oven, op. cit., II, p. 69.   [2] Von Schlabrendorff, op. cit., p. 137.
[3] Dulles, op cit., p. 8.   [4] Von Oven, op. cit., II, p. 86; Zeller, op. cit., p. 246.

exchanges and all of them were in deep air-raid shelters guarded by the SS. Fellgiebel did in fact recover his presence of mind. After Himmler had successfully put a call through to the Prinz Albrecht-strasse, apparently at about a quarter past one, Fellgiebel was able to block all the lines till close on four.[1]

On receipt of Fellgiebel's one and only signal at the Bendler-strasse, Merz von Quirnheim, as Stauffenberg's deputy, ordered a stand-to in preparation for 'Action Walkuere'. But he waited for Stauffenberg's arrival before giving orders to open the sealed dis-patches, a hesitation that seems to have been due to sheer terror as also was the failure or refusal to inform Fromm of Fellgiebel's signal. It was only at a quarter to four, when Stauffenberg telephoned from Rangsdorf airport, that the news was broken to Fromm. By this time Fellgiebel had unblocked the telephone lines, having been tipped off that the SS were watching him. So the incredulous Fromm was able to get through to Keitel at Rastenburg without difficulty. He recovered completely from his rage and excitement and observed laconically that there would be no occasion to operate 'Walkuere'. Without comment Olbricht returned to his office, where he sat with Erich Hoeppner, one of the conspirators of September 1938 and now a conspirator again since his unjust dismissal in December 1941. Hoeppner had brought his uniform to the Bendlerstrasse in a suit-case in case he might need it as Fromm's successor.[2]

Before Stauffenberg could reach the Bendlerstrasse from the air-port, Count Helldorf, the Police President for Berlin, came to find out what was happening. It seems that Helldorf and Nebe, the two essential police chiefs, had been waiting since soon after one o'clock for confirmation that the Walkuere troops had occupied the govern-ment buildings where they were to make their arrests. For three hours Olbricht and his associates had told them nothing. The Walkuere troops had not had their instructions and the Bendler-strasse conspirators had simply waited for a dynamic personality like Stauffenberg to tell them what to do.[3]

When Stauffenberg telephoned from Rangsdorf, there was no car waiting for him. It was half-past four, therefore, before Stauffenberg and Haeften were in the Bendlerstrasse building. Had it not been for Fellgiebel's success in blocking the lines, Stauffenberg's adventures

[1] Zeller, op. cit., pp. 258-9, 368.
[2] IMT Document PS 3881, minutes of trial of Witzleben, etc.
[3] Gisevius, op. cit., p. 533.

would have ended at Rangsdorf airport. The suspicious circum-stances of his departure from Rastenburg had been discovered before two o'clock, but it was nearly four before Himmler could telephone the Prinz Albrechtstrasse, ordering Stauffenberg's arrest, though, as a result of Himmler's first call at a quarter past one, Kaltenbrunner had left for Rastenburg to investigate on the spot. And so it turned out that Colonel Piffraeder and his two plain-clothes detectives on their way from the Prinz Albrechtstrasse to Rangsdorf crossed Stauffenberg's car.[1]

Stauffenberg's arrival at the Bendlerstrasse was closely preceded by that of General Ludwig Beck. Surely this, too, was a very leisurely performance for the new Head of the German State. But Beck, who wore civilian clothes, at least showed resolution in the middle of panic and inertia. He declared that the Putsch must go on, whether Hitler was alive or dead, and he grasped Stauffenberg's hand. As to Stauffenberg, his first concern was to convince the conspirators that Keitel was lying. His next was to see that orders for the operation of Walkuere went out to every part of occupied Europe under Fromm's name. Only then did he confront Fromm with his own story.

Yet Fromm was unmoved by Stauffenberg's description of the effects of the bomb. He ordered Merz von Quirnheim to put himself under arrest and Stauffenberg to shoot himself. The conspirators were compelled to arrest Fromm. It is said that a pistol was pointed at that irritating person's head. It should not have upset Stauffen-berg's moral balance, having just set off a bomb among twenty-four of his service colleagues, to pull the trigger of the pistol, but with a truly memorable exhibition of the old-school-tie spirit Fromm was allowed to stay in his flat in the Bendlerstrasse building under the guard of a single officer, Major von Leonrod; and Hoeppner, who had put on his uniform, came to the flat to apologise.[2]

It was now five o'clock and 'three stagnant hours' had still to be reckoned with before the armoured units, which had received the Walkuere signal, could reach inner Berlin, but the troops in inner Berlin had now opened the sealed orders and were marching on

---

[1] Zeller, op. cit., p. 248. The delayed telephone call is confirmed in the trial minutes PS 3881, p. 319. The version, repeated by Gisevius and Wheeler-Bennett (p. 648), according to which Stauffenberg's arrest was ordered by Kalten-brunner before his departure from Berlin, is wrong on timing.

[2] Von Schlabrendorff, op. cit., p. 143.

their objectives. Soon there arrived the commander of Military Area IV, General von Kortzfleisch, to demand an explanation of the fantastic orders that had been given by von Hase, the Town Commandant. Since they could not let Kortzfleisch see Fromm, they had to lock him up too.

Next came Oberfuehrer Piffraeder of the SS, having hurried from Rangsdorf airport, escorted by only two plain-clothes detectives, a remarkably innocent action for Himmler's former security police commander in the Baltic states, who had spent the past few months exhuming and destroying the bodies of Stahlecker's 221,000 murdered Jews.[1] Piffraeder was a tough man. That a Gestapo official should arrive, all unprotected, to question Hitler's would-be assassin among his own friends was no doubt the way a tough man looked at things, but the careful preservation of Herr Piffraeder was even more extraordinary. They left him, like Fromm, in an adjoining room to turn up before the curtain fell like a character without his trousers in an eight-door French farce.

Count Helldorf had 'frozen' his state police but, having observed no troop movements, telephoned at half past five to 'Gestapo Mueller' at the Prinz Albrechtstrasse. Mueller was only dimly aware that a Putsch was in progress.[2] Kaltenbrunner had left the office at two in the afternoon on receipt of Himmler's telephone call to fly to Rastenburg, leaving Mueller to act for him, but Mueller was even now so little aware of the danger that he allowed one of his section chiefs to visit his home in the country. There was no armed guard at the Prinz Albrechtstrasse and only a dozen automatic pistols in the place. Had the Grossdeutschland Guard Battalion carried out its assignment, the Gestapo would have surrendered without a fight. Willi Hoettl asserts that Mueller telephoned Gottlob Berger's staff office during the afternoon, asking for a Waffen SS detachment.[3] Yet it was not till nearly midnight and on receipt of a special order from Goering at Rastenburg that Skorzeny moved his SS special duties battalion to rescue the imprisoned Piffraeder from the Bendlerstrasse, and Major Remer had got there before him with a detachment from the Army Gunnery School. All this time the Gestapo head office seems to have been unprotected. Willi Hoettl thinks that Mueller was told by Himmler to hold his hand, but this cannot account for the totally unprotected state of the Prinz

[1] Case IX, transcript, p. 1619; evidence of Paul Blobel.
[2] Gisevius, op. cit., p. 547.   [3] Walter Hagen, *Die geheime Front*, p. 96.

Albrechtstrasse. Clearly Mueller had failed to penetrate the camouflage screen of Action Walkuere[1] or even thought about it, but then Mueller despite a reputation for subtlety was a brutal dull dog.

We must now turn to the guard battalion of the Grossdeutschland regiment and its commander, Major Otto Remer. His duty, as von Hase explained to him, was to guard the entire Ministry quarter and see that no general or minister passed the cordon. Two things, however, excited Remer's suspicions. The first was a rumour, which turned out to be false but which showed how the Putsch atmosphere must have spread. It was to the effect that von Brauchitsch, the long-retired Commander-in-Chief, had been seen in his uniform. The second source of Remer's suspicion was the arrival of an unknown liaison officer, a Lieutenant-Colonel Wolters from the Town Commandant's office, who first explained that he was not a spy and then quietly disappeared.[2]

On the strength of his suspicions Remer did two things. A certain Lieutenant Hans Hagen was attached to the battalion as a 'National Socialist Leadership Officer' (NSFO), a form of political commissar which Hitler borrowed from the Russians, just when the Russians were discarding them.[3] Hagen was a lecturer and journalist, employed by the Goebbels Ministry, and through Hagen Goebbels, who had an eye for civil disturbances, had made himself a patron of the regiment. Towards seven o'clock therefore Remer sent Hagen to Goebbels. At the same time Remer went to Unter den Linden to see von Hase, but the Town Commandant refused to tell Remer why he had to guard the Gestapo building. After some argument, however, he withdrew his order to Remer to arrest Goebbels in person.

Goebbels had already known of the bomb through the still un-obstructed Rastenburg telephone exchange before he had sat down to lunch, but only knew of Hitler's escape towards four o'clock.[4] Goebbels told Hagen to bring Remer at once to the office. Remer disobeyed von Hase's instructions and came, but carefully avoided telling Goebbels that he was to have arrested him. Shortly after eight o'clock Goebbels put Remer through on the telephone to Hitler in

[1] Otto Skorzeny, op. cit., p. 209.
[2] Otto Remer, *Die Zwanzigste Juli* (Hamburg, 1951), p. 10.
[3] See *infra*, p. 385.
[4] Rudolf Sammler. *Goebbels, the Man next to Hitler*, p. 132.

person. Whereupon, after a short tirade concerning 'a small ambitious clique of officers', Hitler appointed this unknown major to direct all security arrangements in Berlin till Himmler's arrival.[1]

The Goebbels Ministry was by this time surrounded by troops of the Doeberitz Infantry School and Goebbels himself was in the deep shelter, fingering a revolver. Yet Remer diverted the Walkuere Order with the greatest of ease. In the Fehrbellinerplatz, however, this unknown major was presented with a worse problem, a vast assembly of tanks from the Krampnitz training school. But the problem had already been solved. The Krampnitz commander, Colonel Wolfgang Glasemer, had referred his instructions to the Inspectorate of Armoured Warfare at Zossen. Guderian, the Inspector-General, was on leave at his country house in East Prussia, but his Chief of Staff, General Tomalle, ruled that under no circumstances were the School to march against SS establishments. Glasemer reported this personally at the Bendlerstrasse and Olbricht deemed it advisable to arrest him. But Glasemer's second-in-command took his orders from a Colonel Bolbringer who arrived in the Fehrbellinerplatz from Guderian's office. Heroic scenes have been depicted, both by Remer and some of the Resistance-school writers, but this seems to be the prosaic truth.[2]

During the next few months the party leaders were to make much of Major Remer, who had found himself for an hour or two Hitler's personal deputy in Berlin. He became a major-general and a divisional commander and in March 1952 he was the centre of a libel action which was brought against him by survivors of the Resistance Circle. But Remer escaped the verdict by exile and his Socialist Reich Party was dissolved by the Bonn government. Remer fizzled out like a very damp squib and his trial revealed that he had been by no means a man of destiny on 20 July 1944. It was not Remer that killed the plot, but the active functioning of the Berlin telephone

[1] Von Oven, op. cit., II, p. 78. In the film 'The Jack Boot Mutiny' Remer's action was grossly overdramatised.

[2] Remer, p. 12; Skorzeny, p. 207; Guderian, pp. 305-6; Eberhard Zeller, pp. 265-7; Wheeler-Bennett, p. 654. The legend which reached Switzerland through the Abwehr was that a Major Wolff of the Krampnitz School was about to use the tanks to bombard the Gestapo building. Wolff was dissuaded by Guderian in person, who told him that he would be beheaded. Wolff took his tanks back to Krampnitz, where he found the barracks sacked and looted by the Waffen SS. In fact the tanks remained in Berlin all night. (Dulles, op. cit., p. 190). It is strange that all this could have been believed as late as 1947.

exchange and radio station, both of which the conspirators had failed to blow up.

Here too there had been incredible negligence on both sides. Before Remer arrived in his office, Goebbels seems completely to have lost his nerve. At half past five he received the first telephone call from Hitler, demanding that the news of his survival and a condemnation of the Bendlerstrasse orders be broadcast at once. An hour later, no broadcast having been received, Hitler telephoned Goebbels in such a rage that it was believed at Rastenburg that Goebbels had joined the plotters. The first broadcast went off unimpeded towards seven o'clock, though for the past five hours the Funkhaus had been surrounded by Major Jacob's men from the Doeberitz Infantry School.[1] In the absence of orders they had not dared enter the building, to which the text of the broadcast was telephoned from Goebbels's office over uncut wires.

There are many mysteries about this day of days, 20 July. Doubtless it will be honoured in public holidays and in the names of warships and housing estates on one or other side of the Iron Curtain, if not on both. But among the many Teutonic virtues, praised by Tacitus, the art of making revolutions does not figure, nor is it generally found where industry and obedience are biological necessities. July 20 was a day of muddles and procrastination by loyalists and rebels alike, compared with which Tolstoi's battle of Borodino was something out of a drill-book. What was it that restrained little Remer—so like his patron Goebbels in appearance—from taking his men into the Bendlerstrasse building? He hardly needed a brigade of tanks to interrupt these perspiring old gentlemen. Soon after his conversation with Hitler, Remer learnt that the guard round the Bendlerstrasse building were getting orders from inside it. Instead of marching boldly in, Remer detailed an infantry company to watch the guard and then did nothing more about it till midnight when shots were reported from the building. By that time Fromm and Kortzfleisch had captured and partly murdered their kidnappers without any outside assistance. In fact, things had been so badly managed by the Hitler loyalists that the rebel staff in the Bendlerstrasse building could have made their escape when they realised how desperate was their position.

From six o'clock onwards, with Fromm, Kortzfleisch, Glasemer and Piffraeder locked in different rooms, the conspirators waited

[1] Sammler, op. cit., p. 138; Wheeler-Bennett, op. cit., p. 654; Zeller, op. cit., p. 251.

for the hour when the tanks from the training school should surround the Ministry quarter. At seven o'clock Goebbels began his broadcast from the Funkhaus. Stauffenberg had now to telephone furiously to all commanders throughout Europe, assuring them that Hitler's escape was a lie and Goebbels's broadcast a swindle. At 7.28 he circulated an order of the day in the name of the still absent Witzleben, attributing the broadcast to an ignorant clique of party leaders who had fallen on the rear of the front.[1]

For a moment Stauffenberg's ruse had some result. As Commander-in-Chief of the Western Front, von Kluge actually stopped the V.1 rocket bombardment of England, a preliminary to negotiations. But at eight o'clock Kluge's Chief of Staff Blumentritt learnt the truth from an incorruptible source, a telephone call from Stieff, who was at OKH headquarters at Mauersee near Rastenburg. Soon after half past four Heinrich von Stuelpnagel had received the signal 'Abgelaufen' from Stauffenberg and had given orders for the arrest of the Paris Gestapo. This von Kluge now refused to support and Stuelpnagel went ahead without him. Shortly before their deaths in the Bendlerstrasse, Stauffenberg and his associates knew that the arrests had been carried out.[2]

Even in the Bendlerstrasse it must have been realised by eight o'clock, when von Kluge backed out of the rebellion, that the day was lost. For the Krampnitz and Wuensdorf tanks were long overdue in the Ministry quarter, while dead telephone lines betrayed the flights and defections within the generals' circle. And now at last, as the living image of catastrophe, there arrived from Zossen Beck's appointed Commander-in-Chief for the nine million men who fought for Germany in July 1944. Field-Marshal Erwin von Witzleben had driven into Berlin from Zossen in his own Mercédès, run, as he deprecatingly explained at his trial, on gas. Witzleben stayed exactly three-quarters of an hour, mainly it seems to reproach Stauffenberg for trying to kill Hitler. At his trial Witzleben pleaded that his own plan had been to arrest Hitler by means of a Storm Troop.[3] When Witzleben saw that Beck and Stauffenberg commanded nothing beyond the confines of this hideous building, he returned in the gas-driven Mercédès to his house at Zossen, where the Gestapo picked him up next day, the most broken and pathetic of all the conspirators to face the People's Court.

[1] Wilhelm von Schramm, Die 20. Juli im Paris (Bad-Woerishofen, 1953), p. 133.
[2] Ibid., pp. 119, 136, 139, 157.   [3] Nuremberg Document PS 3881, p. 355.

The choice of Witzleben as Commander-in-Chief shows the true weakness of the Resistance Circle, for Witzleben had on at least three occasions failed to make the Putsch which he had undertaken. He was not an old man—he was sixty-three—but his health had broken down. Himmler described him as a morphine addict. In the first winter of the war, when Hitler had inspected the Siegfried Line, Witzleben had been too ill to come out of his bunker.[1] In March 1942, when Witzleben was in hospital for piles, Hitler replaced him with von Rundstedt.[2] Yet this was the best Goerdeler, Beck and even Stauffenberg could do in their Cabinet making. Not a single serving soldier of general rank, let alone a serving field-marshal, would risk his name on their list. This must be kept firmly in mind when one is told that this or that German general was prepared to march against Hitler.

The culmination of this latest doctoring of history is reached in the claim of Fritz Hesse, the former Foreign Office expert on England, that Eduard Wagner, the Quartermaster-General, had persuaded most of the General Staff to recognise Rommel as the new head of the German state and that Stauffenberg's inept performance thwarted a long-laid plan of the General Staff.[3] Other German writers tell us that, if Rommel had not been wounded in Normandy and sent on leave, he would have acted differently from von Kluge and would have supported the Beck-Stauffenberg Putsch, even when he knew that Hitler had escaped. Von Schramm thinks that Rommel would even have had the support of his two armoured corps commanders from the Waffen SS, Paul Hausser and Sepp Dietrich.[4] Yet Rommel never permitted his name to appear on any of the Resistance lists and he disapproved of killing Hitler. Like most other Nazi generals, Rommel would have taken sympathetic action after a Putsch had been made for him.

At a quarter past eight that night, when Witzleben left the Bendlerstrasse for Zossen, Beck, Stauffenberg and the others might well have gone with him, for Remer's troops did not stop the Field-Marshal. But Stauffenberg continued to telephone useless instructions, while the tanks withdrew from the Ministry quarter and the reputedly loyal guard of Grossdeutschland men melted away from

---

[1] *Vierteljahreshefte fuer Zeitgeschichte*, No. 4, p. 580.
[2] Wheeler-Bennett, op. cit., p. 528; Pechel, op. cit., p. 156.
[3] Fritz Hesse, *Hitler and the English* (London 1954), p. 180-1.
[4] Von Schramm, op. cit., p. 319.

round the Bendlerstrasse building, which had become a volcano about to erupt. The building was full of young staff officers who knew that von Hase, The Town Commandant, had already surrendered to General Hermann Reinecke. They must make a loyalist demonstration or be in the first proscription list, if not murdered by the SS the same night. A certain Lieutenant-Colonel Herber von der Heyde took the lead. Towards half past ten he confronted Hoeppner, who was sitting in Fromm's office.[1] 'Herr Colonel-General, we must know what is going on here. We are here to look after the front, but the flow of reinforcements has been interrupted on account of this Walkuere affair.'

Hoeppner's reaction was to go meekly to Fromm's room and release him. Yet the docile Hoeppner was the only defendant to give his evidence, in the face of Freisler's brutal gibes, in a clear and soldierly manner. For a political general, who had taken part in the Kapp Putsch nearly a quarter of a century before and who had offered to march against Hitler in September 1938, Hoeppner was astonishingly inert. After Olbricht had arrested Fromm, he wasted precious time demanding a written authority from Beck before he would assume Fromm's functions. 'So then your revolution began in a thoroughly bureaucratic style,' Freisler remarked, and he pointed out to the court that Hoeppner, after arriving with a general's uniform in a suitcase, did nothing for six hours.[2]

Except for Beck, who had a Parabellum pistol, the active members of the revolt no longer possessed a weapon between them when Fromm returned to his office. They had been easily disarmed and Stauffenberg had been wounded in a short scuffle with von der Heyde's group, for the latter had smuggled firearms into the building from an armoury in the Zeughaus during the hours of shouting and telephoning.[3] As Fromm entered the room, he addressed the row of battered prisoners who were lined up before him and his words were short and soldierly. 'Well, gentlemen, I am now going to do to you what you wanted to do to me this morning'.

Since all they had done to Fromm was to lock him in his flat, this was not a fair description of the horrible deed Fromm was preparing.

---

[1] PS 3881, p. 417; Zeller, op. cit., p. 231. Von der Heyde, who was 'denazified' on 18 February 1948, is wrongly described on the minutes of the Witzleben trial as Bodo von der Haye.   [2] PS 3881, pp. 403-7.

[3] Gisevius, op. cit., p. 562; Zeller, op. cit., p. 233. There are no true surviving eye-witnesses.

Fromm's savagery is perhaps the strangest aspect of this drama, but his actions can be explained by the single fact that he saw himself a doomed man. He knew already that Keitel had published his dismissal from the command of the Replacement Army. He knew that Himmler was on his way to Berlin, if not there already, and that Himmler would not only supersede him but implicate him in the plot. For weeks past Himmler had sought to step into Fromm's shoes. Only a few days ago Himmler had listened greedily to the tirades of the disgruntled Guderian, who demanded the removal of 'generals who had lived too far from the front'. Oddly enough Himmler had approved a suggestion of Guderian's that Stauffenberg should be promoted to Chief of Staff of the Army.[1]

On 15 July Hitler had authorised Himmler to form fifteen new SS divisions in order to make up part of the losses of the Central Army Group in Russia. This was the danger signal for Fromm. Unless Himmler had full control of the Replacement Army, he could never obtain the necessary drafts of men, since the strength of the Waffen SS could not virtually be doubled through foreign recruitment alone. On that night of 20 July Fromm knew that there would be a proscription and that he himself was the victim most desired by Himmler. Himmler however was the last person to believe in Fromm's alibi. As he put it on 4 August[2] 'Fromm is so cunning and sly that one would not credit him with taking part in this foolish revolution. After his liberation he acted a vulgar film scenario. It was a poor film. No one on earth could believe that things were like that'.

Fromm, Himmler continued, had executed his victims illegally and merely on suspicion of attempted Fuehrer-murder, but of course he had wanted to get them underground, 'quickly, quickly', because they were unfavourable witnesses. And Fromm had ordered the bodies to be burnt and scattered without trace.

So the last act was the only part of this drama in which a military man showed military efficiency. The end came quickly, but for Colonel-General Ludwig Beck, who was sixty-four years old, it was outstandingly horrible. He made two attempts under Fromm's eyes to blow his brains out and with one eye destroyed he had to be finished off by a sergeant. Stauffenberg, Olbricht, Merz von Quirnheim and Werner von Haeften were given a few minutes in order to write messages and then they were shot in the courtyard by the

---

[1] Schwerin von Krosigk, *Es geschah im Deutschland*, p. 346. See also *supra*, p. 262.   [2] *Vierteljahreshefte fuer Zeitgeschichte*, No. 4, p. 588.

light of a lorry's headlamps, the time being a little after midnight. General Kortzfleisch had the right idea. He called for an ancient Teutonic ritual, a shout of 'Sieg Heil' before the blood-spattered bodies.[1]

Yet, even now, mystery attended the doings in the ugly, grey Bendlerstrasse building. Who commanded the shooting party? Who fired the shots? A certain Lieutenant Schlee has been mentioned,[2] but Remer denies with indignation that this was one of his officers. It was only after the shots had been reported to him that Remer sent his men into the building. Skorzeny is equally emphatic that the shooting was over when his detachment arrived. Possibly the execution squad was provided by a detail party in the building itself; polishing tables and peeling potatoes during the day and shooting the General Staff at night.[3]

To resume Hoeppner's evidence, as he gave it before Roland Freisler, President of the People's Court, his own turn came next. Hoeppner, who had been in retirement since the end of 1941, knew little about Fromm. At any rate Fromm thought him a less incriminating witness than the others. He addressed Hoeppner in his heartiest 'it hurts me more than it hurts you' military manner:[4]

Well, Hoeppner, this business upsets me a great deal. You know, we used to be good friends and comrades. You have got yourself caught up in this thing and you must take the consequences. Do you want to choose the same way as Beck or do you want me to arrest you now?

Hoeppner said he didn't feel so guilty; he wasn't (laughter in the court) such a Schweinehund that he had got to shoot himself to death. So Fromm shook hands with Hoeppner and said he understood, and then he shouted to the potato-peeling squad outside to take the Colonel-General to the Wehrmacht Remand Prison.

Fromm was about to execute a half-dozen more conspirators to the flashing of lorry lamps and the shouting of Sieg Heil, when there arrived towards one in the morning first Kaltenbrunner, who had been to Rastenburg and back in the past eleven hours and who was looking for Piffraeder, and then Skorzeny and his men. Kaltenbrunner viewed the bodies with disapproval. He pointed out that Fromm's prisoners would have to be handed over to Himmler, who was responsible for security measures. So Werner von Haeften's

[1] Pechel, op. cit., p. 243.
[2] Pechel, op. cit., p. 343; Zeller, op. cit., p. 234, contradicts Remer.
[3] Remer, op. cit., p. 14, and Skorzeny, op. cit., p. 210.   [4] PS 3881, p. 507.

brother Hans, Witzleben's ADC Peter Yorck, Fritz von der Schulenburg and some other members of the Stauffenberg circle were reprieved for two or three weeks.

And now a curious column of the victorious and of some who
had been spared by Providence converged on to the Goebbels
Ministry in the Hermann Goeringstrasse. Fromm, Kortzfleisch and
Piffraeder went with Kaltenbrunner. They found Goebbels in the
company of Himmler, who had arrived from Rastenburg with his
military Chief of Staff, Hans Juettner. It seems that Reinecke, the
'Oberpolitruk', Remer and Skorzeny sought the same haven of
refuge, while in an adjacent room the imprisoned von Hase loudly
demanded his supper. It was like the gathering of survivors on the
stage in the last scene of a Shakespearean tragedy, to whose unities
the action had singularly conformed.[1]

> Take up the bodies; such a sight as this
> Becomes the field, but here shows much amiss.
> Go, bid the soldiers shoot.

3. HIMMLER AND THE BOMB

For some generations to come Stauffenberg's bomb may provide
a parlour game for winter evenings—that is, provided the march of
science permits conversation between human beings. What would
have happened if Colonel Brant's leg had not tickled, if Hitler had
not got up to look at the map? How would the face of the world
have changed? Would the balance of power have been the same,
ten, twenty, thirty or a hundred years later? Hitler believed in the
intervention of a Higher Power. Nevertheless, the impulse or intuition which took him from his chair at the conference table could
change nothing, neither in Germany's destiny nor in Europe's. This
was because the entirely new problems of a Europe deprived of a
military Germany already existed. For many years to come Germany
would be impotent to intervene in these problems. Stauffenberg's inability to find the combination of circumstances for a foolproof
assassination was a symptom of a national paralysis; and this national paralysis would have remained even if Stauffenberg had
succeeded. One may picture dimly Goering proclaiming himself
Hitler's successor, then ultimatums to Goering from the Bendlerstrasse. No doubt Goering would threaten a march on Berlin and

[1] Von Oven, op. cit., II, pp. 83-5.

Beck and Witzleben would then put themselves in the hands of Rommel and von Kluge. A government by a generals' junta would have followed, a government employing the good offices of the Stauffenberg group to make peace with Russia and the good offices of the Goerdeler circle to make peace with the West. But there would be peace with neither and within a few weeks the disillusioned German armies would melt away like the Russian armies in 1918 after Brest-Litovsk. The war would have been over before the winter of 1944. The Russians and the Western Allies would have met on German territory and they would have been compelled to make a demarcation line little different from the present one. Stauffenberg's bomb could have saved perhaps a half million German lives, the German cities as they were in 1939 would have been left only half obliterated, but the political future of Europe Stauffenberg could not change at all.

Henceforward the Germans were doomed to fight the 'phoney war' of 1939-40 in reverse. Then they had fought for absolute world domination without any bloodshed. Now they fought for nothing at all, but with unparalleled bloodshed. Stauffenberg's failure meant the triumph of the last-ditch mentality, a mentality that had no real existence outside the person of Adolf Hitler and perhaps of Martin Bormann, but now it was too dangerous to exhibit any other mentality. Himmler and Goebbels, the appointed organisers of the fight to the last ditch, were the least convinced last-ditchers of all.

Himmler had been appointed Commander-in-Chief of the Replacement Army when he took leave of Hitler on 20 July, and the confirmation to the military commanders had been sent out by Keitel at eight-twenty in the evening.[1] Under the double threat of invasion this was the key post of the conduct of Germany's war and it was given to a complete civilian. The fall of Fritz Fromm served Himmler precisely as the end of Reinhard Heydrich had served him in 1942, and he owed both advancements to an assassin's bomb, the first because it had killed its man, the second because it had missed. Once more Himmler had greatness thrust upon him and yet he had done singularly little to merit it either before the plot or on the day itself. He had the Dohnanyi and Solf circles in his interrogation cells at Sachsenhausen and Ravensbrueck and yet he was so far off-target that he was ready to believe that the bomb had been laid under the floor by a Communist workman. Himmler was so far from suspecting

[1] The text of one of these orders is given by Zeller, op. cit., p. 368.

Stauffenberg that he had approved a suggestion for making him Hitler's Chief of Staff. In the brief chaos that followed the bomb explosion, the failure of the plot owed much to the strong SS guard posts which were placed at all the vital points in the Rastenburg compound. But it owed still more to the unequivocal attitude of Goering, who could so easily have exploited the situation to his own advantage.

Three months later Goering was to boast, 'Donnerwetter! If the attempt had succeeded I should have had to handle it'. During the last Rastenburg evenings Fegelein used to repeat this story amid roars of stomach laughter and the swelling of choker collars, till one night Himmler turned his solemn myopic gaze on Admiral Doenitz and remarked, 'It is absolutely certain, Herr Grossadmiral, that under no circumstances would the Reichsmarschall have become a successor'.[1]

Himmler's headquarters in East Prussia on 20 July 1944 were not in the Wolfsschanze compound at Rastenburg but twenty-five miles away, at the Villa Hagewald-Hochwald or 'Birkenwald', near Anger-burg on the Maursee. Round the villa there had grown up barracks for troops, but most of the official work took place in the fourteen coaches of a special train. It was better than the villa or the barracks, because you could not shunt *them* into a tunnel during air raids. Here, shortly after the bomb explosion, Felix Kersten saw his patient, preparing to leave for Berlin 'to root out the reactionary breed' and raving that Hitler could not be wounded and that he was protected by destiny. Many months later Himmler told Schwerin von Krosigk that Hitler's escape had taught him to believe in miracles again. He had recovered his faith in God and providence.[2]

Miracle or no miracle, Himmler placed his shilling both ways. He accepted his orders and went to Berlin, but he did not hurry. He was no Piffraeder to go walking into a nest of plotting generals. Between half past three and four o'clock he was with Hitler at the Rastenburg railway siding, waiting for the train that should bring Mussolini. Later Himmler accompanied Hitler and Mussolini on their inspection of the bombed Speer Barracks, after which they

[1] Walter Luedde-Neurath, *Regierung Doenitz* (Goettingen, 1951), p. 39. At his trial in February 1951 Walter Huppenkothen testified that, as a Gestapo commissioner, he had been ordered by Himmler to investigate Goering's connections with the Resistance Circle (*Frankfuerter Abendzeitung*, 13 February 1951).

[2] H. R. Trevor-Roper, op. cit., page 37.

adjourned to the tea-house. Here Himmler was seen by an anonymous observer, standing on the steps as late as five o'clock, while Hitler gave him a parting exhortation to which Himmler replied with a Nazi salute and the audible words 'My Fuehrer, you can leave it to me'.[1]

In Berlin the Putsch ended effectively soon after eight o'clock, when the tanks from the training schools were halted. It is certain that Himmler was not yet in Berlin. For that he would have had to leave the tea-house at Rastenburg well before five. In fact, the earliest instructions which Himmler issued from Berlin were not dispatched till nearly eleven o'clock. These instructions were certainly overdue, for soon after seven Martin Bormann had made an extremely mischievous broadcast from Rastenburg. It was an instruction to all Gauleiters to arrest army officers on suspicion because 'practically the whole General Staff was in league with the Moscow Free Germany Committee'.[2] It was one of Bormann's typical encroachments on Himmler's authority as Minister of the Interior and Chief of Police. One may wonder whether, issued as they were when Himmler was inaccessible in an aeroplane, these instructions to the Gauleiters were not the fruit of deliberate sabotage rather than hysteria. If taken seriously, they might make the task of the appointed pacifier of Berlin unnecessarily difficult. So Himmler got Hitler to countermand Bormann's instructions the same night and to issue on the 24th a directive which was reasonably tactful.[3]

A fortnight later when addressing the Gauleiters in Bormann's presence, Himmler emulated Bormann's language and even attacked the loyalty of the German soldier as well as the loyalty of the General Staff. But on the night of 20 July, when he landed in the chaos of Berlin, the last thing Himmler wanted was to provoke

[1] This detail is reported by Zeller, op. cit., p. 251. The programme of Mussolini's visit will be found in Trevor-Roper, pp. 35 and 114, and in Filippo Anfuso, *Du Palais de Venise au lac de Garde*, pp. 394-5. But it is strange that Filippo Anfuso, in recording Hitler's first telephone call to Goebbels at half past five, says that Hitler shouted, 'Why hasn't Himmler arrived yet?' Had the explosion upset him so much that he had forgotten that Himmler had left him only an hour ago?

[2] *The Bormann Letters*, p. 70. The ridicule of this announcement was made more apparent in October 1955 when after twelve years' captivity Seydlitz was found to be still boycotted by the German generals who returned with him from Russia. And Seydlitz had to wait another nine months before the death sentence passed on him for Hitler: was annulled. (*The Times*, 6.7.56).

[3] Wheeler-Bennett, op. cit., p. 678.

civil war by yelling defiance at the dishonoured Officer Corps. In a moderately worded message he denied the reports of an SS Putsch and declared that his own authority had superseded that of the Bendlerstrasse.[1] The challenge to these instructions came from another quarter. Although he had been told of his suspension, Fromm went back to the Bendlerstrasse from Goebbels's office and, at a quarter to two in the morning of the 21st, von Kluge's staff in France received a teletyped message declaring that Fromm had resumed his command. Kluge was then told by OKH at Rastenburg that Fromm was suspended and, on further inquiries, he received a teletype from Himmler,[2] who evidently was not allowed to go to bed that night.

> The last telephone call from General Fromm is unfounded. In harmony with the Fuehrer's orders I have assumed the command of the Replacement Army. Only orders signed by me are to be carried out.

Yet two days were to pass before Himmler appeared in the Bendlerstrasse. In the meantime the instructions which had lain in Stauffenberg's second brief-case were dealt with by Skorzeny, who had been left virtually in charge of the Replacement Army. Himmler's appointment could scarcely have surprised the Bendlerstrasse survivors. Himmler owed it to Goebbels, who thought on the same lines, and to Bormann, who saw in Himmler's ambitions a chance to ruin him—for Himmler's accumulation of offices had reached the stage when they got beyond him. His nervous stomach cramps were depriving him of his energy and his capacity for pettifogging activity. More than ever before, he sought the refuge of Kersten's clinical sofa and Gebhardt's Hohenlychen Hospital, where wounded soldiers made toys for his second family of children, Helge and Gertrud.[3]

For the relentless proscription of the officers and intellectuals who had been party to the bomb plot Himmler had little time, nor can the horrors of the People's Court trials and the Ploetzensee executions be laid truly at his door. In the late summer of 1944 Himmler had his hands full of infinitely greater horrors, the massing of half a million people into the German concentration camps, the suppression of the Warsaw and Slovakia rebellions, the liquidation of the Lodz ghetto and the abominable bargains with the Allies for the lives of Jewish communities. Himmler's interest in the proscription which followed Stauffenberg's attempt was essentially a

[1] Von Schramm, op. cit., pp. 179, 185.   [2] Von Schramm, op. cit., p. 192.
[3] *The Bormann Letters.*

delaying one. The Gestapo could no longer refrain from arresting Canaris and the Abwehr circle, and these incriminating witnesses of Himmler's double dealing would have to appear in court. Himmler saw to it that the trials were in secret, like that of Popitz and Langbehn, or that they were delayed till a happy peace or a general cataclysm offered opportunities for inconspicuous murder.

But it was essential that the spectacular proceedings of the People's Court against Witzleben, Hoeppner, Stieff, Fellgiebel and their associates should not be repeated. This first of the bomb-plot trials was filmed from every angle and the interrogations, with Freisler's vile insults, were recorded on the sound track. The defendants were shown close to the camera. Collarless, tieless, unshaven, in old pullovers and without braces, they were intended to look like characters from the criminal underworld; but, as the least imagination could have foreseen, they looked like martyrs. The smug officious faces of their persecutors, the inevitable General Hermann Reinecke among them, came out in the film like a backstage crowd in a Peter Breughel Crucifixion. A film was also taken of the executions which were carried out in Ploetzensee prison on the afternoon of the trial itself. Hitler could watch the slow struggles of the almost naked sixty-three-year-old Field-Marshal Witzleben in the strangler's noose, but Goebbels had to hold his hand over his face.[1] The cadets at Gross Lichterfelde walked out when the film was shown to them.

Though Himmler advocated more of this publicity in his Posen address on 3 August, he had to get it stopped. There was no film record of the subsequent trials. The course of retribution became so slow that some of the executions and murders were delayed till the Russians were fighting in the outskirts of Berlin. Such was the case of Albrecht Haushofer, who had known so much about Himmler's contacts with the Allies at the time of the flight of Rudolf Hess.[2] Haushofer was arrested for having been an accomplice of Adam Trott zu Solz in his contacts in Switzerland. He was not found by the Gestapo till 7 December. No attempt was made to carry out Freisler's death sentence. Haushofer's protector saw to it that he was kept among a group who had not been sentenced to death and who were mostly released from the Lehrterstrasse prison as the Russians approached. On 24 April 1945, when Russian troops were in positions as near as the Alexanderplatz, the last of this group to be detained were

[1] Von Oven, op. cit., II, p. 118.   [2] See *supra*, pp. 162-4.

told that they were free to leave, but at the prison gates they were met by an SS section, which had no doubt been sent by Mueller, who now reigned supreme in the Prinz Albrechtstrasse. They were then marched off to the neighbouring Universal Exhibition site, where they were mown down with light machine-guns. One man crawled away to tell the story which led to the discovery of Haushofer's body. His father the 'geopolitician' survived him, but only to commit suicide.[1]

In the nine months following 20 July 1944, some seventy-six persons directly involved in the Resistance Circle and its political plans were executed, but if murders and suicides are included and if victims only indirectly connected with the plot are added, then Dr. Pechel's figure of 147 may stand.[2] There has been some exaggeration of the damage which this proscription caused Germany. If figures worthy of the moral leadership of the nation died, there also died the worst opportunists whom even the 'revolution' of 1933 could produce. And the entire proscription was very small compared with the daily toll of people hanged for grumbling in trams and air-raid shelters or for showing humanity towards deserters and fugitives. In the four weeks beginning 8 August 1944 there were 275 executions which had no connection with the July plot, and in the year 1944 there were 3,427 executions for treason alone.[3]

It is the time-table of the trials that reveals most, for it shows Himmler's efforts to prolong the inquiries of the Gestapo commissioners, Panzinger, Lange, Sonderegger, Stavitsky and Huppenkothen, in order to keep the Abwehr circle of Admiral Canaris hidden away. The month of August saw, besides the mass trial of Witzleben and the men arrested in the Bendlerstrasse, the trials of Schulenburg, Hans von Haeften, Otto Kiepp and Adam Trott zu Solz, Count Helldorf, Elisabeth von Thadden, Ulrich von Hassell and the Paris conspirators, Stuelpnagel and Stauffenberg's cousin, Caesar Hofacker, who was not executed till December. October saw the executions of Langbehn and Reichwein, the former after a secret trial with Popitz. In January 1945 there were the deaths of Julius Leber, von Moltke and Erwin Planck.

The case of Karl Goerdeler deserves a more detailed notice. He had been warned as early as 17 July that there was a warrant out for

---

[1] Hildebrandt, op. cit., pp. 202-7.
[2] Wheeler-Bennett, op. cit., p. 68; Pechel, op. cit., p. 339.
[3] Rudolf Pechel, quoting *Die Lage*, p. 326.

his arrest and at the time of the plot he was hiding in East Prussia. There followed three weeks of aimless wanderings between Berlin and East Prussia. Goerdeler may have been trying to get to Sweden or to pass through the Russian lines, but there was a reward of a million marks for his discovery and on 12 August he was denounced by a member of the women's auxiliary Luftwaffe service at an inn at Konradswalde near Marienwerder.

Goerdeler was sentenced by the People's Court on 8 September after the usual mock trial. Stories that he had been garrulous under the interrogations of the Gestapo and that he betrayed members of the Resistance Circle lack proof. The real harm that Goerdeler caused was done before he was caught. He had a deplorable Prussian bureaucrat's mania for memoranda and lists and these were found in abundance in his old bombed-out apartment in the Askanische Platz as well as in Olbricht's safe in the Bendlerstrasse. While he was an outlaw in hiding, Goerdeler still drew up memoranda for the future of Germany and he drew up still more while waiting the execution of his sentence. Some people were strangled simply because at one time or another their names had been considered for Goerdeler's future Cabinets and he had written them down.

Goerdeler and Popitz were not taken from their cells at Ploetzensee prison to be executed till 2 February 1945. They had waited, Goerdeler from 8 September and Popitz from 3 October. New papers and new witnesses, now brought to light by Goerdeler's friend Professor Gerhard Ritter, make it possible to perceive dimly the conflict of personalities that prolonged their lives. Himmler, it seems, did not want to part so soon with the men whose contacts in Sweden and Switzerland he had so closely followed.

A pretext was found that it was necessary to investigate the plans which the Resistance Circle had drawn up for the economic recovery of Germany after the intended capitulation. Interrogations were begun by Dr. Erhard Maeding of Ohlendorf's Nachrichtendienst or SD. Goerdeler and Popitz were invited to write full-length memoranda and were given facilities to prepare them.[1] Ohlendorf, like everyone except Hitler, foresaw the difficult times after the break-up of the Reich and welcomed the brains of two model bureaucrats. Perhaps, too, he wanted to save their lives. Ohlendorf had known Popitz through his own teacher in economics, Professor Peter Jessen of Kiel University, the father of one of the condemned conspirators.[2]

[1] Ritter, op. cit., pp. 419-20.   [2] See *supra*, pp. 42-3.

As a fellow economist Ohlendorf had nothing against Hitler's former Price Commissioner either. So Goerdeler sat in his cell, helped by an amiable conscripted guard, Wilhelm Brandenburg, who wrote his political testament for him and smuggled letters to his friends which were intercepted by the Gestapo. One of these memoranda contained a list of Goerdeler's acquaintances in high public positions abroad.

It was January 1945. Himmler was Commander-in-Chief of an Army Group and in this distasteful situation Goerdeler's foreign address book stirred up less bellicose memories. According to Brandenburg, who wrote an account of Goerdeler's last days in Ploetzensee prison for Gerhard Ritter in 1950, Himmler made Goerdeler a proposition. He would allow a messenger from Goerdeler to go to Stockholm to interview Jacob Wallenberg, the banker, with whom Himmler had already made contact in the summer of 1943.[1] Wallenberg was to forward peace proposals through the King of Sweden and Dr. Chaim Weizmann, the Zionist leader. But Himmler could not release Goerdeler in order to make the journey himself, nor could he hold out any promises of a pardon. The discussions between Goerdeler and the agent whom Himmler sent to Ploetzensee therefore came to an abrupt end.[2]

This hearsay story—for it is no more—from a Gestapo guard who was not present at any of the meetings is strangely consistent with Himmler's actions in the last months of the war, actions which form the subject of Chapter 15. Moreover, the dates are significant. On 2 February, when the Gestapo had dropped their demand for a suspension of sentence, Thierack signed the execution warrants for Popitz and Goerdeler. It was a little more than a fortnight before Himmler had his first personal interview with Count Bernadotte, the nephew of the King of Sweden.[3]

Goerdeler was by no means the last of the men of 20 July to be executed. Fritz Fromm was not executed till March. He had been arrested within a day or two of his Bendlerstrasse murders, but it took more than six months to find the evidence against him. The only advantage that Fromm derived from his butchery was the right to be shot and not strangled on a hook. The same month they executed Artur Nebe, the ex-commander of an Einsatzgruppe and the reputed father of the gas chambers.[4] Nebe had not even been

---

[1] See *supra*, p. 295.   [2] Ritter, op. cit., pp. 427-8.   [3] See *infra*, p. 413.
[4] Or did they? I have not been able to find any official mention of a Volksgericht trial and Nebe's name is not on Pechel's List of Ploetzensee executions.

suspected at the time of his colleague Helldorf's arrest and he might not have been pulled in at all had he not chosen to hide.

The Abwehr circle were not eliminated till the concentration camps, in which they were confined, were within earshot of Allied or Russian guns. Dohnanyi is said to have been seen alive in Sachsenhausen on 8 April. As to Canaris, the ambiguity of his life extended to his death. It seems that Keitel, who was always singularly loyal to Canaris, contrived to stop the Volksgericht trial which was to have followed Canaris's expulsion from the Wehrmacht.[1] Hitler thereupon ordered Himmler to appoint a summary court. For this a former inspector of the SS judicial section, Otto Thorbeck, was selected. The trial of Canaris was somehow delayed till 9 April, when it took place in Flossenbuerg concentration camp. With Canaris the last of the indicted conspirators were also tried, Hans Oster, Pastor Bonhoeffer, Judge Advocate Carl Sack and the Abwehr officers Struenck and Gehre.

In February 1951 Walter Huppenkothen, who had acted as the Gestapo's prosecutor in this secret trial, was himself tried in Munich for being an accessory to the murder of the five men. The charge was dismissed. Neither Thorbeck nor Huppenkothen had attended the execution. They did not even know whether Hitler had confirmed their findings or whether the sentence had been carried out.[2] It was, however, the belief among the extremely prominent prisoners in the Flossenbuerg bunker that the executions had taken place on the morning after the trial, and the Danish witness Colonel Lunding claimed to have seen Canaris led naked from his cell.[3] The Federal Supreme Court in Karlsruhe quashed the Munich sentence of three and a half years' imprisonment, which had been passed on Huppenkothen for 'extorting evidence and causing bodily harm', and ordered a second trial, this time with Thorbeck as a second defendant; but in November 1952 the Munich court upheld their original verdict. At the second Huppenkothen trial a Gestapo colleague, the famous Criminal Commissar Sonderegger, gave evidence for Huppenkothen. He had seen Hitler's confirmation of the sentences, but they had not been carried out till 10 or 11 April.[4] Other witnesses believed that

[1] Evidence of Dr. Krell, *Frankfuerter Allgemeine Zeitung*, 15 February 1951.
[2] Evidence of Otto Thorbeck, *Frankfuerter Allgemeine Zeitung*, 15 February 1951.
[3] Evidence described by Ian Colvin in *Chief of Intelligence*, pp. 209-14.
[4] *Frankfuerter Allgemeine Zeitung*, 14 October 1952.

Canaris was seen in prison in Berlin as late as 23 April.[1] All this was disposed of in October 1955 when the third Huppenkothen trial was held at Augsburg. New witnesses deposed that they had seen Huppenkothen attend the executions and that these had taken place on the 9th. Huppenkothen was sentenced to seven years' imprisonment, Thorbeck to four. On 19 June 1956 the Federal Supreme Court in Karlsrue dismissed Huppenkothen's appeal but allowed Thorbeck's without hearing any fresh evidence. Yet even after four trials there are legends and doubts concerning the end of the 'Little Admiral'.

The Abwehr circle were not exceptionally badly treated either in the Prinz Albrechtstrasse building, where they remained till the beginning of February when it was destroyed by bombing, or at Flossenbuerg concentration camp. But their death was certainly gruesome and before the end they may have been tortured. The interrogators had an interest in keeping them alive. Abshagen thinks that they prolonged the inquiry in order to avoid conscription. There is a more obvious explanation for the delays, which in the cases of Bonhoeffer, Oster and Dohnanyi amounted to two years from the time of their arrest. This was Himmler's hope that, if Schellenberg and Count Bernadotte failed him, he could still win peace through the men whom he kept behind the wires.

The regular soldiers died quicker, if not in the courtyard of the Bendlerstrasse, mostly by their own hands. The list of suicides and attempted suicides is large and it includes two field-marshals and four colonel-generals, Rommel, von Kluge, Stuelpnagel, Beck, Lindemann and Wagner. Henning von Tresckow sought death by walking into the enemy's field of fire. But the liberation found unexpected survivors living in concentration camps and prisons, among them Franz Halder, the former Chief of Staff, and Georg Thomas of the Armaments Office.

The honoured independence of the old officer class had been a shrivelling plant even before Hitler came to power. Now it was dead. Instead of identifying the conspirators with 'a quite small clique of ambitious officers', the phrase that had leapt to Hitler's lips on the day of the bomb, Himmler, when he addressed the Gauleiters on 3 August 1944, identified the plot with the entire Wehrmacht. A transformation of the army, he said, must be achieved by conducting the trials (but which trials?) in a public and propagandist form. And

[1] *The Times*, 19 September 1955; *Daily Telegraph*, 17 October 1955.

then in the midst of his vituperations Himmler had an access of sensibility and he quoted a moving epitaph which he had heard from a combatant general.[1]

I am convinced that the resources of the German nation will find something new, but that which built up the Reichswehr from the Hundred Thousand Army has gone with it to the grave.

Under so slavish a collection of men as Keitel, Jodl, Burgdorf, Reinecke and Warlimont, the old officer class devoured its own kind. It is true that since the Stauffenberg plot Hitler had a Chief of Staff in Guderian who argued back and even flung scenes, who had openly advocated a new military leadership, and who had listened to Goerdeler and von Tresckow without betraying their confidence; but there were queer limits to Guderian's independence. He consented to sit at the courts of honour which dismissed suspected officers, often without listening to them, in order that they might be handed to the People's Courts, to be exhibited before news cameras in dirty old clothes and to be at the mercy of Freisler, who insulted the army's honour at every sentence with a German general sitting at his side.

Himmler boasted that he had personally proposed this procedure to Keitel in view of the fight for jurisdiction that had taken place after the Rote Kapelle affair.[2] Keitel renounced the armed forces' rights of military trial on 4 August. Ten days earlier he had agreed at Goering's instigation to impose the Nazi salute throughout the armed forces. This step had been delayed exactly ten years from Hindenburg's death on 2 August 1934.[3]

Very very feebly Guderian explains his actions. He only attended two or three sittings; he attended unwillingly; he found the proceedings tragic and shocking; only Keitel, Burgdorf and Burgdorf's deputy, Meisel, found true bills against the officers. Rundstedt, Guderian and three other generals always dissented; and so on. As if all this meant anything at all, compared with the confession that the Chief of Staff of the German Army agreed to act.[4]

Fabian von Schlabrendorff has described how he was tried in absence and dismissed from the army's jurisdiction by one of these courts. But even a military court was now little better than a People's Court. Henceforward generals could be dealt with as easily as privates, and that was very easily indeed. General Heistermann von

[1] *Vierteljahreshefte fuer Zeitgeschichte*, No. 4, pp. 560, 587.
[2] *Vierteljahreshefte fuer Zeitgeschichte*, No. 4, p. 583.
[3] Wheeler-Bennett, op. cit., pp. 678-9.   [4] Guderian, op. cit., p. 312.

Zielburg was arrested at the end of July for disobeying orders. He had permitted his ADC, the deeply implicated Colonel Kuhn, to seek death at the front, but Kuhn chose to get himself captured. Zielburg pleaded forgetfulness. As an army commander during a Russian break-through, he had had five hours' sleep in ten days. The court awarded him nine months' imprisonment. Hitler ordered a re-trial by general court martial which passed a sentence of death with a recommendation to mercy, which Hitler refused to confirm. So Zielburg was shot in Spandau military prison on 2 February 1945. Four days later the Luftwaffe General Weber was shot at the same wall, next to a lorry-driver, six officers, two NCOs and five soldiers. The station commander complained that there were not enough men at the army execution centre to carry out all the sentences and he was told by OKW to order mass executions instead of individual executions, 'not necessarily every day'.[1]

Perhaps Hitler and Himmler were unfamiliar with Voltaire's epigram on the shooting of Admiral Byng—'*pour encourager les autres*'. Hitler was ready to admire some of the civilian conspirators, particularly Trott zu Solz and Schulenburg, if we may trust Fritz Hesse,[2] but for the military conspirators he had nothing but derision. Only in the case of von Kluge, who had been an assiduous courtier at headquarters before his appointment in the West, was Hitler prepared to make allowances and even to refuse to face the truth.[3] As to Rommel, the facts were so damaging to a great Nazi legend that Hitler refused to have them published, and Rommel's suicide *sur commande* was concealed in a state funeral.

Hitler was still capable of a little diplomacy in handling his generals. He had not yet reached the stage when his foremost battle-front was against his own High Command. Proof of this was his hasty correction of the first all-round denunciations which were broadcast from Bormann's office. Himmler closely followed Hitler's lead in these matters. His scorn of the conspiring generals, as poured out before Bormann, Goebbels and the assembled Gauleiters at Posen, was probably an echo of Hitler's intimate conversation. But Himmler's hatred of the professional officer corps, though lifelong and real, seldom descended to this personal plane and Himmler too was capable of diplomatic behaviour among the People's Court

---

[1] Guderian, op. cit., p. 313; Pechel, op. cit., p. 168; Weisenborn, op. cit., p. 129.

[2] Hesse, op. cit., p. 188.

[3] Gilbert, op. cit., p. 97; Von Schramm, op. cit., p. 374.

judgments and the Spandau executions—and never more than in the case of the arrest of the Paris Gestapo.

Many members of the staff of Heinrich von Stuelpnagel, the military governor of France, were involved. Stauffenberg's cousin, Caesar von Hofacker, had set the machinery in motion soon after Stauffenberg's first signal from the Bendlerstrasse. Half an hour before his death Stauffenberg learnt that Major-General Karl Oberg, the higher SS and police leader for France, and Colonel Helmuth Knochen, the Paris commander of the security police, had been arrested with the entire staffs of the Gestapo and SD in the Avenue Foch and Rue de Saussaies. But they spent only three hours in captivity. At one-thirty in the morning, on threats of armed intervention by the naval and Luftwaffe commands, Stuelpnagel released his captives and the affair ended with an all-night drinking party in the Hotel Raphael, where 'Ambassador' Abetz made Stuelpnagel and Oberg shake hands in public.[1] On Oberg's suggestion the troops, who had conducted the arrests and who had got the sand ready for the executions—his own among them—in the Ecole Militaire, were thanked at morning parade for carrying out a practice exercise, 'which had been concerted with the Higher SS Police Leader'.[2]

Himmler allowed Oberg to respect his agreement and before the parade an order had gone out from Himmler's office forbidding reprisals.[3] Stuelpnagel, an unsuccessful suicide, was judicially strangled in Ploetzensee prison, having been dragged from a hospital bed with half his face blown off. Several members of his staff, including Hofacker, received the death penalty too. Yet it is a fact that no charges were brought against the Paris Town Commandant, Boineburg-Lengsfeld, or against the officers who so gladly arrested the Gestapo for him.[4] Of all the inconsistencies of the proscription this is the queerest. Whether it was only Himmler's friendship for Oberg, whether it was Kaltenbrunner's shame at another poor showing by the Gestapo, whether it was fear that such an admission of weakness might stimulate the Paris Resistance leaders, no pressure was put on Himmler by the Bormann-Fegelein-Kaltenbrunner group to make him change his mind.

[1] Von Schramm, op. cit., p. 212. [2] *Ibid.*, p. 219. [3] *Ibid.*, p. 226.
[4] Boineburg-Lengsfeld was relieved of his post and replaced by General Choltitz on 13 August. Choltitz surrendered his men to the Paris Resistance movement and was tried *in absentia* at Torgau in April 1945. Boineburg was to have been charged with failing to order the destruction of the Seine bridges, but escaped to the Americans. Shulman, op. cit., pp. 166, 169.

Fear of the effect on the French Resistance movement certainly played a large part in this decision. Sepp Dietrich, then commanding the 1st Panzer Corps in Normandy, anxiously assured Himmler that there was no need to march the Leibstandarte to Paris to restore order. But Hitler's personal butcher of June 1934 was now such a disillusioned character that he might well have refused to arrest Stuelpnagel and his staff, even had he been called on to do so. The Normandy battlefield had deflated the party fanatic, but long before then Sepp Dietrich had come to terms with the Wehrmacht generals. Shortly before D-day General Geyr von Schweppenburg, who found Sepp Dietrich 'complaisant and comradely', suggested to him that he should use his well-known influence on Hitler to get Ribbentrop replaced as Foreign Secretary by von Hassell[1]— and Sepp Dietrich grinned politely. Dietrich was certainly in the confidence of the 'Resistance' generals. When von Kluge decided to commit suicide, he sent his farewell letter to Hitler through the hands of Sepp Dietrich, 'whom I have come to know and appreciate as a brave and incorruptible man in these difficult weeks'. [2]

Oberg was delighted to be relieved of the responsibility for a proscription of Stuelpnagel's staff. On the day following his own arrest and release, he sent Major-General Boineburg, the Paris Town Commandant, a box of cigars; and three days later he visited Stuelpnagel in Verdun hospital, a mutilated Stuelpnagel who had been fished out of the Morthomme canal only to face death again five weeks later in the Ploetzensee noose. Wilhelm von Schramm, former military archivist to the Western theatre of war, describes the incident thus: 'So there sat not a so-called Gestapist but an officer of the old school by the bed of a seriously wounded comrade in order to talk to him as a comrade'. [3]

To the author, at least, German writing of the Resistance School has few surprises to offer, but, as a piece of *Schwaermerei*, this surely beats everything. Who would suppose that Oberg had conducted for the previous two years a reign of terror, which included the shooting of thousands of so-called hostages and for which he has been twice condemned to death, though alive today? Who would suppose that Stuelpnagel, for all his plotting, did nothing, absolutely nothing, to stand in the way of the torture cellars and shooting walls of the Paris Gestapo?

[1] Von Schweppenburg, *The Critical Years*, p. 204.
[2] Shulman, op. cit., p. 152; von Schramm, op. cit., p. 282.
[3] Von Schramm, op. cit., p. 318.

Perhaps it was too much for Himmler, too. Though Oberg was promoted to lieutenant-general, he was dismissed soon after the fall of Paris. In what was left of France under German rule, the police and Gestapo were taken over by Major-General Richard Jungclaus, the higher SS and police leader for Belgium. As the former armies of Rommel and Kluge streamed north, Jungclaus took over the duties of military governor as well.[1]

Never had an SS police leader infringed so far on the army's prerogative. The appointments of Jungclaus in France and of Karl Wolff in Italy were the climax of the long struggle between Heydrich and Canaris, between Himmler and OKW. But it was a vain climax, for soon Jungclaus was left without a territory. Very few higher SS police leaders fulfilled their functions outside Germany at the end of 1944. The true sequel to Stauffenberg's bomb was not the rise of Himmler nor the extinction of the Junker military families, but the loss of the armies of the West.

[1] Institute of International Affairs, *Hitler's Europe*, p. 491.

13

Rebellion in Eastern Europe

1. HUNGARY; THE GREAT DEPORTATION

The failure of Stauffenberg's plot meant a much longer war. One way and another the German will to resist was stimulated—to such a degree that the Allies were taken by surprise, both by the defence at Arnhem in September and by the attack in the Ardennes in December. But there was no let-up in the growing pace of German disaster. The Normandy front was close to collapse on the day of the bomb explosion and five weeks later Paris fell. On the same day Roumania capitulated and with this event a third door to the Reich lay open and a new front had to be created in Hungary and Croatia by German divisions. Hungary, too, was tottering. As far as possible the Hungarian and Roumanian divisions were replaced by the racial Germans of those countries, who had been conscripted into the Waffen SS. This gave the SS a far more important role than they had fulfilled on the Eastern and Western fronts and it was an SS army which fought the last hopeless battles for Budapest and Vienna.

Both militarily and politically, however, the SS had become involved in Hungarian affairs at an earlier date—in the month of March 1944, when the retreat which had begun in South Russia in July 1943 ceased to be manageable. In that month the Red Army breached the front at Uman and swept up to the River Dniester and the foothills of the Carpathians. The governments both of Roumania and Hungary began secret negotiations with the Allies. Although farther from the front than Roumania, the immediate danger in Hungary was greater. For while the Roumanian line was strengthened with German divisions and the Roumanians defended an annexed territory, the Hungarians were not in the line at all. Since Stalingrad they had withdrawn their troops, an army composed of ten under-strength divisions, and, though they enjoyed the restoration of most of their old territories entirely through Hitler's successes, they had become a neutral country in the rear of the German front, a land of night-clubs and white bread where the privileged could live without rationing or conscription.

It was necessary to get the Hungarian capital and the Regent of the Hungarian throne into German tutelage, but German field divisions could not be diverted in sufficient numbers. Hitler's first idea was to garrison Budapest with Slovak and Roumanian troops. He was dissuaded from a course which would have created internecine war among allies by Walter Hewel, his liaison officer with the Foreign Office. This sleek, rubicund person played a far from negligible role in the last days of Hitler's court. For many years Walter Hewel had been sensible enough to forget his part as a young student in Hitler's Munich Putsch of 1923 by settling down as a planter in Sumatra, but in the end he succumbed to Hitler's appeals for the return of an old party fighter. By the beginning of the war Hewel's success with Hitler as a court entertainer had induced Ribbentrop to bid high for his services. Although Hewel was too timid to use his intimacy with the Fuehrer to become another Martin Bormann, he did not scruple to advise Hitler over Ribbentrop's head and Ribbentrop had to accept this situation. Hewel discovered that Himmler's Abwehr advisers had a better knowledge of East European affairs than the Foreign Office. Having completely failed to recommend to Hitler the plan for autonomy in the Baltic States which had Himmler's approval (see page 205), Hewel now put up another SS proposal and this time with success. Hitler accepted the Hungary plan of Himmler's Abwehr with few modifications. The plan was to lure Admiral Horthy to Hitler's guest castle at Klessheim and there to force him through the threat of kidnapping to accept a mitigated German occupation. There would be a Reich plenipotentiary in the capital, together with a higher SS police leader, a German police force, and a German garrison.[1]

At Klessheim all went well. The seventy-six-year-old Regent, Admiral Horthy, showed even less spirit than might have been expected of a man in his uncomfortable position. He agreed to appoint a pro-German cabinet and to dismiss a whole number of generals and he returned to Budapest in the company of a German watchdog, the Reich plenipotentiary Edmund Veesenmayer. But back in his own capital the Regent felt more confident and the appointment of a pro-Nazi Premier was not made without some opposition. Himmler is believed to have proposed that the Wehrmacht should occupy the royal palace on the Burgberg. In fact seven months were to pass before the Regent submitted to this affront at the hands of Otto

[1] W. Hoettl, *The Secret Front* (London, 1954), pp. 200-2.

Skorzeny.[1] Nevertheless, Horthy's humiliation on 19 March was almost complete. German motor columns drove into the city from Vienna and the surrounding airfields were captured by German parachutists, but a sulky belligerent power had been resurrected. For the moment Hungarian divisions were back in the line, even though that was in their own country.

Horthy dismissed the cabinet of Nicholas Kallay which had made contacts with Tito's partisans, with the Red Army and with U.S. Intelligence officers in Switzerland. Yet, even with a German-approved government in power, the contacts continued under the eyes of a Reich plenipotentiary and an SS police leader. And soon this theatrical show lost its effectiveness. Within a few months there were not enough German troops left in Hungary to keep the Sztojay government in office. Things drifted back to where they had been before, but not till some three hundred thousand innocent lives had been sacrificed to Hitler.

For Hitler's chief motive in securing Hungary was the extermination of European Jewry, the obsession that always transcended his military strategy. In Greater Hungary, as reconstituted between 1939 and 1941, there were seven hundred thousand Jews, more perhaps than had survived in all the remaining countries of occupied and satellite Europe. To some extent the Jews had been persecuted during the past five years of Hungarian rule, but they had not been forced to emigrate. On the contrary, since the opening of Hitler's extermination programme in the summer of 1941, the country had provided a refuge for Jews from Slovakia, Roumania and Poland.

A whole fortnight before Hitler summoned Horthy to Klessheim, an Einsatzgruppe of the security police had been assembled for the Hungarian area in Mauthausen concentration camp,[2] though this was a time when it was still doubtful whether German military intervention in Hungary could be effective. The real purpose of the Einsatzgruppe was to remove all Jews from Hungary when the country became a combat area. Consequently in Hitler's brief to the SS police leader for Hungary this matter came first: 'To perform tasks of the SS and police concerning Hungary and especially duties in connection with the Jewish problem'.[3]

To this position Hitler appointed Otto Winkelmann, a colourless individual who had been Daluege's successor as head of the German

---

[1] Case XI, transcript, 28550.   [2] IMT, III, p. 285; evidence of Wisliceny.
[3] Case XI, Document NG 2957.

regular police. He was not a violently indoctrinated SS man; in fact, Winkelmann was good-natured and lazy and left his nasty responsibilities in the hands of Hitler's plenipotentiary, Edmund Veesenmayer, and of the two Hungarian special commissioners, Endre and Baky. These were two notorious anti-Semites who had been hand picked by Kaltenbrunner and who worked in perfect harmony with the extermination chief from Berlin, Adolf Eichmann. The latter was promoted for the occasion to be commander of the security police for Hungary (Bds. Ungarn). He was put in charge of the Einsatzgruppe, he was installed in Budapest in the Hotel Majestic and for the first time in his career he worked outside his discreet office building in the Kurfuerstenstrasse.

All this had been decided at a very high level and, though there is no record that Hitler ever met Eichmann, it must have been Hitler who decided his new role. Moreover, Eichmann could not have carried out the preparations for a massacre which had been surpassed only in Russia in the autumn of 1941 and in Poland in the summer of 1942 if he had not had the diplomatic cover of Ribbentrop's Foreign Office. Edmund Veesenmayer, the plenipotentiary, although in theory Hitler's personal deputy in Hungary, was really put there for little other purpose than to provide Eichmann with this diplomatic cover. He was only a wartime temporary official, whose career had been made not in the Foreign Office but in the general SS. Veesenmayer had to serve two masters. His immediate chief was Ribbentrop, but he was also responsible to Kaltenbrunner at the Reich Main Security Office for the co-operation of the Hungarian authorities with the German police in carrying out the anti-Jewish measures according to Hitler's brief. His position was thoroughly odious, for this was the time when Kaltenbrunner, having swallowed Canaris's Abwehr, was trying to swallow the Foreign Office too. But, though Veesenmayer's correspondence as produced at Nuremberg shows him often in a ticklish position, on one point there could never be any quarrel between Kaltenbrunner and Ribbentrop, and that was the thoroughness with which both sought to complete the extermination of European Jewry.

For this purpose Veesenmayer was not ill-chosen, being a creature of Wilhelm Keppler,[1] that useful early friend of Himmler's and founder of the 'Friends of the Reichsfuehrer SS'. Keppler's failure to become Minister for Economic Affairs had led him into diplomatic

[1] See *supra*, pp. 28-9.

ambitions. During the plotting that preceded the Austrian Anschluss in 1938, Himmler got him appointed Secretary of the Vienna Embassy alongside the not too certain von Papen. When Keppler fulfilled similar missions in Slovakia and Danzig on the eve of their assimilation, Veesenmayer accompanied him. At the beginning of the war Veesenmayer became a recognised member of the Foreign Office as 'plenipotentiary for Ireland', and early in 1940 he concocted schemes with Admiral Canaris for using members of the Irish Republican Army against England.[1] But sabotage was not destined to be Veesenmayer's wartime activity. He co-signed a report from Belgrade in September 1941, recommending the deportation of the Serbian Jews. Henceforward this was to be Veesenmayer's special province. He composed long reports for Ribbentrop on Hungary's failure to deport Jews in May 1943 and on Slovakia's failure to renew the deportations in December.[2]

It was on the strength of these cold, inhuman and ill-informed documents, which, Veesenmayer insists, were touched up by Ribbentrop before he signed them, that this quite insignificant person became Hitler's deputy in Hungary. In the end it was his insignificance which saved him. Many years after the war Mr. McCloy, the U.S. High Commissioner in Germany, accepted Veesenmayer's pleas which the Nuremberg Court had rejected. It was conceded that the pressure which Veesenmayer had put on Admiral Horthy and his grovelling support of Eichmann's Einsatzgruppe had been just the obedience of a subservient person. Veesenmayer's sentence of twenty-five years' imprisonment was commuted to ten years and in December 1951, at the age of fifty-eight, he was set free, having played a very essential part in the murder of at least three hundred thousand people.

On 8 April 1944 the Russians entered a corner of Carpathian Ruthenia, the region annexed by Hungary from Czechoslovakia in 1939. It was the signal for the first deportations of Jews. Within a week enormous round-ups were staged in the Ruthenian towns of Ungvar and Munkacs. Gradually Veesenmayer gingered up the Sztojay cabinet, while the Eichmann commando forced the hands of the Hungarian commissioners, Baky and Endre. The round-ups spread in a wide ring to all the former Czech, Roumanian and Jugoslav areas. By 15 May more than three hundred thousand Jews, none of whom had been enfranchised in the new Hungary

[1] Abshagen, op. cit., pp. 273-80.
[2] Case XI, Documents NG 2867, NG 4749, and NG 1823-4.

of 1939-41, were held behind barbed wire. They were Hungary's hostages to Hitler in the hope that he would continue as unexacting as before.

Events now followed a familiar pattern. By 20 April the Hungarian commissioners had found that it was impossible to feed the Jews in the hastily improvised ghettos. They begged the Eichmann commando to take these people off their hands.[1] Horthy stood aside in silence. His only concern was for the enfranchised Jews of Budapest and 'Trianon Hungary', who, he expected, would provide him with a hundred thousand labour conscripts. The Premier, Sztojay, struggled with Veesenmayer to preserve this quota for the homeland. It was part of a bargain by which Himmler was to be allowed the same number of labourers to be sent to Germany for the 'Jaeger Plan', the construction of underground aircraft factories which would be proof against Allied bombing raids. Neither Horthy nor Jaross, his Minister of the Interior, concerned themselves with the true implications of the German demand. Yet the special commissioners of the ministry were well aware of the poor physical state of the 'Galician' Jewish communities in Greater Hungary. Experience in Poland had shown that not even a quarter of a deported community was normally preserved by the Germans as fit for labour. Moreover, the number whom the Germans had transported by 30 June was 381,600,[2] and these were to produce a labour force which did not exceed a hundred thousand when they reached their destination, which was Auschwitz.

Horthy had remarkably little difficulty in putting an end to the deportations when it suited his purpose, but in May and June 1944 he renounced all interest in the fate of four hundred thousand people, packed—man, woman and child—in cattle trains, ninety to a truck.[3] And Eichmann with his associates went to work, having no German security police at their disposal, for they left the Einsatzgruppe in Budapest. The operation was conducted by Hungarian gendarmerie and conducted with a callousness which was tempered only by corruption. That very old gentleman, sole survivor of the

[1] Nuremberg Document, affidavit C (Wisliceny).

[2] Case XI, Document NG 2263.

[3] Horthy's published explanation is hardly good enough. 'It was alleged that the deportees were sent to labour camps. Only in August I learned through secret channels the full truth about the extermination camps' (*Ein Leben fuer Ungarn*, 1953, p. 271).

European statesmen of the Versailles era, who lives today in exile at Estoril, should have a heavy weight on his conscience.[1]

Normally the opening of an extermination season at Auschwitz was a routine matter, calling for little or no personal intervention from Himmler. Eichmann could handle the whole thing from booking the special trains to dispersing the ashes from the Auschwitz crematoria. Everything was arranged through his Berlin office, IVA, 4b. But on this occasion the deportations were hurried by the Russian threat to the Hungarian border provinces. Throughout the second half of May the Jews from Greater Hungary arrived at the Birkenau camp siding at the rate of from twelve thousand to fourteen thousand a day in four huge overloaded trains.[2] Even if the four new gas chambers could hold close on ten thousand people between them, which is the implication of these official figures, there would be grave practical difficulties. The crematoria furnaces could not dispose of more than a small fraction of such numbers of bodies in one operation—and it was essential that there should not be more than one. With four trains arriving every day, it was absolutely necessary that the passengers should perceive no trace of bodies or of burning. Due to these considerations, the usual proportion of selections for the gas chambers could not be kept up and masses of people had to be dumped in the uncompleted extensions of Birkenau camp, which became a potential Belsen.

In the depths of Poland these people could just have been left to die in the open, but Auschwitz was under the eye of Pohl's bureaucracy, who became worried about the lack of order and system. It was realised that Hoess alone possessed the experience to deal with such a crisis, but since November 1943 Hoess had been suspended from his functions under a suspicion of peculation and employed in the central office. So Hoess returned to Auschwitz, not as camp commandant but as garrison commander, and from the beginning of June the Hungarian deportation programme became his special assignment under the name 'Action Hoess'. Under his orders burning-pits were dug to supplement the crematoria and shooting places to relieve the gas chambers, while a screen of tree trunks was made

[1] Having refused to extradite Horthy to Hungary, the American occupation authorities eventually decided not to try him as a war criminal and released him in 1948. Veesenmayer tried to pin the whole responsibility for the deportations on to Horthy, but the court accepted Horthy's affidavits on this subject. Case XI, transcript, 28543.   [2] Case XI, NG 2190. Reitlinger, op. cit., p. 423.

to hide it all from the camp. But every night for six weeks the camp inmates could watch the blazing crematoria chimneys, stoked at full pressure.[1]

Himmler was perhaps not aware of this vision of hell. In Hoess he had an executant too unimaginative to find it worth describing and far too German to dream of bothering his chiefs about it—and Himmler did not want to be bothered. But Himmler was interested enough to try to make some money for the SS by selling the lives of the wealthier deportees. He even gave his support to a wild plan for calling off the slaughter against the delivery of war material by the Allies. He also persuaded himself that 'Action Hoess' was providing workers for the aircraft factories.

The intense Allied bombardment of all German factories producing fighter aircraft had begun on 19 February. On 9 April, at the very start of the Hungarian round-ups, Hitler told Field-Marshal Erwin Milch, who was now the real head of the Luftwaffe, that Himmler would find the man-power; but on 26 May at one of Albert Speer's ministerial conferences it was said that only two trainloads of employable Jews had been forwarded from Auschwitz—and this out of 140,000 who had arrived in the past twelve days.[2] Oswald Pohl told Himmler that half the Jews from Hungary who had passed the selection from Auschwitz were women and they could not be used in the Jaeger project. The Hungarian Jewesses must be employed in Poland, digging trenches for the Todt organisation, a work which Himmler thought they could perform if they received a diet of raw garlic to which they were accustomed.[3] Himmler was as always a fanatical herbalist. Later he told Gabor Vajna that the Hungarian Jews had been a great success and that they had increased the Jaeger Plan output by forty per cent.[4] In reality only a few thousands of Jews could be picked for the underground factories, to whose conditions they quickly succumbed. If the Auschwitz selections really spared as many as a hundred thousand Jews from Hungary, they were distributed uselessly in starvation camps, and only a small proportion worked in the factories of the Reich.

But Hitler's startling reversal of policy concerning Jews in the Reich may have given Himmler the idea that he could exaggerate the numbers that had been preserved alive and use them to do a deal

---

[1] Reitlinger, op. cit., pp. 428-9.
[2] Trials of War Criminals, II, p. 555; Nuremberg Document R 134.
[3] Case IV, Document NO. 592.   [4] Case XI, Document NO. 1874.

with the Allies. Such deals had been made in a small way in the past by individual 'resettlement commissioners' and one of them, Dieter Wisliceny, who had sold the lives of many Slovak Jews in 1942, was at work again in Budapest.

Wisliceny's first proposals to the heads of the Hungarian Jewish community were modest, but on 5 May a staggering offer was made by Eichmann to Joel Brand of the Budapest Joint Distribution Committee and this could scarcely have been without Himmler's connivance. The proposal was handled through a certain Colonel Kurt Becher who was employed in Budapest by the SS Personnel Office. A former Hamburg grain salesman, Becher had directed a remount purchasing commission for the SS in the summer of 1942, having been commended to Fegelein's attention through his skill in acquiring the Baron Oppenheim racing stud for the SS.[1] Becher was probably introduced to Himmler's intimate circle of advisers through Schellenberg, but this was only after the 'occupation' of Budapest, when Becher again handled a negotiation for the SS, the acquisition of the Jewish Manfred Weiss Steel Combine.[2]

It is impossible to say whether the fantastic plan, which was put forward by Eichmann to Joel Brand, was Becher's inspiration or Schellenberg's or Himmler's own. Brand was to go to Istanbul and to offer the lives of the seven hundred thousand Jews of Greater Hungary against the payment of ten thousand lorries, to be delivered by the Allies at the port of Salonika. When Brand left in Becher's company on 19 May, Eichmann promised that the Jews who had already been deported to Germany would be kept alive for a fortnight. After that, if he heard nothing from Istanbul, Eichmann would 'let the Auschwitz mills grind'.[3]

In fact the mills were grinding already when Brand and Becher left for Istanbul. Brand tried to make contact with the British Embassy in Ankara and with the Jewish Agency in Palestine. Arrested by British Military Intelligence on the Turkish-Syrian border, Brand was interned in Cairo. He was, however, permitted to see Mr. Moshe Sharett of the Jewish Agency, who transmitted the German proposals to London. On 18 July they were published in the British Press as a revelation of German ignominy. Himmler had to

---

[1] Trials of War Criminals, V, p. 682.

[2] IMT XI, p. 306; evidence of Kaltenbrunner.

[3] Reszoe Kastner, unpublished manuscript, *Der Bericht des Juedischen Rettungs-Kommittees*, etc., pp. 33-7, 48, 55.

live down the discreditable story and it was denied for him by the Goebbels Ministry, but Veesenmayer assured Ribbentrop that the British publication was only a blind to fool the Russians. Himmler's negotiations were still going on.[1]

On 14 June, while Brand was wandering about the Near East, Eichmann made the Budapest Jews a new proposal. Twenty million Swiss francs would save the lives of the first thirty thousand Jews to be deported from the still untouched 'Old Hungarian' communities west of the River Theiss. For a small sum on account they could be kept 'on ice' in a labour camp at Strasshof in the Burgenland, south-east of Vienna.[2] Nine thousand were actually kept at Strasshof and spared the Auschwitz selections, though Kaltenbrunner warned his friend Blaschke, the Mayor of Vienna, that the women and children at Strasshof were not to leave the camp because they were destined for 'special action'.[3] A small portion, consisting of Jews who had paid an individual ransom, were forwarded from Strasshof to the 'exchange camp' at Bergen-Belsen, the Belsen of infamous memory.

In the meantime Jewish international charity found the twenty million francs. In this way 1,684 Jews, mainly from the former Roumanian town of Cluj, were taken from Bergen-Belsen and released in Switzerland in two trainloads on 21 August and 6 December. But only five million Swiss francs were transferred to Himmler and even these he only obtained in the following February, when a further 1,100 Hungarian Jews reached Switzerland.[4]

This portion of the money was released through Roosevelt's personally appointed agency, the War Refugee Board, after fantastic negotiations and incredible difficulties with the U.S. State Department. Himmler received it through the President of the Swiss Republic, on the understanding that it would be used to finance further emigration through the Red Cross. Unfortunately on 6 February, when the third train arrived, the news was published in the Swiss Press and Hitler heard of it. Becher, with the jealousy that was common among Himmler's intimate advisers, accuses his colleague Schellenberg of sending Hitler the Press notice.[5] A stormy interview followed between Hitler and Himmler. Hitler in his fury ordered that no concentration-camp inmate should fall alive into Allied hands.[6]

---

[1] Case XI, Document NG 279.
[2] Kastner, op. cit., pp. 48, 55; Nuremberg Document, Affidavit C.
[3] IMT XI, p. 313.   [4] Kastner, op. cit., p. 113; Document NG 2994.
[5] Case XI, NG 2675; Affidavit, Kurt Becher.   [6] See *infra*, pp. 415, 424.

Nevertheless, in this abortive affair Himmler had made his first contact with the International Red Cross, which led to the Count Bernadotte surrender negotiations.

A few more details concerning Himmler's part in releasing the Hungarian Jews from Bergen-Belsen to Switzerland are given in Felix Kersten's memoirs. The first shipment of 318 Jews on 21 August 1944 had been partly due to a certain Madame Immfeld of St. Gallen, who had sent Himmler a proposal for settling twenty thousand Jews in the south of France. Himmler's first reactions had been hostile and, even after the first train had left, he told Kersten that not a single Jew would thank him for his intervention. After the second train had left, Gottlob Berger taxed Himmler with accepting blood-money for what should have been a humane and generous action. The result was to discourage Himmler altogether. On 2 December he told Kersten that the release of twenty thousand Jews was out of the question. What would Goebbels say to Hitler about it? The most the Swiss could have were two to three thousand Jews and this must not be interpreted by the Allies as a sign of weakening.[1]

In view of Himmler's total lack of fanaticism and his lack of principles in connection with the Final Solution, it is surprising that so few lives were sold. Two thousand seven hundred Jewish lives were redeemed by purchase, but 440,000 were deported from Greater Hungary and less than a quarter survived till the end of the war. One explanation is that the Auschwitz mechanism could not be halted. During the first two weeks, when the Jews arrived at the rate of twelve to fourteen thousand a day, there was no room either in Auschwitz or the other concentration camps to keep them 'on ice'; and not long after the numbers had become manageable, the Regent Admiral Horthy bestirred himself to call off the deportations.

2. HUNGARY: THE FALLEN BASTION
JULY 1944—APRIL 1945

With the successful landing of the Allies in Normandy, followed by the German débâcle on the central Russian front, Horthy began to realise that he had been bluffed and that at the Klessheim meeting he had failed to play his cards. Secretly he now offered the premiership of Hungary to General Lakatos, one of the very commanders whose recall had been exacted by Hitler on the grounds of pacifism.

[1] Kersten: *Memoirs*, p. 219; *Totenkopf und Treue*, pp. 244-5.

For the moment Lakatos refused, but on 26 June Horthy was emboldened to deliver an attack on the conduct of the Hungarian gendarmerie and to demand the recall of the 'resettlement commissioners', Baky and Endre.[1] This was the result of a protest from the Vatican and a diplomatic note from the U.S. State Department, threatening postwar criminal proceedings. The Premier, Sztojay, retorted with a circular to the Corps Diplomatique, claiming that the deportations differed in no degree from normal labour service in Germany, and Horthy might have rested content with that if the bombardment of his conscience had not continued. On 5 July Raoul Wallenberg, a member of the famous Swedish banking family, arrived on a mission from the King of Sweden and there was also a moving personal letter from Karl Burckhardt of the International Red Cross. Two days later the Regent learnt of a statement in the House of Commons by Mr. Anthony Eden and Mr. Brendan Bracken, alleging that seven hundred thousand to one million Hungarian Jews were in the process of extermination at Auschwitz.[2] On 14 July there was another broadcast by Mr. Cordell Hull, again threatening war trials.

The information in the Allies' speeches and broadcasts was derived from secret Polish transmissions, which had begun with the revival of the gassings at Auschwitz and had been picked up as far back as the middle of May. Had the protests been more punctual, they could have saved from two to three hundred thousand lives. They caused Himmler to listen to the views of Madame Immfeld and they caused Admiral Horthy to wriggle out of the clutches of Herr Veesenmayer. Soon there were tangible results. During the first week of July, 17,500 Jews living in the Budapest suburbs west of the Danube were collected for deportation in Budakalacs barracks, but on 8 July, when four trains should have left for Auschwitz, only one sneaked out. During the course of the day General Lakatos had disarmed the Budapest gendarmerie and Baky and Endre had been sent on leave.[3] On the 14th Horthy learnt that Eichmann's German security police had dispatched another train with 1,450 Jews from Kistarcsa camp. The Regent managed to get the train diverted at Hatvan. Thus it came about that in the whole of July, when the 150,000 Jews of Budapest were to have been deported, only three trains reached Auschwitz. The Eichmann commando had lost the fight.

[1] Eugene Levai, *The Black Book of the Martyrdom of Hungarian Jewry* (Zurich, 1948), pp. 235, 243.

[2] *The Times*, 8 July 1944.   [3] Levai, op. cit., p. 250.

Ribbentrop now became very worried and on 17 July he sent Horthy a warning that two German armoured brigades were on the way to Budapest. If Horthy failed to confirm the Sztojay government in office and resume the deportations, the capital would be seized. Himmler followed up Ribbentrop's threat by sending for Eichmann. A new deportation centre was got ready in the suburbs at Bekesmagyar, while a return of clothing for the German concentration camps, dated 1 August, shows that ninety thousand Hungarian Jews were expected to reach Germany.[1] But August saw the German forces in Budapest in no position to carry out Ribbentrop's threats. Eichmann was ordered away to the Roumanian border on 23 August, the day of the capitulation in Bucharest, and his commando left Hungary a few days later. On the 25th Veesenmayer agreed that the Hungarian Ministry of the interior should regain control of the Jews, provided they were kept in labour camps.[2] Finally, on 29 August, Horthy dismissed the Sztojay cabinet and made Lakatos Premier. For three whole months there were no deportations.

For the moment fear of a capitulation to Russia kept the Hungarians in the war. There was even a brief offensive by Hungarian troops, but when it was realised that the capitulation of Roumania had destroyed two German armies, that to postpone surrender was only to turn the country into a battlefront, then on 7 September the Regent authorised peace talks in Moscow. For this Hitler could only blame his intuition. He had failed to take the most elementary sound advice. But even Hitler's obstinacy could not excuse the slackness of generals and ministers who must have seen what was coming. In Roumania two armies were lost unnecessarily, but even while the gap yawned in their front Hitler pursued his obsession. Whole divisions had to be written off for lack of transport, but the procession of trains to the Auschwitz crematoria continued even from Athens and the Island of Rhodes.

After the bomb plot, Himmler had provided himself with duties enough for an entire war cabinet, yet he still had to give the Final Solution, his legacy from the dead Heydrich, the same meticulous attention. For Hitler knew that his Reich and his own person were doomed, whereas the extermination of the Jews was the only part of the New Europe which he could achieve without winning the war. When Roumania surrendered, the only arrangements that the

[1] Nuremberg Document PS 1166.   [2] Levai, op. cit., p. 321.

Germans had made in anticipation of that event were for a deportation of Jews from the border regions of Arad and Temisoara. It was for this purpose that the grand inquisitor Adolf Eichmann had left Budapest.

The lack of interest in Roumanian affairs had been astonishing. Representatives of the Maniu coalition group, who supported the King's surrender negotiations, had been journeying to Malta and Cairo as early as March when the Russians had reached the Dniester. On 5 August, Marshal Antonescu had been received by Hitler at Klessheim. With astonishing realism the Roumanian dictator declared that there was no hope of defending Moldavia and Bessarabia. He proposed a retirement to a line running from the Carpathians to the mouth of the Danube, which would abandon half his country to the enemy.[1] Hitler agreed, but he told General Friessner that the retirement must not begin till the Russians crossed the Dniester, a fatal order because it exposed an entire German army to encirclement if the Roumanians played traitor.

Since he was responsible for Hitler's support of Marshal Antonescu, Ribbentrop was blamed by all Nazi circles for the loss of this army. Ribbentrop complained to Hitler that 'the highest circles of party and state' had made him a scapegoat, and Jodl told Goebbels that Ribbentrop ought to have mentioned the Wehrmacht too.[2] But Hitler would not hear a word against Ribbentrop, though the sight of the man drove him to frenzy. Since his death Ribbentrop has found another champion in Guderian, who writes that Ribbentrop had not trusted the rosy reports which were sent from Bucharest by the idiotic and brutal Freiherr von Killinger. Instead, he had asked Hitler to send an SS armoured division to watch Bucharest. All that Guderian could spare was the 4th SS Division, which had motor transport and was no farther away than Southern Jugoslavia.[3] But Bucharest was not in the front area and Guderian was not competent to make any arrangements there. That would be an OKW matter in the hands of Keitel, who referred everything to Hitler, and so nothing happened.

Three days before the arrest of the two Antonescus and the King's surrender, Roumanian troops already barred the retreating Germans from the Danube bridges. Twenty-one German divisions were confronted with two Russian Army groups, five times their strength. The whole of the Sixth Army and part of the Eighth, a total of sixteen

[1] Guderian, op. cit., p. 330.   [2] Von Oven, op cit., II, pp. 142, 166.
[3] Guderian, op cit., p. 331.

divisions, surrendered. The rest crossed the Carpathians to fight again in Hungary, but the calamity was greater even than this. While the Russians overflowed Western Roumania, there was not a single hostile soldier between them and Budapest and nothing between them and the rear lines of the German Balkan front. The hole that had been made in the defences of the Reich might be plugged from time to time by withdrawing crack divisions from the East and the West, but it always widened again.

A few days after the Roumanian capitulation, a Hungarian force under Varos Dalnoky moved into Transylvania. Had Hitler authorised this sooner, something might have been achieved. But the Hungarians were outflanked from far to the west and they failed to make contact with the Germans retreating from Moldavia. Lakatos asked for five German divisions. He hoped to justify his peace negotiations by the German failure to provide them. But, astonishingly, the Germans moved four divisions into Hungary from the West.[1] Instead of going to the front they were kept in the Budapest region, with the name of the Ninth SS Mountain Corps, under the old Austrian general, Pfeffer-Wildenbruch. Against this dubious background in the middle of September, Horthy dispatched General Farago, who had been a military attaché in Moscow. He was to proceed to Russia, flying via Turkey. Farago was told that only unconditional surrender would be accepted, but for this Horthy and most of the army commanders were now prepared. On 9 October the Russians agreed to halt fifty miles east of Budapest and there receive the Hungarian plenipotentiaries.

The complicated events of 15-16 October show considerable differences of opinion on the course that was to be taken. The Abwehr in Budapest had discovered that Horthy's surviving son, Nikolaus ('Mickey Mouse'), was intriguing with agents of Marshal Tito and they succeeded in planting on him a spurious emissary. The Abwehr believed that the arrest of 'Mickey Mouse' would be sufficient to blackmail Horthy into deferring his surrender. Ribbentrop, however, considered that if Horthy were made to abdicate altogether, a Hungarian government could be formed from the 'Arrow Cross' party of Major Szalasi, a government that would continue the war.[2]

Thirdly, there was Himmler, at this moment less under the influence of Schellenberg and the Abwehr than of his partisan warfare

[1] Case XI, NG 1848; affidavit of Lakatos.   [2] W. Hoettl, *The Secret Front*, p. 218.

expert, Erich von dem Bach-Zelewski. Himmler proposed treating Budapest like Warsaw, smashing all resistance and making the defence of the city against the Russians a purely German affair. As was generally the case when Himmler or Kaltenbrunner tried to dictate foreign policy, Hitler supported Ribbentrop. Approaches were therefore made to Szalasi's party, but, since Ribbentrop mistrusted Veesenmayer as a creature of Himmler's, the negotiations were left to Rudolf Rahn, ambassador to Mussolini's court on the shores of Lake Garda. At the same time Hitler adopted the Abwehr plan for the kidnapping of Nikolaus Horthy, but he put Skorzeny under his own direct orders and not Himmler's.[1]

This action of Hitler's was typical of the state to which he had been reduced by the bomb that blew him out of the Speer barracks. Henceforward, no Ministry, not even the SS, could claim special competence in any special task. The Ministers, *Treuer Heinrich* along with them, must be left to scramble for precedence lest any one of them become too strong. Skorzeny was armed with a sort of Sultan's firman, written on state paper and signed with Hitler's shaky signature. Skorzeny did not rate very highly 'the blind obedience of every office of state to this highest order'. He only invoked it once, and that was in Vienna when he compelled a messing officer to let him have two sausages without surrendering a meat coupon.[2]

Skorzeny and Rahn were helpless for several days. Himmler had declared Budapest an area of partisan warfare and had sent his partisan warfare chief, von dem Bach-Zelewski. Under the terms of the 1941 protocol it was only from him that the Wehrmacht and Waffen SS commanders could take orders. Skorzeny found that Bach-Zelewski's idea was to use a 65-centimetre mortar to bombard the Burgberg.[3] Rahn's experience was no better. When he urged Winkelmann to delay action until he had had his interview with Horthy, Winkelmann declared that he could only take orders from Bach-Zelewski. Rahn had a tremendous row over the telephone with Bach-Zelewski and, as he hung up the receiver, heard the outraged general asking for air.[4] Rahn then suggested that Winkelmann should get his discretionary power confirmed by Himmler, with the result that Himmler recalled Bach-Zelewski to Germany for even higher duties two days later. With Colonel General Walther Wenck in command of the German army in Hungary, the cloak-and-dagger

[1] Skorzeny, p. 230.   [2] *Ibid.*, p. 232.   [3] Skorzeny, op. cit., p. 237.
[4] Rudolf Rahn, *Ruheloses Leben*, p. 264.

diplomatists, Skorzeny and Rahn, were left free to carry out their successful but fruitless coup.

'Mickey Mouse' and two accomplices were successfully ambushed by the Gestapo in the Villa Petoefer on 14 October. They were carried out (rolled in carpets) and shipped to German concentration camps, but some of the Hungarian gendarmerie were alerted and the Gestapo station commander, Otto Klages, was killed in a skirmish.[1]

Rahn waited to hear the result before delivering his ultimatum to Horthy. It was unfortunate, for by one o'clock next day, when Rahn secured an appointment with the Regent, Horthy had already broadcast through Radio Budapest the news of his surrender to the Russians, though this was five days ahead of the date arranged with Marshal Malinovski. Horthy was less overcome by the news concerning his son than Hitler and Ribbentrop had expected. He offered no more than to suspend the capitulation a few days in order that the four German divisions could withdraw from Budapest,[2] a vain promise, because already the Hungarian generals Miklos Bela and Varos Dalnoki had deserted to the Russians, the latter in the Mercédès car presented to him by General Guderian.[3]

This was not all. That afternoon, when Lakatos and his Minister of the Interior, Remenyi-Schneller, met Veesenmayer and Rahn in the embassy to discuss the postponement of the surrender, the Germans learnt that the Burgberg, on which the embassy was situated, had been cut off from the town by Hungarian troops and mined. It seems, however, that the plotters against Hitler, whether German or Hungarian, always forgot the telephone. Rahn was able to keep touch with Skorzeny's troops and even with Ribbentrop, who told him he was out of his mind not to have attacked the Burgberg already.[4]

Pfeffer-Wildenbruch, the commander of the 9th SS Armoured Corps, was himself a prisoner on the Burgberg, but Lakatos knew that forty-two Tiger tanks had been unloaded at the station and were at Skorzeny's disposal. Lakatos received an ultimatum that the Burgberg would be stormed at six in the morning of the sixteenth. During the night there was uninterrupted communication between Horthy and the embassy and at five-thirty, half an hour before the

[1] Skorzeny, op. cit., p. 238; Hoettl, op. cit., p. 220.
[2] Hoettl, op. cit., p. 220; Rahn, op. cit., p. 267.
[3] Guderian, op. cit., p. 342; Skorzeny, op. cit., p. 241; Erich Kern, *Der grosse Rausch*, p. 157.   [4] Rahn, op. cit., p. 269.

attack was due, Horthy offered his abdication. He also gave his approval to the premiership of Ferenc Szalasi, whom the Germans had kept hidden all this time in the embassy. Skorzeny's attack on the Burgberg was little more than a parade, though some shots were fired by guards who had not received the cease fire. Horthy, who complains that his rooms were looted by the Skorzeny commando,[1] had chats which are described as friendly with Rahn and Skorzeny. The latter escorted him to Germany on the 17th, driving unnoticed to the station. It must have caused Mussolini some ironical amusement when a second deposed Axis ruler was given his former residence, the Villa Hirschberg at Waldbichl.[2]

This very briefly is the history of 'Action Horthy' or 'Action Panzerfaust'. As a story of diplomacy and daring in perilous Ruritania it served to ginger German civilian morale, while to the public on the other side of the hill it was a reminder that, if the Germans could not be popular with their friends, they could still be astonishingly stronghanded. Skorzeny's reputation was enhanced so much that he acquired a swollen head. In one statement in 1952 he declared that the march on the Burgberg saved a million German lives.[3] Yet lives were the very last thing this action saved. In October 1944 the four German divisions in Budapest and the scattered remnants fighting to the south, forces which were not a tenth of Skorzeny's figure, could have retired then and there to the 'Alpine Redoubt', had Hitler so willed. Instead of this, Budapest was defended as the key point of an unnecessary occupation of Southern Europe and it was defended with absurdly inadequate means. The Hungarians could offer little help now, beyond the rabble known as the Nyilas or Arrow Cross militia, and the sequel to 'Action Panzerfaust' was another Stalingrad.

There was a second sequel. With a fanatical anti-Semite in power in Hungary, the Eichmann Commando was free to return and the deportation of the Budapest Jews, which had been abandoned during the past three months, could be resumed. On 2 November the Russians gained a temporary footing in the outer suburbs of Pest and all the Jewish labour companies were moved west of the Danube. A few days later they were transferred to the South-east Wall, a defence which was under construction to protect Vienna. This soon provided an excuse for a mass expulsion of any Jewish families the Nyilas

---

[1] Nikolaus Von Horthy, *Ein Leben Fuer Ungarn* (Zurich, 1953), p. 292.
[2] Skorzeny, op. cit., p. 349.
[3] Charles Foley in the *Daily Express*, 17 April 1952.

could round up. The victims, including the aged and infants, were hustled under guard for a hundred and twenty miles, a seven or eight days' march to the nearest German labour camps on Reich territory. Nearly forty thousand were moved in the course of November without welfare arrangements of any kind and soon the death-rate began to mount.[1]

Yet the second deportation of Hungarian Jewry was a lesser tragedy than the first. For one thing Himmler was about to end the Auschwitz selections for good and all. While the Arrow Cross wanted to get rid of every Jew, the Germans wanted only those who could work in the concentration camps. Kurt Becher was sent to Switzerland, where he interviewed M. Saly Meyer of the Joint Distribution Committee, to whom he promised that the selection of Jewish workers in Budapest would be made by the Red Cross, while in the concentration camps these workers would receive the protection of international law.[2] But the news from Hungary gave him the lie, so Becher, finding that the open scandal of the marches from Budapest imperilled the negotiation for five million Swiss francs, flew to Himmler in Berlin. Himmler agreed to send the most respectable member of his Adjutantur to inspect the march. This was Gottlob Berger's successor in the SS Leadership Office, the snowy-haired Hans Juettner. Himmler also sent a less sympathetic observer, for Rudolf Hoess, the executioner of Hungarian Jewry, had been promoted Deputy Inspector of Concentration Camps and the deportations came within his competence. Juettner was shocked at the sight of the bodies of elderly women lying in the road and even the mass-

---

[1] IMT III, p. 286; evidence of Wisliceny.

[2] Kastner, op. cit., p. 115. It must be stressed that the papers of the late Saly Meyer have not been published and that the history of the conferences which he held with Kurt Becher in Switzerland reposes entirely on the typescript narrative of Reszoe Kastner. The latter has since become a centre of controversy. He was a Jewish lawyer from Koloszvar or Cluj who accompanied Kurt Becher on his missions as a kind of hostage for Becher's safety and a guarantee of his credentials. In 1954 Kastner lost an important libel case in Israel and was denounced by the court as a collaborator—very largely for his consent in dealing with Himmler's agent, Kurt Becher. The trial became a political issue and, since the verdict is still subject to an appeal judgment, I prefer to keep an open mind on the lengths to which Kastner was prepared to go in order to save a number of Jewish lives. It is not clear whether he was present when Becher made this promise, but I see no reason to doubt Kastner's account. His narrative is muddled but singularly free from personal prejudices and, until the Joint Distribution Committee chooses to publish the files of these negotiations, it must remain the only evidence.

murderer Hoess objected to the absence of order. In Eichmann's absence Juettner had a row with one of the captains of the SS Commando. Three days later he flew back to Himmler with a strongly worded report, but received no instructions to countermand the orders of the Eichmann Commando and the Arrow Cross militia.[1]

The truth was that Himmler was again vacillating. On learning that Mr. Cordell Hull had been succeeded at the State Department by Mr. Stettinius and that the dispatch of five million Swiss francs had again been deferred, Himmler retracted the promise made by Kurt Becher, and ordered the Eichmann Commando back to Budapest. But on 23 November, a fortnight after the beginning of the march to the South-east Wall, Szalasi himself started to relent, declaring that the Jews remaining in Budapest had ceased to be a political danger. Veesenmayer, however, promised Ribbentrop that he would see to it that the round-ups continued.[2] And on this very day Eichmann returned, swearing that Szalasi had promised him seventy thousand Jews and that he would only stop the press-gangs if another twenty thousand able-bodied Jews came forward voluntarily.[3] So, in the last days of November and the first days of December, a further seventeen thousand Jews were deported to Strasshof and eventually to the German concentration camps. But on 6 December the second train reached Switzerland from Bergen-Belsen. This, so Becher explained to Reszoe Kastner, convinced Eichmann that Himmler's money had been paid up and the deportations ceased.

This was the last deportation from Hungary, but Gabor Vajna, the Minister of the Interior in the Szalasi government, declared that even in December Himmler still promised him deportation trains and Eichmann still threatened to deport old people and children if the quotas were not fulfilled.[4] But by this time the Szalasi government were incapable either of giving orders themselves or of carrying out German orders. Moreover, in the anarchy of the last months of Budapest the Jews came to some extent under international protection. Thus it befell that out of the fifty-five thousand Jews who had been expelled from Budapest, fifteen thousand were rescued by agents of the Papal Nuncio, the International Red Cross and of several neutral powers, who brought them back to the doubtful security of the capital on the eve of a Russian siege.[5]

[1] Case XI, NO. 5218; affidavit of Juettner.   [2] Case XI, transcript, 28743.
[3] Kastner, op. cit., p. 129.   [4] Case XI, NG 1874, affidavit of Vajna.
[5] Levai, op. cit., p. 381.

On 24 December, when the siege began, there were ninety-five thousand Jews in Budapest, of whom thirty-three thousand possessed protection certificates of various kinds. These certificates, which had accumulated under the short-lived Lakatos government, made international protection possible. And so, in spite of a constant threat of massacre and pillage by the unruly Arrow Cross,[1] the losses of the Jewish community in the siege were relatively small. Budapest and Bucharest were the only cities where the invading Red Army found a large Jewish community that had survived all the years of Hitler's Europe,.

It is possible to speculate what would have been their fate if Hitler had recovered Budapest, as he planned to do in January and even as late as March 1945. Himmler told Norbert Masur that he had left 450,000 Jews in Hungary [sic] and that they had shown their gratitude by shooting at the Germans. This shows what pretexts would have been invoked if the Eichmann Commando had come back as conquerors.[2] And perhaps it explains Hitler's fanatical desire to recover Budapest. In Roumania Hitler lost sixteen divisions through sheer fatalism and inanition. But in Budapest he attached an almost mystical significance to the rescue of two Wehrmacht divisions and two dismounted SS cavalry divisions of Hungarian racial Germans, all of them much under strength. To prevent their encirclement a bitter battle was fought south and west of the city shortly before Christmas. In this battle three more SS divisions were committed but the attempt was a failure and a new SS cavalry division, composed of Hungarian racial Germans, the 33rd, was annihilated in the neighbourhood of Lake Balaton.[3] Without consulting his Chief of Staff, Hitler on Christmas Eve ordered Gille's 4th SS Panzer Corps to leave the severely threatened Warsaw front and move four or five hundred miles south to Lake Balaton.[4] The second attack began on New Year's day. Gille's Totenkopf and Viking divisions, supported by an infantry division, made such progress that by 11 January 1945 they had reached Budapest airport and the rescue of forty-five thousand German soldiers, half of them fellow SS men, seemed assured.

[1] On 15 January the Jewish Council discovered a plot by members of the Arrow Cross and the Waffen SS to liquidate the ghetto. Thereafter the ghetto was protected by a Wehrmacht general, Schmidthuber of the Feldherrnhalle division, who lost his life in the final assault two days later (Levai, op. cit., p. 416).

[2] Norbert Masur, *En Jude talar med Himmler* (Stockholm, 1946).

[3] Kern, op. cit., p. 164; Hausser, op. cit., p. 166.   [4] Guderian, op. cit., p. 348.

But General Balck of the 4th Army hoped to surround ten Russian divisions north of the lake and Gille's corps was withdrawn to his sector.[1] It was a tactical error, for Russian resistance stiffened and by the end of January the attack had to be called off. On 17 January the Russians occupied Pest. The German garrison in Buda was too weak to hold out beyond 12 February and altogether only eight hundred men escaped from Budapest. They included 170 men of the 8th SS Cavalry division 'Florian Geyer', whose commander, the thirty-four-year-old Joachim Rumohr, committed suicide during the sortie after he had been wounded.[2] Pfeffer-Wildenbruch, the garrison commander, is still a prisoner in Russia.

Martin Bormann regarded the failure of the sortie as proof of the Fuehrer's wisdom in 1942-3 when he had forbidden the Stalingrad garrison to break out.[3] Hitler did not feel the same certainty. Having approved General Balck's decision to withdraw the Gille Panzer corps from Budapest, he now rounded on the High Command and sacked General Wohler, who commanded the Southern front. And after the Russian occupation of Pest on 17 January he decided to send a second and very much larger force to retake the twin cities, this time from the Ardennes front, where both sides were bogged down after the failure of the Rundstedt offensive. The plan was pursued in spite of Guderian's entreaties to send all available divisions to face the Russians on the Oder. Guderian's opposition provoked the first of those frantic scenes with the half-paralysed Fuehrer which brought about his own dismissal.

Nevertheless, Sepp Dietrich's four SS armoured divisions were re-formed in the Bonn area during February 1945. It was utter madness to dream of a prestige victory at a moment when the next attack must bring the Russians to Berlin itself. It was said that Jodl had promised Hitler the recovery of the Roumanian oilfields as a birthday present and that the Russians were to be caught in pincers between Himmler's offensive in Pomerania and Schoerner's in Northern Hungary'.[4]

The whole of Sepp Dietrich's 6th Panzer Army was moved to Hungary, some ten divisions including the four SS armoured divisions. The battle was opened on 6 March with neither artillery preparation nor air cover.[5] It continued till the end of the month and

---

[1] Kern, op. cit., p. 170; Hausser, op. cit., p. 195.   [2] Skorzeny, op. cit., p. 519.
[3] *The Bormann Letters*, p. 185.   [4] Von Oven, op. cit., II, pp. 245, 247.
[5] Hausser, op. cit., p. 205.

during those precious March days, when the Rhine and Oder fronts needed every man who could walk, Balck and Sepp Dietrich virtually lost their armies. The remnants could create no new front, neither on the unmanned South-east Wall nor in the heart of Vienna itself, where the SS Das Reich division tried pointlessly to hold the Danube canal bridges till 11 April.

On 13 March Sepp Dietrich's four Panzer divisions had retreated into Austria, having failed in an impossible task. There had been symptoms of a rout for the first time among crack SS formations. Hitler, convulsed with fury at the news, ordered Guderian to the Southern front, there to see to the removal of the immensely prized Leibstandarte arm-bands from the men of the four SS divisions,[1] Adolf Hitler, Das Reich, Totenkopf and Hohenstaufen.

Guderian refused and pointed out that Himmler alone was competent in matters concerning Waffen SS discipline, and so it was Himmler who had to give the order to Sepp Dietrich. Guderian records gleefully that 'Himmler did not win himself much love from the Waffen SS over this affair'. Goebbels was very indignant about it and it was believed in his circle that several officers of the Leibstandarte had been driven to suicide. But Paul Hausser writes most positively that the order was never passed on and this was confirmed by Sepp Dietrich himself in an interrogation by Major Milton Shulman. Sepp Dietrich described how he had summoned the four divisional commanders to his headquarters in Vienna, where he had told them that the arm-bands were not to be removed. He then wrote to Hitler that he intended to commit suicide rather than comply with the order. When no reply came from Berlin, he sent all his decorations to Hitler in a parcel. It is doubtful whether Hitler, raving in his deep shelter of the Reich Chancellery and surrounded by frightened men, ever received them;[2] but Sepp Dietrich's rage and disappointment effectively prevented the SS playing the role of

[1] Guderian, op. cit., p. 381. All men who had served in the Leibstandarte had the right to wear the arm-band during their subsequent service. It was worn by Sepp Dietrich himself.

[2] Von Oven, op. cit., II, p. 290; Hausser, op. cit., p. 205; Shulman, op. cit., p. 317. Sepp Dietrich's explanation seems to be the origin of a frequently repeated legend that the Leibstandarte officers sent their decorations to Hitler in a chamber-pot which also contained a human arm complete with Adolf Hitler arm-band. Walter Schellenberg told Mr. Trevor-Roper that Fegelein deliberately advised Hitler to give the arm-band order, hoping thereby to ruin Himmler's popularity with the Waffen SS (*Last Days of Hitler*, pp. 98, 172).

fanatical candidates for self-immolation, the logical consequences of the role for which Hitler had always intended them. Only in Austria was such a concentrated force of crack SS divisions to be found in April 1945, yet Sepp Dietrich's chief aim now was to rescue them from slavery in Russia, and in fact they retreated fast enough to meet the American advance into Upper Austria. It was to the Americans that Sepp Dietrich surrendered his 6th SS Panzer Army at the capitulation, thereby avoiding imprisonment in Russia and most probably a death sentence for his role at Kharkov.[1]

He spent more than ten years in captivity, his actual sentence passed at Dachau in July 1946 being for life imprisonment. When he was liberated in October 1955, Sepp Dietrich was a forgotten man. Even his part in the blood-purge of June 1934 stirred up no vendetta[2] until August 1956 when he was charged with the murder of Roehm.

The Hungarian adventure had swallowed up at least twelve Waffen SS divisions. It had also involved Himmler, Kaltenbrunner, Mueller and Eichmann in the most concentrated of all extermination programmes. Finally, it divided Hitler from his loyal SS. The long diversion has taken us to that moment when Hitler decided that even his Pretorian Guard were against him. There was now no real inner core of loyalty. The German people fought on because they were caught in the cogs of the machine which they had made, but Hitler fought apart from them. He was alone save for a few cringing toadies who took down his orders and shrugged their shoulders.

3. REBELLION IN POLAND AND SLOVAKIA

The personal role of Himmler in these events was a limited one. In spite of the choice of SS men for key positions in Hungary, Himmler was hardly more concerned with the political pressure on Horthy's government than he was concerned with the field dispositions of his Waffen SS divisions in the final Hungarian battles. Only in the field of racial extermination he reigned supreme. One incident, however, suggests other possibilities. When Himmler dispatched Bach-Zelewski from Warsaw to Budapest, he expected

[1] The exception was the Totenkopf division, which, having retreated in a northerly direction, was led by its commander Helmuth Becker to the relief of Prague. The whole division fell into Russian hands at the capitulation and Becker is still a prisoner. Sepp Dietrich appears to have deserted his men in an attempt to smuggle his wife into Switzerland. (General Karl Koller, *Der letzte Monat*).

[2] See *supra*, p. 141, and *infra*, p. 395, footnote 1; *The Times*, 24 October 1955.

that the efforts of the diplomats and the ambush-planners would fail and that Budapest would become, like Warsaw, an anti-partisan theatre of war. In that case it would not have been Bach-Zelewski who commanded the operations; it would have been Himmler himself. Although in December 1944 the appointment of Himmler to command an army group was to outrage the soul of the High Command, Himmler had, in a sense, been a field commander since 1941.[1]

Himmler's position as chief of anti-partisan warfare was a logical outcome of Hitler's plans for the SS. Himmler was no ordinary police chief. Hitler intended him to be the head of a force concerned with the struggle in the rear, a force which was to make a repetition of the so-called 'stab in the back' of 1918 impossible. His policemen were soldiers and his police chiefs had the rank and in some cases the experience of generals. They had fought for Himmler the only war he had been allowed to direct and it was natural that in 1945, when he commanded an army group himself, Himmler should prefer his police generals to the men whom he had completely failed to know after their years of experience as Waffen SS divisional commanders under Wehrmacht control.

These police generals had fought since 1941 a shadow war without publicity, a war with its own standards, in which Himmler had a greater personal share than appeared. Up till the end of 1942 anti-partisan actions, conducted by any units which happened to be available in the Rear Area Command zones, came nominally under the direction of Himmler's higher SS police leaders, one of whom was attached to each army group. In fact there was little central direction and the conditions of partisan warfare were anarchic both on the Russian and on the German side. They resulted in Himmler appointing a special staff at his field headquarters to supervise anti-partisan warfare. The first commander of this staff was the higher SS police leader to the Central Army Group, Erich von dem Bach-Zelewski.[2]

This controversial figure found favour with his captors when he was interned in an SS camp after the war and he appeared as a prosecution witness not only at the Nuremberg trials but at several subsequent trials, including the Warsaw trial of Governor Ludwig Fischer. This circumstance protected him from extradition to Russia and reserved him for a nominal sentence by a German court, a

---

[1] Westphal, op. cit., p. 285.   [2] IMT IV, p. 32.

sentence which he never served.[1] In Bach-Zelewski's own testimonies he is always a humanitarian, lecturing Himmler on one occasion and persistently intervening for the doomed Russian Jews. In the literary works of other Nazi eminences he appears in a different light. The most important accusation is perhaps that of Peter Kleist, who describes a propaganda organisation of Russian officer prisoners known as the Drushina, which was formed in 1942 by Schellenberg's Foreign Intelligence Branch of RSHA. According to Kleist, Bach-Zelewski secured control of the Drushina and used them in 'bloody police measures against the partisans', with the result that the Drushina murdered their German commanders and deserted.[2]

Guderian, writing on Bach-Zelewski's role at Warsaw, Rudolf Rahn on his role in Budapest, and Skorzeny on his conduct on the Oder front in 1945, give an equally bad impression. Bach-Zelewski says that Himmler hated and suspected him, but that cannot always have been the case. This handsome, typically military East Prussian, a professional soldier of the Hundred Thousand Army, joined the SS in 1930 and commanded in East Prussia and Pomerania from 1934. Early issues of *Das Schwarze Korps* show him in 1935-6 very much in Himmler's company. Hitler himself had a high regard for him and, when he confirmed his appointment as chief of anti-partisan warfare, he dilated on Bach-Zelewski's special qualities.

That Bach-Zelewski is one of the cleverest persons. Even in the party I only used him for the most difficult things. When the Communist opposition in a locality seemed too strong to break down, I brought him there and he beat them to pulp.[3]

At Nuremberg Bach-Zelewski, the prosecution witness, was feather-bedded and allowed to get away with a deliberately misleading account of his appointment. In particular he was allowed to gloss over his direct responsibility to Himmler. Yet he kept a permanent staff at Himmler's headquarters and some of their gruesome reports have survived.

Two of the anti-partisan actions, which were handled by Himmler through this staff, stand out with special prominence, namely the first and second Warsaw rebellions. Himmler's part in these actions is perfectly clear; he was the ultimate authority over Bach-Zelewski and Juergen Stroop, because theirs was a dirty business of which the High Command tried to wash its hands.

[1] Ten years' special labour, sentence of the Munich Hauptspruchkammer, 31 March 1951.   [2] Kleist, op. cit., p. 201.   [3] Gilbert, op. cit., p. 8.

The first Warsaw rebellion took place in the rigidly enclosed ghetto. Between 22 July and 3 October 1942 this immense warren had been 're-settled'. Of the 310,332 persons who were removed, four-fifths went to Treblinka, a death-camp on a lonely branch line barely sixty miles away. During this period there was no resistance, but in October Himmler revised his plans and called off the action in order to convert the ghetto into a concentration camp. In January Himmler changed his plans again. The able-bodied Jews were to be sent to other labour camps, the remainder were to be killed. This time, however, there was resistance and in April Lieutenant-General Juergen Stroop, the higher police leader in Greece, was sent to Warsaw to remove the fifty-six thousand surviving Jews.

As an anti-partisan commander, Stroop was empowered to draw on all troops in the Warsaw area, in addition to the security police. Stroop's 2,096 men included two SS training battalions and some Wehrmacht details. The massacre was treated as a campaign, Stroop sending daily situation reports to Himmler at Zhitomir. Himmler himself did not go to Warsaw, but he sent Stroop personal orders. He also sent the police leaders Krueger and von Herff to act as observers. Furthermore, Himmler reported on the action to Hitler at Rastenburg and tried by means of photographs to convince the High Command that military emplacements had been built in the ghetto.[1]

Himmler was determined that this desperate resistance, at the fag-end of the extermination of two million Polish Jews, should figure as a genuine campaign and a battle honour for the SS and police. It was for this reason that Stroop's dispatches, though they were nothing but a record of daily killings, were bound as a sumptuous illustrated album for presentation to Himmler, who does not seem to have considered that, in treating the affair this way, he was helping the Jews in the creation of a national epic. But with the second Warsaw rebellion Himmler faced a task which was neither so simple nor so free of the criticisms of his rivals.

The second Warsaw revolt broke out on 1 August 1944, when Russian troops were already on the opposite bank of the Vistula in the suburb of Praga. General Komorowski's Polish partisans fought in the German front area and this time the High Command were not at first disposed to wash their hands of the butchery by leaving it

[1] Nuremberg Document PS 1061, containing Stroop's report in full. IMT XV, p. 308; evidence of Jodl.

entirely to Himmler's anti-partisan command. But barely twelve days had passed since Stauffenberg's bomb and the High Command were in disgrace. In the words of the newly appointed Chief of Staff, Heinz Guderian:[1]

I requested the inclusion of Warsaw in the army's operation area but the ambition of Governor-General Frank and Reichsfuehrer Himmler obtained from Hitler that Warsaw—though it was in the actual front line—was not assigned to the army as an operational area but was placed under the Governor-General. The Reichsfuehrer SS was commissioned to put down the revolt, and he dispatched for that purpose SS Gruppenfuehrer von dem Bach-Zelewski and a number of SS and police formations.

These formations were many times bigger than those available against the ghetto rebellion. They included four thousand men of the Dirlewanger penal brigade, three or four battalions of German regular police under the police general Reinefarth and part of the 22nd SS Cavalry Division, which was recruited in Hungary from racial Germans and which Admiral Horthy begged Guderian to withdraw on account of Hungary's ancient friendship for Poland.[2] But the largest individual force was the SS Kaminski brigade. This consisted of 6,500 Russian prisoners of war serving under a White Russian officer called Kaminski. At one time the German High Command had permitted Kaminski to run his own government at Lokot, behind the lines of the Central Army Group.[3] Kaminski had won Hitler's praise in July 1943 by his skill in rounding up Russian peasants to follow the retreating Central Army Group as slave labourers.[4]

Himmler only incorporated this dubious character and his still more dubious men in the Waffen SS during the Warsaw rebellion, when they came under his orders. Kaminski's chief merit was that he had lived under Polish rule and hated the Poles. His further merit was that his men had existed for the past month on loot and pillage. This was in keeping with Himmler's theory, which dated from the first days of the concentration camps, that political enemies could only be kept in order by regular criminals. At the beginning of the Warsaw rebellion, on 3 August, Himmler's Posen speech contained very special mention of the Kaminski and Dirlewanger contingents.[5]

They have come back with more weapons than they had before. I must find out from my German Leadership Staff how many cigar-cases belonging to the

[1] Guderian, op. cit., p. 322.   [2] Guderian, op. cit., p. 333.
[3] Kleist, op. cit., pp. 196, 201.   [4] Gilbert, op. cit., p. 65.
[5] *Vierteljahreshefte fuer Zeitgeschichte*, No. 4, p. 577.

General Staff these Russians have brought back as souvenirs. My units are never so well off for underwear as when such a break-through as this takes place. Why, another group of two or three thousand Russians under Lieutenant-Colonel Sickling of the SS and police arrived in absolutely new German uniforms, having plundered the clothing depots that the Wehrmacht had left behind.

Mysteriously, the Russians had ceased to be sub-human; mysteriously, Russian prisoners of war who had once been allowed to die like flies were praised for stealing German stores. Himmler had travelled a long road since the days of the 'Commissar Order'. Still, these Russians made Himmler vulnerable in party circles and soon he learnt it. The futile and unintelligent bravery of the Warsaw civil population and the ghastly, long-drawn agony of this city were too much under the eyes of the world to remain pigeon-holed for ever on the files of OKW and OKH, as if they were an SS matter that only concerned Jews. Guderian writes that he was so shattered by what he learnt that he tried to persuade Hitler in person to remove the Dirlewanger and Kaminski brigades from Warsaw. Hitler at first refused, but was persuaded when even Himmler's liaison man, Hermann Fegelein, admitted that Kaminski's men were 'real bandits'.[1]

There may be another side to this story. Alfred Jodl stated at Nuremberg—and his story was confirmed in the affidavit of the OKW archivist, Captain Wilhelm Scheidt—[2] that it was Fegelein in the first place who ratted on Himmler and reported the Kaminski atrocities to Guderian and Jodl. Probably the Bormann-Kalten-brunner-Fegelein cabal had been at work on Himmler again, but there was also another motive for this uncharacteristically humane and sensible action of Fegelein's. As an international display rider before the war Fegelein had often competed with Colonel Komorowski (General Bor), the leader of the rebels, and Fegelein continued to protect Komorowski after his surrender. This is the somewhat fortuitous explanation of the end of the régime of terror by the SS in Warsaw and of Hitler's decision to treat the rebels as prisoners of war, things for which Jodl, Guderian and Bach-Zelewski tried to gain credit.[3]

---

[1] Guderian, op. cit., p. 322.   [2] IMT XV, p. 285; IV, p. 19, affidavit 13.

[3] Guderian, op. cit., pp. 323-4. Nevertheless, on 17 May 1954, when Guderian died, *The Times* obiturist referred to him as 'the general who in 1944 extorted from Hitler permission to withdraw two SS brigades which had committed monstrous atrocities in Warsaw'.

The Dirlewanger and Kaminski units were not disbanded, but only removed from Warsaw. The Kaminski brigade were incorporated as Russian liberators in Vlassov's 2nd Division. On 16 October, Oskar Dirlewanger, now a brigadier-general and bearer of the Knight's Cross, was entertained to lunch by Governor Frank and thanked for the 'model employment of his combat troops in the Warsaw fighting'.[1] Kaminski fared less well. The well-informed Peter Kleist says that he was killed either in the Warsaw fighting or while trying to desert.[2] But Bach-Zelewski claims that he had Kaminski tried and executed.

In Guderian's view Bach-Zelewski only acted this way 'to get rid of a not irreproachable witness', and that he had been quite prepared to carry out Himmler's order to treat Warsaw as the ghetto had been treated in 1943 by levelling it completely to the ground and removing all property.[3]

This order, too, was frustrated by the High Command and within a few days Bach-Zelewski was in Hungary. He was now regarded by Himmler as the most reliable of his police generals, even if it was true that Himmler kept a file about Bach-Zelewski and that he had discovered that Bach-Zelewski and Himmler's bugbear, Manstein, were not only both called Erich but had a common ancestor—a Slav at that—in the sixteenth century.[4] Hitler made Bach-Zelewski a full general with command of an army corps, and he took him from the Rhine front to the Vistula.

During the early days of the Warsaw rebellion Himmler was concerned in a further large-scale anti-partisan campaign. On 23 August, the black day that saw the loss of Paris and the surrender of Roumania, rebellion broke out in the small republic of Slovakia, where a portion of the cabinet under the Defence Minister, General Catlos, backed by part of the army under General Golian, declared against the Germans at Neusohl in the Carpathians. This was a still more dangerous situation than that of Warsaw, because the rebellion

[1] IMT XX, p. 310, and Document PS 2233.

[2] Kleist, op. cit., p. 200; Case XI, transcript, 28380.

[3] IMT VII, pp. 216-17. Letter from Ludwig Fischer, Governor of Warsaw, to Governor Frank, dated 10 October 1944. Unfortunately Bach-Zelewski's own account in a Russian prosecution affidavit was not admitted in evidence at Nuremberg or printed. Equally, I am unable to follow the recriminations between Bach-Zelewski and Ludwig Fischer in the latter's trial in Warsaw in March 1947

[4] Unpresented affidavit of von dem Bach-Zelewski, published in *Aufbau* (New York, 1946), No. 34. Vol. 12.

cut off the retreat of the routed German Eighth Army in Galicia. At first only an improvised armoured regiment, formed from the SS training schools in Bohemia-Moravia, was available against the rebels, who had the assistance of two Russian airborne brigades which landed behind the German lines, as well as General Viest and his staff who were flown from England. Later, the 18th SS division (Horst Wessel) extricated itself from Galicia and with the remains of the Ukrainian SS division attacked the rebels from the east.[1] Himmler only took over the operation as an anti-partisan front after the capture of Neusohl by the armoured regiment and the surrender of Golian and Viest.

The pacification of Slovakia after the surrender of the main army of the rebels was not at first an out-and-out man-hunt. The commander whom Himmler sent out on 31 August was Gottlob Berger himself, who had played a large part in forcing the government of Father Tiso on the country in March 1939. Berger's task was to save the remains of the puppet state, but he only stayed three weeks. Himmler replaced him with Hermann Hoefle, a typical higher SS police leader.[2] For the special task of pacification he sent five commandos of security police under Colonel Witiska. The era of mass executions had begun.

At the end of September Himmler arrived in Bratislava in person. He had a lot to keep him busy at this moment, creating a new Replacement Army, acting as policeman in the rear of the German troops retreating from France and trying at the same time to get possession of the Rhine Army. One would have thought that Himmler had enough to do besides fussing over a rebellion that had receded to remote mountain strongholds. But the matter went deeper. Why had a country, not as yet menaced with Russian occupation, welcomed British-trained parachutists? And why had part of the army been willing to go over to the enemy? For Hitler there could only be one answer. In Slovakia the Jews had been allowed to survive. In March 1942 Slovakia had set a good example to other satellite countries by deporting her own Jews to Poland. But later in that year, when fifty-six thousand had been sent, it was discovered that re-settlement in Poland meant the gas chambers of Auschwitz, Treblinka, Belsec and Sobibor. Henceforward, under cover of a complicated codex of laws, thirty-five thousand Jews had remained in the country.

---

[1] Hausser, op. cit., p. 165; Kraetschmer, op. cit., SS, pp. 371, 375.
[2] Case XI, Document NG 5921.

In September 1944 Himmler was required to resume these deportations and his conscience was not clear in the matter. In 1942 he had listened to a proposal from the Bratislava Zionist Relief Committee, which was conveyed to him through his Resettlement Commissioner, Dieter Wisliceny.[1] It was a matter of two million dollars' worth of foreign currency. The money had not been produced, but the offer was a bridge not only towards immense international funds which might be exacted from World Jewry, but also towards peace discussions with the West. And so the government of Father Tiso was allowed to cheat over its Nuremberg laws and the 35,000 Jewish survivors remained in the country.

After Himmler's visit to Bratislava in September 1944 a last-minute attempt was made by the Bratislava Relief Committee to approach him through the accessible Kurt Becher.[2] But Becher learnt from Himmler that no Jews from Slovakia could be exempted from deportation, because Gottlob Berger and Kaltenbrunner had represented the military situation in Slovakia as too dangerous. Becher returned to Bratislava at the beginning of October to find one of Eichmann's resettlement commissioners already at work.[3] And so the business of pacifying the Slovak rebellion proceeded. Colonel Witiska's figures show that by 9 December he had made 18,937 arrests in this little country and over half were Jews; 8,975 Jews had been sent to German concentration camps, while 722 had been 'specially handled' on the spot.[4]

Yet the remainder of the Slovak Jews survived the war. They were saved by the same grouping of circumstances as the remnants of Hungarian Jewry. The Germans could not afford to keep troops for purely security police duties in a small country and with the approach of the Russians many Germans stationed in Slovakia tried to establish an anti-Nazi record for themselves. There was also international intervention. M. Georges Dunand of the Swiss Red Cross stayed in the Bratislava lion's den and one way and another was able to organise the forces of humanity.[5]

Slovakia, Hungary and Roumania passed behind the Iron Curtain. Under the conditions of today there are doubtless many

[1] Reitlinger, op. cit., p. 391; and see *supra*, p. 356.

[2] Case XI, NG 2866; affidavit of Hoefle.

[3] Kastner, op. cit., p. 97; Nuremberg Document NO. 4824; Reitlinger, op. cit., p. 393.

[4] Frederic Steiner, *The Tragedy of Slovak Jewry* (Bratislava, 1949), Facsimile Document.   [5] Georges Dunand, *Ne perdez pas Leur trace!* (Neuchatel, 1951).

blameless people who wish that the German armies in South-east Europe had been better prepared and better led in the autumn of 1944, and that these countries had been defended till the Allies had a chance of winning the race with Russia. Those who think so would do well to reflect that, had Hitler retained his hold on South-east Europe till the end of the war, the gas chambers would have claimed at the very least another half-million victims.

14

Himmler the War Lord

JULY 1944 TO MARCH 1945

1. THE REPLACEMENT ARMY; VLASSOV

The Stauffenberg bomb had been intended to kill Goering and Himmler as well as Hitler. Stauffenberg's failure should therefore have advanced the position of the two 'successors', but Goering was too far gone in decline to profit by the plot and Himmler shared his promotion with Goebbels, with whom there was the semblance of a working alliance. It had been slow in coming, for in the winter of 1942 Himmler had not supported Goebbels's plan for a War Cabinet and as late as the time of the Badoglio capitulation Goebbels could note in his diary the settlement of an unspecified difference with Himmler with the sour comment, 'He'll be careful in future not to send me insolent teletyped messages'.[1] In November, however, Himmler and Goebbels had an exceptionally friendly conversation, and three days before the bomb plot Goebbels declared to Werner Naumann: 'The army for Himmler, and for me the civilian direction of the war! That is a combination which could rekindle the power of our war leadership, but it will probably remain a wonderful dream'.[2]

On 25 July, after Goebbels's visit to Rastenburg, a place that had become so steeped in fear that even the Minister for Propaganda was searched at the entrance, the wonderful dream seemed to have come true. Whether or not Hitler had read Goebbels's fifty-page memorandum, whose drafting had been interrupted by 'Action Walkuere', he made Goebbels Plenipotentiary for Total War. Goebbels was to have the widest powers to move and direct the civilian population and even to redistribute manpower within the armed forces. A million men were to be conscripted by November, a hundred divisions were to be added to the field strength of the Wehrmacht. The Luftwaffe were to disgorge half a million men who performed no fighting duties, and all were to pass through the mill of Himmler's Replacement Army. Goebbels would fill the barracks with civilians and

---

[1] *The Goebbels Diary*, p. 354.   [2] Von Oven, op. cit., II, p. 94.

non-combatants and Himmler would empty them as fast towards the battlefronts.

One by one the partnership brought new offices and positions to Himmler. In September, when it appeared that General Buhle, who had been wounded in the Speer barracks, would not recover, Himmler achieved a long-cherished ambition, the control of the production of mystery weapons. The V.1 rockets had now almost ceased to figure as a war weapon. The V.2 rockets were still to come and they were, as we recall, nasty things. But no war could have been won with them, least of all a war so undermatched as Germany's. Nevertheless, the still unfulfilled secret weapons were the mainstay of party orators, and only to be connected with these Delphic mysteries made Himmler's appointment almost sacred.

Himmler's command included the Volksgrenadiere divisions which had been planned in the early summer. These were new formations with grandiloquent names, built up on the basis of party leadership without officers of experience, where Himmler, as head of the Replacement Army, had full liberty to make political appointments. Then in October came the Volkssturm, the German invasion Home Guard, and in November the last hope, the future resistance army of an occupied Germany, the Werwolf. All these were within Himmler's nomination and competence.

On 16 October Goebbels suggested that Himmler should be made Minister of War.[1] That office had been abolished in February 1938 and largely through Himmler's machinations, but to all intents and purposes Himmler in October 1944 performed a Minister of War's functions. The only thing that Hitler would not let him have was the title. But when Hitler's usual commemoration speech was delivered in the Munich Bierbraeukeller on 9 November by Himmler, it was an acknowledgment that Himmler was the second man in the state.

Between Goebbels and Himmler the limits of competence were indistinct. For instance, on 10 December, shortly before the last German offensive of the war, Goebbels was empowered as Reich plenipotentiary to examine the man-power situation in Wehrmacht units and to recommend postings and transfers, an encroachment on Himmler's office.[2] But Himmler raised no objection and till the very end these two men worked in remarkable unison. Utterly dissimilar in background, they shared in common a strict Catholic education.

[1] Von Oven, op. cit., II, p. 161.   [2] Von Oven, op. cit., II, p. 184.

Both were incapable of exercising authority except by intimidation, punishment and repression. Both believed in shooting *pour encourager les autres*. Both could work themselves up to the pitch of readiness to kill entire races or social orders, Goebbels because he hated the privileged and the clever, and Himmler because he romanticised the physical blond Nordic body.

But there was another and perhaps stronger bond between Himmler and Goebbels. Both were 'Westerners', both believed in their capacity to confront British and American statesmen with the spectre of Bolshevism. Goebbels maintained that the English way of thought was very near to him; 'I could manipulate my good and friendly relations with many important Englishmen'. And what better way than through Himmler and his Abwehr contacts in Switzerland.

I will be frank. After 20 July, when the rescue of Germany was still possible, a rescue, be it understood, that implied the sacrifice of the Fuehrer, I had frequent hesitations, above all, when I discovered someone of the same views in so immaculate and exemplary a character as the Reichsfuehrer SS. Himmler and I were in a position to rule a Hitlerless Germany in a future that was certain, though not perhaps such as we dreamed of. I resisted the temptation. My choice between Hitler and Germany could not have turned out other than it was, although I was quite clear about it that thereby both would be destroyed.[1]

Thus on 16 April 1945, a fortnight before his suicide, Goebbels told von Oven how he had become reconciled to *Goetterdaemmerung*, the final nihilism of a German soul in search of a theory to embrace the whole of life. Himmler had not helped him to it. He had been a materialist and an optimist and he had half carried Goebbels with him in these secret councils, which could not have been so different from the councils of Beck, Goerdeler and Popitz, and of Stauffenberg, Schulenburg and the Kreisau circle after them. Yet they were the background to the recruitment of new armies whom Goebbels and Himmler hustled, untrained and unequipped, to the battlefronts.

To these conscripted masses it was a background of treachery and listlessness. Over them loomed the shadows of a half-million-strong army group that had melted away in White Russia and of the six brigades that had been exploited by the opposition in 'Action Walkuere'. Himmler spoke of these six brigades, who had been kept in Germany to conduct a civil war, as if this role had been of their

---

[1] Von Oven, op. cit., II, p. 297.

own choosing, and he boasted that he had improved on the Walkuere Order by sending the six brigades to the front.[1]

An old favourite of Himmler and Goebbels was resurrected as an example to the new armies. Ferdinand Schoerner was known variously as 'The People's General', 'The Bloodhound' and 'The Gendarme of Kurland'. He was an ugly Bavarian policeman of a general, who had been overlooked in the days of the proud and independent Reichswehr and who had been thwarted of his ambition to join the General Staff. He used to go about with a cudgel, chasing his men back to the line, and his visits were always accompanied by a spare lorry to cart off victims for his 'Flying Courts martial'.[2] He was a general of the new slave warfare, who shot privates and colonels with impartial zeal.

Promoted in January 1945 from the command of the stagnant Kurland pocket to the vital Silesian front, Hitler made Schoerner a field-marshal in expectation of the wonders he never performed. For Schoerner ended the war in ignoble flight and on his return from captivity in Russia in January 1955 there was a demand in Bavaria for his trial.[3] It is significant that this last hope of the last-ditchers was not a Waffen SS general, though Schoerner had been noticed by Himmler since the early days of the war. For all Himmler's admiration of Schoerner's brutality, the democratic traditions of the Waffen SS would not have accepted him. It was felt that something else besides the large Germanic tribe of Schoerners and their drum-head courts martial was needed, something more than festoons of deserters swinging from the girders of bridges, to induce Germans to fight like the army of a Paraguayan dictator after the eleventh hour.

Plans to give the entire Wehrmacht a political indoctrination, similar to that of the SS, dated back to the Blomberg period. General Hermann Reinecke, head of the General Wehrmacht Office, the

[1] *Vierteljahreshefte fuer Zeitgeschichte*, NO. 4, p. 589.

[2] Von Oven, op. cit., I, p. 225.

[3] In fact it proved impossible to challenge the legality of the summary courts martial of 1944-5 in the West German courts of 1955. The case against the SS General Max Simon collapsed. Two charges against Schoerner were, however, sustained for a short time, because, though the victims were never executed, Schoerner had demanded their death in spite of the fact that the Standgericht had delivered a different verdict. He had ordered the execution of Colonel Sparre and Major Jungling for abandoning the encircled town of Neisse when it could not be defended. The two officers were saved by the action of the army commanders, Heinrici and Schulz. It appears that the charge against Schoerner will not be proceeded with (*Abendzeitung*, Munich, 12 August 1955).

Oberpolitruk, was particularly concerned with them. In December 1943 he had introduced the National Socialist Leadership Officers, the NSFO, and these in turn had produced Lieutenant Hagen at a critical moment on 20 July. Wilhelm Burgdorf, who had been Hitler's military adjutant since that fatal day, pressed for more and more NSFOs. A few days after the plot Himmler addressed a concourse of NSFOs at Bad Schachen.[1]

I give you the authority to seize every man who turns back, if necessary to tie him up and throw him on a supply wagon. You should take such people at once to the Pioneer Company and there put them to hard labour. Believe me, there will be no more detail parties at the base in the area of this division. I give you the authority and the order to halt everything that streams back. Put the best, the most energetic and the most brutal officers of the division in charge. They will soon round up such a rabble. They will put up anyone that answers back against a wall.

After this display of the Jenghiz Khan spirit by a man whose soldiering had been limited to a few months as a cadet in 1918, it is odd to discover that neither Goebbels, Himmler, Reinecke nor Burgdorf controlled the NSFO, but only Martin Bormann. Burgdorf, a disgruntled man who was known as 'the grave of the German Officer Corps', shared with Fegelein the honour of being the only person at the Fuehrer's headquarters who could provoke Bormann to jollity of an evening. Consequently Burgdorf had been got at by that sinister individual. On the Eastern Front the NSFO sent their reports direct to Bormann, who used them to impose his views on Hitler.[2]

In fact, from the beginning of their alliance, Himmler and Goebbels found that their plans depended on the goodwill of the doorkeeper of the ante-room. At the end of August Albert Speer, a rapidly rising star in the Nazi universe, objected strongly to Goebbels's first monthly quota of conscripts, for half of the three hundred thousand men were to come from Speer's armaments industry. Hitler supported Goebbels and Himmler in this dispute, but only because the call-up measures were in the hands of the Gauleiters, who were under the authority of Bormann's party office. Bormann went to Hitler and on 3 September Goebbels learnt that he had been victorious over Speer. But this victory had only come about because Bormann's competence had been attacked.[3]

[1] Karl Paetel, *Beitrag zum Soziologie des Nationalsozialismus* in *Vierteljahreshefte fuer Zeitgeschichte*, Vol. 2; January 1954, p. 20.
[2] Guderian, op. cit., p. 328.   [3] Von Oven, op. cit., II, p. 124.

Bormann's greatest triumph was the Volkssturm. The proposals for a levy *en masse* of the civilian population had begun, after the Russian break-through on the Central Army front, with a plan by General Adolf Heusinger, the chief of the Operations Section of the General Staff. This was rejected in August 1944, together with a more limited proposal made by Guderian and based on the party organisations in the invasion area. Hitler objected that it meant a revival of the SA. Eventually Hitler accepted Guderian's recommendation of Wilhelm Schepmann, the Chief of Staff of the SA, to be director of weapon training for the new mass levy. Hitler's memories of Roehm and Pfeffer made him suspicious of an SA revival, but there were many old SA leaders who had survived the Roehm affair and had become respectable as Gauleiters under the vigilant eye of Martin Bormann. Consequently Guderian's plan was discarded in favour of a levy conducted by the Gauleiters. The model was to be the Volkssturm which Erich Koch had created in East Prussia.[1]

The decree creating a national Volkssturm was issued on 18 October, the date of the anniversary of Leipzig, the battle of the nations against Napoleon. Himmler, as Commander-in-Chief of the Replacement Army, was to be responsible for overall organisation, training and equipment, and Bormann for recruiting and political leadership.[2] In reality Himmler's position was quite nominal and even the Wehrmacht had no authority except in tactical dispositions. Bormann had already given his instructions to the Gauleiters on 26 September.

Historically the value of a levy *en masse* has been shown to be very small, except as an expression of national will. In this case it was an outright encumbrance. Keitel declared at Nuremberg that Bormann refused to give military authorities either advice, co-operation or information concerning the Volkssturm, and that, when army commanders encountered Volkssturm units in their area, they either incorporated them or sent them home.[3] But with a really puffed-out Gauleiter the situation could be even worse. Before the military catastrophe in Poland in January 1945, Erich Koch used to confiscate for his Volkssturm the munition trains which were intended for Hans Reinhardt's Central Army Group.[4]

---

[1] Guderian, op. cit., p. 327; Juergen Thorwald, *Es begann an der Weichse* (Stuttgart, 1950), p. 29 (Hereafter referred to as *Thorwald, I*).

[2] Institute of International Affairs, *Hitler's Europe*, p. 44.

[3] IMT XI, p. 57.   [4] Thorwald, I, p. 29.

In this way the encroachments of Bormann's party office weakened Himmler's powers as head of the Replacement Army. The only answer was to divert as many of the new conscripts as possible into the Waffen SS. The Goebbels-Himmler recruiting drive, which produced twenty Volksgrenadiere divisions and fifteen divisions formed from the old Luftwaffe, added fourteen divisions to the Waffen SS, almost doubling its field strength. But of the fourteen new SS divisions which were established by the end of 1944, only two, 'Goetz von Berlichingen' and 'Horst Wessel',[1] were German, whereas seven were recruited in South-east Europe, three in the Low Countries and two in the Italian Alps. Of the twenty-nine SS divisions in existence at the beginning of 1945, sixteen were foreign and this foreign preponderance made it all the harder for other party agencies to penetrate the organisation of the Waffen SS. Moreover, in addition to foreign SS divisions, a large part of the floating population which made up Himmler's personal command, the Replacement Army, was foreign, too, and of former Russian allegiance.

The manipulation of these Russian troops had played a large but obscure part in Stauffenberg's plans. Adam Trott zu Solz tried to suggest to Mr. Allen Dulles that the Resistance Circle would use the Red Army deserters as a bridge towards negotiations with Stalin.[2] It is difficult to see how the deserters could have served this purpose, even if they numbered more than 650,000. The Russian government regarded these men as traitors; it was not interested whether they lived or died and, after the war, only demanded their repatriation in order to send them to punishment camps. But the idea that mercenaries without a country could be used equally well to fight against anyone must have crossed Stauffenberg's mind and also Himmler's. After the July plot, Himmler was sufficiently struck with it to revise his attitude towards General Vlassov and his plan for a Russian Liberation Army.[3]

The Vlassov movement had been openly countenanced by the High Command and by the Foreign Office at a time when the order

[1] Hausser, op. cit., pp. 184-5.   [2] See *supra*, p. 310.

[3] Stauffenberg had been responsible for the original plan to concentrate the Vlassov volunteers round Prague. According to an officer who had some part in the matter, Stauffenberg's purpose was to save them from service on the Russian front, where their capture meant death. (Karl Michel, *Ost und West, der Ruf Stauffenbergs*, 1947, pp. 127, 156.)

for the execution of commissars was still being carried out. But German policy in Russia, when confronted on the one hand with collaborationist minority nations and on the other with prospects of pillage, annexation and abundant slaves, was incapable of facing in any one direction. In this state of confusion there was still some value in a man like Vlassov, who was not just a Cossack or Tartar light cavalryman, ready to fight against any government because he disliked all governments, but a thoroughly indoctrinated Marxist soldier. Only seventeen years old at the time of the Revolution, Vlassov had served in no army but the Red Army. He had organised the workers' militia in the defence of Moscow and, when captured in the spring of 1942, he was deputy commander of an army group.

For many weeks before his capture, Vlassov had been cut off behind the German lines. During these weeks he realised that his starving and doomed Second Shock Army had been written off by the Russian High Command as expended. In this way he became disillusioned with his masters and their cause. A 'Political Gremium' of Russian generals in German captivity had been formed as early as 1941. And this the captured Vlassov joined. In August 1942 he was permitted to tour the rear area of the Northern Army Group and to make recruiting speeches among the prisoners of war. The propaganda section of the Wehrmacht installed him in a villa in Dahlem and even let him go to Brussels and Paris.[1] The Foreign Office were interested in this Russian equivalent of von Paulus and on 12 April 1943 Vlassov's committee in Smolensk issued an appeal to the Russian people on the lines of the Free Germany Committee.

It was an injudicious move. The appeal criticised German policy in occupied Russia, it made no concession to the Russian separatist movements, which the Germans thought they were encouraging, and it opposed the cession of any territory. Nevertheless it had the backing of Ribbentrop's Foreign Office. Himmler and Rosenberg were outraged. They had always opposed the Bolshevist system, but they were not so anxious to 'liberate' anyone from it. One member of the Vlassov committee, General Shilenkov, had been the chief *Politruk* of an army group and had only escaped execution under the Commissar Order by disguising himself as a lorry driver.[2] In August Himmler denounced Ribbentrop to Hitler for countenancing such

[1] Kleist, op. cit., pp. 209-10.   [2] *Ibid.* pp. 214, 259.

things and for a time Vlassov was confined again in the Russian generals' internment camp.

In his first Posen speech on 4 October Himmler let fly at Vlassov:[1]

With a conceit which is characteristic of the Slav, Herr Vlassov has told a story to the effect that Germany will never be in a position to conquer Russia in war and that Stalin can only be defeated by Russians. Herr Vlassov has made speeches in Berlin, Paris and Brussels criticising the German treatment of the Russian nation, which abolished corporal punishment decades ago. Abolished indeed! Why, the general who accepted the surrender of von Paulus had been tortured by the GPU for years on end. Perhaps it is only generals whom the Russians beat nowadays.

A few weeks later at Danzig Himmler declared that the High Command had recommended a Bolshevik journeyman butcher to Hitler as an ally.[2]

Himmler was right to distrust Vlassov. Even had he been given his opportunity, Vlassov was not the man to rally 650,000 deserters to a common cause. He was tragically Russian in temperament and tragically devoid of political sense. Nevertheless, it is likely that Himmler would have accepted the Vlassov movement even in 1943 as another department of the SS, had he not associated it with the opposition circle in the High Command and the insufferable Ribbentrop. After the bomb plot, when there were such overrriding reasons for securing the support of the Russian mercenaries, Himmler modified his view of the Russian Liberation Committee, but he still balked at the personality of Vlassov himself.

Soon after the bomb plot Himmler commissioned Gunter d'Alquen, now head of the Army Propaganda Department, to run a Russian deserters' recruiting campaign. Since no less than twenty-five Russian divisions were spoken of in these addresses, it was thought that Hitler himself had changed his mind.[3] Hitler, however, had the lowest opinion of the Russian volunteers. At a staff conference in January 1945 he declared that Vlassov was nothing at all, but at least he would not personally go over to the enemy—and even there Hitler turned out to be wrong.[4]

In any case Himmler never intended Vlassov to have command over any but pure 'Muscovite' Russian troops who alone might be amenable to Vlassov's form of propaganda. Himmler wanted the

[1] Nuremberg Document PS 1918. Full version of the speech in Bayle, op. cit., p. 429.

[2] Kleist ,op. cit., p. 209.   [3] Thorwald, *Die Unerklaerte Faelle*, p. 219.

[4] Gilbert, op. cit., p. 162.

Russian minorities as his own province. At the beginning of 1945 five divisions of Latvian, Estonian, Ukrainian and White Russian troops were established or in formation for the Waffen SS. Improvised brigades from Turkestan and the Caucasus had also been absorbed in the SS, and Himmler had his eye on the three Cossack divisions of the Pannwitz Corps. This covered most of the deserters. A twenty-five-division command for Vlassov could only come about if the great majority of the remaining Russian prisoners turned traitor, and this they were little likely to do when the Red Army was about to invade Germany.

In the end Vlassov was destined to command less even than two divisions of troops. On 14 November 1944 he held a conference of the various Russian leaders in Prague, addressing them as if he were the head of a future Russian state, a sort of German-sponsored de Gaulle. But there were serious absences from Vlassov's meeting. The representatives of the German Ministries of the Interior and Propaganda, the International Corps Diplomatique and the Foreign Office never arrived and the delegates for the Russian civilian labourers were not permitted to attend. Himmler sent Vlassov a vague congratulatory telegram and Vlassov declared that Himmler had promised him in his one and only conversation that the labourers would be liberated.[1]

The conference ended with a banquet given in true Russian style at the Czernin Palace, but dissension could not have been more complete. Three of the minority leaders, Kajum Khan the Crimean Tartar, Bandera the Ukrainian, and Bangerskis, the Commander of the 20th Latvian SS Division, refused absolutely to regard themselves as Russians.[2] Nor would the Wehrmacht abandon to Vlassov their Cossack divisions and their Russian auxiliary battalions (ROA). In the end it was decided to create not twenty-five Vlassov divisions but three. Only one division, numbered the 600th, was ever brought to strength. It was moved from Muensingen to Beran near Prague in February 1945. A second Vlassov division, the 605th, was formed at Heuberg, but it contained such unsavoury elements as the remains of the Kaminski brigade and it was never completed.

At one of Hitler's daily staff conferences in the Reich Chancellery on 27 January 1945 Fegelein stated that Himmler expected to be

---

[1] Thorwald, *Die Unerklaerte Faelle*, pp. 224-6.   [2] Kleist, op. cit., p. 216

given command of both Vlassov divisions.[1] In the confusion of the next three months the matter was overlooked. The Vlassov army was never incorporated in the Waffen SS. In fact the Waffen SS were the only enemy it ever fought and the story is one of the queerest of the whole war.

At the beginning of May 1945 the first Vlassov division numbered eighteen thousand men. With a few tanks, inherited from the Kaminski brigade, and some German equipment which it picked up on the road, it was marched by General Bunichenko from its cantonments at Beran into Prague. Most of the city was in the hands of Czech insurgents, though Karl Frank, the Protector, still held the Hradcín citadel with a strong force of SS and police. The Czechs begged Vlassov to allow them the help of Bunichenko's division to disarm the SS. Vlassov as a fellow-Slav ordered Bunichenko to halt, though he might have joined the general westward rush of German divisions seeking to surrender to the U.S. forces. For a few days Vlassov's Russians contained the SS in the Hradcín quarter, fighting as it were between the lines and for neither side. On 6 May an American armoured patrol entered Prague, but only to inform the insurgents that the boundary agreement forbade U.S. forces to occupy the town. The Vlassov men left Prague on the following afternoon and were interned by the Americans on the demarcation line. On the 13th they were disarmed and handed over to the Russians, who are said to have hanged large numbers on the spot. Vlassov and his staff were surrendered by the Americans two days later. The Vlassov Liberation Army shared the fate of the mass of repatriated deserters, that is to say a very obscure one. The punishment of the generals was delayed. On 1 August 1946, Radio Moscow announced the execution of Andrej Vlassov, Shilenkov, Bunichenko, and nine others.[2]

. . . .

The story of the Italian SS was even more dismal than the Vlassov fiasco. In the last great man-hunt of Hitler's Reich, when sixty-year-old Volkssturmers were incorporated in line regiments, when there were brigades and divisions of ex-officers, sailors and convicts, when Warsaw and Walcheren were defended by battalions of men with gastric ulcers, when such honorary Aryan races as Kalmucks, Armenians and Tartars fought in the SS under their own banners,

[1] Gilbert, op. cit., p. 162.
[2] Juergen Thorwald, *Die Unerklaerte Faelle*, pp. 187, 230-3.

Himmler balked at the Italians. Partly it was his old dislike, dating from Mussolini's intervention in Austrian affairs in 1934, and partly it was the fear which the Badoglio treachery had inspired in him. The Italian troops who were disarmed by the Germans in September 1943, the IMIs, were sent to labour camps indiscriminately and the Italian volunteer labourers in Germany, who then numbered 170,000, were enslaved and treated as Eastern workers. Till October 1944 there were press-gang round-ups for the slave camps, which were conducted on behalf of the Sauckel organisation in northern Italy; that is to say they were slave raids on the territory of an ally, Mussolini's Fascist republic.[1]

Nevertheless, when Mussolini made his journey to Rastenburg on the fateful 20 July, he was to discuss the future of four new Italian divisions which had been carefully picked from the prisoner camps and trained by German instructors in Wehrmacht establishments. Hitler promised Mussolini that they should fight under General Graziani's command against the British and Americans. But when he became head of the Replacement Army, Himmler arranged a different fate for them. On the ground that they could not be trusted in the line, he directed that the Italian divisions should be used against Italian partisans, just as the Kaminski and Drushina units had been used in Russia. As might be expected, they deserted. In the words of Filippo Anfuso, the last Italian ambassador to Hitler's Reich:

> The instigators of ideological war have not yet got the right book (and why shouldn't it be a novel?) telling the story of a boy of eighteen, shall we say a Calabrian, who begins the war in Libya against the British, then fights for a fortnight against the Germans, enlists again with Mussolini against the British, has a year's instruction in Germany, returns to fight the British but finds himself fighting the Italians.[2]

In addition to these four resoundingly named Wehrmacht Italian divisions, one Italian division was recruited for the SS. It was called the 29th Volunteer Grenadier SS Division 'Italien'. This too was used entirely against partisans and was included in the capitulation of the German armies in Italy on 29 April 1945. They were not the only Italians to serve in the SS, for after the Badoglio armistice of September 1943 the South Tyrol, Friuli and Istria were virtually incorporated in the Reich. In this way a further batch of racial Germans of Italian nationality became available for conscription

---

[1] Anfuso, op. cit., p. 370.   [2] Anfuso, op. cit., p. 403.

into the SS. A battalion was formed at Predazzo for service against partisans in the Julian Alps. Late in 1944 this battalion was expanded into an SS division, the 24th SS 'Karstjaeger' Division or Carso Scouts. The German-speaking part of this division remained loyal till the end. Together with the SS Officer Cadet School from Klagenfuerth and the Replacement Battalion of the Prinz Eugen Division, they tried to hinder the 8th Army's advance into Austria after the capitulation of all German troops in Italy and they were in action before Villach as late as 6 May 1945.[1] As to the rest of the Carso Scouts, Paul Hausser may be quoted for a typical portion of the dreary annals of slave warfare in the last days of the Reich and a typical record of the latter-day SS.[2]

The more or less volunteer mixture of nations, Germans, Italians, Slovenes, Croats, Serbs and Ukrainians, formed no true combatant unit. It befell that somewhere in March or April 1945 they offered an armistice to Tito's partisans.

2. HIMMLER WITH THE RHINE AND VISTULA ARMIES DECEMBER 1944—MARCH 1945

More than one reason has been advanced for Himmler's appointment as Commander-in-Chief of the Army Group 'Rhine' on 10 December 1944. Hausser and Guderian have suggested that Himmler's appointment was part of a plan by Bormann to ruin him. General Westphal thinks that Himmler was appointed because it was the only way of sending his Replacement Army to the front. 'This was the one advantage of the singular choice of a man who had been no more than an NCO in the old Bavarian Army and who possessed *Weltanschauung* as his only qualification to be the commander of an army group.'[3] It has also been said that Hitler made a political appointment to show the High Command what he could do with them. But there was a still more cogent reason why Himmler had to have a command at the front. It was the only way to keep him off the Ardennes counter-offensive, which Hitler planned in October 1944. Rundstedt's spearhead was to be a newly equipped Panzer army, the first to be commanded by an SS man; this was the Sixth Army of Sepp Dietrich, now once more the hero of the hour.

Hitherto Himmler had accepted the role by which SS divisions came under Wehrmacht corps commanders and SS army corps or armoured groups under Wehrmacht army commanders. But now for

[1] Hausser, op. cit., p. 192.   [2] *Ibid.*, p. 161.   [3] Westphal, *Heer im Fesseln*, p. 285.

the first time a whole army came under the control of an SS officer and a large part of it consisted of SS formations. There was a danger of far-reaching encroachments by Himmler and the SS Leadership Office into the Wehrmacht's strategic control. Moreover, there was a chance that the malicious incitement of Martin Bormann might lead Himmler into other excesses. In company with Josef Buerckel, the Gauleiter for Saarland-Lorraine, Himmler spent much of September inspecting the old Siegfried Line defences.[1] During this inspection General von Rundstedt was astonished to receive orders issued by Himmler under the title of 'Supreme Commander, Westmark'.[2]

It was the first warning that Himmler had achieved the command of an Army Group. Himmler had sent part of his Replacement Army to block the huge gap in the defence of the German frontier south of Karlsruhe which had been created by the mainly northward retreat of the German troops in France. In this way Himmler secured a sector which was quite independent of von Rundstedt, the Commander-in-Chief in the West. Equally, Von Rundstedt had freed himself of the danger of Himmler's interference in the Ardennes. Himmler did, however, have an opportunity of addressing his SS commanders before the Ardennes offensive. He is said to have used the familiar language of Metz and Kharkov: 'I rely on you to prove yourselves worthy of your SS runes and to guarantee victory *so oder so.*'[3]

As usual the words were unfortunate for Himmler's men, particularly on 16 July 1946, when Sepp Dietrich, Commander-in-Chief of the 6th SS Panzer Army, Kraemer, Commander of the 1st SS Armoured Corps, Hermann Priess, the Commander of the Adolf Hitler division and Jochen Peiper, Commander of a combat group, together with sixty-nine others were on trial at Dachau. They were found guilty of the murder on 17 December 1944 of seventy-one unarmed American prisoners of war, south-east of the Malmédy cross-roads. It was said that Jochen Peiper, who was only twenty-nine years old, had been an adjutant of Himmler's and that he commanded a terror unit. This was not true and it was not the lesson of the trial. Peiper's men formed a combat group like any other combat group of the SS and the incident could have taken place in

[1] *The Bormann Letters*, pp. 96, 103.
[2] Siegfried Westphal (English ed.), p. 172; *The German Army in the West* (London, 1951).   [3] Frischauer, op. cit., p. 232.

any sector where SS officers with Russian experience were in command.[1]

Himmler's part in the Ardennes offensive was limited to the creation of a special brigade for Skorzeny, who had been given no rest after his return to Germany with Admiral Horthy. He went at once to the Wolffschanze at Rastenburg, which Hitler did not finally quit till 20 November. Here Skorzeny was initiated into the mysteries of the second German invasion of the West. His own part was to be nothing more nor less than the plan that had been concocted at the end of 1939 by Heydrich and Canaris, namely the seizure of the Meuse bridgeheads by units wearing allied uniforms.[2] The plan was to be known as 'Unternehmen Greif'.

Such an undertaking could only succeed if it was followed up by a rapid armoured thrust. In 1939 the intention had been betrayed by the theft of Dutch frontier guard uniforms. In 1944 history seemed to repeat itself. The Allies learnt, though without drawing the right inference, of a circular which had gone out to Wehrmacht units, asking for English-speaking volunteers for Skorzeny's Oranienburg regiment.[3] Skorzeny as a result wanted the whole plan to be recast, but was told by Himmler and Fegelein, 'The stupidity has taken place. The action must be carried out notwithstanding.'

Skorzeny succeeded in recruiting some two thousand English-speaking individuals for his 150th Panzer Brigade, as this unit in

[1] The Malmedy Cross-Roads trial lasted from 16 May to 16 July 1946. Forty-three defendants were condemned to death, twenty-three to prison for life, and eight received shorter sentences. Sepp Dietrich received a twenty-five-year sentence, Priess eighteen years, and Kraemer ten. Jochen Peiper was among those condemned to death.

The trial attracted attention on account of the extreme irregularity of the interrogations which had preceded it, and the demand for revision was headed by the Chief Prosecutor himself, Colonel W. M. Everett of Atlanta. A Senate Committee of Investigation, the Baldwin Committee, on which sat the famous Senator McCarthy, created so much adverse publicity that the Dachau trials were stopped altogether. In March 1948 thirty-one of the death sentences were remitted. In April 1948 General Lucius Clay reduced the death sentences from twelve to six. Under the McCloy amnesty of January 1951 these six death sentences were commuted to prison for life. By April 1952 only those serving life sentences remained in Landsberg; they numbered thirteen. At the time of writing, Jochen Peiper, together with Major Diefental and Captain Preuss, are still in Landsberg prison, but are likely to be released shortly. Kraemer was freed in 1948, Priess in 1954 and Sepp Dietrich not till October 1955. (Dietrich Ziemessen, *Der Malmedy Prozess*, Munich, 1952.)   [2] See *supra*, p. 146.

[3] Skorzeny, op. cit., p. 260. Full text in Shulman, op. cit., p. 239.

American uniform and equipment was called. Although a few men in captured American vehicles penetrated great distances and were captured even as far away as Paris, not one position was held by the 50th Panzer Brigade long enough to be relieved by the main force, because Sepp Dietrich's 6th SS Panzer Army failed to maintain the pace. Very few members of the 150th Panzer Brigade got back to their own lines, and many were summarily shot according to the uses of war, or condemned to death by field court-martial, as at Henri Chapelle in Belgium on 22 December. One member of the 150th Panzer Brigade, Lieutenant Collonia, received the Knight's Cross for having functioned for a number of days as 'First Lieutenant George P. Ward'.[1]

Skorzeny and the responsible members of his staff were not tried till September 1947, when they were acquitted by the American Dachau Tribunal. Hitler had forbidden Skorzeny to take personal part in 'Unternehmen Greif', but it was fitting that the organiser of this affair should share the fate of so many of his men. This, however, could no longer be regarded as a legitimate reason for condemning Skorzeny. There were precedents on the Allied side for the use of enemy uniforms, but there was no precedent whatever for continuing the treatment, customarily awarded to enemy saboteurs, when the war had been over for more than two years. So Skorzeny continues to sell cement in Brazil.[2]

Sepp Dietrich's slow start on 17 December ruined not only 'Unternehmen Greif' but also any limited successes the Ardennes counter-offensive might have achieved. For its purpose in the broken Ardennes country the 6th Panzer Army was overloaded with vehicles, and this at the moment when the yawning gap in South-east Europe cried out for more equipment. The armoured columns were bogged down on the first day in the narrow lanes of the Eiffel, though one of Skorzeny's groups was already fifty miles ahead beyond the Meuse near Liége.[3] Moreover Sepp Dietrich, who had been chosen for the place of honour, was the last to appreciate it. When interrogated after the war, he blamed Guderian and Jodl for th- ailure of his tanks to deploy, of which he had warned them in advance. He had, he said, attacked Jodl with these words.[4]

[1] Kraetschmer, op. cit., p. 365.·
[2] Shulman, op. cit., p. 229; Skorzeny, op. cit., pp. 410-12.
[3] Westphal, *Heer im Fesseln*, p. 183.
[4] Georges Blond, *L'agonie del'Allemagne*, 1944-5, (Paris, 1952), p. 118. Also, but less picturesquely, in Shulman, op. cit., p. 229.

Very well then. I shall protest to the Fuehrer himself. He could not possibly have been seriously informed when he took these decisions. Do you know what they mean for me and my army? Reach the Meuse in two days, cross it, take Brussels, go on and then take Antwerp? Simple. As if my tanks could advance in a bog. And this little programme is to be executed in the depths of winter in a region where there are nine chances out of ten that we will have snow up to our middles. Do you call that serious? Out of all the original Adolf Hitler Division there are only thirty men today who are not dead or prisoners. Now I have re-created a new Panzer army and I am a general and not an undertaker. I tell you that it is impossible to execute these orders in this form and I shall tell this to the Fuehrer.

But the days were past when Hitler could discuss the next move with his old chauffeur. Sepp Dietrich was refused an audience.

Sepp Dietrich also complained of his troops. It was the first time that an SS army had taken the field, yet it was an SS army only in name. Four of his six armoured divisions belonged to the Waffen SS, but two of them were soon withdrawn from the right flank in order to strengthen the Fifth Army. Their place was taken by the poorest material of all, the Volksgrenadiere divisions from Himmler's Replacement Army. Nevertheless, Sepp Dietrich's failure was regarded as the failure of the SS. Von Rundstedt, Hitler's reluctant Commander-in-Chief in this affair, felt particularly malicious about it. He declared in captivity, 'I received few reports from Sepp Dietrich of the Sixth Panzer Army and what I did receive was generally a pack of lies. If the SS had any problems, they reported them directly to the Fuehrer, who would then make them known to Model.'[1] Hitler himself did not as yet express openly his disappointment with the Waffen SS, but the breach which culminated in the insulting armbands order of 27 March had begun.

A few days before the opening of the Ardennes offensive Himmler took up his duties as Commander of the Upper Rhine Army Group, that is to say all forces south of Karlsruhe and as far as the Swiss border. In addition to the Nineteenth Army, Himmler's command included a new and completely improvised army of frontier guards, Eastern workers' battalions, Volkssturm and former anti-aircraft units, which were shuffled into divisions and spread like cards on a table. They formed the XIVth and XVIIIth SS Army Corps under the command of the heroes of Warsaw, the police generals Reinefarth and von dem Bach-Zelewski.[2] This army had been created in a matter of six weeks and, while it was a triumph of improvisation, it was

[1] See Shulman, op. cit., p. 247.   [2] Hausser, op. cit., p. 185.

fortunate that it served in a sector where the Allies never attacked. But to Hitler the phantom army had a mystical importance. It represented the triumph of the amateur over the professional, of corporals like himself over the officer caste. He thoroughly regretted it when Bach-Zelewski was sent East and the menaced Rhine front was deprived of his services.[1]

Hitler: If Bach-Zelewski were here, I would be entirely at ease. He would scrape up prisoners of war, convicts, everything. By the way, where is he now?
Keitel: The Reichsfuehrer took him with him.

Himmler, however, felt that he ought to be doing something more glamorous than holding a dead sector with the scrapings of the barrel. He wanted nothing less than a new offensive across the Rhine to relieve the pressure on the bulge which had been created by the failure of the German offensive in the Ardennes. The opportunity came on New Year's Eve when the battle in the Ardennes had already lasted a fortnight. To relieve some of the enemy's pressure, von Rundstedt had ordered a small attack by two SS armoured divisions and six Volksgrenadiere divisions south of Bitsch through Hagenau towards Strasbourg. Himmler at once persuaded Hitler to withdraw the 6th and 10th SS divisions, which Rundstedt had used in this attack, in order that he might borrow them himself. He wanted the glory of capturing Strasbourg from the east, using the Nineteenth Army's bridgehead across the Rhine. General Westphal, Himmler's bitterest critic, says that so much time was lost moving these two divisions that the enemy had leisure to strengthen his position in Strasbourg.

General Westphal is not quite accurate. It was not the enemy's military position which was strengthened but his resolution. As soon as Himmler had gained a bridgehead towards Strasbourg at Herresheim, Eisenhower decided to abandon the city and withdraw the entire Allied right flank behind the Vosges Mountains. Himmler might have been hailed as the conqueror of Alsace, the civilian who had won a victory while the High Command floundered on the fruitless Ardennes battlefield. But fate was seldom kind to the Reichsfuehrer in his last few months. Charles Fey, the newly reinstated mayor of Strasbourg, begged General de Gaulle to intervene with Mr. Churchill and, through Churchill, Eisenhower was persuaded that the political value of Strasbourg to the French was worth a little risk.[2] And against the threat of Himmler's offensive Strasbourg

1 Gilbert, op. cit., p. 134.
2 *The Times*, 15 October 1955: Obituary of M. Fey.

was held without the diversion of a division. Soon Himmler's upper Rhine Army Group could no longer defend the bridgeheads. On 20 January the French and Americans counter-attacked and within three weeks there were no German troops left west of the Rhine.[1]

On 23 January Himmler quitted the Black Forest, having been posted to the Eastern Front to command the Vistula Army Group. Paul Hausser took over the Upper Rhine Command, which once more came under von Rundstedt's orders as Commander-in-Chief, West. 'There was naturally no question of an orderly transfer,' the sour Westphal writes, for Himmler as Commander-in-Chief Upper Rhine, had left behind him 'a laundry-basket full of unsorted orders and reports. That too was apparently part of his new methods of leadership.'[2]

In the five or six weeks that he spent as 'Ob.Oberrein', Himmler handled his office of Commander-in-Chief much as he handled his other offices, that is to say, without vision, without grasp of essentials, but with sudden bursts of energy concerning trifles. He made his Army and Army Corps Commanders turn out to watch the firing of a new type of heavy gun and the subservient Keitel made everyone observe that 'the Reichsfuehrer's new methods of leadership were very worthy of note.'[3] Otherwise it was merely a transference of Himmler's court from East Prussia to South Germany. Early in December Hitler had moved his Reich Chancellery to von Rundstedt's headquarters, a deep shelter called the 'Adlerhorst' at Ziegenburg near Bad Nauheim. Himmler's headquarters were behind his own front near the tourist resort of Triberg in the Black Forest, where he kept his special train close to a convenient railway tunnel.[4] He was a good 150 miles from Bad Nauheim, but the coming and going seems to have been continuous. On Christmas Eve Himmler entertained Guderian to dinner at Ziegenburg and told him that he was almost convinced that nothing was going to happen in the East.[5] Two days previously he had entertained von Rundstedt and Jodl at his own headquarters in the Black Forest. Jodl had danced after supper and Rundstedt had returned the invitation, just as if they were attending peace-time manœuvres.[6] And all this time the last

---

[1] Hausser, op. cit., p. 186; Westphal, op. cit., p. 288; Chester Wilmot, *The Struggle for Europe* (London 1952), p. 606.

[2] Westphal, op. cit. 289.　　　[3] *Ibid.*, p. 286.　　　[4] *The Bormann Letters*, p. 158.

[5] Guderian, op. cit., p. 347.　　　[6] *The Bormann Letters*, p. 155.

German offensive was evaporating in the snow-drenched woods of Malmédy and Bastogne.

There was to be no dancing at Deutsch Kroner, whither Himmler was now bound. He went to a place of gloom and fear which was to destroy finally all that was left of his moral fibre. Yet it is hard to accept Luedde-Neurath's view that Himmler's appointment was a punishment and a sign of Hitler's displeasure. Hitler could hardly have given the man the greatest military responsibility in the gravest of crises for the sake of punishing him, or merely to gratify the mischievous impulses of Martin Bormann.[1] Once again Himmler's position as head of the Replacement Army decided his appointment, for it was a question of building another improvised army group, this time to fill the gap created by the Russian attack across the Vistula which had begun at Baranov on 12 January.

Within ten days this tremendous attack reached the Baltic east of Danzig and cut off twenty-five German divisions in East Prussia. To scrape together a new army, the Vistula Army, and to lead it into the gap, Guderian recommended the Austrian General Weichs, whose own front in Croatia had dissappeared. Hitler might have agreed, had not Alfred Jodl upset him by describing Weichs's religious background. Himmler, Hitler declared, was clearly the only man for the job. Hitler even vetoed Guderian's sensible suggestion that Himmler should use Weichs's General Staff which was kicking its heels in Zagreb. Himmler was to choose his own General Staff.[2]

And so, for the first time, an SS man was chosen to be Chief of Staff to an army group. This was Major-General Heinz Lammerding, the commander of the SS division, Das Reich. Lammerding had been chief staff officer in Eicke's Totenkopf division in Russia before commanding a division himself at the age of thirty-nine, but his reputation was founded on other qualities. In May 1944 he had been the hero of the 'Blood and Ashes action', a drive against the French partisans in the mountains of Auvergne. In the small town of Tulle alone ninety-nine victims, including some women, were hanged. A month later Lammerding had to conduct a long march from the Bordeaux region to the Allied bridgehead in Normandy. On this occasion the Das Reich division lived up to its Russian reputation even more thoroughly. At Oradour-sur-Glane, near Limoges, an SS captain was shot at and killed. For this the entire village of 642

---

[1] Luedde-Neurath, *Regierung Doenitz*, p. 43.
[2] Guderian, op. cit., p. 366; Thorwald, I, p. 273.

inhabitants was exterminated. The women were separated from the men and, with 207 children, were mown down by machine-guns in the church. Two days later the bodies of fifteen children were found packed behind the altar.[1]

The fate of Major-General Heinz Lammerding, Himmler's Chief of Staff for two months, has not been an onerous one. After the war he concealed his identity so well in the prison camps that in July 1951 a Bordeaux court finally condemned him to death for the Tulle affair *in absentia*.[2] Shortly afterwards Lammerding began to live under his own name in Duesseldorf in the British zone. In January 1953, when the Bordeaux court began proceedings against twenty-one men of the Das Reich division for their part in the Oradour affair, Lammerding felt so confident of his position as to write a letter of encouragement to the men who had served under him.[3] M. Pleven, the French Minister of Defence, now asked for his extradition, but, since September 1948, extradition of war criminals had become practically a dead letter. The British Control Commission and the Foreign Office showed a rousing want of enthusiasm, when questioned on the subject. On 12 March 1953, a month after the extremely controversial Oradour sentences, M. Francois Poncet, the French High Commissioner in Germany, requested a search for Lammerding in the American zone. It seems that the general had moved discreetly to Mittenwald on the Austrian border.[4] That was three years ago. Today the German courts have no desire to proceed against SS generals who carried out Himmler orders. A former Chief of Staff to the Commander-in-Chief of an army group—even a bad one as Lammerding was—may soon find himself in demand among the nascent High Command of the West German Army.

Himmler established his headquarters at Deutsch Kroner on 24 January. The Russians had then reached a line running from Elbing on the Baltic through Thorn and Posen to Breslau. North of Posen there was no German front, for the remains of the Central Army Group were cut off in East Prussia. Quite large parts of Germany were in the hands of an invading army whose standard of living was low, whose discipline had been deliberately relaxed and who had every reason to feel vengeful. Himmler drove to his new command through a mass of panic-stricken refugees. He had an out-of-date

---

[1] *The Times*, 29 January 1952 and 2 February 1953.
[2] *The Times*, 2 February 1953.   [3] *Ibid*. 30 January 1953.
[4] *The Times*, 13 March 1953.

map in his car when he arrived at Deutsch Kroner and he had no idea that his Second Army was reduced to a fraction, or that his Ninth Army was no longer a fighting force.[1]

Six days later Himmler's notions of the situation seem to have been equally hazy. Skorzeny, who had recovered from the wound he had received in the Ardennes offensive, was ordered by Himmler to move the remains of his Commando Force to Schwedt on the Oder and to build up a bridgehead beyond the river. On the way he was to relieve the town of Freienwalde, which was beseiged by the Russians. To Skorzeny it seemed odd enough that a unit, on its way to take up position, should be told to defeat a besieging force of unknown size merely *en passant*. And still more extraordinary the news that a town, not thirty miles from Berlin and well west of the Oder, should be in Russian hands. In fact Skorzeny's men drove through Freienwalde in perfect peace and at Schwedt they discovered the Russians were as yet nowhere near the Oder.[2]

In sheer eating-up of territory this last Russian attack had been even more devastating than the Bobruisk break-through of the previous July, but again it had outdistanced its supplies. During the two months that Himmler commanded the Vistula Army Group, the front was actually to become stabilised but this was not till well into March. When Himmler arrived at Deutsch Kroner there was no front at all. Immediate decisions had to be made which might alter the whole course of the war. It was not a place like the lower Rhine, where an enemy, who was certain to make his own attack somewhere else, could be teased with an amateur local offensive. Within two days of his arrival, acting without consulting Guderian, Keitel or Jodl, Himmler made a serious mistake. He withdrew the isolated garrisons which extended beyond the lower Vistula at Thorn, Kulmm and Marienwerder. By doing so he lost the bridgeheads for any offensive in the direction of the isolated army of East Prussia.[3]

Having perceived his error, Himmler went to the other extreme and imitated Hitler in defending fortresses that were already doomed and useless. The great communications centre of Posen was surrounded on 25 January. Within a few days the Russians occupied all but a corner of the town. Himmler thereupon dismissed Mattern, the elderly garrison commander, and appointed Colonel Gonell in his place. Gonell was the commander of a force composed of two

[1] Thorwald, I, p. 275.   [2] Skorzeny, op. cit., pp. 325-9.
[3] Guderian, op. cit., p. 368.

thousand officer cadets from the 5th SS Training School, the Welfenschloss in Brunswick, and therefore to be relied on as a fanatical last-ditcher. Himmler forbade Gonell to break out to the west and so the defence of Posen continued in conditions of inconceivable ghastliness till 23 February; but, a week before this, Gonell permitted his two thousand cadets to make their way out in groups. He then took his own life rather than face Himmler's court martial, so that the final surrender of Posen was offered by General Mattern.[1]

Himmler had once been extremely popular with his Waffen SS, for whose welfare he had worked assiduously, and perhaps no part of the Waffen SS had been more congenial to him than the Officer Cadet Schools which he had founded in 1934-5. Incidents like this and the notorious 'armbands order' five weeks later made Himmler odious throughout the Waffen SS. When he became a general in the field, Himmler ceased to be a fairy godmother.

On 24 January, when Himmler reached Deutsch Kroner, the very name Vistula Army Group had become ridiculous. West of beleaguered Posen the gap in the front, caused by the dissolution of the Ninth Army, was filled by the Vth SS Mountain Corps from Jugoslavia under Lieutenant-General Walter Krueger.[2] This corps held a portion of the old German-Polish frontier which had been fortified in 1934. In the course of a local offensive General Bellauf of the 21st SS Division—the Albanian Skandar Beg division—had to abandon his car to the Russians. In that car were the plans of the fortified frontier. With their aid Russian pioneer units found the openings in the defences, with the result that the enormous Warthe-Oder river loop, which was straddled by this relatively short line, fell entirely into Russian hands. On 31 January the Russians even established a bridgehead across the Oder at Wriezen near Kuestrin, only forty-five miles from Berlin.[3]

Perhaps the Russians might have achieved still more, had there not been a sudden thaw on the frozen River Oder. Three months later Himmler told Schwerin von Krosigk that this was a miracle which,

[1] Thorwald, I, pp. 95-100.

[2] Walter Krueger, who committed suicide in Libau in May 1945, was actually the commander of the VIth SS volunteer corps in the Kurland pocket and only served temporarily on the Vistula Army Group front. He was one of the older SS generals with a long military career and must be distinguished from Friedrich Krueger, also from Strasbourg, who had been higher SS and police leader in Poland. (See *supra*, p. 234.)   [3] Thorwald, I, p. 277.

like the Fuehrer's escape in the Speer barracks, had brought him back to God.[1] But in the early days of February Himmler took no chances with miracles. He lined the banks of the Oder with companies of security police and regular police and gave them orders to shoot at any German soldiers whom they saw trying to get back across the river. This did not stop the Russians establishing several new bridgeheads, though on 15 February, when Goebbels visited the front, Wilfrid von Oven's first glimpse of the Oder Line was of the bodies of German deserters swinging from the steel girders of mined railway bridges.[2]

To retrieve the situation Himmler turned to the offensive. In the first days of February he attempted to roll up the much-extended Russian right flank by an attack from Deutsch Kroner towards Schneidemuehl. The attack was led by Demelhuber, who was one of the officers who had risen entirely in the ranks of the Waffen SS. Westphal writes contemptuously that in the Regular Army Demelhuber had been a cavalry groom. The Russian counter-attack not only pushed back Demelhuber's corps, but it also sent Himmler himself scuttling out of his first headquarters at Deutsch Kroner. He had to move to a fantastic building, the Ordensburg at Crossinsee, built by Robert Ley for the Labour Front.[3]

Himmler was now forced to withdraw almost his whole force to the Oder. Most of his isolated garrisons had anticipated this already by breaking out on their own and their commanders had faced courts martial. General Gerhard Kegler, who abandoned Landsberg, was reduced by Himmler to the rank of private. He recovered his rank only in September 1953, in order to qualify for a Bonn Government pension of £200 a year.[4]

Thus the Russians now lined the Oder almost as far downstream as Stettin. Nevertheless, Hitler under the obstinate influence of Admiral Doenitz was determined to hold the Baltic U-boat bases at any cost. Himmler was compelled to waste more than a third of the Vistula Army Group, including some of the best foreign SS troops, in defending a far-extended flank along the Baltic from Stettin past Danzig to Elbing. Berlin itself became open to the enemy at the end of January. In spite of Himmler's optimism on Christmas Eve, the Russians had advanced four hundred miles and made the Reich capital a frontier.

---

[1] Trevor-Roper, op. cit., p. 37.   [2] Von Oven, op. cit., II, p. 245.
[3] Thorwald, I, p. 280.   [4] *Daily Telegraph*, 1 September 1953.

There had been the beginnings of panic in Berlin as early as 20 January when the Russians entered Silesia. On the 21st the alarm signal 'Gneisenau' was given to the Berlin Volkssturm, in anticipation of riots by the Eastern workers, and Frau Goebbels was already talking of the suicide of her family.[1] On the 31st a hundred Russian tanks were reported across the Oder, two hours' drive from the Wilhelmstrasse. But the training schools of Krampnitz and Wuensdorf manned two hundred German heavy tanks which they unloaded on the sidings. In the next few days the Russian Oder bridgehead at Wriezen was sealed off. It may have been the case that the Russians could bring no more heavy tanks to the Oder front or there may have been some dark unfathomed cause, connected with the untrustful character of inter-Allied politics. Whatever the explanation, the Russians attempted no general offensive across the river till 16 April.

Naturally, as soon as there was a lull, party leaders began to talk hopefully of a counter-offensive. The huge Russian salient was to be pinched off in simultaneous attacks by Himmler in Pomerania and Schoerner in Silesia.[2] Even Guderian favoured the design, provided that Sepp Dietrich's 6th Panzer Army, which was still in the West, was sent to the Oder; provided also that every available division was taken from Kurland, Italy, Jugoslavia, Norway and Denmark.[3]

But Hitler, against the opinion of Sepp Dietrich himself, decided to send the 6th SS Panzer Army to Hungary and to defend all the foreign lands that were in German occupation, even though the Russians were forty-five miles from Berlin. Guderian was taken out by Goering and calmed with cups of coffee, but the most he could achieve was to persuade Hitler to force a professional general on Himmler as Chief of Staff in place of Heinz Lammerding, whom he considered a mere policeman and amateur divisional commander. Guderian recommended his own second-in-command, General Walter Wenck, but Hitler retorted that 'Himmler was man enough for it'. For two hours and a half Himmler sat in the room, embarrassed and speechless, while Hitler and Guderian argued about his merits in the presence of a hostile and sullen Sepp Dietrich. In the end Hitler turned to the wretched man and said, 'Very well, Himmler, Wenck is coming to you this evening. The attack begins on the 15th.'

[1] Von Oven, op. cit., II, p. 229.   [2] Von Oven, op. cit, II, p. 242.
[3] Guderian, op. cit., p. 375.

Guderian considered that he had won 'the last Battle of the General Staff'.[1]

On 13 February Himmler again moved his headquarters. He was now in a wood near Prenzlau, well behind the Oder and some sixty miles from the Arnswalde sector where the attack on the great Russian salient was to begin. Wenck coldly refused to lunch with Himmler next day and proceeded to make his way to the front. But it was not Wenck who directed the attack. Summoned to report at the Reich Chancellery on the 17th, Wenck was driving down the Stettin-Berlin road when his driver fell asleep. Wenck took the wheel but he was so exhausted that he fell asleep too, hit a tree and broke his shoulder. He was immobilised till the last four weeks of the war. [2] Wenck's place was taken by Hans Krebs, who was destined to be Hitler's last Chief of Staff and whose only merit (apart from having been kissed by Stalin when a military attaché in Moscow) was that he was a companion of Burgdorf's and a member of the Bormann-Fegelein caucus.

In the meantime the attack had to go on. Himmler dealt with the situation by making the first of his retirements into hospital at Hohenlychen. There Skorzeny saw him about 15 February and listened to another repetition of the opinion that the Russians did not possess enough reserves to stand a flank attack from Pomerania on the Oder bulge.[3] Perhaps Himmler still believed this; perhaps it was only one of his dutiful slogans, like the future German frontier in the Urals.

Before the offensive of 15 February Himmler addressed a stirring Order of the Day to his troops from his hospital bed at Hohenlychen: 'Forward through the mud! Forward through the snow! Forward by day! Forward by night! Forward for the liberation of German soil!'[4] Steiner, too—Felix Steiner, the founder of the first of the SS divisions of European volunteers, the defender of Narva, and the only SS general apart from Hausser and Sepp Dietrich to command an army—believed in the offensive he had to direct. He told his divisional commanders at Panke on 13 February that huge reinforcements were arriving. At Landsberg the Russians on the Oder would be taken in the rear; at Lodz the front would be encircled and contact made, both with Schoerner advancing from

[1] Narrative of Colonel Eismann in Thorwald, I, p. 285.
[2] Guderian, op. cit., p. 377.   [3] Skorzeny, p. 444.
[4] Leon Degrelle, *Die verlorene Legion* (Stuttgart, 1955), p. 408.

Breslau and with Sepp Dietrich advancing from Hungary through Slovakia. Before the year was out the Germans would be once more on the Dnieper.[1]

The Steiner attack was launched by four Wehrmacht and four SS divisions on the short sector between Stargard and Arnswalde. These divisions included the IIIrd SS Armoured Corps, but most of that corps was armoured only in name. The immense concentrations of Russian tanks east of the Oder were to be met by not more than 250 German tanks, all told. Practically without air cover or artillery support, neither tanks nor infantry could advance more than a few miles through the muddy wooded country. By the 19th the Russians had recovered Arnswalde, encircled Graudenz and reduced the German base at Stargard to rubble. Steiner had captured the small town of Brallentin and two villages. The official military communiqué dismissed the matter as a minor engagement, but in fact the four-day battle had cost Himmler's Vistula Army Group immense casualties among the few divisions which could still be relied on for an attack. The remains of the tank units were moved to the Oder front and the least mauled SS division, the 4th Police, was shipped off by sea for the defence of Danzig.[2] Steiner, an army commander for a few days, emerged from his experience a complete defeatist, though party propaganda still built him up in Hitler's eyes as the hope of the future, together with Schoerner 'the bloodhound'.

The latter had not been able to attack at all. The Russians had forced his men out of their assault-bases beyond the Silesian Oder and a part of his army was surrounded in Glogau. As to Sepp Dietrich, neither he nor the bulk of his 6th SS Panzer Army had reached Hungary. There the offensive was mounted more than a fortnight too late. Thus died the great Himmler-Schoerner pincer movement. Martin Bormann, concealing some of the pleasure with which he watched Himmler's failure, wrote drily to his wife, 'Uncle Heinrich's offensive did not succeed; that is to say, it did not develop properly'.[3]

Early in March the situation on Himmler's absurdly extended coastal flank grew more critical. The Russians established two more bridgeheads south of Stettin and on 7 March broke through to the sea at Colberg and so isolated Danzig from land access. Colberg itself was surrounded. Himmler had sent Colonel Fullriede to

---

[1] Degrelle, op. cit., pp. 411-13.
[2] Thorwald, I, p. 287; Hausser, op. cit., p. 209.   [3] *The Bormann Letters*, p. 189.

organise a defence to the finish, but such orders were becoming more and more ignored. Fullriede held on just long enough to get the civilians shipped off and then embarked his own force.[1] The defence of the coast was now a strategic absurdity to everyone except Hitler and the exclusively naval-minded Admiral Doenitz. Lammerding and Colonel Eismann tried to get Himmler to put a plan to Hitler for the abandonment of all Pomerania beyond the Oder. Himmler agreed in principle, but he was too frightened of Hitler to approach him.[2]

Probably at all periods of his career Himmler had been in terror of Hitler. He had never had any private entrée to Hitler's presence, like Goebbels or Speer, and his conversations with him were always official. At this period, when he was on paper the most powerful person in the Reich, Himmler's fear of Hitler became pathological. He had seen how his own 3rd Panzer Army commander, the Austrian Raus, had been dismissed, simply because Hitler had mistaken his accent for that of an East Prussian and presumably a Junker.[3] He may have feared that Hitler suspected his foreign contacts, for on 18 February Himmler had his first interview with Count Bernadotte. Above all, Himmler was afraid because he knew that Hitler's only personal adviser was Martin Bormann, and that if he, Himmler, tried to advise his Fuehrer, Bormann would know what use to make of that.

Of Bormann's malicious powers Himmler had seen a recent example and it was singularly near home. One of Himmler's oldest SS adherents was Artur Greiser, who had been the Nazi leader in Danzig when it was a Free City, and was now the governor of the new province Warthegau with a capital at Posen. Here on 20 January 1945 Greiser received a telegram from Bormann, ordering him to evacuate all German civilians and to report in Berlin for new duties. On reaching Frankfurt-on-Oder, Greiser learnt that Bormann had tricked him. Hitler had just declared that Posen must be held at all costs, while Goebbels and the party bravoes were demanding Greiser's blood as a coward and a deserter. The most that Himmler could do for his friend was to advise him to retire to Karlsbad. Hitler had stopped Bormann proceeding against Greiser, but now, at the beginning of March, Greiser turned up in Himmler's headquarters, demanding to be allowed to challenge Bormann over the forged telegram. Himmler was so frightened that he forbade him to

---

[1] Thorwald, I, p. 338.   [2] *Ibid.*, p. 305.   [3] Guderian, op. cit., p. 382.

reopen the matter and Greiser retired to the Bavarian Alps, where later he surrendered to the Americans. Artur Greiser, the former President of the Danzig Senate, was tried in 1947 by a Polish court in Posen. Before they hanged him in front of his former palace, they paraded him round the town in a cage.[1]

So instead of going to Hitler to demand the evacuation of Pomerania, Himmler went to bed. For the second time within three weeks he retired to his favourite room in Hohenlychen hospital and to the tender care of Kersten and Karl Gebhardt. Hohenlychen was in any case no further from the front than Himmler's so-called field headquarters.

During the fortnight that Himmler spent in hospital the Russians were very kind to him, for very little happened on the Oder front between 6 and 22 March. The Army Group Vistula had grown to a normal size, thirty-three divisions.[2] Whatever else was lacking, there was no want of man-power in the last weeks of Hitler's Reich. Officially there were still ten million men wearing German uniform, well over a million of them foreigners, but of what use were these masses without tanks, motor transport, artillery or ammunition? The Vistula Army Group included aerodrome staffs, sailors, frontier guards, schoolboys from the Hitlerjugend, convicts, Eastern workers and elderly Home Guards or Volkssturmers. On the 3rd Panzer Army front, which had been intended for the counter-offensive, there were a few tried divisions of the Wehrmacht and the SS and a few more on the Second Army front in Pomerania. But the greater part of the Oder front from Guben almost to Stettin was held by Himmler's creation, the re-formed Ninth Army, which consisted of the two improvised army corps of Reinefarth and Bach-Zelewski and the Albanians and Slovenes of Krueger's Vth SS Mountain Corps.[3]

In Bach-Zelewski's corps Skorzeny served. A lieutenant-colonel without experience in handling large bodies of troops, he had to build up a new division in the Schwedt bridgehead from any fugitives who came his way. Skorzeny did not love Bach-Zelewski, with whom he had clashed over the attack on the Burgberg. Skorzeny therefore has little good to say about Hitler's favourite improviser, the man who could make divisions out of anything. He accused him of failing to visit the front or to maintain the flow of supplies. The

---

[1] Narrative of Walter Petzel, in Thorwald, I, pp. 89-91.

[2] Guderian, op. cit., p. 373.

[3] But not the Bosnian Moslem division 'Handschar', which was in Hungary.

Schwedt bridgehead, which extended many miles east of the Oder, was hard pressed by the Russians in the middle of February. Attacks at Grabow and Nipperwiese nearly eliminated it. Skorzeny was summoned to Himmler's presence at Hohenlychen to explain his conduct. Skorzeny declared that Bach-Zelewski had sent not a pound of supplies nor a single reinforcement to the bridgehead, but only a mass of idiotic orders. All Himmler could reply to the torrent of invective was, 'But you have kept me waiting four hours.' In the end Himmler promised Skorzeny some tanks and invited him to dinner, but Bach-Zelewski retained his post and he ended the war as an Army Commander.[1]

Skorzeny's description of Himmler's front does not conceal the sense of helplessness and doom, but it completely glosses over the loathsome cruelties. The last fragmentary report of Hitler's military conferences in the Reich Chancellery, dating from the middle of March, mentions a request by Gauleiter Forster that the special commando of 450 security policemen of the SS be retained in Danzig.[2] Even during the siege of the city this commando was at work, rounding up all who left their posts, such as schoolboy A.A. gunners who visited their parents in the town, and delivering them to the Station Tribunal. The trees of the Hindenburg Allee were used as gibbets and the dead carried placards: 'I hang here because I left my unit without permission.'[3]

Commanders like Skorzeny may have tried to whip up some sort of enthusiasm, but it must have been hard when the daily sight of refugee columns showed the German soldier the doom to which Hitler had consigned the Reich. As to Himmler, he had long ceased to be an effective scoutmaster and his brutal nagging speeches had long ceased to offer any hope or inspiration. All he offered now was punishment. One of his orders of the day threatened to extend to the German army the Gestapo practice of Sippenhaft, the arrest and even the execution of the relatives of delinquents.[4]

It is an act of racial duty according to Teutonic tradition to exterminate even the kinsmen of those who surrender themselves into captivity without being wounded.

This order was issued from the front of the Vistula Army Group, but in fact it was impossible anywhere to escape from Himmler's

---

[1] Skorzeny, op. cit., p. 241.   [2] Gilbert, op. cit., p. 153.
[3] Thorwald, I, p. 328.   [4] Pechel, op. cit. (Frankfurt, 1948), p. 170.

notions of discipline.[1] In the besieged cities the special commandos of the security police ignored the garrison commanders and were a law unto themselves. The conditions in besieged Danzig were repeated in Koenigsberg and Breslau. Moreover, as Commander of the Replacement Army, Himmler was in charge of all military prisons and penal units. In the Field Justice Sections (Feldgerichts-abteilungen or FGA) soldiers who had been found guilty of cowardice in the face of the enemy could be beaten, a punishment unknown in the Prussian army for more than eighty years. Soldiers were condemned to death and then made to watch the execution of their companions before they were told of their own pardons. In the FGA the sick died under a diet which could not support life, while soldiers on duty were worse fed than concentration-camp inmates. Most of the FGA sections were determined to go over to the enemy. And it was during Himmler's period with the Vistula Army Group that the Spandau executions were at their liveliest.[2]

But at the end of March 1945 Himmler cared little about any of these things. He was sick at heart and listless and even when at his headquarters rose at eight o'clock, rested three hours after lunch and went to bed at ten. He was, according to Colonel Eismann, quite exhausted and without concentration towards evening. Yet Himmler was only forty-four years old and he had till recently been the hardest-working of Hitler's leaders.[3]

We must now follow the struggles of Himmler's conscience, which had led him to this pass.

[1] According to Milton Shulman the 3rd U.S. Army Staff obtained a copy of a Himmler order, dated as far back as 10 September 1944, in which it is declared that 'on examination of the circumstances a deserter's family will be summarily shot'. (*Defeat in the West*, p. 218.) In practice, examination of the circumstances seems to have meant proof of harbouring or connivance. I can find no record of the shooting of a deserters' family merely as an act of symbolic reprisal.

[2] Weisenborn, op. cit., p. 121.   [3] Quoted in Thorwald, I, p. 280.

15

Eclipse

1. HIMMLER WORKS HIS PASSAGE WITH THE ALLIES

It was 18 March 1945. A whole month had passed since Wenck had been sent to Himmler to direct his Vistula offensive. Guderian, who had received no reports from Prenzlau, believed that Himmler was no longer taking orders from the High Command. He did not know, as Goebbels had known as far back as 7 March, that Himmler was in hospital.[1] So Guderian drove to Prenzlau and was greeted by Lammerding's cheerful words, 'Can't you get rid of our Commander-in-Chief for us?'[2] Guderian went on to Hohenlychen, where he found the invalid doing so well that he reproached him for leaving his post for such a trifling indisposition. Guderian told Himmler that he must be breaking down under the strain of his five appointments and that he had already done his job in creating a new army group. But Himmler, who dared not hand in his resignation to Hitler, was quite pleased when Guderian offered to do it for him.[3]

Hitler accepted Himmler's resignation with equanimity. It suited him well enough, for, according to Albert Speer, Himmler's insistence in commanding an army group had removed him from Hitler's favour. At this period, says Speer, not only did Bormann and Fegelein have more influence than Himmler, but also Goebbels and Ley.[4] But the Bormann-Fegelein alliance had been all for recommending Himmler as a soldier and the record of a Fuehrer conference, held a day or two before Himmler's resignation, shows Fegelein still gunning for Himmler pretty assiduously.[5]

A more likely cause of Hitler's disappointment was the 'wonder weapon'. In 1944 Himmler had used his position as head of the Replacement Army to wrest the control of production of V.2 rockets from the Luftwaffe. Production in the final stages and the launching of the weapons from Holland were put in the charge of Lieutenant-General Heinz Kammler, the head of the SS Construction Office in

---

[1] Von Oven, op. cit., II, p. 25   [2] Guderian, op. cit. 384.
[3] Juergen Thorwald, *Die Ende an der Elbe* (Thorwald. II), p. 15.
[4] IMT VII, p. 54; evidence of Albert Speer.   [5] Gilbert, op. cit., p. 153.

Oswald Pohl's WVHA organisation. Kammler was an absolutely ruthless, thoroughly efficient technician—he was the man who carried out the construction of the super-gas-chambers at Auschwitz—but even Kammler could not make an important weapon out of V.2. It was too costly, too erratic and produced in too small quantities to have the least effect on the outcome of the war. Hitler and Goebbels had ordered an extensive propaganda campaign to precede the first launchings of V.2. And Hitler had hypnotised himself into believing it. Now Kammler, Himmler and the SS bore the full burden of Hitler's depression.

So Hitler agreed to Guderian's recommendation of General Gotthard Heinrici to succeed Himmler. Heinrici reached Prenzlau on 22 March and found Himmler sitting at a large desk under a portrait of Frederick the Great, looking unusually white and puffy. Himmler began with a long account of his command, which gave Heinrici the impression that 'in four months Himmler had failed to grasp the most basic elements of generalship'. A whole hour elapsed and the stenographer stopped taking notes; the staff officers, Eismann and Kinzler, slipped out of the room, but Himmler went on for another hour till the telephone rang. It was General Busse, who commanded the Second Army, reporting that the Russians had linked up two Oder bridgeheads and cut off Reinefarth's corps in Kuestrin. Himmler, with a surprised and helpless expression, gave Heinrici the receiver and said, 'You command the army group now; please give the appropriate order.' Himmler then started again on his reminiscences, but Heinrici at last cut him short; he wanted to visit the Ninth Army front; he wanted to hear the reports of members of Himmler's staff. Himmler looked at him suspiciously and then risked it: 'The time has come to enter into negotiations with our Western enemies. I have initiated steps. My agents have established contact'.[1]

By 'contact' Himmler surely meant Count Folke Bernadotte, the nephew of the King of Sweden and vice-chairman of the Swedish Red Cross, though Himmler's first meeting with Count Bernadotte on 18 February had been no more than a breaking of the ice, the subject being the repatriation of Danes and Norwegians from the German concentration camps.[2] Nevertheless the contact had been made and Count Bernadotte was kept in his mind as an emissary to the West if Hitler should collapse or die and Himmler succeed him.

---

[1] Thorwald II, p. 25, narrative of General Heinrici.
[2] Bernadotte, *The Curtain Falls*, p. 42.

At this time Himmler became more than ever interested in Hitler's health. But, since he never saw Hitler, he had to pump those who were frequently in Hitler's company. A week after the Bernadotte meeting Himmler left his headquarters to attend a party at the Goebbels Ministry. He sounded Goebbels by describing the bad physical impression Hitler had created on Gauleiter Forster of Danzig, when on a visit to the Reich Chancellery. But Goebbels was in his worst hero-worshipping mood and blethered about a 'fiery spirit that rose above drugs and narcotics'.[1] Nor would Goebbels entertain the project of negotiating with the West except under Hitler's orders and Hitler, he understood, was more in favour of negotiating with the East. At this Himmler murmured something which sounded like 'Madness!' Three days later, on 28 February, Goebbels went to Hohenlychen and returned, once again impressed with Himmler's realism and good sense. But now Goebbels was no longer a party to Himmler's plans; he had made his choice 'between Germany and Hitler'. He had decided on *Goetterdaemmerung*.

Such inner diplomacy was not for everyone's ears. On the day before his parting words to Heinrici, Himmler had been button-holed by the blustering and hostile Guderian in the garden of the Reich Chancellery. The two men walked to and fro among the ruins and, though Hitler saw them, he did not interfere. Guderian begged Himmler to go to Hitler and demand a discussion on surrender terms. Himmler refused with the words, 'Dear general, it is still too early', to which Guderian retorted, 'It is no longer five minutes to twelve but five minutes past. If we don't negotiate now it will be useless.' And Guderian comments, 'There was nothing to be done with this man. He was afraid of Hitler'.[2]

But Guderian did not know that in his own devious way Himmler had been trying to negotiate for the past two months. Early in February Hitler himself had approved of an approach to the Western Allies on the basis of a memorandum of Ribbentrop's. It was a threat to hand Germany over to the Russians. Alternatively Germany would surrender to the West but transfer all her troops to the East to stem the Bolshevist flood. The National Socialist Government would resign; the persecution of Jews and political opponents would cease.

The ridiculous proposal was actually submitted to the Swiss government and the Vatican, both of whom declined to intervene.

[1] Von Oven, op. cit., II, pp. 252-4.   [2] Guderian, op. cit., p. 387.

From Switzerland Ambassador von Schmieden reported that much stronger assurances from the SS on the matter of Jews and concentration camps would be needed before any emissary could make contact with the enemy.[1] Only Himmler could give this assurance. Ribbentrop is said to have seen Himmler on 15 February—presumably at Hohenlychen. A week had passed since Hitler's order to evacuate the concentration camps before they fell into Allied hands, and Himmler professed himself ready to ignore this order. Himmler had in fact been in negotiation with the Swiss Red Cross since the end of January on a proposal of Karl Burckhardt's to put the concentration camps under International Red Cross inspection.[2]

On 2 February Swiss Red Cross officials had actually been admitted to the concentration-camp inspectorate at Oranienburg, but the publication in the Swiss Press on 6 February of the arrival of a train from Bergen-Belsen had, as we have seen, disrupted these negotiations.[3] But Ribbentrop's interest in the concentration-camp plan enabled Himmler to recover from some of the fright caused by his scene with Hitler. At any rate, Himmler approved of Ribbentrop's dispatch of Fritz Hesse to Stockholm on 17 February.

In Stockholm Hesse spent three weeks in fruitless and misguided interviews, and on 13 March the British Press published Hesse's peace proposals in all their ridicule. Hesse, however, had made a number of contacts and one of them is interesting. He had seen Dr. Hillel Storsch, the Stockholm representative of World Jewish Congress, who knew a great deal about Schellenberg and Becher and their bartering of bodies. Storsch was astonished to learn from Hesse that Himmler would act with the Foreign Office in a plan to hand over *all* the Jews in German-held territory, or alternatively to put them under neutral protection.[4] Storsch was incredulous and with good reason. For, before Hesse's return to Germany, the first news reached him of the incredible conditions at Belsen.

On 17 March, having returned from Stockholm, Hesse had an interview with Ribbentrop who, he found, had come to mistrust Himmler too much to join him in any negotiation without Hitler's knowledge. The interview between Himmler and Bernadotte on 18 February had annoyed Ribbentrop, because Himmler had discussed

[1] Fritz Hesse, *Hitler and the English*, p. 199.
[2] *Documents sur l'activite du CIRC en faveur des detenus civils* (Geneva, 1946), p. 94.   [3] See *supra*, p. 357.   [4] Hesse, op. cit., p. 204.

Ribbentrop's plan for the protection of the surviving Jews as if it was his own.[1] Ribbentrop correctly identified the hand of Schellenberg in this affair and he believed that it was Himmler's intention, if the West recognised him as a negotiator, to get rid of Ribbentrop and put Schellenberg in his position.

Henceforward Ribbentrop abandoned his faintly awakened interest in concentration camps, about which he had never felt a minute's concern in all his years of office. Himmler, however, found his interest in the plan rekindled by his father-confessor. For some months past Himmler had permitted Felix Kersten to practise his craft in Stockholm, where Kersten had heard from Hillel Storsch of the reports from Belsen. Kersten flew back to Germany early in March and saw the invalid of Hohenlychen. Himmler was very difficult at first. Hitler had told him that the concentration-camp inmates must not survive liberation by the Allies to emerge as victors. They must share the collapse of Germany.[2] However, on 10 March Himmler sent a circular to Kaltenbrunner, Pohl and Gluecks, as well as to Grawitz the medical inspector, demanding measures against the typhus epidemic at Belsen. Finally, on 12 March Himmler defied Hitler's secret order of February. He decided that the camps should be surrendered intact on the approach of the enemy, and that the Jews in the camp should have equality of treatment with other internees—for what that was worth in the conditions of 1945. By 17 March Himmler had been persuaded by Kersten to receive a visit from Hillel Storsch or some other representative of World Jewish Congress. Kersten left again for Stockholm on the 22nd.[3]

On 21 March Himmler, still an invalid at Hohenlychen and still the Commander-in-Chief of the Oder front, wrote in person to Hillel Storsch, a letter from the omnipotent Reichsfuehrer to a Jew. It was a ridiculous letter, full of the carefully thought-out phrases which Himmler was to repeat, parrot-fashion, to Norbert Masur four weeks later. The release of 2,700 Jews to Switzerland in three trains had been, according to Himmler, nothing but a continuation of his work to assist Jewish emigration which he had begun in 1936.[4] As to the Belsen typhus epidemic, he was already taking the proper steps.

---

[1] Hesse, op. cit., p. 216.   [2] Kersten, *Totenkopf und Treue*, p. 342.
[3] Kersten, *Totenkopf und Treue*, p. 351.
[4] *Memoirs of Felix Kersten*, p. 228; and see *supra*, p. 361.

On 23 March Karl Burckhardt of the International Red Cross went in person to the headquarters of RSHA and interviewed 'Gestapo Mueller'. He was told that Belsen would be given up and that the Jews in German territory would be taken to another camp where relief could be distributed.[1] Yet, even now, not a single concentration camp had been opened to Red Cross inspection and at Belsen trainloads of Jews kept pouring in from all camps. Nothing whatever had been done to provide more food or medical care. On 19 March Oswald Pohl, accompanied by Hoess, brought Himmler's new instructions to Captain Jakob Kramer of the SS, the camp commandant. More than sixty thousand concentration-camp inmates from all over Germany had reached Belsen and, as Hoess recollected at Nuremberg, 'tens of thousands of corpses lay everywhere'.[2] And yet transports continued to arrive in Belsen till the first week in April. Someone, possibly Eichmann but more probably the jealous and crazy Kaltenbrunner, was sabotaging Himmler's well-laid plan to become a mediating angel.

Such, then, was the situation on 22 March when General Heinrici came to Prenzlau to relieve Himmler of his military duties. Himmler was afraid to reveal his game even to Guderian, and still more was he afraid to approach Hitler. But he had begun to build up a position abroad, starting with Count Bernadotte and Hillel Storsch. If he could still achieve some form of international protecting power for the Jews in Germany, following the lines of the 'protected Jews' in Budapest, Himmler believed that the Western Allies would recognise him as a peace emissary. He was such a practised self-delusionist that he failed to see, right up to the moment of his suicide at Lueneburg, that the Allies knew him only as a mass murderer.

Full of this idea, Himmler had a considerably longer interview with Count Bernadotte in Hohenlychen Hospital on April 2nd. This time Himmler asked the Count for his good offices with General Eisenhower, but the reply was that nothing could be done unless Himmler himself established an interregnum government in Germany.[3] But Himmler had not reached this point. He refused to treat with Count Bernadotte as if he were *de facto* head of the state until Hitler had announced that he would never emerge again from

---

[1] International Red Cross, *Documents der l'activité du CIRC en faveur des detenus civils* 1939-1945, pp. 97.

[2] Reitlinger, op. cit., pp. 463-4; Nuremberg Document D 749; affidavits of Hoess.   [3] Bernadotte, op. cit., pp. 97-103.

the Reich Chancellery bunker. That is to say, not until 24 April.

Till then Himmler kept his oath to Hitler after his fashion. He resisted the persistent prompting of Schellenberg, who wanted him to murder or depose his Fuehrer. He indulged instead in the wishful thought that Hitler would die soon enough for him to save Germany. And with Himmler this was quite an old self-delusion. As long ago as December 1942, he had shown Kersten an elaborate case-history which explained Hitler's recurrent throat polyp, the hysteric blindness from which he suffered in Paswalk military hospital in the First World War, the trembling left arm and dragging left foot which had become apparent long before Hitler was blown up. Naturally there could be only one explanation in the medical jurisprudence of Himmler's information service: Hitler was a syphilitic who would become progressively paralysed.[1]

Himmler has been accused in the still unpublished diary of Walter Schellenberg of trying to murder Hitler in the Reich Chancellery bunker and Willi Hoettl has repeated his former chief's charges.[2] Schellenberg was struck with the positive assurance with which Himmler declared to Count Bernadotte on 24 April that Hitler would die in a day or two of a cerebral hæmorrhage and he linked this in the knowing manner of the Gestapo with the presence in the bunker of a surgeon whom Himmler had recommended to Hitler's notice, Ludwig Stumpfegger. But Fritz Hesse had learnt about this hæmorrhage from one of Himmler's adjutants as early as 18 March.[3] The explanation may be as follows. Himmler had been told by a certain Professor de Crinis of the Charité Hospital in Berlin that Hitler's movements, as shown in news films, suggested Parkinson's disease. Himmler may have supposed that, if you had that, you were sure to die of a cerebral hæmorrhage. In reality Stumpfegger, who replaced Karl Brandt, was far from a mystery figure or a paid assassin. From his arrival at Rastenburg in September 1944 Hitler took strongly to him and it is doubtful whether Stumpfegger even observed for Himmler. Mr. Trevor-Roper has adequately disposed of this romantic hypothesis.[4]

If Himmler made no efforts to get rid of Hitler, it may be wondered what he did between his retirement from Army Group Vistula on 22 March and his armistice proposals to Count Bernadotte on 29 April, five weeks of chaos in which all Himmler's offices and the

---

[1] *Memoirs of Felix Kersten*, p. 194.   [2] Trevor-Roper, op. cit., p. 147.
[3] Hesse, op. cit., p. 216.   [4] Trevor-Roper, op. cit., p. 97.

Reich itself fell to pieces. The answer is that he did very little. He stayed in the country north of Berlin, hovering between Hohenlychen Hospital and the country house, Schloss Zieten, near Jastrow. He tried to get medical reports on Hitler but, ever since the unhappy scene of 13 February, 'The Last Victory of the General Staff', Himmler avoided audiences with Hitler. He tried to continue his role as mediator with the International Red Cross and he listened to Schellenberg, Schwerin von Krosigk and other tempters.

Himmler was also Minister of the Interior, Chief of Police and Reichsfuehrer of the SS. He may even have considered interesting himself in some of these duties while waiting to become the hero of an honourable peace. He certainly continued to sign orders of the most bellicose kind. On 14 April a brand-new Himmler Order was intercepted and it appeared in the Intelligence summary of the 1st Canadian Army. In it Himmler declared that field commanders who failed to hold German towns, together with civilian officials who abetted their treachery or negligence, would be punished with death, the only punishment Himmler now recognised.[1] One may wonder in what capacity Himmler gave this order. As Commander-in-Chief of the Replacement Army he had no authority over any commanders in action against the enemy. Presumably this was a decree issued in Himmler's dual capacity of Minister of the Interior and Chief of Police. It is certain that many such executions took place in pursuance of the sentences of Himmler's Standgerichte. These were emergency courts which any SS commander, who happened to be on the spot, was entitled to set up. Such was the court with which Max Simon, commanding the 16th SS division, carried out the iniquitous Brettheim executions of 7 April, the subject of another trial held as late as October 1955. Such were the Standgerichte which were set up in Berlin during the final battle under the commander of Himmler's bodyguard, the SS Major-General Wilhelm Mohnke.[2] They were the last signs of Himmler's administrative activity.

In the meantime another high SS dignitary tried to negotiate surrender, but with the good sense to see that Himmler must be kept out of it at all costs. This was Karl Wolff, formerly Himmler's liaison officer with Hitler and now military governor of Northern Italy. Early in February Wolff obtained access through the Abwehr to Mr. Allen Dulles in Zurich. At first Wolff sent Colonel Eugen

[1] Shulman, op. cit., pp. 280, 429; and see *infra*, p. 450.
[2] See *supra*, p. 411, and *infra*, p. 439.

Doltmann,[1] his liaison officer with Field-Marshal Kesselring, the Commander-in-Chief in Italy. Early in March, having achieved a passive consent from Kesselring, Wolff went to Zurich in person. The terms were simple and such as need not conflict with the unconditional surrender formula of Casablanca. The Germans would put up a purely token resistance in the Po Valley if the Allies would refrain from bombing civilian targets in North Italy. The Alpine Redoubt would not be defended, since the surrender of all the available forces would take place in the Italian plain. Almost the only other condition asked for—and it served Himmler's former adjutant in good stead after the war—was immunity from criminal prosecution for the negotiators. Mussolini, whose person Wolff was supposed to guard and protect, was not included in the deal. He was not even informed. [2]

On 11 March Field-Marshal Alexander learnt of the offer and, a week later, Generals Lyman Lemnitzer and Terence Airey arrived incognito in Switzerland. They were to meet Kesselring's emissaries at Berne and discuss with them the preliminaries for an armistice conference which would be held at Allied headquarters in Caserta. It was this incident which caused the disastrous misunderstanding with Stalin, that embittered the last days of President Roosevelt's life. Mr. Molotov wanted to send three Russian officers to Berne to take part in the first talks. With astonishing lack of tact the Combined Allied Chiefs of Staff turned down the request because the Russians were to be invited to Caserta, where the real negotiations were to take place. As might have been expected, there followed a crescendo of Russian accusations that peace talks with the Germans had been undertaken without consulting them. The climax was a personal note from Stalin to Roosevelt, declaring that Germany had been offered easier peace terms by Britain and the U.S.A. in return for Kesselring's military assistance. Kesselring, be it noted, had never been an active partner in Wolff's missions and would certainly not have negotiated at all so long as Hitler was alive. On 11 April, after a further exchange of notes, Roosevelt thought it expedient to write to Stalin that he was glad the unfortunate incident was over. Stalin never withdrew his charge. [3]

It is not true, however, that the Russian accusations caused the Combined Allied Chiefs of Staff to abandon the negotiations. The

---

[1] See *supra*, p. 191.   [2] Rahn, op. cit., pp. 282-3.
[3] James Byrnes, *Speaking Frankly*, London, 1947, p. 57.

two Allied generals waited in Switzerland till the end of the month, but no German emissaries appeared, even though Kesselring had been superseded by the far more pacifist General Scheel von Vietinghoff. Some version of the surrender offer had leaked out in Germany. Rahn was recalled by Ribbentrop and Wolff by Himmler. Wolff, it seems, had attracted Himmler's suspicion by writing a letter, reminding him that his duty was to Germany and not to 'a single individual'.[1] Wolff denied to Himmler the nature of his negotiations and pretended that he had been concerned only with an exchange of prisoners as a tactical game to drive a breach between the Allies and the Russians—and this at least Himmler could believe and approve. But on Hitler's instructions Himmler had to forbid Wolff to undertake any more journeys to Switzerland.

According to Hoettl, it was Kaltenbrunner who denounced Wolff's negotiations to Himmler. Kaltenbrunner had charge of the Red Cross negotiations with Karl Burckhardt concerning the concentration camps, and Himmler insisted that Wolff must regulate his alleged exchange of prisoners with Kaltenbrunner. But with that unsavoury character Dulles had no desire to traffic. And so the two Allied generals waited in Switzerland in vain and Field-Marshal Alexander opened his offensive in North Italy.

It was now a straight fight between two members of the SS Higher Command, Kaltenbrunner and Wolff. At the end of March Himmler made Kaltenbrunner Chief of Security in the southern half of the Reich in order to prepare the 'mountain redoubt'. But Kaltenbrunner was suspected by Himmler of negotiating on his own account, so he sent Gottlob Berger to Innsbruck to double Kaltenbrunner's functions and to watch him.[2]

In this propitious state of anarchy Wolff tried to renew the negotiations. On 25 April he returned to Switzerland with two members of Vietinghoff's staff who were flown on to Caserta. But Kesselring came back to take command in Italy, deposed Vietinghoff and appointed Kaltenbrunner in Wolff's place as military governor. Wolff threatened to defend his headquarters with armoured cars if his SS colleague Kaltenbrunner came to Verona. At Vietinghoff's headquarters there were arrests and counter-arrests and, amid the glorious chaos of *Untergang*, Wolff had his last telephone conversation with Himmler at Hohenlychen on 27 or 28 April. With that burning passion for the inessential which had now completely

[1] Rahn, op. cit., p. 285.   [2] Hoettl, *The Secret Front, p.* 294.

mastered the Reichsfuehrer, Himmler demanded angrily to know how Wolff had dared evacuate his wife and children from St. Wolfgang in Austria. It was a very bad example for a higher SS police leader to set. 'Wolffchen' must bring them back at once.[1]

But two days later Hitler was dead and Kesselring, like Himmler himself, was relieved of his oath. On 2 May he allowed Vietinghoff to conduct the surrender of the army of Italy according to the protocol agreed at Caserta three days earlier. It can be said that Wolff's negotiation, which earned him so much credit with the Allies, had not shortened the fighting by a single day.

We return now to Germany. On 7 March the collapse of the Western Front had begun when the Americans obtained an intact bridge over the Rhine at Remagen. On 22 March, the day of Himmler's resignation from the Vistula Army Group, this bridgehead was thirty miles deep and threated to roll up the rest of the Rhine front. After the British crossings of the Rhine in the Wesel area on the 23rd there was no cohesive front left in the West. And by the end of the month the eastward-moving columns had surrounded the Ruhr. On 16 April, when the long calm on the Oder front was at last broken by an almost unopposed Russian drive towards Berlin, British patrols were sixty-five miles from that city and the Americans were at Nuremberg. In the Ruhr Model's encircled army group was in the process of surrender.

On the Eastern front, however, nothing had happened for the past month except for the capitulation, far behind the lines, of the long-beleaguered cities of Danzig and Koeningsberg. In this way it came about that, while the American Ninth Army reached the demarcation line on the Elbe on the 11th, a whole fortnight passed before they made contact with the Russians. Many reasons have been sought for this, ranging from sinister deals between Stalin and Hitler down to plain Slav procrastination, but in fact the Russian delay was tactically sound. Since the Russians welcomed no Allied assistance within their demarcation lines, it was to their advantage to delay the final struggle till the Allied advance had left fewer Germans to face their front.

The Allied advance to the Elbe and the Czechoslovak border in the first three weeks of April overwhelmed the three largest and most overcrowded of the German concentration camps, Belsen, Buchenwald and Dachau. Into these three camps alone were packed

[1] *Mittag*, 17 May 1946; narrative of a former Intelligence officer.

more than a quarter of the surviving *Haeftlinge*. Nothing that the
Western world read about concentration camps could equal what
British and American soldiers were to see with their own eyes. And
this had clearly been foreseen by Goebbels. On 5 April Wilfrid von
Oven noted this observation of his master.[1]

I fear that the concentration camps have grown a bit above Himmler's head.
Just suppose that these camps should be overrun by the enemy in their present
condition. What an outcry will be heard. Even among our own people no one
will speak any more of the advantages derived from them by the greater part of
the German nation; for instance that since 1933 and throughout the war there
were no disturbances in Germany, no strikes, no sedition, no rowdyism, no Jews
and no gipsies; that the man in the street could live more freely and more tran-
quilly than ever before. Instead they will point at bestial Nazis, without reflecting
that all these atrocities were necessary to the war and practically inevitable as the
price of their own tranquillity.

It may be thought that Goebbels was unduly pessimistic about
German reactions to the freeing of the camps. It may be thought
that the smug postwar pleas of *ignoramus* by the leaders of German
society were an acknowledgment in themselves of the advantages of
concentration camps. But in one respect Goebbels was right.
Himmler had underestimated the outcry among the enemy. Himmler
was to learn of the rejection of his surrender terms with genuine
disappointment, but, many days before he received that news, the
Allied newspapers had told him that he was the most execrated man
in the world. Although he could not bring himself to believe it, one
result of that undesired publicity was a reversal of Himmler's policy.
As he told Norbert Masur, he had handed Belsen to the Allies intact
but he 'got no thanks for it'.[2] On the approach therefore of the
Russians to Berlin, he ordered the evacuation of Ravensbrueck and
Sachsenhausen camps, leaving only the bedridden sick. It was not
till 3 May, three days after Hitler's death, that the last survivors of
the notorious Sachsenhausen death march reached the British lines
at Schwerin.

There were cogent enough reasons why Himmler did not want
the Russians to inspect another Lublin or Auschwitz, but his final
action in regard to the concentration camps lacked even this degree
of consistency. What happened was determined entirely by circumstance. Belsen was handed over to the British intact and closely
cordoned, because the military commanders dared not let loose

[1] Von Oven, op. cit., II, pp. 287-9.
[2] Norbert Masur, *En Jude talar med Himmler* (Stockholm, 1946).

fifty-five thousand potential typhus cases on the countryside. On the other hand, more than half the forty-eight thousand inmates of Buchenwald were evacuated and left to starve for days on end in sealed trains which wandered aimlessly over the bombed Reich railway system. And this took place between 3 April and 10 April, when Himmler was supposed to be keeping his word with the International Red Cross. On 24 April, when the Americans overran Dachau, Himmler no longer felt bound to honour his agreement, but the mass evacuation towards the Alpine redoubt had already been stopped by Gottlob Berger.

Hitler had told Pister, who was in command of the camps in the south, that Dachau, Mauthausen and Theresienstadt were to be blown up together with their inhabitants if they could not be evacuated before the arrival of the Allies,[1] but in fact there was little will left to carry out such orders. Schellenberg and Becher agreed in their depositions that the evacuation of 28,285 inmates of Buchenwald, most of them Jews from Poland and Hungary, was ordered by Kaltenbrunner without Himmler's knowledge and that Himmler stopped it on a complaint by the Swiss President, M. Musi, whose son arrived to inspect the camp while evacuation was in full swing.[2]

On 10 April, when Himmler allegedly telephoned Buchenwald to stop the evacuations, the SS guards were already leaving and the illegal prisoners' committee was about to take over the camp. It seems therefore unlikely that Himmler seriously intervened to stop the evacuation or that it had been ordered without his knowledge by Kaltenbrunner. For Kaltenbrunner had no motive for seeing that Hitler's murderous order was carried out. He wanted to get Himmler out of the way and save his own hide by stepping into Himmler's place as the recognised mediator with the International Red Cross. That Kaltenbrunner should have given orders for the bombing and mining of Dachau and Mauthausen is even more improbable. The story that he intended to bomb Dachau from the air reposes on the affidavit of an assistant of the Munich Gauleiter, Paul Giesler, who

---

[1] In Eugen Kogon's view, Pister only carried out the terrible evacuations from Buchenwald under pressure from the higher SS and police leader, Prince Waldeck-Pyrmont who had persistently sheltered the worst Buchenwald criminals. The Prince received a life sentence. Pister committed suicide (Eugen Kogon, *The Theory and Practice of Hell*, p. 256).

[2] IMT III, p. 295; Document NG 2675; affidavit of Becher.

was himself an implicated man. The plan, which was typical of the brutish and drunken Gauleiterschaft in the last days of the collapsing Reich, was almost certainly Giesler's.[1]

The Mauthausen case is on the same footing. A Red Cross observer, the Swiss M. Haefliger, had been finally allowed to stay in the camp. Somewhere between 23 April and 8 May M. Haefliger learnt that the camp commandant, Ziereis, planned to blow up all the inmates in a subterranean aircraft-construction hanger at Gusen. Ziereis never attempted to put the plan into action. He disguised himself and hid in the camp, and was shot after the liberation while trying to get away. In a dying testimony, taken down by a camp inmate in the presence of American officers who spoke no German, Ziereis denounced Kaltenbrunner as the author of the Gusen plan. In fact Kaltenbrunner had signed an order that the camp should be handed over intact to Patton's troops.[2]

No concentration camp was destroyed with its inmates, yet the death marches from Ravensbrueck and Sachsenhausen, the ghost trains from Buchenwald and even the blowing up of the Gusen hanger, had it ever taken place, could not have equalled the horror of Belsen, where Himmler's officials tried to hand over a concentration camp intact and in an orderly manner. On 15 April the British troops found thirteen thousand corpses in camp Number 1. The number who had died in Belsen since February and the first typhus outbreak was hardly less than forty thousand. They had not been exterminated, nor was their death due to Allied bombing which had paralysed the railways and disrupted the German supply system. The evidence at the Lueneburg Trial showed that the bakeries and flour stores of the Panzergrenadier School at Bergen-Belsen could have kept the uninfected inmates of the camp alive for many weeks, had authority been given to use them.[3] Forty thousand people died in Belsen as a result of twelve years of tolerated incompetence in the overblown offices of Oswald Pohl and Richard Gluecks.[4]

In between the Buchenwald and Belsen revelations Schellenberg tried to stir Himmler into action again. Kersten had been in Stockholm since 22 March but still there was no permit for an emissary of

[1] IMT III, p. 241.

[2] IMT, PS 3870 and International Red Cross, *Documents*, etc. (Geneva, 1946), p. 134.   [3] *The Belsen Trial* (London, 1948), p. 178.

[4] Oswald Pohl was hanged in Landsberg prison in June 1951. Gluecks disappeared before the end of the war and has never been traced.

World Jewish Congress to visit Himmler. On 13 April, when app-
roached by Schellenberg, Himmler said, 'But how am I going to do
that with Kaltenbrunner about? I shall be completely at his mercy.'[1]
Yet four days later Himmler authorised the journey of Dr. Norbert
Masur and on 19 April, in earshot of the Russian guns, the first
Jew to pay an official visit to the rulers of Germany landed at
Tempelhof airport. Dr. Masur had no passport, but a special pass
signed by Schellenberg awaited him, together with a police guard.
The guard halted by the aeroplane, clicked their heels and shouted
'Heil Hitler!' The passenger politely removed his hat and bade them
Good-day. Kersten and Masur then drove to Kersten's property at
Harzwalde, forty miles north of Berlin, but Himmler did not arrive
till half past two in the morning of the 21st.[2]

Himmler arrived straight from Hitler's presence. Besides aug-
menting the irony of the situation, the fact was important in other
respects. It was Hitler's official birthday dinner-party, celebrated by
as many high dignitaries as could be squeezed into the Reich Chancellery bunker. After dinner there was a conference, where it was
decided who should stay in Berlin and who should move to the new
headquarters in the south, for already the Russians were shelling the
city and at any moment the land corridor between the Eastern and
Western fronts would be closed. Hitler had not yet decided to remain
in Berlin and Himmler was one of those who pressed him to go to
Bavaria.[3]

Himmler's conversation with Kersten and Masur lasted till daylight. He was not in the least exhausted, and Masur found him
fresh and lively, quiet and self-possessed, evidently a different
Himmler to that described by Colonel Eismann. The end of his
military career had done him good. But it is difficult to believe that
Himmler thought he was fooling the man who sat opposite him.
He must have been fooling himself. And what was Himmler trying
to achieve? Dr. Masur had taken an enormous personal risk in the
hope that Pharaoh might relent and let the survivors of his people
go. Yet Himmler, who took a risk almost as great as Masur's, struck
no bargain and demanded no concession. The most that he could
seek from this journey into the night were a few good-conduct marks
with the conquerors to offset his huge notoriety.

---

[1] Nuremberg Document PS 2990; affidavit of Schellenberg.
[2] Masur, op. cit.; Kersten, *Totenkopf und Treue*, p. 271.
[3] Trevor-Roper, op. cit., p. 120.

Dr. Masur asked formally for the evacuation to Sweden and Switzerland of the Jews in the remaining camps, or, if they were too far from the frontier, their delivery to the Allies in good health and without further movements from camp to camp. According to Himmler's figures there might still be seventy-five thousand Jews, distributed between Ravensbrueck, Theresienstadt and Mauthausen. After withdrawing for twenty minutes with Schellenberg and Rudi Brandt, Himmler came out with an offer for the release of a thousand Jewesses in Ravensbrueck to Sweden and a rather larger number of Dutch Jews in Theresienstadt to Switzerland, the International Red Cross providing the transport.

Dr. Masur returned to Sweden with little confidence in the outcome, but two days later Himmler permitted the Swedish Red Cross lorries to remove seven thousand women from Ravensbrueck, about half of them Jewish. It seems that Himmler had gone straight to Hohenlychen Hospital, which was close to Kersten's property, and there breakfasted with Count Bernadotte, with whom he arranged the details.[1] At this interview Himmler made no attempt to seek Bernadotte's intervention with the Western powers, for Hitler had not announced his approaching self-immolation and Himmler was still a frightened man.

2. HIMMLER'S TREACHERY, AND THE DEATH OF HITLER

Himmler's dismissal from the command of the Vistula Army Group on 22 March had been followed in a few days by that of Guderian. The occasion was the arrival of General Busse at the Reich Chancellery to report the impossibility of relieving Reinefarth's four SS battalions in Kuestrin. When Hitler abused Busse to his face, Guderian interrupted. There was a famous hysterical screaming match, which terminated in Guderian's going off to a sanatorium at Ebenhausen and the servile Hans Krebs taking his place.[2]

With Guderian's departure Hitler had no soldier to take his orders, save the yes-men, the 'last-ditchers', Krebs and Burgdorf, Keitel and Jodl. Though these four men could get no intelligible

---

[1] Bernadotte, op. cit., p. 102.
[2] Juergen Thorwald, *Das Ende an die Elbe* (Thorwald II), p. 37; Guderian, op. cit., p. 389.

instructions out of the Reich Chancellery bunker, they strove, like some industrious and totally blind species of insect, to see that all orders, however contradictory, should be followed and that all gestures of independence should be punished. Not one army group or army commander shared the confidence that these four men professed in their Fuehrer, not even Schoerner in Silesia, for the 'bloodhound' was in the secret of Karl Wolff's negotiations and was already planning to avoid personal capture by the Russians;[1] not even Felix Steiner who, since the dismissal of Paul Hausser and the insult delivered to Sepp Dietrich, was the only SS general to have Hitler's confidence. Steiner on the contrary was surrounded by a circle of resentful SS Obergruppenfuehrers who talked quite openly of a plan to kill Hitler and put Himmler in his place.[2]

Accounts of the last days of Hitler tend to present a picture of dark night and utter chaos in which Hitler fought non-existent battles in his deep shelter, while the armed forces of Germany wriggled helplessly like a catch of fish in a huge net. It is not quite a true picture, for inside the contracting net there was some element of design or rather there were two conflicting designs. The official strategy, which was transmitted from Hitler through Jodl almost to the hour of his death, was to relieve Berlin from the south-west and the north-east. But the army commanders were concerned that their men should surrender to the Western Allies rather than to the Russians, so that they tended to bypass Berlin. The battle of Berlin was fought by a force, not as big as a normal German army corps, which had been detached from the Army Group Vistula.[3] This force received no support from the Wenck and Steiner armies which failed to converge on Berlin, because Hitler's desire for a last battle in the capital meant their delivery to the Russians.

[1] Hoettl, op. cit., p. 293; Thorwald, II, pp. 363-7.

[2] Trevor-Roper, op. cit., p. 186.

[3] The troops who defended Berlin consisted of Mummert's LVIIth Corps of two under-strength Wehrmacht divisions, and the remains of the SS volunteer division Nordland, to which was attached a French battalion, part of a projected SS French volunteer division, named Charlemagne. On the day before his death Hitler awarded three Knight's Crosses to Frenchmen who fought an action within a few hundred yards of the Reich Chancellery. Mohnke's SS battalion, dispatched by Himmler at the last moment, was known as the Ersatztruppen and formed a separate command. It may be remembered that the Russian broadcasts described the battle in Berlin as the greatest of the war, yet it is doubtful whether the Germans could muster twenty-five thousand trained men apart from half-armed Volkssturm and Hitlerjunge (see Kraetschmer, op. cit., p. 411, etc.).

In this dual design it is almost impossible to make any sense out of the movements of the armies, and indeed these movements are less interesting than the conflicts of personality in Hitler's Reich. The last stage of Himmler's career and the last role of the SS can only be presented like the battles in Shakespeare's plays. The stage direction reads, 'Another part of the field', and the characters meet in front of a stage backcloth, from behind which there come the rumblings of a huge and complex Armageddon of which they seem no part.

We left Himmler breakfasting with Count Bernadotte at Hohenlychen on 21 April. On the following day Hitler learnt that the Russians had broken into the northern suburbs of Berlin and that Steiner had deliberately ignored Hitler's orders. Steiner's troops, a mere skeleton army consisting of the 3rd Marine Division and the 4th SS which had been reported at Eberswalde thirty miles northeast of the city, were avoiding Berlin by a retreat through Brandenburg. Hitler refused the advice of his military staff which was to go at once to Berchtesgaden, there to organise the resistance of the intact Schoerner and Kesselring army groups, while the northern plain of Europe was abandoned to the Russians and the Allies. Late that night Hitler announced that the whole of Germany had betrayed him and that he meant to die in Berlin.[1]

But, when the hysteria had subsided, it seemed that Hitler had a plan beyond merely immolating himself in the ruins of the Reich. Facing the Americans, who had halted voluntarily on the Elbe since 11 April, was a new reserve army, the Twelfth, under the command of General Wenck, who was to have led Himmler's offensive at the time of his motor accident. Wenck's army was composed of Volksgrenadiere divisions with grandiloquent names from German military history, but with scarcely any weapons except rifles and hand grenades. Having first ordered these divisions to face westwards where Model's army group had been encircled in the Ruhr,[2] Hitler now faced them towards the Russians so as to join the defenders of Berlin. Keitel and Jodl were to direct the operations in person. Thus the greater part of the staffs of OKW and OKH, instead of going southward where four-fifths of the German strength lay, had to stop as close to Berlin as the battle would permit. So next day the two generals left for Krampnitz, never to see Hitler or the Reich Chancellery again.

[1] Trevor-Roper, op. cit., p. 129.
[2] Narrative of General Heinrici, Thorwald, II, p. 75.

That night at Hohenlychen Fegelein brought Himmler the news of Hitler's decision. It could not have been a surprise to Himmler, for he had been in the ante-room of the Reich Chancellery on 16 April, when Schoerner was flown in from Sudetenland and he had learnt from the laconic and not very friendly 'bloodhound' that Hitler had refused his entreaty to join him in his headquarters.[1] But at Hohenlychen Himmler received the news in the presence of the ultra-loyal Gottlob Berger. Filled with Fuehrer-love, Berger implored Himmler to go with him to the Reich Chancellery and to send his own escort battalion of the Leibstandarte under Major-General Mohnke to join the defence of Berlin.

To the second proposal Himmler agreed, but to the first he pleaded illness. So Berger and Fegelein left for the Reich Chancellery without him. Having failed to persuade Hitler by telephone to go south, Himmler decided to hold another conference on the subject after Fegelein's return. For this purpose he drove to Nauen, halfway to Berlin. Fegelein did not return that night from the Reich Chancellery and Himmler sent Karl Gebhardt with further pledges of his loyalty. Himmler himself never saw Hitler again.

These were Himmler's movements on the fateful night of 22-23 April as checked by Mr. Trevor-Roper.[2] That Himmler waited at Nauen in order to hear the result of a poisoning attempt on Hitler may be dismissed as a fantasy of Schellenberg and Hoettl.[3] What else could Himmler have done but wait for Fegelein's report? It would have been madness to have gone to the Reich Chancellery bunker, from which every soldier and civilian with a grain of sense escaped that night. Whether or not the halt at Nauen was passed by Himmler in the dramatic agonies of doubt which Mr. Trevor-Roper describes, it enabled him to make up his mind. By breakfast time Fegelein and Gebhardt had rejoined Himmler at Hohenlychen and their report from the bunker convinced him that a matter of days or even of hours must see the Reich Chancellery—and Hitler in it—firmly cordoned off by Russian troops. Soon no order from Hitler would have any effect in the remains of the Reich. Himmler could now present himself to Bernadotte as a plenipotentiary who believed himself Hitler's legal successor. He was relieved of his terrible SS oath.

[1] Thorwald, II, p. 307, narrative of General Natzmer.
[2] Trevor-Roper, op. cit., pp. 134-9.   [3] Ibid., p. 47; Hagen, op. cit., p. 99.

At that very moment Schellenberg was with Bernadotte in Flensburg. He was charged with a message that Himmler would be willing to see General Eisenhower in person if Count Bernadotte could prepare the ground.[1] Bernadotte consented to see Himmler in the Swedish consulate at Luebeck, and there, late that night, in a candlelit shelter to the inevitable off-stage accompaniment of an air raid, Himmler made his offer.

So far as the Western Allies were concerned, the offer meant unconditional surrender, but on the front against the Russians Himmler would fight till his troops had been relieved by the Allies. Bernadotte gave Himmler no cause for optimism, but Himmler was calmly convinced that the Allies would treat him as a saviour of Europe from the hordes of Bolshevism. And in this mood Himmler spent the next five days waiting for the Allies' answer.

At first the omens seemed very propitious. At one moment during the theatrical session in the Reich Chancellery bunker on 22 April, Hitler had remarked, 'If it is a question of negotiating, Goering can do it better than I'. This had been repeated by Jodl to General Karl Koller, Chief of Staff of the Luftwaffe, and Koller had thought it his duty to fly to Berchtesgaden and inform Goering.[2] With the agreement of Lammers of the Reich Chancellery Goering drafted a telegram to be sent to Hitler. In this telegram Goering assumed that he was the chosen delegate for the powers that the immured Hitler no longer possessed. Goering proposed to use these powers, failing a reply from Hitler by ten o'clock that night. While Himmler was on the road to meet Bernadotte at Luebeck, this telegram exploded in the Reich Chancellery bunker. Bormann called it an ultimatum and a proof that Goering was plotting treason. Hitler sent telegrams ordering Goering's immediate arrest and his demission from office and from the succession. So, on his return from Luebeck, Himmler knew that there could be no other legal successor to Hitler but himself.

This was the morning of the 24th. Berlin was almost cut off from access to the south, though it was not till next day that the Americans and Russians met at Torgau on the Elbe. North-east of Berlin a Russian armoured thrust threatened to cut the city off from the Baltic as well. Himmler moved from Hohenlychen, which was dangerously near the advancing front, to Schwerin, where Admiral Doenitz had set up a new command headquarters known as the 'Nordraum'.

[1] Bernadotte, op. cit., pp. 105, 113.   [2] Trevor-Roper, op. cit., p. 140.

Awkwardly Hitler, though dedicated to death, refused to die. Up till 28 April, when communication was lost, orders still chased each other out of the Reich Chancellery. Keitel and Jodl kept moving their headquarters away from the Russians, from Zossen to Krampnitz, then to Fuerstenberg, then to Reinsberg, still trying to link the armies retreating from the Oder, the Ninth and the Eleventh, with the shadowy Twelfth of General Wenck moving north-east from the Elbe. The two generals raced about with great energy, tracing an imaginary semi-circle of defence with Berlin tucked inside it. Since the 20th Hitler had planned that General Felix Steiner should drive a passage between the Oder and Elbe armies and so keep the communications open between Berlin and the rest of the Reich and avert a blockade of the capital. But from the confusion of the various military narratives it seems to emerge that there never was a Steiner army except in Hitler's imagination, and that Steiner himself did not know where he was to attack or with what troops. Since the failure of his Stargard-Arnswalde offensive in February, Steiner had abandoned the SS creed of blind obedience to the Head of the State; a conversion all the more remarkable since Steiner, as the former Head of the Education Staff at the old War Office, had been responsible since 1934, more even than Paul Hausser, for the indoctrination courses of the Waffen SS. It seems, however, that Steiner, like Himmler, had persuaded himself in 1945 that the Western Allies would fight the Russians as soon as they made contact. For this purpose they would need the German army; therefore the quicker the German divisions escaped from the Eastern front to surrender to the West the better the chances. Early in April Steiner told Léon Degrelle that the British and Americans should be greeted with large hoardings declaring 'Here is the anti-Soviet Front'.[1]

Nevertheless, since the end of March Steiner had set up an army group staff at Oranienburg, with a view to the creation of a reserve army which was to defend Berlin when the Oder front gave way. On 21 April Hitler believed that the 'Steiner group' really existed and that it lay immediately north of Berlin, ready to roll up the Russian advance west of the Oder. In fact, as Steiner testified in captivity, the five divisions, which were promised him from Heinrici's Vistula army group, never reached him. Steiner's command consisted of the 4th SS Police Division, which had escaped from the siege of Danzig without its equipment, and a division composed of naval ratings.

[1] Degrelle, op. cit., p. 456.

Steiner was also given a few thousand men of the Luftwaffe ground staff from the Berlin area whom Hitler furiously ordered General Karl Koller, Goering's Chief of Staff, to dispatch to an army that did not exist. 'I refused,' Steiner declared, 'to use the indescribable bands of soldiers which had been so hurriedly assembled; I did not want to lose a single man in an enterprise which was doomed to crushing disaster from the beginning. The plan of attack had been established on bases which existed only in the imaginations of the Reich Chancellery Bunker.'[1]

Already, on 22 April, when Krebs explained to him that Steiner had received no reinforcements except the wretched unarmed Luftwaffe ground staff, Hitler had had an outburst against the SS. It was the occasion when he announced his decision to die in Berlin. So when Keitel and Jodl left the bunker, it was their task to make contact not only with Wenck but with Steiner. This Keitel succeeded in doing on the night of the 25th, when he ordered Steiner's so called IIIrd Corps, that is to say his only two organised divisions, to advance on Nauen. But Steiner made no attack. His small group was merely caught up in the westward migration of Heinrici's army group which swept towards the Allied lines leaving Berlin to its fate. Steiner, the former ultra-loyalist, acted no differently from any other general.[2] Keitel persevered. On the 28th he overtook Heinrici himself, seventy miles north of Berlin, and accused him of trying to deliver his troops to the Americans beyond the Elbe.[3] Keitel told Heinrici that he should have imitated the example of General Rendulic in Vienna and hanged a few thousand deserters. Heinrici says that he pointed to the practically unarmed columns on the road with the words, 'Herr Feldmarschall, if you want to shoot them please begin'.[4] Keitel then had a Hitlerian outburst in the middle of the road and threatened Heinrici with execution. Heinrici was, in

[1] Steiner's interrogation in Georges Blond, *L'agonie de l'Allemagne* (Paris, 1952), p. 287. Koller describes his orders from Hitler in *Der Letzte Monat* (Mannheim, 1949), pp. 21-7. Gerhard Boldt, ADC to Krebs, adds the interesting detail that in conference on 23 April Hitler declared, 'I have no use for these dull, undecided SS leaders. In no circumstances whatever do I want Steiner to be in command' (*In the Shelter with Hitler* (London, 1948, p. 52).

[2] Kraetschmer in an endeavour to save Steiner's reputation says that before retreating to the American lines on the Elbe he attempted an attack towards Kremmen on 1 May, the day of Hitler's death (*Die Ritterkreuztraeger der Waffen SS*, p. 22). [3] J. Schultz, Die *letzten dreizig Tage* (Stuttgart, 1951), p. 46.

[4] Narrative of General Heinrici in Thorwald, II, p. 198.

fact, superseded that night by the Luftwaffe parachute-troop General, Kurt Student, as if such changes could any longer mean anything.

But in Hitler's eyes it was the corps nearest Berlin that bore the full responsibility for treachery and disobedience. Moreover, the commander of this corps belonged to the discredited SS who had failed him in Hungary and whom he had disgraced. One of Hitler's orders to Keitel which never got through, was that Steiner should be replaced by Holste, a corps commander in Wenck's army. On the 27th Himmler sent the last of the famous 'Fuehrerbefehle' which by passed the High Command. It was addressed to the 25th Panzer Grenadier Division which was to join Holste's corps because Hitler had lost faith in Steiner.[1]

It is unlikely that Himmler had anything to do with Steiner's action, which was no different from that of other corps and army commanders. But when Hitler learnt of Himmler's negotiations, he assumed that Steiner had taken Himmler's orders and this belief was responsible for an incredible last act of savagery, Hitler's execution of Fegelein in the garden of the Reich Chancellery.[2] Far from giving Steiner tactical orders, Himmler had had enough of meddling in military operations for many weeks past, but it was a fact that on 28 April he attended one of Keitel's last staff conferences at Reinsberg. It was also a fact that Himmler sat in the chair which should normally have been occupied by Hitler, because he took it for granted that he was Hitler's personal deputy and successor. Yet by the following midnight Hitler had ordered Himmler's arrest as well as Goering's.

The news of Himmler's negotiations with Count Bernadotte had been released that morning and had appeared in a Reuter's dispatch from San Francisco, which had not failed to mention the cerebral hæmorrhage of which Himmler expected Hitler to die. Hitler might not have known of it but for one of his few remaining contacts with the outside world, Otto Dietrich's Press Ministry, for the news was brought to the bunker at nine o'clock that night by Dietrich's liaison officer, Heinz Lorenz.[3]

Himmler himself had learnt through Schellenberg on the previous day that his overtures had been rejected, but had not been unduly disheartened. Himmler still continued to discuss his plans for ruling Germany with one whom he regarded as essential to his

---

[1] Schultz, op. cit., p. 39.   [2] Trevor-Roper, op. cit., p. 185.
[3] Trevor-Roper, op. cit., p. 79.

cabinet, in spite of his dislike of his person. This was Ohlendorf, the head of the SD.[1] Apparently, too, Doenitz as military governor of the Nordraum had accepted Himmler's succession as inevitable. Still, at five twenty that afternoon Doenitz telephoned Himmler at Reinsberg asking for information on the English story about his negotiations. Himmler answered that the Grand Admiral had already been told that the news was false, but that he, Himmler, would order no counter-declaration on the wireless. He would simply ignore the report.[2]

Thus, between midnight on the 28th and the afternoon of 30 April, while the tremendous final drama played itself out in the Reich Chancellery bunker, Himmler lived in a realm of unreality. That had been Himmler's condition since the July plot had doubled the number of his offices and functions. Some may prefer to think that this realm of unreality dated from the days when the expense book of two hundred part-time SS men had provided something which the mind of the Waldtrudering poultry-keeper could encompass.

Hitler lived some forty hours after his first outburst of rage against Himmler's treachery, yet Himmler seems to have run very little risk of its consequences. Firstly Hitler entrusted the arrest of Himmler to the first person to leave the bunker, and then forgot about it. Secondly, all telephonic communication between the bunker and the outside world ceased within a few hours and thirdly Hitler's written testament did not reach Admiral Doenitz in time. Hitler entrusted the arrest of Himmler to Field-Marshal Ritter von Greim, Goering's successor as head of the Luftwaffe, who was urged by Hitler to see to it that 'a traitor shall never succeed me as Fuehrer'.

Von Greim reached Doenitz's headquarters at Ploen in Schleswig in the afternoon of the 29th, in a midget plane piloted by the woman aviator Hanna Reitsch. The latter actually encountered Himmler at Ploen and claims to have taxed him with his treachery. It is not clear, however, how soon this occurred after the arrival of Hanna Reitsch in Ploen.[3] Nor is it clear whether von Greim told Doenitz of Hitler's wishes. In any case it was a moment when Doenitz was too over-awed by Himmler's control of the police to dare arrest his person.

Hitler's will was drawn up in the early hours of the morning of the 29th, after von Greim's departure. It provided successors for Himmler. Karl Hanke was to be Reichsfuehrer SS and head of the

---

[1] Trevor-Roper, op. cit., p. 183.   [2] Schultz, op. cit., p. 48.
[3] Trevor-Roper, op. cit., pp. 187-9.

police, while Paul Giesler was to be Minister of the Interior. These men were the Gauleiters of Breslau and Munich, both notorious for their brutality and corruption, but neither was destined to succeed to office. Giesler, hunted by armed bands of Bavarian separatists, took his own life. Hanke flew from besieged Breslau ostensibly to take up his appointment with Doenitz in Flensburg, but in fact to find refuge at Schoerner's headquarters at Kronenberg and there to disguise himself. He is said to have been shot by the Czechs while escaping from arrest soon after the capitulation.[1]

Late that night Hitler sent Colonel Claus von Below, his Luftwaffe adjutant, through the Russian cordon with a postscript to his will, which was intended for Keitel, and even in this flood of reproaches there was no specific demand for Himmler's arrest.[2] At three-fifteen on the morning of the 30th Bormann sent Doenitz a telegram on his own account: 'The Fuehrer orders you to proceed immediately and mercilessly against all traitors, as fast as lightning and as true as steel'.[3] But the telegram did not mention Himmler by name and the implication of the wording was that the traitor was Keitel, who had failed to move the Wenck army into Berlin.

Such was the famous 'Bormann telegram', which can hardly have been intended to ruin Himmler, greatly though Bormann had wanted to do this when power still mattered. It was an ambiguous telegram which deliberately concealed from Doenitz his succession under Hitler's will. Bormann was playing some obscure game by which he hoped to secure his own position and he may have thought of playing Himmler against Doenitz. Even the telegram which Bormann dispatched in the afternoon, shortly after the burning of Hitler's body in the Reich Chancellery garden, though it spoke for the first time of Doenitz's nomination, failed to mention Hitler's death.[4] Bormann's last telegram of all was sent on the morning of 1 May before he set out to cross the Russian cordon to reach Doenitz in person. Something very secret was in the mind of the former ante-room king, who still would not admit Hitler's death. Mr. Trevor-Roper gives the text of the last telegram as follows:[5] 'Grand Admiral Doenitz. The testament is in force. I will join you as soon as possible. Till then I recommend the publication to be held up. Bormann.'

But Bormann never reached Admiral Doenitz. It was believed by

[1] Thorwald, II, p. 319; *Wiener Library Bulletin*, May-June 1949.
[2] Trevor-Roper, op. cit., p. 211.   [3] *Ibid.* p. 216
[4] Trevor-Roper, op. cit., p. 226.   [5] *Ibid.*, p. 228.

the counsel who represented him at Nuremberg that he had been blown to pieces when a Russian rocket hit the German tank which he had followed through the Ziegelstrasse. The same story was repeated by Hitler's valet, Heinz Linge, after his repatriation from Russia on 9 October 1955. Mr. Trevor-Roper, however, had an opportunity soon after the capitulation to interview another of the men who escaped from the bunker, Artur Axmann, the Hitler Youth leader. Axmann declared that he came upon Bormann's body in the Invalidenstrasse, north of the River Spree, hours after the alleged explosion. There were no signs of violence and he concluded that Bormann had taken poison.[1] There are still some survivors from the Reich Chancellery bunker in captivity in Russia who may one day cast further light on Bormann's last journey. That he is dead can no longer be doubted, and with Bormann's departure from this world there vanishes the clue to his last mysterious and frantic bid to survive in power politics. And part of that mystery is Himmler's immunity to Bormann's vendetta.

[1] Trevor-Roper, op. cit., footnote to p. 236.

16

Extinction

1. RETIREMENT AND DEATH OF THE REICHSFUEHRER

We must turn for a moment to the thunder behind the stage back-cloth. The loss of all telephone communication with the Reich Chancellery bunker on the morning of 29 April corresponded with a strategic fact. Wenck's Twelfth Army, which had at one moment made contact with the Potsdam garrison, was now desperately on the defensive and was being pushed away from Berlin. General Weidling, commanding the Berlin garrison, reported that night at the bunker that the Russians must occupy the Reich Chancellery at the latest on 1 May. Resisting the plan of Axmann, the Hitler Youth Leader, to smuggle him to Wenck's army through a gap in the Russian lines in south-west Berlin, Hitler decided to end his life not later than next day.[1] And wisely so, for apart from the hundred thousand men who slipped into American captivity across the Elbe between 5 and 7 May, the Russians swallowed the Wenck and Busse armies whole.[2]

Twelve hours after Hitler's death Hans Krebs, the last Chief of Staff of the German Army, the man who knew Russian and who had been embraced by Stalin, was in the Immelmannstrasse in the presence of General Chuikov (not the more famous marshal Zhukov). Krebs hoped to bargain the lives of Hitler's court against the surrender of Berlin—in vain. One of the three officers who accompanied Krebs has recorded what must have been one of the most strained conversations in modern history. It opened as follows:[3]

Krebs: Today is the 1st of May, a great holiday for our two nations.
Chuikov: We have a great holiday today. How things are with you over there it is hard to say.

Chuikov demanded that the persons in the bunker be surrendered unconditionally and Krebs was allowed to go back to the bunker

---

[1] Hitler was to have escaped under the protection of the remains of the SS Nordland division through Gruenwald. Hitler was so enraged that he relieved the divisional commander, Joachim Ziegler, of his command and kept him under arrest in the bunker. After Hitler's death Ziegler was killed while trying to negotiate a truce (Kraetschmer, op. cit., p. 393).

[2] Thorwald, II, p. 259.　　　　[3] Thorwald, II, p. 224.

with this ultimatum. Goebbels, Burgdorf and Krebs himself decided on suicide; Bormann, Hewel, Rattenhueber and a group of minor courtiers and officers on escape.[1] In the general panic no one thought of the fate of the men fighting in Berlin. The arrangements for a cease-fire had to be undertaken by Hans Fritsche, the head of the broadcasting service, a mere civilian. These arrangements did not become fully effective till as late as 4 May, for the defence of Berlin was a 'soldiers' battle' of small units and groups of men who resisted in scattered buildings and shelters.[2]

With this last battle Himmler had no concern. The remnants of RSHA and the SS Leadership Office were busy enough fending for themselves as they picked their way from Schwerin to Luebeck in the last pocket of the Reich. Himmler, however, had prepared in advance the role of his SS in the defence of Berlin. On 23 April, when the Russians held northern and eastern Berlin and Himmler was still at Hohenlychen planning to meet Count Bernadotte, he ordered the creation of 'flying field and station tribunals' similar to those he had appointed for the menaced cities of Danzig, Koenigsberg, and Breslau. Supported by 'Sperrkommandos' formed of men of the security police and SD, the field gendarmerie and party organisations, these tribunals were conducted by young and fanatical SS men, mostly from Mohnke's Leibstandarte Regiment—Himmler's personal escort—which cordoned inner Berlin and stopped the flow of stragglers through the city. So, while in the Chancellery bunker Hitler prepared his last betrayal of the German nation, these Flying Tribunals dragged wounded men and schoolboys out of cellars in order to string them up as an example to the disloyal.[3]

But General Mummert, commanding the LVIIth Infantry Corps which sustained the greater part of the defence, announced that he would shoot down any Flying Tribunal that invaded his sector. 'A division that has the greatest number of bearers of the Knight's Cross with Oak Leaves does not have to be persecuted by these young louts'.[4] Before the end the fanatics of the SS were betrayed by their own leaders. Major-General Wilhelm Mohnke, who was in the bunker when Hitler died, joined one of the escape groups on the night of 1 May and was captured by the Russians while hiding

---

[1] Rattenhueber returned from Russia on 10 October 1955. Hewel's fate is not known.

[2] IMT VII, p. 238.   [3] Narrative of General Karl in Thorwald, II, p. 141.

[4] Narrative of General Karl in Thorwald, II, p. 183.

in a cellar in the Schoenhauser Allee.[1] After the capitulation Mohnke was wanted by the Canadian Government as an accomplice to Kurt Mayer in the massacre of prisoners at the Ancienne Abbaye, Ardenne.[2] Although Mohnke was eventually traced to a Russian POW camp at Strausberg, the Russian authorities denied all knowledge of him. Recently Mohnke, together with several of the last occupants of the bunker, has been reported to be surviving in Russian captivity.

At ten o'clock on the night of 1 May, while Hitler's court assembled for their attempted escape, Fritsche broadcast the news of Hitler's death and Doenitz's accession. At once all pretence of a last-ditch battle was abandoned. Next day Doenitz received the news of Kesselring's surrender orders for the army of Italy. He ordered the Vistula Army Group to make its way as best it could into British or American captivity, and in the afternoon Keitel arranged for a delegation to Montgomery's headquarters to conduct surrender negotiations for the 'Nordraum'. Admiral von Friedeburg's delegation left next day, and on the 4th Field-Marshal Montgomery's terms were accepted at Doenitz's new headquarters on board the liner *Patria* at Flensburg. Norway and Denmark were to be handed over at once. No mass surrender of troops escaping from the Russians would be accepted, but no surrender by individual soldiers would be refused.[3]

We must now briefly follow Himmler's actions since his surrender proposals were published in the Allied Press on 28 April. No khalif's black executioner arrived in Luebeck or Ploen to cut off Himmler's head and on the morning of the 30th, still unaware from Bormann's ambiguous telegram whether Hitler was alive or dead, Doenitz visited Himmler, who was quartered in the police barracks at Luebeck, loyally to seek the co-operation of the future head of the German state. It seems that Ohlendorf, still the faithful Gestapist, had tapped the telephone conversations of Gauleiter Kaufmann in Hamburg and discovered a plot to surrender the city. Doenitz needed Himmler's joint authority to overawe Kaufmann, for Doenitz believed that if the British troops were allowed across the Elbe, the last escape route from the Russians in North Germany would be closed. Luedde-Neurath describes how Himmler started to take down an exhortation to Kaufmann in his own handwriting. This

---

[1] Trevor-Roper, op. cit., p. 237.   [2] See *supra*, p. 196.
[3] Schultz, op. cit., pp. 65-70.

Doenitz tried in vain to stop with the words 'Luedde will do it for you'. But Himmler's effusion was 'of a more pathetic than practical nature' and Doenitz sent off his own draft without Himmler's signature. While Luedde-Neurath was telephoning the message to Hamburg, Doenitz, mindful of Bormann's ambiguous telegram to proceed against traitors 'as fast as lightning and as true as steel', again taxed Himmler with his negotiations and showed him the telegram which had been dispatched at 3.15 a.m., and again Himmler said it was all enemy propaganda.[1]

But that afternoon Doenitz learnt to his amazement that he was himself the appointed successor and not Himmler. He at once asked Himmler to come and see him, but, fearful of what the head of the German police might do to a Grand Admiral without an army, Doenitz took the advice of Gauleiter Paul Wegener of Bremen and posted U-boat crews at his headquarters as Himmler with an enormous staff approached from Luebeck. He also hid his Browning under a pile of papers on his desk. But the vapid exhibition which Himmler now put on was worthy of the jelly-man whom Doenitz had interviewed in the morning. At the sight of Bormann's last telegram Himmler went pale and Doenitz was emboldened by this sight to refuse Himmler's request to be made the second man in the State. In Doenitz's own words:[2]

Himmler continued to tell me the great advantages that I should derive from his own person. He amazed me with his belief that he had a great reputation abroad. He left me between two and three in the morning with the knowledge that he would not be employed by me in any post of importance. On the other hand I could not entirely separate from him while he had the police in his hands. Be it noted that as yet I knew nothing of the concentration camp atrocities and the extermination of the Jews.

At next day's military conference Himmler admitted that he had put out peace feelers through Sweden, and this revelation that Himmler had lied carried more weight with the strictly service-minded Grand Admiral than did Himmler's loathsome reputation. He declared pompously that 'he who has committed treachery once is ready for it a second time'.[3] Himmler therefore could have no part in the proposed surrender negotiations. Nevertheless, after a brief return to his 'field headquarters' near Wismar, Himmler followed Doenitz's train to Flensburg in the far north of Schleswig-Holstein, the last capital of the Reich.

[1] Luedde-Neurath, op. cit., pp. 34, 43.   [2] *Ibid.*, p. 93.
[3] Luedde-Neurath, op. cit., p. 96.

At this moment Himmler received an awkward reminder that his faithful SS men, whose 'oath was loyalty', regarded him as a father and that there are moments when fathers are expected to do something. This awkward reminder was Léon Degrelle, the former Belgian fascist leader and nominally the commander of the SS Army Corps 'West', which comprised the three Belgian and French SS volunteer divisions. The actual situation of Léon Degrelle was, however, less inspiring than this. His command during the last fighting month of the war never amounted to anything more than three improvised Belgian storm battalions, the remains of which joined the general rout from the River Oder after the Russian crossings of 19-21 April. In a column of fleeing soldiers and civilians, Degrelle and his Belgians passed through Schwerin and Neustrelitz and on 30 April, when he heard the Allied broadcasts on Himmler's surrender-offer, he was in Luebeck. Here a member of Doenitz's staff told Degrelle, 'Listen to this, tomorrow the Fuehrer's death will be announced'.[1]

Like most facsist leaders, Léon Degrelle was one of Nature's great simplifiers. Hitherto he had kept a collection of false identity papers to enable his men to escape screening by the Allies. Now he wanted to put them at Himmler's disposition, to present them to this second Fuehrer who would dispose benevolently of their fate. So Degrelle drove through the night among the milling refugees and in the small hours of the morning of 1 May he reached the hideous late-Victorian castle on the road from Luebeck to Wismar, where Himmler had his 'field headquarters'. During the morning Himmler arrived from Ploen, pale and unshaven, but only to spend a few minutes at the castle before removing his staff to the neighbourhood of Admiral Doenitz. Himmler left word for Degrelle that he was to assemble his men at Bad Segeberg, west of Luebeck. Late in the afternoon, after the announcement of Hitler's death, Degrelle received a personal summons to Himmler's presence. He was to be next day at Malente near Ploen.

Degrelle now set about planning the unplannable. He would offer to surrender his own person to the Belgian police if his men got a safe-conduct. Alternatively, his Belgian SS would fight a war of their own at Bad Segeberg, like the Goths on Vesuvius. Himmler should decide. But at Luebeck Degrelle learnt that there was no possibility of a last stand at Bad Segeberg. The British were there

[1] Degrelle, op. cit., p. 473.

and would soon be in Luebeck. In spite of Admiral Doenitz's orders, General Ernst Busch and Gauleiter Kaufmann had made Hamburg an open city, thereby opening the sluice gate for the British into Schleswig-Holstein. Luebeck had been cut off and Degrelle's men were behind the British lines. So now Degrelle set off for Copenhagen, whither some of his Belgian SS had been directed by sea.

Travelling in a Volkswagen, driven on potato schnaps, Degrelle caught up Himmler's car on the road to Ploen. Himmler in person, wearing a leather crash-helmet, was at the wheel. Degrelle followed him to Malente, where at last, on the afternoon of 2 May, he obtained his interview in the presence of Karl Gebhardt and Werner Best. Himmler was friendly but completely cold-blooded. There was nothing to be done about anything, he said. Indifferently, he agreed that Degrelle might as well take command of his men in Copenhagen. Then Degrelle pursued Himmler's train of fifteen lorries as it followed Doenitz's court in its retreat from Ploen to Flensburg. Outside Kiel the column were ordered off the road during a British daylight raid which reduced the last naval base of the Reich to shapeless rubble. Police generals and women typists threw themselves over garden walls in wild confusion, leaving their shoes in the deep mud. Only Himmler, to whom the experience of being in the open during an aerial bombardment was probably quite new, remained self-controlled, shouting from his car, 'Discipline, gentlemen, discipline!' Gradually the last of the SS Leadership Office crawled back to their cars and lorries and the cumbrous convoy turned back south to seek a way to Flensburg, avoiding Kiel. Degrelle took the direct road north through the bombed city. 'I had left Himmler for ever', he writes; but he makes this observation with a singular lack of valedictory curses on the man who had abandoned the SS to their fate. For Degrelle, writing from a Spanish hospital in San Sebastian, was in no position to throw stones, having escaped from Norway in Albert Speer's aeroplane.[1]

Himmler established himself in Flensburg. On 4 May he was still permitted his say when Field-Marshal Montgomery's terms were discussed by the Doenitz 'cabinet'. Himmler disputed Doenitz's view that no concessions were to be gained by continuing the defence of Norway, Denmark, Czechoslovakia, Holland, Crete, Rhodes and the Channel ports. On the contrary, Himmler argued, these places

[1] The whole of the preceding narrative is derived from Leon Degrelle, op. cit., pp. 473-502.

were 'fist-pledges'. In particular the troops in Norway might be surrendered to Sweden, a fellow-Nordic nation, and so saved from Russian captivity. Schellenberg, who had gone to Sweden to buy steamer-coal for the evacuation of the Kurland army, had been engaged for the past two days in this negotiation. Doenitz was not convinced that Sweden would undertake such a role in defiance of the British, but he hesitated to call off Schellenberg's mission.[1]

And now another circumstance arose to discredit Himmler with the not very knowledgeable Grand Admiral. It seems that Doenitz did not believe in concentration-camp stories. He knew that they were lies, because he had once seen an ill-informed Allied report that his favourite U-boat commanders, Prien and Schulze, were being so detained. But on 3 May Admiral Friedeburg brought illustrated papers from Montgomery's headquarters which showed photographs of Belsen and Buchenwald. Even these were regarded as atrocity propaganda in Flensburg and 'likened to Katyn', but within a day or two a ship reached Flensburg which was crammed with the last survivors of Strutthof concentration camp, all of them in a deplorable condition. On 16 May, eight days after the capitulation, Doenitz tried to gain credit with Eisenhower with the information that he was conducting an inquiry into concentration-camp atrocities. At this date Doenitz must have known perfectly well where Himmler could be found, and Himmler's arrest would have been the first step to such an inquiry. Yet Doenitz swore at Nuremberg that he would never have let Himmler escape had he known the truth—a story which one may believe or not as one wishes.[2]

Between the relatively simple negotiation with Field-Marshal Montgomery on 4 May and the prolonged negotiations with the Combined Allied Command which culminated in total surrender at Reims on 8 May, Doenitz purged his cabinet of the remaining Nazi leaders who had been left to him under Hitler's will. At the same time Doenitz notified Himmler of his dismissal. On the evening of 6 May he sent for Himmler and handed him a letter terminating with the words, 'I thank you for the services which you have given the Reich'.[3]

Although Doenitz had held out no promises, the dismissal was a shock to Himmler, who had moved to Flensburg on 3 May, bringing with him a staff of a hundred and fifty officials, a fleet of cars, and a radio detachment. On the 5th, accompanied by his adjutant

[1] Luedde-Neurath, op. cit., p. 84; Schultz, op. cit., p. 70.
[2] Luedde-Neurath, op. cit., pp. 97-9.   [3] Trevor-Roper, op. cit., p. 246.

Grothmann, who had succeeded Fegelein, and by the unshiftable secretary Rudi Brandt, Himmler held a staff conference. Himmler's speech was heard by Ohlendorf and the heads of the Leadership Office, the Obergruppenfuehrers Hans Juettner, von Woyrsch, and von Herff, all of whom have been interrogated by Mr. Trevor-Roper. Himmler announced the dissolution of the Leadership Head Office; nevertheless he intended to keep them on as advisers. Himmler still believed that he would keep control of the police, since he ordered Obergruppenfuehrer Alfred Wuennenberg, who had succeeded Daluege and Winkelmann as head of the Ordnungspolizei, to remain in his functions. And in complete disregard of his notice of dismissal Himmler declared that he intended to head a reformed National Socialist administration in Schleswig, which would negotiate with the West as an independent power.

There had been a time when Goebbels had described Himmler as a political realist, a time when even the astute Count Ciano had regarded him as a person with his ear well to the ground who understood the German people. Himmler's dizzy speeches about the Watch on the Urals had never been anything more than a propaganda device. But propaganda devices were surely the last thing needed now. Either Himmler meant what he said, in which case he was mad, or he said it to impress his hearers, in which case he was a fool. The plot of July 1944, which had shot Himmler upstairs with the force of a rocket, had initiated the rapid decay of his faculties. For his opponent Doenitz Himmler could be no match. The mind of this strait-laced, unimaginative Grand Admiral was as one-track as his own, but it was a mind fed on the naval tradition. Unlike the traditions created by elderly boy scouts at Bad Toelz and at the Welphenschloss in Brunswick, the naval tradition was based on the supposition that ships may sink, and it provided for such events, requiring the captain to remain on the bridge.

It was Doenitz who was the realist now. On the day of Himmler's conference he learnt from General Kinzel that the personnel of a Luftwaffe squadron were taking Himmler's orders and forming themselves into a Werwolf Association. Doenitz sent for Hans Pruetzmann, a jack-booted relic of the SS occupation of Russia, who for the past six months had been in charge of these day-dreams, and warned him that he had forbidden Werwolf to function because the end of resistance by the regular troops had made it superfluous.[1]

[1] Luedde-Neurath, op. cit., p. 72; Schultz, op. cit., p. 76.

Werwolf was indeed the very embodiment of Himmler's muddled thinking. If he believed that within a few months the Western Allies would ask him to restore order in Europe and would need his SS to fight the menace of Bolshevism,[1] what was the sense of the SS sabotaging the Western Allies? To Doenitz, surrender was a less complicated proposition than this. It was in the regulations. You took the enemy's orders and there was an end to it, so long as honour was not infringed. But, when the British occupation authorities in Norway required the Wehrmacht to arrest the SS and the party, Doenitz intervened. The Wehrmacht were not to carry out 'defamatory orders'. These must be left to the enemy.[2]

Himmler left Doenitz's headquarters on the evening of 6 May, a dazed, dejected man, but nevertheless a free one. As a rebel against Doenitz's authority, as a traitor against the late Fuehrer, no execution squad in a back garden and no political bunker in a concentration camp awaited him. Yet if we are to believe Rosenberg's death-cell memoirs, Doenitz and Gauleiter Wegener had agreed to arrest Bormann the moment he set foot in Flensburg.[3] Himmler could count himself lucky, for to him his survival was a reality and the puppet state of Flensburg still an object to be striven for. He could not comprehend that Flensburg was a mere convenience for the Anglo-American Command and that Doenitz could not avoid handing him over to any power that asked for him.

As Himmler hesitated outside the office where Doenitz had given him his notice of dismissal, he was button-holed by Schwerin von Krosigk, the worldly Rhodes Scholar who had once thought Himmler the destined saviour of his country. Himmler told him that for the time being he was going into hiding. He still believed that the great conflict between East and West would break out in three months at most. 'We shall then become the tremor in the scales and achieve what we could not achieve in the war'.

Schwerin von Krosigk had been chosen by Doenitz to succeed Ribbentrop as Foreign Minister and only a day had passed since Himmler had begged him to accept the same post under a Himmler government. Schwerin now upbraided Himmler for his decision to go underground. 'It must not happen that the Reichsfuehrer decks himself out with a false name and a false beard. There is no other way for you but to go to Montgomery and say "Here I am".

[1] Luedde-Neurath, op. cit., p. 216.   [2] Ibid., p. 115.
[3] Alfred Rosenberg, Memoirs, p. 299.

It is then that you must assume the responsibility for your men'.[1]

This must have been very disturbing to the Reichsfuehrer at so comfortless a moment. Amid the icy politenesses of Doenitz's conferences no one had told him in all simplicity not to be an ass. How much better if they had. Now this tiresome person was adjuring him to search his conscience. The Reichsfuehrer mumbled something about waiting till Schellenberg came back from Sweden and broke off the conversation. He did not go to Montgomery to offer himself up as the vindicator and chief defendant of the SS. He wrote the Field-Marshal a letter instead, but there was no reply.

After 6 May it is difficult to trace Himmler's movements. According to Mr. Frischauer, Himmler stayed, together with the adjutants Macher and Grothmann, in the apartment of his mistress, apparently the woman known as Haeschen, who was the mother of Himmler's second family, the children Helge and Gertrud.[2] Himmler was not actually in concealment, nor was there much room in the state of Flensburg in which to hide. Part of the time Himmler spent with Field-Marshal Ernst Busch, the Commander-in-Chief of the forces in Schleswig and Denmark.[3] Busch had been made the scapegoat for the collapse of the Central Army Group in July 1944, but as an out-and-out Nazi general had received another command. Even this good party man could not fall in with Himmler's high-flying schemes. Busch had already been negotiating surrender before the news of Hitler's death.[4] So Himmler drifted back to the dwindling band of SS Gruppenfuehrers, in particular to the company of Karl Gebhardt, a lifelong friend, and Otto Ohlendorf, an object of particular dislike. Ohlendorf declared at his own trial that he saw Himmler every day between 8 and 21 May.[5]

Apparently it was an onslaught by that insufferable man on Himmler's conscience all the time. Ohlendorf wanted Himmler to surrender so that in his own person he could vindicate the calumnies against the SS.[6] And Gebhardt joined in. He wanted Himmler to use the Flensburg radio station in order to broadcast messages to SS men in captivity or hiding from captivity. Himmler was to absolve

---

[1] Thorwald, II, op. cit., p. 299.   [2] Frischauer, op. cit., p. 255.
[3] Trevor-Roper, op. cit., p. 247.
[4] Chester Wilmot, *The Struggle for Europe*, p. 704.   [5] Bayle, op. cit., p. 41.
[6] Case XI, transcript, 504.

the SS from their oaths; above all he was to declare the dissolution of Werwolf.[1]

But Himmler did none of these things, for he no longer wanted to attract attention. He knew that his captured colleagues had been segregated by the Allies for trial, among them Goering. And as to honourable capitulation on terms, that was what Rosenberg had offered, yet on 18 May the British had merely entered Murwik hospital and arrested him.[2]

On 21 May, two days before the arrest of the entire Doenitz government, Himmler left Flensburg accompanied by his two military adjutants from the Waffen SS. Colonel Werner Grothmann had more or less stepped into Karl Wolff's shoes in the autumn of 1943 and was an old hand at court. Major Heinz Macher dated only from Himmler's appointment to the Replacement Army and was a young tank commander with a distinguished record. They had false papers and formed part of a group of twelve members of the Secret Field Gendarmerie on their way to seek passage through the British cordon to Bavaria. Himmler's papers were made out in the name of Heinrich Hitzinger. He had shaved his moustache and he wore a black patch over his left eye. That Himmler should choose to assume this identity of all others was a strange indication how little he realised even now the way the world regarded his activities, for the Secret Field Gendarmerie, originally the creation of Admiral Canaris, had become in May 1942 a branch of the Gestapo,[3] and was on the Allies' list of indicted organisations whose members must be detained at sight.

The party, wearing a mixture of civil and military dress from which all badges had been removed, reached the British control point at Meinstedt between Hamburg and Bremerhaven the same day. Had their papers been those of ordinary members of the Wehrmacht, they would have been passed through, but since they purported to be members of the Secret Field Police they were screened at three successive camps, Bremervoerde, Zeelos and Westertimke. From this point onwards accounts vary considerably. Only one published statement may be accepted with confidence. It is that of Captain T. Sylvester, who commanded the last camp, where the twelve men arrived some eighteen to twenty hours later. Soon after his arrival Himmler asked to see Captain Sylvester privately and disclosed his identity. Captain Sylvester then kept Himmler in his personal

[1] Bayle, op. cit., p. 498.   [2] Rosenberg, op. cit., p. 300.
[3] See *supra*, pp. 94, 210.

custody till the 23rd, when he was taken to the British Second Army Headquarters at Lueneburg.[1] Published accounts, declaring that Himmler spoke to members of the staff at the British screening camp and that he demanded to see Field-Marshal Montgomery, would seem to be apocryphal.[2]

It is still a mystery why Himmler revealed himself. It may be that Macher and Grothmann were going to turn him in; it may be that he was misguided enough to think that he would get better treatment as Heinrich Himmler than as a private; it may be that he still thought he could drive some sort of bargain. If Himmler kept any of these illusions, his reception in Lueneburg at the special interrogation centre in the Uelznerstrasse removed them. He was stripped, thoroughly searched and made to change into British Army clothing.[3] He was then kept in a cell till Colonel N. L. Murphy arrived from Montgomery's Intelligence Office. Murphy was not satisfied with the search that had been made and ordered the medical officer to re-examine Himmler's mouth. It is possible that, if this had been done earlier, history would have been enriched by a public trial of Heinrich Himmler among the Nuremberg defendants. But seeing that his last escape gap was closing, Himmler bit his 'Zyankali' capsule of potassium cyanide, an object that every Nazi leader carried at the end of the war, and which was wedged in a cavity of his gums.

Another twelve minutes passed before Himmler was dead. Captain Wells, the medical officer, wrestled with him in an attempt to wrench the poison from his mouth. Emetics were administered and a stomach-pump, but to no purpose. Finally the body of the Reichsfuehrer was photographed, doubled up on the floor of the interrogation room among the grisly litter of swabs and basins which testified to the struggle. It looked a satisfying portrait of the Grand Inquisitor of the Twentieth Century. Few could have seen in this photograph, or in the grim death-mask published in the magazine *Life*, the timid, hesitant, muddle-headed mediocrity that had been Heinrich Himmler.

2. THE SS ON TRIAL

Erich Kern, an officer in the Waffen SS, who was interned by the Americans after the capitulation, describes the suicide of a brother

---

[1] *Daily Mail*, 11 March 1953.   [2] Musmanno, *Ten Days to Die*, p. 260.
[3] Sergeant-Major Edwin Austen, quoted in Willi Frischauer, op. cit., p. 257. Himmler arrived at Lueneburg at night. By 11 p.m. he was dead.

officer. This man, a bearer of the Knight's Cross, had hanged himself in a camp latrine, leaving a note declaring that he could no longer live since his Reichsfuehrer had betrayed him.

One of my best comrades parted from life because he loved his wife so dearly that he could not endure her unfaithfulness. My Reichsfuehrer forbade him burial with military honours, and after his death erased his name from the SS with insult and shame. And yet he himself tried to slip through the cordon, dressed as a character in a bad detective story. And when he was caught, he swallowed Zyankali instead of accepting responsibility before the victor's court and saving from the gallows a hundred poor devils who had done nothing but carry out their duty.[1]

This comment on Himmler by one of his own men explains why in the Germany of today there is no SS legend of any serious consequence. Paul Hausser and Gottlob Berger may still write from time to time, urging NATO to consider the claims of the men who trained the first European army in the struggle against Bolshevism. But to most Germans the SS is a name to be forgotten, not because of the concentration camps, gas chambers and extermination commandos, but because of Himmler's breakdown and ignoble end.

On 8 June 1951 the last seven Germans to be condemned to death under the International Nuremberg Statute, were hanged in Landsberg prison. During a wave of hysteria throughout Western Germany there was a strong disposition to regard these men as martyrs. A year later at Otto Remer's trial, the prosecution declared that Remer's SRP party venerated them as 'The Seven Great Germans'. Yet everyone of the hanged men had been in the SS; two of them, Pohl and Ohlendorf, had been very high in the hierarchy and all had been professional mass murderers.[2]

It would be a mistake, however, to suppose that in 1952 it was a title to credit to have been Himmler's Concentration Camp King. As late as October 1955 a court at Ansbach was willing to try one of Himmler's Waffen SS generals. This was Max Simon, the commander of the 16th Panzer SS Division, who had established a drumhead court martial on 7 April 1945 in the Swabian town of Brettheim. Among others he had condemned to death an elderly farmer who had disarmed a mob of Hitlerjugend boys, believing that to allow children to shoot at American troops was sheer lunacy. What Simon had done was to carry out a Himmler order[3] and the

---

[1] Erich Kern, *Der grosse Rausch* (Zurich, 1948), p. 184.
[2] For the Remer trial see *supra*, p. 325.
[3] For this Himmler Order see *supra*, p. 419.

court ruled that it had been legal. Dr. Hoegener, the Minister-President of Bavaria, protested strongly at a verdict which was certainly dangerous, yet it was surely remarkable that in 1955 it was still possible to accuse an SS general, particularly one whom the British had once condemned to death for killing Italian partisans and who had earned the title to martyrdom of a ten-years' stretch in Werl prison.[1]

In a Germany determined to forget history, this case stirred up few passions. The SS was not a subject of conversation and the words which the SS officer had written on the latrine wall were of no interest to unindoctrinated German youth. Yet there had once been an SS oath and to SS men who were neither careerist knaves nor indifferent conscripts it had meant something. On their badges had been the words, 'Our oath is loyalty', and they had been told that these words were the sum and all of their existence. Permitted neither religion nor political philosophy, nothing but the bleak party line, their oath became an abstraction and a religion in itself.

Such were the hard-core SS, as distinguished from the great mass who had been conscripted simply because they were Germans born outside Germany, or who were foreigners who had been bought or crimped for Himmler's last outlandish SS divisions. For years to come the hard-core SS in captivity were the despair of liberal-minded persons who tried to re-educate them in accordance with democratic dogma. They were the solid tree-stump where once there had been a huge and untidy tree; but without the tree the stump is not of much significance and today the importance of the political antics of hard-core SS men is habitually exaggerated. What cannot be exaggerated is the danger that Germany will always produce such men; and that men like these, well rooted in the ground though their loyalty may be, will always be governed from light and lofty tree-tops, well swayed in the wind.

The Allied lawyers, civil and military, who set themselves the task of segregating the leaders of the SS, of judging their degree of responsibility and of exacting retribution for what they had done, had little idea of the immense complications that were in store for them. The prosecutors accepted a hypothesis which had been created before the war by German refugees, their Press and their writings. According to this hypothesis the SS was a state within a state, responsible only to itself, the terror of German bureaucrats and the force that

[1] *The Times*, 19 and 20 October 1955.

impelled them to tyranny and cruelty. Ten years of Allied war trials have not killed this view; on the contrary, they have encouraged it. For though the mass of prosecution documents have refuted the myth, the pleas of German defendants, who had no part in the active SS, have perpetuated it as the basis of their defence.

Himmler himself has been dethroned from the position of a cold, mechanical grand inquisitor. The rather amiable fool depicted in Felix Kersten's books, though far from giving the complete picture, is probably the most credible one. But even if Himmler has been debunked, the Gestapo has lost none of its awesome prestige. It is not realised how little the Gestapo was an independent agency, and how much its powers depended on the co-operation of the entire German bureaucracy.[1] It is not realised that the massive machinery, by which more than four million Jews were dragged from their homes to die in often very distant concentration camps, ghettos, and gas chambers, could never have been handled by a single obscure department of the Gestapo, could never have been secret and could not have happened at all without the minute interlocking of the Ministry of the Interior, the Ministries of Transport, Finance, and Economics, the two High Command Offices, the Ministries of Labour and Armaments, and above all the Foreign Office. The first Nuremberg Tribunal set itself the task of judging the SS in bulk and deciding whether it was a criminal organisation, mere membership of which could be made an indictable offence. It judged affirmatively and through this judgment membership of the SS constituted some degree of complicity in the atrocities that had been committed. Psychologically it was the most dangerous of errors. If such a judgment were to be made at all, it should have been made on the German nation as a whole, instead of providing the German nation with a convenient scapegoat.

The better-informed SS leaders foresaw that this would happen. Hence the appeals which they made to Himmler's conscience after the capitulation. But the world has lost no masterly exposition of the facts through Himmler's Zyankali capsule. Whether Himmler would have chosen at his trial to accept personal responsibility for his many offices or whether he would have pleaded that they acted without his knowledge, he was not capable of explaining the inter-

[1] I have however to admit that since this book went to press Mr. Edward Crankshaw has striven hard to drive this lesson home in his valuable study, *The Gestapo: Instrument of Tyranny* (London, 1956).

locking of his 'dirty work' departments with the various Ministries. It may be doubted, too, whether the vainglorious Karl Wolff, who asked at one moment to stand trial in place of Himmler, could have shown the world clearly how the Ministries had required and used the unpopular agencies of RSHA, VOMI, RUSHA and the rest. Something of the objectivity of Albert Speer was needed, but the SS had no Albert Speer. Some notion of the truth was provided in the many testimonies of Otto Ohlendorf, but, though Ohlendorf's SD reports had once been famous for their objectivity, he proved a dishonest, muddled, and pedantic witness.

The plain question 'What was the SS?' cannot be plainly answered. The SS is commonly compared with the political police agencies of Communist governments. It can be said that in such agencies all Communist states possess the equivalent of RSHA, to which normal police activities are subordinated in the same way. Heinrich Mueller, who organised the political police of the Weimar Republic into the Gestapo, was a student of the Russian police system. But there are limits to this comparison. The Cheka, later the GPU, the NKVD and later still the MVD, was the creation of a revolution, the necessary tool of a government that only tolerated one system of political thought. The political police under Himmler and the SD under Heydrich were created for the same purpose but there was this essential difference, the difference stated in the first chapter of this book. In Germany there was no revolution. Capital and the monopolistic power of German capitalism remained in precisely the same hands as before. The bulk of the civil service stayed in their jobs and were not even required to join the party. Hitler used his SS not to consolidate his revolution but to nip it in the bud.

After June 1934 there was no reason why the SS should have continued to exist, unless it was to be the kernel of a new citizen army. The few armed SS Standarte could have turned in their arms with the SA, and Himmler could have been awarded the control of the unified German police without the mystic combination 'SS und Polizei'. But Hitler, who had cheated his followers of revolution, had to keep up the trappings of revolution to the end. His Ministers were therefore induced to wear the black uniform and silver insignia of SS Gruppenfuehrers. Hitler had to tolerate the messy infiltration of the SS into the army and civil service, but he did no more than tolerate it and he never showed that he liked this state of affairs. Yet the SS oath and the SS *mystique* impressed Hitler. Himmler, he declared, was his Ignatius Loyola who had created a Jesuit order for him. It was not to turn them into crack armoured divisions or watchdogs over the labyrinth of German bureaucracy that he wanted these men of exceptional loyalty. He wanted them for secret tasks and these were not the tasks of revolution but the tasks of frenzied racial intolerance.

It is for these tasks that the SS will be remembered. The machinery of the SS as a state within a state will be forgotten because it never achieved its end. The successes of the SS in the field will be forgotten because the SS never fought as an army and its leaders never achieved more than local tactical control. The idealism of the SS will be forgotten because it meant nothing beyond loyalty to one man. But the racial transplantations, the concentration camps, the interrogation cells of the Gestapo, the medical experiments on the living, the mass reprisals, the manhunts for slave labour and the racial exterminations will be remembered for ever.

Bibliography

1. Documents

Documents mentioned in the footnotes under serial numbers refer exclusively to the Nuremberg trial conducted by the International Tribunal in 1945-6, and the twelve Nuremberg trials conducted by the American Tribunal in 1947-9. The documents used in the International trial will be found in extracts printed in English in *Nazi Conspiracy and Aggression* (Washington, State Department, 1946-8, 11 volumes). The German text will be found, printed much more fully but in many cases only in extracts, in *The Trial of the Major War Criminals* (Nuremberg, 1946-52, 42 volumes). The documents used in this book all bear the initials PS, L, M, EC, USSR or RF, but the USSR and RF documents (French series) were mostly not printed, and these are quoted from other sources. The proceedings of the trial are quoted from the British (H.M. Stationery Office) version (23 volumes, 1946-51) and are referred to throughout under the initials IMT.

Documents used in the later Nuremberg trials are quoted under the initials NG or NO, in rare cases NI or NOKW. Only a very small selection of them was printed in the official publication, *Trials of War Criminals before the Nuremberg Military Tribunals* (Washington, 1951-3, 14 volumes), in spite of the enormous scale of that work. When the documents are to be found in *Trials of War Criminals*, volume and page references are given, but in many cases stencilled court copies or photostats have been used. In some cases the documents have been printed in private publications which will be found listed in the bibliography.

The British military trials, held at a number of places in Germany, the trials of the American Dachau Tribunal, the Russian, French, Dutch, Belgian, Italian, Polish, Czechoslovak, Jugoslav and Greek war trials have not been published as a series and, except in the case of a few special monographs on individual trials, information is hard to obtain, apart from references in the daily press. For the German trials of war criminals the author has been helped to some extent by court copies of the charges and the summing-up.

A strong word of caution is necessary in the case of the numbered Nuremberg documents. Not all were put in evidence and of those that were put in evidence not all were accepted by the court. Many of them only served to show that the German bureaucrats who wrote them had been informed wrongly. There is an unfortunate tendency to regard any numbered Nuremberg document as established evidence, on the analogy of the camera which it is said cannot lie. They are, of course, only of comparative value and the author has hesitated to use them where no corroborative evidence exists.

2. Published Works

It has been considered advisable not to separate primary sources, such as the memoirs of German leaders and collections of illustrative official documents, from secondary sources. Many so-called primary sources are of little value, because the authors never wrote them. They permitted others to 'ghost' or edit them or their posthumous papers have been so edited. The work of a professional historian, who has been engaged for many years in sifting the material, is often preferable. Some of the German memoir writers, who have been quoted with great frequency in this book, are of indifferent value, but they cannot be dispensed with. A few of the German biographies which have appeared since the war are extremely scholarly and the sources of each sentence are given with an accuracy bordering on pedantry, but all seem to suffer from a lack of appreciation of the rules of evidence.

ABSHAGEN, KARL HEINZ — *Canaris, Patriot und Weltbuerger*, Stuttgart, 1949.

ANFUSO, FILIPPO — *Du palais de Venise au lac de Garde*, Paris, 1949.

ARON, ROBERT — *Histoire de Vichy*, Paris, 1954.

BACH-ZELEWSKI, ERICH VON DEM (affidavits by) — *Leben eines SS Generals*, 'Aufbau-reconstruction', Vol. 12, pp. 34-6, 1946, New York.

BAYLE, FRANCOIS — *Croix gammée ou caducée*, Freiburg, 1950. *Psychologie et éthique du national-socialisme*, Paris, 1953.

BAYNES, NORMAN H. — *The Speeches of Adolf Hitler*, 1922-1939, Oxford, 1942.

BERNADOTTE, COUNT FOLKE — *The Curtain Falls*, New York, 1946.

BLACK BOOK OF POLISH JEWRY — New York, 1943.

BLEICHER, HUGO — *Colonel Henri's Story*, edited by Ian Colvin, London, 1954.

BLOND, GEORGES — *L'agonie de l'Allemagne*, 1944-5, Paris, 1952.

BORMANN, MARTIN — *The Bormann Letters*, edited by H. R. Trevor-Roper, London, 1954.

BULLOCK, ALAN — *Hitler, a study in tyranny*, London, 1952.

CIANO, GALEAZZO — *Ciano's Diary*, 1939-1943, edited by Malcolm Muggeridge, London, 1947.

COLVIN, IAN — *Chief of Intelligence* (Canaris), London, 1952.

CRANKSHAW, EDWARD — *The Gestapo, Instrument of Tyranny*, London, 1956.

DEGRELLE, LÉON — *Die verlorene Legion*, Stuttgart, 1955.

DIELS, RUDOLF — *Lucifer ante Portas* (Zwischen Severing und Heydrich), Zurich, 1949.

D'ALQUEN, GUNTER — *Auf Hieb und Stich*, Berlin, 1937. *Die SS*, Berlin, 1939.

DOCUMENTS ON GERMAN FOREIGN POLICY — Official series, Vols. D1 and D5, 1952 and 1954.

DOKUMENTY I MATERIALY — Central Jewish Historical Commission, Lodz, 1946, 3 volumes.

DORNBERGER, WALTER, MAJOR-GENERAL — "*V*2", London, 1953.

DULLES, ALLEN — *Germany's Underground*, New York, 1947.

DUNAND, GEORGES — "*Ne perdez pas leur trace*", Neuchatel, 1950.

FRANK, HANS — *Im Angesicht des Galgens*, Graefelfing, 1953.

FRIEDMAN, FILIP — *This was Oswiecim*, London, 1946.
FRISCHAUER, WILLI — *Himmler, the Evil Genius of the Third Reich*, London, 1953.
GERMAN CRIMES IN POLAND — Government publication, Warsaw, 1946-7.
GILBERT, FELIX — *Hitler Directs his War* (Minutes of Hitler's military conferences), New York, 1950.
GILBERT, G. M. — *Nuremberg Diary*, New York, 1947.
The Psychology of Dictatorship, New York, 1950.
GISEVIUS, HANS BERND — *To the Bitter End*, London, 1948.
GOEBBELS, JOSEF — *The Goebbels Diaries*, edited by Louis P. Lochner, London, 1948.
GREINER, HELMUTH — *Die Oberste Wehrmachtfuehrung, 1939-1943*, Wiesbaden, 1952.
GUDERIAN, HEINZ — *Erinnerungen eines Soldaten*, Heidelberg, 1951.
HAGEN, WALTER — See Hoettl, Wilhelm.
HASSELL, ULRICH VON — *The von Hassell Diaries, 1938-1944*, London, 1948.
HAUSSER, PAUL — *Waffen SS im Einsatz*, Goettingen, 1953.
HEIDEN, KONRAD — *Der Fuehrer, Hitler's Rise to Power*, Boston, 1944.
HESSE, FRITZ — *Hitler and the English*, London, 1954.
HEYDRICH, REINHARD — *Wandlungen unseres Kampfes*, Berlin, 1935.
HILDEBRANDT, RAINER — *Wir sind die Letzten, Aus dem Leben des Widerstandskampfers, Albrecht Haushofer und seiner Freunde*, Neuwied-Berlin, 1947.
HIMMLER, HEINRICH — *Rede der RFSS im Dom zu Quedlinberg*, 1936.
Die SS als antibolschewistische Kampforganisation, Berlin, 1936.
Die Rede Himmlers vor den Gauleitern am 3.8.44.
Vierteljahreshefte fuer Zeitgeschichte, Stuttgart, 1953. Vol. 4, pp. 357-94; other speeches quoted under Nuremberg Documents.
HITLER, ADOLF — See Picker, Henry.
HOETTL, WILHELM (Walter Hagen) — *Die geheime Front*, Linz, 1950; translated and enlarged as *The Secret Front*, London, 1954.
Hitler's Paper Weapon, London, 1955.
HOFFMANN, HEINRICH — *Hitler was my Friend*, London, 1955.
HORTHY, NIKOLAUS VON — *Ein Leben fuer Ungarn*, Zurich, 1953.
HOSSBACH, FRIEDRICH — *Zwischen Wehrmacht und Hitler*, Wolfenbuettel, 1949.
JERK, WIKING — *Endkampf um Berlin* (translated from the Swedish *Rangeroek*), Buenos Aires, 1947.
JOLLY, CYRIL — *The Vengeance of Private Pooley*, London, 1956.
KASTNER, RESZOE — *Das Bericht des juedischen Rettungskommittees aus Budapest, 1942-45.* Privately circulated stencil, Geneva, 1946.

KERN, ERICH — *Der grosse Rausch, Russlandfeldzug* 1941-1945, Zurich, 1948.

KERSTEN, FELIX — *The Memoirs of Dr. Felix Kersten*, New York, 1947.

Totenkopf und Treue, Heinrich Himmler ohne Uniform, Hamburg, 1953.

KIENAST, E. — *Der grossdeutsche Reichstag*, 1943.

KLEIST, PETER — *Zwischen Hitler und Stalin*, Bonn, 1950.

KOGON, EUGEN — *Der SS Staat*, Berlin, 1947. (English translation, *The Theory and Practice of Hell*, London, 1951.)

KOLLER, KARL, GENERAL OF THE LUFTWAFFE — *Der letzte Monat*, Nauheim, 1949.

KORDT, ERICH — *Nicht aus den Akten*, Stuttgart, 1950.

KRAETSCHMER, ERNST — *Die Ritterkreuztraeger der Waffen SS*, Goettingen, 1955.

KRAUSNICK, HELMUT — *Wehrmacht und Nationalsozialismus*, 1934-9, supplement to *Das Parlament*, Bonn, 9 November 1955.

KROSIGK, GRAF LUETZ SCHWERIN VON — *Es geschah im Deutschland*, Tuebingen, 1951.

LEBER, ANNEDORE — *Das Gewissen steht auf*, Berlin, 1953.

LEDERER, ZDENEK — *Ghetto Theresienstadt*, London, 1953.

LEVAI, EUGENE — *The Black Book of the Martyrdom of Hungarian Jewry*, Zurich, 1948.

LEVERKUEHN, PAUL — *German Military Intelligence*, London, 1954.

LINGENS-REINER, ELLA — *Prisoners of Fear*, London, 1948.

LOSSBERG, MAJOR-GENERAL BERNHARD VON — *Im Wehrmachtfurungsstab*, Hamburg, 1949.

LUEDDE-NEURATH, WALTER — *Die letzten Tage des dritten Reichs*, Goettingen, 1951.

McDONALD, B. J. S. — *The Trial of Kurt Meyer*, Toronto, 1954.

MASUR, NORBERT — *En Jud talar med Himmler*, Stockholm, 1946.

MAU, HERMANN — *Die zweite Revolution*, 30. *Juni*, 1934. *Vierteljahreshefte fuer Zeitgeschichte*, Stuttgart, Vol. 1, No. 2, 1953.

MITSCHERLICH, A., AND MIELKE, F. — *Wissenschaft ohne Menschlichkeit*, Heidelberg, 1949.

(English version *Doctors of Infamy*, New York, 1949.)

MONNERAY, HENRI (edited by) — *Les persecutions des juifs:* (1) *France et les pays de l'Ouest*, Paris, 1947.

Les persecution des juifs: (2) *Les pays de l'Est*, Paris, 1949 (trial documents).

MOYZISCH, C. W. — *Operation Cicero*, London, 1950.

MUSMANNO, MICHAEL A. — *Ten Days to Die*, London, 1951.

OVEN, WILFRID VON — *Mit Goebbels bis zum Ende*, Buenos Aires, 1949.

PAETEL, KARL — *Ein Beitrag zur Soziologie des National-sozialismus. Vierteljahreshefte fuer Zeitgeschichte*, Stuttgart, 1954, Vol. 2, 1.

PAPEN, FRANZ VON — *Memoirs*, London, 1952.

PAYNE-BEST, CAPTAIN S. — *The Venlo Incident*, London, 1950.

PECHEL, RUDOLF — *Deutscher Widerstand*, Zurich, 1947.

PHILIPS, RAYMOND — *The Belsen Trial*, London, 1949.

PICKER, HENRY — *Hitler's Table Talk*, translated by Norman Cameron and R. H. Stevens, London, 1953.

PLATTEN-HALLERMUND, ALICE — *Die Toetung Geisteskranker im Deutschland*, Frankfurt, 1949.

RAHN, RUDOLF — *Ruheloses Leben, Aufzeichnungen und Erinnerungen*, Dusseldorf, 1949.

RED CROSS COMMITTEE — *Documents sur l'activite de la Croix Rouge: Serie II, camps de concentration*, Geneva, 1946.

REITLINGER, GERALD — *The Final Solution: The Attempt to Exterminate the Jews of Europe*, 1939-1945, London, 1953.

REMER, OTTO — *Die zwanzigste Juli*, 1944, Hamburg, 1951.

RIBBENTROP, JOACHIM — *Zwischen London und Moskau, Erinnerungen und letzte Aufzeichnungen*, Leoni am Starnberger See, 1953.

RITTER, GERHARD — *Karl Goerdeler und die deutsche Widerstandsbewegung*, Bonn, 1954.

ROEDER, MANFRED — *Rote Kapelle, Aufzeichnungen des Generalrichters Dr. M. Roeder*, Hamburg, 1952.

ROSENBERG, ALFRED — *Letzte Aufzeichnungen*, Goettingen, 1955. (Part translation, *Rosenberg's Memoirs*, New York, 1949.)

ROTHFELS, PROFESSOR HANS — *The German Opposition to Hitler: an Appraisal*, Chicago University, 1949.

ROZANSKI, ZENON — *"Muetzen Ab"*, Hanover, 1948.

SALOMON, ERNST VON — *The Answers of Ernst von Salomon*. London, 1954. (In the German edition, 1953, called *Fragebogen*.)

SAMMLER, RUDOLF — *Goebbels: the Man Next to Hitler*, London, 1947.

SCHAUMBURG-LIPPE ZU, PRINZ FRIEDRICH CHRISTIAN — *Zwischen Krone und Kerker*, Wiesbaden, 1952.

SCHELLENBERG, WALTER — Edited memoirs, published as *Die grosse Moerder GmbH, aus den Aufzeichnungen des Oberst Z von SD* in *Quick*, Nos. 37-44, Munich, 1953.

SCHLABRENDORFF, FABIAN VON — *Offiziere gegen Hitler*, Zurich, 1945.

SCHRAMM, WILHELM VON — *Der 20 Juli in Paris*, Bad Woerishofen, 1953.

SCHULTZ, JOACHIM — *Die letzten 30 Tagen, aus dem Kriegstagebuch des OKW*, Stuttgart, 1951.

SCHWEPPENBURG, GEYR VON — *The Critical Years*, London, 1952.

SEABURY, PAUL — *The Wilhelmstrasse*, Berkeley, California, 1955.

SHULMAN, MILTON — *Defeat in the West*, London, 1947.

SIEGLER, FRITZ FREIHERR VON — *Die hoeheren Dienststellen der deutschen Wehrmacht, 1933-1945*, Munich, 1955.

SKORZENY, OTTO — *Geheimkommando Skorzeny*, Hamburg, 1950.

SONNTAG, R. J., AND BEDDIE, J. S. — *Nazi-Soviet Relations*, Washington, 1948.

THORWALD, JUERGEN — *Die ungeklaerten Faelle*, Stuttgart, 1950.
Es begann an der Weichsel. Stuttgart, 1950 (Thorwald I).
Das Ende an der Elbe, ditto (Thorwald II).

TOYNBEE, ARNOLD AND VERONICA (edited) — *Hitler's Europe*, London, 1954.

TREVOR-ROPER, H. R. — *The Last Days of Hitler*, London, 1947.

WAITE, ROBERT — *Vanguard of Nazism; the Free Corps Movement in Post War Germany*, 1918-1923, Cambridge, Mass., 1952.

WEISENBORN, GUNTER — *Der lautloses Aufstand*, Hamburg, 1953.

WESTPHAL, SIEGFRIED — *Heer im Fesseln*, Bonn, 1950.

WHEELER-BENNETT, J. W. — *The Nemesis of Power: the German Army in Politics 1918-1945*, London, 1953.

WHITE BOOK COMMITTEE — *Weissbuch ueber die Erschiessungen des 30. Juin.* Paris, 1934.

WIENER LIBRARY BULLETIN — *Vols. III-IX*, 1949-55.

WILMOT, CHESTER — *The Struggle for Europe*, London, 1952.

ZELLER, EBERHARD — *Geist der Freiheit*, Munich, 1953.

Dramatis Personae

A guide to some of the more important personalities mentioned in this book

ABETZ, OTTO (1903-   )

Hitler's ambassador in Paris after the fall of France; sentenced to twenty years' hard labour in July 1949; released from a French prison, April 1954.

ANFUSO, FILIPPO

Mussolini's ambassador in Berlin after his re-establishment in September 1943. See bibliography.

ANTONESCU, ION, MARSHAL (1882-1946)

Rumanian Premier, 1939-44; executed in Bucharest, 1 June 1946.

AXMANN, ARTUR

Reich leader of the Hitler Youth; one of the last to escape from the Reich Chancellery bunker in May 1945.

BACH-ZELEWSKI, ERICH VON DEM, LIEUT.-GENERAL SS (1899-   )

Himmler's Chief of Partisan Warfare and commander of an army corps at the end of the war; sentenced in Munich, 31 March 1931 to a suspended sentence of ten years' 'special labour'.

BANDERA, STEPAN

Founder of a Ukrainian militia working for the Germans; still directing 'Benderovce' activities (1955).

BECK, LUDWIG, COL.-GENERAL (1880-1944)

Chief of General Staff; resigned 1938; nominated by the Resistance Circle as future Head of the German state; committed suicide 20 July 1944.

BECHER, KURT, COL., SS (1909-   )

Head of SS remount purchasing commission; Himmler's negotiator for the lives of Jews in 1944-5.

BEHRENDS, HERMANN, MAJOR-GENERAL, SS (1907-1946)

First head of Berlin SD. In charge of Tuchachewski forgeries; directed racial German office in Jugoslavia, VOMI; hanged Belgrade, 1946.

BENDER, BRIG.-GENERAL, SS

Head of the Waffen SS Judge Advocate's department.

BERGER, GOTTLOB, GENERAL, SS (1876-   )

Head of the SS main leadership office and for some months virtual administration of the Rosenberg Ministry in Russia; sentenced to twenty-five years' imprisonment in April 1949; released at end of 1951.

BEST, KARL WERNER, LIEUT.-GENERAL, SS (1903-   )

First legal adviser to the SD and Gestapo. Plenipotentiary to Denmark, 1942-5; death sentence of 1946 commuted; released from prison, Copenhagen, 29 August 1951.

BLANKENBERG, WERNER, HON. BRIG.-GENERAL, SS

Head of the secret Euthanasia Office in the Fuehrer's Chancellery; whereabouts unknown.

BLOMBERG, WERNER VON FIELD MARSHAL (1870-1946), — Minister of Defence, January 1933-February 1938, field-marshal, April 1936; dismissed on account of his scandalous marriage; died in the witness wing, Nuremberg prison, 1946.

BOCK, FEDOR VON, FIELD MARSHAL (1880-1945) — Army group commander in Russia of semi-Resistance sympathies; killed in an air raid near Hamburg at the end of the war.

BONHOEFFER, PASTOR DIETRICH — Arrested April 1943 after attempting peace contacts in Sweden, and executed at Flossenbuerg camp, 9 April 1945.

BORMANN, MARTIN (1900-45) — Chief of the Party office from May 1941, and Hitler's personal secretary from April 1943; the most powerful man in Germany at the end of the war; last seen alive 2 May 1945; fate unknown. See bibliography.

BOUHLER, PHILIP, HON. GENERAL, SS (1899-1945) — Chief of the Fuehrer's Chancellery and head of the Euthanasia section; committed suicide Zell am See, May 1945.

BRACK, VIKTOR, COL., SS (1905-48) — Official in Fuehrer chancellery; took part in setting up extermination camps in Poland; hanged in Landsberg prison, 2 June 1948.

BRANDT, RUDOLF, GENERAL, SS 1909-48) — Himmler's 'personal referent' and Head of the Ministers' office: hanged in Landsberg prison, 2 June 1948.

BRANDT, KARL, LIEUT.-GENERAL, SS (1897-1948) — Hitler's private surgeon and Reich Commissioner for Health; hanged, 2 June 1948, for his medical experiments.

BRAUCHITSCH, WALTER VON, FIELD MARSHAL (1881-1948) — Commander-in-Chief from February 1938 to December 1941; was to have been tried in connection with illegal military orders, but this was abandoned in 1948, Brauchitsch being then practically blind; died in British internment camp.

BURCKHARDT, PROFESSOR KARL (1891-   ) — Former League of Nations commissioner in Danzig and during the war years president of the Swiss Red Cross.

BUERCKEL, JOSEF (1895-1944) — Nazi leader during the Saar plebiscite, 1935; first Gauleiter of Vienna; Gauleiter Lorraine-Palatinate, 1939-44; committed suicide, November 1944.

BUCH, MAJOR WALTER, HON. GENERAL, SS (1883-1949) — President of the Party tribunal and father-in-law of Martin Bormann; committed suicide in an American internment camp, 1949.

CANARIS, ADMIRAL WILHELM (1887-1945) — Director of German Military Intelligence, 'Abwehr', January 1935-February 1944; hanged in Flossenbuerg camp, 9 April 1945, for his part in the July 1944 plot.

CIANO, COUNT GALEAZZO (1903-44)

Mussolini's son-in-law and Foreign Minister; executed at Verona, January 1944. See bibliography.

CLAUBERG, KARL, BRIG.-GENERAL, SS (1898-   )

Director of a women's clinic; joined the SD; employed by Himmler in experiments in the mass sterilisation of Jewish women from July 1942, at first at Ravensbrueck and then at Auschwitz; returned from imprisonment in Russia, October 1955; again charged in November by the Kiel Landgericht.

CONTI, LEONARDO, LIEUT.-GENERAL, SS (1900-45)

Early Party member and Hitler's 'Reich Health Leader' till August 1944; a protégé of Bormann; committed suicide in an internment camp, October 1945.

DALUEGE, KURT, GENERAL, SS (1897-1946)

First SS Fuehrer, Berlin, and from 1934 to 1942 head of the Ordnungspolizei; Heydrich's successor as protector of Bohemia-Moravia; hanged Prague, 20 October 1946.

D'ALQUEN, GUNTER, BRIG.-GENERAL, SS (1910-   )

Himmler's propagandist; first editor of *Das Schwarze Korps*, 1935; Head of Armed Forces propaganda section at end of the war.

DARRÉ, WALTER RICHARD HON. GENERAL, SS (1895-1953)

Early friend of Himmler and founder of RUSHA bureau; Minister of Agriculture, 1933-42.

DIELS, RUDOLF, HON. COL., SS (1900-   )

Official of the Prussian political police; became first head of the Gestapo. See bibliography.

DIETRICH, OTTO, HON. LIEUT.-GENERAL, SS

Head of the Press section in the Ministry of Propaganda from 1937; released from Landsberg prison, December 1949.

DIETRICH, JOSEF (SEPP), COL.-GENERAL, SS (1892-   )

Commander of Hitler's SS bodyguard, 1928; Army commander, 1944-5; sentenced to twenty-five years' imprisonment in 1946; released, 25 October 1955.

DIRLEWANGER, OSKAR MAJ.-GENERAL, SS (1895-   )

Commanded a brigade of ex-convicts against Russian partisans, protégé of Gottlob Berger; disappeared in May 1945.

DOENITZ, GRAND ADMIRAL KARL (1876-   )

Commander-in-Chief Germany Navy, 1943; Head of the German state, 1 May 1945; to be released from Spandau prison, October 1956.

DOHNANYI, HANS (1902-45)

Austrian lawyer; arrested by Gestapo in April 1943 and condemned for treason after the bomb plot; executed, 8 April 1945.

DOLLMANN, EUGEN, COL., SS

SS police attaché in Rome embassy 1941-3; then adjutant to Karl Wolff as Military Governor, North Italy.

EBERSTEIN, FRIEDRICH KARL, FREIHERR VON, LIEUT.-GENERAL, SS
Higher SS and police leader for Munich and Lower Bavaria; SS man since 1928 and spokesman for the SS at Nuremberg.

EICHMANN, KARL ADOLF, LIEUT.-COL., SS (1906-   )
Head of office 'IVA4b', Jewish resettlement department of Gestapo, 1939-45; boasted of five million murders; escaped from American internment camp, 1945.

EICKE, THEODOR, GENERAL, SS (1882-1943)
First head of the concentration camps, 1934; Commander of the Totenkopf division from 1940; killed in action, March 1943.

EHRHARDT, CORVETTE-CAPTAIN
Freikorps leader; took part in Baltic expedition and Kapp Putsch; created a Fatherland Bloc to which Hitler once belonged; escaped death in June 1934 and died in Germany during the war.

EPP, FRANZ, FREIHERR RITTER VON, GENERAL (1868-1947)
Commander Munich war area; made by Hitler Reichstatthalter for Bavaria; pioneer of the Freikorps movement, but a cipher after 1933; died in a U.S. camp, 1947.

ERNST, KARL (1904-1934)
Head of the SA in Berlin under Roehm; executed, 30 June 1934.

FEGELEIN, HERMANN, GENERAL, SS (1906-45)
Himmler's liaison officer with Hitler from the beginning of 1943; executed by Hitler a few days before his own death.

FELLGIEBEL, ERICH FRITZ, COL.-GENERAL (1896-1944)
Army Chief of Signals; took part in 20 July 1944 plot; executed, 10 August 1944.

FOERSTER, ALBRECHT, HON. LIEUT.-GENERAL, SS (1902-   )
Former leader of Nazis in Danzig Free City; Gauleiter Danzig-Westpreussen; condemned to death Danzig, 28 April 1948; sentenced commuted to life imprisonment.

FRANK, HANS (1900-46)
Reichskommissar for German Law; Governor-General of Poland; executed at Nuremberg, 16 October 1946. See bibliography.

FRANK, KARL HERMANN LIEUT.-GENERAL, SS (1898-1946)
Leader of German minority in Czechoslovakia; Protector, Bohemia-Moravia, 1943-5; hanged in Prague, 22 May 1946.

FREISLER, ROLAND (1893-1944)
Former Communist; President of People's Court, 1942-4; killed in a bombing raid, October 1944.

FRICK, WILHELM (1877-1946)
The first Nazi bureaucrat; Reich Minister of the Interior, January 1933-August 1943; hanged, Nuremberg, 16 October 1946.

FRIEDEBURG, ADMIRAL HANS VON
Introduced Himmler to High Command Circle, 1933; committed suicide, May 1945, after signing the capitulation.

FRITSCH, BARON WERNER VON, COL.-GENERAL (1880-1939)
Commander-in-Chief, 1934-8; sought death in the Polish campaign, 18 September 1939.

FROMM, FRITZ, COL.-GENERAL (1888-1945)

Commander-in-Chief, Replacement Army; tried for his ambiguous role in the July 1944 plot and executed, March 1945.

FUNK, WALTER (1890-)

Minister of Economic Affairs, 1936-45; sentenced 1 October 1946 to life imprisonment; removed to hospital, 14 October 1955.

GALEN, CLEMENS VON, CARDINAL ARCHBISHOP OF MUENSTER (1876-1946)

Made public attack on the killing of the insane in 1941.

GEBHARDT, PROFESSOR KARL, LIEUT.-GENERAL, SS (1898-1948)

Boyhood friend of Himmler; head of Hohenlychen Hospital and chief consultant SS and police; hanged for his medical experiments, 2 June 1948.

GIESLER, PAUL (1895-1945)

Gauleiter for Munich on the death of Adolf Wagner, March 1943; suicide, May 1945.

GISEVIUS, HANS BERND (1903-)

Official in the Gestapo, 1933; later in police department of Ministry of the interior, and during the war in the Abwehr; now living in U.S.A. See bibliography.

GLOBOCNIK, ODILO, MAJOR-GENERAL, SS (1904-45)

Austrian Nazi leader; SS and police leader, Lublin and Trieste; head of 'Einsatz Reinhard', the Jewish extermination programme in Poland; suicide in Carinthia alleged, May 1945.

GLUECKS, RICHARD, LIEUT.-GENERAL, SS (1889-)

Head of Concentration Camp Inspectorate, 1939-45; went underground in April 1945; not traced.

GOEBBELS, JOSEF (1897-1945)

Reich Propaganda Minister and Gauleiter for Berlin; from July 1944 plenipotentiary for total war; suicide in Hitler's bunker, 1 May 1945. See bibliography.

GOERDELER, KARL (1884-1945)

Reich Price Control Commissioner in Hitler's first government; the chief force behind the Resistance Circle from 1937; executed Ploetzensee prison, 2 February 1945.

GOERING, HERMANN, REICHSMARSCHALL (1893-1946)

Minister President of Prussia, 1933; Chairman of Reich Defence Council and Commander-in-Chief Luftwaffe; Senior officer of armed forces; suicide in Nuremberg prison, 15 October 1946.

GRAWITZ, ERNST, LIEUT.-GENERAL, SS (1899-1945)

Chief of SS medical services from 1936; head of German Red Cross; committed suicide, end of April 1945.

GREIM, ROBERT RITTER VON, FIELD-MARSHAL

Head of 6th Air Fleet; made a field-marshal and Goering's successor as C.-in-C. Luftwaffe shortly before Hitler's death; committed suicide, 24 June 1945.

GREISER, ARTUR, LIEUT.-GENERAL, SS (1897-1946)

President Danzig Senate till 1939; Gauleiter of the Warthegau (Posen-Lodz province); hanged Posen, 20 June 1946.

GROTHMANN, WERNER, COLONEL, SS (1915-   )

Himmler's military adjutant from September 1943; accompanied his attempted escape in disguise, 23 May 1945.

GUDERIAN, HEINZ, COL.-GENERAL (1886-1954)

Inspector-General armoured troops, 1943; Chief of the Army General Staff, July 1944; dismissed by Hitler, March 1945. See bibliography.

GUERTNER, FRANZ (1881-1941)

Reich Minister of Justice, 1932; retained his post under Hitler till his death.

HAEFTEN, WERNER VON, LIEUTENANT

ADC to Stauffenberg; murdered by Stauffenberg's side, 20 June 1944; his brother Hans von Haeften was executed later.

HALDER, FRANZ, COL.-GENERAL (1884-   )

Chief of the Army General Staff, 1938-42; in correspondence with the Resistance Circle; arrested July 1944, but not brought to trial.

HAMMERSTEIN, KURT VON, COL.-GENERAL (1878-1943)

Commander-in-Chief, 1930-4, when he was succeeded by Fritsch; inconclusive evidence that he wanted to oppose Hitler in January 1933; flirted with Resistance Circle.

HANKE, CARL, HON. LIEUT.-GENERAL, SS (1903-45)

Gauleiter of Silesia; named by Hitler as Himmler's successor; shot by Czech partisans, June 1945.

HARNACK, ARVID (-1942)

Official in Economics Ministry; conveyed information to Russia by secret transmitter in 1941-2; executed after the second Rote Kapelle trial, December 1942.

HASE, PAUL VON, LIEUT.-GENERAL (1885-1944)

Town commandant Berlin; took part in plot of 20 July 1944; executed, 8 August 1944.

HASSELL, ULRICH VON (1881-1944)

Ambassador in Rome till 1938; member of Goerdeler-Beck Resistance Circle; executed, 8 September 1944. See bibliography.

HAUSHOFER, ALBRECHT (1903-45)

Son of Hitler's 'geopolitician', Professor Carl Haushofer; member of Resistance Circle; not tried but murdered, 24 April 1945.

HAUSSER, PAUL, COL.-GENERAL, SS (1880-   )

First director of training to Field SS, 1934; first SS man to command an army, July 1944; Commander army group, Rhine, March 1945; apologist for the SS. See bibliography.

HEIDEN, ERHARD, MAJOR, SS

Member of Hitler's 'Stosstruppe', 1922; commanded SS, 1927-9.

HEINES, EDMUND (1898-1934)

SA leader in Silesia as deputy to Roehm, 1931-4; murdered at Wiessee at Hitler's orders, 30 June 1934.

HEINRICI, GOTTARD, COL.-GENERAL — Took over Army Group 'Vistula' from Himmler, March 1945; repatriated from Russia, 8 October 1955.

HELLDORF, HEINRICH WOLFF, COUNT VON, GENERAL, SS (1896-1944) — Deputy SA leader for Berlin in 1933; Police President for Berlin after 1934; executed for his part in the July 1944 plot, 15 August 1944.

HENLEIN, KONRAD, HON. LIEUT.-GENERAL, SS — Leader of Sudeten Germans in Czechoslovakia till 1939, then Gauleiter, Sudetenland; committed suicide, May 1945.

HESS, RUDOLF (1894-) — Hitler's deputy and head of the Party office till his flight to Scotland, May 1941; sentenced to life imprisonment October 1946; still in Spandau prison (July 1956).

HESSE, FRITZ — 'Referent' on British affairs in the Foreign Office during the war; entrusted with a peace mission to Stockholm, February 1945. See bibliography.

HEWEL, WALTER, HON. LIEUT.-GENERAL, SS (1904-45) — Ribbentrop's liaison officer with Hitler throughout the war; probably killed escaping from the Reich Chancellery, 2 May 1945.

HEYDRICH, REINHARD, GENERAL, SS (1904-42) — Chief of SD, 1931-4; Chief of security police and SD, 1934-9; Chief of RSHA, which also included criminal police and Gestapo, 1939-42; Protector of Bohemia-Moravia, September 1941; died of wounds from a bomb, 6 June 1942.

HILDEBRANDT, RICHARD, LIEUT.-GENERAL, SS — Higher SS police leader, Danzig-Westpreussen, 1939-43; Head of RUSHA, race and settlement office, SS 1943-5; sentenced to twenty-five years' imprisonment, 10 March 1948; at present in Landsberg prison (July 1956).

HIMMLER, HEINRICH, REICHSFUEHRER, SS (1900-45) — Reichsfuehrer SS, 1929; Police President, Bavaria, 1933; Chief of Reich Political Police, 1935; Chief of German Police, 1936; Minister of the Interior, 1943; Commander-in-Chief, Replacement Army, July 1944; Commander-in-Chief, Rhine and Vistula armies, December 1944-March 1945; committed suicide at British Interrogation Centre, Lueneburg, 23 May 1945.

HINDENBURG, FIELD-MARSHAL PAUL VON (1847-1934) — Last President of the German Republic; confirmed Hitler's succession to him as Head of the German State in his will, August 1934.

HITLER, ADOLF (1889-1945) — Reich Chancellor, January 1933; Head of the German State, August 1934; Minister of Defence, February 1938; Supreme Commander in the Field, December 1941; committed suicide in the Reich Chancellery bunker at 3.30 p.m., 30 April 1945.

HOEPPNER, ERICH, COL.-
GENERAL (1886-1944)

Armoured warfare commander; cashiered by Hitler, December 1941; hanged 8 August 1944 for his part in the July 1944 plot.

HOETTL, WILHELM, LIEUT.-
COLONEL, SS (1915-   )

Austrian member of the SD from 1938; Director of Intelligence for SS, South-east Europe and Italy, 1943; defence witness for Kaltenbrunner at Nuremberg. See bibliography.

HOESS, RUDOLF, LIEUT.-
COLONEL, SS (1900-47)

Sentenced to life imprisonment for murder, 1923; Commandant, Auschwitz camp, 1940-3; Deputy-Inspector concentration camps, 1944-5; hanged in Auschwitz camp, 2 April 1947.

HORTHY, ADMIRAL MIKLOS
(NIKOLAUS) VON NAGYBANIA
(1868-   )

Regent of Hungary, 1919-44; forced to abdicate by the Germans, October 1944, and interned; lives at Estoril in Portugal (July 1956).

HOSSBACH, FRIEDRICH,
COL.-GENERAL

Hitler's military adjutant, 1934-8; dismissed from command of Fourth Army, 30 January 1945; living. See bibliography.

HUPPENKOTHEN, WALTER,
COLONEL, SS

Criminal commissar of the Gestapo; tried three times 1951, 1952, and 1955 for his part in the condemnation of Admiral Canaris.

JODL, ALFRED, COL.-
GENERAL (1890-1946)

Chief of Staff of the High Command armed forces (OKW) and chief of the High Command land operations department (OKH), 1938-45; hanged Nuremberg, 16 October 1946.

JOST, HEINZ, MAJOR-
GENERAL, SS (1905-   )

Head of Amt VI, Foreign Intelligence section of SS, 1938-42; liaison officer at Southern Army Group Headquarters; sent by Himmler to the front as 2nd lieutenant, May 1944; sentence of life imprisonment commuted; released December 1951.

JUETTNER, HANS, GENERAL,
SS (1884-   )

Head of SS main leadership office in succession to Berger, 1943-5; released and 'de-nazified', 1950.

KAHR, GUSTAV VON

Minister-President of Bavaria, 1921-4; failed to support Hitler's Munich Putsch; murdered during the blood-purge, 30 June 1934.

KALTENBRUNNER, ERNST,
GENERAL, SS (1903-46)

Helped to engineer Austrian Anschluss; SS police leader, Vienna 1938-43; then Head of Reich Security main office till end of the war; hanged Nuremberg, 16 October 1946.

KAMINISKI, BRIG.-GENERAL,
SS

Russian deserter who formed an anti-partisan brigade; said to have been executed after his part in quelling Warsaw rebellion, September 1944.

KAMMLER, HEINZ, LIEUT.-
GENERAL, SS

Head of the SS works department, WVHA(c); head of guided missiles programme, 1943-5; built the gas chambers at Auschwitz; disappeared during the battle of Berlin.

KAPPLER, HUBERT, COLONEL, SS

Commander of security police, Rome, 1941-4; sentenced in Rome to life imprisonment, 1947, in connection with Ardeatine tunnels massacre.

KEITEL, FIELD-MARSHAL WILHELM (1882-1946)

Chief of the High Command, Armed Forces (OKW) February 1938-May 1945; hanged Nuremberg, 16 October 1946.

KEPPLER, GEORG, LIEUT.-GENERAL, SS (1894-)

First commander of SS Standarte 'Deutschland'; Commander of division 'Das Reich'; commanded 1st SS Armoured Corps, Normandy, August 1944.

KEPPLER, WILHELM, HON. LIEUT.-GENERAL, SS (1882-)

Hitler's economic adviser, 1932-6; helped engineer Anschluss as embassy secretary in Vienna; ran Keppler bureau in Ministry of Economics as liaison with Himmler; released from Landsberg prison, January 1951.

KERSTEN, FELIX (1898-)

Himmler's masseur; of Baltic German origin, but Finnish nationality. See bibliography.

KESSELRING, FIELD-MARSHAL ALBERT

Luftwaffe general who commanded an army group in Italy and West Germany; sentenced to death by British Military Court, Venice, July 1947, for Ardeatine tunnels massacre; sentence twice commuted; released October 1952.

KIEP, OTTO (1886-1944)

Foreign Office official, employed in the Abwehr; arrested, January 1944, for treasonable contacts in Switzerland and hanged the following September.

KILLINGER, MANFRED VON (1886-1944)

Former SA leader; escaped death in June 1934; ambassador to Rumania, 1941-4; committed suicide on approach of the Russians.

KLEIST, EWALD VON, FIELD-MARSHAL (1881-1954)

Commander-in-Chief of Southern Army Group, Russia; died in a Russian prison camp, October 1954, having been extradited from Jugoslavia in 1949.

KLEIST, PETER

Foreign Office expert on Russian affairs; charged with peace contacts with Russian agents in Stockholm, 1942-3. See bibliography.

KLUGE, GUENTHER VON, FIELD-MARSHAL (1882-1944)

Army Goup commander in Russia and France; in correspondence with Resistance Circle from November 1942; committed suicide to avoid arrest at Dombasle, 19 August 1944.

KNOCHEN, HELMUTH, COLONEL, SS (1910-)

Commander of security police, Paris, 1940-4; sentenced to life imprisonment by British Wuppertal court, June 1946, for execution of captured airmen; sentenced to death, Paris, October 1954; in Cherche-Midi prison (July 1956).

KNOECHLEIN, FRITZ, LIEUT.-COLONEL, SS (1911-49)

Officer of the Totenkopf division who shot a hundred British prisoners at Le Paradis, 27 May 1940, hanged, Hamburg, January 1949.

KOCH, ERICH, HON. LIEUT.-GENERAL, SS (1896-)

Gauleiter of East Prussia, 1930-45; and Reichskommissar Ukraine, 1941-4; extradited to Poland, 1950, but not since heard of.

KOERNER, PAUL, HON. LIEUT.-GENERAL, SS

State Secretary to Goering as Prime Minister of Prussia, 1939, and as Head of Four-Year Plan, 1936; chairman of Hermann Goering works; released from Landsberg prison, December 1951.

KORHERR, RICHARD (1903-)

Himmler's Inspector for Statistics, 1940-4.

KREBS, HANS, COL. GENERAL

Hitler's last Chief of Staff and successor to Guderian, March 1945; committed suicide 1 May 1945.

KRUEGER, FRIEDRICH, GENERAL, SS (1894-1945)

Higher SS police leader, Cracow, 1939-4; killed in Austria while commanding a division, May 1945.

LAHOUSEN, ERWIN VON, BRIG.-GENERAL (1897-)

Head of Section II of the Abwehr under Canaris; Nuremberg prosecution witness.

LAMMERDING, HEINZ, LIEUT.-GENERAL, SS (1895-)

Commanded SS division Das Reich, 1944; Himmler's Chief of Staff, Vistula Army Group, January-March 1945; condemned to death *in absentia*, Bordeaux, 1951; still wanted for Oradour massacre.

LAMMERS, HANS, HON. LIEUT.-GENERAL, SS (1879-)

Chief of Reich Chancellery, 1933-45; Rank of Minister from November 1934; sentenced to twenty years' imprisonment at Nuremberg, but released November 1951.

LANGBEHN, CARL (1901-44)

Lawyer and friend of Himmler, with whom he maintained contacts on behalf of the Resistance Circle; arrested September 1943 and executed 12 October 1944.

LANGE, LEO, COLONEL, SS

Criminal Commissar of the Gestapo in charge of Rote Kapelle and Solf Circle prosecutions; apparently not tried.

LEBER, JULIUS

Former Social Democrat deputy, nominated by Stauffenberg to be Reich Chancellor on Hitler's death; executed January 1945.

LEY, ROBERT (1894-1945)

Head of the German Labour Front, which extinguished the trade union movement in 1933; committed suicide on the eve of the Nuremberg trial.

LOHSE, HINRICH (1898-)

Gauleiter, Schleswig-Holstein; Generalkommissar for Baltic States and White Russia, 1941-4; released from a German prison in 1951 and awarded a pension by the Bonn government.

LUDENDORFF, ERICH, FIELD-MARSHAL (1853-1937)
The Commander-in-Chief who forced 'the November criminals' to sign the capitulation of Germany in 1918; nevertheless a Nazi hero because he joined Hitler's Putsch in 1923.

LUETZE, VIKTOR
Head of the SA after the murder of Roehm, related through his wife to Brauchitsch, with whom he conspired to revive the armed SA. A one-eyed man, killed driving a car May 1943.

LUTHER, MARTIN (1896-1945)
Head of Deutschland section in Foreign Office, 1938-43, where he acted as Himmler's agent; sent to Sachsenhausen concentration camp, February 1943, and died soon after his release in May 1945.

MACHER, HEINZ, MAJOR, SS (1919-   )
Adjutant to Himmler together with Werner Grothmann when he was captured by the British in May 1945.

MANSTEIN, FRITZ ERICH FIELD-MARSHAL (1888-   )
Army Group commander, twice dismissed by Hitler and reinstated; Himmler's *bete noire;* sentenced by British court 19 December 1949 to eighteen years' imprisonment for failing to protect civilian lives; released, August 1952.

MAURICE, EMIL, COLONEL, SS (1897-1945)
Early companion of Hitler and member of first SS; credited with murder of Edmund Heines and Father Stempfle in June 1934.

MEISSNER, OTTO, HON. LIEUT.-GENERAL, SS (1880-1953)
Chief of President's Chancellery under Hindenburg and Hitler, 1920-45; acquitted at Nuremberg April 1949; died, 28 April 1953.

MEYER, KURT, MAJOR-GENERAL, SS (1911-   )
Commanded SS Hitlerjugend division Normandy 1944, where he murdered Canadian prisoners of war; death sentence of December 1945 commuted; released, 7 September 1954.

MILCH, ERHARD, FIELD-MARSHAL (1892-   )
Inspector-General of the Luftwaffe from 1943; sentenced to life imprisonment, 1947, for procuring slave labour and human guineapigs; released from Landsberg, 4 July 1954.

MOHNKE, WILHELM, MAJOR-GENERAL, SS
Took part with Kurt Meyer in the Normandy massacre; In the Fuehrer's bunker as eibstandarte commander on 30 April 1945; said to be a prisoner in Russia (1955).

MOLTKE, HELMUTH GRAF VON (1907-45)
Legal adviser to the Abwehr; involved in the 'Solf Tea-party' affair; leader of a Socialist group in the Resistance Circle; executed, 24 January 1945.

MORGEN, GEORG KONRAD LIEUT.-COLONEL, SS
Judge of the SS police courts; conducted investigation for Himmler, 1943-4, into concentration-camp abuses; Nuremberg witness.

MUELLER, HEINRICH,
GENERAL, SS (1900-   )

Official of Munich political police under Weimar Republic; head of the Gestapo, 1935-45; last heard of in Hitler's bunker, 29 April 1945; may be alive.

MUGROWSKI, JOACHIM,
LIEUT.-GENERAL, SS
(1905-48)

SS man from 1931; professor of bacteriology; head of SS Health Department, 1939-45; hanged at Landsberg, 2 June 1948.

MUSSOLINI, BENITO
(1883-1945)

Duce or head of the Italian government; rescued from the Badoglio party, 13 September 1943; head of a puppet Italian government till end of the war; murdered, May 1945.

NAUJOCKS, ALFRED,
COLONEL, SS

Official of AMT VI of the Security Service; concerned in the *agent provocateur* incidents at Gleiwitz and Venlo; also concerned in faking British bank notes; escaped from U.S. internment camp; probably alive.

NEBE, ARTUR, GENERAL, SS
(-1945)

Head of criminal police, 1933-45; commanded an extermination group in Russia; took part in July 1944 plot; executed, 21 March 1945 (alleged).

NEURATH, FREIHERR
CONSTANTIN VON (1873-   )

Foreign Minister till 1938; Protector, Bohemia-Moravia, 1939-43; released from Spandau prison, 7 November 1954.

NOSKE, GUSTAV (-1946)

Minister of Defence, 1919-20; although a social democrat, Hitler paid him a pension of 800 marks a month throughout the war.

OBERG, KARL, GENERAL, SS
(1896-   )

Sentenced by a British court in 1946 for illegal execution of captured airmen while SS police commander France 1942-4; sentenced to death in Paris, October 1954; still in Cherche-Midi prison (July 1956).

OHLENDORF, OTTO, LIEUT.-
GENERAL, SS (1907-51)

Head of the SD of Amt II in the Main Security Office (1939-45); Section Leader for overseas trade in Ministry of Economics, 1943; commanded an extermination group in Russia, 1941-2; hanged at Landsberg, 8 June 1951.

OLBRICHT, FRIEDRICH,
COL.-GENERAL (1886-1944)

Head of the General Wehrmacht Office or Supply Section in Fromm's Replacement Army Command; murdered in the Bendler-strasse building on the day of the plot, 20 July 1944.

OSTER, HANS, MAJOR-
GENERAL (1895-1945)

Chief of Staff to Admiral Canaris as Head of the Abwehr; suspended, April 1943, and arrested after the bomb plot; executed in Flossenbuerg camp, 9 April 1945.

PAPEN, FRANZ VON (1879-)

Reich Chancellor in 1932 and Vice-Chancellor to Hitler, 1933-4; then ambassador to Vienna till 1938, and then to Ankara; acquitted at Nuremberg, but not cleared by German authorities till 1948. See bibliography.

PAULUS, FRIEDRICH (1890-)

Field-Marshal; surrendered with the Sixth Army to the Russians at Stalingrad; broadcast for the Russian Free Germany Committee; gave evidence at Nuremberg for the Russian prosecution; permitted by the Russians to live in East Germany, 1953.

PAYNE-BEST, MAJOR

British Intelligence officer; kidnapped at Venlo, 9 November 1939, and accused of the Bierbraeukeller plot; released at end of the war. See bibliography.

PEIPER, JOCHEN, COLONEL, SS (1915-)

Commander of a combat group of armoured SS who murdered seventy-one American prisoners at the Malmedy crossroads, 17 December 1944; condemned to death, 16 July 1946, but later reprieved; at present in Landsberg prison.

PFEFFER, FRANZ VON, CAPTAIN

Chief of Staff of the SA, 1928-31; escaped death in the blood-purge of June 1934; commanded a Volkssturm division at the end of the war.

PHILIP OF HESSEN, PRINCE (1896-)

Obergruppenfuehrer of the SA; married to Princess Mafalda of Italy and employed by Hitler as a good Party man on missions to Italy; sent to Sachsenhausen concentration camp, September 1943, and liberated at end of the war.

PHLEPS, ARTUR, LIEUT.-GENERAL, SS (1890-1944)

Former Austrian officer who became a Roumanian general, but transferred to the Waffen SS in 1941 and commanded the SS mountain corps in South-east Europe; disappeared mysteriously in Transylvania, October 1944.

POHL, OSWALD, GENERAL, SS (1892-1951)

Head of the economic administration of the SS (WVHA), including the concentration-camp inspectorate, 1942-5; hanged at Landsberg, 8 June 1951.

POPITZ, PROFESSOR JOHANNES (1884-1945)

Acting Finance Minister for Prussia, 1933-44; member of the Resistance Circle who tried to gain Himmler's adherence; executed, February 1945.

PRUETZMANN, HANS, LIEUT.-GENERAL, SS (1901-45)

Higher SS police leader, Ukraine, 1942-4; head of the 'Werwulf' organisation, 1944-5; committed suicide Lueneburg 21 May 1945.

QUIRNHEIM, GRAF MERTZ VON, MAJOR — Strauffenberg's deputy, killed by his side in the Bendlerstrasse building on the failure of the plot, 20 July 1944.

RAEDER, GRAND ADMIRAL ERICH (1876-   ) — Commander-in-Chief of the German navy till 1943; released from Spandau prison on remission of life sentence, 26 September 1955.

RAHN, RUDOLF (1900-   ) — Ambassador to Italy, 1943-5; in charge of negotiations for Admiral Horthy's abdication, October 1944; party to Karl Wolff's peace negotiations with Allies, March 1945; denazified, February 1950.

RASCHER, SIGMUND, MAJOR, SS (1909-45) — Authorised by Himmler to conduct high-altitude and freezing experiments for the Luftwaffe on Dachau inmates; liquidated by Himmler as an awkward witness at the end of the war.

RATTENHUEBER, JULIUS, MAJOR-GENERAL, SS (1897-   ) — Hitler's personal security officer till his death; captured by Russians while escaping from the Reich Chancellery, 2 May 1945, and repatriated to Germany, 18 October 1955.

REICHENAU, WALTER VON, FIELD-MARSHAL (1884-1942) — Played an uncertain role in the blood-purge of 1934 as head of the Army Supply Office; a Party general; died of a mysterious infection, 17 January 1942, soon after being made a field-marshal.

REICHWEIN, ADOLF, PROFESSOR — Socialist member of Resistance Circle; arrested before the July plot when contacting Berlin Communists; executed August 1944.

REINECKE, HERMANN, COL.-GENERAL — Chief of the General Wehrmacht Office throughout the war and chief of the National Socialist Guidance staff (NSFO) from 1943 (the 'Oberpolitruk'); sentenced to life imprisonment, 28 October 1948; still in Landsberg.

REINECKE, GUENTHER, BRIG.-GENERAL, SS — Head of department 'SS courts' and Chief Judge highest court 'SS and Police'.

REMER, OTTO, MAJOR-GENERAL — Promoted to divisional commander for his part in restoring order in Berlin on July 20 1944; sentenced in March 1952 to three months' imprisonment for a collective libel on the Resistance Circle; sentence not served. See bibliography.

RIBBENTROP, JOACHIM, HON. GENERAL, SS (1893-1946) — Ambassador to London, 1936-8; Foreign Minister, 1938-45; hanged Nuremberg, 16 October 1946. See bibliography.

ROEDER, MANFRED, MAJOR-GENERAL, LUFTWAFFE — Generalrichter or Judge Advocate-General; in charge of Rote Kapelle case, 1942, and Dohnanyi-Bonhoeffer inquiry, April 1943; released by Americans, January 1949; denazified, December 1951. See bibliography.

ROEHM, ERNST, CAPTAIN (1887-1934) — Adjutant to Ritter von Epp, 1919-28; Chief of the SA, 1931-4; made a cabinet minister, December 1933; executed in Stadelheim prison, Munich, 6 July 1934.

ROMMEL, ERWIN, FIELD-MARSHAL (1891-1944) — Commanded the Afrika Corps, the reserve army in Italy, and an army in Normandy; made contact with the 'Resistance General' Heinrich von Stuelpnagel, May 1944, but was opposed to the bomb plot; forced by Hitler to commit suicide, 14 October 1944.

ROSENBERG, ALFRED, HON. GENERAL, SS (1893-1946) — Chief of foreign political section in Party office, 1930-41; Minister for Eastern territories from April 1941; hanged, Nuremberg, 16 October 1945. See bibliography.

RUNDSTEDT, KARL GERD VON, FIELD-MARSHAL (1875-1953) — Army Group commander; dismissed by Hitler in 1941, and at the end of 1944; saved by his age from trial in 1949 for orders to execute Commando troops.

SAUERBRUCH, FERDINAND, PROFESSOR (1875-1952) LIEUT.-GENERAL — Chief surgeon of the German army and head of the Charité Hospital, Berlin; mildly involved in the Resistance Circle, but not arrested.

SAUCKEL, FRITZ, (1894-1946) — Gauleiter for Thuringia; made plenipotentiary for labour recruitment, March 1942; conducted slave raids in Russia and other occupied countries; hanged, Nuremberg, 16 October 1945.

SCHACHT, HJALMAR (1877-   ) — Minister for Economic Affairs, August 1934 to November 1937; remained president of Reichsbank till 1939 and Minister without Portfolio till 1944; arrested for contacts with the Resistance Circle, but not tried; acquitted by Allies at Nuremberg, but not denazified till November 1950.

SCHELLENBERG, WALTER, LIEUT.-GENERAL, SS (1910-52) — Deputy chief of Amt VI, foreign Intelligence section of SD, 1939-42; then Chief till 1944, when he became head of the united SS and Wehrmacht military Intelligence and Himmler's personal adviser; released from prison December 1950. See bibliography.

SCHLABRENDORFF, FABIAN VON, MAJOR (1909-   ) — Staff officer in correspondence with Resistance Circle; arrested after the July 1944 plot; acquitted in the following March, but kept in a concentration camp till the liberation. See bibliography.

SCHLEGELBERGER, FRANZ — Acting Minister of Justice, January 1941 to August 1942; sentenced to life imprisonment, 4 December 1947; released as incurable, February 1951.

SCHLEICHER, KURT VON, COL.-GENERAL (1879-1934) — Reich Chancellor for a few weeks, end of 1932; planned to get back by intriguing with Roehm and Gregor Strasser; murdered by Hitler, 30 June 1934.

SCHMIDT, ANDREAS (1912-   ) — Son-in-law of Gottlob Berger and leader of German Nazi Party in Rumania 'Bonfert'.

SCHMUNDT, RUDOLF, MAJOR-GENERAL — Hitler's military adjutant, 1938-44; died of injuries from the bomb which was to have killed Hitler, 20 July 1944.

SCHOERNER, FERDINAND, FIELD-MARSHAL (1893-   ) — Commanded an Army Group in Czechoslovakia and Silesia at the end of the war, which was expected to relieve Berlin; returned from captivity in Russia, 24 January 1955.

SCHULENBURG, FRITZ VON DER (1904-44) — Deputy to Graff Helldorf as Police President, Berlin, 1938, and to Josef Wagner as Gauleiter of Silesia, 1939-40; executed for his part in the plot as an officer on Fromm's staff, 10 August 1944.

SCHULENBURG, WERNER VON DER (1875-1944) — Ambassador in Moscow till 1941; executed for his part in the bomb plot, 1944.

SCHUSCHNIGG, KURT VON (1897-   ) — Chancellor of Austria 1934-8; in concentration camps from 1938 to 1945.

SCHULZE-BOYSEN, HARRO (1910-42) — Official in the Luftwaffe Intelligence service who played a leading role in the Communist Rote Kapelle spy network; executed, December 1942.

SCHWEPPENBURG, LEO GRAF GEYR VON, COL.-GENERAL — Military attaché, London, 1934-7; commanded army in France, 1944; contacts with Resistance Circle.

SCHWERIN VON KROSIGK, GRAF LUETZ (1887-   ) — Minister of Finance, 1932-45; Foreign Minister in Doenitz government, May 1945; released from Landsberg prison, January 1951. See bibliography.

SEECKT, HANS VON, COL.-GENERAL (1866-1936) — Commander-in-Chief, 1919-30; creator of the post-war 'Reichswehr'; signed training pact with Russian General Staff in 1926.

SEVERING, KARL (1875-   ) — Prussian Minister for Interior, 1921-32; removed by von Papen; like Noske, a Social Democrat who received a pension from Hitler.

SEYDLITZ, WALTER VON, LIEUT.-GENERAL
Chief of Staff to Paulus at Stalingrad; first German officer to broadcast from Moscow, 1943; nevertheless imprisoned by the Russians till October 1955.

SIMON, MAX, MAJOR-GENERAL, SS (1899-)
Commanded Totenkopf division, 1943, and 16th SS Division, 1944; acquitted of illegal executions (carried out in 1945), 19 October 1955.

SIX, PROFESSOR FRANZ, BRIG.-GENERAL, SS (1909-)
Joined the SD as a pupil of Professor Hoehn in the 'thirties; served in the extermination groups in Russia, 1941; transferred from SD to Foreign Office as an anti-Semitic expert; life sentence commuted; released, 30 September 1952.

SKORZENY, OTTO, MAJOR-GENERAL, SS (1908-)
Commanded commando unit 'Oranienburg' in Amt VI of the RSHA from April 1943; divisional commander on Oder front, January 1945; acquitted of illegal practices in Ardennes offensive, 9 August 1947. See bibliography.

SOLF, HANNA, WIDOW OF WILHELM SOLF, AMBASSADOR TO JAPAN
Arrested in January 1944 for complicity in a treasonable correspondence with Switzerland but not tried; liberated at end of war.

SONDEREGGER, COLONEL, SS
Criminal commissar of the Gestapo; charged with investigation of Oster-Dohnanyi circle from April 1943.

SPEER, ALBERT (1905-)
Hitler's architect; Minister of Armaments and War Production, 1942-5; convicted of procuring slave labour, 1 October 1946; at present serving life sentence at Spandau.

SPRENGER, JAKOB (1884-1945)
Former postmaster and Gauleiter, Hessen; fanatical agent in euthanasia killings and Jewish deportations; committed suicide, April 1945.

STAHLECKER, FRANZ WALTER, MAJOR-GENERAL, SS (1900-42)
Head of Section VIa of the Reich Main Security Office; led an extermination group to the Baltic States which claimed 221,000 executions; killed by partisans, March 1942.

STAUFFENBERG, CLAUS, SCHENCK VON, COLONEL (1907-44)
Chief of Staff to Fritz Fromm, commanding Replacement Army; tried unsuccessfully to blow up Hitler in his staff conference room, 20 July 1944; murdered by Fromm the same night in the Bendlerstrasse.

STEENGRACHT VON MOYLAND, GUSTAV (1903-)
Succeeded von Weizsaeker as Chief Secretary of State in Foreign Office, 1943; released from Landsberg prison, February 1950.

STEINER, FELIX, GENERAL, SS (1896-)
First commander Viking Division, 1940; commanded an army corps which was intended to relieve Berlin at the end of war.

STEVENS, R. H., COLONEL — British officer, kidnapped at Venlo, 9 November 1939. See Payne-Best.

STRASSER, GREGOR (1890-1934) — Founder of the Berlin SA and Hitler's deputy in Berlin; quarrelled over policy from 1926 onwards; may have conspired with von Schleicher; murdered, 30 June 1934.

STRASSER, OTTO (1897-   ) — Younger brother of the same; left the Party in 1930 and formed 'Black Front' in Prague; lived in Switzerland during the war; and later in Canada; recovered German citizenship, November 1954.

STRECKENBACH, BRUNO, LIEUT.-GENERAL, SS (1902-   ) — Heydrich's deputy as chief of RSHA and head of Amt I; Commander of 19th Latvian SS Division; serving a prison sentence in Russia (August 1956).

STREICHER, JULIUS (1885-1946) — Gauleiter of Franconia till 1936, and editor of *Der Stuermer*; although arranged among the first twenty-one Nuremberg defendants he was a person of no consequence and a private individual after his dismissal.

STROOP, JUERGEN, MAJOR-GENERAL, SS (1895-1951) — SS and police leader, Warsaw, during ghetto rebellion, 1943; SS and police leader, Greece, 1943-4; condemned to death by American court, Dachau 22 March 1947; condemned again and executed Warsaw, 8 September 1951.

STUCKART, WILHELM, HON. LIEUT.-GENERAL, SS — Permanent Secretary of State in Ministry of the Interior; drafted Nuremberg laws, 1935; released from Nuremberg prison, April 1949.

STUELPNAGEL, OTTO VON, COL.-GENERAL (1878-1948) — Military Governor, France, 1940-2; committed suicide in a French prison, February 1948.

STUELPNAGEL, HEINRICH VON, COL.-GENERAL (1886-1944) — Military Governor, France, 1942-4; took part in July 1944 plot; tried to commit suicide near Verdun; hanged, August 1944.

SZALASI, FERENC — Premier of Hungary, October 1944-March 1945; head of Arrow Cross Party; executed Budapest, 1946.

SZTOJAY, ANDOR (1883-1946) — Premier of Hungary, March-August 1944; executed Budapest, January 1946.

TERBOVEN, JOSEF (1898-1945) — Gauleiter, Duesseldorf, and Reichskommissar for Norway, 1940-5; committed suicide in Norway, May 1945.

THADDEN, EBERHARD VON — Foreign Office official in charge of Department Inland II and concerned with Jewish deportation questions, 1943-4; two charges in German courts, 1950-2, never proceeded with.

THADDEN, ELISABETH VON (1890-1944) — Liaison between ex-Chancellor Josef Wirth and General Halder in the 'Solf Tea-party' conspiracy; executed, 15 August 1944.

THIERACK, OTTO (1889-1946) — President of the People's Court till July 1942, then Minister of Justice till end of the war; committed suicide in an U.S. camp, October 1946.

THOMAS, GEORG, COL.-GENERAL — Chief of the Armaments section at OKW (WI-Ru Amt); member of the Resistance Circle; arrested in July 1944, but not brought to trial; liberated by Allies.

THOMAS MAX, MAJOR-GENERAL (1891-1944) — SS police leader, France, 1940-2, then SS police leader, Ukraine; said to have been killed in action, 1944.

TRESCKOW, HENNING VON, MAJOR-GENERAL (1894-1944) — Successive Chief of Staff to the Army Group commanders, Kluge, Bock, and Manstein; the creator of the Walkuere plan for a Putsch against Hitler; walked into the Russian field of fire after the failure of the plot.

TROTT ZU SOLZ, ADAM VON (1909-44) — Foreign Office and Abwehr official; involved in Stauffenberg's plot-plans; executed, August 1944.

TUCHACHEWSKI, MARSHAL OF THE RED ARMY (1892-1937) — Signed the 'Seeckt-Tuchachewski protocols' in 1926 for co-operation with the German General Staff; accused of a pro-German plot after Hitler's access to power and condemned to death, 12 July 1937.

VEESENMAYER, EDMUND, COLONEL, SS (1894-   ) — SS official transferred to Foreign Office as a protégé of Keppler's and engaged in anti-Semitic activities; plenipotentiary in Hungary, March-October 1944; released from Landsberg prison, December 1951.

VIETINGHOFF, HEINRICH VON, COL.-GENERAL (-1952) — Commander Tenth Army, Italy, and then Commander-in-Chief who signed the capitulation of all German forces in Italy.

VLASSOV, ANDREJ, COL.-GENERAL (1900-46) — Russian army commander; captured in 1942; was allowed to set up a Free Russia Committee and eventually to command two divisions of Russian deserters; executed, Moscow, 1 August 1946.

WAGNER, ADOLF (1890-1943) — Member of the 'Braunehaus' clique, who helped engineer the massacre of Roehm's followers, 1934; Gauleiter of Munich till the beginning of 1943.

WAGNER, EDUARD, COL.-GENERAL — Quartermaster-General for the armed forces; joined the Resistance Circle in the autumn of 1943; committed suicide on the day of the plot, 20 July 1944.

WAGNER, GERHARDT (1888-1938) — Plenipotentiary for Health in the Party Office and Leader of the National Socialist Chamber of Medicine; possibly the originator of the euthanasia plan.

WAGNER, JOSEF
(1899-1945)

Gauleiter of Silesia, dismissal by Hitler, 1940. Executed after the bomb plot, 1945.

WAGNER, ROBERT
(1895-1946)

Early Party member who was tried with Hitler after the November 1923 Putsch; Gauleiter for Baden, 1925, and for Alsace as well, 1940; shot by the French at Strasbourg, 1946.

WALDECK-PYRMONT,
ERBPRINZ-JOSIAS ZU,
GENERAL, SS (1896-   )

Himmler's first blue-blooded recruit, 1929; higher SS and police leader for Cassel-Mainfranken from 1939; for his jurisdiction over Buchenwald camp sentenced to life imprisonment at Dachau, 14 August 1947; still in Landsberg prison.

WARLIMONT, WALTER,
LIEUT.-GENERAL

Led the German volunteers for General Franco; chief of National Defence section in OKW, 1938-44; sentenced to life imprisonment, 28 October 1948; commuted to eighteen years: may be released from Landsberg shortly (July 1956).

WEBER, CHRISTIAN
MAJOR-GENERAL, SS (1883-1945)

A bookmaker and publican; one of the first members of Hitler's Stosstruppe (later the SS); took part in June 1934 murders; killed by Bavarian Separatists, 1945.

WEIZSAECKER, ERNST VON
(1882-1951)

Chief Secretary of State in Foreign Office, 1938-43, where his role was peculiarly shabby; released from Landsberg prison, October 1950; died, 6 August 1951.

WINKELMANN, OTTO,
MAJOR-GENERAL, SS (1894-   )

Commanded the Ordnungspolizei, 1942-4; higher SS police leader Hungary, 1944-5.

WIRTH, CHRISTIAN, LIEUT.-
COLONEL, SS

Head of an organisation of four extermination camps for Jews in Poland under Odilo Globocnik, whom he accompanied to Trieste in September 1943; said to have been killed by Tito partisans, but he may be alive.

WISLICENY, DIETER, MAJOR,
SS (1899-1948)

Official of Eichmann's Jewish resettlement Office, part of the Gestapo; made several collective bargains for Jewish lives in Slovakia, Hungary, and Greece; prosecution witness, Nuremberg; hanged at Bratislava, July 1948.

WITZLEBEN, ERWIN VON,
FIELD-MARSHAL (1881-1944)

Retired by Hitler, April 1942; after which he became the military head of the Resistance Circle, who intended him for Commander-in Chief; executed after the bomb plot, 8 August 1944.

WOLFF, KARL, COL.-
GENERAL, SS (1900-   )

Himmler's liaison officer with Hitler till 1943; then Military Governor, North Italy, and plenipotentiary to Mussolini; tried to negotiate surrender of troops in Italy at end of the war; freed from prison, August 1949.

Maps

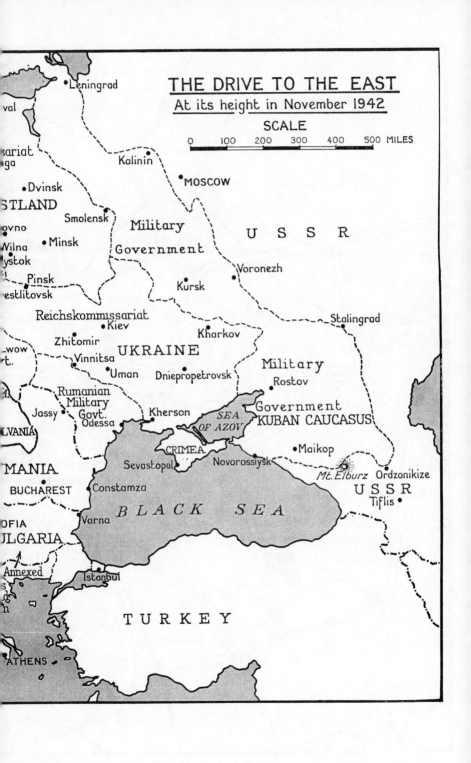

THE DRIVE TO THE EAST

At its height in November 1942

SCALE

0   100   200   300   400   500 MILES

• Leningrad

val

sariat
iga

• Dvinsk

• Kalinin

• MOSCOW

STLAND

ovno

Smolensk

Military

U   S   S   R

Wilna   • Minsk

ystok

• Pinsk

estlitovsk

Government

• Voronezh

Kursk

Reichskommissariat

Zhitomir   • Kiev

Kharkov

• Stalingrad

wow

rt.

UKRAINE

• Vinnitsa

Military

• Uman

Dniepropetrovsk

Rostov

Rumanian
Military
Jassy   Govt.

Kherson

Government

• Maikop

KUBAN CAUCASUS

Odessa

SEA
OF AZOV

VANIA

CRIMEA

MANIA

Sevastopol

Novorossiysk

Mt. Elburz   Ordzonikize

BUCHAREST

• Constamza

U   S   S   R

Tiflis •

OFIA

ULGARIA

Varna

B L A C K   S E A

Annexed

Istanbul

T U R K E Y

ATHENS

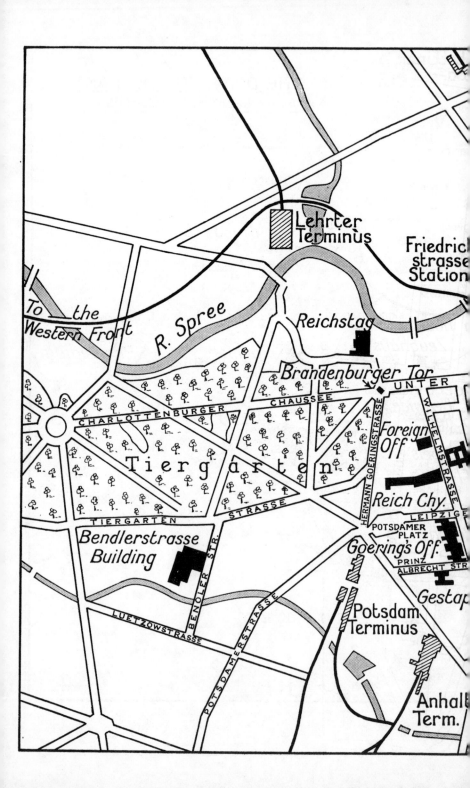

Lehrter
Terminus

Friedrich
strasse
Station

To the
Western Front

R. Spree

Reichstag

Brandenburger Tor

UNTER

Charlottenburger
Chaussee

Foreign
Off

WILHELMSTRASSE

HERMANN GOERINGSTRASSE

Tiergarten

Strasse

Reich Chy.

LEIPZIGE

POTSDAMER
PLATZ

Tiergarten
Str.

Goering's Off.

Bendlerstrasse
Building

PRINZ
ALBRECHT STR.

Gestap

BENDLER STR.

Luetzowstrasse

Potsdam
Terminus

POTSDAMERSTRASSE

Anhalt
Term.

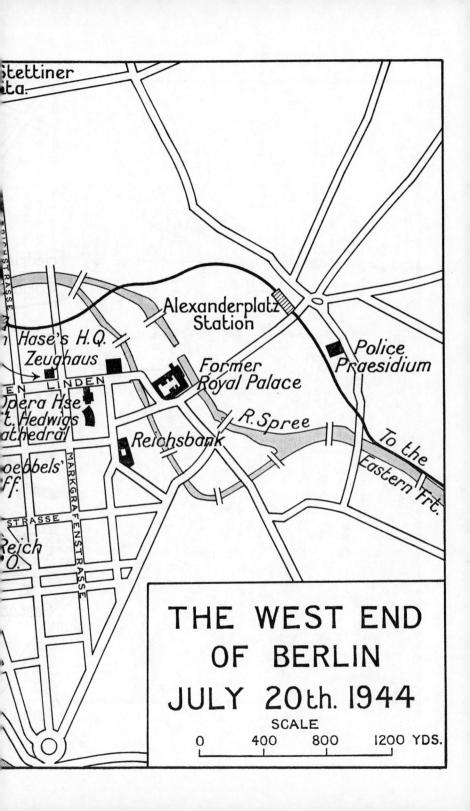

tettiner
ta.

Alexanderplatz
Station

Hase's H.Q.
Zeughaus

EN LINDEN

Police
Praesidium

Former
Royal Palace

pera Hse
t. Hedwigs
athedral

R. Spree

oebbels'
ff.

Reichsbank

STRASSE

To the
Eastern Frt.

Reich
O.

MARKGRAFENSTRASSE

THE WEST END
OF BERLIN
JULY 20th. 1944

SCALE

0   400   800   1200 YDS.

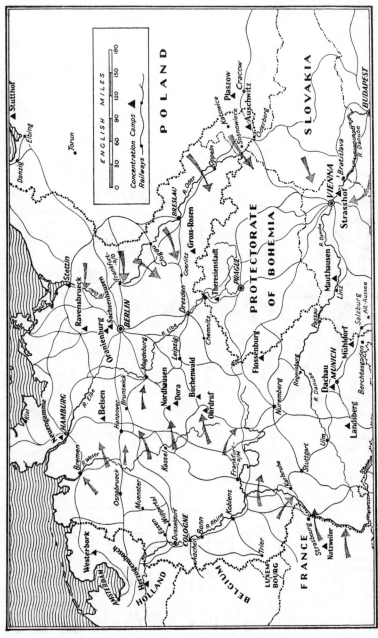

Germany, showing position of main concentration camps at the end of the war: arrows denote approximate position of Allied spearhead on 10 April 1945, when neither Belsen nor Buchenwald had been liberated.

Index